Approaching Apollonius

Approaching Apollonius

An Introduction to Apollonius of Tyana
for Students and Teachers in Biblical Studies

Floyd O. Parker Jr.

PICKWICK *Publications* · Eugene, Oregon

APPROACHING APOLLONIUS
An Introduction to Apollonius of Tyana for Students and Teachers in Biblical Studies

Copyright © 2025 Floyd O. Parker Jr. All rights reserved. Except for brief quotations in critical publications or reviews, no part of this book may be reproduced in any manner without prior written permission from the publisher. Write: Permissions, Wipf and Stock Publishers, 199 W. 8th Ave., Suite 3, Eugene, OR 97401.

Pickwick Publications
An Imprint of Wipf and Stock Publishers
199 W. 8th Ave., Suite 3
Eugene, OR 97401

www.wipfandstock.com

PAPERBACK ISBN: 979-8-3852-3039-6
HARDCOVER ISBN: 979-8-3852-3040-2
EBOOK ISBN: 979-8-3852-3041-9

Cataloguing-in-Publication data:

Names: Parker, Floyd O., Jr., author.

Title: Approaching Apollonius : an introduction to Apollonius for students and teachers in biblical studies / Floyd O. Parker Jr.

Description: Eugene, OR: Pickwick Publications, 2025. | Includes bibliographical references and index.

Identifiers: ISBN 979-8-3852-3039-6 (paperback). | ISBN 979-8-3852-3040-2 (hardcover). | ISBN 979-8-3852-3041-9 (ebook).

Subjects: LCSH: Apollonius, of Tyana. | Pythagoras and the Pythagorean school. | Biography—To 500. | Jesus Christ—Miscellanea.

Classification: BT304.93 P37 2025 (print). | BT304.93 (ebook).

VERSION NUMBER 08/01/25

I am grateful to Oxford University Press for permission to use "One Remarkable Life" from Bart Ehrman, *A Brief Introduction to the New Testament* (New York: Oxford University Press, 2004).

I dedicate this book to my wife, Angel,
to my three daughters, Tara, Jessica, and Alexa,
and to my grandchildren.

Contents

Preface | ix
Acknowledgments | xi
Abbreviations | xv

Part 1: Introductory Issues

1. Introduction: Why Apollonius Matters | 3
2. Devising Criteria for the Apollonian Decalogue | 29
3. Apollonian Studies: From Antiquity to Modern Times | 57

Part 2: Philostratus II and His Literary Corpus

4. Philostratus II and His World | 101
5. An Introduction to Philostratus's Writings | 123
6. An Introduction to the *VA* | 153
7. A Summary of the Contents of the *VA* | 164

Part 3: Investigating the Apollonian Decalogue

8. Items 1–2: Pre-Philostratean Sources and Sources Contemporaneous with Philostratus Not Used or Mentioned in the *VA* | 187
9. Items 3–4: Pre-Philostratean Sources Used or Mentioned in the *VA* | 211
10. Item 5: Damis and His Memoirs | 232
11. Item 6: Historical and Geographical Errors in the *VA* | 261
12. Item 7: Potential Political, Philosophical, Pagan Religious, and Literary Agendas of the *VA* | 309

13 Items 8–9: Potential Anti-Christian Agendas and Borrowing of Christian Texts or Ideas | 339
14 Item 10: The Temporal "Gap" between Apollonius and the Composition of the *VA* | 370
15 Summary and Concluding Remarks Concerning the Apollonian Decalogue | 380

Part 4: Apollonius and Jesus

16 The Sources for Apollonius and Jesus Compared | 387

Bibliography | 427
Index | 443

Preface

My first conscious encounter with Apollonius of Tyana was when I attended a regional SBL meeting in Gainesville, Florida in the late 1990s. Standing in the book exhibit, I perused and then purchased a copy of G. R. S. Mead's *Apollonius of Tyana*. Although this work was not the best entry point for the serious study of Apollonius—I was a New Testament professor who knew nothing about this arcane topic at the time or about Mead's theosophical views—the book did a reasonable job of acquainting me with the story of this ancient holy man who so closely resembled Jesus. After reading the book, I had intended to locate a few academic works about Apollonius, but I did not immediately follow up on this investigation. The topic of Apollonius resurfaced in 2010 when a student called my attention to a passage in Bart Ehrman's *New Testament Introduction* in which this author underscored several similarities between this pagan holy man and Jesus. Since this was a secondary text for the course, I had not yet thoroughly read the book and was caught off guard by the force of Ehrman's assertions that Jesus was just one of several such teachers and miracle workers of the first century AD. As a Christian, I was disconcerted by Apollonius's resemblances to Jesus. As an academic, I felt that I should address this issue in print but, due to a heavy teaching load at the time and the responsibility of raising a family, it was easy to put this major research project on the back burner once again. Yet, the nagging questions raised by these two encounters remained. Was Jesus just one among many first-century, itinerant holy men? What ancient sources and modern sources were available for investigating the historical Apollonius? Was Philostratus's biography of Apollonius an accurate depiction of the Tyanean?

PREFACE

In 2017, when Dr. Scott Gleaves—Dean of the Kearley Graduate School of Theology at Faulkner University—gave me a semester off to work on a research project, I began collecting materials for a book on Apollonius. I quickly discovered several things. First, I did not know as much about the Greco-Roman world as I thought; although I had a good grasp of the first century AD, it took several years for me to become familiar with the history and literature of the second and third centuries. The amount of classical scholarship about Apollonius and his biographer, Philostratus, was overwhelming. In addition to that barrier, progress on this book was slowed because many of these resources were written in German, Dutch, and French. Second, I realized that many New Testament scholars who had written about Apollonius were as unaware as I had been of the many difficult historical issues surrounding Apollonius of Tyana and of the classical research that had been written on this topic. It seemed to me that many professors and students in biblical studies also needed a guide to lead them through this vast and confusing area of study. Therefore, I wrote the book for them that I wish someone had written for me. Third, I discovered, to my great shame, that I had already encountered Apollonius many times before I read Mead's book. Many of the books in my library that I had read cover-to-cover mentioned the Tyanean, even though I could not recall reading about him. Perhaps some of my readers will find that they have also crossed paths with this ancient magician but have forgotten the encounter. I hope that this book will serve as a guide to those who are approaching Apollonius for the first time and for those who may need to approach him a second time to take a closer look.

Acknowledgments

This book is the product of the prayers and encouragement of numerous people. I am indebted to my father, Floyd O. Parker Sr., who surrounded me with hundreds of books in my early years and instilled in me a love for reading. My mother, Oleta, taught me to read, cleaned a church building with me to help pay for my college education, and encouraged me to take a master's level course in Bible, the course that set me on the path to earning a PhD in New Testament. These two were my first Bible instructors and role models. Their examples of faith, courage, perseverance, and marital commitment (even through Alzheimer's disease) have served as a beacon when the fog of life envelops me. They did not live to see the completion of this book, yet without them, it would not have been written.

I am tremendously grateful for the support of my extended family during the composition of this book. These dear people have prayed for the completion of this book and my health during my cancer treatments on the last leg of my publication journey. My children, siblings, their children, and their grandchildren have prayed for me regularly as I struggled to complete this project. Some, who shall remain nameless at their request, have even contributed financially to this project. A few of them read and offered advice in the earliest stages of the book's composition: my wife Angel, my daughter Jessica Parker, and my son-in-law Sam Boshell. Family is one of the greatest gifts in my life.

From an academic perspective, I would like to express my gratitude for my many teachers along the way. Larry Boling, my sixth-grade Sunday school teacher at Panama Street Church of Christ drilled me on the basic facts of the Bible and introduced me to the world of ancient

Egypt. Marie Echols (Alabama Christian High School), my high school history teacher, showed me that history could come alive in the hands of a master teacher and storyteller. At Southern Christian University (now Amridge University), Dr. John Mark Hicks always modeled excellence in the classroom, gave me the confidence to attempt a PhD, and set before me the goal of completing that degree before age thirty, as he had done. The teachings of Dr. Randall Bailey on the Psalms and Job have strengthened me and blunted my fears on many occasions, especially as cancer threatened to force me down into the valley of the shadow of death. The harsh tutelage and flaming eyes of Dr. Kalyon Dey (Drew University) taught me to get the facts straight before presenting a seminar paper. Dr. Herbert Huffmon (Drew University) gently mentored me and, through his infectious love of learning, instilled in me a deep interest in ancient Near Eastern religion, culture, and language. Some of these instructors are now dead. Of those who still live, most do not know that I was writing this book. Nevertheless, they paved the way for it.

Administrators are also worthy of my gratitude. I would like to thank my former Dean, Dr. Scott Gleaves (Faulkner University), who in 2017 encouraged me to write a book and granted me a semester off to conduct the initial research. I would also like to recognize my current president, Dr. Michael Turner (President of Amridge University) for his unwavering support in completing this book, encouraging me as I endured numerous chemotherapy infusions, and joining with me in several long and uncomfortable fasts prior to these treatments.

My list of supporters is long; time would fail me to tell of the students, friends, and librarians who have contributed to this book. I am grateful for the support of many of my former students, but two are worthy of note in accomplishing this project. Dr. David Stark (Faulkner University) graciously read an early draft of this manuscript, suggested several ideas that improved it, and encouraged me to press on toward its completion. Dr. Daniel Roberts (minister of the Cameron Avenue Church of Christ), who has recently published with Wipf and Stock, patiently answered my questions about the process of publishing with this company. Dr. Mark Sneed (Lubbock Christian University), my classmate at Drew University, showed me the ropes around campus in the late 1980s and, more recently, advised me as I sought a publisher for this manuscript. I am grateful for the help of the library staff at Faulkner University's Gus Nichols Library—especially Angie Moore and Lyla Broadway—for helping me find obscure texts and enduring endless interlibrary loan requests.

ACKNOWLEDGMENTS

Most of all, I am grateful for my wife Angel, the wife of my youth, who has listened to my complaints, doubts, and theories—often with feigned but loving interest. She has been my support and partner through this project and, as she promised me years ago, she has remained steadfast in sickness and in health ὅτι κραταιὰ ὡς θάνατος ἀγάπη (Song of Songs 8:6, LXX).

Abbreviations

AB	Anchor Bible
ABD	Anchor Bible Dictionary
ACME	Annali della Facoltà di Filosofia e Lettere dell'Università Statale di Milano
Aev	*Aevum: Rassegna de scienze, storiche, linguistiche, e filologiche*
AGJU	Arbeiten zur Geschichte des antiken Judentums und des Urchristentums
AJP	*American Journal of Philology*
AJT	*The American Journal of Theology*
ANF	Ante-Nicene Fathers
ANRW	Aufstieg und Niedergang der römischen Welt
BASP	*Bulletin of the American Society of Papyrologists*
BICS	*Bulletin of the Institute of Classical Studies*
BSR	*Bulletin for the Study of Religion*
ByzZ	*Byzantinische Zeitschrift*
Cels.	*Contra Celsum*
CJ	*Classical Journal*
ClAnt	*Classical Antiquity*
ClQ	*Classical Quarterly*
CQ	*Church Quarterly*
CSEL	Corpus Scriptorum Ecclesiasticorum Latinorum
CSHB	Corpus Scriptorum Historiae Byzantinae

ABBREVIATIONS

Demon.	*Demonax*
DJG	*Dictionary of Jesus and the Gospels*
DMBI	*Dictionary of Major Biblical Interpreters*
DLNT	*Dictionary of the Later New Testament and Its Developments*
ECNT	Evangelical Commentary on the New Testament
Epp. Apoll.	*Epistulae Apollonii* (*Letters of Apollonius*)
FBBS	Facet Books Biblical Series
GCRW	Greek Culture in the Roman World
GRBS	*Greek, Roman and Byzantine Studies*
Gymn.	*De gymnastica* (*Gymnasticus*)
Her.	*Heroicus*
Hier.	*Against Hierocles*
Hist. Aug.	*Historia Augusta* (*Augustan History*)
Hist. rom.	*Historia Romana* (*Roman History*)
HSCP	*Harvard Studies in Classical Philology*
Il.	*Ilias* (*Iliad*)
Imag.	*Imagines*
JAC	*Jahrbuch für Antike und Chistentum*
JBL	*Journal of Biblical Literature*
JCS	*Journal of Cuneiform Studies*
JETS	*Journal of the Evangelical Theological Society*
JHS	*Journal of Hellenic Studies*
JOCBS	*Journal of the Oxford Centre for Buddhist Studies*
JRH	*Journal of Religious History*
JRS	*Journal of Roman Studies*
JSNTSup	Journal for the Study of the New Testament Supplement Series
JTS	*Journal of Theological Studies*
LCL	Loeb Classical Library
Nat. an.	*De natura animalium* (*Nature of Animals*)
NICNT	New International Commentary on the New Testament
NIGTC	New International Greek Testament Commentary
NTS	*New Testament Studies*

ABBREVIATIONS

PG	Patrologia Graeca
PGM	*Papyri Graecae Magicae*
Phil	*Philologus*
Philops.	*Philopseudes* (*The Lover of Lies*)
Praep. ev.	*Praeparatio evangelica* (*Preparation for the Gospel*)
Quaest. conv.	*Quaestiones convivialum*
RE	Realencyklopädie für protestantische Theologie und Kirche
REA	*Revue des études anciennes*
SBLDS	Society of Biblical Literature Dissertation Series
SEERI	St. Ephrem Ecumenical Research Institute
Syr. d.	*De syria dea* (*The Goddess of Syria*)
TAPA	*Transactions of the American Philological Society*
TS	Texts and Studies
VA	*Vita Apollonii* (*Life of Apollonius*)
Ver. Hist.	*Vera Historia* (*True History*)
Vit. Phil.	*Vitae philosophorum* (*Lives of the Eminent Philosophers*)
VS	*Vitae sophistarum* (*Lives of the Sophists*)
WBC	Word Biblical Commentary
WUNT	Wissenschaftliche Veröffentlichungen der deutschen Orient-Gessellschaft
YCS	*Yale Classical Studies*
ZDMG	*Zeitschrift der deutschen morgenländischen Gesellschaft*
ZPE	*Zeitschrift für Papyrologie und Epigraphik*

Part 1

Introductory Issues

1

Introduction

Why Apollonius Matters

THE NAME APOLLONIUS OF Tyana is unlikely to ring a bell with many students of the Bible. Among the writers who have echoed this sentiment, two experts on Apollonius are particularly noteworthy. Bart Ehrman, a prolific New Testament scholar, assumes that those who attend his lectures and read his books have probably had no prior exposure to this ancient holy man.[1] Erkki Koskenniemi, who has written extensively about the Tyanean, suspects the same nescience within other groups: "The Cappadocian miracle worker Apollonius of Tyana is unknown to the ordinary reader of the Bible, and most pastors have forgotten that they ever read anything about him."[2] Most likely, ignorance concerning this ancient figure extends beyond the casual Bible student or pastor to include most biblical scholars, theologians, and church historians. A Bible professor might vaguely recall from a passage in a textbook or a graduate school lecture that Apollonius was a miracle-worker or philosopher, but, if put on the spot, would probably be hard-pressed to remember the sage's philosophical school, primary biographer, timeframe, miracles, or most faithful disciple.

Absolution should be quickly granted to anyone who might be ashamed of their ignorance on this topic for there are legitimate reasons

---

1. Ehrman, *Did Jesus Exist?*, 208; Ehrman, *How Jesus Became God*, 12; Ehrman, *The New Testament* (2016), 46.

2. Koskenniemi, "Apollonius of Tyana," 455.

why even well-read students of the Bible might be unacquainted with Apollonius. Perhaps the most likely reason for not knowing about him is that no pagan, Jewish, or Christian source from the first century AD mentions him. A further reason for overlooking him is that only a few New Testament scholars have conducted substantial research on Apollonius or his biographer, Philostratus, in recent times; many of the most insightful and detailed works touching on Apollonius belong to a long-forgotten era of biblical scholarship. To compound this problem, the German language, in which the bulk of these rare and detailed studies by biblical scholars have been written, erects an inadvertent barrier to many monolingual readers.[3] A final reason for not encountering Apollonius could be that those who seem to show the most interest in researching this figure work within the domain of classical studies rather than biblical studies. In contrast to the meager literary output of New Testament scholars in this area, classical scholars have produced a vast literature on both Apollonius and Philostratus.[4] Regrettably, these studies have apparently escaped the notice of many New Testament scholars, even some of those who have intentionally set out on a quest to find the Tyanean. These are but a few good reasons that account for why Apollonius is largely unknown to the current generation of churchgoers, students, and biblical scholars.

MAKING THE CASE FOR WHY APOLLONIUS MATTERS

At first blush, no persuasive reason presents itself for investing time in a study of Apollonius of Tyana. Since no first-century author took note of him, one might conclude that he was an insignificant figure. Most present-day lay readers have probably gotten along quite well in their Bible study without having ever heard of him and, if the literary output on Apollonius within academia serves as a gauge of his perceived value, many modern biblical scholars must also deem him irrelevant. Even instructors who are aware of Apollonius may find it difficult to justify lecturing extensively on the Tyanean or asking their students to invest time in reading an entire book or article about him when there are so

---

3. Baur, *Apollonius von Tyana*; Petzke, *Die Traditionen*; Koskenniemi, *Der philostrateische Apollonios*; Koskenniemi, *Apollonios*.

4. Meyer, "Apollonius von Tyana," 370–424; Phillimore, *In Honour*; Dzielska, *Apollonius*; Anderson, *Philostratus*; Flinterman, *Power*; Demoen and Praet, *Theios Sophistes*; Bowie and Elsner, *Philostratus*; Miles, *Philostratus*.

INTRODUCTION

many other ancient figures whose contributions to understanding the New Testament rank much higher than that of this seemingly peripheral figure (e.g., Josephus, Philo, Herod the Great, or Domitian). Of what value, then, is a study of Apollonius of Tyana to New Testament students or scholars? In truth, there are several excellent reasons for wanting to know about him.

Reason One: Apollonius Closely Resembles Jesus

Gospel scholars seem fascinated by figures from antiquity who resembled the Nazarene. The ancient Mediterranean world was peopled with miracle workers,[5] exorcists,[6] prophets,[7] sages,[8] itinerant teachers,[9] and divine humans[10] who resembled Jesus in some way or another. Yet, Apollonius and Jesus are unique in that their chroniclers attributed all the aforementioned roles to both of them.

There can be no disputing that Apollonius, at least as he is presented by Philostratus in his *Life of Apollonius* (hereafter referred to as the *VA*),[11] resembles Jesus more than any other person in antiquity. Both ancient figures were renowned holy men, miracle-workers, and teachers who lived in the first century AD. According to their respective biographers—the authors of the four canonical Gospels and Philostratus[12]—their mighty

---

5. E.g., Hanina ben Dosa (Ber. 1.9d, 34b; Maʿaś 5.56a; Eccl. Rab. 1), Honi the Circle Drawer (*Ant.* 14.22–29), and Simon Magus (Acts 8:9–24; Justin, *1 Apol.* 1.26).

6. E.g., Eleazar (Josephus, *Ant.* 8.46–48) and Simon b. Yoḥai (Meʿil 17b). See also Origen, *Cels.* 68.

7. E.g., John the Baptist (Josephus *Ant.* 18.116–119), the Samaritan (Josephus, *Ant.* 18.85–89), the Egyptian (Josephus, *Ant.* 20.169–171; Acts 21:38), Jesus ben Ananias (Josephus, *J.W.* 6.300–309), and Jonathan the Weaver (Josephus, *J.W.* 6.437–450).

8. E.g., Hillel the Elder and Gamaliel I.

9. E.g., Pythagoras (Iamblichus, *Vit. Pyth.*, 2–7), Empedocles (Diogenes Laertius, *Vit. Phil.* 8.61), Peregrinus (Lucian, *Pereg.*), and several unnamed itinerants (Plato, *Resp.*, 364b–365a).

10. E.g., Dionysus (Hesiod, *Theog.*, 940, Euripides, *Bacch.* 1, 90) and Caligula (Dio Cassius, *Hist. rom.* 59.24.4, 59.25–28.8).

11. *VA* will be used as the abbreviation for *Vita Apollonii*, the Latin title for Philostratus's *Life of Apollonius*. Although this work is sometimes abbreviated as *Vit. Apoll.*, the current study adopts the shorter and more commonly employed abbreviation, *VA*.

12. Although there are several earlier references to Jesus (e.g., Paul) and Apollonius (e.g., Lucian, Maximus of Aegae, and Moiragenes), the four Gospels and the *VA* are the earliest extant biographies of the two men.

deeds included raising a young girl from the dead,[13] casting out demons by merely speaking to them,[14] controlling the waves of the sea,[15] disappearing at will,[16] knowing the thoughts of others,[17] possessing knowledge of current events in remote places,[18] and foretelling future events.[19] Both men were unmarried.[20] Both were itinerant teachers,[21] who led a group of disciples.[22] Both figures on occasion taught in an enigmatic fashion to prevent the uninitiated from understanding their doctrines.[23]

---

13. Luke 8:40–42, 49–56; *VA* 4.45.

14. Mark 1:21–28; 9:25–27; *VA* 4.20.

15. Mark 4:35–41. *VA* 4.13 indicates that Apollonius was impervious to storms at sea.

16. Luke 24:31; Luke 4:30?; John 8:59?; *VA* 8.5.4.

17. Matt 9:4; 12:25; Luke 9:47; John 2:23–25; *VA* 1.19.2; 7.22.2.

18. John 1:48; *VA* 4.34.4; 8:25–27.

19. Matt 17:22–23; 24:1–2; John 2:19–22; 13:38; *VA* 4.6; 4.18.2; 4.24.2–3; 5.11; 5.18; 5:31; 6.32.2; 7:10.

20. Philostratus records that Apollonius was celibate (*VA* 1.13.3). The Gospels are silent on Jesus's marital status. However, the evidence seems to favor that Jesus was single for, had he been married, it is unlikely that his wife and children would have escaped mention in the Bible. A wife would have surely been mentioned along with his brothers (Acts 1:14), mother (Acts 1:14), male disciples (Mark 3:13–19; Acts 1:13), and female followers (Luke 8:1–3). Even though marriage was the norm for Jewish men of that era, there are several who were unmarried (Simon ben Azzai, some Essenes, and, presumably, John the Baptist) or who married late in life (Josephus, *Vita* 414–415, 427). The apostle Paul serves as another example of an unmarried Jewish man, at least at the time of his composition of 1 Corinthians (1 Cor 7:7–8; 9:5). Paul may have always been celibate, but it is also possible that he was a widower or that his wife had separated from him (perhaps due to his conversion to the Way). Clement of Alexandria argued that Paul was married (Eusebius, *H.E.* 3.30.1), although this was an unusual view among early Christian writers. Occasionally, the unproven claim is still circulated that Paul would have had to have been married because he was a member of the Sanhedrin (Acts 7:57). The difficulties with this argument are that (1) there is no certain evidence that the council required its members to be married during the time of Paul, (2) Acts does not explicitly state that Saul was a member of the Sanhedrin (Bruce, *Acts*, 180; Marshall, *Acts*, 150); even Saul's "casting a vote" against Stephen (Acts 26:10) is not clear proof of membership (Bruce, *Acts*, 443), and (3) a rabbinic passage (Sanh. 19a) indicates that members of the council had to be of advanced age; the description of Saul as a young man (Acts 7:57) would have barred Paul from being a member of this body, if this late rabbinic text preserves the first century requirements for membership.

21. Matt 4:23; Luke 8:1; 9:58; *VA* 6:18.

22. Mark 3:13–19; Koskenniemi discusses Apollonius's disciples in detail and collects the relevant passages ("Philostratean," 325–26). For passages discussing Apollonius's disciples, see *VA* 1.16, 1.19, 4.17, 20, 37, 39–40, 47; 5.43; 7.14; 8.31; *Epp. Apoll.* 42, 43, 77, 85, 92–93; Lucian, *Alex.* 5.

23. Matt 13:10–17, 34–35; *VA* 7.27.

INTRODUCTION

According to their chroniclers, some of the major episodes of their lives also mirrored each other. Celestial omens accompanied their nativities.[24] Both men were rejected by their own *patriae*,[25] accused by their opponents of using magic or demonic powers to perform wonders,[26] imprisoned with malefactors,[27] humiliated by Roman authorities,[28] and tried by Roman officials.[29] They invited their disciples to touch them as confirmation that they were not dead,[30] ascended into heaven,[31] and granted postmortem appearances to doubters as confirmation of their continuing existence.[32] A further significant similarity was that their followers regarded them as divine in some sense.[33] After all, each was rumored to be the offspring of a god.[34] So much do these two figures mirror each other that it is no wonder that some have referred to the Tyanean as a "pagan Christ,"[35] a "Hellenistic Christ,"[36] or even as "Apollonius the Nazarene."[37]

One would suspect that if the numerous similarities between Apollonius and Jesus were more widely known they would attract the attention of biblical scholars, Christian apologists, critics of Christianity, and historians interested in the first century AD. Yet, as it stands, Jesus is well known, being the subject of thousands of books and peer-reviewed articles, while Apollonius has faded into obscurity in most circles of scholarship. Academics who prefer a purely historical or literary approach to the study of antiquity would surely find Apollonius significant for research

---

24. Luke 1:11–38; Matt 2:2, 9–10; *VA* 1.4–5.

25. Luke 4:24; John 4:44; *Epp. Apoll.*, 44.

26. Matt 10:25; 12:24–28; *VA* 7.17.1

27. Mark 15:7; *VA* 7.34.

28. Mark 15:16–20; *VA* 7.34.

29. Mark 15:1–15; *VA* 35; 8.1–5.

30. The Gospels claim that Jesus offered his disciples an opportunity to touch his wounded body after his resurrection (Matt 28:9; Luke 24:39–40; John 20:27). Apollonius allowed his disciples to touch him to confirm that he had not died at the hand of Domitian (*VA* 8.12). Both figures presented their hands to their disciples to demonstrate that they were not ghosts or spirits (Luke 24:39; *VA* 8:12).

31. Luke 24:51; Acts 1:9; *VA* 8.30.2–3.

32. John 20:24–29; Acts 9:3–6; 22:6–10; 26:12–18; *VA* 8.31.

33. *VA* 3.15; 7.21; 7.38.2; 8.13.2.

34. *VA* 1.4 (Proteus), 1.6 (Zeus); Luke 1:32–35.

35. The subtitle of a book by Réville, *Apollonius of Tyana*, called the Tyanean the pagan Christ of the third century.

36. Copleston, *Greece and Rome*, 449.

37. One book about Apollonius by Bernard was entitled *Apollonius the Nazarene*.

in such topics as ancient philosophy, first-century holy men, and ancient biography. Christian apologists would likely be eager to distinguish the biblical sources about Jesus, which they believe accurately portray him, from Philostratus's *VA*, which they would probably dismiss as an exaggerated tale about the Tyanean. Similarly, skeptics, who reject the claims of Jesus's divinity, would find Apollonius useful in making the case that Jesus was not the only first-century figure whose disciples claimed their leader was a "divine man"; they might argue that either both men were supernatural figures, undermining Jesus's uniqueness, or both men were later mythologized by their disciples. Although the people engaged in biblical studies are a diverse lot, many of them would likely be interested in these similarities between the Tyanean and the Nazarene, the debates surrounding these two figures, and the nature of the sources that spoke of them if only they were aware of these issues.

A person's initial opinion about how Apollonius relates to Jesus will understandably be influenced by such things as their religious convictions (or lack thereof) and the first materials that they have read about him. Some readers will favor the view that both Apollonius and Jesus were mere men. Others will hold the position that Jesus was Lord, but that Apollonius was a liar and lunatic. Rarely, someone may attribute genuine paranormal abilities to Apollonius[38] or regard Apollonius as a genuine historical figure and Jesus as largely fictional.[39] A very few may contend that neither figure existed at all.[40] Whichever view a person initially favors, good historical methodology would dictate that an investigator become thoroughly familiar with all sides of the debates and complex issues related to Apollonian research before formulating a firm conclusion.

Reason Two: First Contact with Apollonius is Likely

In the last decade or so, Apollonius has begun to reemerge from the shadows. A resurgence of interest in Apollonius by a few New Testament scholars, especially in works intended for non-specialists, insures that contact with this ancient sage is more likely than ever before for the casual Bible student as well as for those at work in the academy and the church.

---

38. Mead, *Apollonius of Tyana*, 110–18.

39. Bernard, *Apollonius of Tyana: The Nazarene*, 7–68.

40. Price, *Deconstructing Jesus*, 15; Price, "Was There a Historical Apollonius of Tyana?," 4–40.

Apollonius is featured in several recent studies of the historical Jesus, such as in Reza Aslan's NYT bestseller *Zealot* and at least four widely-read works written by Bart D. Ehrman.[41] The former author contends that Apollonius, like Jesus, was viewed by his followers as a first-century wonderworker; the latter presents him, along with Jesus, as one of many figures of that age whose disciples regarded them as miracle-working sons of God.[42] Popular works like those written by Aslan and Ehrman, prominent in bookstores and highly ranked on online sites like Amazon, are where first contact with this Cappadocian holy man is most likely to take place for the nonspecialist.

In academia, however, a chance encounter with Apollonius has always been a possibility. Since Apollonius closely resembles Jesus in his roles as a first-century teacher, holy man, and miracle-worker, there are frequent points of contact between the two men in New Testament research. References to him are scattered over a wide range of older and current texts, all of which are still cited by scholars and make their way into bibliographies of books and assigned reading lists for university courses. An undergraduate student in biblical studies will likely first encounter the sage of Tyana in an introduction either to the New Testament[43] or to the Greco-Roman world,[44] where Apollonius is often trotted out as an example of a first-century holy man or the quintessential Neopythagorean philosopher. Yet, serendipitous meetings can also occur in more specialized areas of study. Apollonius is frequently referenced in historical Jesus research.[45] Due to his roles as a miracle-worker or sor-

---

41. Aslan, *Zealot*, 106; Ehrman, *The New Testament*, 44–46, 48, 99, 184, 252–53, 287–88; *A Brief Introduction*, 2004), 15–16, 22, 173, 174; Ehrman, *Did Jesus Exist?*, 208–10, 215, 217; Ehrman, *How Jesus Became God*, 11–12, 150.

42. Ehrman, *The New Testament*, 46, 48.

43. Norman Perrin, *The New Testament*, 316–17; Freed, *The New Testament*, 179–84; David L. Barr, *New Testament Story*, 226–27; Spivey et al., *Anatomy of the New Testament*, 2007, 195; Powell, *Introducing the New Testament*, 38–39; Johnson, *The Writings*, 2010, 25; Puskas and Robbins, *An Introduction*, 21; Boring, *An Introduction*, 149, 468, 511; Ehrman, *The New Testament*, 44–46, 48, 99, 184, 252–53, 287–88.; Landry and Martens, *Inquiry*, 56.

44. Cartlidge and Dungan, *Documents*, 205–8; Roetzel, *The World That Shaped*, 1985, 103; Koester, *Introduction*, 2:375–76; Martin, *Hellenistic Religions*, 111; Barrett, ed., *New Testament Background*, 82–85; Bell., *Exploring*, 175–76; Ferguson, *Backgrounds*, 226–27, 381–83.

45. Hengel, *The Charismatic Leader*, 9–10, 26–27, 29–30; Blomberg, *The Historical Reliability*, 83, 85–86, 89; Meier, *Mentor*, 576–81; Eddy and Boyd, *The Jesus Legend*, 151–54; Boyd and Eddy, *Lord or Legend*, 57–58.

cerer, he often appears in studies on such topics as miracles (or magic),[46] exorcism,[47] and the resurrection of the dead.[48] Studies on the genre, agendas, or formation of the Gospels sometimes refer to Philostratus's biography of Apollonius.[49] One might even cross paths with the Tyanean in oblique areas like Church history,[50] New Testament commentaries,[51] Pauline studies,[52] archaeology,[53] Greek language resources,[54] and, of course, apologetics.[55] Apollonius is frequently mentioned in academic writing. Yet, he may be easy to miss because he is normally mentioned in passing as an illustration of or support for some aspect of biblical studies, but he is rarely studied in detail as a historical figure.

Although this book will not deal with digital sources in any significant way beyond the material mentioned in this paragraph, Apollonius has a strong online presence. Although many of these sources are unscholarly, inaccurate, or heavily biased, a few gems can be spotted among the rubble. Platforms such as YouTube feature numerous videos about Apollonius. Some of these recordings compare Apollonius to Jesus,[56] while others mention him in debates between Christian apologists and

---

46. Kee, *Miracle*, 256–65; Luck, *Arcana Mundi*, 11, 35–36, 43, 103–7, 137, 153–56, 173, 238, 290, 302; Smith, *Jesus the Magician*, 84–93; Habermas, "Did Jesus Perform Miracles?," 117–40; Geivett and Habermas, *In Defense of Miracles*, 207–8; 211; Keener, *Miracles*, 1:30–31, 46, 48, 50–56, 66, 579; 2:782–83.

47. Ferguson, *Demonology*, 55–56; Twelftree, *Jesus the Exorcist*, 16, 21, 22–27, 46–48, 52, 70, 74, 96, 146, 148, 156–60, 227.

48. Wright, *The Resurrection*, 74–75; Licona, *The Resurrection of Jesus*, 146–47, 173, 178–79, 282.

49. Sanders and Davies, *Studying the Synoptic Gospels*, 293–94, 254–55, 269; Bird, *The Gospel of the Lord*, 49, 231, 233–34; Köstenberger, *A Theology*, 113–15. Burridge, *What Are the Gospels?*, 75, 116, 137, 151, 160, 165, 167, 172, 180, 184, 259, 324; Keener, *Christobiography*, 46–48.

50. Frend, *The Rise of Christianity*, 272, 275–76, 443, 479; MacMullen, *Christianizing the Roman Empire*, 17, 23; Chadwick, *The Early Church*, 110, 277; Fox, *Pagans and Christians*, 189, 191, 196, 245, 253–54.

51. Reimer, *Miracle and Magic: A Study of the Acts of the Apostles and the Life of Apollonius of Tyana*.

52. Georgi, *The Opponents of Paul*, 157–58; Bruce, *Paul*, 35, 239; Roetzel, *The Letters of Paul*, 24–25; Beker, *Paul the Apostle*, 115, 296; Hooker, *Paul: A Short Introduction*, 52.

53. Unger, *Archaeology*, 240; McRay, *Archaeology*, 235, 299, 304.

54. McLean, *Hellenistic and Biblical Greek*, 387–96.

55. Geisler, *The Big Book*, 23–24. Indeed, Apollonius even made a cameo appearance in G. K. Chesterton's work, *The Everlasting Man*, 205–6.

56. Winger, "The 'Other Jesus' Story," 56:40. Also see Horn, "Bart Ehrman's Bad Arguments," 4:50—8:09.

INTRODUCTION

their opponents.[57] An occasional podcast will focus on Apollonius as a historical figure.[58] Likewise, the social media network, Facebook, contains several pages dedicated to this ancient philosopher. Amazon Prime features a streamed video, *Bible Conspiracies*, that identifies Apollonius with Paul's companion Apollos (1 Cor 1:12) and argues that the facts from the life of the historical Apollonius were cobbled together by Christians to create the mythical story of Jesus.[59] The LibriVox Audiobooks collection is perhaps the most useful online tool to date since it provides a full reading of several of the primary texts: Philostratus's *The Life of Apollonius of Tyana*, the *Epistles of Apollonius*, and Eusebius's *Response to Hierocles*. These electronic materials demonstrate that a chance encounter with this mystic sage could even take place in cyberspace.

Reason Three: First Contact with Apollonius Is Likely to Be Unsettling

Quite possibly, the first encounter with the Tyanean will be unsettling for certain types of people. A person of the Christian faith, whether an undergraduate student or a church member, could understandably be disturbed by learning about this pagan counterpart to Christ because of the challenge Apollonius poses to Jesus's unique status. Some believers might even seek private counsel with their professor or pastor after hearing a class lecture or reading a passage about Apollonius. Thus, an educator or minister might benefit from some preparation in this area so

---

57. Ehrman, "Ehrman vs. Craig," 1:12:54—1:13:25.
58. Fontainelle, "Graeme Miles on Apollonius."

59. Gardiner, *Bible Conspiracies*. This factually challenged film tangles itself up in several historical contradictions within the first few minutes of it that are dedicated to Apollonius. The film asserts that no ancient historian of the Augustan age mentioned Jesus but fails to realize that this statement was also true concerning Apollonius. Indeed, Apollonius of Tyana is absent from the historical record for a far longer time than was Jesus; the Tyanean is first mentioned by Lucian in the second century AD and not again until the early third century. The narrator also mistakenly attributes Marcus Aurelius's philosophical instruction (*Meditations* 1.8) to Apollonius of Tyana rather than to Apollonius of Chalcedon, a Stoic philosopher (Dio Cassius, *Hist. rom.* 71.35; *Hist. Aug.* Antonius Pius, 10; Lucian, *Demon.* 3.31). An identification of this emperor's instructor with the Tyanean is also rendered impossible because Apollonius would have died (ca. AD 100) before Marcus Aurelius's birth (ca. AD 121). This video also attributes a quote about Apollonius's talismans to Justin Martyr (ca. AD 100–165), although Eusebius (ca. AD 312) was the first author to mention these magical devices (*Hier.*, 44.2).

that they may counsel or console those who have had their faith shaken by an encounter with this previously unknown figure. Likewise, a bit of advanced preparation would aid counselors in suggesting a few scholarly resources to those whose worldview has been challenged but who prefer to research Apollonius on their own.

In another scenario, the Tyanean might make a public appearance in the university classroom or a Sunday morning Bible study. Should Apollonius become the topic of discussion in either venue, the chances are good that this would make for a more disturbing experience than would a conversation about other extrabiblical figures such as Josephus or Philo of Alexandria. A first encounter with Apollonius might be exciting for some people, but unnerving for others. Such a situation might even become unsettling for a professor, who is suddenly thrust into the role of referee or blindsided by a barrage of questions about Apollonius from that rare, overzealous student who actually read the assigned chapter of the textbook on the topic of ancient philosophers or god-men. Even instructors who have no faith commitment might want to learn to handle aright the historical sources and claims about Apollonius, so that they might lead better classroom discussions, direct interested students to the best resources, and avoid making inaccurate statements about this complex topic. Perhaps most professors are prepared to field questions about Apollonius on the spot; most likely they are not. To be fair, no professor can be conversant on every topic that might arise during a class session or be prepared fully for how certain students may react to new information that might challenge their worldview. Yet, taking in a modicum of information about Apollonius in advance could be a good investment if there is a possibility that this pagan, holy man might visit the lecture hall.

One can only imagine the sorts of questions that students or church members might generate based on their first encounter with Apollonius, some of which may be driven by rage, confusion, or by genuine curiosity and excitement:

- Did Apollonius really exist?
- Can you provide me with a list of ancient sources that mention him?
- What do we know about his biographers, their historical veracity, and their agendas?
- Do the sources about Apollonius agree on the crucial details of his life?

- Can you recommend a few reliable books or seminal articles for me to read on this topic?
- Did other godmen like Apollonius and Jesus supposedly exist in the first century?
- Is Apollonius mentioned in the New Testament?
- Could the story of Jesus have been reliant upon that of Apollonius or vice-versa?
- Why hasn't my minister ever mentioned Apollonius?
- May I meet with you privately to discuss my recent crisis of faith?

Whether one works in an academic institution or a church environment the current book will supply its reader with fundamental background knowledge about Apollonius. It has the goal of providing answers to questions like those listed above and aiding curious instructors and students in conducting further research in this area.

Reason Four: Apollonius Is Valuable in His Own Right

Although most reader of this book are probably interested in how Apollonius compares to Jesus, the Tyanean is a fascinating figure to study in his own right. For instance, the extant sources are sometimes contradictory in their descriptions of and opinions about Apollonius, which invites the reader to determine the historical merit of each piece of evidence while formulating a theory of what the historical Apollonius was like. This study will discuss and evaluate these often-contradictory traditions about Apollonius. Likewise, an investigation of Philostratus, Apollonius's most famous biographer, compels a serious investigator to take a side concerning the historicity of his account, his claims that his account is truly based on an eyewitness source, and whether his agenda (or that of his imperial sponsor) may have had a major influence on the work. Furthermore, whatever one decides about the matters just mentioned, a researcher cannot help but be impressed by Philostratus's as an author, his enormous literary output, and his ability to compose both history and fiction. Finally, the *VA* is an important but often neglected piece of literature; it is the longest biography to have survived from ancient times, providing valuable insight into that genre, and it claims more about Apollonius of Tyana than any other source. In addition to these academic facts, it is a sheer delight to read. *Approaching Apollonius* will introduce the reader to the major issues in Apollonian scholarship, Philostratus the biographer, the Philostratean corpus, the *VA*, and the other ancient sources that reference Apollonius.

IMPROVING HOW WE TEACH ABOUT APOLLONIUS: LESSONS FROM *ONE REMARKABLE LIFE*

In this section, Bart Ehrman's clever piece, *One Remarkable Life*, will serve as a vehicle for illustrating several ways in which instructors and authors might improve on how they educate others about Apollonius of Tyana. In several of his books, Erhman has employed a variation of the passage entitled *One Remarkable Life*[60] to introduce Apollonius of Tyana to his students on campus[61] and to those who read his books:

> From the beginning his mother knew that he was no ordinary person. Prior to his birth, a heavenly figure appeared to her, announcing that her son would not be a mere mortal but would himself be divine. This prophecy was confirmed by the miraculous character of his birth, a birth accompanied by supernatural signs. The boy was already recognized as a spiritual authority in his youth; his discussions with recognized experts showed his superior knowledge of all things religious. As an adult he left home to engage in an itinerant preaching ministry. He went from village to town with his message of good news, proclaiming that people should forgo their concerns for the material things of this life, such as how they should dress and what they should eat. They should instead be concerned with their eternal souls.
>
> He gathered around him a number of disciples who were amazed by his teaching and his flawless character. They became convinced that he was no ordinary man but was the **Son of God**. Their faith received striking confirmation in the miraculous things that he did. He could reportedly predict the future, heal the sick, cast out demons, and raise the dead. Not everyone proved friendly, however. At the end of his life, his enemies trumped up charges against him; and he was placed on trial before Roman authorities for crimes against the state.

---

60. This title and the content of *One Remarkable Life* appear to imitate *One Solitary Life*, a poem based on a portion of a sermon preached by James Allen Francis in 1926 that detailed the significance of the life of Christ; Francis, *The Real Jesus*, 123–24.

61. Ehrman, *Did Jesus Exist?*, 208.

INTRODUCTION

> Even after he departed this realm, however, he did not forsake his devoted followers. Some claimed that he had ascended bodily into heaven; others said that he had appeared to them, alive, afterwards, that they had talked with him and touched him and become convinced that he could not be bound by death. A number of his followers spread the good news about this man, recounting what they had seen him say and do. Eventually some of these accounts came to be written down in books that circulated throughout the empire.
>
> But I doubt that you have ever read them. In fact, I suspect you have never heard the name of this miracle-working "Son of God." The man I have been referring to is the great neo-Pythagorean teacher and pagan holy man of the first century C.E., Apollonius of Tyana, a worshipper of the Roman gods whose life and teachings are still available for us in the writings of his later (third-century) follower Philostratus in his book, *The Life of Apollonius*.[62]

This cunningly crafted passage does several things well. The presentation of the material ensures a memorable introduction to Apollonius; at first, it appears to relate the familiar story of Jesus, but then, in a shocking reversal of expectations, reveals his pagan counterpart, Apollonius of Tyana. This piece also provides a novice with a fairly accurate[63] summary of Apollonius's life as it is presented in Philostratus's *VA*. In addition, it does a good job of underscoring the numerous similarities between Philostratus's version of Apollonius and the Jesus of the canonical Gospels. Yet, despite what *One Remarkable Life* does well by way of introducing and piquing interest in Apollonius, there are several things that it does not do well. A brief examination of its deficiencies will help to identify several obstacles that the neophyte is likely to encounter when studying

---

62. The version above is taken from Ehrman, *A Brief Introduction*, 15–16. Variant versions of this account appear in several of his books (*The New Testament*, 44–46; *Did Jesus Exist?*, 208; *How Jesus Became God*, 11–12).

63. Although largely correct, Ehrman is a bit off on a few of his statements about Apollonius. There are no accounts of Apollonius being touched by his disciples after his departure from earth. However, while he was still alive he appeared to Damis, who believed him to be dead, and Apollonius invited this disciple to touch him in confirmation that he was not a ghost (*VA* 8.12). Apollonius appeared in a dream to a young man after his departure, but there is no indication that he was physically touched in that account (*VA* 8.31). Further, there is no indication that Apollonius's disciples were convinced he was the "Son of God" for this title is never used in the *VA*. However, Philostratus reports that the people of Tyana referred to Apollonius as the son of Zeus (*VA* 1.6), and Damis, his closest disciple, was said to have become aware of Apollonius's divine nature at almost the end of his ministry (*VA* 7.38).

Apollonius and provide an opportunity to offer a few suggestions as to how future authors and instructors might fill in these gaps when teaching others about this ancient sage.

Obstacle One: The Lack of Full Disclosure about Critical Problems in the *VA*

One would expect that those who write and teach about Apollonius of Tyana would be both knowledgeable concerning the topic and would shoulder the burden of bringing their readers up to speed on key aspects of research in this field of study. As a rule, NT scholars, Ehrman included, do an excellent job of educating their readers about the important historical issues within their own discipline of biblical studies; their careful attention to such details can be observed in their meticulous treatment of the sources for the historical Jesus, Paul, and select extrabiblical figures. Therefore, in an introduction to the New Testament or a textbook on New Testament backgrounds, one would expect to find at least the same careful treatment when introducing the lesser-known extrabiblical figure Apollonius of Tyana. Such texts would be expected to provide a clear summary of his life and significance as well as broach a few of the critical issues currently debated by modern scholars. Even more attention to such issues is to be hoped for in detailed studies comparing the historical Apollonius to the historical Jesus in their roles as "divine men," holy men, or miracle workers. Scholars writing technical works about Apollonius would be expected to provide a comprehensive list of the ancient historical sources that mention him. In introducing these sources, an author should include a discussion of their dates, contents, veracity, and agendas so that these sources may be carefully investigated alongside similar data collected from the Gospels. Unfortunately, such expectations about the Apollonius research conducted by biblical scholars often do not match reality.

As the next chapter in this study will demonstrate, several of the articles and books that treat Apollonius that are produced by New Testament scholars do not communicate to their readers the vast number of historical and literary problems related to this topic. This curious phenomenon of passing over critical matters is difficult to explain. Perhaps the reason why some authors fail to disclose these issues to their readers is that they are unaware of them themselves. Perhaps others deem these matters will be too irrelevant, complex, boring, or distracting for their intended audience.[64] Hopefully, such omissions are not intentional. In the end, speculation is pointless about why these matters are often neglected, but that they are often overlooked is easily demonstrated, as chapter 2 will show.

Instead of sharing a brief critique of the historical veracity of the *VA* with their readers, most New Testament scholars who write about Apollonius simply provide the reader with a précis of Philostratus's biography. Such a synopsis of his *VA* helps orient the novice, but it is inadequate without some analysis of the historical merit of the document itself. As J. S. Phillimore, a classical scholar from a more plainspoken era writes, "The main questions at issue about Apollonius are questions of historical criticism; . . . any book which takes Philostratus' work at its face value and makes no inquiry about the author, his sources, his motives, and his times, is negligible for the discovery of the truth."[65] By merely summarizing the *VA* but not critiquing it for their readers, scholars risk giving the impression, perhaps inadvertently, that they accept the historical accuracy of the Philostratus's work. They also do a disservice to their readers, who are likely to be unaware of the historical problems with the *VA* or who may be somewhat informed about these matters but do not know where to begin conducting an examination of them on their own.[66] In either situation, those who are new to this topic would benefit from a little expert guidance from those who are introducing them to Apollonius.

---

64. The reasons for omitting a discussion of critical issues that were proposed above are largely unpersuasive, for many scholars who write about Apollonius and Jesus take up a good deal of space treating critical issues related to the New Testament and even sometimes briefly address such critical issues when teaching about extra-biblical topics. For instance, Ehrman frequently employs boxes or sidebars in his introduction that touch on historical figures (e.g., Alexander the Great, Josephus, Plutarch, Honi; Ehrman, *The New Testament*, 43, 70, 78, 99) and ancient texts (e.g., the Septuagint, the *Gospel of the Ebionites*, the *Epistle of Barnabas*, and the *Martyrdom of Polycarp*; Ehrman, *The New Testament*, 65, 217, 488, 509). In these text boxes he discussed the political agenda of Josephus and the origin—both historical and legendary—of the Septuagint (Ehrman, *The New Testament*, 65, 70). Such a sidebar would have been ideal for introducing a few of the historical issues of the *VA* and Philostratus's agendas for writing it.

65. Phillimore, *In Honour*, v–vi.

66. Even Ehrman, who warns of the possibility of legendary accretion in the *VA*, ends up presenting a summary of the historical Apollonius that is essentially the same as that of Philostratus, minus the supernatural and mythical elements. See Ehrman, *How Jesus Became God*, 13.

PART 1: INTRODUCTORY ISSUES

The "Socratic problem" (or "Socratic question") provides an extrabiblical example of why a biographical summary of a historical figure is often insufficient in trying to reconstruct a figure from the past. Most studies of Socrates do not merely summarize the views that Plato attributed to his master or assume that the Platonic dialogues preserve the most accurate information on his life or teaching.[67] Rather, responsible researchers will communicate to their readers that one must (1) take into account the sometimes confusing and contradictory perspectives about Socrates that were recorded by other writers of his day,[68] (2) recognize and attempt to account for the apparent contradictions within Plato's dialogues where Socrates defended one position in a dialogue and a contrary view in another,[69] and (3) interact with or at least mention some of the major modern theories that have attempted to solve the Socratic problem. After such a brief tutorial, the neophyte will have been alerted to several options: Plato may have accurately passed on the teaching of Socrates, only the earliest strata of Plato's writings may represent the ideas of his master, or Plato may have shaped Socrates into a mouthpiece for his own ideas. This example makes clear why an accurate summary of the life and teachings of Socrates would be incomplete without mentioning the historical problems involved in this area of study.

Like in the case of Socrates, studies about Apollonius ought to pose questions about biographical sources. Is Philostratus the sole voice concerning Apollonius or did others from antiquity speak about him? On what points do available sources agree or disagree with each other about this historical figure? Did Philostratus turn Apollonius into a mouthpiece for some of his own political or religious views (or those of his patron)? Hopefully, by now it has become clear that it is inadequate to merely

---

67. For examples of such a treatment of the "Socratic problem," see Copleston, *Greece and Rome*, 1:99–104; Nails, "Socrates," para. 7–16.

68. For instance, Xenophon, Aeschines of Sphettos, Antisthenes, and Aristippus of Cyrene were disciples of Socrates; all of these men wrote about Socrates. Other important sources for reconstructing Socrates are Aristotle—a student of Plato—and Aristophanes, who was a critic of Socrates and happens to be the earliest source of all. Motto demonstrates the importance of listening to multiple voices when evaluating ancient figures: "Think of the barren image we should have of Socrates, had the works of Plato and Xenophon not come down to us and were we wholly dependent upon Aristophanes' description of this Athenian philosopher. To be sure, we should have a highly distorted, misconstrued view. Such is the view left to us of Seneca, if we were to rely upon Suillius alone" (Motto, "Seneca on Trial," 257).

69. Nails, "Socrates," para. 14–16.

INTRODUCTION

summarize Philostratus's version of Apollonius without at least alerting the reader to a few of the historical issues that plague it.

It is rather odd that the same New Testament scholars that are so energetic and thorough in their investigation of the historical sources about Jesus,[70] often do not conduct equally rigorous investigations of the Apollonian sources. The consequences of neglecting these matters are severe. Whether intended or not, such an approach grants Philostratus's biography of Apollonius a privileged status over the sources for Jesus in historical comparisons of the two figures. When the *VA* gets a free pass in terms of its veracity, but the Gospel materials are heavily interrogated, this practice risks creating the impression that the former is an example of a good biography, while only the latter material about Jesus is problematic. A more equitable approach is to examine rigorously the historical sources for both Apollonius and Jesus.

Rather than perpetuating such asymmetrical treatments of the historical sources used for understanding these two figures, New Testament scholars would do better to apprise their readers of the historical problems within the *VA* and perhaps even attempt to grapple with a few of them. Below is a sampling of a few matters that an author could present that would aid the uninitiated reader in making an initial assessment of the veracity of the Philostratus's *VA* as a historical source:

- Some ancient sources before and contemporaneous with Philostratus's *VA* contradict his portrayal of Apollonius on several points.
- The *VA* claims to be based on the diary of Damis, a first-century disciple of Apollonius, yet it is riddled with numerous historical and geographical errors that challenge this claim of eyewitness testimony.
- Although a minority of scholars believe that Damis's memoir was an actual document (or a pseudepigraph), the majority believe that Philostratus was the true author of the material that he attributed to Damis.
- The *VA* contains a menagerie of magical beasts (e.g., unicorns, a phoenix, a satyr, gigantic snakes that can drag away elephants, and serpents with magic jewels in their heads) and recounts supernatural phenomena (e.g., a talking tree, a talking statue of a pharaoh,

---

70. Most critical scholars evaluate Gospel claims of apostolic authorship, critique claims of eyewitness testimony, investigate the various Gospel sources, and point out historical improbabilities and contradictions.

and two vampires), thus raising the question of whether the work was intended as fiction or as a serious biography.

- Philostratus wrote his work over a century after the death of the historical Apollonius, thus allowing for the possibility of the legendary accretion in oral and written sources about this figure.[71] This raises the question of whether Philostratus's third-century portrayal of Apollonius is an accurate description of the historical Apollonius who lived in the first century.

- Some scholars suggest that Philostratus, perhaps at the direction of his imperial patron Julia Domna, may have intended the *VA* as anti-Christian propaganda–perhaps consciously modeling Apollonius's life on earlier biographies about Jesus–or that he may have distorted the historical Apollonius to align him with his preferred religious or philosophical agendas.

Readers of this book who are just now coming to learn about Apollonius should pause to ask themselves whether they would have preferred reading a summary like *One Remarkable Life* by itself or whether they would have liked this passage to have been supplemented afterward by a few issues like those mentioned in the list above. More likely than not, readers will agree that this additional information is valuable in thinking through the historical value of Philostratus's account. Further, a list like this might take some of the shock out of the initial encounter with Apollonius for some Christian students. An approach that combines a summary of the *VA* with an evaluation of its claims would appear to be a more helpful way to introduce the man from Tyana than merely giving an unexamined summary of Philostratus's biography. To alter the Socratic dictum, an unexamined "Life"—understood in the sense of a biography—is not worth reading, at least if one is seeking solid historical information. As the most frequently consulted source of information about Apollonius, the *VA* must be subjected to the same rigorous historical analysis as the Gospels have been.

The importance of asking historical questions like these about the *VA* can be illustrated by revisiting *One Remarkable Life*. In its context, this passage prepares the way for Ehrman's assertions that belief in divine humans was common in antiquity and that Jesus was just one of many

---

71. To his credit, Ehrman does address this issue after presenting a version of *One Remarkable Life* in his *Did Jesus Exist?*, 288.

figures believed by ancient folk to be sons of God. Ehrman's assertions may be correct, yet without demonstrating a few fundamental historical points, his arguments become vulnerable. Since the *VA* was composed so much later than the Gospels, sometime after AD 217, how can Ehrman know for certain that the stories about Apollonius embedded in this biography date to the first century rather than to the second or third centuries? Since the *VA* postdates the canonical Gospels, how can Ehrman be certain that Philostratus has not consciously or unconsciously modeled the events of Apollonius's life after the stories of Jesus? To his credit, Ehrman does mention this latter possibility in an endnote in one of his studies, but he neither pursues this topic nor seems to view it as a challenge to his hypothesis.[72] Since, as Ehrman claims, Apollonius and Jesus were the only two examples of "divine men" in which previously existing deities had taken up residence,[73] what would happen to this aspect of the "divine man" model if Philostratus's account of Apollonius proved to be unhistorical and Jesus remained as its sole representative of this category? Further, since the *VA* contains many historical errors and legendary elements, what criteria would Ehrman recommend to his students for separating the historical wheat from the fictional chaff so that a more accurate picture of Apollonius could be reconstructed? In at least one work, immediately following a version of *One Remarkable Life*, Ehrman distinguished between Philostratus's tale about Apollonius and the different description of Apollonius that is generally agreed upon by scholars of Roman religion, but he did not indicate the method he used to detect and "to weed through the later legendary accretions" in the story of Apollonius.[74] These are fundamental historical questions that a reader may have. *One Remarkable Life* is remarkably silent on all such matters.

Obstacle Two: *One Remarkable Life* Lacks Follow-up Resources for Further Research

A reading of *One Remarkable Life* generates many fascinating questions about Apollonius, but it offers little guidance to those who want to find satisfying answers to these same queries. Ehrman, to his credit, lists two primary sources, but he does not include all the primary materials available

---

72. Ehrman, *How Jesus Became God*, 373.
73. Ehrman, *How Jesus Became God*, 18.
74. Ehrman, *How Jesus Became God*, 13.

for Apollonius (the *Letters of Apollonius*), lists no secondary literature at all to assist the interested reader in follow-up research,[75] and does not interact with the writings of other New Testament scholars or classicists on this topic. Although generating a bibliography on an unfamiliar topic is not difficult for those who have been trained to conduct research, it might prove a daunting task to someone new to this area of scholarship. Those unfamiliar with the topic of *Apollonica* (Apollonian studies) would find a cursory list of primary and secondary sources helpful as they begin their research. Indeed, secondary material is crucial for acquainting the beginner with the multiplicity of ancient opinions about Apollonius, the sources used by Philostratus in composing the *VA*, Philostratus's reason for writing the biography, and the debate over the historical accuracy of *VA*. Access to good academic resources early on would also aid the beginner in formulating a sound methodology for research.

Obstacle Three: *One Remarkable Life* Does Not Note the Differences Between Jesus and Apollonius

At first glance, the lives of Apollonius and Jesus appear to mirror each other concerning the most minute details, as Ehrman's *One Remarkable Life* seeks to illustrate. Yet, just as the image in a mirror appears to be flipped from the perspective of the observer, so also Jesus and Apollonius can appear as opposites. *One Remarkable Life* focuses only on the similarities between these two holy men, obscuring the truth that their biographers often indicate that they were opposite from or dissimilar to each other in several rather profound ways.

Jesus and Apollonius were born into different worlds and had different upbringings. In terms of race and religion, Jesus was a Jew who revered the one God of Israel,[76] whereas Apollonius was a gentile, who revered the traditional Greek gods but emphasized the worship of the supreme god.[77] They also differed in social status: Jesus was born into a

75. Ehrman mentions only two works in his various treatments of Apollonius, both of which are versions of the *VA*. The first work he mentioned was a Loeb Classical Library translation of Philostratus's *VA*. This translation is accompanied by an introduction that addresses several of the key historical problems, but Ehrman did not alert the reader to the presence of this additional information. The second work he refers to was by Cartlidge and Duncan, *Documents*, which he cites in two works (*The New Testament*, 59; *Did Jesus Exist?*, 357).

76. Matt 22:37.

77. Porphyry, *Abst.* 2.34.2; Eusebius, *Praep. ev.* 4.12–13.

peasant home,[78] while Apollonius was born into great wealth, which he later chose to renounce.[79] In terms of education, Apollonius had several instructors along the way,[80] but Jesus, so far as the Gospels indicate, had none.[81] Apollonius was the more privileged of the two figures.

Their messages and lifestyles were also distinct. Jesus's mission was to announce the coming kingdom of God to the Jews, whereas Apollonius sought to restore the correct practices of the Greek cults in the numerous cities he visited. The two sages used different methods to select their disciples: Jesus selected his own,[82] while Apollonius's followers sought him out as their master.[83] Their diets were also dissimilar in some ways: Apollonius was a vegetarian and abstained from strong drink,[84] while Jesus occasionally partook of animal flesh and wine.[85] As to miracles, Jesus reportedly expelled many demons[86] and performed multiple resurrections;[87] Apollonius, although famous for various other wonders, performed only one exorcism and one resurrection.[88]

The geographical extent and length of their ministries differed significantly as well. In contrast to Jesus, who conducted most of his ministry in Galilee and only occasionally ventured to Jerusalem and its environs during major feasts, Apollonius visited the major cities of the Roman Empire and reached the boundaries of the known world, traveling as far

78. Luke 2:22–24 (cf. Lev 12:8).

79. *VA* 1.13.2

80. Apollonius's teachers were Euthydemus (*VA* 1.7.1), Euxenus (*VA* 1.7.2–1.8.1), the Arabs (*VA* 1.20), the Babylonian *magoi* (*VA* 1.26), and the Indian Brahmans (*VA* 3.11–49). See Koskenniemi, "Philostratean," 324.

81. John 7:14–15; Acts 4:13. Some scholars suggest that Jesus was a disciple of John the Baptist. It is doubtful, even if this were true, that John would have been regarded as a teacher in a formal sense of the word rather than as a prophet, hermit, or preacher.

82. Mark 1:20; Matt 9:9.

83. *VA* 1.19.2; 6.15–17.

84. *VA* 1.8, 21.3.

85. For Jesus's consumption of animal flesh, see Luke 22:7–8, 11, 15; 24:42–43. For his drinking—or making—wine, see Luke 7:34, 22:17–20, and John 2:1–11. Although some have claimed that Passover wine was unfermented because of the feast's prohibition of yeast, this prohibition only applied to certain grains—wheat, rye, oats, spelt, and rye—and thus wine was not considered a leavened product.

86. Mark 1:21–28; 5:1–20; 7:24–30; 9:14–29; Matt 12:28–29.

87. Luke 7:11–17; 8:40–56; John 11:1–44.

88. In *VA* 4.45, Apollonius may have raised a maiden from the dead, although Philostratus was open to the possibility that the girl was still alive. The *VA* also mentions two exorcisms (*VA* 3.38; 4.20).

east as India,[89] as far west as the Pillars of Hercules in Spain,[90] and as far south as the third cataract of the Nile.[91] During his travels, Apollonius hobnobbed with some of the most famous people of his day: Emperors (e.g., Nero, Vespasian, Titus, and Domitian), philosophers (e.g., Dio of Prusa, Euphrates), foreign kings, and Roman governors.[92] By way of contrast, Jesus's contacts were limited to figures of lesser import in Judea and Galilee, such as Jewish religious officials,[93] Herod Antipas,[94] and Pontius Pilate.[95] Although Jesus's ministry was brief, usually reckoned to be about three years, the career of Apollonius spanned most of the first century AD. Despite the brevity of Jesus's mission, his movement eventually grew into a major world religion that still exists today. Apollonius, however, founded no lasting movement,[96] is revered today by only a few Theosophists and New Agers, and has been all but forgotten even in academic circles.

Although *One Remarkable Life* draws attention to the similarities of the final days of these two figures, there are also stark contrasts between how their missions ended. During his trial, Jesus remained largely silent before the high priest, Herod Antipas, and Pilate,[97] whereas Apollonius not only spoke during his defense but composed a speech—which he did not have an opportunity to deliver—that took up the better part of one book of the *VA*.[98] Unlike Jesus, who was tried and crucified by the Romans, Apollonius supposedly disappeared during his Roman trial and resumed his travels. Jesus died in his thirties,[99] whereas Apollonius may have lived to be a hundred years old.[100] The Gospel narratives assert that Jesus died, was buried, and rose from the dead in Jerusalem,[101] while Philostratus sets forth three separate traditions about how and where Apollonius met his

89. *VA* 2.4–3.50.
90. *VA* 5.1.1–5.
91. *VA* 6.26.1–2.
92. *VA* 5.1.10.
93. Matt 26:57–65; John 18:13, 24.
94. Luke 23:8–11.
95. Mark 15:1–15; John 18:28—19:16.
96. Koskenniemi, "Philostratean," 326.
97. Matt 26:62–63, 27:12–14; Mark 14:60–61, 15:4–5; Luke 23:9; John 19:9–10.
98. *VA* 8.5–7.
99. Luke 3:23.
100. *VA* 1.14.2. Philostratus recorded variant traditions that claimed Apollonius died when he was eighty, over ninety, or a hundred years old (*VA* 8.29).
101. Luke 24:18–24.

end.¹⁰² The story of Jesus ends with an empty tomb and resurrection; the tale of Apollonius ends with no tomb at all (*VA* 8.31.3).

Considering the similarities and differences that exist between Jesus and Apollonius, it is difficult to decide whether these sages are spitting images of each other or rather "splitting" images. *One Remarkable Life* frames the story of Apollonius so that it resembles the life of Jesus, yet when their differences are included, Jesus and Apollonius are certainly more distinct. *One Remarkable Life* certainly captures one's attention. Yet, as an accurate summary of the *VA* (and, by implication, the story of Jesus as told in the Gospels) it should perhaps be renamed *One Half of One Remarkable Life*, for, to modify the words of the Queen of Sheba, "the (other) half" of the story "has not been told."

THE PURPOSE OF THIS BOOK

The overarching purpose of *Approaching Apollonius* is to equip the reader with the tools necessary for understanding or researching Apollonius of Tyana, whether one is interested in studying him as a historical figure in his own right or in conducting a comparison of the historical Apollonius to the historical Jesus.

More specifically, this study seeks to determine whether Philostratus's biography is a reliable historical source and whether his portrayal of the historical Apollonius as a philosopher and holy man is more accurate than the alternative picture of him as a charlatan and magician preserved by the earlier authors (e.g., Lucian and Moiragenes) and sources contemporaneous with Philostratus (i.e., Dio Cassius). This new study is significant in that it questions the commonly held assumption in biblical studies that the *VA* is the most reliable guide for investigating the historical Apollonius. This research also asks to what extent the *VA* should still be utilized in the exploration of first-century topics such as the historical Jesus, "divine men," miracles, and other topics ancillary to biblical studies.

In this study, the exploration of the Apollonius of Tyana is broken into three parts.

Part One demonstrates the importance of a proper understanding of Apollonius in New Testament research, highlights obstacles a novice may encounter in Apollonian studies, and reviews past scholarly

---

102. *VA* 8.30.1–3.

PART 1: INTRODUCTORY ISSUES

successes and failures in this endeavor. This section also demonstrates that there is often a lack of rigor in the way in which Apollonius is taught today in biblical studies. The current chapter, chapter 1, has already made the case that, although Apollonius is likely to be unknown to most contemporary scholars, he resembles Jesus more than any other first-century figure and is therefore worthy of study. This chapter also discussed obstacles to learning about Apollonius and introduces the objectives of this book. Chapter 2 identifies ten criteria (the Apollonian Decalogue), a list of ten vital issues about Apollonius often cited by classical scholars who study Apollonius, and surveys thirty-one works written by New Testament scholars to see how often these ten items are mentioned in their discussions about Apollonius. After demonstrating that New Testament authors often fail to note these criteria, the chapter makes recommendations for how researchers can do a better job of teaching about Apollonius in the future. Chapter 3 conducts a chronological survey of Apollonian studies from Antiquity until modern times. The primary goals of this chapter are to (1) demonstrate how the picture of Apollonius in the *VA* has dominated scholarly research on Apollonius from antiquity down to the present day (mostly to the exclusion of other ancient sources), (2) acquaint the reader with seminal works in Apollonius research whose findings have sometimes been overlooked or ignored by New Testament scholars, and (3) note when the ten items included in the Apollonian Decalogue were proposed in the history of research.

Part Two of this study introduces the reader to Philostratus and the entirety of his writings while showing how some of the agendas and trends found in his other writings may question the historicity of his biography about Apollonius. Chapter 4 examines the rulers of the Severan dynasty that Philostratus served, discusses his profession as a sophist, and concludes with a biographical sketch. Chapter 5 provides a brief introduction to eight works of Philostratus's literary corpus (*Lives of the Sophists, Heroicus, Gymnasticus, Nero, Erotic Letters, Imagines I,* and two brief discourses) and demonstrates how an awareness of the contents of his broader corpus assists in evaluating the historicity of the *VA*. Chapter 6 introduces Philostratus's biography of Apollonius, the *VA*, treating issues of its origin, date, genre, and intended audience. Chapter 7 summarizes the *VA* for those who have never read it or need a quick review of its contents.

Part Three takes on the task of addressing the ten crucial issues, identified in chapter 2, that scholars should touch upon when dealing with Apollonius. Chapter 8 examines the pre-Philostratean sources and sources contemporary with Philostratus that mention Apollonius but that were not mentioned or utilized by Philostratus in the composition of the *VA*. This study notes the similarities and differences between the portrayal of Apollonius in these sources and the *VA*. Chapter 9 examines the pre-Philostratean sources that mention Apollonius and were utilized in the composition of the *VA*, while noting the similarities and differences between the portrayal of Apollonius in these sources and the *VA*. Chapter 10 discusses whether Damis, the alleged disciple of Apollonius, and his first-century diary truly existed. Chapter 11 catalogs and evaluates the major historical and geographical errors within the *VA*. Chapter 12 addresses whether the philosophical, pagan religious, and political agendas of Philostratus or his patron, Julia Domna, altered his portrayal of Apollonius. Chapter 13 determines whether the *VA* had an anti-Christian agenda and whether the *VA* borrowed New Testament texts or ideas. Chapter 14 discusses whether the chronological gap between Apollonius and Philostratus was too great for the latter to have written an accurate biography of the sage. Chapter 15, discusses the findings of the entire study.

Part Four of the study treats Apollonius and Jesus. Although these two figures are compared and contrasted in the earlier chapters of the book, chapter 16 sharpens the study by comparing the historical materials about Apollonius to those available about Jesus with respect to their (1) quantity (do sufficient sources exist so that traditions can be compared to one another?), (2) date (were the sources composed near to the time of the events they describe?), (3) independence (did the authors of these works collude with other sources?), (4) consistency with other traditions (do the sources contradict one another?); (5) internal consistency (does a source contradict itself?), and (6) biases (are the sources relatively free of bias?).[103]

This work is primarily intended for professors and students in Biblical studies who are interested in learning about Apollonius of Tyana, but it may also be of interest to classical scholars, ministers, apologists, or even the curious layperson. The book is written in non-technical language so that the non-specialist can read it and get the lay of the land while approaching Apollonian studies. All quotations from foreign languages have been limited to the footnotes or have been translated when they appear in the text to make this information accessible to a broader readership.

103. These criteria were proposed by Ehrman for the evaluation of ancient, historical sources (Ehrman, *The New Testament*, 236).

PART 1: INTRODUCTORY ISSUES

No monograph in the English language is aimed either at introducing professors and students in biblical studies to Apollonian studies in general or at discussing the role of Apollonius within the context of biblical studies.[104] Although classical scholars have authored books about Apollonius and Philostratus, these texts are normally written for specialists and infrequently engage with biblical materials and themes. While New Testament scholars sometimes mention Apollonius in their books and articles, these treatments are usually brief and tend to mine his biography to illustrate topics in biblical studies rather than providing a systematic introduction to the sage and the other ancient sources that reference him. *Approaching Apollonius* (1) provides a thorough introduction to Apollonian studies, Philostratus and his corpus, and the VA, (2) investigates whether the VA should be regarded as a reliable source for studying the historical Apollonius, (3) sets Apollonius within the context of biblical studies, especially concerning his relationship to the historical Jesus, and (4) provides numerous resources for follow-up research.

---

104. Only two monographs, to my knowledge, have been written on Apollonius as he relates to New Testament studies. One of these is fifty-five years old (Petzke, *Die Traditionen*) and the other is thirty (Koskenniemi, *Apollonios von Tyana*). Both of these works were written in German.

2

Devising Criteria for the Apollonian Decalogue

DEVELOPING CRITERIA FOR WHAT STUDENTS (AND SOME OF THEIR PROFESSORS) NEED TO KNOW

WHAT SHOULD BE THE criteria for selecting the central issues that scholars should mention when writing or teaching about Apollonius? On the one hand, these issues are not difficult to identify for they are of the same sort as those normally employed by historians in examining any ancient biblical or classical source. Scholars in both fields normally evaluate the primary texts in terms of their authorship, date, sources, recipients, and agendas. On the other, fine-tuning such a list of critical issues so that it addresses problems unique to the study of Apollonius and Philostratus is more challenging. Fortunately, Apollonius researchers have already done the heavy lifting for this portion of the project; they have been fine-tuning the most crucial questions for over a century, even though they have not always agreed upon the answers to them. The criteria for what to teach or what questions to ask about Apollonius should be formulated from the data highlighted by these specialists.

PART 1: INTRODUCTORY ISSUES

THE APOLLONIAN DECALOGUE: TEN ITEMS "THOU SHALT TEACH" ABOUT APOLLONIUS

Numerous technical studies on the Tyanean provide their readers with a brief orientation that includes a history of research and a discussion of several key controversial issues. Presumably such information is routinely provided because the authors suspect that their readers are unfamiliar with it. If Apollonius scholars deemed such precautions necessary for the benefit and guidance of fellow classicists or biblical scholars, who were likely to be familiar with the history and literature of the ancient world already, it becomes all the important for current authors to provide such information to their readers, some of whom—undergraduates or lay readers—are unprepared to negotiate the critical minefields of this arcane region of scholarship.

These specialists in Apollonian scholarship have customarily informed their readership of several of the following issues, hereafter referred to in this study as the Apollonian Decalogue:

1. Apollonius is mentioned by a few sources that are earlier than (Lucian) or contemporary with (Dio Cassius) Philostratus's *VA*.[1] These sources were not mentioned by Philostratus.

2. Some of these sources disagreed with Philostratus's positive portrayal of Apollonius (both Lucian and Dio Cassius disparaged Apollonius as a magician and charlatan).[2]

3. Philostratus relied upon several earlier sources in the composition of his biography of Apollonius (the biographical materials of Maximus of Aegae and Moiragenes).[3]

---

1. In classical studies see, Phillimore, *In Honour*, l–lv; Bowersock, Introduction to *Life of Apollonius*, 11; Dzielska, *Apollonius*, 85–91; Francis, *Subversive Virtue*, 86; Anderson, *Philostratus*, 123–24; 185–90; Philostratus, *Apollonius of Tyana*, 1:4, 17; Harris, "Apollonius of Tyana," 189–90; Taggart, "Apollonius," 33–44; Flinterman, *Power*, 67, 72, n. 73. In NT studies see, Petzke, *Die Traditionen*, 154–55; Koskenniemi, *Apollonios*, 3–6, 177; Koskenniemi, "The Philostratean Apollonius," 322, 330.

2. Phillimore, *In Honour*, li–lii, liv–lvi; Bowersock, Introduction to *Life of Apollonius*, 11; Dzielska, *Apollonius*, 91; Anderson, *Philostratus*, 138; Francis, *Subversive Virtue*, 86, 90; Philostratus, *Apollonius of Tyana*, 1:4; Ferguson, *The Religions*, 181; Taggart, "Apollonius," 42; Petzke, *Die Traditionen*, 155; Koskenniemi, *Apollonios*, 5; Koskenniemi, "The Philostratean Apollonius," 330–31.

3. Phillimore, *In Honour*, xxii–xxix; Philostratus, *The Life of Apollonius*, 1.vi; Bowersock, Introduction to *Life of Apollonius*, 10–11, Dzielska, *Apollonius*, 130, 185; Anderson, *Philostratus*, 123–24; Francis, *Subversive Virtue*, 86; Philostratus, *Apollonius*

4. Philostratus differed strongly from Moiragenes's perspective on Apollonius, which resulted in his disparagement of that source.[4]

5. Scholars disagree concerning the veracity of Philostratus's claim that he had access to the memoirs of a first-century eyewitness and disciple of Apollonius named Damis.[5]

6. Numerous verifiable historical and geographical errors appear in the VA.[6]

7. Researchers debate whether the philosophical, political, pagan religious, or literary agendas of Philostratus or the Empress Julia Domna, his patroness, may have influenced the portrayal of Apollonius in the VA.[7]

8. Scholars disagree over whether the VA was intended as a counterblast to the Gospels or Christianity.[8]

---

of Tyana, 1:4, 7; Harris, "Apollonius," 191; Taggart, "Apollonius," 62–98; Flinterman, Power, 68–70; Petzke, Die Traditionen, 65, 73; Koskenniemi, Apollonios, 5, 175–78.

4. Phillimore, In Honour, xxiv–xxv; Philostratus, The Life of Apollonius, 1:vii, viii; Bowersock, Introduction to Life of Apollonius, 11; Dzielska, Apollonius, 44, 88, 185. Anderson, Philostratus, 123; Francis, Subversive Virtue, 86, 94–95; Harris, "Apollonius," 191–92; Taggart, "Apollonius," 62; Flinterman, Power, 69–70; Petzke, Die Traditionen, 67, 155; Koskenniemi, Apollonios, 170, 175–76.

5. Gildersleeve, Essays, 260; Phillimore, In Honour, xxvii–xxix, cxvii–cxix; Philostratus, The Life of Apollonius, 1:vii; Bowersock, Introduction to Life of Apollonius, 10, 17–19; Meyer, "Apollonius von Tyana," 390; Dzielska, Apollonius, 19–49; Anderson, Philostratus, 124, 155–73; Francis, Subversive Virtue, 86–89; Philostratus, Apollonius of Tyana, 1:5–6; Ferguson, Religions, 182; Taggart, "Apollonius," 68–77, 220; Flinterman, Power, 2, 80–88; Petzke, Die Traditionen, 67–74; Koskenniemi, Apollonios, 4, 27, 138, 173–74; Koskenniemi, "The Philostratean Apollonius," 322; Miles, Philostratus, 4.

6. Gildersleeve, Essays, 259, 266, 268–69; Phillimore, In Honour, xv, n. 2, xviii; Bowersock, Introduction to Life of Apollonius, 10, 17–19; Dzielska, Apollonius, 86; Anderson, Philostratus, 176–84, 199–220; Francis, Subversive Virtue, 87; Philostratus, Apollonius of Tyana, 1:14–17; Harris, "Apollonius," 192, 198; Taggart, "Apollonius," 70, 73, 99–100, 153; Flinterman, Power, 80–81, 101, 103–4; Petzke, Die Traditionen, 63, 67, 84–85, 152–53; Koskenniemi, Apollonios, 178–83.

7. Gildersleeve, Essays, 254–55; Phillimore, In Honour, xxi–xxii, lxxi–lxxii; Bowersock, Introduction to Life of Apollonius, 12, 14; Dzielska, Apollonius, 91–94, 188–91; Anderson, Philostratus, 227–28; Francis, Subversive Virtue, 90, 94–97, 128–29; Harris, "Apollonius," 190, 192; Ferguson, Religions, 181; Taggart, "Apollonius," 58, 73, 100, 154, 215–16; Flinterman, Power, 1, 22–27, 66; Praet, "Pythagoreanism," 311; Koskenniemi, Apollonios, 50, 184–87.

8. Gildersleeve, Essays, 251–52, 293–96; Phillimore, In Honour, lxxvi, lxxx–lxxxiii; Bowersock, Introduction to Life of Apollonius, 21; Philostratus, The Life of Apollonius, 1:xiii; Ferguson, Religions, 51, 181–82; Bider, "Literature and Philosophy," 614; Taggart, "Apollonius," 212; Petzke, Die Traditionen, 64–65; Koskenniemi, Apollonios, 6, 90, 185;

9. Experts disagree over whether the Philostratus was consciously or unconsciously influenced by the Gospels[9] or later Christian sources.[10]

10. Philostratus (third century AD) may have been too far removed from the time of Apollonius (first century AD) to ensure his access to accurate information.[11]

Although this list is not comprehensive, these ten items accurately reflect the issues that are commonly discussed and debated by Apollonius and Philostratus specialists. Although not written on tablets of stone by the finger of God, these ten issues—the near consensus of classical and biblical experts—constitute an Apollonian Decalogue that should be known, used, and mentioned by scholars who teach and write about the Tyanean.

Although classical scholars agree that these ten items should be grappled with when writing about Apollonius, they have not always agreed upon how to deal with some of them. While there is a near consensus concerning the first four items in the list—sources earlier than and contemporary with Philostratus existed and these sometimes differed with his presentation of Apollonius—a wide range of opinions emerges over how to address items five through ten. Thus, the point of developing the Apollonian Decalogue for this study is not to dictate the conclusions at which a scholar should arrive but to demonstrate that these are the sorts of issues that scholars should address. The Apollonian Decalogue was also developed as tool to measure whether New Testament scholars broach these issues when they write about Apollonius.

KEEPING AND BREAKING THE COMMANDMENTS: EXAMPLES OF WHAT HAS BEEN TAUGHT ABOUT APOLLONIUS IN NEW TESTAMENT STUDIES

How well, then, have New Testament scholars communicated these ten critical issues to their academic and non-academic readers? In an attempt

---

Miles, *Philostratus*, 15–16.

9. Gildersleeve, *Essays*, 272–73, 276, 292–93; Phillimore, *In Honour*, lxxvi; Anderson, 144; Harris, "Apollonius," 193; Petzke, *Die Traditionen*, 62, 141; Koskenniemi, *Apollonios*, 27–29, 31–34, 37, 63, 131.

10. Phillimore, *In Honour*, lxxvi–lxxvii, lxxix; Harris, "Apollonius," 196–97.

11. Parker, *Roman India*, 3; Anderson, *Philostratus*, 124; Petzke, *Die Traditionen*, 154, 234; Koskenniemi, *Apollonios*, 31, 53, 54, 58–60, 63, 84, 98, 170–73, 187–88; Beck, "Mystery Religions," 141, n. 41.

to answer this question, the writings of several biblical scholars that reference Apollonius were checked against the items listed in the Apollonian Decalogue.[12] This study sampled thirty-one books that span several fields of biblical scholarship: New Testament introductions,[13] the Historical Jesus,[14] the Gospels,[15] Paul,[16] Acts,[17] Greco-Roman backgrounds for the New Testament,[18] Christian apologetics,[19] exorcism,[20] and miracles (or magic).[21] While this study is a mere sampling of academic writing on Apollonius, it provides a glimpse of how Apollonian material is often treated in Biblical Studies and exposes several gaps in the coverage of critical matters with respect to Apollonius and Philostratus.

Before presenting the findings of this survey, a word needs to be said about the scholars who were unwittingly included in this study. Unlike the Israelite community who heard their Ten Commandments before they agreed to accept the covenant (Exod 24:3), these scholars did not have the benefit of such an advanced warning about these ten items before participating in this study. Much like students who are surprised by a pop quiz, the participants in this study may feel that they are the

12. The monographs written by Petzke and Koskenniemi—full-length works dedicated to the study of Apollonius and the New Testament—were excluded from this study for two reasons: they had already been utilized along with classical sources above in the creation of the Apollonian Decalogue and they were substantially longer than the other materials studied (with the one exception of Reimer's *Miracle and Magic*).

13. Koester, *Introduction*, 2:375–56; Barr, *New Testament Story*, 226–27; Spivey et al., *Anatomy*, 195; Powell, *Introducing the New Testament*, 38–39; Boring, *Introduction*, 149, 468; Ehrman, *The New Testament*, 44–46, 99; Landry and Martens, *Inquiry*, 56.

14. Meier, *Mentor*, 576–81, 602–4; Evans, *Jesus and His Contemporaries*, 245–50; Aslan, *Zealot*, 106, 247–48; Ehrman, *Did Jesus Exist?*, 208–10, 288; Ehrman, *How Jesus Became God*, 13–18, 373; Eddy and Boyd, *The Jesus Legend*, 151–54; Boyd and Eddy, *Lord or Legend*, 57–58.

15. Votaw, *The Gospels*, 15–29; Sanders and Davies, *Synoptic Gospels*, 39, 169–70, 254–55, 269, 293–94; Bird, *Gospel of the Lord*, 49, 231, 233–34; Keener, *Christobiography*, 46–48.

16. Roetzel, *Letters of Paul*, 24–25.

17. Reimer, *Miracle and Magic*, 14–23.

18. Dungan and Cartlidge, *Documents*, 205–8; Roetzel, *The World That Shaped*, 103–4 (abbreviated as WTS in the chart below); Klauck, *The Religious Context*, 168–77; Bell, *Exploring*, 131, 176; Ferguson, *Backgrounds*, 384–86.

19. Geisler, *The Big Book*, 23–24.

20. Twelftree, *Jesus the Exorcist*, 23–27.

21. Kee, *Miracle*, 256–65; Habermas, "Did Jesus Perform Miracles?," 121–24; Keener, *Miracles*, 1:53–56; Smith, *Jesus the Magician*, 84–93. Smith's book could have been categorized as a study of the historical Jesus, but its precise designation will not matter at all for the following investigation.

victims of an academic ambush. Yet at the same time, scholars writing about Apollonius would be expected to be conversant with the primary and secondary sources concerning this figure and to mention a few of the items that appear in the Apollonian Decalogue. Hopefully, the lessons learned from the successes and failures of these earlier scholars will improve how future scholars write and teach about Apollonius.

The following chart indicates how often the authors included in this study touched on the ten issues customarily mentioned by Apollonius scholars. The numbers, one through ten, ranging across the top of the chart correspond to the ten items of the Apollonian Decalogue. If an author mentioned one of these items, a shaded box containing the page number in the book where that detail was mentioned appears under the corresponding number. An empty white box indicates that an author did not address an item. The system of assessment for determining whether an item was touched upon was rather generous in that it gave scholars credit for merely mentioning an issue even if it was not discussed in any detail. The chart also recorded data on additional issues in the two columns to the far right: authors who made factual errors about Apollonius (the column marked "Error")[22] and the approximate number of pages employed by authors for their discussion of Apollonius (the column marked "Pages").

---

22. The page numbers for these errors are not included on the chart since each of them is discussed below in the analysis.

Author[23]	1	2	3	4	5	6	7	8	9	10	Error	Pages
Aslan			247								x	2
Barr									226		x	2
Bell									131, 176	131		2
Bird					49, 231?			234			x	2
Boring			149, n. 17									3
Dungan & Cartledge						206	205?					2
Eddy & Boyd[LOL]			58			58	57	58	58	57		4
Eddy & Boyd[dT]L					153	152	151			151–53	?	4
Ehrman[DJE]							288?			288	x	4
Ehrman[HJBG]									373, n. 3			6
Ehrman[TNT]												4
Evans												6
Ferguson		384, 384, n. 106, 385, n. 111				385	385	385	385	385		3

23. Books penned by the same author are distinguished from each other in the chart by a superscripted abbreviation of the book's title next to the author's name (e.g., Ehrman[DJE]; Ehrman[HJBG]).

PART 1: INTRODUCTORY ISSUES

											x	
Geisler										24	x	2
Habermas					123	123		123–24		123		4
Kee			257		256	256–57		264	264			9
												5
Keener^C	48, n. 137	46, 47, 48, n. 137, 48, n. 142	47, 48	47	46, 48, n. 142	47			48	43, 44		4
Keener^M		1:55, n. 186				1:54, n. 175, 1:55, 1:56		1:54	1:55	1:53, 1:55		2
Koester		2:374										9
Klauck	169	169	169					170–71	171	170		1
Landry & Martens									56	56		8
Meier	577–78, 602, n. 6, 603, n. 10	577	578, 603, n. 12	579, 603, n. 16, 604, n. 18	578–80, 602, n. 17	577		580, 604, n. 23 and 24	580	578		2
Powell												4
Reimer			18–19	20	23, 198, n. 134			22, n. 69		19–22		2
Roetzel^{LP}										25?	x	

36

DEVISING CRITERIA FOR THE APOLLONIAN DECALOGUE

										103?	x	2
Roetzel[WTS]												
Sanders & Davies			169						294			8
Smith	85	88	86		86	86	86–87						9
Spivey et al.												1
Twelftree			23, n. 4, 24 n.5		24, n. 5	24, n. 5				24		5
Votaw	15, n. 4?		18–20, 27	19–20		16, n. 1, 21, 27	29	28	29	21		14

Although this study did not assign a score to each book, a glance at the numerous blank, white spaces on the chart indicates that only a few authors did an adequate or superior job of broaching these topics. The following sections cite examples of some of the better and poorer responses to the Apollonian Decalogue.

Items 1–4

Since items 1–4 are all concerned with various pre-Philostratean sources about Apollonius, they were evaluated here as a group for the sake of brevity. The chart indicates that sixteen of the works surveyed failed to mention any earlier sources at all.[24] One of the more surprising observations from this section was that few of the works with a strong apologetic agenda (e.g., Eddy & Boyd[TJL], Geisler, and Habermas) indicated an awareness of these contradictory sources about Apollonius or grasped their utility in challenging the veracity of Philostratus's biography.

A few scholars evinced an awareness of these other early materials about Apollonius yet failed to mention the names of these authors or their sources. For instance, Ehrman noted that Philostratus's *Life of Apollonius* was "our chief source of information about Apollonius,"[25] by which he seemed to hint that there were less significant sources of information. Yet, if this was indeed his intention, he failed to mention what those sources were or their nature (e.g., textual or archaeological). Likewise, he mentioned that "books" about Apollonius circulated throughout the empire, but, once again, he did not provide their titles or authors.[26] In these instances, no credit was given because these statements were vague. However, two authors received credit for listing the *Letters of Apollonius* in a footnote or endnote even though they did not discuss the significance of this ancient source.[27] Unfortunately, budding scholars would likely miss these vague allusions to other ancient texts and might skip over the references in the footnotes.

---

24. The percentages for those who did not mention earlier sources are 87 percent for column 1, 87 percent for column 2, 58 percent for column 3, and 80 percent for column 4.

25. Ehrman, *Did Jesus Exist?*, 217.

26. Ehrman, *The New Testament*, 46; Ehrman, *How Jesus Became God*, 12; Ehrman, *Did Jesus Exist?*, 208.

27. Aslan, *Zealot*, 247; Koester, *Introduction*, 2:374.

Other scholars went the second mile in listing and discussing the significance of earlier sources and authors such as Lucian,[28] Dio Cassius,[29] the fragment *On Sacrifices*,[30] a *Life of Pythagoras*,[31] the *Letters of Apollonius*,[32] Apollonius's testament,[33] Moiragenes,[34] Maximus of Aegae,[35] and the memoirs of Damis.[36] Some of these authors further noted the importance of these sources for identifying two distinct versions of Apollonius: a disreputable magician (e.g., Lucian and Moiragenes) and a noble sage or philosopher (e.g., Philostratus). Meier wrote,

> One of the purposes of the *Life* seems to have been to rehabilitate the reputation of Apollonius as a divinely guided philosopher and sage. If we may judge from the politics of the sophist Euphrates in the 1st century and of Lucian and (presumably) Moiragenes in the 2d century, Apollonius was viewed instead by many of the educated class as a fraud and magician (see, e.g., *Life* 1.2). Such an apologetic purpose need not exclude, however, the rhetorical intent of a sophist to display his talent and entertain a cultured audience.[37]

Similarly, Klauck noted that "Philostratus takes a critical distance from those who had written before him, and from the traditions on which he draws, since he wishes at all costs to prevent Apollonius from being seen as a mere magician—something that had clearly been the case."[38] Likewise, Ferguson, although uncharacteristically reticent here to name specific sources or traditions, reiterates the point made by these scholars:

---

28. Smith, *Jesus the Magician*, 88; Klauck, *Religious Context*, 169; Meier, *Mentor*, 577; Keener, *Christobiography*, 48, n. 137.

29. Smith, *Jesus the Magician*, 88; Keener, *Christobiography*, 48, n. 137.

30. Smith, *Jesus the Magician*, 85; Klauck, *Religious Context*, 169; Meier, *Mentor*, 602, n. 6.

31. Klauck, *Religious Context*, 169.

32. Smith, *Jesus the Magician*, 85, 86; Klauck, *Religious Context*, 169; Meier, *Mentor*, 177; Keener, *Christobiography*, 48.

33. Smith, *Jesus the Magician*, 86.

34. Smith, *Jesus the Magician*, 86; Klauck, *Religious Context*, 169; Meier, *Mentor*, 577; Keener, *Christobiography*, 47–48.

35. Smith, *Jesus the Magician*, 86; Meier, *Mentor*, 577; Keener, *Christobiography*, 48, n. 137.

36. Smith, *Jesus the Magician*, 86; Klauck, *Religious Context*, 169–70; Meier, *Mentor*, 577.

37. Meier, *Mentor*, 577–78.

38. Klauck, *Religious Context*, 169.

"Rival traditions about Apollonius were circulated in the ancient world, but the only full account to be preserved is the *Life of Apollonius* by Flavius Philostratus (c. A.D. 170–249). Behind Philostratus are two older views of Apollonius–as a magician and charlatan or a wonderworker and theosoph."[39] These authors, with a knack for good pedagogy, have informed their readers of specific pre-Philostratean sources and have explained their significance for understanding the historical Apollonius.

To sum up, the importance of communicating the first four items in the Apollonian Decalogue to a reader is to show that the *VA*, as valuable as it is, was not the only source to speak about Apollonius in the ancient world and that there were earlier, varying opinions about Apollonius against which Philostratus was reacting in the *VA*. To omit these details gives the impression that the *VA* is the sole record concerning Apollonius that survived antiquity, prevents the reader from spotting the two distinct versions of Apollonius, and conceals the possibility that Philostratus's agenda was to rehabilitate the image of Apollonius. No responsible New Testament historian would merely expose a student to the material about Jesus found in the Gospel of John, while withholding what was said about him by the Synoptic Gospels, Paul, Josephus, Tacitus, Suetonius, patristic authors, and the Talmud. Likewise, scholars writing about Apollonius should consider how important it is to allow non-specialists to hear what all these ancient voices had to say about him. The writers who mention these other materials allow their readers to begin sorting out which of the two versions of the Tyanean is most plausible; the earlier, negative version of him as a magician (or huckster) based on fragmentary sources or the later, positive portrayal of him as a holy man that is based on the multivolume *VA*. Awareness of these pre-Philostratean sources may well prevent a future generation of scholars from dancing ecstatically around the golden image of the *VA* like some of their academic forefathers did as if this source were the only god in the camp.

Item 5

Much like the biblical story of Hilkiah's rediscovering the Book of the Law and bringing it to King Josiah (2 Kgs 22:8–11), a relative of Damis supposedly brought the previously unknown memoirs of this first-century disciple of Apollonius to Empress Julia Domna. Yet the scholarly

---

39. Ferguson, *Backgrounds*, 384.

treatment of these two accounts differs markedly when it comes to the evaluation of their authorship and historical worth. While biblical scholars have vigorously debated the Mosaic authorship, date, and content of Josiah's book for years,[40] oddly the authorship and date of Damis's diary has often been either implicitly accepted without evaluation or, if critical issues were raised, accepted anyway as if it still preserved valid historical information about Apollonius.

The existence of Damis and his memoirs is one of the most controversial issues involved in evaluating the VA as a source for Apollonius. Since Philostratus asserted that the core of the VA is based on this document, the historian must decide how much weight to put on the truth of this claim. Scholarly opinions range from the wholesale acceptance of the existence of this first-century disciple and his diary to disbelief in the existence of Damis and the acknowledgment of a forgery attributed to him, to the belief that both the diarist and diary were the literary creations of Philostratus. To state the importance of mentioning Damis's diary in the idiom of the Decalogue, it is imperative that contemporary researchers and authors "remember the memoir to evaluate it wholly."

Informing readers about this debate over the authenticity of Damis's *Scrapbook* is important for several reasons. This issue is foundational for all who study Apollonius, for they must decide at some point in their research whether they will regard the VA as a work based on a reliable first-century source, an unreliable pseudepigraph of uncertain date, or a fiction concocted entirely by the third-century sophist Philostratus. Much of Apollonian scholarship hinges on the date and nature of the Damis memoir. If this diary is early and authentic, then it would be the only first-century source to reference the Tyanean. If it is not, no other early details can be known about Apollonius, for he was not mentioned at all in the first century and is referred to only once with certainty in the second century (Lucian).[41] This matter is important for historians in general because it impacts any reconstruction of the historical Apollonius. This issue is also of tremendous import to those who wish to compare Apollonius to the historical Jesus. If the Damis material dates from the

---

40. For instance, some scholars regard Josiah's book as the entire Torah, while others think that it was the book of Deuteronomy (or an early version of it). Yet others regard the text as a creation of the priests of Josiah's time.

41. Other early sources that mentioned Apollonius may also date to the second century (Moiragenes, Maximus of Tyre). Since their dates are uncertain, only Lucian is listed as a second century source.

first century, a better case can be made for comparing the third-century portrayal of Apollonius in the *VA* to the depiction of Jesus in the four Gospels. But if the Damis source proves to be a pseudepigraph from a later period or a fiction hatched from the fertile imagination of Philostratus, the *VA*'s value in such comparisons is vastly diminished or altogether negated. So, from a historical perspective, experts in this area would do well to make their readership aware of the available options from the very beginning.

Item 5 on the chart above recorded which scholars noted the Damis controversy, regardless of which view they endorsed. In this study, 68 percent of the sources failed to raise this issue. Some authors noted that Philostratus relied upon a source, but they did not discuss it in any detail.[42] Others accepted Philostratus's claim that he used eyewitness testimony. Boring argues that scholars can know much more about Apollonius than about Jesus because of the diary of Damis, "Apollonius's traveling companion and pupil for forty years, kept a journal carefully recording his teacher's sayings and deeds."[43] Boring's implication that scholars have access to more historical information about Apollonius than Jesus might be true, but such a view is contingent upon whether Damis and his diary existed and whether, assuming it existed, the information contained within it is accurate. Ehrman, taking a different approach from Boring, shifted the burden of proof for the Damis source from his shoulders to those of Apollonius's biographer. He stated that Philostratus "had done considerable research for his book, and his stories, he tells us, were largely based on the accounts recorded by an eyewitness and companion of Apollonius himself."[44] Oddly, as much as Boring[45] and Ehrman[46] have doggedly in-

---

42. Boyd and Eddy, *Lord or Legend*, 58.

43. Boring, *Introduction*, 468.

44. Ehrman, *How Jesus Became God*, 12.

45. Boring dismisses the anonymous authors of Matthew (*Introduction*, 534–36), Mark (*Introduction*, 520–22), and John (*Introduction*, 630) as eyewitnesses, but he allows for some material embedded in the Gospels to have derived from eyewitnesses (*Introduction*, 468). He likewise rejects the possibility that the "we" passages of Acts represent eyewitness testimony, favoring the view that they were a literary device (*Introduction*, 573–75). For his analysis of the claims of eyewitness testimony in 2 Peter, see his *Introduction*, 455, 461.

46. Ehrman, *The New Testament*, 88, 93, 120–30, 189–90; Ehrman, *Did Jesus Exist?*, 46–50, 72–73, 179, 181–82; Ehrman, *How Jesus Became God*, 90–93. Ehrman disregards the "we" passages of Acts as genuine eyewitness testimony and, while not settling on a particular theory, sets forth the claim that the author was slyly implying that he was an eyewitness and could be trusted concerning his account; *The New Testament*,

vestigated and challenged the claims of eyewitness testimony about the Gospels, the "we" passages of Acts, and the eyewitness claims of 2 Peter, neither of them questioned Philostratus's nearly identical claim that he possessed an eyewitness source nor mentioned that numerous scholars have questioned the existence of this account.

At the other end of the spectrum, several scholars in this study who were conversant with these alternative views either mentioned their doubts about the validity of this eyewitness claim or the skepticism of other scholars concerning it. Some authors regarded the Damis document as a pseudepigraph. Smith, for instance, believed that the memoir was the fabrication of someone posing as Damis's relative; it had been presented to Julia Domna as an authentic work but was really composed to receive a financial reward from the Severan family.[47] Similarly, Keener informed his readers of his position and responsibly reported other views, writing that "[a] clearly greater number of scholars . . . contend that even Damis is a fiction of either Philostratus or (as I think somewhat more likely) an earlier pseudepigrapher."[48] Other writers in this study favored the view that the diary sprang entirely from the imagination of Philostratus. Meier, after noting the views scholars ranged on both sides of this issue, comments that if one concludes "that both Damis and his diary are inventions of Philostratus, the gap between the historical Apollonius and the *Life* appears almost unbridgeable."[49] Likewise, Klauck provided a summary of scholars who either accepted or dismissed the existence of Damis's diary, and he also shared his own opinion that this work was the creation of Philostratus:

> But it is not difficult to perceive that this is a transparent fiction intended to make Philostratus' own book more credible (this is the view of the majority of scholars, at least since Meyer; cf. e.g., Bowie, Mumprecht, Dzielska and Koskenniemi; Anderson is confident of the existence of memoirs by Damis, while Speyer assumes a forgery, which would however be earlier than Philostratus himself).[50]

329–30. For his rejection of 2 Peter's claims to be written by an eyewitness, see his *The New Testament*, 524–25.

47. Smith, *Magician*, 86.
48. Keener, *Christobiography*, 47.
49. Meier, *Mentor*, 579.
50. Klauck, *Religious Context*, 170.

This latter group of Apollonius scholars has done a service to their readers by alerting them to the various scholarly perspectives on the memoirs of Damis, discussing the outcomes of these views, and supplying them with the bibliographical resources requisite for conducting follow-up research so that they can make an informed decision on this matter.

Item 6

Specialists in this study have often adhered to the spirit of the sixth Apollonian commandment to "bear witness" to the numerous historical and geographical errors within the VA. Their appraisal of the impact of these errors on the historical worth of VA varies. Some believe the work to be largely fiction, whereas others maintain that the historical blunders within it do not detract from its value as a historical source. Whatever one's opinion on this issue, some scholarly guidance on this topic would be a boon to novices and seasoned researchers alike in approaching several questions. Does the VA provide a historically accurate description of the first century in general? Does it provide an accurate description of Apollonius? What damage is done to the claim of the accurate, eye-witness testimony of the Damis material on the VA, which claims to be heavily reliant upon it, when historical inaccuracies occur within materials explicitly attributed to this memoir of Apollonius's disciple? What ramifications might such historical errors in the VA have for comparing the historical Apollonius to the historical Jesus? Asking questions like these should be of obvious importance to those interested in investigating the historical Apollonius.

Item 6 on the chart above identified the authors that noted historical and geographical errors in the VA. About 55 percent of the scholars surveyed failed to mention this issue. Of those who did, some provided vague details such as that the VA contained fictional or legendary components. For example, Ferguson, who drew attention to fictional components within the VA, but did not provide any concrete examples, wrote "As a travel romance of a saint and a wonder-worker and as a collection of lore from many places the *Life of Apollonius* is of a piece with the Christian apocryphal Acts."[51] Likewise, some authors did not address matters of historicity apart from generic warnings about "several blatant

---

51. Ferguson, *Backgrounds*, 386.

historical errors"[52] or legendary accretions and miraculous occurrences within the account.[53] Although these authors have at least warned the reader that the *VA* cannot be taken at face value, they have not given concrete examples of such details, indicated the great frequency at which they occur, or indicated whether they are problematic for investigating Apollonius as a historical figure.

A handful of scholars claimed that the *VA* was still reliable despite its historical problems. Roetzel, although designating the *VA* as a "highly romanticized biography,"[54] nevertheless believed it was still a fairly accurate account. In like spirit, Smith noted that the travel stories in Philostratus "are full of fantasies that resemble Pythagorean fictions. But this does not prove they were pure fabrications."[55] Votaw also opined that "The *Life* contains not a little that is romantic in its descriptions of the adventures of Apollonius on his journeys through many countries, and much miracle as regards Apollonius' own life and deeds. But in the main it is to be regarded as a historical account."[56] Although all these authors alerted their readers to the romantic features of the *VA*, they neither educated them as to the extent of the historical problems it contained nor gave specific examples of them.

Other scholars did a superb job of providing their readers with concrete examples of historical errors in the *VA*. Habermas offered the specific detail that the cities of Nineveh and Babylon, regarded as inhabited cities by Philostratus, had been in ruins for centuries.[57] Keener, providing even more detail, lists several geographical mistakes and historical implausible events that challenge the claim that this was an eyewitness source (e.g., Babylonian and Indian rulers debated philosophy in the Greek language).[58] Kee also drew attention to the significance of the blunders within the Damis account, commenting, "The material allegedly drawn from Damis is so full of historical anachronism and gross geographical errors that one could not have confidence in Damis as a reporter if there actually were a diary."[59] This statement is followed by a

---

52. Boyd and Eddy, *Lord or Legend*, 59.
53. Ehrman, *How Jesus Became God*, 13–14, 17; Ehrman, *Did Jesus Exist?*, 209.
54. Roetzel, *The Letters of Paul*, 24–25.
55. Smith, *Jesus the Magician*, 86.
56. Votaw, *The Gospels*, 16, n. 1.
57. Habermas, "Did Jesus Perform Miracles?," 123.
58. Keener, *Miracles*, 1:56.
59. Kee, *Miracle*, 1:256.

helpful list that includes two historical errors, one geographical blunder, and a list of exotic or mythological creatures (e.g., dragons and satyrs).[60] Meier, after summarizing Kee's list of historical errors and supplementing it with a few more examples from the classicist Ewen Bowie for good measure, concluded that, "All this should make one very leery of citing the *Life of Apollonius* as a reliable report about what exactly a miracle-worker similar to Jesus was doing in the 1st century."[61] After exposure to several specific examples of blunders like these, a new reader is better equipped to evaluate the historical merit of the *VA* and knows to watch for historical oddities along the way. Although authors should not leave novices with the impression that Philostratus's historical information is always inaccurate, they should make them aware that the *VA* contains numerous errors and that a greenhorn explorer must stay alert while navigating this strange new world.

Item 7

Items seven and eight of the Apollonian Decalogue both dealt with the agendas of the *VA*. While item 8, treated in the next section, dealt with whether the *VA* had an anti-Christian agenda, item 7 sought to discover whether any political, philosophical, pagan religious, or literary agendas of Philostratus or that of the Empress Julia Domna, his patroness, might have influenced the portrayal of Apollonius in the *VA*. Only 32 percent of the works surveyed touched on this matter. Meier and Keener briefly touched on this topic but did not spell out its ramifications with any specificity.[62] Other scholars were more specific with their theories about Philostratus's agendas. Ferguson noted that the *VA* was written at the instigation of the empress Julia Domna: "Some of the apparent parallels may be due to syncretistic tendencies already present in Severan circles. Indeed, Apollonius may be the spokesman of Philostratus's own religious views and so represent third-century thought rather than the first century."[63] Boyd and Eddy wrote, "Apollonius's biographer (Philostratus) was paid by a wealthy empress to compose a positive account of Apollonius, giving him a motive to make Apollonius look good. Those

---

60. Kee, *Miracle*, 1:256–57.
61. Meier, *Mentor*, 580.
62. Meier, *Mentor*, 577; Keener, *Christobiography*, 47.
63. Ferguson, *Backgrounds*, 285.

who preached and wrote about Jesus do not seem to have had these sorts of financial or political motives."[64] Even though some of these writers postulated various agendas, none of them fleshed them out in a way that showed how Philostratus's portrayal of Apollonius was shaped in a significant way, thereby disobeying the commandment issued by the Apollonian Decalogue to investigate the various agendas of the *VA*.

Item 8

The scholars in this study differed over whether the *VA* had an antireligious agenda of attacking either Christianity as a whole or the Gospels in particular. Bird, who voiced the strongest support for this view, wrote "the 'divine man' as depicted in Philostratus's account of Apollonius seems to have been deliberately intended and marketed as a pagan rival to the Gospels."[65] The majority of authors were less adamant about the presence of such an agenda but were still open to this possibility. As a representative of this view, Klauck writes, "In view of the period of its composition, one must ask whether perhaps Philostratus himself intended to create an alternative to the Christian tradition about Jesus."[66] Keener expressed a similar opinion:

> Philostratus's portrait suits a late second- or third-century setting (i.e., the author's own) much better than a mostly late first-century setting (i.e., Apollonius's); his accounts of Apollonius even resemble reports from Christian gospels, though especially of the "apocryphal" variety. This is very possibly deliberate; by the fourth century, pagan writers were explicitly using Apollonius as an alternative to Jesus, claiming that the pagan world offered its own healers . . . Although scholars today often doubt the nineteenth-century view that Philostratus tried to offer Apollonius as an alternative to Jesus (apart from the case of the strongest parallels), it seems clear that Christian stories were at least among the serious influences on his storytelling approach, including by offering literary fodder for his miracle stories.[67]

---

64. Boyd and Eddy, *Lord or Legend*, 57.
65. Bird, *Gospel of the Lord*, 234; also, Habermas, "Did Jesus Perform Miracles?," 123–24.
66. Klauck, *Religious Context*, 170.
67. Keener, *Miracles*, 1:54.

Kee also noted that some aspects of the *VA* suggest its author "was writing consciously a pagan Gospel" and that it had been commissioned by an opponent of Christianity, but he did not specifically mention the role of Julia Domna.[68] In a similar statement, Habermas argued, "The similarities between Apollonius and Jesus may well be more than coincidence. Philostratus was commissioned to write this work by Julia Domna, the wife of the Roman emperor Septimius Severus, and it is popularly held that she did so to in order to orchestrate 'a counterblast to Jesus.'"[69] Boyd and Eddy also note that "it may very well have been that certain aspects of the Jesus story were incorporated into the Apollonius story for competitive-evangelistic purposes."[70] Meier alone explicitly rejected the notion that the *VA* was created to challenge to the Gospels, but rather saw it as influenced by the stories found within them.[71] Despite the wide range of beliefs espoused by these authors, they have at least alerted their followers to the possible influence of agendas of the author and patroness of the *VA*, unlike the eighteen participants in the study who did not mention this point at all.

Item 9

Scholars disagree over whether the Philostratus was consciously or unconsciously influenced by materials in the Gospels or in later Christian sources. Of the works surveyed above, 58 percent did not address this issue. Yet, several allowed for the possibility that Gospel materials were an influence on the *VA*. Ehrman writes, "Since Philostratus was writing after the Gospels were in circulation, it is entirely possible—as many critics have pointed out—that he was influenced by their portrayal of Jesus and that, as a result, he himself created the similarities between his account of Apollonius and the Gospel stories"[72] Bell, who is also open to the possible influence of the Gospels on Philostratus's *VA*, wrote "As already noted, the written account of his life is later than the Gospels and Acts, so we cannot be sure how much the picture of Apollonius is influenced by stories about Jesus and Paul, which were relatively well known by A.D.

---

68. Kee, *Miracle*, 264.
69. Habermas, "Did Jesus Perform Miracles?," 123–24.
70. Boyd and Eddy, *Lord or Legend*, 58.
71. Meier, *Mentor*, 580.
72. Ehrman, *How Jesus Became God*, 373, n. 3.

200."[73] Meier, allowed for this possibility as well, although he believes Gospel influence was indirect. He suggests that Philostratus may have drawn on a few Gospel stories (Mark 5:21–43; Luke 7:11–17) to flesh out the story of Apollonius (*VA* 4.45), but he cautions that "since many of the motifs are found in other ancient miracle stories as well, no firm proof is possible."[74] Keener believes that many accounts in the *VA* resemble the Gospels, "although most frequently of the apocryphal variety . . . Given the relative dates, Christian stories would have been at least among the significant potential influences on his storytelling approach (offering literary fodder for miracle stories)."[75] Although none of these scholars are willing to commit entirely to the view that Philostratus has directly or indirectly borrowed ideas from the Gospels, they are to be commended for at least placing this option before their readers.

Item 10

Travelers in the London Underground are familiar with the automated warning to "mind the gap" that cautions them about the dangerous space between the platform and the train door. In Apollonian studies, the hazardous gap the historian must be wary of is temporal rather than spatial. The gap in time separating the third-century Philostratus from the first-century Apollonius could have affected the accuracy of his source material in several ways. For instance, is there any guarantee that the oral and written sources that were available to Philostratus in the third century (e.g., *Letters of Apollonius*, Maximus, or oral traditions) accurately portrayed the first-century Apollonius? If these Apollonian legends existed in the first century, could they have grown from history into hagiography by the time of Philostratus? Is it possible that these stories about Apollonius were created in the second or third centuries and were hagiographic from the beginning? Questions of this nature ought to be considered when investigating Apollonius as a historical figure. A New Testament scholar writing on the topic of Apollonius should heed the commandment of earlier experts on Apollonius: "thou shalt mind the gap."

In studies about the historical Jesus, many scholars assume that changes were made to the oral and written traditions about him within

---

73. Bell, *Exploring*, 176.
74. Meier, *Mentor*, 580.
75. Keener, *Christobiography*, 48.

just a few decades. First, scholars often assume that oral and written sources that stand behind the canonical Gospels were altered to some degree by early Christian tradents. Second, scholars often assume that the Gospel writers themselves edited these materials to suit their own agendas. Third, the clutch of extrabiblical sources that mention Jesus are sometimes deemed less valuable with time because they are further from the event described and more vulnerable to hearsay or the insertion of legendary elements (e.g., Josephus, Suetonius, Tacitus, the Talmud, and non-canonical Gospels).[76] Fourth, scholars often note that few extrabiblical sources mention Jesus until the late first century (Josephus) and early decades of the second (Tacitus, Suetonius, and Pliny);[77] the paucity of such material deprives scholars of valuable outsider perspectives concerning Jesus that could serve as a correction to material written by his followers. Whether all these points are valid, they at least demonstrate that New Testament scholars are aware of the possible effects that this minuscule, temporal gap of a few decades could have had on information about the historical Jesus.[78] Oddly, about 45 percent of the books in this study that were written by New Testament scholars neither show an awareness of nor an interest in the yawning chasm between the death of Apollonius (c. AD 100) and the composition of the *VA* (sometime after AD 217) or its potential impact on the case for the historical Apollonius.

A few works included in this study noted the temporal distance between Apollonius and Philostratus but did not take the final step of discussing whether such distance could have had an impact on the factuality of his statements. For instance, Boring mentions the brute fact that Apollonius's "biography was not written until more than a hundred years later."[79] Likewise, Aslan, mentions the gap: "The earliest work on Apollonius is the third-century text by Philostratus."[80] Yet, neither of these authors minded the gap enough to comment on the problem that the great gulf fixed between Apollonius and the time of his biographer could present for historical research.

---

76. Ehrman, *The New Testament*, 237–40. Aslan notes that Josephus, Tacitus, and Pliny are late. See Aslan, *Zealot*, xxv.

77. Ehrman, *The New Testament*, 237–40; Boring, *Introduction*, 135; Spivey et al., *Anatomy*, 188; Aslan, *Zealot*, xxiv–xxv.

78. Aslan claims that the canonical Gospels were written many years after the events they describe (xxvi) by people who had never known Jesus; *Zealot*, 170.

79. Boring, *Introduction*, 149.

80. Aslan, *Zealot*, 246.

Others did a slightly better job of weighing in on the impact of the gap between Apollonius and the late date of composition for the *VA*. Roetzel acknowledged this issue, but indicated that he did not view this gap as overly problematic:

> Although his highly romanticized biography was not commissioned until A.D. 216 (over a century after his death), the piety reflected in it conforms rather well to Apollonius' actual first-century outlook... Although the biography of Apollonius is late, his activity as a wonder worker, wise man, lawgiver, and patron of the mysteries is in tune with the spirit of the age. Whereas the literary portrait of Apollonius painted by Philostratus reflects some later concerns, the basic outline of his sketch closely resembles the picture of first-century Neo-Pythagoreanism presented by others."[81]

Elsewhere Roetzel states almost the same idea, "Although Philostratus' biography was late (3d century C.E.), most scholars see in it traditions and forms of piety shared with much of first century religious expression."[82] What was important for Roetzel was that the *VA* seemed consistent with the era in which Apollonius is said to have lived, not that the work could just as easily have been a description of circumstances in the second or third centuries. Likewise, Votaw showed no concern for the late date of the biography for he was convinced that Philostratus possessed a first-century source. He explains, "As Damis' journal had been written in Apollonius' lifetime ... the interval of about 120 years between the death of Apollonius and Philostratus' biography of him did not much affect the trustworthiness of the main information concerning him."[83] Yet, even if one allows Votaw's assumption that Philostratus had access to a first-century source, such a source should not be admitted into evidence without a thorough vetting simply because it is early. If the Gospels writers could not be trusted to preserve reliable facts about Jesus at forty to eighty years from the events they described, as Votaw himself argues,[84] at

---

81. Roetzel, *Letters of Paul*, 25.

82. Roetzel, *The World that Shaped*, 103.

83. Votaw, *The Gospels*, 21. Petzke was also noted the difficulty posed by the tremendous gap between the death of Apollonius and the *VA*. Although he thought the Gospel materials were early, being edited 40–70 years after the death of Jesus, he argued similarly to Votaw that the temporal distance between Apollonius and the *VA* could be bridged by the early pre-Philostratean sources used in its composition. See Petzke, *Die Traditionen*, 234.

84. Votaw, *The Gospels*, 3.

least the same degree of skepticism should be applied to the hypothetical first-century source used by the *VA*. Even so, these two scholars, to their credit, have at least noted the gap and alerted their readers to it, even though they did not regard it as unbridgeable.

Others in this investigation did regard this temporal gap as a serious problem. Meier concisely summed up how the distance between Apollonius and the time of Philostratus is problematic, while at the same time showing how the sources for Jesus do not encounter the same sort of issues: "Despite his careful use of sources about Apollonius outside of the *Life*, it remains true that we know very little about Apollonius before Philostratus' work. Hence, we are faced with a serious gap of information between the time of Apollonius' death toward the end of the 1st century A.D. and the composition of the *Life* ca. 217–20."[85] In this same entry, Meier contrasts traditions in the late-coming *VA* for Apollonius with those of Jesus: Paul wrote about Jesus two or three decades after Jesus's death, and the Gospel of Mark (and perhaps Q) appeared within four decades.[86] Keener, whose focus was on examining the antiquity of the miracle traditions associated with Apollonius and Jesus, also touched on this matter: "The period between Jesus's crucifixion and Mark's Gospel, usually estimated to be at roughly forty years, may be less than a third of the period between Apollonius's death or disappearance and Philostratus's story about him."[87] Boyd and Eddy not only noted the gap but also spoke about the opportunity it afforded for legendary development:

> The only account we have of Apollonius's life was written more than a century after Apollonius lived, giving ample time in the environment for stories about his life to expand. In the case of Jesus, however, we have five sources (the four Gospels and Paul) written within several decades of his life. Not only this . . . each of these accounts gives us indications they are passing on reliable oral material that predates them.[88]

These latter scholars have argued that the gap between Jesus and his biographers is a narrow ditch when compared to the mighty canyon separating Apollonius from Philostratus. In so doing, they have shown their readers why they too should mind the gap in Apollonian studies.

---

85. Meier, *Mentor*, 578–79.
86. Meier, *Mentor*, 579.
87. Keener, *Miracles*, 1:53.
88. Boyd and Eddy, *Lord or Legend*, 57.

Errors in Material about Apollonius

Most of the errors in material about Apollonius were relatively minor and may seem like nitpicking to some readers. Nevertheless, such mistakes may betray a scholar's carelessness, ignorance of the ancient and modern sources, or unfamiliarity with the basic contours of Apollonius's life as told by his primary biographer, Philostratus. The errors that were detected in this study and noted on the chart above fell into three categories: errors concerning the life of Apollonius as it was related in the *VA*, errors caused by misreading secondary material, and errors concerning the ancient sources that speak about Apollonius.

The factual or historical errors concerning the life of Apollonius as related by Philostratus may have been due to a careless or hasty reading of the *VA*. In relating the various theories proposed for the end of Apollonius's life, Ehrman states that some claimed he ascended, while others said that he had appeared to his followers alive, spoke with them, and allowed them to touch him.[89] Ehrman is correct that Philostratus recorded the ascension of Apollonius (*VA* 30.2), but he is mistaken that the holy man was touched during a postmortem appearance. Ehrman appears to have conflated two accounts here.[90] In addressing another tradition, Ehrman writes, "Apollonius of Tyana came to one of his followers after he ascended to heaven, as we have on the basis of eyewitness testimony."[91] Although Ehrman's intention here is not to claim that this eyewitness claim was accurate, he does attribute the claim to an eyewitness. This assertion, however, is not accurate for Damis was the only figure for whom an eyewitness claim was made in the *VA*, yet the ascension account to which Ehrman referred (*VA* 8.31) was not a part of Damis's eyewitness testimony; Philostratus claimed that Damis's account came to an end at *VA* 8.29. Most likely, both errors were simply due to a hasty reading of the primary source.

89. Ehrman, *The New Testament*, 45–46.

90. The two accounts that Ehrman appears to conflate here both appear in the eighth book of the *VA*. In the first story, Apollonius demonstrated to two disciples that he had not been executed by the emperor Domitian by offering to let them touch him; this confirmation to them that he was not a spirit (*VA* 8.12). This episode occurred before the death of Apollonius. In the second, Apollonius appeared after his departure from earth to a sleeping man in hopes of convincing him of the doctrine of immortality (*VA* 8.31), but the sage remained invisible and inaudible to others who were present. There is no indication in this latter account that Apollonius was physically present or that he was touched by anyone.

91. Ehrman, *How Jesus Became God*, 150.

More serious problems arise when authors have not read the *VA* for themselves or have misread secondary literature about Apollonius. In two of his books, Roetzel claimed that Apollonius was martyred in Rome.[92] Yet, according to Philostratus—the only ancient source cited by Roetzel—Apollonius of Tyana was not martyred in Rome (or anywhere else), as anyone who had consulted the eighth book of the *VA* could have easily ascertained.[93] Perhaps Roetzel confused Apollonius of Tyana with a Christian martyr of the same name who was executed in Rome.[94] Boring, apparently misreading a passage from a secondary source, writes that Apollonius, like Pythagoras and Iamblicus, "calmed the waves of the sea in order to grant safety to those in danger."[95] Yet, Iamblicus (AD 245–325), the Neoplatonic philosopher and biographer of Pythagoras, was never said to have performed such a feat, but rather Iamblicus had attributed this miracle to Pythagoras.[96] In a final example of this type of error, Geisler claimed that Philostratus reported Apollonius's postmortem appearance to a sleeping man "two hundred years after Apollonius is to have lived (AD 275)."[97] Philostratus does not give a clear timeframe for this appearance of Apollonius, but the chronology proposed by Geisler is certainly incorrect, for it would have been impossible for Philostratus to have recorded an event in the *VA* that occurred after its publication and after Philostratus had died (ca. AD 240s). Errors such as these do not inspire confidence in an author's mastery of the material.

Finally, three authors made incorrect statements about the ancient sources that speak of Apollonius. Aslan can perhaps be forgiven for his claim that the earliest work written about Apollonius was the *VA*. In truth, the *VA* is merely the earliest *extant* work,[98] although at least two works

---

92. Roetzel, *Letters of Paul*, 25; Roetzel, *The World that Shaped*, 103–4.

93. Three accounts of Apollonius's end are related at *VA* 30.1–2. One tradition said he died at Ephesus, another that he died at Lindos, and the last records that he ascended into heaven from Crete.

94. Eusebius, *Hist. eccl.*, 5.21.

95. Boring, *Introduction*, 149.

96. Iamblichus, *Vit. Pyth.* 28.

97. Geisler, *The Big Book*, 24.

98. Aslan, *Zealot*, 247. Philostratus indicates that several authors had written prior to the composition of his own work: Moiragenes (*VA* 1.3.2), Maximus of Aegeae (*VA* 1.3.2), and Damis (*VA* 1.3.1). Eddy and Boyd were granted a question mark on an issue very similar to that of Aslan, for they claim that "we have only one source for the life of Apollonius—Philostratus's *Life of Apollonius*—written more than a century after he lived"; Eddy and Boyd, *The Jesus Legend*, 151. If by this they intend that there is only one extant biography of Apollonius, they are correct, but there are numerous materials

antedated it as Philostratus himself indicated (*VA* 1.2). However, Aslan must be held accountable for the statement that the text of Hierocles's *Lover of Truth*, which employed the *VA* to attack Christian ideas, was preserved, for it is no longer extant.[99] In a final example, Ehrman repeatedly and perplexingly comments that he doubts that his students have read any of the ancient books about Apollonius.[100] His statement is accurate, for no one has read these works, including Ehrman himself. This is because no books that were written about Apollonius still exist except for the *VA*. The pre-Philostratean works of Moiragenes and Maximus of Aegae have perished, as have the post-Philostratean books penned by Hierocles and Sidonius. Perhaps Ehrman had in mind Apollonius's letters, but this was not a book written about Apollonius but a collection of letters supposedly written by the sage himself.

Errors are certain to occur in writing and some of these errors are less serious than others. Yet, most of the ones discussed in this section could have been avoided by taking the time to read the primary and secondary material with a bit more care.

The Number of Pages Needed to Mention the Ten Items

A final item was included in the study in anticipation of the objection that it would be impossible, in a short space of text, to address the ten items of the Apollonian Decalogue. The examples of several authors that were included in this survey quash such an objection. Several authors covered five (Ferguson, Geisler, Kee, Keener[M], Reimer), six (Eddy & Boyd[LOL], Klauck), seven (Smith), or eight items (Keener[C], Votaw) in just a few pages. Meier covered all ten items within the space of eight pages. The value of recording the number of pages taken to address the issue is significant; the authors that covered the most items in the study were often able to raise and discuss multiple issues within the course of a few paragraphs, pages, or footnotes, thereby demonstrating for future writers

---

that serve to reconstruct the life of Apollonius, some of which were written by others (Lucian, Dio Cassius) and some of which are attributed to Apollonius himself (*Letters of Apollonius, On Sacrifices*).

99. Aslan, *Zealot*, 247. Here, Aslan is under the impression that Conybeare's translation of the *VA* included the work of Hierocles, a work which is no longer extant, rather than Eusebius's *Reply to Hierocles*.

100. Ehrman, *The New Testament*, 46; Ehrman, *How Jesus Became God*, 12; Ehrman, *Did Jesus Exist?*, 208.

that mentioning all or most of the items of the Apollonian Decalogue is neither an unreasonable expectation nor an unattainable goal.

CONCLUSION

The root of the problem concerning how Apollonius has been treated by many NT scholars appears to be either unfamiliarity with the excellent research on both Apollonius and Philostratus that has already been conducted by New Testament and classical scholars or a hesitancy to share this earlier research with the reader. The next chapter will attempt to remedy this deficiency to a degree by walking the reader through some of this important material and revealing some of the scholarship from which the items codified in the Apollonian Decalogue derive. By following the lead of earlier scholars who have specialized in the study of Apollonius, non-specialists in this area can do a better job of formulating and grappling with pertinent questions about Apollonius, the *VA*, and Philostratus in future research. Perhaps this will also aid professors in transmitting this information to those they teach in the classroom and through their writings.

―――――― 3 ――――――

Apollonian Studies

From Antiquity to Modern Times

The history-of-research chapter in a dissertation or book is often considered boring or irrelevant, even by the academic who wrote it. Nevertheless, New Testament scholars who write about Apollonius and those who wish to study about him must be conversant with the research that preceded them. The story of Apollonian research is filled with tales of scholars who made brilliant observations, created tremendous blunders in logic, and traveled down blind alleys in scholarship.

The examples of such studies that follow in this chapter are written for the admonition of future scholars. If the work of previous generations is studied, it will inform and may inspire new generations of researchers; if ignored, a future researcher may well suffer the indignity of finding that their hasty comment or brilliant argument about the Tyanean was rebutted by a scholar who died a century ago; if ignored, a future researcher will likely repeat some of the blunders of the past and may miss out on rich material that could spark new ideas. Hopefully, exposure to some of the material in this chapter will prevent future scholars from making similar mistakes and oversights. Therefore, this chapter unapologetically presents a rudimentary history of research on the topics of Apollonius and the *VA*.

This chapter has two agendas. First, it will demonstrate that earlier scholars were aware of the ten items that constitute the Apollonian Decalogue that was set forth in chapter two. The following history of research will note when most of the items from the Decalogue were discovered and will note them within parentheses. Second, this chapter will highlight just how dominant the *VA* has been as a source for learning about Apollonius from the time of its composition down to the current day, often to the exclusion of lesser-known sources. Although these two agendas will be the primary foci of the survey, hopefully, the reader will also find the history of Apollonian studies informative and enjoyable as well.

PRE-PHILOSTRATEAN SOURCES FOR APOLLONIUS

Apollonius was mentioned by several ancient authors before the time of Philostratus. Some of these comments about the sage were brief, (e.g., Lucian and *On Sacrifices*), but there were at least two substantial biographies of Apollonius (e.g., Moiragenes and Maximus of Aegae) and various collections of letters that were supposedly written by Apollonius himself (*Letters of Apollonius*). The earliest of these authors was critical of Apollonius (Lucian), and all but one of these writers (Maximus of Aegae) regarded him as some sort of magician. The sources just mentioned will be treated in detail in upcoming chapters, but these lesser-known materials are mentioned here simply to contrast them with the most famous tome of Apollonian lore: Philostratus's *VA*.

If the previous chapter is a good measure of the state of knowledge on Apollonius, these pre-Philostratean sources have been forgotten by or are unknown to numerous New Testament scholars. This phenomenon is forgivable because many of these sources do not seem to have been widely known even in antiquity. The reason for the neglect of these materials in ancient and modern times is likely the same; they were all eclipsed by Philostratus's *VA*.

THE NON-SORCERER'S APPRENTICE: PHILOSTRATUS PUBLISHES HIS *LIFE OF APOLLONIUS*

Although Philostratus defended Apollonius against the accusations of earlier writers that he was a magician, he became a bit of a sorcerer in his own right. Sometime after AD 217, Philostratus performed one of the greatest tricks in ancient history by publishing his *Life of Apollonius* for, by this single act, he transformed the memory of Apollonius from that of a magician into a philosopher, made the rival biographers of the

Tyanean disappear, and bestowed the gift of literary immortality upon the pagan sage.

Although Philostratus was not the first author to write extensively about Apollonius in ancient times his biography of the holy man surpassed its two predecessors in both popularity and scope. The *VA* effectively drove its earlier competitors "off the market"[1] (Item 3) by disparaging the account of Moiragenes (Item 4) and incorporating the work of Maximus of Aegae into its own narrative, thereby rendering it redundant. Philostratus claims to have drawn on other earlier sources as well, such as Apollonius's letters and various traditions he had gathered from cities that had honored the sage.[2] Philostratus's massive, eight-book collection of Apollonian lore dwarfed the Gospel accounts in length and provided later pagan apologists with ample material for their attacks against Christianity's founder–this despite the *communis opinio* of modern scholars that Philostratus himself had no anti-Christian agenda for its publication.

Philostratus's biography also insured that the name of the wonder-working Tyanean did not perish. As Gildersleeve wrote,

> Apollonius of Tyana is a great name; but if it had not been for Philostratus, he would not even be the puzzling shadow that he is now . . . We should have still known that Caracalla raised a monument in his honor, that Alexander Severus set up his image in the Imperial chapel beside Abraham, Christ, and Orpheus, and that Aurelian made vows to him of temples and statues. But of all his wonderful travels we should have known as little as Apollonius himself; of his miracles we should be almost totally ignorant. One historian would have preserved one specimen of his gift of second-sight . . . But blot out Philostratus and the traditional Apollonius is blotted out with him."[3]

Philostratus almost singlehandedly preserved the story of Apollonius's career for posterity–or at least he succeeded in perpetuating his unique version of the tale. Yet, the effects of its publication were delayed, for in the decades immediately following its release the work appears to have done little to revive interest in the man from Tyana.[4] Although it was not

---

1. C. P. Jones, "Apollonius of Tyana in Late Antiquity," 55.
2. *VA* 1.2.3; Eusebius, *Hier.* 3.
3. Gildersleeve, *Essays*, 253.
4. Taggart writes, "In fine, in the period of roughly eighty years following the publication of Philostratus' *opus magnum*, Apollonius seems to have remained a figure of

appreciated in its day, the *VA* lay dormant until Hierocles resurrected it for his attack upon Christianity.

THE LOVER OF TRUTH: HIEROCLES AND HIS CHRISTIAN DETRACTORS

The first attested systematic comparison of Apollonius and Jesus appeared on the cusp of Diocletian's persecution of the Christians.[5] In AD 302, an anti-Christian Roman official named Sossianus Hierocles wrote a two-part tract entitled *The Lover of Truth* (Φιλαλήθης λόγος πρὸς Χριστιανούς). Supposedly its aim was not to attack the Christians, but rather to persuade them of the falsity of their Scriptures (Lactantius, *Inst.* 5.2) but its message was perceived by several leaders as an attack upon the faith. This work has not survived,[6] but the contours of its argument can be reconstructed from the responses to it by the Christian leaders Eusebius and Lactantius.

These two writers indicate that Hierocles developed at least two major lines of argumentation. The first was a generic attack, borrowing from the ideas and works of earlier critics of Christianity (Eusebius, *Hier.* 1.1), that pointed out the contradictions in Christian Scripture and accused

---

little importance and to have returned to that limbo of forgotten wise men from which Philostratus and Julia Domna attempted in vain to rescue him." Taggart, "Apollonius of Tyana," 170. As possible evidence for the unimportance of Philostratus's biography, Origen of Alexandria mentioned Moiragenes's book about Apollonius in his *Contra Celsum* (c. AD 248), but did not mention the *VA*; Duliére, "Protection permanente," 249.

5. Some have suggested that Porphyry was the first to compare Apollonius and Jesus. See the discussion by Barnes ("Sossianus Hierocles," 241). Although Porphyry compared Apollonius and the apostles of Christ, (Jerome, *Tract. Ps.* 81), evidence for his comparison of Apollonius to Jesus is uncertain. See Philostratus, *Apollonius of Tyana*, 3:157, n. 4. If Porphyry had written such comparisons, there could be several reasons why Eusebius did not mention them. Perhaps Eusebius was simply unaware of Porphyry's work (Barnes, "Sossianus Hierocles," 241). Alternately, Eusebius may have known of such comparisons, but did not consider them thoroughgoing enough to warrant a detailed response. As it stands, clear evidence of such a comparison by Porphyry remains theoretical. Whatever the case, Eusebius regarded the work of Hierocles as the first "formal contrast and comparison with our savior" (*Hier.* 1.2). Bowersock also believed that Hierocles was the first to compare the two men (Bowersock, Introduction to *Life of Apollonius*, 13).

6. Reza Aslan has apparently confused Hierocle's work with Eusebius's reply to it: "Conybeare's book also includes a translation of a later work on Apollonius by Hierocles titled *Lover of Truth*, which expressly compares Apollonius to Jesus of Nazareth" (Aslan, *Zealot*, 247).

its authors (Peter and Paul) of being deceivers, unskilled, and unlearned men (Lactantius, *Inst.* 5.2; Eusebius, *Hier.* 2.2).[7] The second line of argumentation, which had never been employed before (Eusebius, *Hier.* 1.2), consisted of a detailed comparison (σύγκρισις)[8] of Apollonius to Christ that demonstrated the superiority of the former figure (Eusebius, *Hier.* 1.1; Lactantius, *Inst.* 5.3).[9] This second type of attack was novel in another way; Hierocles appears to have been the first critic to employ Philostratus's *Life of Apollonius* as a polemical tool.[10] Although the publication of Hierocles's tract does not answer the question of whether the *VA* had an anti-Christian agenda, it does show how easily this biography of Apollonius could be weaponized by pagans for polemical purposes.

---

7. Although earlier pagan apologists developed generic critiques that demeaned the intellect of Christians (Celsus) or attacked the apostles themselves, Hierocles more narrowly focused his attack on the Gospel writers' lack of skill, truthfulness, and accuracy when compared to Philostratus, Damis, and Maximus (Eusebius, *Hier.* 2.2). Taggart correctly observed that Hierocles "not only attacked the Christian scriptures but also attempted to demonstrate the superiority of Hellenic culture over the Christian" (Taggart, "Apollonius of Tyana," 172).

8. Schirren explains that, although Plutarch had compared various Greeks and Romans with a view toward "giving both cultures equal esteem," Hierocles had the goal of elevating the pagan religious view and denigrating the Christian one. See Schirren, "Irony," 178.

9. Hierocles presented Apollonius as a wise man, but not a god, who had performed his miracles through wisdom rather than sorcery (Eusebius, *Hier.* 2.1). Jesus, he argued, had performed fewer spectacular feats than the Tyanean and some of them had been exaggerated by his biographers (Eusebius, *Hier.* 2.2) but Jesus was considered a god nonetheless by his gullible followers (Eusebius, *Hier.* 2.2).

10. As noted above, some scholars would argue that Porphyry was the first author to employ the *VA* but this claim is unproven. Other works appear to have been in play at this time of crisis between paganism and Christianity, but these tended to promote Apollonius rather than compare him to Jesus. Soterichos of Oasis Magna in upper Egypt (c. AD 300) wrote a poem entitled, *Life of Apollonius of Tyana* during the time of Diocletian according to the *Suda*. Jones thinks it was probably based on the *VA* and perhaps *Lover of Truth* by Hierocles. See Philostratus, *Apollonius of Tyana* 3:109, n. 21. Dzielska also thinks he might have had more than the *VA* before him; Dzielska, *Apollonius*, 97. Jones suggests that this work related to the emperor's anti-Christian policies; see C. P. Jones, "Apollonius of Tyana in Late Antiquity," 55. Shortly after AD 303, Arnobius's *Adversus Nations* lists Apollonius among several other individuals, like Zoroaster, who had some "repute in the magical arts." Arnobius calls on the pagans to see if they or their gods can perform what was done by "uneducated Christians using simple commands." Jones notes that this passage, or that of Lactantius, is the first mention of Apollonius in Latin literature. See Philostratus, *Apollonius of Tyana*, 3:111, n. 22.

PART 1: INTRODUCTORY ISSUES

Around AD 312,[11] Eusebius[12] wrote a rejoinder to this work entitled, *Against Hierocles*. He chose to address only the portion of the work that specifically contrasted Apollonius to Christ because he felt that Hierocles's other charges against Christianity had already been adequately fielded by Origen (*Cels*.1.1).[13] Therefore, Eusebius concentrated his efforts upon the *VA* and its author, Philostratus, on whom Hierocles had lavished so much praise for his "very high level of culture and honored truth" (Eusebius, *Hier.* 2.2; 4.3). Perhaps mirroring Hierocles's technique of enumerating contradictions within Christian writings (Lactantius, *Inst.* 5.2), Eusebius cataloged numerous self-contradictions,[14] absurd events (especially during the Indian and Ethiopian travels of Apollonius),[15] and implau-

---

11. Philostratus, *Apollonius of Tyana*, 3:149. Barnes argues that Eusebius's response was almost immediate (before AD 303). See Barnes, "Sossianus Hierocles," 240, 242.

12. Some scholars believe that the *Reply to Hierocles* differs too much from Eusebius's works to have been written by him. See Schwartz, "Eusebios von Caesarea," 1394; Hägg, "Hierocles," 138–50; Barnes, "Scholarship or Propaganda?" 60. Jones, however, rebutted these arguments and defended Eusebian authorship. See C. P. Jones, "Apollonius of Tyana in Late Antiquity," 49–52. Despite some ambiguity concerning authorship, *Reply to Hierocles* claims to have been written shortly after *Lover of Truth*; C. P. Jones, "Apollonius of Tyana in Late Antiquity," 52.

13. Eusebius listed the items that he thought Origen had already adequately covered in *Contra Celsum* (*Hier.* 1.1). Indeed, this list does resemble several topics raised by Origen in his *Contra Celsum*: Jesus had better divine credentials than other figures (*Cels.* 3.26–31), did numerous (*Cels.* 1.68) and incomparable miracles (*Cels.* 2.57), was prophesied years in advance of his coming (*Cels.* 1.34, 3, 49; 3.4), currently performed miracles (*Cels.* 1.6, 67; 2.33, 3.36), had disciples who were willing to die for the faith (*Cels.* 2.10, 45), and possessed a vast number of followers (*Cels.* 2.46; 3.10).

14. For instance, Philostratus claimed that: (1) Apollonius's ability to understand the language of animals was learned from the Arabs, yet this would have required him, a vegetarian, to have consumed the heart or liver of a snake (*Hier.* 10.1); (2) Apollonius knew all languages yet needed to learn Attic Greek from teachers (*Hier.* 9) and to have an interpreter in India (*Hier.* 14); (3) Apollonius had numerous teachers and learned from the teachings of Pythagoras, even though he was a god and consequently would not need to be taught anything (*Hier.* 9); (4) Apollonius perceived everything by "second sight," yet several times in the *VA* this ability failed him (*Hier.* 15; 28.1; 28.2; 33.1; 35.2; 37; 41); and (5) Apollonius was not a sorcerer, yet the Indian philosophers were sorcerers and had taught the Tyanean (*Hier.* 31.1–2).

15. For example, Philostratus mentioned a vampire (*Hier.* 13), a sighting of a women who was half white and half black (*Hier.* 19.2), dragons with jewels in their heads (*Hier.* 19.2), urns that moved automatically (*Hier.* 19.2; 24), wine servers made of bronze that passing round cups at a feast (*Hier.* 24), thunders and winds in jars (*Hier.* 24), an elm tree spoke with a feminine voice, and a violent satyr (*Hier.* 34). Eusebius claimed that these events surpassing those in the fictional work *The Wonders Beyond Thule* (*Hier.* 17).

sible miracles[16] found throughout all eight books of the *VA*. He likewise noted Philostratus's shortcomings as a biographer for not providing a witness for the miraculous events surrounding Apollonius's birth (*Hier.* 8.1; 12.1), for being uncertain about the manner of Apollonius's death (*Hier.* 44.3), for slandering the philosopher Euphrates—considered by many of his day to be a great man—merely for having a different opinion than Apollonius (*Hier.* 33), and for plastering a mask of a Pythagorean lifestyle on Apollonius (*Hier.* 5). As a barb, Eusebius echoed verbatim Hierocles's charge that Christians were naïve, uncouth, and fabricators (*Hier.* 1.21; 2.2), as he showed that Hierocles and Philostratus were the ones who were "suspect and gullible" (*Hier.* 4.1; 4.4; 17, 20) for believing such nonsense about Apollonius. These two pagan authors proved themselves to be "liars, ignoramuses, and sorcerers" by their contradictions and inconsistencies (*Hier.* 43.4). Eusebius mocked Hierocles's praise of high pagan "culture," for it was nothing more than tall tales with no regard for "truth" (*Hier.* 4.3; 17).

In actuality, the *Reply to Hierocles* was an attack upon Philostratus and Hierocles rather than upon Apollonius himself.[17] Eusebius did not object to several of the less fantastic claims about Apollonius[18] but rejected their claims that Apollonius was a divine figure (*Hier.* 8.1; 8,2; 8.3; 12.3), a holy man (*Hier.* 48.2), and a Pythagorean (*Hier.* 5). Eusebius even accused Apollonius's adherents of portraying Apollonius as a hypocrite (*Hier.* 43.4).[19] In raising several important questions about Philostratus's sources, contradictions within the *VA*, and the historical implausibility of the account, Eusebius anticipated item 6 of the Apollonian Decalogue.

---

16. Eusebius observed that Domitian and his officials would have surely heard of the resurrection of a girl from a consular family in Rome (*Hier.* 30.2; 35), yet this did not appear as one of the charges of sorcery against Apollonius during the trial (*Hier.* 30.2). On top of this, even Philostratus expressed doubt about this tale (*Hier.* 30.2). Eusebius also accused Philostratus of fabricating the story in which Apollonius thwarted a plague at Ephesus; he provided a naturalistic explanation of the event (*Hier.* 27.2–3).

17. Dzielska writes, "Lactantius attacks Apollonius himself, but Eusebius turns against his biographer" (Dzielska, *Apollonius*, 156).

18. Eusebius accepted that Apollonius was a philosopher (*Hier.* 5; 48.2), came from an old and wealthy family (*Hier.* 12.2), cured patients by giving sound medical advice (*Hier.* 12.2), was celibate (*Hier.* 12.3), and spent five years in silence in imitation of Pythagoras (*Hier.* 12.3).

19. Eusebius pointed out that these authors slandered Apollonius because they claimed that the sage praised Domitian to his face but condemned him privately (*Hier.* 43.2, 4).

Eusebius not only accused Philostratus and Damis of reshaping the story of Apollonius in the *VA*, but he also argued that it contradicted communal memories about Apollonius: "At the same time we need not devote too much attention and study to the gentleman's career, seeing that those of our contemporaries among whom his memory survives at all, are so far from classing him among divine and extraordinary and wonderful beings, that they do not even rank him among philosophers."[20] He also noted that past and contemporary people regarded Apollonius as an exceptional sorcerer (*Hier.* 44.2), in part because of the magical devices purportedly set up by him throughout the Roman world. By these arguments, Eusebius showed that the memory of Apollonius alive in his time did not match Philostratus's portrayal of him and by so doing appreciated the importance of earlier and contradictory sources, somewhat like items 1 and 2 of the Apollonian Decalogue, although he did not name the precise sources he had in mind. Eusebius's thorough and devastating response is noteworthy for being the first critique of the claims of the *VA*.

Lactantius embedded his rebuttal of Hierocles within his apologetic treatise *The Divine Institutes* (ca. AD 315). Sometime after Hierocles had been appointed governor of Bithynia, Lactantius had attended a public reading *The Lover of Truth* by its author, and he felt compelled to refute its sacrilegious claims.[21] His refutation was not as lengthy as that of Eusebius and did not focus exclusively on the comparison of Apollonius and Christ. Instead, it aimed at an array of charges raised by Hierocles such as the contradictions in the Scriptures (*Inst.* 5.1), the attacks upon the ignorant and deceitful apostles who authored them (*Inst.* 5.1), and the assertion that Christ was a mere magician. In this latter section, he responded to Hierocles's comparison of Jesus to Apollonius (*Inst.* 5.3).[22]

20. *Hier.* 32 (Conybeare, LCL). Conybeare's translation, quoted here, has this passage at section *Hier.* 32, while Jone's translation in the Loeb Classical Library places it at *Hier.* 36. Eusebius's statement challenges the accuracy of Philostratus's portrayal of Apollonius and may bear witness to another strain of tradition that held the Tyanean was a charlatan and magician.

21. Lactantius, *Inst.* 2.1; 4.2; see also the discussion of Dzielska. See Dzielska, *Apollonius*, 154.

22. One of Hierocles's complaints was that Christ was a magician and was, consequently, regarded as a god, yet Apollonius had performed equal or greater miracles (Lactantius, *Inst.* 5.3.8). Lactantius claimed that Apollonius was a better magician than Jesus because he had disappeared from his trial. Lactantius crowned his case with the argument that Christ was believed to be God neither because of his own testimony nor because he had performed miracles, but because of the testimony of the prophets who foretold his deeds and his suffering, a thing that had never happened in the case of any sorcerer, including Apollonius (Lactantius, *Inst.* 5.3.21).

The Hierocles controversy had several important results. One of them was that it renewed interest in traditions about Apollonius.[23] Another outcome was that it helped preserve and promote the *VA*, for all three participants in this literary debate had relied on it to make their cases. Dzielska points out that the *VA* had not been widely popular in the third century and that "Without Hierocles, Apollonius would remain for us only a figure from the biographic work of Philostratus, the figure shaped according to the abilities of this moderately gifted writer."[24] An additional result was an increase in pagan literary output concerning Apollonius: Latin translations or paraphrases of the *VA*[25] appeared and, perhaps inspired by the *VA*, new biographies of Apollonius were produced.[26] Finally, despite the renewed interest in Apollonius in the pagan

---

23. Shortly after the time of Hierocles, statues and effigies of Apollonius appeared and, in the fourth century, circular medallions of Apollonius were issued (Dzielska, *Apollonius*, 157, 172).

24. Dzielska, *Apollonius*, 15.

25. The first of these translations appeared in the last decades of the fourth century when Virius Nicomachus Flavianus either translated the *VA* into Latin or adapted it, perhaps for promoting his religious and political views. See Dzielska, *Apollonius*, 153, 181. Dzielska writes, "Such an outstanding politician as Nicomachus Flavianus would not have put so much effort into his translation of the *VA* if he had not aimed at popularizing the views of the Tyanean among the less educated classes of Roman society who did not know Greek" (Dzielska, *Apollonius*, 181). The fifth century Christian writer Sidonius Apollinaris was aware of two versions of the *VA* in Latin: the translation of Nicomacus and that of Tascius Victorianus, which had been based on the manuscript of Nicomacus. See Dzielska, *Apollonius*, 170, 180; Elsner, "A Protean corpus," 7. In addition to these works, Sidonius created a third version that was based on the work of Victorianus. Scholars are uncertain whether Sidonius referred to a Latin translation, an abbreviation of an extant Latin version, or a Greek transcription. Taggart writes, "It would stretch credence to believe that a Catholic chaplain from Narbo who lived in the court of a Visigoth king would know Greek. Yet the term *exscribere* which Sidonius uses to describe the manuscript he sent should be taken to mean 'copy' or 'transcribe' rather than 'translate'" (Taggart, "Apollonius of Tyana," 211). For a brief treatment of the various options laid out above, see C. P. Jones's comments in Philostratus, *Apollonius of Tyana*, 3:140, n. 47.

26. The author of the *Historia Augusta* (late fourth or early fifth century) spoke of Greek biographies of Apollonius's life—Philostratus's *VA* perhaps among those mentioned—and expressed his own desire to write of his deeds, if time permitted (*Hist. Aug.* Aur., 24.8–9). Taggert comments, "Whether anything ever came of "Vopiscus'" plan to compose a Latin biography of Apollonius is unknown. But apparently biographies of Apollonius were in circulation in certain literary circles as late as the late fourth and early fifth century A.D" (Taggart, "Apollonius of Tyana," 210). Basil of Seleucia (d. after AD 468) also mentions many had written lives of Philostratus. For this claim of Basil, see Philostratus, *Apollonius of Tyana*, 3:134.

world, the rebuttals of Eusebius and Hierocles appear to have shut down further pagan attempts to promote Apollonius as a rival to Christ.[27]

PAGAN AND CHRISTIAN *TESTIMONIA* ABOUT APOLLONIUS IN ANTIQUITY

Although the arguments of Eusebius and Lactantius appear to have effectively neutralized the arguments of Hierocles, in later times "Apollonius by no means disappears entirely from view."[28] Even though late antiquity saw more no heated debates between or large-scale literary comparisons of the followers of the Tyanean and the Nazarene, brief and sporadic comparisons of the two figures still appeared and the fame of Apollonius did not quickly wane.

Pagan opinions about Apollonius in this era varied. The majority of pagan texts remembered him as a philosopher, a portrayal that was based to a large extent on the presentation of him as such in Philostratus's *VA*.[29]

---

27. Taggart, "Apollonius of Tyana," 200. Moses Hadas argues that these Christian refutations "left Apollonius with a bad reputation as a wizard and charlatan;" Hadas, *Greek Literature*, 277. In actuality, the opinion that Apollonius was a disreputable magician existed long before any conflicts with Christianity (e.g., Lucian and Dio Cassius).

28. Taggart, "Apollonius of Tyana," 200.

29. Porphyry (c. AD 234–305) described Apollonius as a philosopher ("a wise man"; *On Abstinence* 2.34.2). Libanius (AD 314–c. 393) relied on the *VA* for his comments about Apollonius as a philosopher. In a discussion of several famous philosophers and orators, he asks who would say that the famous man from Tyana did not "know himself" (Libanius, *Oration* 4.4)? This latter remark is perhaps based on one or several instances in the *VA* where this Delphic maxim is mentioned (*VA* 4.44; 6.35; cf. 2.27; 7.14). In *Oration* 16.56, Libanius described Apollonius as he "who pilloried our city in two lines" (a reference to *VA* 1.16). Themistius (c. AD 317–c. 388) listed Apollonius along with Plato and Musonius Rufus as the three philosophers that distinguished themselves by fighting against tyranny (Themistius, *Or.* 6.72). He also mentioned the attempt by Domitian, the "the fratricide," to imprison Apollonius (cf. *VA* 6.32). Ammianius Marcellinus (c. AD 330–c. 395) assumed that Apollonius and others (Homer, Pythagoras, Socrates, Numa Pompilius, Scipio the elder, Marius, Octavian, Hermes Trismegistos, and Plotinus) were assisted by familiar spirits (Ammianius Marcellinus, *Hist.* 23.6.19). He also classed Apollonius as "that greatest of philosophers" (*amplissimus ille philosophus*), a title he also ascribed to Plato (Dzeilska, *Apollonius*, 176). In this same passage, his description of the temple of Asbamaean Jupiter and its spring resemble the details of the account in *VA* 1.6, yet with some discrepancies. Finally, a fourth or fifth century AD shield portrait of Apollonius was discovered among the remains of a philosophical school in Aphrodisias of Caria. Only the name of Apollonius and a torso survive. Apollonius was featured here along with several philosophers (Pythagoras, Pindar, Socrates, Aristotle) and leaders (Alexander of Macedon, and Alcibiades). Most likely the inscription referred to Apollonius of Tyana rather than Apollonius of Rhodes, because of the

Some pagans, however, regarded Apollonius as divine in some sense, a view that was also promoted in the *VA*.[30] Another pagan perspective, perhaps a residuum from the pre-Philostratean era, recalled Apollonius as a sorcerer.[31] Yet, most surprising of all are the great champions of paganism that did not mention the Tyanean at all: Libanius (AD 314–93), Julian the Apostate (AD 332–63), and Himerius (AD c. 315–c. 386). Even Iamblicus, who wrote a good deal about the Pythagoreans, did not list Apollonius among their most illustrious practitioners or refer to him in his *Life of Pythagoras*.[32]

Tyanean's eminence and its pairing with a portrait of Pythagoras, whom he followed. See Smith, "Late Roman Philosopher Portraits," 127–55.

30. Eunapius of Sardis (c. 345–414), a sophist in the court of Julian the Apostate, described Apollonius in his book, *The Lives of the Philosophers and Sophists* (2.1.4), as not a philosopher, but rather as something between a god and a human being. He suggested that Philostratus should have entitled his account *The Visit of a God to Mankind*. Eunapius later described Apollonius, Pythagoras, and Archytas as men who only seemed to possess bodies and to be men (23.1.8). The *Historia Augusta*, in its treatment of the *Life of Severus Alexander* (29.2), recorded that each morning the emperor sacrificed in a sanctuary that contained images of the deified emperors, his ancestors, and other holy men (Apollonius, Christ, Abraham, and Orpheus). In the same work's treatment of the *Life of Aurelian,* the long dead Apollonius appeared to Emperor Aurelian as he was considering the sacking of Tyana and told that he should spare the city if he wanted to be emperor and wanted to live. In response, the emperor spared Tyana and promised Apollonius an image, statues, and a temple. In describing Apollonius, Aurelion claimed that Apollonius should be worshipped for he of all mortal was like a god, for he had raised the dead and said things of which humans were incapable of uttering (*Hist. Aug.* Sev. 22.2–9). However, the *Historia Augusta* is not historically reliable in many respects. On this, see Bowersock, Introduction to *Life of Apollonius*, 12–13. Indeed, Jones regards this account as largely fictional but suggests portions of the story might be true since Orpheus often appears in Christian art as a prototype of Christ. See his comments in Philostratus, *Apollonius of Tyana*, 3:119, n. 32. Taggart views these as apocryphal stories, even though the author claims to have gotten them from trustworthy men and to have read the same account in the Ulpian library (Taggart, "Apollonius of Tyana, 208). As a final piece of evidence, a fragmentary *Inscription from Mopeuestia* (Cilicia) from the fourth or fifth century AD may hint at Apollonius's divinity by claiming either he was sent from heaven or now resides there. For this text, see Philostratus, *Apollonius of Tyana*, 3:131, n. 43; Burian and Richardson, "The Epigram on Apollonius," 283–85.

31. A Greek Magical Papyrus (fourth century AD) mentioned Apollonius as a magician (*PGM*, 2.54–55.11a). This spell appears to summon a goddess and transform her into the spellcaster's servant; Dzielska, *Apollonius*, 93, n. 19; Philostratus, *Apollonius of Tyana*, Philostratus, 3:131, n. 45.

32. Phillimore, *Philostratus*, xcv–xcvi, xcviii. Réville implausibly argues that the Alexandrian philosophers chose Pythagoras as their patron rather than Apollonius because Philostratus had disparaged the wisdom of Egypt; Réville, *Apollonius*, 80, 89. Actually, Philostratus's critique was not of the Alexandrians, the Pythagoreans, or even philosophers in general, but of the Ethiopian Gymnosophists, who most closely

PART 1: INTRODUCTORY ISSUES

Like their pagan counterparts, Christians also expressed a wide range of opinions concerning Apollonius. Some Christian writers regarded Apollonius as a mere magician.[33] Others regarded him as both a philosopher and a magician,[34] but even so, they did not place the magical deeds of Apollonius on par with the miracles of Christ and the apostles. For example, Jerome could speak well of Apollonius at times,[35] but he sharply distinguished between the power of the Lord and the tricks of the "magicians" (*magorum*), such as the feat of Apollonius's sudden

---

resembled the Cynics. Philostratus also rebuked the Ethiopian philosophers for straying from their Indian origins, which were essentially Pythagorean, a point at which the Alexandrian philosophers would not have taken offence. Perhaps, then, the reason these philosophers rejected Apollonius was because Pythagoras was more ancient, universally recognized, and was the founder of their movement, as Réville himself conceded (Réville, *Apollonius*, 90). Although Philostratus favored Apollonius because he lived closer to the time of his readers than Pythagoras (*VA* 1.2), for many thinkers, antiquity would have bestowed authority on Pythagoras and trumped the novelty of Apollonius. Yet, there must have been more to the issue than this, for there seems no good reason why the Alexandrians could not have embraced both holy men, rather than ignoring Apollonius altogether.

33. Origen (c. 185–255), in a discussion about sorcery, referred to Moiragenes's now lost memoirs of Apollonius. He remarked that notable philosophers were beguiled by Apollonius's magic (μαγείας), whom they had initially come to him as if he were charlatan sorcerer (ὡς πρὸς γόητα αὐτὸν εἰσελθόντας). Origen also mentioned that Euphrates, the opponent of Apollonius later featured in the *VA*, was in this company of philosopher (*Cels.* 6.41). The Bordeaux Pilgrim (AD 333) passed through Tyana, the city of the sorcerer Apollonius (*Appollonius magus*), on his way to Jerusalem (*CSEL* 39.16). Cyril of Alexandria (c. 376–444) paraphrased an episode from the visit of Apollonius to the Gymnosophists recounted in the *VA* (*VA* 6.10.3; *Against Julian* 3). Pseudo-Ambose (fourth or fifth century) relates another story from the *VA* (8.5.4 and 8.8) in which the "magician" (*magus*) Apollonius disappeared during his trial before Domitian, (*On the Trinity*, 29).

34. Jerome (AD 347–420), in his *Chronicle* on Olympiad (218.4), allowed that some regarded Apollonius and Euphrates as notable philosophers (*insignes philosophi habentur*). Augustine (AD 354–430), in *Letter* 102.32, stated that, if what had been said about Jonah's three day stay in the belly of the fish had been said about Apollonius and Apuleius, who are called "magicians or philosophers" (*magos uel philosophos*), pagans would have responded not with laughter but with pride. He further noted that even though the miraculous claims of those two pagan men were not supported by reliable testimony, demons may have given the impression of having performed real miracles like those of holy angels. Synesius of Cyrene (c. 373–c. 414) included Apollonius in his catalogue of bald sages, although he conceded that Apollonius had long hair; he also classed him with sorcerers and those adept at demonic practices (*Eulogy of Baldness* 6.2).

35. Jerome, *Epist.* 53.1.3–4. Here, Jerome praised Apollonius, "that great man," for finding something to learn wherever he travelled and for seeking to improve himself.

disappearance from Domitian's courtroom.[36] A similar theme emerges in Augustine's exchange with his friend Marcellinus (*Letter* 136) in which Augustine was asked to respond to the false charge that the Lord had done nothing more miraculous than Apollonius, Apuleius, or other men acquainted with the magical arts had done. In his reply (*Letter* 138), Augustine first dismissed their comparison of such men as these with Christ as ridiculous but also jests that it is more tolerable that they compare the Lord to a chaste man like Apollonius than to Jupiter, with his many indecencies. In contrasting the libidinous head of the Roman pantheon with the celibate Apollonius, Augustine likely shows his dependence on the *VA*, for that text stressed Apollonius's chastity (*VA* 1.13.3).[37] Like their pagan counterparts, most of these Christian authors drew upon the *VA* for information about Apollonius.[38]

However, on occasion, alternative traditions that cast Apollonius in the role of a magician resurfaced in Christian references. Apollonius was linked to talismans located in several cities that allegedly warded off wild animals and provided protection against earthquakes (Eusebius, *Hier.* 44.2). Eusebius had also referred to contemporary opinions about Apollonius that he was not a holy man (*Hier.* 36) but an exceptional magician (*Hier.* 44.2). John Chrysostom (AD 349–407), in one passage, contrasts the unsuccessful attempts of Apollonius to establish a movement that matched the success of Christ's church. He argued that Apollonius's attempts at reform failed, largely due to his miracles being counterfeit.[39]

---

36. Jerome, *Jo. Hier.*, 34; Dzielska, *Apollonius*, 178. Jerome also defended the apostles, Paul and Peter, from Porphyry's charge that they used magical arts by countercharging that the Magi of Egypt, Apollonius, and Apuleius worked miracles by means of magical arts (*magis artibus*) to extract money from wealthy women whom they had duped (Jerome, *Homily on Psalm 81*). Although there are no known charges of stealing from women were leveled against Apollonius, Apuleius was charged with using spells and charms to gain affections of Pudentilla and wrote his *Apologia* as a defense against these allegations.

37. For translations of these letters, see Philostratus, *Apollonius of Tyana*, 3:125, 127.

38. Jerome, *Epist.* 53.1.3–4. In this epistle, Jerome seems to rely on the *VA* for the basic itinerary of Apollonius (e.g., Persia, the Caucuasus, India, Alexandria, Ethiopia) and he meets the same groups and figures (e.g., Brahmans, Iarchus, Chaldeans, Parthians, Arabs, Gymnosophists), yet his list of Apollonius's travels is filled with details that differ somewhat from Philostratus's account (e.g., Apollonius did not visit Scythia or Palestine in the *VA*).

39. Chrysostom writes, "To help you see the truth of this, consider how many men wished to introduce their teachings among the Greeks and to establish a new commonwealth and way of life. Think of such men as Zeno, Plato, Socrates, Diagoras,

In another passage, Chrysostom used the argument from the efficacy of Christ's miracles to account for the church's survival in the face of tyrants and whole peoples who rose against it, and he refused to allow a comparison of Christ to Apollonius as a mere magician, for he was a "cheat and a charlatan" who was famous in "a tiny part of the world, and for a short time" before being snuffed out without a legacy.[40] Perhaps it could be argued that Chrysostom deemed Apollonius a fraud from his reading of the *VA*, yet his assertion that Apollonius was famous in a tiny area of the world and for a short time appears to contradict the *VA*'s picture of him as a world-renowned globetrotter. Jerome (AD 347–420), who knew of the *VA*, also indicates an awareness of contradictory traditions about Apollonius when he ponders "whether he was a magician (*magus*) as the vulgar say, or a philosopher, as the Pythagoreans say."[41] This negative evaluation of Apollonius as a fraud and a magician closely resembles the pre-Philostratean opinions of Lucian or Dio Cassius and suggests that this variant tradition, although its sound was dampened, could still occasionally be heard alongside the positive portrayal of the *VA*.

Macarius of Magnesia (fifth century), an eastern writer,[42] mentioned Apollonius in two passages of his *Apocriticus*. This work provides

---

Pythagoras, and countless others. Yet they fell so far short of success that many people do not even now know them by name. But Christ not only wrote a constitution but even brought a new way of life to the whole world. How many miracles do they say that Apollonius of Tyana worked? But all his deeds were a fraud, a vain show, and devoid of truth. And you may learn this from the fact that, in an instant, they vanished and disappeared. Let no one consider it an insult to Christ that, while speaking of him, I mentioned Pythagoras, Plato, Zeno and the man from Tyana. I am not doing this of my own choice but out of consideration for the weakness of the Jews, who see in Christ a mere man." (*Adv. Jud.* 5.3.1–2). For this translation, see Chrysostom, *Discourses*, 104–5.

40. Chrysostom states, "From where then, tell me, does such a great power come?' 'He was a magician,' someone says. Well, then, he was the only magician that has turned out like this. Surely you have heard that among the Persians and the Indians there have been many magicians, and that there are still some now. But not even their name is known anywhere. 'But what about the man from Tyana?' someone says. 'That man was a cheat and a charlatan and he was renowned.' Where, and when? In a tiny part of the world, and for a short time, then he was quickly snuffed out and perished, leaving behind neither a church nor a people, nor any other such thing. And why do I mention the magicians and charlatans whose lives have been snuffed out? From what power did all the cults of the gods cease, both the Dodona and the Claros, and all these wicked workshops fall silent and be muzzled?" (*Hom.* 4.7.197–94.8.198). This translation is taken from Mitchell, *The Heavenly Trumpet*, 461.

41. Jerome, *Epist.* 53.1.3–4. Just which Pythagoreans Jerome had in mind here are unclear, for the extant literature of that school does not reference Apollonius at all.

42. The author of the Apocriticus appears to have shown particular interest in Asia Minor, eastern heretics (Montanus of Phrygia; Dositheus of Cilicia, and the Encratites

the most substantial comparison of Apollonius with Christ from this later era. The *Apocriticus* contains a dialogue that supposedly took place between Macarius and an anonymous pagan opponent. Some scholars believe that the questions of the pagan interlocutor in this work are based on a lost work of the Neoplatonic philosopher and critic of Christianity, Porphyry (*Against the Christians*).[43] The significance of this view, if it were correct, would be that Porphyry predated Hierocles and thus would have been the first to use the *VA* against the Christians. Other researchers believe, with good reason, that these questions were addressing issues raised by Hierocle's *Lover of Truth*.[44] Whatever the origin of the queries in the book, the work indicates the sorts of questions pagans asked (or at least those that Christians thought pagans might ask) about Apollonius and provided the appropriate Christian response to them.

The two passages in the *Apocriticus* reflect either direct or indirect knowledge of the *VA*, perhaps via Hierocles. In the first passage, the unnamed pagan interlocutor asked why Christ did not instruct Pilate during his trial, as Apollonius did during his interrogation by Domitian, rather than remaining silent and being mocked (*Apocriticus* 3.1). Both the pagan's question and Macarius's response in this passage reference

---

of Asia Minor), church leaders (e.g., Polycarp of Smyrna), and other natives of the area (e.g., Apollonius of Tyana and Aratus of Cilicia). Crafer, *The Apocritucus*, xvi.

43. Beginning with Harnack, several scholars have espoused the view that the *Apocriticus* addressed the arguments of Porphyry. For this view, see Petzke, *Die Traditionen*, 21; Dzielska, *Apollonius*, 98; Hoffman, *Porphyry's Against the Christians*, 18–19; Schirren, "Irony," 162, n. 4. Yet, Barnes points out that "if Macarius was quoting Porphyry, he was totally unaware of the fact. His *Apocriticus*, only half of which is still extant, consists of questions or problems posed by an adversary, usually in groups, and of Macarius' answers. The dialogue is depicted as a historical event witnessed by a crowd of onlookers, the adversary as a contemporary–and at one point he is referred to Porphyry" (Barnes, "Porphyry," 428). The quotation from Porphyry to which Macarius referred is in Eusebius *Praep. ev.* 4.6.3. Unfortunately, the evidence is not sufficient now in scholarship to conclusively support the view that Porphyry's material stands behind questions in the *Apocriticus*.

44. Other scholars have argued that the pagan content derives from Hierocles, partially because the content and wording of several passages within the *Apocriticus* that closely resemble *The Lover of Truth*. Macarius's statement that Apollonius disappeared from before the judgment seat is echoed Eusebius and Lactantius in their refutation of has Hierocles. Further, "whereas the language of the objector in the Apocriticus has nothing in common with the extent words of Porphyry, there are a few sentences given by Eusebius as occurring verbatim in the *Philalethes* of Hierocles, in which, out of eleven words of a distinctive king, no less than seven are found in the Apocriticus" (Crafer, *Apocriticus*, xiii–xv). This argument is made more plausible by the numerous references in the *Apocritucus* to events in the *VA* on which *The Lover of Truth* was based.

events from the *VA*: Apollonius's bold speech before Domitian (*VA* 8.1–7), his disappearance from Domitian's courtroom, (*VA* 8.4.4; 8.8) and his supernatural journey from Rome to Dicaearchia in a few hours (*VA* 8.10–12). In the second passage (*Apocriticus* 4.5), the critic argued that Christ's warning that many would come in his name and lead many astray (Matt 24:4–5) was never fulfilled: "Why look, three hundred or more years have passed, and no one of that sort has appeared, unless you mean to say Apollonius of Tyana, a man adorned with every kind of wisdom; you cannot find another. Yet he does not talk of one person but of many, (saying) 'They will arise.'" Macarius responded to this objection by pointing to Manes, Montanus, Cerinthus, Simon Magus, Marcion, and others who had fulfilled this prophecy of Christ. Nevertheless, his pagan interlocutor noted that Apollonius's wisdom resembled that of Christ (*VA* 3.58; 4.1, 25.1; 6.11.3; 8.7.39; 8.13.2) and, implicitly, identified the Tyanean as a rival of the Nazarene. The first example above from *Apocriticus* draws on details from the *VA*.

After the time of the Hierocles controversy, Christian references to Apollonius were rarely polemical in the west[45] or the east.[46] By that time, the Tyanean seems to have been more of a curiosity than a threat. Bishop Sidonius Apollinaris (c. 430–86), the final figure from the west to show tremendous interest in the man from Tyana, sent a copy of his work the *Life of Apollonius the Pythagorean* to his friend Leo[47] and recommended that he read the work for its philosophical and ascetic value. His only caveat was that Leo read it "with deference to the Catholic faith."[48] So, sometime between the era of Eusebius and Sidonius, Christians lost their fear of Apollonius and some even saw value in some of the principles he taught and exhibited in the *VA*.

---

45. Taggart observed that, "[t]he Latin Fathers are much less harsh in their treatment of Apollonius than had been their counterparts in the Greek-speaking East, and this is due, perhaps, simply to the passage of time and to the continuing success of Christian polemicism" (Taggart, "Apollonius of Tyana," 205).

46. Petzke, *Die Traditionen*, 28.

47. Leo served in the court of the Visogothic king Euric.

48. Taggart, "Apollonius of Tyana," 210.

THE "TALISMANIAN" DEVIL: CHRISTIAN REACTIONS TO THE ΤΕΛΕΣΜΑΤΑ OF APOLLONIUS

A study of Apollonius in antiquity would be incomplete if it did not address the talismans (τελέσματα) that Apollonius allegedly installed in numerous eastern cities (e.g., Byzantium and Antioch of Syria) to protect their inhabitants against disease, earthquakes, and wild beasts.[49] Although the evidence for these devices is entirely literary,[50] their existence is confirmed by a number of pagan and Christian references to them. The public nature and apparent effectiveness of these magical devices helped keep the memory of Apollonius alive and, perhaps more than anything else, forced Christians to interact with his legend. The sheer number of inquiries sent to and replies from Christian authorities on the topic of these talismans demonstrates that this is one of the more troublesome aspects of Apollonius with which the church had to contend.

The origin of these talismans is still a mystery. The earliest sources do not report that Apollonius constructed such devices.[51] The *VA* did not mention such devices and, consequently, it is unlikely to have been the source of this legend,[52] for the word *telesma* does not occur in the *VA*,[53] and Philostratus never recorded a visit of Apollonius to Byzantium where several of these objects were erected.[54] Perhaps Philostratus intentionally omitted that Apollonius had manufactured talismans from the *VA* for such devices might have complicated the case that the Tyanean

---

49. Hesychius of Miletus (sixth century) reported that Apollonius fashioned a statue of three storks at Byzantium. Malalas (sixth century) records several Apollonian talismans near Byzantium, and he made some against the north wind and against scorpions (a scorpion on a column) at Antioch of Syria. The *Chronicon Paschale* (seventh century) mentions the consecration of talismans of turtles, horses, and others at Byzantium. George Cedrenus (eleventh century) was still relating the stories of these objects that warded off scorpions and snakes in Byzantium and scorpions and mosquitoes in Antioch. For a more detailed treatment of the sources mentioned in this note, consult Duliére, "Protection permanente," 253–55, 258; Martí-Aguilar, "Talismans against Tsunamis," 975.

50. According to Nicetus, the talisman of an eagle and serpent still existed in the Hippodrome of Constantinople until 1204 when it was eventually melted down (*Ann.* 10.649–51). For an English translation of this work, see Nicetus, *O City of Byzantium,"* 357–60.

51. Dzielska, *Apollonius*, 100.

52. Photius, *Bibliotheca*, 44; Dzielska, *Apollonius*, 100.

53. Taggart, "Apollonius of Tyana," 203.

54. Duliére, "Protection permanente," 247.

was a sage and not a wizard.⁵⁵ It could be that the *VA* provided the raw material for constructing a bridge between the legend of Apollonius and these talismans. The Tyanean reportedly rescued cities from disasters⁵⁶ and visited at least one talismanic site⁵⁷ but there is no hard evidence for the proposal that the *VA* suggested a connection between Apollonius and these objects.

Another theory is that the talismans first emerged in the wake of the publication of Hierocles's *The Lover of Truth*.⁵⁸ This view is possible: these magical devices (περιέργους μηχανὰς) were first mentioned by Eusebius a mere decade after the publication of this tract.⁵⁹ Yet it is also possible that the talismans existed at the time of Hierocles and that Eusebius just happened to be the first author to refer to them.

Another proposal is that such devices were indeed constructed by the historical Apollonius. Yet, his construction of the talismans of Byzantium is questionable for no early record of his visit to the city exists and many of the legends surrounding the creation of these devices are plagued with historical problems.⁶⁰ Perhaps Apollonius's talismans were based on the earlier example of the devices created by the pre-Socratic philosopher Empedocles.⁶¹ At this point, there is insufficient evidence to account for the origin of the talismans.

What is indisputable, though, is that many pagans and Christians acknowledged the effectiveness of these objects.⁶² In light of their efficacy, it is no surprise that Christians saw these objects as a challenge

---

55. Anderson suggests this possibility ("Folklore," 222).

56. *VA* 4.4, 10.

57. The *VA* details Apollonius's visit to the temple of Hercules at Gadiera, which contained cubit-high pillars that possibly performed talismanic functions: these bound earth and sea together so that the elements were in harmony (*VA* 5.5). However, Apollonius was merely a visitor to this site and had nothing to do with its construction. For a detailed discussion of the temple and these pillars, see Martí-Aguilar, "Talismans," 968–93.

58. Dzielska, *Apollonius*, 99, 124.

59. Eusebius, *Hier*. 44.2.

60. Hesychius of Miletus claimed that Apollonius erected a talisman in Constantinople, consisting of a statue of three storks, to prevent birds poisoning wells by dropping snakes into them; see Martí-Aguilar, "Talismans," 975.

61. Empedocles made bags from donkey skins and placed them on hilltops to prevent the etesian winds from destroying crops (Diogenes Laertius, *Empedocles*, 60). In *VA* 1.2, Empedocles, like Apollonius, is said to have associated with magicians without having been corrupted by them.

62. Dzielska, *Apollonius*, 107.

to the validity of the Christian worldview. After all, how could Christ, who was Lord of all creation, allow the talismans of a mere magician to continue to exert power in the world when his miracles were relegated to the time of his ministry in the distant past?

Christians attempted to account for the efficacy of these talismans in several ways. One approach, taken by such figures as Nilus of Ancyra (d. ca. AD 430),[63] and Basil of Seleucia (d. after AD 468),[64] was to attribute their powers to sorcery.[65] A second Christian explanation for the potency of these objects was that their magic was benefic. For instance, Pseudo-Justin (fifth century?) surmised that Apollonius had created talismans through his understanding of natural powers. He pointed out that, on the one hand, God did not annul their effects because they did not conflict with nature but that, on the other hand, God had silenced the oracular demon within an image of Apollonius that had once led people to worship him as a god. Pseudo-Nonnus (ca. AD 500) made a similar case for Apollonius's use of beneficent magic: "Magic differs from sorcery and sorcery from witchcraft. Magic is calling on beneficent demons who do good for the attainment of some good purpose, as the talismans of Apollonius of Tyana exist for a good purpose" (*On Gregory of Nazianzen*, Against Julian 1.70 [Jones, LCL]).[66] Finally, some Christian authors attempted to disassociate Apollonius from the talismans: Eusebius was skeptical of the rumors that Apollonius had set up such devices,[67] while Isodore of Pelusium (d. ca. AD 450) denied that Apollonius had fashioned these talismans because Philostratus, who had accurately recorded the history of Apollonius, said nothing about his creation of talismans and had cleared Apollonius of the malicious charge of magical practices. Significantly, none of these figures argued against the efficacy of these devices.

---

63. Nilus of Sinai (*Letter* 148) encouraged his readers not to admire or be disconcerted by these talismans that were the product of Apollonius's magical powers.

64. Basil of Seleucia, *Life and Miracles of Saint Thecla* 22.

65. Basil used elements of the *VA* to argue this point. He recalls that Apollonius was not welcomed by the Gymnosophists in Egypt and India, thereby showing that he was not a philosopher or holy, but rather was tainted by sorcery. Although he was incorrect about Apollonius's reception by the Indians, who according to the *VA* gave him a hearty welcome, he was also initially rejected in Ethiopia. However, this rejection was not because Apollonius was a sorcerer but because of a false report that he was arrogant (*VA* 6.7).

66. For this passage, see Philostratus, *Apollonius of Tyana*, 3:135.

67. Eusebius, *Hier.* 44.2.

PART 1: INTRODUCTORY ISSUES

These talismans constituted a unique strand of Apollonian tradition in the ancient world. Their placement within the Apollonian traditions is ambiguous: do they fit best with the view that Apollonius was a benevolent wonderworker of the VA[68] or with the earlier tradition that he was a magician? At any rate, the talismans of Apollonius continued to be discussed by later Christian writers (Hesychius of Miletus, sixth century; Malalas, ca. AD 491–578) and even passed into Arabic traditions, where Apollonius came to be known by the name Balinas.

APOLLONIUS IN THE EAST: BYZANTIUM AND BEYOND

In the East, interest in Apollonius continued throughout the Byzantine period and even after Byzantium fell to the Ottoman Turks in 1453. Much like in antiquity, the authors of this period varied quite a bit in their opinions of Apollonius.

Two types of positive assessments of Apollonius are attested by church writers. The first was that Apollonius was not a magician, just as the VA had argued. Photius (c. AD 815–97), the patriarch of Constantinople, spoke of Apollonius as a benevolent philosopher (*Bibliotheca*, 44).[69] In his summary of the VA, Photius indicated that Philostratus intended to prove that Apollonius was not a wonderworker, but rather that he was an enemy of magicians and performed his amazing feats employing his philosophical knowledge. Although Photius did not dispute these claims and is not critical of Apollonius himself, he offered a severe critique of the absurdities that occurred during the visit to India, thereby anticipating item 6 of the Apollonian Decalogue. George Cedrinus (eleventh century), a Byzantine historian, presented a second type of positive view of Apollonius as a benevolent magician. In his *Synopsis historion*, Cedrinus referred to the practice of invoking beneficent demons for good purposes, "just as in the matters of Apollonius of Tyana" (ὥσπερ τὰ τοῦ Τυανέως Ἀπολλωνίου)[70] and illustrated the good that such magic could do by mentioned the talismans of Apollonius in Byzantium and Antioch of Syria.[71]

---

68. Petzke, *Die Traditionen*, 156.
69. Photius, *The Library of Photius*, 37–38.
70. For the Greek text, see Cedrenus, *Georgius Cedrenus*, 73.
71. Duliére, "Protection permanente," 258.

Yet, occasionally, negative presentations of Apollonius as a black magician resurfaced along with a negative critique of his interaction with demons. Anastasius Sinaita, in his *Questions and Answers* (PG 89.524D–525B), told an apocryphal tale about the three magicians Apollonius, Apuleius, and Julianus, who competed to see who could rescue Rome from a plague. Julianus, who was closer to the Devil, bested his rivals.[72] After this tale, Anastasius related several acts of Apollonius that were done through the agency of demons while he was alive (e.g., diverting harmful animals and flowing rivers) and even listed miracles that were performed in his name at his tomb.[73] In the *Chronicle* written by the Byzantine monk George Harmartolos (c. AD 867), the iconoclastic Patriarch John VII (AD 838–843) was described as "the chief conspirator or rather chief sorcerer and chief demon" and as the new Apollonius of Tyana and Balaam.[74] Even in this era, the negative view of Apollonius persisted alongside the positive one.

In post-Byzantine times, a curious transformation took place in Orthodox circles as Apollonius of Tyana seems to have been confused or conflated with a much earlier figure named Apollo. According to Pseudo-Athanasius,[75] a certain wise man named Apollo (σοφός τις ὀνόματι Ἀπόλλων), who lived long before the time of Christ, was moved by God to build a temple in Athens along with an altar dedicated to the unknown god. Seven philosophers—Titon, Bias, Solon, Cheilon, Thucydides, Menander, and Plato—gathered to ask him about the temple, prophecy, and the advent of this new god. At that time, Apollo prophesied that the Logos would be conceived in a maiden named Mary and that he would take the whole world captive. Oddly, the Apollo of this story also seems to fit the description of a philosopher named Apollonius given by Dionysius of Fourna (ca. AD 1670–1744). Fourna authored a manual on

72. The tale is suspect because Apollonius was a first century figure, while Apuleius and Julianus lived in the second century. See Penella, "An Overlooked Story," 414; Anderson, "Folklore," 222.

73. This tradition appears to contradict Philostratus's claim that he had never seen a tomb of Apollonius (*VA* 8.31.3). Philostratus may have denied the existence of a tomb because he wanted to leave the impression that the philosopher had vanished or ascended to heaven (*VA* 8.30.2–3). Alternately, the monument or tomb to Apollonius that Anastasias mentioned (1) may have been constructed after the time of Philostratus, (2) may have been a building misidentified in later times as the sage's tomb, or (3) may have been a fiction altogether.

74. Barber, *Contesting the Logic of Painting*, 8.

75. Ps.-Athanasius, *On the Temple at Athens*. For the Greek text of the commentary, see Delatte, "Le déclin de la Légendes," 97–111.

iconography in which he placed Apollonius first in the list of the wise men of Greece who foretold the incarnation of Christ. He states that Apollonius is to be represented in the following fashion: "Apollonius: An old man, with a large beard separated in two, wearing his turban on his head, he says on a scroll: 'I announce in a trinity, a single God reigning over all things. His incorruptible Word will be conceived in the womb of a virgin. Like a person who throws fire, he will pass through space, he will seize the whole universe alive, and present himself to his father.'"[76] Just such a depiction of Apollonius and a similar inscription can be seen on the monastery gate at Vatopaidi (by Nikephoros, ca. 1858, 1870).[77] Is this a description of Apollonius of Tyana, who was transfigured into a saint[78] (or at least into a pagan prophet who predicted the coming of Christ), or another figure altogether who was named Apollos or Apollonius? On the one hand, this Apollo (or Apollonius) predated the seven Greek sages who also predicted Christ's coming, thereby ruling him out as Apollonius of Tyana. On the other, this figure was also a philosopher like the Tyanean, and he supposedly established a temple in Athens to the unknown god (cf. Acts 17:3). Although Philostratus never indicated that Apollonius of Tyana constructed such a temple, he did mention altars in Athens dedicated to unknown gods (*VA* 6.3.5).

APOLLONIUS IN THE WEST: THE MIDDLE AGES

Scholars frequently state that Sidonius was the last major writer to mention Apollonius in the Latin West until the Renaissance.[79] However, such statements are not quite accurate. Porreca is closer to the truth with his remark that "this is the final instance where Philostratus's biography of Apollonius is mentioned firsthand in the Western tradition until its recovery during the Renaissance."[80] Yet, even this statement does not tell

---

76. Dionysios of Fourna, *Manuel D'Iconographie Chretienne*, 148. For the Greek texts, see Didron, *Manuel D'Iconographie*, 148.

77. Icons of Apollonius can be seen in the narthex of some churches (St. Nicolas church on Joannina Island, Epirus from c. AD 1560); Dzielska, *Apollonius*, 182; Petzke, *Die Traditionen*, 35.

78. Koskenniemi, *Apollonios*, 9.

79. Phillimore, *In Honour*, ci; Philostratus, *Apollonius of Tyana*, 3:20; Petzke, *Die Traditionen*, 10.

80. Porreca, "Apollonius of Tyana," 165–67.

the whole tale, for Apollonius (or Balinus) and the *VA* were still mentioned in a few texts of the Middle Ages.[81]

At least two historical texts of the Medieval period mention both Apollonius and the *VA*. The anonymous editor of Paul the Deacon's (ca. AD 720–799) *Roman History* retold a few episodes from the *VA* and recalled that Philostratus was the biographer of Apollonius. This later point was repeated in Ekkehard of Aura's (1126) *Universal Chronicle*.[82] Although these texts yield minimal information, they demonstrate that Apollonius, the *VA*, and its author were still remembered by some.

Several magical texts mention Apollonius and may even draw upon Philostratus's biography. Hugo of Santalla's (twelfth century) Latin translation of the Arabic text *Kitāb sirr al-ḫalīqa* (*Book of the Secret of Creation*) may allude to the *VA*.[83] Although much of its description of Balinus (Apollonius) contradicts the information in the *VA*,[84] its tale of Balinus's descent into an underground chamber to retrieve the Emerald Tablet (*Tabula smaragdina*) from Hermes is reminiscent of the *VA*'s account of Apollonius's descent into the cave of Trophonius from which he returned with a book of Pythagorean teachings (*VA* 8.19).[85] Another magical text, the *Ars Notoria*,[86] claims to have had Apollonius as its author. Within its pages, Apollonius instructed the reader on how to acquire knowledge of all the arts without study and to gain a perfect memory of all that is learned. The Apollonius of the *Ars Notoria* and the *VA* are similar in several ways, suggesting a garbled transmission of traditions between the two works. For instance, the *Ars Notoria* places Apollonius in the role of a teacher (Magister) who is knowledgeable in all fields of study,[87] which resembles the Philostratus's portrayal of the

---

81. Cassiodorus (c. AD 485–c. 585) regarded Apollonius as a notable philosopher (Apollonius Tyaneus philosophus insignis) in his *Chronica*, 9.

82. Porreca, "Apollonius of Tyana," 172–73.

83. Porreca, "Apollonius of Tyana," 166.

84. For instance, the *Book of the Secret Creation* contradicts the *VA* in describing Balinus (Apollonius) as an orphan of Tyana, destitute, and possessing the art of talismans. For the translation of this Arabic work, see Colavito, "Book of the Secret Creation," paras. 4–67.

85. Porreca, "Apollonius of Tyana," 166.

86. The *Ars Notoria* may be the earliest portion of the *Lemegeton Clavicula Salomonis*, which in turn belongs to the Medieval "Solomon Cycle" that dates back at least as far as the thirteenth century. For a discussion of this material, see Peterson, *The Lesser Key of Solomon*, xvii.

87. *Ars Notoria*, 2.

sage. Another similarity is that the Apollonius of the *Ars Notoria* did not acquire his knowledge through study, but by direct infusion of knowledge from God, much like the Apollonius of the *VA* simply knew things from his guardian spirit or the gods (e.g., *VA* 1.18; 8.7.31).[88] Yet another resemblance is that the *Ars Notoria* employs several languages–Chaldee, Hebrew, Greek, and Latin–in teaching this pure science;[89] such skills are befitting the Apollonius of the *VA*, who knew all human languages without having to study them (*VA* 1.19.2). Finally, Apollonius is associated with astronomy in this work (*Ars Notoria*, 13, 18.20b), as he is in *VA* (3.41.1–2), although Philostratus went to great lengths to distance him from such questionable practices. So then, Apollonius seems to have been remembered in some quarters after the time of Sidonius. In these later texts, Apollonius appears to be a hybrid of the Philostratean philosopher and the pre-Philostratean sorcerer.

THE RENAISSANCE AND THE ADVENT OF THE *VA* IN THE WEST

The introduction of new works of classical literature into Western Europe during the Renaissance sparked interest in Apollonius in intellectual circles.[90] Occult texts, which in the opinion of some included the *VA*, created tension between those who held fast to a traditional Christian worldview and scholars who were open to a synthesis of ancient pagan and Christian ideas. Thinkers who favored the latter position did not pit Apollonius against Christ, as had been done in earlier eras, but rather blended the teachings of the Tyanean with their beliefs about Christianity, philosophy, Hermeticism, and Kabbalah. In their discussions about the supernatural, these scholars were careful to distinguish natural

---

88. Much as Apollonius in the *VA* received information from his guardian spirit, so the *Ars Notoria* claimed that God revealed esoteric skills to Solomon through his holy angel (*Ars Notoria*, 1). No angel is mentioned as an intermediary in the biblical account of Solomon's reception of wisdom (1 Kgs 3:4–15), but Solomon's ability to gain information from and control angels (and jinn) is mentioned in later traditions (Josephus *Ant.* 8.42; Q al-Naml 27:17–19), perhaps most notably in the *Testament of Solomon*. Since Apollonius was the successor of Solomon in these arts, the author of the *Ars Notoria* may have assumed an angel was the source of Apollonius's wisdom or may have interpreted the guardian spirit in the Philostratean tradition as an angel (*Ars Notoria*, 7, 18).

89. *Ars Notoria*, 3, 8, 13, 14, 19, 63, 81.

90. Dzielska, *Apollonius*, 193.

magic, a beneficent type of magic based on a manipulation of natural forces (e.g., astronomy and alchemy), from harmful, ceremonial magic. Marsilio Ficino, even though a priest, saw no conflict between Christianity and the practices of astrology and natural magic; he referenced Apollonius frequently and with approval.[91] Pico della Mirandola, unlike Ficino, rejected the validity of astrology.[92] Yet, in his *Oration on the Dignity of Man* (1486), he included Apollonius with philosophers like Pythagoras, Empedocles, Plato, and Democritus who practiced a form of "magic" (μαγεία), the highest form of natural philosophy, but who had no truck with the other form of "magic" (γοητεία), which relied upon the operations and powers of demons.[93] Most of Pico's[94] and Ficino's[95] references to Apollonius were based on material found in the *VA*.

Perhaps the most significant event of the Renaissance period related to the man from Tyana was the publication of several editions of Philostratus's *Life of Apollonius*. Aldus Manutius (ca. 1449–1515), a Venetian humanist and publisher, was the first to print Philostratus's *Life of Apollonius* in Greek (1501–1502), and the text was accompanied by Alemano Rinuccini's Latin translation of the work.[96] The date of its publication coincided with the Vatican's attack on occult arts and the persecution

---

91. At the insistence of Cosimo de Medici, Ficino translated the *Corpus Hermeticum* into Latin in 1463. It was printed in 1471; see Rudolph, *Gnosis*, 26.

92. Burckhardt, *The Civilization*," 319.

93. Pico, *Oration on the Dignity of Man*, 55. For a brief discussion of Pico's distinction between the two types of magic, natural and criminal and its use in Butzbach's later defense of Trithemius, see Zambelli, *White Magic, Black Magic*, 53–55.

94. Pico's argument in *Oration* suggests familiarity with the *VA*, for Philostratus also listed many of the same philosophers (Pythagoras, Empedocles, Democritus, and Plato), discussed their travels to study "magic" abroad with foreigners, and made a distinction between acceptable and unacceptable magical or supernatural practices (*VA* 1.1.2–1.2.2).

95. E.g., in *On obtaining life from the heavens*, Ficino quotes the Indian Iarchus (*VA* 3.42) in chapter 3, mentions Apollonius's unmasking of Lamiae (*VA* 4.25.2–6) in chapter 21, and references the story of the plague-demon disguised as an old man (*VA* 4.10) in chapter 23. For English translations of these three passages, see Voss, *Marsilio Ficino*, 121, 152, 168. However, not all his references to Apollonius were from the *VA*. In a letter to the physician Tommaso Valeri, mentioned that "Pythagoras, Empedocles, and Apollonius of Tyana are said to have cured diseases with chants rather than with herbs" (Ficino, *Meditations on the Soul*, 205). Although Pythagoras was known to have used music to heal both body and soul (Iamblicus, *Vit. Pyth.* 15; Porphyry, *Vit. Pyth.* 30), there is no clear example of Apollonius using this technique in the classical literature. In *Epp. Apoll.* 9, Apollonius directs Dio to sooth with music, not with language. However, healing is not technically in view in that context.

96. Manutius, *Philostrati*; Boter, "Critical Edition," 22–23.

of certain humanists, who were suspected of dabbling in them. Therefore, Aldus's book was published along with Eusebius's *Reply to Hierocles* to prevent, as he put it, the "pagan poison" of the *VA* from spreading without the remedy; this decision may have had the secondary purpose of protecting him from censure by the church.[97] He also wrote disparagingly of the *VA* in the preface to the work, "I do not remember ever reading anything of lower quality or less deserving of attention."[98] Whether his motive for publishing Eusebius along with the *VA* was genuine or merely a ploy to shake church officials off his scent, it did set the precedent of publishing the two works together.[99] Aldus's text was followed by translations of the *VA* in Italian[100] and French,[101] as well as by Morel's publication of the complete Greek corpus of Philostratus (1608) which was largely based on the Aldine text.[102]

However, Apollonius was not appreciated by all scholars of the Renaissance. French philosopher Michel de Montaigne (1533–1592) mentioned Apollonius within his *Essais*, several times disparagingly or as a negative example.[103] In the context of discussing the ease with which people are manipulated by leaders, he wrote, "I am no longer amazed at those who are hoodwinked by the monkey tricks of Apollonius and Mohammed."[104] In another passage, alluding to episodes in the *VA*, Apollonius heads the list of several ancients who claimed to be able to communicate with and understand animals.[105] Given Montaigne's views on miracles and religion in general, he probably did not believe Apollonius possessed such supernatural powers. As an example of an openly hostile view of Apollonius, Polish Renaissance writer Stanislaw Poklatecki spilled much ink in portraying the Tyanean as a sorcerer and, while admitting

---

97. Dzielska, *Apollonius*, 194–96.

98. Demoen and Pratt, *Theios Sophistes*, vii.

99. Dzielska wrote, "Thanks to Aldus, till this day Philostratus' work has been published together with Eusebius of Caesarea's treatise," *Apollonius*, 197.

100. Baldelli, *Filostrato Lemnio*; Dolce, *La vita del gran philosopho*; Gualandi, *Filostrato greco scrittore elegantissimo*.

101. Vigenère, *Philostrate*.

102. Boter, "Critical Edition," 22.

103. However, Montaigne quoted Apollonius at least once with approbation: "Apollonius said that it was for slaves to lie, and for free men to speak the truth" (Montaigne, *Complete Essays*, 491).

104. Montaigne, *Complete Essays*, 775.

105. Montaigne, *Complete Essays*, 331.

that some earlier Christian authors regarded him as a practitioner of natural magic, he thought that the sage was in league with the devil.[106]

PHILOSTRATUS AMONG THE PLATONISTS

A few of the seventeenth-century Cambridge Platonists interacted with Philostratus's biography of Apollonius. These men combined their appreciation for certain ancient philosophers (e.g., Plato and Plotinus) with a defense of theism. Since several of these scholars had theological backgrounds and were supportive of the Bible, it comes as no surprise that they held a negative view of Apollonius.

Several of these intellectuals made comparisons of Christ to Apollonius. Henry More (1614–1687), whose interests included biblical interpretation, dedicated a section of one of his books to a rather extensive comparison of Apollonius and Jesus.[107] In the introduction to this work, he wrote that he should,

> touch a little upon the circumstances of the Birth of that famous Corrival of our Saviour, Apollonius Tyaneus; whose story writ by Philostratus, though I look upon it as a mixt business partly true and partly false, yet, be it what it will be, seeing it is intended for the highest Example of Perfection, and that the Heathen did equalize him with Christ, you shall see how ranck his whole History smells of the Animal Life, and how hard a thing it is either in actions or writings to counterfeit that which is truly holy and divine. For which end I shall make a brief Parallelisme of the Histories of them both in the chief matters of either, that the Gravitie and Divinitie of the one and the ridiculousness and Carnality of the other may the better be discerned.[108]

More, although holding some unorthodox Christian beliefs himself, argued for the superiority of Christ to Apollonius. Ralph Cudworth (1617–1688), who was both an Anglican clergyman and a Cambridge Platonist, also compared Jesus and Apollonius in his work, *The True Intellectual System of the Universe*. He believed that Apollonius had been assisted by

---

106. Dzielska, *Apollonius*, 199. See also Poklatecki, *Pogrom*. Just beyond the era under discussion, Piotr Skarga, a Polish Jesuit writer of the Counter-Reformation, regarded Apollonius's activities as devilish, basing a good deal of what he thought on stories taken from Philostratus's *VA*. See Dzielska, *Apollonius*, 199–200.

107. More, *An Explanation*, 102–52.

108. More, *An Explanation*, 102.

Satanic powers and that Philostratus in particular had dressed him up "in such a garb and manner as might make him best seem to be a fit cor-rival with our Saviour Christ, both in respect of sanctity and miracles."[109] Both of these intellectuals assumed that the VA had an anti-Christian agenda of rivaling and parodying Christ (item 9) and that many of Apol-lonius's deeds reported therein were either fictitious or were done by the power of the devil.

DEISTS VERSUS THEISTS[110]

One of the most heated exchanges concerning the Tyanean and the Nazarene took place between the deists and Christians. One of the major tenants of deism was that God did not perform miracles after he had created the cosmos. Christians, of course, held that God had continued to perform miracles after the creation of the world. In an unexpected move, the miracle-denying deists used the miracle-working Apollonius of Tyana to challenge the position of the miracle-affirming Christians.

In deist hands, Apollonius was like an apologetic multi-tool, whose functions allowed the deists several options for attempting the disas-sembly of the Christian worldview. One deist stratagem, endorsed by Legrand d'Aussy and Voltaire (François-Marie Arouet), was to claim that Apollonius had performed mighty works not by magic but by his superior knowledge of and ability to manipulate nature. They took a ra-tionalist view of Apollonius's feats, either detecting nothing magical in his deeds because his wonders were performed in harmony with natural law[111] or attributing any miraculous claims to the elaborations of Damis, Philostratus, or later disciples.[112] Deists also praised Apollonius as a noble

109. Cudworth, *The True Intellectual System*, 437.

110. Although the term "deist" and "theist" can be used as synonyms in some con-texts, a distinction is made between them here. As John Orr explains, the terms "deism" and "deist" were differentiated from "theism" and "theist" after the sixteenth century: "Prior to the 17th Century the terms were used interchangeably with the terms 'theism' and 'theist', respectively . . . Theologians and philosophers of the 17th Century began to give a different signification to the words . . . Both asserted belief in one supreme God, the Creator . . . But the theist taught that God remained actively interested in and operative in the world which he had made, whereas the Deist maintained that God endowed the world at creation with self-sustaining and self-acting powers and then surrendered it wholly to the operation of these powers acting as second causes" (Orr, *English Deism*, 13).

111. D'Aussy, *Vie d'Apollonius de Tyane*, 1.xxxii–xxxiii. Dzielska, *Apollonius*, 208.

112. Voltaire, *Essai*, 1:146.

philosopher; Voltaire claimed he was temperate, chaste, and just,[113] while Cotta described him as wise, irreproachable in conduct, and a promoter of a religion of tolerance and goodness from which all natural religion derived.[114] This line of argumentation cohered well with the deist view that miracles do not occur because Apollonius, according to this view, was merely a skilled manipulator of the natural order. The objective of this argument may have been to show that Jesus's displays of power were like those of Apollonius and were not divine in origin or that Jesus was not unique.

Another deist strategy attacked Christianity from the opposite angle in which "Apollonius of Tyana was paraded as a figure who invited comparison with Jesus, suggesting the implication that Jesus was just another none-too-reputable ancient holy man."[115] Réville similarly explains of the deists that, "[r]esting their arguments on the undeniable similarity between the Christ of the Gospels and Apollonius of Tyana, they maintained that both histories were equally apocryphal."[116] By stressing the similarities between Apollonius and Christ, deists could argue that either Jesus's stupendous works were in accord with natural law (and not miraculous at all) or, alternately, that Christ was merely a false magician.

In response to such claims, Christians asserted the superiority and uniqueness of Christ's miracles. Samuel Clarke (1675–1729) argued that the miracles of Christ were plausible for the dual reason that they illustrated a particular Christian doctrine and could be confirmed by eyewitness testimony. By way of contrast, the works supposedly performed by Apollonius and other pagans were poorly attested (shades of item 5) and "were worked either without any pretense of confirming any new Doctrine at all; or else to prove absurd and foolish Things; or to establish Idolatry and the Worship of False Gods."[117] Samuel Chandler (1693–1766), in his response to deists, dismissed Philostratus's reports as romance or fable.[118] Thus, Christians took their stand largely on two

---

113. Voltaire, *Essai*, 16:146.

114. Cotta, *Gewißheit der Beweise*, 54–55.

115. Brown, *Miracles*, 53; see also Cragg, *The Church*, 77.

116. Réville, *Apollonius of Tyana*, 58.

117. Clarke, *A Discourse*, 387–88.

118. Chandler, *A Vindication*, 82. Unfortunately, the fabulous event Chandler references was not said to have been performed by Apollonius but was an unusual event that Apollonius supposedly witnessed while in India.

arguments: the superiority of the eyewitness testimony for Christ's miracles and the fictional nature of the VA.

Thomas Woolston's (1668–1733) opinion was a compromise between the deistic and theistic positions. Although he has often been classified as a deist,[119] Woolston more likely held unorthodox Christian views that merely resembled the deist ideology in some respects. He argued that Christ's miracles in the Gospels were merely illustrations or parables, not literal supernatural deeds. Of the miracle at Cana, he wrote: "If Apollonius Tyanaeus, and not Jesus, had been the author of the Miracle, we should often have reproached his Memory with it."[120] To be clear, Woolston's point was not to disparage Christ, in whom he believed, but to show that any miraculous claim, whether pagan or Christian, should equally be met with derision.

The centrality of the VA in the deist agenda should not be overlooked. In 1680, Charles Blount published the first English translation of a portion of Philostratus's *Life of Apollonius*. Although Blount claimed to have translated the entire VA, he only published its first two books presumably because the backlash from the publication of these initial volumes discouraged him from releasing the remainder of the work.[121] As Bowersock notes, its "publication in the vernacular was considered a threat to the Christian religion."[122] Blount's text was accompanied by Lord Herbert of Cherbury's introduction and commentary, which compared the miracles in the Gospels to those performed by Apollonius.[123] Yoder writes, "The effect was to ridicule Jesus by undermining the uniqueness of his miraculous powers."[124] Réville explains that Blount, in

---

119. Orr, *English Deism*, 45–52.

120. Woolston, *A Discourse*, 51.

121. Blount, *The Two First Books of Philostratus*.

122. Bowersock, Introduction to *Life of Apollonius*, 20.

123. Lord Herbert's notes critiqued not only at the founder of Christianity, but related topics such as church practices, the failure of biblical prophecies, and materials in the Pentateuch that he thought did not differ substantially from pagan mythology. His notes not only compared the miracles of Jesus and Apollonius, but also other aspects of their thoughts and actions. For instance, Herbert believed that the judicial decision of Apollonius about the owner of a hidden treasure to be superior to the position of Christ that was presented in the parable of the hidden treasure in Matt 13:44; Blount, *Philostratus*, 242–43.

124. Yoder, *Hume on God*, 66. As an example of such ridicule, Herbert derided the miraculous birth of Jesus by comparing it to the supernatural events of Apollonius's nativity: "But to conclude this Subject, I question not but *Hierocles* in his Parallel, did impiously compare this Miracle of the Swans and Lightning, at *Apollonius*'s Birth, with

essence, claimed that "we must either admit the truth of the miracles of Apollonius as well as those of Jesus Christ, or if the former are untrue, he maintained that there was no better ground for believing the latter to be true."[125]

Blount's work was met with sharp critiques from Christian writers shortly after its publication.[126] Yoder reports that "in the ensuing uproar, it was alleged that Blount's book was the most dangerous attack levied against revealed religion in his century, quite a charge indeed considering that he shared the century with Hobbes and Spinoza."[127] Although Blount's life was cut short by suicide—perhaps because he was refused permission to marry the sister of his deceased wife—at least his translation enjoyed a long life both in England and on the continent. Other deists, such as Tindal and Bolingbroke may have borrowed directly from this work.[128] B. Castillon, a French scholar and philologist, re-published the two volumes of Blount's *Life of Apollonius of Tyana* in 1774 and translated the remaining portion of the *VA* that Blount had not printed.[129] In France, J. B. Legrand d'Aussy, who was not particularly impressed by Castillon's work, revised and expanded the *VA*.[130] In addition to its continued influence on the continent, back in England Blount's translation was still viewed as a live threat to Christianity as late as the time of John Henry Newman, who wrote a rebuttal of it in 1826.[131]

THE "QUEST" OF THE HISTORICAL APOLLONIUS

Students of the New Testament are familiar with the quest for the Historical Jesus,[132] but most are probably not familiar with the somewhat similar

---

that melody of holy Angels, and new Star appearing at Christ's Nativity, as being both equally strange, but not alike true. For to believe any Stories that are not approved of by the publick Authority of our Church, is Superstition; whereas to believe them that are, is Religion" (Blount, *Philostratus*, 13).

125. Réville, *Apollonius of Tyana*, 58–59.
126. Leslie, *A short and easy method*, i–xiv, 42.
127. Yoder, *Hume on God*, 66.
128. Orr, *English Deism*, 45.
129. Dzielska, *Apollonius*, 205, 207.
130. Dzielska, *Apollonius*, 208; D'Aussey, *Vie d'Apollonius*, 1.xlvii.
131. Newman, *The Life of Apollonius*. This work was first published in 1826, while Newman was still an Anglican.
132. The first quest began with the posthumous publication of Reimarus's *Fragments* in 1778 and ended with Schweitzer's *The Quest of the Historical Jesus* which

quest of the Historical Apollonius. To be fair, this is because the word "quest" was never formally applied to this study of Apollonius, although this descriptor has sometimes been applied to this period of Apollonian research.[133] While the parallels between the two quests should not be exaggerated, a few general similarities do exist. For instance, just as some scholars set out to expose the real Jesus of Nazareth and to question the historical foundations of Christianity,[134] others took the parallel course of developing more rigorous historical methodologies to discover the true nature of the sage from Tyana. This approach marked a new era in Apollonian studies, for it signaled a transition from the religious debate between Christians and the defenders of Apollonius[135] to the adoption of a critical approach to the sources that would for the first time challenge the veracity of the *VA* on historical grounds. Another similarity is that the two quests began at approximately the same time. Hermann Samuel Reimarus's posthumously published *Fragments* marked the beginning of the first quest for Jesus (1778). F. C. Baur (1832) is often credited with the first thoroughly scientific study about Apollonius many years after this time,[136] but, in truth, the quest for the historical Apollonius began much

---

appeared in 1906. This period of investigation and debate was followed by the second (1953–1970s) and third quests (1980s–2010s).

133. Danny Praet distinguished between the "old quest" and an implied "new quest" for Apollonius. He writes, "The two main topics of the "old quest" in the literature on Apollonius—comparisons of the *Vita Apollonii* with New Testament writings and the source-critical search for the "historical Apollonius"—have gradually been replaced by research that focuses on the role of Philostratus as an author in his own right" (Praet, "Pythagoreanism," 283).

134. Wright points out that that First Quest for the historical Jesus "began as an explicitly anti-theological, anti-Christian, and anti-dogmatic movement. Its initially agenda was *not* to find a Jesus upon whom Christian faith might be based, but to show that the faith of the church (as it was then conceived) could not in fact be based on the real Jesus of Nazareth" (Wright, *Jesus*, 17).

135. Several authors continued their attacks on Apollonius from a religious perspective. For instance, Godeau believed that the church had no greater enemy that Apollonius, whose reputation grew at the expense of Christianity because of his prediction of Domitian's assassination. He noted that even the pagans identified him as a trickster and magician and that Philostratus's biography was fable rather than history. See, Godeau, *Histoire de l'Eglise*, 1:368, 372. Fleury questioned the reality of Apollonius's miracles and argued that, if true, they were performed with the assistance of the devil. He argued that Apollonius's resurrection of a maiden was a false miracle and that even the devil had apostles among the pagans. See Fleury, *The Ecclesiastical History*, 1:110, 138, 150, 155. Petzke gives an overview of other writers who engaged in such religious attacks (*Die Traditionen*, 12–13).

136. Petzke, *Die Traditionen*, 13; Koskenniemi, *Apollonios*, 11.

earlier. Many seventeenth- and eighteenth-century writers were already asking and answering the same sorts of questions that Baur later posed and addressed in more detail.

These pre-Baur era "questers" were hard at work slightly before and around the time of Reimarus (1694–1768). One of the earliest of these figures was Samuel Parker (1681), Bishop of Oxford, who raised the question of whether Damis's diary was a forgery or whether the document ever existed at all (item 5).[137] In 1709, M. J. C. Herzog wrote a brief Latin tract that aimed at discovering the true form of the practical philosophy of Apollonius.[138] In 1754, P. D. Huetius, a bishop of Avranches, expressed the view that Philostratus copied the Gospels and matched Apollonius's life to that of Christ; he was the first to ask whether the *VA* relied on the Gospels (item 9).[139] In 1796, Christoph Martin Wieland used his first-century fictional characters to explore several critical themes in his philosophic novel *Agathodämon*: the possibility that Damis's account was filled with well-intentioned fairy tales about his master; the difficulty of selecting the correct the most accurate portrayal of Apollonius from several options; the view that Apollonius was a mere human being rather than as a god. In this dialogue, the miracles of Apollonius were given a rationalist interpretation.[140]

Perhaps the most notable of these pre-Baur scholars was Nathaniel Lardner (1766), for he asked a wide range of questions about Apollonius. He made an important observation, often overlooked by modern scholars, that almost all knowledge of Apollonius is based on a single source, the *VA*,[141] thereby raising the question of whether a single source can be trusted to tell the Tyanean's story. He further drew attention to earlier historical sources (item 1) that portrayed Apollonius as a

---

137. Parker, *A Demonstration*, 293–94. Parker, like some before him, asked whether the *VA* should be classified as romance rather than history because of its mythical beasts and childish stories. He also noted its lack of reliable eyewitness testimony. For instance, Apollonius was alone when he witnessed to the shade of Achilles at Troy. Further, it would have been impossible for witnesses to have failed to report Apollonius's disappearance from his Roman trial. See Parker, *A Demonstration*, 295–300).

138. Herzog, *Philosophiam practicam Apollonii Tyanei*.

139. Dzeilska, *Apollonius*, 203.

140. Wieland, *Agathodämon*. In the final chapter of this work, Christ is shown to be the reality of which Apollonius was only a shadow. For further discussion of Wieland's full agenda in the book, see McCarthy, *Christoph Martin Weiland*, 149–51; Dzielska, *Apollonius*, 210.

141. Lardner, *Large Collection*, 3:246–48.

magician and fraud (item 2).[142] Lardner also pointed out that since only a few ancient people mentioned the Tyanean and Celsus was silent about him—although Celsus mentioned other magicians—this was proof that Apollonius "was not a man of much consideration among the Heathen people" as Philostratus had asserted.[143] Upon investigating the *VA*'s claims, Lardner found them wanting because the *VA* itself was composed a hundred years after the time of Apollonius (item 10), Damis was an obscure person, and Damis's diary was delivered to Julia Domna by an unknown person (item 5). He also noted that the *VA* contained incorrect or questionable historical data (item 6).[144] Concerning earlier influences upon the *VA*, he concluded that it had been modeled after the biography of Pythagoras,[145] not the Gospels[146] (items 8 and 9). Lardner himself anticipated at least seven items of the Apollonian Decalogue, although he did not investigate them all in detail. Lardner and his contemporaries, along with the publication of the first complete translation of the *VA* in English in 1809 by Edward Berwick,[147] were harbingers of the era of the critical study of Apollonius. This phase of research, if not a part of the "quest" proper, might at least be regarded as the "proto-quest" for the historical Apollonius.

Whether or not the quest originated with Baur, as is often asserted, he was a major contributor to it in that he wrote one of the earliest scientific studies of Apollonius.[148] He was aware of the work of some of his predecessors and mentioned their contributions (e.g., Wieland).[149] He noted that the *VA* and the life of Christ had numerous and indisputable

---

142. Lardner, *Large Collection*, 3:247. The earlier authors he cited that referenced Apollonius were Lucian, Apuleius, and Origen.

143. Lardner, *Large Collection*, 3:247–48.

144. Lardner, *Large Collection*, 3:251. For instance, Euphrates, Apollonius's backbiting enemy in the *VA*, was highly regarded by other writers such as Pliny the Younger, Epictetus, and Eunapius.

145. Lardner, *Large Collection*, 3:244–70.

146. Lardner, *Large Collection*, 3:252–57.

147. Edward Berwick translated the entire *VA* into English in reaction to what he interpreted as disparaging comment of Edward Gibbon about Jesus. In reality, Gibbon's comment had been directed at Apollonius, an impostor about whom little could be known due to the mythical tone of the surviving sources. Bowersock, Introduction to *Life of Apollonius*, 20; Dzielska, *Apollonius*, 205).

148. Koskenniemi, *Apollonios*, 11; Petzke, *Die Traditionen*, 13.

149. Baur, *Apollonius von Tyana*, 10–13.

similarities.¹⁵⁰ Both Christ and Apollonius had unusual births, performed exorcisms, raised the dead,¹⁵¹ experienced similar Passions, and ascended into heaven.¹⁵² After investigating the agenda of Philostratus, Baur concluded that the *VA* had been written as anti-Christian propaganda (item 8).¹⁵³ He also noted gross historical errors in this work (item 6) and suspected that Philostratus had embellished the story.¹⁵⁴ He believed that the work had little basis in history; otherwise, much like Lardner had already pointed out, such a noteworthy figure like Philostratus claimed Apollonius to have been would have been mentioned earlier and more widely in ancient records.¹⁵⁵ Baur, like Parker before him, suspected that Damis and his notebook were inventions of Philostratus (item 5).¹⁵⁶ Petzke claims that Baur was also the first to show how the Pythagoras legend had influenced the *VA*,¹⁵⁷ even though Lardner had briefly explored this idea earlier. Baur's study laid a firm foundation for the quest by highlighting several important problems with the Apollonius legend.

From the end of the nineteenth century through the early twenty-first century, classical scholarship had taken up this quest. Researchers continued the exploration of the themes raised by Baur and his predecessors such as the reality of Damis and his notebook, the historical problems in the *VA*, and whether there was an anti-Christian bias in the *VA*.¹⁵⁸ In investigating the historical and geographical problems in the *VA*, some took a hard look at the historicity of Apollonius's travels to

---

150. Baur, *Apollonius von Tyana*, 101.

151. Baur believed that the story of Apollonius's activity as an exorcist had an unmistakable correspondence to Luke 7:1 and Mark 5:39; Baur, *Apollonius von Tyana*, 138–39.

152. Baur, *Apollonius von Tyana*, 141–47.

153. Baur, *Apollonius von Tyana*, 102; Bowersock, Introduction to *Life of Apollonius*, 21.

154. Baur, *Apollonius von Tyana*, 106.

155. Baur, *Apollonius von Tyana*, 109–10.

156. Baur, *Apollonius von Tyana*, 112–13.

157. Petzke, *Die Traditionen*, 14. Baur dedicates a good deal of the last part of his book to Pythagorean influences on the *VA*'s vision of Apollonius; Baur, *Apollonius von Tyana*, 161–225.

158. The bibliographical information for the ten items of the Apollonian Decalogue can be found in chapter 2.

Mesopotamia,[159] India,[160] Egypt,[161] Ethiopia,[162] and Spain.[163] Some have suggested that the geography of the VA was never intended to be accurate but was designed to convey a philosophical or spiritual meaning.[164] Some have continued the investigation of the possible influence of Pythagoras on the story of Apollonius, an idea that was suggested earlier by Lardner and Baur.[165]

New areas of research not prompted by Baur have emerged concerning Philostratus, Apollonius, and the VA. A handful of monographs have been dedicated to the life, career, and writings of Philostratus[166] along with several articles about him as a writer of fiction.[167] A few other studies that are dedicated to the VA itself,[168] have attempted to discover whether the agenda in the VA was political, national, philosophical, or religious.[169] One book has investigated the relationship in the VA between philosophers and monarchs.[170] Apollonius has also had his fair share of books written about him, some of which are more generic studies[171] while a few German works are finetuned to investigating his rela-

---

159. C. P. Jones, "Passage to India," 185–99.

160. Priaulx, *The Indian Travels*, 2–3; Smith, "The Indian Travels," 329–44; Charpentier, "The Indian Travels," 1934), 1–66; Marshall, *Taxila*; Bernard, "L'Aornos bactrien," 475–530; Cobb, "Apollonius in India," 440–73.

161. Bowersock, "The Miracle of Memnon," 21–32.

162. Robiano, "Les gymnosophistes éthiopiens," 413–28.

163. Gasco la Calle, "El viaje de Apolonio," 13–22.

164. Elsner, "Hagiographic Geography," 22–37; Abraham, "The Geography of Culture," 465–80.

165. Nielsen, *Apollonios fra Tyana*; Miller, "Die Beziehungen,"137–45; Flinterman, "Pythagoras and Pythagoreanism," 155–75.

166. Anderson, *Philostratus*; Bowie and Elsner, *Philostratus*; Miles, *Philostratus*.

167. Harris, "Apollonius," 189–99; Bowie, "Philostratus: Writer of Fiction," 181–99; Francis, "Truthful Fiction." 419–41.

168. Demoen and Praet, *Theios Sophistes*.

169. See the summary of sources in Koskenniemi, *Der philostrateische Apollonius*, 27. In this work, Koskenniemi used redactional criticism on the Philostratean corpus to discover the intention of the author. He concluded that Philostratus was not attempting to promote a religion and was not anti-Christian. However, the VA's political-national agenda shone through in Apollonius's praise and censure of different rulers. Philostratus may have even consciously or unconsciously included and critiqued events from the time of the Severans in the VA. Koskenniemi also showed that Philostratus demonstrated an interested in sophistic themes and Attic rhetoric in the VA, as he did in his other writings; see Koskenniemi, *Der philostrateische Apollonius* 27–30, 80–82.

170. Flinterman, *Power*.

171. Dzielska, *Apollonius*; Koskenniemi, *Der philostrateische Apollonios*.

tionship to the New Testament.¹⁷² A few researchers have turned their attention to the legend of Apollonius's talismans.¹⁷³ Several new translations of the *VA* were produced (i.e., those by Phillimore,¹⁷⁴ Conybeare,¹⁷⁵ and Jones¹⁷⁶), along with several other books of the Philostratean corpus.¹⁷⁷ In addition, translations of the *Letters of Apollonius*, a collection of testimonia about Apollonius, and Eusebius's *Reply to Hierocles* have been produced.¹⁷⁸ These are positive signs, at least within the domain of classical studies, that the quest for Apollonius continues.

THE PHILOSTRATEAN APOLLONIUS AND NEW TESTAMENT STUDIES

Koskenniemi has helpfully identified three major areas in which the Apollonian material has been utilized in New Testament studies: questions of the literary relationship of the *VA* to the NT, form criticism, and the "divine man" theory.¹⁷⁹ Each of these areas will be briefly surveyed below.

Koskenniemi notes that scholars investigated two possibilities related to the literary dependence between the *VA* and the NT. The first of these was whether the NT was directly reliant on the *VA*. Eduard Norden, an advocate of this view, proposed that Paul's Areopagus speech (Acts 17:22–31) had been based on a hypothetical speech of Apollonius of Tyana (*VA* 6.3.5).¹⁸⁰ Because this theory was rejected by subsequent

---

172. Petzke, *Die Traditionen*; Koskenniemi, *Apollonios*.

173. Duliére, "Protection permanente," 247–77: Marti-Aguilar, "Talismans," 968–93.

174. Phillimore, *In Honour*.

175. Philostratus, *The Life of Apollonius*.

176. Philostratus, *Apollonius of Tyana*.

177. The entire corpus of Philostratus is now available in the Loeb Classical Library. See also Maclean and Aitken, *Flavius Philostratus*.

178. Volume 3 of Philostratus, *Apollonius of Tyana* in the Loeb Classical Library contains these three works. See also the excellent earlier work of Penella, *The Letters of Apollonius*.

179. Koskenniemi, *Apollonios*, 13–15.

180. Norden, *Agnostos Theos*, 1–124. For an excellent summary of this issue, see Koskenniemi, *Apollonios*, 20–27. Koskenniemi concludes this section in his book with these words concerning Norden's proposal: "Heute ist die Diskussion über die These beendet. Es gibt keine Veranlassung mehr zu glauben, daß Lukas die Worte des Paulus von der Apollonios-Tradition übernahm" (Koskenniemi, *Apollonios*, 27).

scholarship[181] and since this topic concerns Apollonius's relationship to the book of Acts rather than to Jesus and the Gospels, it will not be considered further in this survey of literature. The second possibility was that the *VA* might betray evidence of dependence on the NT (item 9). As Koskenniemi notes, there was no consensus on this question.[182] He noted that some researchers argued for reliance on NT passages, while others claimed none can be detected (e.g., Gerd Petzke and Graham Anderson). Of the advocates endorsing the reliance hypothesis, some claimed that the *VA* borrowed directly from certain NT texts (e.g., Johannes Hempel, Arnold Ehrhardt, and Erkki Koskenniemi), some that the *VA* and NT may have shared a common Hellenistic miracle source (Hans Joachim Schütz), and others that the stories from the *VA* made their way into the *VA* because Philostratus was influenced by Christian culture. This question of the relationship of the *VA* to the NT will be taken up in chapter 13's treatment of item 9 of the Apollonian Decalogue.

Apollonius's miracle stories in the *VA* played a central role in the development of form criticism. As Koskenniemi points out, most of the early developers of this discipline, such as Martin Dibelius, Rudolf Bultmann, and Karl Ludwig Schmidt drew heavily upon miracles stories in the *VA* for parallels to the miracle accounts in the Gospels.[183] This was true even of later researchers in form criticism, such as Gerd Theissen[184] and Gerd Petzke.[185]

Although the *VA* provided the best and most numerous examples of miracle accounts from pagan sources,[186] these researchers never seri-

---

181. Conzelmann, *Acts*, 147.

182. For an overview of the authors mentioned in this paragraph, see Koskenniemi, *Apollonios*, 27–36.

183. Interestingly, Taylor only referenced one story about Apollonius in his book about form criticism. See Taylor, *The Formation*, 127.

184. Theissen, *The Miracle Stories*.

185. Perhaps the most extensive treatment of the forms of Apollonian material found in the *VA* (and their redaction to some extent) was conducted by Petzke. The purpose of his book was to make the traditions about Apollonius more accessible to NT scholars (Petzke, *Die Traditionen*, 230). In addition to his investigation of various forms (e.g., miracle stories, proverbs, and legends), he explored the similarities in themes between the *VA* and the NT, although he himself did not detect a literary dependence between the two bodies of material (Petzke, *Die Traditionen*, 62).

186. Koskenniemi helpfully listed the number of times the *VA* and other sources were cited by these authors in their research; Koskenniemi *Apollonios*, 43–44, 57). Blackburn pointed out that the early authors who worked on the miracle accounts often neglected Old Testament and extrabiblical Jewish parallels about healings,

ously addressed the possibility that the accounts in the *VA* might have originated too late to compare well to the first-century miracles in the Gospels. In contrast to these earlier scholars, Koskenniemi contended that the date of the material in the *VA* is a central issue in this discussion, for (1) if these miracle stories date to the second or third century rather than preserving first-century material, the comparison of the *VA* to the Gospels may be invalid (item 10) and (2) if the Gospel stories influenced the *VA*'s miracle accounts, such comparisons in the field of form criticism are likewise invalid (item 9).[187] Koskenniemi astutely observed that, if not for the Apollonius material, there would have been very little to speak by way of pagan parallels to resurrections or exorcisms found in the Gospels. This underlines the importance of establishing that the material in the *VA* is early and independent if it is to be taken seriously in the study of form criticism or any other discipline that touches on the study of Apollonius.

Perhaps most significantly, Apollonius became central to the discussions about the "divine man" (θεῖος ἀνήρ).[188] Several researchers (e.g., Richard Reitzenstein, Gillis Wetter, and Hans Windisch) contributed to the development of this idea, although their starting points and definitions of the term "divine man" were not identical.[189] Nevertheless, the concept of the "divine man" eventually gained acceptance and was incorporated into New Testament studies by key figures like Bultmann,[190]

---

resurrections, and exorcisms that provided much closer analogues to the Gospel miracles that the pagan material in terms of form and content. He further noted that the form of the pagan miracles did not often match that of the Gospel stories well; only three pre-Christian miracle accounts resemble the material in the Gospels. See Barry L. Blackburn, "Miracle Working ΘΕΟΙ ΑΝΔΡΕΣ, 196–97; 199–201.

187. Koskenniemi, *Apollonios*, 63.

188. Blackburn sums up the essence of the term "divine man" as follows: "In NT scholarship, the term *Divine Man*, or its Greek form *Theios Anēr*, designates an alleged type of religio-philosophical hero, legendary or historical, which was more or less indigenous to Greece or at least Hellenism and whose representatives were characterized by moral virtue, wisdom and/or miraculous power so that they were held to be divine" (Blackburn, "Divine Man," 189). He notes that ancient figures like Pythagoras, Empedocles, Apollonius, and Alexander of Abonoteichos normally comprised the core of these models or types. See Blackburn, "Miracle Working ΘΕΟΙ ΑΝΔΡΕΣ," 192.

189. Koskenniemi, "Apollonius of Tyana," 458.

190. Bultmann, *John*, 101–2, 104, 106, 180, 187–88, 269. Most of Bultmann's examples in John are those in which Jesus has supernatural knowledge of certain situations or of a person's thoughts.

Dieter Georgi,[191] and Theodore Weeden.[192] As Koskenniemi put it, these scholars were essentially claiming that early Christians, whether orthodox or heterodox, had to "re-package" Jesus as a divine man to market him to the Gentile world.[193] Not surprisingly, the example of Apollonius as he is depicted by Philostratus was one of the chief proofs of the existence and popularity of such divine men, whose ranks Jesus had just recently joined.

However, the "divine man" theory has met with strong criticism for a host of reasons. In general, (1) the definitions and criteria for a "divine man" were imprecise, varying from scholar to scholar;[194] and (2) the identification of Paul's opponents in 2 Corinthians as "divine men" and in Mark as promoting Jesus as a "divine man" was not plausible to many New Testament scholars.[195] A more specific problem was that of all the proposed candidates for the category of "divine man," only Apollonius

---

191. Georgi, *The Opponents of Paul*, 229–83. Georgi identified the Corinthian interlopers as "divine men" who promoted themselves by their rhetorical skills and miraculous powers (2 Cor 2:14—7:4; 10–13).

192. Weeden proposed that Mark's Gospel attempted to counter the preachers of a *theos-aner* Christology (a *theologia gloriae*) with a gospel of the suffering Son of Man (a *theologia crucis*). See Weeden, *Mark: Traditions in Conflict*.

193. Koskenniemi, "Apollonius of Tyana," 456.

194. Blackburn lists several reasons for the rejection of this category in his "ΘΕΟΙ ΑΝΔΡΕΣ," 185–92, among which are (1) θεῖος ἀνήρ did not function as a *technicus terminus* at the time of the composition of the Gospels and was not widespread in its usage; the term was only used of three figures, once of Epimenides, once (perhaps twice) of Moses, and four times of Apollonius; (2) the ancient sources mined to construct the definition of divine men did not uniformly classify the divinity of the candidates, but rather displayed a spectrum of ideas (e.g., θεοί, δαίμονες, heroes, seers, healers; offspring of major gods, the muses, the nymphs); Pythagoras was even called Hyperborean Apollo, thus disqualifying him as a human; (3) the date of the sources for figures that best represent the type were late (Philostratus for Apollonius and Iamblicus for Pythagoras). Other scholars can be added to Blackburn's list, for they have pointed out that (4) some of these representatives of divine men were late, such as Alexander Abonoteichos (Klauck, *Religious Context*, 176–77); (5) the divine man model may have been influenced by Christianity in some cases (Klauck, *Religious Context*, 176–77; Hengel, *Son of God*, 31–32; and (6) the term θεῖος ἀνήρ does not appear to be interchangeable with υἱὸς τοῦ θεοῦ (Hengel, *Son of God*, 31–33).

195. For instance, Holladay has challenged the position of Georgi that the opponents in 2 Corinthians were "divine men." Holladay convincingly argued that Jews like Philo and Josephus preserved the distinction between their human heroes (e.g., Moses) and the divine. His findings reduced the likelihood that the divine man was mediated to Christianity by Hellenistic Judaism. For a summary of his views, see Holladay, *Theos Aner*, 233–42. Weeden's proposals concerning Mark were approved by some; see Perrin, "The Christology of Mark," 95–108. However, others have been critical of his "divine man" hypothesis; Betz, "Concept," 229–40; Holladay, *Theos Aner*, 237–38.

and Jesus truly fit the pattern.[196] As Koskenniemi sums up, "When the Christian texts and the late work of Philostratus are removed from the pattern, the whole θεῖος ἀνήρ pattern collapses."[197] Once again, the problem of the date of the VA (item 10) and the independence of the material found within it reappears (item 9).

Koskenniemi noted that even in more recent decades, scholars are still divided over whether the divine man is a legitimate category (e.g., Thiessen, Betz, and Koester), an illegitimate one (Koskenniemi), or one that is partially correct (Klauk). For those who would still promote the theory, Koskenniemi's observation still stands firm: without the Apollonius of the VA, there is no basis for this type of figure within the first century apart from Jesus himself. This point is important, for if one could demonstrate that the VA was unhistorical (item 6), the Damis diary was not from the first century (item 5), and that the sources of the VA were too far late to be accurate (item 7), then Apollonius would be out of contention for the category of a divine man and Jesus would serve as the sole example of the type from the first century.

CONCLUSION

This survey of scholarship has highlighted the sorts of critical questions raised by a previous generation of researchers that were used to create the Apollonian Decalogue employed in this study. These of course should be combined with many classical scholars of the past and present who have observed the same ten items.[198] Unfortunately, many recent biblical scholars who write about Apollonius have either ignored or were never aware of the work done in this area by earlier scholars. This situation is understandable, for it is difficult enough to keep abreast of the past and current research on even a handful of topics within New Testament studies. Nevertheless, some awareness of these issues is important for

---

196. Pythagoras and Alexander of Abonoteichos are often suggested as examples of divine men. However, little is known about Pythagoras as a historical figure (Klauck, *Religious Context*, 176) and the extant sources, like that of biography of Iamblicus, are late (Blackburn, "ΘΕΟΙ ΑΝΔΡΕΣ," 176). In some traditions, Pythagoras would be disqualified as a divine man because he was identified with the Hyperborean Apollo, who was a full-blown deity (Blackburn, "ΘΕΟΙ ΑΝΔΡΕΣ," 186). Alexander is questionable as well since he was a figure from the second century AD.

197. Koskenniemi, "Apollonius of Tyana," 462.

198. For a list of several classical scholars who also contributed to the formulation of the Apollonian Decalogue, see the footnotes in chapter 2 for each of the ten items.

the New Testament scholars who write about Apollonius, for this might prevent them from making mistakes, overstating evidence, or recreating the wheel. An author who uncritically accepts the validity of the "divine man" theory, the genuineness of Damis's account, or the historical accuracy of the *VA* likely has not conducted adequate background research on Apollonius. The principles that comprise the Apollonian Decalogue were formulated long ago, although they were not formally listed together, and those who study Apollonius ignore them at their peril.

So then, there is a need for New Testament scholars to acquaint or reacquaint themselves with the key issues in Apollonian research. Just such a study will be conducted in part three of this book where each item of the Apollonian Decalogue will be investigated in detail. But in laying a foundation for approaching that task, all those interested in learning more about Apollonius would benefit greatly from an introduction to Philostratus, his literary corpus, his literary agendas, and the *VA* itself. These will be the topics of the next section.

Part 2

Philostratus II and His Literary Corpus

4

Philostratus II and His World

IF THERE IS A figure that is less well-known to Biblical scholars than Apollonius of Tyana it may well be his biographer, Philostratus II. Indeed, a few classicists have lamented that Philostratus and his writings, while not altogether ignored, have not received the attention they are due even within their own discipline.[1] Fortunately, within the last few decades, several excellent studies in classical scholarship have begun to fill this gap in Philostratean research. Because these resources are technical and intended for specialists, they are probably not the best entry point into Philostraean or Apollonian studies for the novice. Therefore, this chapter will attempt to fill this role by introducing newcomers to the political and sophistic contexts of Philostratus, as well as to the key details of his life.

---

1. Classical scholar Graham Anderson begins his 1986 monograph on Philostratus with these lines: "'Not another book on Philostratus!' is a cry unknown in the history of classical scholarship. There is nothing that could be called a general study of this author of any length in any language, let alone an available one in English; and the deterrents against writing and reading about Philostratus at all are considerable. Of the two major German surveys, the more recent will soon be half a century old" (Anderson, *Philostratus*, vii). Since then, Rusten noted an upswing in interest in Philostratus between the 1980s and the 2000s. See his comments in Philostratus, *Heroicus*, 3–4. In 2018, Miles wrote that there has been an increased interest in the study of almost all of texts of the *Corpus Philostrateum* recently (Miles, *Philostratus*, 3).

PART 2: PHILOSTRATUS II AND HIS LITERARY CORPUS

THE POLITICAL WORLD OF PHILOSTRATUS II

Philostratus's career as a sophist lasted from about AD 200 until his death sometime in the 240s. The first part of his professional life (ca. AD 200–217) was spent in the service of the Severan rulers: Septimius Severus (AD 193–211), Caracalla (AD 211–17),[2] and Julia Domna, the wife of the former figure and the mother of the latter. Although evidence is lacking for Philostratus's connections with the royal household after AD 217, a good portion of his career transpired during the reigns of the two remaining Severan rulers, Elagabalus (218–22) and Severus Alexander (AD 222–35). The last segment of his career (AD 235–40s) took place during the first portion of the Crisis of the Third Century. Because Philostratus worked closely with several rulers and lived during the time of others, a brief overview of the rulers and events that occurred during his career will provide some context for Philostratus II and his writings.[3] The vignettes of the monarchs presented below will also familiarize the reader with names, events, and academic theories related to these rulers that will be encountered in the upcoming chapters of this study.[4]

---

2. The name Caracalla will be used in this book to refer to the second Severan ruler. His birth name Lucius Septimius Bassianus was later changed to Marcus Aurelius Antoninus. His nickname Caracalla was given to him because of the foreign-looking (Gallic) cloak that he wore and required soldiers and visitors to court to wear (Dio Cassius, *Hist. rom.* 79; Aurel. Vict. *Epit.* 21).

3. For readers that are interested in a more detailed account of these rulers and this era, see Schultz and Ward, *A History*, 514–27.

4. For instance, some scholars believe that Philostratus alluded to or critiqued the behavior of the Severan rulers in the *VA*, disguising them as the first century Julio-Claudian and Flavian emperors of Apollonius's day. Scholars commonly accept that Philostratus alludes to the Severan rulers periodically in the *VA*. However, not all agree to more speculative theories. For instance, Göttshing believed that Vespasian, Titus, and Domitian in the *VA* corresponded to Septimius Severus, Geta, and Caracalla respectively; Nero, of course, corresponded to Elagabalus. Since he believed that Philostratus would not have risked criticizing current rulers, he proposed that the *VA* was written in the time of Severus Alexander as a guide for the young ruler; a rehearsal of the virtues and vices of the Severans would aid Alexander's moral formation. See Göttshing, *Apollonius von Tyana*, 80–89. Flinterman, however, deems this view implausible. First, most of the alleged parallels between the Flavians and Severans are superficial. Second, he notes that, in most instances, the alleged parallels between the *VA* and the Severan rulers may be coincidental; the events in both periods can be verified by historical sources so that "there is no need to assume that the writer deliberately created these parallels in order to hold a mirror up to the faces of his contemporaries, including Severus Alexander" (Flinterman, *Power* 218). For a full discussion and evaluation of this and similar theories, see Flinterman, *Power*, 216–30.

Septimius Severus

Septimius Severus was a capable ruler and military leader. His road to the throne was difficult because he rose to power after a time of crisis[5] and because he faced Senatorial opposition due to his birth in a province and his equestrian rank.[6] Once the Senate acknowledged him as the legitimate emperor,[7] he consolidated his rule by systematically eliminating rival claimants to the throne (i.e., Pescennius Niger and Clodius Albinus), increasing the wages of his troops, and reforming the Praetorian Guard. These actions ensured that Italy would no longer be privileged in the selection of an emperor or capable of governmental interference.[8] Severus also fought several wars[9] and strengthened the frontiers of the empire in Britain,[10] Arabia, Syria, Numidia, and Mauretania.[11] Although Severus was an able warrior and administrator, he was unsuccessful in resolving the conflicts that arose within his own household.

The problems that plagued the royal household stemmed from two somewhat related issues. The first source of conflict was Plautianus, who was Severus's cruel and ambitious relative.[12] Because Severus's expertise was in the area of military affairs, he had turned the administration of the government over to Plautianus,[13] who soon gained so much power

---

5. When the emperor Pertinax was killed by the Praetorian Guard, these soldiers held an auction for the position of emperor, which was purchased by a wealthy ex-consul named Didius Julianus (Herodian, *Hist.* 2.6). When Severus, who was the governor of Pannonia at the time, heard of this scandalous arrangement, his own legion declared him emperor (Herodian, *Hist.* 2.9.11; 2.10.9). Thereafter, he quickly marched to Rome to claim the throne and avenge the murder of Pertinax.

6. Septimius was born in Leptis (or Lepcis) Magna in the province of Africa. In an apparent attempt to legitimate his rule, he made what associations he could to the Antonine rulers before him. For instance, he had himself adopted into the family of Marcus Aurelius and even named his son, later known as Caracalla, Marcus Aurelius Antoninus. For these details, see Schulz et al., *A History*, 516.

7. Herodian, *Hist.* 2.12.6–7.

8. Schultz and Ward, *A History*, 514–15.

9. I.e., the Second Parthian War (AD 197–198) and the Caledonian Campaign (AD 208–211).

10. Severus rebuilt Hadrian's Wall that had been razed to the foundation by the Caledonians. See Dudley, *Civilization of Rome*, 207–8.

11. Schultz and Ward, *A History*, 520–21.

12. Herodian, *Hist.* 3.10.6–7. In this passage, Herodian noted that Plautianus was one of the most feared prefects of all time.

13. Schultz and Ward, *A History*, 519.

that he technically possessed the authority of an emperor.[14] Some even referred to him as a "fourth Caesar."[15] This imperial grant of administrative latitude to Plautianus, his recently increased power in his position of prefect of the Praetorians,[16] and his brutal personality combined to fracture several relationships within the Severan family. He drove a wedge between Septimius and Julia Domna, his spouse, cruelly isolating her from AD 200–205.[17] To strengthen his position further, Plautianus forced the marriage of his daughter Plautilla to Severus's son, the fourteen-year-old Caracalla, in AD 202.[18] Consequently, Julia and her two sons, Caracalla and Geta, hated Plautianus. By AD 205, Caracalla had had his fill of Plautianus's meddling and framed the prefect for plotting the murder of Severus and his sons.[19] After Plautianus's execution, Caracalla summarily divorced Plautilla. One scholar proposed the implausible theory that Julia Domna had commissioned Philostratus's *VA* as a warning to Severus to beware of wicked counselors like Plautinius.[20]

The second source of conflict in the royal family was sibling rivalry, for Severus's two sons despised each other. The removal of Plautianus[21] allowed the brothers to give full vent to their mutual animosity, and they

---

14. Dio Cassius, *Hist. rom.* 76.14–15; 77.4.5. Two modern sources also describe him as "almost autocratic" (Parker and Warmington, "Plautianus," 519).

15. This designation refers to Plautianus's possession of status that rivaled that of Severus and his two sons, Caracalla and Geta. Dio Cassius, *Hist. rom*.76.15.2

16. The praetorian prefect "was in charge of the grain supply and was commander-in-chief of all armed forces stationed in Italy. He was also vice-president of the Imperial Council, now the supreme court of the Empire and its highest policy-making body" (Schultz and Ward, *A History*, 517).

17. Parker and Warmington, "Julia Domna," 567. Dio Cassius recorded that Plautianus conducted investigations of Julia, gathering evidence against her by torturing women of the nobility; *Hist. rom.* 76.15.6.

18. Herodian, *Hist.* 3.10.8.

19. Parker and Warmington, "Plautianus," 842.

20. Caldarini, "Teoria e pratica politica," 213–41. Calderini's argument has not met with much approval. Flinterman found fault with his view for it requires an exceedingly early date for the *VA* during the reign of Severus and because the *VA* presents some counsellors, like the prefect Aelianus, in a favorable light. (Flinterman, *Power*, 219). This latter point is not blunted by the negative portrayal of the prefect Tigellinus in the *VA*, for he does not bear much resemblance to Severus's prefect Plautianus and, consequently, would not have served as a warning to emperor of such men serving in his court.

21. Dio Cassius records that, with Plautianus out of the way, the brothers felt as if they had gotten rid of a pedagogue (*Hist. rom.* 77.7.1).

sided against each other in even the most trivial matters.[22] Later, during the campaign in Britain, Caracalla plotted to kill Geta but was prevented by his father and the troops, who were affectionate towards his younger sibling.[23] Shortly before Severus's death from gout in Eboracum (York) in AD 211, he supposedly enjoined his two sons to "[b]e harmonious, enrich the soldiers, and scorn all other men."[24] As Dudley wryly remarked, Severus's first admonition was disregarded, while the last two were obeyed by Caracalla, the son that survived the fraternal conflict.[25]

Philostratus may have alluded to details of the life of Septimius Severus in a few passages within the VA, but he never mentioned the ruler by name.[26] Philostratus's portrayal of the first-century emperor Vespasian is reminiscent of Severus, for both men patiently performed their duties under bad rulers early in their careers, seized power in a chaotic situation, and had two sons who were at odds with each other.[27] Also, the story of Darius II Ochus and his children, related in the VA, may allude to Severus and his two hostile sons.[28] However, it is also possible that the resemblance of these two rulers to Severus was coincidental, for the details about Vespasian and Darius are historically accurate.

Caracalla

After the passing of their father, tensions between Caracalla and Geta came to a head. They were made co-emperors upon their father's death, yet they each amassed supporters and plotted to kill their sibling to claim

22. Dio Cassius, *Hist. rom.* 77.7.

23. Dio Cassius, *Hist. rom.* 77.14.1; 78.1.3.

24. According to Dio Cassius, the above quote preserved Severus's exact words (*Hist. rom.* 77.15.2). Schultz, however, writes, "Probably these words are rhetorical inventions, but they are significant in their emphasis on favoring the military and their contrast with the failure of the heirs to work together" (Schultz and Ward, *A History*, 522).

25. Dudley, *Civilization of Rome*, 208.

26. Philostratus did mention Severus in the VS (e.g., VS 601, 606, 610, 614).

27. Göttsching, *Apollonius*, 86. Koskenniemi, *Der philostrateische Apollonios* 41.

28. In VA 1.28.2, the tale of king Darius II Ochus and Severus are similar in their details: both rulers were about sixty years old, both had quarrelling sons, and one son killed the other. See Koskenniemi, *Der philostrateische Apollonios*, 41. However, the differences in the story might challenge this idea. For instance, in the VA Darius is said to have *reigned* sixty years or so, while Severus *lived* sixty-five years but *reigned* only eighteen years.

the throne.²⁹ The brothers divided the palace and fortified their apartments, allowing no one to pass between the two halves of the building. Their fear of each other was so great that they even contemplated dividing the empire in half, with Caracalla retaining Europe (and western Africa) and Geta ruling Asia (and Egypt), but this plan was thwarted by their mother Julia, who still held out hope for their reconciliation.³⁰ Driven by his desire to rule alone, Caracalla's soldiers finally succeeded in murdering Geta murdered as he attempted to take refuge in the arms of his mother.³¹ After the assassination of his rival, Caracalla took the throne, put to death many of his brother's supporters, promised many gifts to his soldiers and the Senate to pacify them,³² and subjected Geta to *damnatio memoriae*.³³ Some researchers believe that Philostratus alluded to this unhappy tale of brotherly discord and fratricide in several of his writings.³⁴ Others have noted that the tensions between Titus and Domitian detailed in the *VA* closely resemble the conflict between Caracalla and Geta.³⁵

29. Herodian, *Hist.* 4.3.1–4. Herodian even mentions that the brothers tried to poison each other (*Hist.* 4.4.2).

30. Herodian, *Hist.* 4.3.5–9.

31. Because Geta was constantly guarded by soldiers and athletes, Caracalla could find no opportunity to kill his sibling (Herodian, *Hist.* 4.4.2). Therefore, Caracalla asked his mother to invite Geta to come with him to her quarters. Once all three family members were present, Caracalla's troops rushed in and stabbed Geta to death.

32. Dio Cassius, *Hist. rom.* 78.3. Herodian, *Hist.* 4.4.7–8; 4.6.1–5.

33. This modern scholarly term refers to the attempt to remove the name of an enemy of the state from all records. In the case of Geta, his name was removed from inscriptions and statues; busts of him were destroyed, and coins with his image were melted down or defaced. See Schultz and Ward, *A History*, 522; Dudley, *Civilization of Rome*, 208.

34. As mentioned earlier in this section, the tale of king Darius II Ochus and Severus are similar in their details. Both rulers had sons that hated each other; in both cases, one son killed his sibling (*VA* 1.28.2). In his *Erotic Letters*, Philostratus criticized Caracalla (*Epistle* 72). Although the letter did not explicitly mention fratricide, at the same time its contents did not exclude it. See Koskenniemi, *Der philostrateische Apollonios*, 39. This letter may never have been delivered to Caracalla or may it have been written as a literary exercise after the death of Caracalla.

35. In *VA* 6.32, there seems to be a correspondence between Domitian and Caracalla: both men were the sons of a powerful, dynastic head (i.e., Vespasian and Severus), both killed a ruling sibling (i.e., Titus and Geta) after the deaths of their respective fathers, and both were assassinated. See Göttsching, *Apollonius*, 86; Koskenniemi, *Der philostrateische Apollonios*, 41; Flinterman, *Power*, 220. However much these stories resemble each other, the details of both seem to confirmed by other historical sources. This leaves open the question of whether Philostratus intended a comparison between rulers here or if the similarities are coincidental.

The reign of Caracalla was a mixed bag. His most lauded achievement was the *Constitutio Antoniniana* (AD 212), an edict in which he granted citizenship to all free members of the Roman Empire.[36] Although "[m]odern scholars are inclined to regard it as a landmark in Roman constitutional history, and to commend its liberal spirit,"[37] Caracalla may have enacted it for the less noble reasons of reducing "the privileged position of Italy and the old senatorial elite,"[38] creating additional taxable citizens,[39] and generating recruits for the army.[40] Philostratus does not appear to have alluded to this legislation in the *VA*.[41] Caracalla also seems to have been a fairly skilled military man, leading campaigns against the Alameni and other German tribes (AD 213) and also against the Parthians (AD 216). Yet, Caracalla's detractors point out that he debased the currency (AD 215),[42] killed Vestal Virgins,[43] slaughtered Geta along with his numerous supporters, and massacred numerous inhabitants of Alexandria because they claimed that Caracalla was involved in an incestuous relationship with Julia Domna, his own mother.[44] Philostratus may have alluded to some of Caracalla's crimes and misbehavior under the guise of discussing nearly identical acts performed by Domitian,[45] but it is difficult to determine whether these events were indeed veiled references to Caracalla's behavior.

36. Parker and Warmington, "Aurelius," 153; Schultz and Ward, *A History*, 522.
37. Dudley, *Civilization of Rome*, 208.
38. Schultz and Ward, *A History*, 522.
39. Parker and Warmington, "Aurelius," 153; Dudley, *Civilization of Rome*, 208.
40. Schultz and Ward, *A History*, 523.
41. Koskenniemi, *Die philostrateische Apollonios*, 55.
42. Dudley, *Civilization of Rome*, 208.
43. Dio Cassius *Hist. rom.* 78.16.1.

44. Herodian *Hist.* 4.9 (cf. Dio Cassius, *Hist. rom.* 78.22). One surprising insult mentioned by Herodian appears to insinuate that Caracalla had an incestuous relationship with his mother (Phillimore, *Philostratus*, lxiii), a rumor also attested in other sources. This accusation appears to be false for Dio Cassius did not mention it, it only appeared in later sources, and it inaccurately describes Julia Domna as Caracalla's stepmother (*Hist. Aug.*, Sev. 21:6-7; Car. 10.1-4, 11.5). This charge may have developed from a misunderstanding of the close mother-son relationship the two had. See Galimberti, "La Vita," 132. Another possibility is that this was an accusation concocted by Plautianus during his reign of terror. For this view, see Magie's comments in *Scriptores historiae augustae*, 415, n. 134.

45. For instance, several sources claimed that Domitian executed Vestal Virgins (Dio Cassius, *Hist. rom.* 67.3; Pliny the Younger, *Ep.* 4.11; Suetonius, *Dom.* 8.4) like Caracalla did (Dio Cassius, *Hist. rom.* 78.16.1). See also Koskenniemi, *Der philostrateische Apollonios*, 41.

Caracalla was fascinated by the tales of the ancient hero Achilles, enamored of Alexander the Great,[46] and had high regard for Apollonius of Tyana. Like his father,[47] he was superstitious, and he took delight in magicians and sorcerers (τοῖς δὲ μάγοις καὶ γόησιν), including Apollonius of Tyana.[48] At the Hellespont, he honored Achilles at his tomb with sacrifices and races, like Alexander[49] and Apollonius had done centuries before him (*VA* 4.11–16). Philostratus featured the Homeric hero cult in both the *VA* and *Heroicus*, both of which may be occasioned by or allude to Caracalla's visit to Troy.[50] Perhaps Caracalla's desire to invade Parthia was inspired by the Persian campaign of Alexander.[51] Phillimore suggested that Julia encouraged Philostratus to write so much about Apollonius and Alexander the Great in the *VA* because these characters appealed to Caracalla.[52]

Yet, unlike Alexander the Great, Caracalla never completed his Persian campaign. After a successful invasion of Media, he withdrew to Edessa for the winter, hoping to resume the campaign in the spring.[53] While en route to offer sacrifice at the Temple of the Moon at Charrhae, he stopped to relieve himself by the side of the road and was fatally stabbed

---

46. Caracalla collected items supposedly used by Alexander and even dressed like him (Dio). He modelled the army after Alexander's troops, creating phalanxes like those once used by the Macedonians and naming his commanders after Alexander's generals (Dio Cassius, *Hist. rom.* 78.8; and Herodian, *Hist.* 4.8.3). He filled Rome and other cities with statues and pictures of Alexander, sometimes putting atop a single body a head that was one half Alexander and the other Caracalla (Herodian, *Hist.* 4.8.1–2).

47. Severus was regarded as a competent astrologer, for was able to determine that Julia Domna was destined to be his wife by looking into her horoscope (*Hist. Aug.*, Sev. 3.9). Severus also believed in dream divination and even wrote a book on the topic (Dio Cassius, *Hist. rom.* 72.23). He also experienced the power of dreams in his own career, for they predicted his rise to power (Herodian, *Hist.* 2.9.5–6) and added weight to the accusation of Plautianus's attempt to assassinate him (Dio Cassius, *Hist. rom.* 76.3).

48. Dio reports that Caracalla erected a shrine in Apollonius's honor (Dio Cassius, *Hist. rom.* 78.4. Although Herodian does not specifically mention Apollonius, he mentions that Caracalla consulted magicians, astrologers, experts in sacrifice, and sorcerers (Herodian, *Hist.* 4.12.3). Some scholars have attributed Caracalla's interest in Apollonius to his mother's love for the sage. See C. P. Jones, "Apollonius of Tyana, Hero," 78.

49. Green, *Alexander of Macedon*, 167–68; Dio Cassius, *Hist. rom.* 78.16.7.

50. Galimberti, *La Vita*, 128–29; Solmsen, "Some Works of Philostratus," 559.

51. Dudley, *Civilization of Rome*, 208.

52. Phillimore, *In Honour*, lxiv; Galimberti, "La Vita," 125–36.

53. Schultz and Ward, *A History*, 522.

by a tribune named Martialis.⁵⁴ The army was without an emperor for a few days. Because they were under threat of attack by the Parthians, they hastily chose Macrinus as the new emperor. Unbeknownst to the troops, Macrinus had been the mastermind behind Caracalla's assassination.⁵⁵

The enthronement of Macrinus seemed to signal the end of the Severan dynasty. Both male heirs to the throne were dead, Julia Domna had committed suicide upon learning of Caracalla's death,⁵⁶ and Macrinus had ordered Julia Maesa, Julia Domna's sister, to return to Edessa.⁵⁷ Yet, against all odds, the Severan house did not fall. The army turned on Macrinus after a mere fourteen-month reign, and, thanks to the efforts of Julia Maesa, the Severan family was restored. But, before relating this tale, the narrative must backtrack to tell the story of Philostratus's patroness, Julia Domna, whose rule spanned the eras of both her husband Severus and her son Caracalla.

Julia Domna

Julia Domna was arguably the most significant woman of Philostratus's era. She was the daughter of Gaius Julius Bassus, the high priest of Baal (Elagabalus) at Emesa in Syria. After the death of Septimius Severus's first wife, Paccia Marciana (AD 186), he married Julia, who bore Caracalla and Geta. Julia possessed great importance in the early years of Severus's reign.⁵⁸ Yet, as Plautianus rose to power around AD 200,⁵⁹ Julia was marginalized when he began to mistreat her, Caracalla, and the other noblewoman. Julia took refuge from her tormentor and "for this reason she began to study philosophy and passed her days in company with sophists."⁶⁰ She created for herself a "salon" or "circle" (κύκλος)⁶¹

---

54. Dio Cassius, *Hist. rom.* 79.5. Herodian, *Hist.* 4.13.3–5.

55. The architect of this assassination was Macrinus, the prefect of the Praetorian Guard. Caracalla had insulted Macrinus for cowardice, lack of military experience, and dislike of army food. Macrinus conspired with the centurion Martialis, who hated the emperor for insulting him and for executing his brother.

56. Herodian adds that Julia Domna may have killed herself on her on initiative or because she was ordered to do so (*Hist.* 4.13.8).

57. Herodian, *Hist.* 5.3.2–3.

58. Schultz and Ward, *A History*, 524.

59. Taggart, "Apollonius," 49.

60. Dio Cassius, *Hist. rom.* 76.15.7.

61. *VA* 1.3.

by assembling a group of rhetoricians,[62] mathematicians (γεωμέτραις),[63] and philosophers.[64] Although some rather extravagant claims have been made concerning the membership of this circle,[65] Bowersock makes a convincing case that "[m]ost of the persons of Julia's will have been lesser philosophers and sophists, whose names, if we had them, would be unfamiliar to us."[66] Of this circle, Harris states, "Philostratus was its chief literary ornament, and the *Life of Apollonius* its best literary product."[67] After the execution of Plautianus in AD 205, Julia returned to prominence.[68] She accompanied Severus on his Caledonian campaign, attempted to reconcile her sons before Geta's assassination, and, when this plan failed, continued to assist her remaining son, Caracalla. She traveled with him during his Parthian campaign as far as Antioch, where she oversaw his Greek and Latin correspondence[69] until the time of her suicide by starvation in AD 217.

Elagabalus

Julia Maesa, the sister of Julia Domna, can be credited with restoring the fortunes of the Severan house in the aftermath of Macrinus's assassination of Caracalla. She had a grandson from each of her two daughters: the fourteen-year-old Bassianus, the son of Julia Soaemias Bassiana, and the nine-year-old Alexianus, the son of Julia Mamaea. While still in Syria, Julia Maesa finagled to set Bassianus on the throne by spreading the rumor among the soldiers that he was the illegitimate son of Caracalla and by promising them wealth for helping her to restore the dynasty through his enthronement.[70] Many troops defected to Bassianus's banner and, after

62. *VA* 1.3; Dio Cassius, *Hist. rom.* 76.15.7.

63. *VS* 622. This Greek term most likely refers to astrologers or Pythagorean/Platonic mathematicians. See Maclean and Aitken, *Flavius Philostratus*, xlvi; Philostratus and Eunapius, *The Lives of the Sophists*, 301, n. 4.

64. *VS* 622. Dio Cassius, *Hist. rom.* 76.15.7.

65. For instance, Galen and Dio Cassius are sometimes said to have belonged to this group (Luck, *Arcana Mundi*, 35. Harris, "Apollonius of Tyana," 192). Yet, only Gordian (I or II), Philiscus, and Philostratus are known to have belonged to this group with any certainty.

66. Bowersock, *Greek Sophists*, 109.

67. Harris, "Apollonius of Tyana," 192.

68. Schultz and Ward, *A History*, 524.

69. Dio Cassius, *Hist. rom.* 78.18.2; 79.4.2–3.

70. Herodian, *Hist.* 5.3.9–11; 5.4.1–3.

Macrinus's execution, the entire army proclaimed Bassianus as emperor, thereby rehabilitating the Severan dynasty.

Bassianus (AD 218–22), better known as Elagabalus,[71] did not live up to the expectations of Julia Maesa and the inhabitants of Rome. His practices of wearing Phoenician clothing, applying cosmetics, and dancing in worship to his deity were off-putting to the Senate, army, and people of Rome. His grandmother, correctly anticipating how his behavior would be received by the Romans, tried in vain to curtail it.[72] Elagabalus also attempted a reform of Roman religion by bringing the image of the Emesene deity to Rome, building a temple to it on the Palatine, and elevating this god above all other gods, including Jupiter.[73] Some believe that Philostratus hinted at these reforms of Elagabalus in the *VA*,[74] although others disagree.[75] Even more troublesome than Elagabalus's

---

71. Bassianus had been a priest of the Syrian sun god, Elagabal, since childhood (Herodian, *Hist.* 5.3.6). Eventually, he took this very name as his own in honor of the deity.

72. Herodian, *Hist.* 5.4–5.

73. Dio Cassius, *Hist. rom.* 79.11.1; Herodian, *Hist.* 5.6.5, 8.

74. Flintermann allows that the reference to a foolish king who claimed that he was the same as the Sun (*VA* 3.28) was probably an allusion to Elagabalus (Flinterman, *Power*, 220–221). Koskenniemi points out that several renowned scholars regard Apollonius's daily and exclusive worship of the Helios in the *VA* as references to the religious propaganda of Elagabalus's religious reforms. See Koskenniemi, *Der philostrateische Apollonios*, 71.

75. Koskenniemi himself thinks that there is little that could be construed as speaking about Elagabalus or his religious reforms in the *VA*. Apollonius acknowledged other gods and even prayed to them. Although Koskenniemi claims that Apollonius only prayed to one deity other than the Sun, namely Apollo (*VA* 8.13; Koskenniemi, *Der philostrateische Apollonios*, 71, n. 8), the sage also prayed to Heracles (*VA* 7.28–29) and claimed to live under Zeus (*VA* 7.5; Dio Cassius, *Hist. rom.* 70.11). Koskenniemi also believes the *VA* was composed before the religious reform of Elagabalus because he never alludes to it (Koskenniemi, *Der philostrateische Apollonios*, 81). Indeed, according to him, there is no particular religious trend promoted in the *VA* (Koskenniemi, *Der philostrateische Apollonios*, 79). Apollonius does indeed show special affinity to the Sun (e.g., *VA* 1.31; 2.38; 6:10; 7:10, 31). However, other characters in the narrative do the same: King Vardanes (*VA* 1.31, although with inappropriate sacrifices), Phroates (*VA* 26.3), and the Wise Ones (*VA* 3.2). Yet, Apollonius did not discourage the worship of other gods, for he wrote a book on how to offer sacrifice appropriately for each one of them (*VA* 3.41) and lectured on this topic (*VA* 4.19). Indeed, he himself swore by Athena (*VA* 8.26) and poured out libations to the Ionian gods (*VA* 4.6). He does not advocate for the cult of Helios (Koskenniemi, *Der philostrateische Apollonios*, 74), as one might have expected if Elagabalus was in mind. Philostratus himself does not appear to have been an advocate of Helios, since he rarely mentioned this god outside of the *VA* (Koskenniemi, *Der philostrateische Apollonios*, 75). Koskenniemi believes it is impossible to determine whether the historical Apollonius really worshipped the sun or if this was attributed to him later (Koskenniemi, *Der philostrateische Apollonios*, 78).

un-Roman appearance and religious innovations were the tales of his extravagance, human sacrifice, and sexual perversion.[76] Because of his un-Roman behavior, he was hated by the soldiers and the populace.[77] Maesa, fearing that he would lose the support of the army attempted another intervention. She encouraged Elagabalus to adopt his cousin Alexander (formerly Alexianus) as Caesar. She planned that Elagabalus would devote himself to cultic matters while Alexander[78] would tend to matters of state. Initially, Elagabalus agreed to this arrangement, but when the favor of the people shifted to Alexander[79] he twice tried to murder him. Maesa and Mamea, being wise to palace intrigues,[80] thwarted both attempts. After the second attempt on Alexander's life, the Praetorians hunted down Elagabalus and his mother. They were slain, beheaded, dragged through the city, and thrown into the sewers that lead to the Tiber, from which Elagabalus posthumously earned the name, Tiberinus. So dreadful was his reign that Göttsching proposed that the *VA*'s portrayal of the decadent tyrant Nero had been modeled on the recently assassinated Elagabalus.[81]

---

76. Ancient sources report that Elagabalus threw extravagant banquets (Dio Cassius, *Hist. rom.* 80.9.2), sacrificed of boys in religious rites (Dio Cassius, *Hist. rom.* 80.11), married and defiled a Vestal Virgin (Dio Cassius, *Hist. rom.* 80.9.3–4; Herodian, *Hist.* 5.6), and appointed actors to important imperial posts (Herodian, *Hist.* 5.7). His sexual exploits seem to have been a favorite target of his chroniclers: having intercourse with women for the purpose of learning how to act with his male lovers (Dio Cassius, *Hist. rom.* 80.13.1), playing the part of a female prostitute who solicited male passers-by at brothels and at home (Dio Cassius, *Hist. rom.* 80.1), having a husband he wanted to appoint as Caesar (Dio Cassius, *Hist. rom.* 80.14.1), and promising to pay physicians vast sums if they could surgically fashion a vagina for him (Dio Cassius, *Hist. rom.* 80.1–14, 17). Some of these stories may have been exaggerated by "hostile and sensationalistic sources" (Schultz and Ward, *A History*, 525).

77. Dio Cassius, *Hist. rom.* 80.17.1; Herodian, *Hist.* 5.8.

78. Herodian claims that his name was changed to Alexander because his alleged father, Caracalla, had admired the Macedonian leader (*Hist.* 5.7.3).

79. Although Elagabalus wanted Alexander trained in matters pertaining to the Syrian cult—dancing, leaping, and to wear garments like his—Alexander's mother privately had him trained in self-control, Greek and Latin studies, and wrestling (Herodian, *Hist.* 5.7.5–6). The soldiers and the people grew bitter toward the effeminate Elagabalus, preferring the modest Alexander to him (Herodian, *Hist.* 5.8.1–2).

80. Herodian, *Hist.* 5.7–3. Maesa would have likely known to watch for assassinations for she had lived in the imperial court during the reigns of Severus and Caracalla (Herodian, *Hist.* 5.3–4).

81. Göttsching, *Apollonius*, 86.

Alexander Severus

Alexander Severus (AD 222–35) appears to have been successful as a ruler. He was crowned immediately after Elagabalus's death but, since he was only fourteen at the time, Julia Maesa and Julia Mamea took charge of the administration and imperial policy.[82] During his reign, reforms were enacted to restore a more moderate form of government that included the appointment of respectable senators, the restoration of traditional Roman religion, and the removal of the corrupt officials Elagabalus had appointed. The first part of Alexander's rule was peaceful, but because he failed to deal with military mutinies, win a war against Parthia, and purchase peace from invading Germanic tribes, the army killed him and his mother.[83] Alexander's death marked the end of the Severan dynasty and the beginning of the Crisis of the Third Century (AD 235–84), a period characterized by civil war, barbarian invasions, and a succession of short-lived emperors.

As noted earlier, there is no strong evidence that Philostratus had contact with rulers after the deaths of Caracalla and Julia in 217. Yet, it is almost certain that Philostratus lived through the times of Elagabalus and Alexander, lived to see the first portion of this period of the Crisis of the Third Century, and died sometime during the reign of Philip the Arab.[84] One notable scholar has proposed that the *VA* was intended to instruct Severus Alexander through the virtues and vices of various rulers.[85] Perhaps a hint of Philostratus's influence on the royal family can be detected in the time of Alexander, for the *Historia Augusta* (second half of the fourth century) recorded that each morning this ruler sacrificed in a sanctuary that contained images of the deified emperors, his ancestors, and other holy men (i.e., Apollonius, Christ, Abraham, and Orpheus).[86] Yet, evidence is insufficient to determine whether Alexander's veneration

---

82. Herodian, *Hist.* 5.8.10; 6.1.1–2. Maesa died ca. AD 225, leaving Mamaea in control of the government. Even when Alexander reached maturity, he was still easily dominated by his mother.

83. Schultz and Ward, *A History*, 526–27.

84. After the Severans, Philostratus would have lived through the reigns of several rulers: Maximinus (AD 235–238) Gordian I (AD 238) Gordian II (AD 238), Pupienus Maximus (AD 238), Balbinus (AD 238), Gordian III (AD 238–244), and Philip (AD 244–249).

85. Göttsching, *Apollonius*, 80–89.

86. Göttsching argues that either Philostratus or the *VA* had direct influence on Alexander Severus. See Göttsching, *Apollonius*, 88–89. For the reference to the worship of Apollonius, see *Hist. Aug.*, Sev. 29.2.

of Apollonius was due to the direct influence of Philostratus within the court, the reading of Philostratus's *VA*, or some other source unrelated to the sophist. The only certain connection of Philostratus to a figure of this later period is found in his *Lives of the Sophists*, which he dedicated either to emperor Gordian I or Gordian III (*VS* 479).

As we have seen in this survey, several scholars have suggested that Philostratus had drawn parallels between the persons and events of the third century and the events of the first century in the *VA*. Although these suggestions remain theoretical, the reader should at least be alert to the possibility that Philostratus altered elements of the *VA* to match those of his era. If Philostratus did at times base some of his narrative on rulers of his time, such modifications are not particularly problematic from a historical perspective. However, such adaptations, if proven, might suggest that Philostratus would have also felt free to alter the story of Apollonius to some degree based on the models of other historical figures (e.g., the sophists) closer to his era.

THE SOPHISTIC PROFESSION OF PHILOSTRATUS II

Since Philostratus was a sophist by profession, a brief introduction to the sophistic lifestyle is in order before moving to the particulars of his life. Unfortunately, the precise definition of "sophist" is somewhat elusive, for sometimes it appears to overlap with the occupations of philosophers and orators,[87] as Philostratus himself indicates (*VS* 479, 484, 492). Yet, several features help to distinguish the sophists from these other groups. Forensic orators were generally more audacious, self-confident, and less easily flustered than sophists; the sophists were more accustomed to interacting with younger, inexperienced men (*VS* 614). Political orators avoided "emotional effects and poetical allusions" that were commonly employed by sophists.[88] Unlike philosophers, sophists were not necessarily interested in philosophical truth or morality, for they could argue either side of an issue as an oratorical exercise with equal proficiency. Sophists also differed from many philosophers in that they were experts in improvisation and were sought out for their public declamations.

---

87. Anderson, *Philostratus*, 8–10.

88. Philostratus and Eunapius, *The Lives of the Sophists*, xviii. In *VS* 621, Philostratus noted that the sophist Quirinus may have been better suited for the courtroom even though he participated in declamations.

Another distinction between the sophists and these two other professions was that "[p]hilosophers and rhetors are treated as conscientious and austere professionals, whereas the sophist has broken into the media"; consequently, from Philostratus's "point of view philosophers and rhetors are somehow a little *manqués*."[89]

A sophist was expected to be the master of several skills. He would need to be an expert in all genres of Greek literature (e.g., poetry, oratory, drama, philosophy, and history),[90] for he might be called upon to extemporize on a broad spectrum of ancient themes. For recalling the details of these subjects, the rhetor would also need a capacious and accurate memory. Much like a modern politician, standup comedian, or street preacher, a successful sophist would need to be an expert in the art of verbal self-defense and debate. A speaker often had to fend off attacks from sophistic rivals, the arrogant disciples of another sophist, or an educated listener in the audience; ideally, a sophist would end such an encounter by delivering a sharp rejoinder to an opponent.[91] In their presentations, sophists had to utilize proper Attic style, avoid barbarisms or solecisms, and, at the same time, form a coherent argument.[92] They could not lose their temper or nerve because of the misbehavior of the audience; delayed applause or a haughty expression on a listener's face were among the trials a speaker might have to endure (*VS* 614). Further, they must avoid a bad start to a speech, misquoting a classical source, making a *faux pax* in the presence of a patron, or, worst of all, a breakdown in public.[93] In this cutthroat occupation, an emotional, stylistic, or factual mistake could be fatal to a sophist's career, as could the displeasure of an emperor like Caracalla.[94]

One might wonder why a career based largely on one-upmanship and filled with the pressure of public speaking would have been such a popular occupation. Fame, of course, would have been one reason, but there are others as well, as Wright indicates in his description of second and third-century sophists:

89. Anderson, *Philostratus*, 10.

90. Philostratus and Eunapius, *The Lives of the Sophists*, xvi.

91. Philostratus and Eunapius, *The Lives of the Sophists*, xvi; Anderson, *Philostratus*, 47–48.

92. Anderson, *Philostratus*, 44.

93. Anderson, *Philostratus*, 46–47. The sophist Heracleides the Lycian broke down before Severus, the court, and the royal bodyguard (*VS* 614).

94. The situations of Antipater (*VS* 607) and Philiscus (*VS* 621–23) illustrate this point.

> For the only time in history professors were generally acknowledged as social leaders, went on important embassies, made large fortunes, had their marriages arranged and their quarrels settled by emperors, held Imperial Secretaryships, were Food Controllers, and high priests; and swayed the fate of whole cities by gaining for them immunities and grants of money and visits from the Emperor . . . and not least by attracting thither crowds of students from the remotest parts of the Empire. No other type of intellectual could compete with them for popularity, no creative artists existed to challenge their prestige at the courts of phil-Hellenist Emperors, and though the sophists often show jealousy of the philosophers, philosophy without eloquence was nowhere.[95]

So then, despite the great risk of failure and humiliation, the successful sophist had much to gain by way of influence, wealth, and reputation in his chosen occupation. A further factor in choosing a sophistic career may have been the social position of these figures. Sophists tended to come from elite Greek families. Young men from such families who did not desire a political career may have found a sophistic path more to their liking.[96] For all these reasons, one might have chosen to pursue the career of a sophist.

Apart from individual notoriety, the broader sophistic movement, called by Philostratus the Second Sophistic,[97] appears to have had an agenda of its own. This movement or outlook had a strongly pro-Hellenic agenda of reviving all aspects of Greek culture, but it was at the same time loyal to the Roman Empire.[98] As a later chapter on the literary corpus of Philostratus will demonstrate, his works are shot through with themes of Greek revivalism and nationalism, whether his topic was religion (*Heroicus*), biography (*VS* and *VA*), fiction (*Nero*), art (*Imagines I*), athletics (*Gymnasticus*), or letter writing (*Erotic Letters*). As this applies to Philostratus's portrayal of the Tyanean in the *VA*, one should at least be open to the possibility that Philostratus transformed the historical Apollonius to some degree into an apostle of Hellenism in the service of the Second

---

95. See Wright's comments in Philostratus and Eunapius, *The Lives of the Sophists*, xv.

96. Bowie, "The importance of sophists," 29–59; Flinterman, *Power*, 35.

97. Philostratus claimed that the sophists from Nicetes (mid–first century AD) until the days of Philostratus (early third century AD) belonged to the "Second Sophistic." Philostratus coined the phrase "Second Sophistic" as a way of distinguishing this phase from an earlier sophistic movement in the fifth century BC.

98. Anderson, *Philostratus*, 8.

Sophistic. Not only does Philostratus's Apollonius frequently discourse on several sophistic themes, but several of the details of his life and many of his attributes closely resemble some of the sophists described in the *VS* (i.e., *Vitae sophistarum* or *Lives of the Sophists*).

PHILOSTRATUS II: A SKETCH OF HIS LIFE

Although little solid biographical information about Philostratus II survives, enough evidence remains to sketch the general contours of his life. Lucius Flavius Philostratus, also called "the Athenian"[99] or "the Second,"[100] was probably born on the island of Lemnos around AD 170.[101] If he was a native of this island, as most historians suspect, he would have been born an Athenian citizen since Lemnos was a territory of Athens at that time.[102] Scholars also differ about whether Philostratus was raised on Lemnos or in Athens.[103] Whatever the case, he must have spent some time on the island early on, for he mentioned an incident from his youth that transpired there and was familiar with various details of the island.[104]

After moving to Athens, Philostratus studied rhetoric and soon became an accomplished sophist. There he claims to have studied under the tutelage of several orators, one of whom was Proclus of Naucratis.[105] His

---

99. Anderson, *Philostratus*, 3; 18, n. 6.

100. Bowie, "Philostratus: the life of a sophist," 19.

101. Philostratus and Eunapius, *The Lives of the Sophists*, ix; Petzke, *Die Traditionen*, 5. Some scholars have placed his birth as early as AD 165 and as late at AD 190/1. For a discussion of these theories, see Maclean and Aitken, *Flavius Philostratus*, xlv.

102. Flinterman, *Power*, 15.

103. Several scholars favor Lemnos (Anderson, *Philostratus*, 3; Maclean and Aitken, *Flavius Philostratus*. xlv), whereas Bowie favors Athens ("Philostratus: the life of a sophist," 20).

104. Flinterman notes two references to Lemnos (*VA* 6.27 and *VS* 515; *Power*, 15, n. 66). Bowie suggests that Philostratus grew up in Athens, but "probably spent some time on family estates on Lemnos"; Bowie, "Philostratus: the life of a sophist," 20. If one includes *Dialexis II* as a Philostratean writing, it mentions a geological formation that resembled a dragon on the island of Lemnos.

105. *VS* 602–4. Philostratus admits to having had other teachers of rhetoric (*VS* 585). Several candidates have been proposed for these additional instructors: Damianus of Ephesus (*VS* 605), Antipater of Phrygian Hierapolis (*VS* 606–7), and Hippodromus of Larissa (*VS* 616–17). Bowersock placed Hippodramus among Philostratus's other teachers. See Bowersock, *Greek Sophists*, 1969, 4. Bowie deems Philostratus's association with Hippodramus likely as well ("Philostratus," 19), given the "detail and enthusiasm" he shows in chronicling him, but concedes that even if he were not an official instructor Philostratus at least must have heard him at Athens ("Philostratus," 24).

career as a sophist can be confirmed by several sources. An inscription from Erythrae, calls Flavius Philostratus—almost certainly a reference to Philostratus II—the "sophist" (τοῦ σοφιστοῦ Φλ[αβίου] Φιλοστράτου),[106] as does another inscription from Olympia that the Athenians had dedicated there in his honor.[107] Moreover, the *Suda* indicates that he "was a sophist in Athens and in Rome, under the emperor Severus and until Philip."[108] Assuming that this latter source is correct, the *Suda* helps to establish a rough time frame for Philostratus's floruit as an orator in these two cities; it would have stretched from some point during the reign of Septimius Severus, between AD 205–7, until his death sometime during the rule of Philip the Arab (AD 244–49).[109]

Philostratus also became a high-ranking politician in Athens before he served the Severans.[110] An inscription, dated somewhere between AD 200/1 and 210/11, provides several details of Philostratus's political career in Athens.[111] Lucius Flavius Philostratus is described as "hoplite general" (Στρατηγοῦντας ἐπὶ τὰ ὅπλα Λ. Φλ. Φιλοστράτου Στειριέως). Bowie explains that "by this period the office had nothing to do with weaponry or warfare, but was a magistracy especially involved with securing the city's food supplies."[112] This title also indicates that Philostratus ranked second within the Athenian hierarchy.[113] The use of the *tria nomina* in this inscription—Lucius Flavius Philostratus—provides the additional

---

However, Anderson points out that "Philostratus evidently did not hear Hippodramus as a teacher; he taught the Lemnian Philostratus," as *VS* 617 seems to confirm. See Anderson, *Philostratus*, 18, note 13. Flinterman allows that Philostratus studied under Proclus and perhaps Damianus but is skeptical that there is sufficient evidence that he studied under Antipater and Hippodramus. He does, however, acknowledge that Philostratus had more than one teacher (*VS* 585). See Flinterman, *Power*, 16, n. 68.

106. This inscription also preserves the name of Philostratus's wife, Aurelia Melitine, the name his son, L. Flavius Capitolinus, and the provides the detail that an unnamed "son" and one of his relatives both held senatorial rank. See Philostratus and Eunapius, *The Lives of the Sophists*, xi; Anderson, *Philostratus*,18, note 6; Bowie, "Philostratus: the life of a sophist," 20.

107. Flinterman, *Power*, 18; Miles, *Philostratus*, 11.

108. Anderson, *Philostratus*, 4.

109. Anderson, *Philostratus*, 3; Philostratus and Eunapius, *The Lives of the Sophists*, xi; Petzke, *Die Traditionen*, 5.

110. Flinterman, *Power*, 18.

111. Koskenniemi, *Apollonios*, 1–2; Bowie believes that he would have held this position in Athens around AD 203–5. See Bowie, "Philostratus: the life of a sophist," 20, n. 10, and 25.

112. Bowie, "Philostratus: the life of a sophist," 20.

113. Koskenniemi, *Apollonius*, 6; Anderson, *Philostratus*, 6.

detail that Philostratus was a Roman citizen, although just when in his family's history this occurred and by whom it was granted remains a mystery.[114] Finally, Philostratus was one of the *prytaneis* of his tribe, representing them in the Athenian council.[115] The picture of Philostratus as a combination of orator and politician that emerges from this data is consistent with the roles played by some of the other sophists that he wrote about in the *VS*.[116]

Within the first few years of the third century,[117] Philostratus had moved from Athens to Rome where he was welcomed into the Severan court.[118] Just how he gained access to imperial circles is unclear. One popular theory proposes that his admission was aided by the endorsement of his former teacher and fellow sophist, Antipater of Hierapolis.[119] This is a plausible explanation, since Antipater himself had several connections within the imperial court,[120] and the Syrian ancestry that he shared with the empress Julia Domna might have made her favorable to his recommendation of Philostratus.[121] Another conjecture is that Philostratus "may have owed his first steps of preferment to Septimius Severus, for Septimius was a patron and amateur of letters."[122] A final possibility is

114. Flinterman, *Power*, 17, n. 76.

115. Bowie, "Philostratus: The Life of the Sophist," 20.

116. Flinterman, *Power*, 17.

117. Bowie places Philostratus's arrival at Rome after AD 205 or 206 before the end of 207. See Bowie, "Philostratus: the life of a sophist," 20, n. 10, 24–25. Flinterman places his arrival at Rome and introduction to the royal court around AD 203, certainly before 207/8. The royal family was in Britain between AD 208 and 211 and, since Philostratus was with them in Gaul (c. AD 213; *VS* 625) and had regularly heard Antipater speak (before his death in AD 212), his entry into the circle of Julia Domna would have been more likely to have occurred early on. See Flinterman, *Power*, 20. The other option was that Philostratus entered into royal service during the brief window of time between AD 211–213, when the imperial family had returned from Britain and Julia left for Gaul.

118. Bowie, "Philostratus: the life of a sophist," 20. Petzke is vaguer about this date, placing it somewhere around the turn of the century, *Die Traditionen*, 5.

119. Philostratus and Eunapius, *The Lives of the Sophists*, x.

120. Antipater was appointed secretary in charge of the Greek correspondence of Septimius Severus (*ab epistulis graecus*) in the 190s (*VS* 607). For this date, see Flinterman, *Power*, 19. Philostratus was also appointed "tutor of the Gods," a title which refers to his job as the instructor of Severius's sons Caracalla and Geta (*VS* 607).

121. Philostratus and Eunapius, *The Lives of the Sophists*, x; Lesky, *Greek Literature*, 837; Anderson, *Philostratus*, 4.

122. Phillimore proposed and retracted this theory, preferring to attribute Philostratus's rise to power to Julia Domna instead. See Phillimore, *In Honour*, lxi–lxii; Dio Cassius, *Hist. rom.* 77.11.

that Julia Domna herself drew Philostratus into her company because of their common interests in philosophy and rhetoric.[123] Whatever the circumstances of his entry into Julia's private literary circle, Philostratus quickly rose to prominence within it.[124]

Philostratus appears to have been directly associated with the Severans for a little over a decade. He may have traveled with the imperial court during Severus's campaign in Britain (AD 208–211).[125] He was certainly with them in Gaul when Heliodorus the Arab presented his case to Caracalla (AD 212/13).[126] One of these two occasions likely allowed Philostratus to view the Atlantic coast from France or Spain.[127] Later, the sophist may have accompanied Caracalla and Julia during the eastern campaigns, which began in 214.[128] If so, their itinerary would have included several sites that Philostratus would later feature in the journeys of Apollonius in the *VA*: the Hellespont, Ilium, Pergamum, Tyana, and Antioch of Syria (AD 215).[129] The empress's visit to Tyana may have been the occasion on which she commissioned Philostratus to write the *VA*. He may have stayed with Julia Domna in Antioch of Syria, for this was the base from which Julia Domna oversaw administrative matters for Caracalla during the Parthian campaign.[130] In all this time of close association with the imperial family, Philostratus appears to have "stayed on the right side of the emperor"[131] and to have thrived in his position.

Yet, after the assassination of Caracalla in 217 and the suicide of Julia Domna later in that same year, little is known of Philostratus's career.

123. Interestingly, Philostratus notes a much earlier sophist, Philostratus the Egyptian, who studied with Queen Cleopatra; this Egyptian took great pleasure in her as a lover of learning (*VS*, 486).

124. Meier, *Mentor*, 577.

125. Anderson, *Philostratus*, 5; Flinterman, *Power*, 24.

126. *VS*, 625; Bowie, "Philostratus: the life of a sophist," 20, 25; Flinterman, *Power*, 20.

127. *VA* 5.2; Philostratus, *Apollonius of Tyana*, 2:3; Miles, *Philostratus*, 10. Flinterman prefers to place this event during Septimius Severus's invasion of Britain, since Caracalla's movements do not suggest proximity to the Atlantic coast. See Flinterman, *Power*, 24.

128. Flinterman, *Power*, 24.

129. Bowie, "Philostratus: the life of a sophist," 20; Petzke, *Die Traditionen*, 5; Flinterman, *Power*, 24; Miles, *Philostratus*, 11.

130. Dio Cassius, *Hist. rom.* 78.18.1; Flinterman, *Power*, 24.

131. *VS* 608; Anderson, *Philostratus*, 6. Unlike Philostratus, Antipater fell from grace because he was too eager to use the sword in his role as governor of Bithynia and he had written a letter criticizing Caracalla for executing his younger brother. Antipater probably committed suicide around AD 212 (Flinterman, *Power*, 20).

Perhaps, with the death of Julia, her circle of scholars dispersed[132] and he exited royal service. Perhaps Philostratus found favor in the eyes of the last of the Severan rulers (e.g., Elagabalus or Severus Alexander) and continued to serve in the court.[133] There is a rumor of his residence at Tyre[134] and much stronger evidence of his return to a career as a sophist in Athens.[135] He appears to have published several of his works, including the *VA*, in the period after Julia's death.[136] The *Suda* claims that Philostratus was a sophist until the reign of Philip the Arab (AD 244–249) during whose reign most historians presume he died.[137]

In modern times, if Philostratus is remembered at all outside of the classics department, he is probably known for his literary legacy. Some have probably heard of the literary renaissance known as the "Second Sophistic,"[138] although they may not realize that Philostratus coined that phrase,[139] that the modern use of this designation differs somewhat from the meaning that he intended by it,[140] or that he recorded the history of many of its participants in the *VS* (*Lives of the Sophists*). Some of

---

132. Phillimore, *In Honour*, lxxxiii–lxxxiv.

133. Anderson, *Philostratus*, 7. Anderson notes that the legend that Severus Alexander had an image Apollonius in a private chapel might hint that Philostratus's hero at least was still held in high esteem.

134. This tradition may be due to confusion of Philostratus II with Philostratus of Tyre. See Galimberti, "La Vita," 126.

135. Lesky, *Greek Literature*, 837; Anderson, *Philostratus*, 7; Maclean and Aitken, *Flavius Philostratus*, xlvi. Flinterman argues that Philostratus's title *Philostratos Tyrios*, employed by several late writers (i.e., Photius, *Bibliotheca* 44, Arethas, and Johannes Tzetzes, *Chiliades* vi.303–8), does not constitute solid evidence of his residence in Tyre. He does, however, deem it "reasonably certain" that Philostratus returned to Athens. See Flinterman, *Power*, 26. Bowie, bolstering the case for a later Athenian residence, writes, "His remarks about the sophistic quarrel between Aspasius and Philostratus of Lemnos gaining strength in Ionia and about his friendship with the Athenian Nicagoras and the Phoenician Apsines (who taught in Athens) point rather to his spending much, perhaps most, of his time in Athens and Ionia in the 220s and 230s" (Bowie, "Philostratus: the life of a sophist," 25).

136. Elsner argues that the *VA* and the *VS* may have been written after the death of Julia in Athens; Elsner, "Protean corpus," 4.

137. Anderson, *Philostratus*, 7.

138. Elsner, "Protean Corpus," 14.

139. Miles, *Philostratus*, 11.

140. Bowie, "Philostratus: the life of a sophist," 29–30. Anderson explains that the Second Sophistic is not so much a movement as a mindset: it was a pro-Hellenic literary outlook that drew strongly on the rich heritage of the Greeks. He explains that "It embodied a cultural nationalism in an international milieu, while remaining loyal to the Roman Imperial system." See Bowie, *Philostratus*, 8.

PART 2: PHILOSTRATUS II AND HIS LITERARY CORPUS

Philostratus's works have been mined by classical[141] and biblical scholars for use in other projects,[142] but they have been rarely studied as literature or examined within the context of the overall canon of Philostratus although this trend in classics has changed in the last decades.

The next two chapters will bring the newcomer up to speed by introducing the literary corpus of Philostratus, displaying his skill and creativity as an author, and exploring his wide range of interests. Yet, the primary goal of these next chapters is to explore the question of whether Philostratus's depiction of Apollonius is historically accurate.

---

141. Miles notes that scholarship has not been interested in books like the *VA* and *Heroicus* in their own right, but for ulterior motives: "This is true in fact of the *Corpus Philostrateum* as a whole, which has until relatively recently been more often mined than read" (Miles, *Philostratus*, 6–7).

142. Biblical scholars occasionally reference the works of Philostratus in their studies of early fiction (*Heroicus*), biography (*Lives of the Sophists*), or epistles (*Erotic Letters*). As was seen in the previous chapter, the *VA* was frequently ransacked by form critics for miracle stories and by "divine man" advocates for support of their theories.

5

An Introduction to Philostratus's Writings

THE ADVANTAGES OF BEING FAMILIAR WITH THE ENTIRE PHILOSTRATEAN CORPUS

THOSE WHO ARE INTERESTED in learning about the historical Apollonius may not see the value of getting acquainted with all of Philostratus's writings. Because the VA is the only work of Philostratus to address Apollonius at length,[1] readers might have the impression that it can be studied in isolation from his other writings. Indeed, the VA is indisputably the most important work for investigating the Tyanean and can be studied on its own, but a good case can be made that the VA is best studied in conjunction with Philostratus's other works.[2]

This chapter will demonstrate that even a modicum of familiarity with the rest of the Philostratus's corpus can be invaluable in assessing the historical worth of the VA and the accuracy of what it claims about Apollonius. One such advantage is that a brief survey of Philostratus's entire corpus reveals his favorite topics, overarching agendas, and biases.[3] Just as a Pauline scholar who is investigating the book of Romans would

---

1. Apollonius is briefly mentioned in a few passages in the VS (521, 570).
2. E.g., Koskenniemi, *Der philostrateische Apollonios*, 29.
3. Cazemier, "Apollonius en magie," 29–30.

want to compare similar vocabulary and themes occurring in the rest of the Pauline corpus, so a student of the *VA* will benefit from familiarity with the various topics found elsewhere in the writings of Philostratus. For instance, readers who are familiar with Philostratus's broader corpus will probably note that several of his works promote anti-magical and pro-Hellenic ideas along with elements of political advisement or critique. These same readers will likely also notice the nearly identical themes recur in the *VA*, where Apollonius is depicted as a non-magical miracle worker,[4] an advocate of Hellenism, and a close advisor to Roman emperors and foreign kings. Although this may be an accurate portrayal of the historical Apollonius, the discovery of several of Philostratus's favorite themes in the *VA* might also suggest that he has brought earlier traditions about Apollonius into alignment with his interests.

Another benefit of familiarity with the *Corpus Philostrateum* is that one will spot the repetition of nearly identical stories that may challenge the historicity of the *VA*. The phenomenon of twice-told tales (and sometimes thrice-told ones) shared by the *VA* and Philostratus's other works, might help in assessing the historicity of the *VA*. Retelling a story in multiple contexts is not necessarily problematic, but when such a story is presented as a historical event in the *VA* and it also appears elsewhere in a fictional dialogue or once more in a totally different context, this raises the question of whether Philostratus was as interested in relating accurate history as he was in good story-telling. This phenomenon also raises the question of sequence: were such repeated tales borrowed from Philostratus's earlier texts to flesh out the tale of Apollonius's journeys or were historical events from Apollonius's life later placed in fictional contexts in his other works? These examples, along with the one in the previous paragraph, illustrate how the rest of Philostratus's literary corpus might be used to evaluate or at least to prompt questions concerning the historical validity of the *VA*.

Yet, before these other works of Philostratus can be used as tools for historical inquiry, one must first determine which of the several works attributed to Philostratus are genuine. Thus, this chapter will have the dual task of (1) introducing the books of the Philostratean corpus and considering issues of authorship and (2) discussing how the authentic works might aid in evaluating the trustworthiness of the *VA*. Just as New Testament scholars must determine which books truly belong within the

---

4. In the *VA*, Philostratus claimed that Apollonius performed his wonders by means of philosophy and his understanding of the natural world, not by means of magic.

Pauline corpus before making certain historical and theological judgments about the apostle Paul, those who would speak authoritatively of Philostratean concepts, themes, or language must also make informed decisions about which works belong within his canon.[5] Therefore, this chapter will begin with a discussion of which books belong within the Philostratean canon.

THE PROBLEM OF THE PHILOSTRATI: THE *SUDA*'S ACCOUNT OF WHICH AUTHOR WROTE WHAT

The Philostrati were a Greek, literary family that spanned three or four generations of the late second and early third century AD. All these men bore the name "Philostratus," appear to have been of Lemnian origin, and seem to have written on similar topics.[6] These commonalities, coupled with a confusing entry in the *Suda*, a tenth-century Byzantine encyclopedia, have made it difficult to determine which of these men authored some of the works that are included in the Philostratean literary corpus. Therefore, one of the most perplexing problems in establishing the corpus of Philostratus II is that of distinguishing him from other members of his family and sorting out which of their writings should be attributed to him.

The initial step in trying to assign the appropriate works to Philostratus II begins with trying to make sense of a rather lengthy entry in

---

5. Students of the New Testament will note that much of the process of assigning authorship and date in the case of Philostratus resembles the method used by New Testament scholars when addressing the authorship and date of the Pauline epistles. For instance, many of the same criteria for determining authorship are used for both corpora: e.g., internal and external evidence, language/style, and content, such as a consistent point of view on particular themes or topics. Scholarly opinions on which works were written by Philostratus also resemble the views of Pauline scholars. In the Philostratean corpus, works are often divided into the categories of uncontested, likely, and questionable. Likewise, in the Pauline collection, scholars generally accept seven books as authentic (i.e., Romans, 1 Corinthians, 2 Corinthians, Galatians, Philippians, 1 Thessalonians, and Philemon), are about evenly divided on two (i.e., Colossians, 2 Thessalonians), and mostly reject several as inauthentic (i.e., Ephesians, 1 Timothy, 2 Timothy, Titus, and Hebrews). However, occasionally a reputable scholar breaks with the consensus view and accepts most (or all) of the books in the NT attributed to Paul; For examples of the latter view, see Johnson, *The Writings*, 240–42; Witherington III, *Invitation*, 237–53.

6. For instance, at least two of these authors wrote works about the interpretation of painting (*Imagines I* and *Imagines II*).

the *Suda*, for it provides the most complete description of the lives and accomplishments of the Philostrati:

> Philostratus, the son of Philostratus also named Verus, a sophist from Lemnos, and himself a second sophist, having been a sophist in Athens, then in Rome, under Severus the king and until the reign of Philip. He wrote declamations, *Erotic Letters*, *Imagines*, which are descriptions in four books, *Agora*, *Heroicus*, *Dialexeis*, *Goats* or *Concerning the Flute*, *The Life of Apollonius of Tyana* in eight books, *The Lives of the Sophists* in four books, *Epigrams*, and some other compositions. Except, he ought to be placed first.
>
> The first Philostratus, a Lemnian, son of Verus, and the father of the second Philostratus, also a sophist himself, after being a sophist in Athens, lived under Nero. He wrote many panegyric speeches and four Eleusinian speeches, declamations, *Questions among the Orators*, *Oratorical Resources*, *Concerning the Noun*; this is a response to the sophist Antipater; *On Tragedy* in three books, *Gymnasticus*; it concerns what was accomplished at Olympia; *Lithognomicus*, *Proteus*, *The Dog* or *The Sophist*, *Nero*, *The Spectator*, forty-three tragedies, fourteen comedies, and many other worthy works.
>
> Philostratus, son of Nervianus, nephew of the second Philostratus, a Lemnian, also a sophist himself; he also taught in Athens, but died and was buried in Lemnos, a student and son-in-law of the second Philostratus. He wrote *Imagines*, *Panathenaicus*, *Troicus*, *Paraphrase of Homer's Shield*, five declamations, and some ascribe *The Lives of the Sophists* to him.[7]

What may appear at first glance to be a straightforward biographical entry contains numerous, knotty interpretive problems. Since some of the arguments presented later in this study hinge on which works are attributed to Philostratus II, it is important to summarize at least three of these esoteric issues at this point in the investigation.

First, the entries in this passage from the *Suda* are not in chronological order.[8] Although the reason for this unusual order is unclear,[9]

---

7. This is the author's own translation.

8. Philostratus, *Heroicus*, 5, note 1.

9. The phrase "he ought to be placed first" is ambiguous. If this phrase refers to the father (i.e. Philostratus I), it may represent an attempt by the author of this entry or by a later hand to correct the chronological issue of placing the son before his father. See Anderson, *Philostratus*, 292; Phillimore, *In Honour*, xli. Alternately, if the phrase refers to the son (i.e., Philostratus II), it may justify placing the son before his father in

the three figures mentioned in it can, fortunately, be placed in proper sequence. In chronological order, the three Philostrati are Philostratus I (the son of Verus, second half of the second century AD), Philostratus II (the son of the Philostratus I and author of the *VA*; ca. AD 170–249), and Philostratus III (the son of Nervianus, and great-nephew and son-in-law of Philostratus II; ca. AD 190–ca. 230).[10] So then, to be clear, the first figure mentioned in the *Suda* entry above is Philostratus II, the author of the *VA*.

Second, three issues are amiss in the *Suda*'s treatment of Philostratus I—the father of Philostratus II—concerning his time frame, literary works, and occupation as a sophist. The first issue is that Philostratus I could not "have lived in the time of Nero,"[11] as the *Suda* claims, and at the same time have been the father of Philostratus II.[12] Rather, as Flinterman puts it, "it is obvious that Philostratus I must have lived in the second century, perhaps surviving into the early years of the third."[13] The most likely explanation for this odd claim is that the chronicler mistakenly placed Philostratus I in the first century during the reign of Nero because of a discourse attributed to him that was entitled *Nero*, which critiqued that first-century emperor.[14] The second matter is that the *Suda* credits Philostratus I with writing *Gymnasticus*. This attribution is unlikely for it records the victories of the famous wrestler named Helix who won two events in AD 213 and 217 (or possibly in AD 209 and 213).[15] That *Gymnasticus* was composed around or after AD 220 "practically rules out the possibility that it was written by Philostratus I."[16] If the *Suda* is incorrect about the authorship of *Gymnasticus*, it might also be wrong about assigning other works to the various authors and thus allow for the possibility that Philostratus II was the author of this work. The third issue is that the *Suda* describes Philostratus I as a sophist, yet Philostratus II never mentions him in his vast catalog of orators in the *VS*. This

---

the list because of his greater literary achievements. See Anderson, *Philostratus*, 292; Phillimore, *In Honour*, xliii.

10. For a more detailed discussion of this chronological issue, see Anderson, *Philostratus*, 292.

11. If true, Philostratus I would have lived over a century before the birth of Philostratus II.

12. Phillimore, *In Honour*, xli

13. Flinterman, *Power*, 6.

14. Petzke, *Die Traditionen*, 1.

15. Flinterman, *Power*, 6, n. 12.

16. Flinterman, *Power*, 6.

could indicate that Philostratus I was not a sophist as the *Suda* claims, but rather a lesser author.[17] This discovery could be significant because, if Philostratus I was not a sophist, this allows for the possibility that some of the works attributed to him may have been penned by his son Philostratus II[18] or by an even later family member named Philostratus.

Third, the relationship between Philostratus II and Philostratus III is perplexing, largely due to potentially conflicting data collected from other ancient sources. The *Suda* attributes the authorship of *Imagines II* to Philostratus III, the great-nephew and son-in-law of Philostratus II. Yet, the author of *Imagines II* attributes the first *Imagines* to his grandfather, who is usually identified with Philostratus II. Most classicists reject the notion that Philostratus III could have been at the same time the great-nephew, son-in-law, and grandson of Philostratus II.[19] Because of this conflict, some have proposed the addition of a fourth Philostratus to the three men already listed in the *Suda*.[20] Another solution that has been proposed is that the chronicler has skipped a generation.[21] Yet, Anderson warns that the *Suda* might be correct after all and that scholars must wait for further data.[22] This issue is significant because it impacts

17. Petzke, *Die Traditionen*, 2; Flinterman, *Power*, 9. The omission of the accomplishments of Philostratus's father may not be significant and, in the end, an opinion formulated upon this observation is an argument from silence. Still, the fact that Philostratus II had no qualms about praising the achievements of his younger relative named Philostratus (*VS* 617, 623, 625, 627–28) suggests that he did not omit his father out of modesty.

18. Flinterman, *Power*, 9–10.

19. Anderson, *Philostratus*, 293.

20. Phillimore, *In Honour*, xli, xliii; Petzke, *Die Traditionen*, 2; Harris, "Apollonius of Tyana," 192.

21. Flinterman, echoing Schmid's theory about the *Suda* entry writes, "It is not inconceivable that the numeral in the first case is used to refer to the Philostratus whom the lexicographer dealt with second, i.e. Philostratus I, while in the second case it is used to refer to the author of the *VA* and the *VS*, who was the first to be discussed by the lexicographer, but who is referred to with chronological correctness as 'the second sophist [with the name Philostratus]' in the article on him. In that case, Philostratus I is the great-uncle of Philostratus III, while only one generation separates each of them from Philostratus II, the teacher and father-in-law of the Lemnian Philostratus" (Flinterman, *Power*, 10–11).

22. Anderson, cautioning against too hastily dismissing the *Suda*'s information, notes that a single adoption might resolve this difficulty. For example, if Philostratus II adopted his nephew (the son of an elder brother) and that nephew later married Philostratus II's daughter, "before his marriage he would naturally have regarded Philostratus II, adoptive father of his own father, as grandfather first and foremost." At the time of composition of *Imagines II*, Philostratus III would "need not yet be his relative's son-in-law" (Anderson, *Philostratus*, 293).

whether *Imagines I* should be included in the corpus of Philostratus II or attributed to another figure.

This entry in the *Suda* underscores the difficulty of assigning the various works of the Philostrati to their proper authors. It is difficult to determine whether the *Suda* is largely correct in the information it provides or whether it is as confused about its attribution of works to the correct author as it was on the matters of chronology and the relationships of the Philostrati. To find more satisfying answers about which books belong within the corpus of Philostratus II, a deeper investigation into the list of books composed by the Philostrati is necessary.

ESTABLISHING THE CORPUS OF PHILOSTRATUS II

The Philostratean corpus is comprised of nine works: the *VA* (*Life of Apollonius*), the *VS* (*Lives of the Sophists*), *Heroicus, Gymnasticus, Nero, Erotic Letters, Imagines I*, and two brief discourses. The consensus of modern classical scholars is that Philostratus II authored all or most of these works.[23] Much of the evidence for common authorship is based on the recurrent wording, themes, and identical examples found throughout the collection,[24] although some do not place much stock in such

---

23. Elsner summarizes this scholarly perspective with the words, "suffice it to say that most authorities currently go for a broad view that incorporates the majority of these into the corpus as written by one man," "Protean corpus," 4. For instance, de Lannoy accepts the *VA, VS, Gymnasticus, Nero, Heroicus, Imagines I*, and *Letters* as the work of Philostratus II. See de Lannoy, "Le problème des Philostrate," 34.3:2363. Although Flinterman accepts the *VA, VS, Gymnasticus*, and *Nero* as authentic, he is uncertain about the authorship of *Heroicus, Imagines I*, and the discourses. See Flinterman, *Power*, 13–14. For an excellent, brief overview of this entire issue, see Koskenniemi, "Philostratean Apollonius," 322, n. 6.

24. Philostratus, *Heroicus*, 6. A few of the unifying ideas in the *Corpus Philostrateum* are (1) an emphasis on the interpretation of various objects (e.g., paintings, dream, oracles, and statues; Miles, *Philostratus*, 16, 27, 28, 37); (2) the endorsement of the belief in physiognomy; e.g., *VA* 2.22; *Imagines* 2.9; Miles, *Philostratus*, 24, 33, 94, 130, 139, 148, 152; König, "Training athletes," 254; (3) a strong emphasis on Hellenic tradition, history, and mythology; Miles, *Philostratus*, 129, 146, 164, 166; Elsner, "Protean corpus," 17; (4) a focus on the theme of wisdom (*sophia*), whether the topic be painting, sculpture, or gymnastic training; e.g.,*Gymn.* 1.261.1–15; Miles, *Philostratus*, 81, 149; Elsner, "Protean corpus," 15; (5) a trend of correcting mistaken views, whether they be about Apollonius as a magician (*VA*), the sophists (*VS*), Homeric legends (*Her.* 26.10; 30; 48.17; 51), athletic training (*Gymnasticus*), or legends about Alexander the Great (*VA* 2.9.4); (6) a theme of pitting philosophers or sophists against tyrants (*VA* 4.38.1–2; 5.35.4; 7.1–3; *VS* 488; 500, 625; *Nero*; *Letter* 72?); (7) an interest in renovation of the shrines of gods and heroes (*VA* 4.1.2; 4.5; 4.11; 4.18.2 and *Her.* 9.5); (8) the use

similarities as a reliable method for determining authorship.[25] There will always be doubts about the authorship of some of these works, but on the whole, the conclusion that Philostratus II is likely to have been the author of all the works in the corpus seems to be well-founded and it will be the position adopted in this investigation. Like Elsner, this introductory study has "no intention of entering into the critical maelstrom of precise attribution and dating in respect of these works."[26] Yet, the neophyte will still profit from a brief treatment of each work concerning authorship, date, and content. Such an overview will also acquaint the reader with Philostratus's wide range of interests and his extraordinary literary talent.

The reader may also note a few abnormalities in the following study. Most notably, the *VA* will be excluded from this study since it will be examined in detail in the very next chapter. Also, since the *VS* and *Heroicus* arguably have the most promise of evaluating the historicity of the *VA*, much more space will be allotted for their examination below.

Gymnasticus

The non-fictional *Gymnasticus* is a treatise on athletic training. This handbook was intended as a corrective to the declining skill of athletic instruction in the author's time by encouraging a return to the tried-and-true techniques of more ancient times.[27] This training manual covers a variety of topics such as (1) the skills required of athletic trainers (e.g., the ability to motivate and to match an athlete to a sport based on physiognomy); (2) the training of athletes (e.g., various regimens, individual

---

of a "prompter" as a foil for the more educated speaker (Damis for Apollonius in the *VA*, Menecrates for Musonius in *Nero*, and the Phoenician for the Vintner in *Heroicus*); (9) the motif of a travelling scholar (Apollonius of the *VA* along with the narrators of *Erotic Letters* and *Imagines I*; Miles, *Philostratus*,143); (10) an optimism about reversing the decline of Hellenism and the return to (or the hope to exceed) the Golden Age of athletics (*Gym*), virtue and cult (*VA*), or the age of heroes (*Heroicus*; see Miles, *Philostratus*, 150, 157, 166); (11) the theme of time, particularly that of the "experience of the past within the present" (Elsner, "Protean corpus," 11; also see Anderson, *Philostratus*, 8); and (12) a fascination with gigantic heroes (*VS* 552; *Her.* 142; *VA* 3.20.2; 4.16.2; *Her.* 7.9, 12; 8.1–17).

25. Phillimore argued that because the Philostrati explored similar themes, assigning authorship to the various works on this basis alone was practically impossible. See Phillimore, *In Honour*, xxxiv.

26. Elsner, "Protean corpus," 4.

27. Swain noted that restoration of the traditional standards in sport in *Gymnasticus* demonstrates the importance of the role the gymnasium played in Greek education and society. See Swain, "Culture and nature," 39.

techniques, and the dangers related to diet and lifestyle); and (3) the history of the Olympic Games and other athletic events. For the author of *Gymnasticus*, a trainer was not a mere technician but an instructor in *sophia*, who taught and conserved the practices of the Hellenistic, athletic tradition. As König sums up this point, a trainer was "constantly concerned with mediating between the heritage of the Greek past and the realities of the Greek present."[28] The theme of wedding the Greek past with the present and of preserving the treasures of Greek heritage resemble those found elsewhere in the Philostratean corpus.[29] Such similarities with the uncontested works of Philostratus II would make him an attractive candidate for the authorship of this text.[30] Indeed, there is now "almost universal agreement"[31] that Philostratus II was the author of this work—despite the *Suda*'s claim to the contrary—because of the similarities of language, style, and content to *VA* and *VS*, the two uncontested works of the author. *Gymnasticus* also resembles other works within the corpus.[32] The date of the book also favors composition by an author later than Philostratus I.[33]

28. König, "Training athletes," 283.

29. Examples of this principle can be seen in several of Philostratus's works: the *VS* stressed the link between the First and Second Sophistic movements, the *VA* highlighted Apollonius's restoration of correct forms of worship during his travels, and *Heroicus* valued the remembrance of ancient heroes in the present age.

30. The most likely candidate for the authorship of *Gymnasticus* is Philostratus II. Yet, according to the *Suda*, this work was written by Philostratus I. This view has been occasionally championed by modern scholars See Phillimore, *In Honor*, xlii.

31. Flinterman, *Power*, 6–7. Many scholars endorse Philostratus II as the author of this work. See Philostratus, *Heroicus*, 6, 335; Philostratus and Eunapius, *The Lives of the Sophists*, xi; Hadas, *Greek Literature*, 278. Bowie, making a strong claim to authorship by Philostratus II wrote, "It fits his persistent concern with Hellenic values and identity and with the prestige of the Greek city elites, and linguistic parallels support this attribution" (Bowie, *Philostratus*, 30). Others, although uncertain, favor Philostratus II as author. See Elsner, "Protean corpus," 4. Miles seems to favor it as a work of Philostratus II because of its similarities to the rest of the corpus, but notes that "we are dealing with probabilities rather than certainties" (Miles, *Philostratus*, 10).

32. *Gymnasticus* resembles other Philostratean works in several ways in that it displays (1) an interest in sports (Koskenniemi, *Die philostrateische Apollonios*, 5; Anderson, 243, 268–72; König, "Training athletes," 280–282); (2) an apologetic that various Greek traditions (e.g., athletics [*Gymnasticus*], oratory [*VS*], painting [*Imagines I*], and farming [in *Heroicus*]) are repositories of wisdom; and (3) a focus on surpassing the standards of an earlier age: much like Apollonius surpassed his sophistic and philosophical rivals, so the athletic trainer will surpass the trainers of the past (Miles, *Philostratus*, 150).

33. Like *Heroicus*, *Gymnasticus* mentions the famous athlete, Helix. However, *Gymnasticus* may allude to Helix's Capitaline later victories in AD 219, thereby placing

PART 2: PHILOSTRATUS II AND HIS LITERARY CORPUS

Nero

Nero is a brief dialogue that highlights two aspects of that infamous emperor's reign: his unsuccessful attempt to dig a canal through the Corinthian Isthmus and his equally disastrous tour of Greece as a singer. The setting for the story seems to have been the Aegean Island of Gyara around AD 68,[34] where a conversation transpires between Menecrates[35] and Musonius, a Stoic philosopher who had once been forced to participate in Nero's failed engineering project. Musonius is the primary speaker in dialogue, while Menecrates merely feeds him the questions that advance the story. After describing several examples of Nero's hubristic behavior at the canal, Musonius shifted to several events that occurred during the emperor's musical tour: a revolt against Nero in the West, mockery of the emperor's mediocre singing voice (*Nero* 6), and Nero's murder of a more skilled rival for not yielding a musical contest to him (*Nero* 9–10). The work concludes when the conversation is interrupted by the arrival of a ship that bore the joyful news of the tyrant's death (*Nero* 11). This work, which was probably written by one of the Philostrati,[36] probably

---

the work in the 220s or 230s when Helix's fame would likely have been at its peak. See Philostratus, *Heroicus*, 334. Flinterman explains, "The fact that the *Gymnasticus* was completed after ca. 220, practically rules out the possibility that it was written by Philostratus I" (Flinterman, *Power*, 6).

34. *Lucian* (Macleod, LCL), 506; Elsner, "Protean corpus," 5.

35. The identity of Menecrates is uncertain, but there is some evidence that this was a family name belonging to the friends of the Philostrati. For a further discussion of this and other theories, see Whitmarsh, "Greek and Roman," 142, n. 4.

36. MacLeod details several reasons why scholars tend to assign *Nero* to someone within this literary family: (1) the style is unlike Lucian but resembles the *VA*; (2) some Lucianic manuscripts are known to have contained works of Philostratus and other sophists; (3) *Nero* and the *VA* claim that Musonius was involved in digging the canal in Corinth; (4) a work called *Nero* is attributed to Philostratus I in the *Suda*; and (5) Lemnos, the island home of the Philostrati, is mentioned in the dialogue as well (*Nero* 6). See MacLeod's comments in *Lucian* (MacLeod, LCL), 506.

by Philostratus II,[37] has a significant overlap in content with the *VA* that suggests the common authorship of the two works.[38]

Erotic Letters

The *Erotic Letters* consist of seventy-three short letters, both amatory and non-amatory. Most of the love letters were addressed to unnamed boys[39]

---

37. Some scholars favor Philostratus I as the author of *Nero* because it is attributed to him in the *Suda* and because one passage in *Nero* appears to contradict the *VA*; *Nero* 9 claims that the emperor sought to win the tragic contests at the Isthmus, while the *VA* claims Nero's competed there in contest for lyre and herald and received a tragic victory at Olympia (*VA* 4.24). See MacLeod's comments in *Lucian* (MacLeod, LCL), 517, n. 2. Neither of these arguments is entirely persuasive because the *Suda* entry appears to be confused on some points and Philostratus II is also known to have contradicted himself within writings clearly attributed to him. For instance, in the *VA* 5.37.2, Apollonius is presented as superior figure to Dio Chrysostom, but in the *VS* 488, Dio the superior person; several contradictions within the *VA* itself will be discussed in an upcoming chapter. The similarity in content between *Nero* and the other books in the corpus has convinced other scholars that it likely to have been written by Philostratus II. See Koskenniemi, *Der philostrateische Apollonios*, 5; Miles, *Philostratus*, 9; Elsner, "Protean corpus," 4.

38. The numerous similarities between *Nero* and the *VA* strongly suggest a borrowing between the two works. The major features shared by them are that (1) the cutting of the Isthmus canal was compared to Xerxes's bridging of the Hellespont (*VA* 5.7.4, *Nero* 2); (2) Nero's motive for beginning this engineering marvel was so that ships would not have to sail around Malea (*VA* 4.24.2; *Nero* 1); (3) Musonius the philosopher was in chains while he was forced to dig the canal (*VA* 5.19; *Nero*, 4); (4) Nero's Egyptian engineers advised against finishing the canal for fear that the Aegean would be flooded because of the disparity of water levels on both sides of the Isthmus of Corinth (*VA* 4.24.3, *Nero* 4); (5) Vindex and the western nations revolted against Nero (*VA* 5.11; *Nero* 5); (6) the aforementioned revolt forced Nero to leave Greece and suspend the digging of the Corinthian canal (*VA* 5.7.4; *Nero* 5); (7) Nero conducted a singing tour of Greece (*VA* 5.10.2); (8) Nero's stage presence and voice were mocked (*VA* 5, *Nero* 6); (9) Nero was compared to Orestes and Alcmaeon as a matricide, but the latter two were excused because they were avenging their fathers' deaths (*VA* 4.38.3, *Nero*, 10); and (10) Nero's matricide is discussed in the broad context of the rebellion of Vindex (*VA* 5.10.2; *Nero*, 5, 10). Although this list is not exhaustive, it is sufficient to demonstrate that the numerous similarities are not coincidental. In addition to these similarities, Anderson detects three *topoi* from *Nero* that are developed in the *VA*. See Anderson, *Philostratus*, 273.

39. Letters 1, 3–5, 7–11, 13–19, 24, 27, 46, 56–58, and 64. One of these boys is called a prostitute (*Letter* 19).

and women.[40] The non-amatory letters, that "are barely connected"[41] to the love letters in this collection, were written to members of the Severan household (*Letters*, 72, 73), to a sophistic rival named Epictetus (*Letters*, 42, 65, 69), and perhaps to the long dead novelist Chariton (*Letter* 66). These epistles display an interest in persuasive rhetoric and sophistic themes, topics that would be consistent with Philostratus II as the author of both the amatory[42] and non-amatory[43] portions of the collection.

The interpretation of the amatory letters poses several problems. According to Miles, one barrier to understanding them is simply that

40. *Letters* 2, 6, 12, 20–23, 25–26, 28–39, 47–48, 50, 53–55, 59, and 60–63. Some of these recipients were further described as a married woman (*Letter* 30), a female prostitute (*Letter* 38), a companion (*Letter* 4, Ἑταίρῳ τινί), and a hostess at an inn (*Letter* 60).

41. Goldhill, "Constructed identity," 302.

42. The authorship of at least some of the *Erotic Letters* is contested, with some scholars attributing the entire collection to Philostratus II (Philostratus and Eunapius, *The Lives of the Sophists*, ix) and others attributing some of the non-amatory letters to him (Koskenniemi, *Der philostrateische Apollonios*, 4–5, 322). As early as the *Suda*, this collection of letters was attributed to Philostratus II (Bowie, "Philostratus: the life of a sophist," 31). One of the manuscripts of the epistles bear the title "Letters of Philostratus the Athenian" (Φιλοστράτου Ἀθηναίου ἐπιστολαί), which helps to situate the collection within the family, but it does not identify which of the Philostrati was intended (Benner and Fobes, *Letters*, 391). Even though many have cast doubt on Philostratean authorship of the amatory letters, a substantial case can be made for them as well. First, the author of *Letter* 55 indicates that he had been to Rome, a detail that would fit well with Philostratus II (Benner and Fobes, *Letters*, 394.). Second, the thematic connections between the love letters and other works in the Philostraean corpus are numerous, especially with the themes in the undisputed ones, thereby suggesting that they are all the work of a common hand. A few themes shared by the *Letters*, the *VA*, and the *VS* are that they mention (1) a Scythian altar used for human sacrifice and their foreign rites (Letter 8; *VA* 6.20.3, 5); (2) exotic animals and people: the phoenix of India (Letter 8; *VA* 3.49), elephants (Letter 8; *VA* 2.6, 11, 15, 16; 6.25), and the Magi (Letter 8; *VA* 1.18, 25, 29, 32, 41; see Miles, *Philostratus*,143); and (3) the Phoenician origin of letters of the alphabet (Letter 8, *VS* 587). As Lesky's much earlier assessment of the *Erotic Letters* concludes, "no decisive grounds against their authenticity have been put forward" (Lesky, *Greek Literature*, 838).

43. Unlike the fictional and unidentified author of the amatory letters, the author of these last few letters appears to have written them as the historical Philostratus. For instance, the author of the collection (1) refers to himself as a Lemnian (*Letter* 70); (2) addressed the empress Julia (*Letter* 73) and the emperor Caracalla (*Letter* 72), two figures of the royal household with whom Philostratus II certainly had close contact (*VA* 1.3.1; *VS* 607); (3) addressed Ctesidemus (*Letter* 68), who is perhaps the same figure mentioned by Philostratus II at *VS* 552; (4) mentioned Gorgias, a favorite sophist of Philostratus II (*VS* 481–83), using him to further the sophistic cause (*Letter* 33); and (5) believed that the dead can still be contacted (e.g., Plutarch [*Letter* 73] and Chariton [*Letter* 66], if this name belongs to the long-dead novelist), a theme found also in the *VA* and *Heroicus* (Miles, *Philostratus*, 76).

AN INTRODUCTION TO PHILOSTRATUS'S WRITINGS

"[t]he letters of Philostratus are the least studied part of the *corpus*"[44] and that this lack of familiarity may have led to some interpreters drawing hasty conclusions about them or even developing an overt bias against them. Another obstacle to their proper interpretation is that readers may not be able to resist the temptation to identify distinct love stories within the collection. Several experts in this literature warn that "the collection as a whole and many of the individual letters resist narrativization"[45] and that "[i]t is impossible to determine any coherent love story (or stories) from them."[46] A related issue that experts warn against is that of identifying the voice of the epistolary author with Philostratus himself.[47] The identification of a real, single author behind these compositions seems unlikely because (1) there are so many tensions and contradictions within the collection;[48] and (2) it is implausible that a single author would have sought to woo such a diverse group of lovers (e.g., male, female, married, single, Hellenes, foreigners, slaves, and freemen). Yet, if these are not genuine letters written to Philostratus's paramours, then what was he seeking to accomplish by writing these epistles?[49] Miles answers that these letters were a vehicle for flaunting Philostratus's great learning.[50] Goldhill answers differently, suggesting that "These are not letters for sending, but for helping the reader express 'a correspondence of

---

44. Miles, *Philostratus*, 137.

45. Goldhill, "Constructed identity," 296.

46. Miles, *Philostratus*, 9.

47. Miles contends that it would "be a mistake to equate this voice straightforwardly with Philostratus as empirical author, though it is certainly the case that a distinctive, albeit contradictory, persona does emerge from the collection: obsessive, tendentious in amatory argument, on occasion inclined to present himself as an exile or fugitive" (Miles, *Philostratus*, 8). Likewise, Elsner noted that it is difficult to tell whether the lover in the letters is Philostratus or not, but one of the problems with the view that a single voice is depicted in this collection is that many lovers of both genders are addressed in the work (Elsner, "Protean corpus," 9).

48. Does the author prefer his youthful, male lover be still beardless (Letter 13) or that he have a beard (*Letter* 14)? Is the male lover more interested in whether a boy is from Sparta, Thessaly, or Athens (*Letter* 5) or whether a woman is Spartan, Corinthian, or Elian (*Letter* 47)?

49. Goldhill opines, "The most insistent question provoked by these texts is 'what on earth are they for?', 'what do they do?'" (Goldhill, "Constructing Identity," 287).

50. Miles explains that "[t]he speaking voice of the *Letters* is a learned lover, who expects a learned addressee (whether *puella docta* or *puer doctus*)," and that Philostratus expects that the addressees and the eavesdropping readers "will be swayed by his seduction through erudition" (Miles, *Philostratus*, 137).

feeling.'"[51] In short, the letters were exempla of how to write love poetry in different contexts; this was at least the use to which the English poet Ben Jonson later put portions of the Philostratus's letters (*Letters* 2, 32, 33, and 46) in his "Song: To Celia."[52] Whatever the intended purpose of these letters, the author displayed a deep knowledge of Greek literature, the gift of persuasion, and perhaps a talent for creating fictive scenarios. These traits are certainly consistent with those displayed by Philostratus II elsewhere in the corpus.

Imagines I

The work entitled *Imagines I* purports to be a record of sixty-five lectures that were delivered by an art historian on a collection of paintings displayed in the portico of a villa at the Bay of Naples. In this text, this master interpreter addressed a ten-year-old boy, along with a group of older youths, as they moved from picture to picture in this gallery. The author of this work keeps the reader in the dark by withholding the names of the adult interpreter, the boy who is addressed throughout the piece, and the painters whose masterpieces were under consideration.[53] One cannot even be certain whether the paintings described here were real or imaginary.[54] One thing for certain is that the author of *Imagines I* was well-versed in the elements of painting and art interpretation.[55] Although many scholars have opined on whether these paintings were real or imaginary, Elsner points out that the real purpose of the work is that "this is a commentary on whether the *phantasia*—or vivid visualization—evoked by the sophist can replace or even outdo in the hearer's or reader's mind the actual impression of a real gallery, a real painting, a real landscape seen directly."[56] Perhaps, then, this ancient author's experiment should be deemed a success, for scholars continue to be intrigued

---

51. Goldhill, "Constructed identity," 301.
52. Goldhill, "Constructed identity," 300–301; Phillimore, *In Honour*, lxviii. Johnson's poem "To Celia" was first published in 1616.
53. Miles, *Philostratus*, 2, 83.
54. Several have argued that it is unknown whether the pictures were real; Hadas, *Greek Literature*, 279; Elsner, "Protean Corpus," 10–11. Miles deems them "likely imaginary images" (Miles, *Philostratus*, 2, 7–8).
55. Lesky observed, "whether the collection existed or not—there is no doubt of its relation to actual painting" (Lesky, *Greek Literature*, 838).
56. Elsner, "Protean corpus," 10–12.

by his vivid descriptions of paintings that may have existed only in his imagination.[57]

Dialexis I and II

Two short discourses (*Dialexis I* and *Dialexis II*) have also been included in the Philostratean canon. Some experts do not think that certainty can be attained concerning the authorship of these two works.[58] Others reject the first discourse as a work of Philostratus II[59] (it is not a discourse in reality) but have accepted his authorship of *Dialexis II* for several reasons.[60] First of all, the *Suda* claims that Philostratus wrote "discourses" and "this implies that he had published a collection of them."[61] Second, although *Dialexis II* is brief, it still "contains a remarkable number of ideas which recur in the Philostratean *corpus*."[62] The most compelling connection between the short discourse and the *VA* is the mention of a natural rock formation on Crete shaped like a lion.[63]

---

57. Scholars have not reached a consensus on the authorship or date of *Imagines I*. For a summary of this issue, see Koskenniemi, "Philostratean Apollonius," 322, n. 6. Some have assigned this text to a later author such as Philostratus III. For this view, see Hadas, *Greek Literature*, 278–79; Philostratus and Eunapius, *The Lives of the Sophists*, ix; Bowie, "Philostratus: the life of a sophist," 31. Others assign it to Philostratus II (Philostratus, *Heroicus*, 6; Koskenniemi, *Der philostrateische Apollonios*, 5) or at least believe it was likely to have been written by him (Elsner, "Protean corpus," 4). In favor of the last two views, the *Suda* attributes a work called *Imagines* to Philostratus II and the style and content of *Imagines I* resembles that of the *VA*. A few themes shared by the *VA* and *Imagines I* are (1) an interest in art and its interpretation (*VA* 2.22; 4.7; 6.19; Anderson, *Philostratus*, 128; Platt, "Virtual Visions," 135; Koskenniemi, *Der philostrateische Apollonios*, 5); (2) the mention of the god Proteus (*VA* 1.4; 3.24.1; 4.16.5; 7.22.2; *Imag.* 2.17.20–21); (3) the creation of islands accompanied by earthquakes (*VA* 4.34.4; *Imag.* 2.17.19–24); and (4) speculation about volcanology (*VA* 5.17; *Imagines* 2.17.5–15) that dismisses the hypothesis that such phenomena are caused by the giant Typho being held captive within the earth (*VA* 5.16 *Imagines* 2.17.15–20). Neither internal nor external evidence appears to shine any light on the issue of date of this work.

58. Koskenniemi, *Der philostrateische Apollonios*, 5.

59. Miles does not regard *Dialexis I* as a true discourse. Further, he attributes it to the later Philostratus of Lemnos (*VS* 628); Miles, *Philostratus*, 9.

60. Swain, "Culture and nature," 43.

61. Swain, "Culture and nature," 43.

62. Miles, *Philostratus*, 154. *Dialexis II* explores the relationship between human creativity and non-human nature (stones, statues, clouds;), and it also touches on the rejuvenation of Hellenistic culture (Miles, *Philostratus*, 153–57).

63. *Dialexis* II.2; *VA* 4.34.3; Bowie, "Philostratus: the life of a sophist," 31.

VS (*Lives of the Sophists*)

The authorship of the VS (*Vitae Sophistarum* or *Lives of the Sophists*) is rather easy to determine, for only it and the VA can be attributed to Philostratus II with absolute certainty. This claim has not been challenged by any author[64] because two passages within the VS assure the correct identification of the author of these two biographies.[65] These passages are doubly significant for, in addition to establishing the common authorship of these works, they also indicate the order in which these two works were composed: the VA was published before the VS.

Unfortunately, the exact date of the VS cannot be determined. Its dedication to "Antonius Gordian, consul" (VS 479) would give a rough indication of its date of publication if only the identity of the Gordian to whom it was dedicated could be established. Two candidates have been proposed for the identity of this figure: the consensus seems to be that the passage refers to Gordian I (c. AD 159–238),[66] but Gordian III (AD 223–44) is also a possibility.[67] Either figure would have lived within the time frame of Philostratus II; either of their deaths is potentially a *terminus ad quem* for the VS. Beyond these generalities, a solid date for the VS cannot currently be determined.

The VS, as its title suggests, is a collection of biographical sketches of prominent Greek sophists from antiquity. Philostratus's work is selective in terms of the orators treated and uneven in several other respects as well. One example of this spotty coverage is that he limited the study to eighteen sophists of the First Sophistic (fifth through fourth centuries BC) and forty-one of the Second Sophistic (from the time of Nero down to Philostratus's era), while for some reason ignoring several significant Hellenistic orators situated between these two movements.[68]

---

64. Petzke, *Traditionen*, 3; Philostratus and Eunapius, *The Lives of the Sophists*, xi.

65. Flavius Philostratus identified himself as the author the VS in its dedication (VS 479), and later within the same work he claimed authorship of the VA as well (ἐν τοῖς ἐς Ἀπολλώνιον, VS 570).

66. Phillimore, *In Honour*, lxxxvi.

67. Schmitz, "Narrator and audience," 50, n. 6. Yet, if Gordian's relationship to the sophist Herodes was based on his academic pedigree rather than blood relation (VS 480), as Anderson suggests, only Gordian I would qualify as the dedicatee. Gordian I, age eighty at his proclamation in AD 238, was barely old enough to have been a student of Herodes Atticus, who died in AD 179. See Anderson, *Philostratus*, 297–98.

68. Adams, *The Genre of Acts*, 99; Bowie, "Philostratus: the life of a sophist," 29. Philostratus's most notable omission from the Hellenistic era was Lucian of Samosata. See Bowie, "Philostratus: the life of a sophist," 26. Yet, there are good reasons to think

AN INTRODUCTION TO PHILOSTRATUS'S WRITINGS

Another example of incomplete treatment of this topic is that Philostratus did not produce comprehensive biographies of the orators he did treat, but rather crafted vignettes that focused on their "anecdotes and personal characteristics."[69] A final example of unbalanced coverage can be observed in the amount of space dedicated to the various sophists; some figures receive superficial, cursory treatment while a handful tend to dominate the work.[70] A first impression of the VS might well be that Philostratus was more interested in collecting tales of scandal and gossip than in writing true biographies of these sophists. Yet, first impressions are probably misleading in this case.

In the quest to discover Philostratus's real purpose in the VS, scholars have puzzled over several questions. Was his approach to the topic of sophistic history serious or flippant? Was he attempting to write genuine history[71] or merely seeking to entertain his readership (VS 479–80)?[72]

---

that Philostratus knew about Lucian but that may have ignored him because he had satirized other sophists (Philostratus and Eunapius, *The Lives of the Sophists*, xiv, xvii, xxv, xxxii, xxxix), because Lucian's originality might have taken away from that of Philostratus (Bowie, "Philostratus: the life of a sophist," 26–27), or because was better known as a writer than a performer (Miles, *Philostratus*, 12). Philostratus appears to have used and reworked Lucian's material without naming the author. See Miles, *Philostratus*, 167.

69. Philostratus and Eunapius, *The Lives of the Sophists*, xii. Bowie notes five elements that are somewhat regularly followed when dealing with the sophists: their students, teacher, chair, statue, and burial. See Bowie, "Geography of the Second Sophistic," 76–81.

70. Herodes Atticus is treated with the most detail in the VS, perhaps because of his connection to Philostratus and Gordian (VS 480, 546–66). See Miles, *Philostratus*, 125. Buck notes that Herodes's name "at least is cited in eleven of the thirty-three biographies in Book II, and even in Book I, he makes an appearance in four of the twenty-six lives" (Buck, "Eunapius of Sardis," 80).

71. Philostratus at times appears to be concerned with correcting misperceptions about the sophists, such as sorting out the true birthplace of Polemo (VS 530). See Schmitz, "Narrator and audience," 53. Philostratus also attempted to sort out the truth of the various reports of Herodes lifting his hand against Emperor Antonius Pius (VS 554–55; Schmitz, "Narrator and audience," 54, n. 18) and the various accounts of Polemo's death (VS 543–44). This approach can also be seen in the VA, where Philostratus is keen to set the record straight on Apollonius as a magician (VA 1.2.1–3) and to sort out the various accounts of his death (VA 8.29–30). Similarly, Philostratus defended the sophists against slanderers (VS 596; Schmitz, "Narrator and audience," 60), although he himself censured them at times (VS 605).

72. Adams notes that main agenda of Philostratus's VS was not biography, although biographical details were included in it, but rather its agenda was the defense of being a sophist. He notes that the work was "also full of scandalous events and stories that often have little to do with the overall presentation of a sophist's character. It appears that these stories are provided to entertain the reader, rather than to promote a particular

Why was he so haphazard in terms of methodology and style?[73] Did Philostratus have a clearly defined agenda and, if so, did he fail to achieve it or did he successfully execute a carefully crafted strategy?[74] Although scholars agree that he intended to write a biography of the sophists,[75] several recent studies suggest that his agenda was interested in more than the mere preservation of sophistic history. Two of these studies suggest that the *VS* was intended as a manual to help its readers understand, evaluate, and appreciate the art of rhetoric.[76] Other scholars have suggested that Philostratus may have intended the *VS* as a monument to himself as the paragon of the Second Sophistic movement.[77] So then, although writing a sophistic biography appears to have been Philostratus's overarching agenda, the genre may have been placed in the service of self-aggrandizement, for it positioned him both as the authoritative interpreter of the sophists and as the culminating figure of the Second Sophistic.

As indicated above, the *VS* promises to be one of the more important texts in evaluating the historicity of the *VA*. In part, this is because the two works share a common author (Philostratus II), possess an identical genre (biography), and treat similar content. A reading of these two texts side by side affords historians with an opportunity to observe Philostratus at work as a biographer on two different subjects: Apollonius and

lifestyle or to elicit a positive change within the reader" (Adams, *The Genre of Acts*, 100).

73. With respect to the *VA*'s careless style, Miles believes "The appearance of casualness, even haphazardness, is a cultivated effect" (Miles, *Philostratus*, 121).

74. Schmitz, "Narrator and audience," 49.

75. E.g., Keener, *Christobiography*, 94. Votaw claims that these Lives "belong to the type of popular biography in the period, a eulogistic and didactic method of writing about famous teachers, of which Plutarch's *Lives* and Diogenes Laertius' *Lives and Opinions of the Ancient Philosophers* are the best examples" (Votaw, *The Gospels*, 18).

76. Miles argues that the *VS* is "anything but an attempt at neutral history of the cultural movement it documents. Rather it teaches its readers how to appreciate and interpret sophistic rhetoric, and how to be seen to do so appropriately" (Miles, *Philostratus*, 134). Similarly, Schmitz believes that Philostratus created an environment in which readers are invited to evaluate the sophists, but in which they too are put on trial to see if they qualify as cultured interpreters. Schmitz further notes that Philostratus never revealed the criteria by which his readers should evaluate these sophists, thereby placing himself in the authoritative position to "impress and intimidate his readership" (Schmitz, "Narrator and audience," 65, 68).

77. Elsner notes that the *VS* was somewhat "self-serving" in that it emphasized the contributions of Philostratus, his family, and Philostratus of Lemnos. See Elsner, "Protean corpus," 8. Miles similarly notes that the *VS* is not just a record of sophistic history but that Philostratus "positions himself as the culmination of it" (Miles, *Philostratus*, 124).

the sophists. Researchers can compare the types of sources he collected for the two works,[78] how these sources are cited,[79] observe the kinds of mistakes he made because of these sources,[80] and gauge his willingness to insert fictional elements into a text.[81]

Reading these texts side-by-side allows for the highlighting of their differences. A few of the more obvious differences between the two texts are their length (the VA is much longer) and the number of figures investigated (e.g., the VS deals with fifty-nine men and the VA with only one). A subtler difference is that Philostratus largely stuck to relating history in the VS but did not hesitate to insert fictional elements into the narrative

---

78. One type of source used in the VS is oral tradition about the sophists (e.g., "older men" in VS 579) or Philostratus's teachers (VS 585). See Schmitz, "Narrator and audience," 55; Keener, *Christobiography*, 94. Another source was Philostratus's personal experience (VS 617). See Schmitz, "Narrator and audience," 56; Keener, *Christobiography*, 94. However, Philostratus does appear to have used some published works in the VS as well (e.g., VS 568), where he claims to have had access to written material about Herodes (Schmitz, "Narrator and audience," 56–57) and where he refers to various accounts of the declamation (VS 583), which were largely declamations of the sophists. See Bowie, "Philostratus: the life of a sophist," 30. In contrast to the VS, the VA claims to have relied mostly on written materials and, to a lesser degree, on oral traditions.

79. Adams notes that Philostratus was hesitant to cite his sources in the VS. Speaking of the VS, he wrote that "[f]irst is his treatment of sources. Whereas one of the defining characteristics of Diogenes Laertius' work is his near obsessive citation of sources, Philostratus is markedly different in that he is quite reluctant to identify the source of his information or quotations. It appears that Philostratus' most consistent source was personal reminiscences, notably those of 'his former teacher' Damianus, Ctesidemus the Athenian, and one of Philostratus' older colleagues, Aristaeus" (Adams, *The Genre of Acts*, 100, n. 179). Here, Adams references VS 524, 550, 552, 579, 605. Philostratus is mostly consistent with this technique in the VA, informing his readers that he is using a source but not always clarifying what the source was. He also often employed the vague introductory formulae "they say" (e.g., VS 514; VA 1.25.3; 2.2.2), "some say" (e.g., VS 482; VA 8.30.1), "others say" (e.g., VS 482; VA 8.30.2) in both works.

80. Swain shows that in Philostratus's use of sources in the VS, he makes mistakes, is sometimes gullible, and may have sometimes fallen prey to the nature of oral sources. Yet, he argues that one should still believe Philostrastus unless there is a good reason to doubt him. See Swain, "The Reliability," 163. Philostratus had similar problems with some of his historical sources in the VA. However, his accounts of Apollonius's journeys to Mesopotamia, India, and Ethiopia, which are often supposedly rooted in Damis's eyewitness testimony, are clearly fictional at points.

81. Apart from historical statements in the VS that can be confirmed by external sources, one must wonder about those that are beyond external confirmation. Miles warns that, due to Philostratus's use of oral sources, one can only guess how these rather detailed conversations and stories were gathered. Further, he warns that is impossible to know whether Philostratus invented some of this material (Miles, *Philostratus*, 127).

of the *VA*.⁸² Although such differences between these works are important, the similarities between them can also be instructive.

One oft-noted resemblance between the two biographies is that Philostratus's portrayal of the sophists and Apollonius seems to be cut from the same cloth.⁸³ Anderson points out that the sophists of the *VS* are practically holy men, while Apollonius is often depicted as an ideal sophist who resembles the sophists Scopelian, Polemo, and Herodes.⁸⁴ Anderson follows this observation with several pages of correspondences between Apollonius and various sophists.⁸⁵ Indeed, many other striking similarities could be added to Anderson's list.⁸⁶ Yet, of all the sophists, Apollonius resembles Scopelian the most. Anderson notes that "they share similar birth-miracles, similar difficulties over inheritance,

---

82. Bowie identifies the *VS* and *Gymnasticus* as Philostratean works "where 'non-fiction' is preponderant" (Bowie, "Philostratus: Writer of fiction," 181). Examples of such fictional elements are Apollonius's undelivered speech (Swain, "Reliability," 163) and talking trees (Anderson, *Philostratus*, 124).

83. Miles, *Philostratus*, 14, 124.

84. Anderson, *Philostratus*, 124.

85. Anderson, *Philostratus*, 126–29. For instance, Apollonius, Scopelian, and Hermocrates each proved the innocence of young men who had been falsely accused by a stepmother or a concubine (*VA* 6.3; *VS* 517, 610). Apollonius and Herodes both discussed Nero's attempt to cut the Corinthian Isthmus (*VS* 547; *VA* 4.3) and gave advice about such things as the use of wealth (*VS* 548; *VA* 1.38), buried treasure (*VS* 547–49; *VA* 2.39), and were accused of plotting against Roman officials (*VS* 560; *VA* 7.9). Like Apollonius, Dionysius of Miletus and Adrian the Phoenician were accused of dabbling in magic, a charge that Philostratus denies in the case of all three men (*VS* 523, 590; *VA* 1.1–3). Both Apollonius and Polemo managed to speak from beyond the grave: the former in a dream (*VA* 8.31) and the latter through a letter (*VS* 539–40). Whereas Onomarchus delivered a speech about a man who had fallen in love with a statue (*VS* 598), Apollonius corrected a man who had fallen in love with an image of Aphrodite (*VA* 6.40). On this last point, see also Gyselinck and Demoen, "Author and Narrator," 103, n. 25.

86. Herodes had an inner circle of students who were called "the thirsty ones" (διψῶντας), which was the exact title used for the pupils of Apollonius (οἱ διψῶντες); *VS* 585, 594; *VA* 4.24. Like Antiochus of Aegae, Apollonius stayed in the temple of Asclepius (*VS* 568; *VA* 1.8.2) and conversed with the healing god there (*VS* 568, *VA* 1.9.1). Like Alexander (Clay Plato), whom some allege was Apollonius's love child, Apollonius visited the Naked Ones of Ethiopia (*VS* 571; *VA* 6.6–23). Dio praised and censured cities (*VS* 7), as did Apollonius (*VA* 5.20; 6.34). Favorinus quarreled with and survived an emperor (*VS* 8), while Apollonius resisted and endured both Nero and Domitian. Apollonius's memory at age 100 surpassed that of Simonides (*VA* 1.14), as did the memory of Proclus at the age of 90 (*VS* 604; cf. *VS* 494–95). Philostratus related multiple legends concerning the deaths of Polemo (*VS* 543–44) and Apollonius (*VA* 8.30.1–3), evaluating them in detail.

connection with the vine edict and interest in the Eretrians."[87] How, then, does one account for these striking correspondences? Did the historical Apollonius genuinely resemble these sophists, or did Philostratus clothe him in the garb of an orator with material borrowed from his fertile imagination or his memory of the sophists?

The answer to this question is not a straightforward one. One must be open to the possibility that some of the sophistic material attributed to Apollonius is authentic.[88] In defense of Philostratus's depiction of the sage, Apollonius often resembles the Greek philosophers more than he does the sophists.[89] Even so, the vast number of similarities between the Tyanean and the sophists are still rather suspicious. One reason to suspect that Philostratus is sometimes guilty of transforming Apollonius into a sophist is that in the *VA* he had shaped Apollonius so that he was also described in ways similar or superior to many famous historical (Alexander the Great), philosophical (Pythagoras, Plato), and divine figures (Hercules, Dionysus) from the Greek past. Another reason to suspect Philostratus's reimagining the Tyanean as a sort of sophist is that this portrayal differs from the earliest extra-Philostratean sources that did not associate Apollonius with sophistry (e.g., Lucian, Dio Cassius, and Moiragenes). Finally, at times, Philostratus seemed unable to make up his mind as to whether Apollonius was a sophist or a philosopher.[90]

---

87. Anderson, *Philostratus*, 194, n. 63. In this note, Anderson listed several such connections between Apollonius and Scopelian: (1) lightning nearly strikes them both near the time of their births (*VS* 515; *VA* 1.5); (2) they were mentioned in the context of the vine edict under Domitian (*VS* 520; *VA* 6.42); (3) in the context of discussing their loss or renunciation of their inheritance, they refer to the story of Anaxagoras's lost property (*VS* 518; *VA* 1.13.2); (4) Scopelian had Cappadocian and Assyrian disciples (*VS* 518) like Apollonius, the Cappadocian, had an Assyrian follower; *VA* 1.19.1–2); (5) both were interested in the Eretrian problem (*VS* 518; *VA* 1.23); (6) the rival of Scopelian, Timocrates (*VS* 536), was the pupil of Apollonius's rival Euphrates. One could add to this list that both figures; (7) allude to Plato's claim that men are playthings of the gods (*VS* 518; *VA* 4.36.2); (8) mention the gardens of Tantalus (*VA* 4.25; *VS* 513); and (9) are paired in several passages (*VA* at 1.24.5; *VS* 521).

88. By way of comparison, many Christian apologists and commentators accept as authentic traditions about Jesus in which he resembles Old Testament figures: Jesus and Moses fed people in the wilderness with bread, Jesus was born in Bethlehem like David, and Jesus raised the dead like Elijah and Elisha.

89. Philostratus's Apollonius is clearly classified as a philosopher rather than a sophist. Unlike the sophists, he was not concerned with his appearance, wealth, depilation, or collecting fees from students. See Harry Sidebottom, "Philostratus," 76, 78, 81, 82, 84, and 85.

90. Dzielska observes, "Philostratus contradicts himself when he describes Apollonius' sophistic activity. On the one hand he insists that Apollonius was not a sophist

Therefore, Apollonius's likeness to the sophists raises interesting questions concerning the historicity of the *VA* and whether the traditions of the lives of the historical sophists mentioned in the *VS* served as the material for constructing Philostratus's version of Apollonius.

Of course, someone might rightly object that the *VA* could not have drawn on the stories in the *VS* because the *VA* was published first. Yet, there are other ways to explain how sophistic traditions that later found their home in the *VS* could have influenced Philostratus's depiction of Apollonius. One plausible explanation is that Philostratus was working on these two books simultaneously,[91] thereby allowing for a cross-pollination of ideas. This would help to explain why the two works share so many of the same elements[92] and why Apollonius and the sophists in the *VS* seem to be cut from the same cloth. An alternative explanation that does not demand borrowing directly on the material in the *VS* is also possible. Long before Philostratus composed either the *VA* or the *VS*, he was well-versed in oral or written sophistic lore.[93] He may have molded

---

but only a φιλόσοφος (I 2; 7; II 20–26; 40), and he criticizes rhetoric as a means used by those sophist who seek glare and cheep [sic] popularity (IV 27; VII 16; VIII 21); he tries to pose Apollonius as a pre–Socratean sage ... infatuated with the old regime and the old customs (I 38; IV 18; 22; 32; VI 20–21; VIII 7,7). On the other hand he describes typically sophist appearances of Apollonius in various cities of Asia Minor and he holds what characterized Apollonius's every–day practice was διάλεξις ἐς πάντας (I 16; IV 41; VIII 26), and he regards otherwise despised sophistry as an art of the first rank (τεχνῶν σοφαί VII 7,4)" (Dzielska, *Apollonius*, 53).

91. Elsner, "Protean corpus," 4, n. 6.

92. A few examples of material shared between the two works are (1) the allusion to a hymn called *In Honour of Memory* (*VA* 1.14.1; *VS* 523); (2) the proverb that a lover does not approach his beloved with a sword (*VS* 2; *VA* 7:36); (3) the proverb about "the ox of silence" (*VS* 21; *VA* 6.11); (4) the story of Python of Byzantium from Demosthenes's *On the Crown*, 136 (*VS* 2; *VA* 7:37); (5) a reference to the same passage in Herodotus 1.47.3 (*VS* 481; *VA* 6.11.16) (6) an allusion to Helen's cup with Egyptian potions from Homer's *Odyssey* 4.220 (*VS* 480; *VA* 7.22.1); (7) an allusion to the gardens of Tantalus, mentioned in *Odyssey* 11.588, gardens "which are and are not" (*VA* 595; *VA* 4.25); (8) the story of a man falling in love with a statue (*VS* 18; *VA* 6.40); (9) an evaluation of the accent of Cappadocian orators (*VA* 1.7; *VS* 594); (10) matricides listed in the same order: Nero, Orestes, and Alcmaeon (*VS* 481; *VA* 4.38); (11) a comparison of philosophy itself (*VS* 481) or of Apollonius as a philosopher (*VA* 1.2) to the arts of the Egyptians, Babylonians, and Indians; (12) the mention of the friendship of Dio Chrysostom and Apollonius (*VS* 488; *VA* 5.33, 37); (13) the story of Domitian forcing philosophers to flee Rome (*VA* 7.4; *VS* 488); (14) a mention of the gymnosophists of Ethiopia (*VS* 571; *VA* 1.2.1; 6.4.3–23); and (15) a reference to the temple of Daphnean Apollo in Ephesus (*VS* 480; *VA* 1.16).

93. In the introduction to the *VS*, Philostratus refers to conversations that he had with Gordian about the sophists while they were in Antioch of Syria, which probably

Apollonius into the image of the sophists that he so admired by drawing on his vast knowledge of sophistic history and personal experiences with the orators of his own era. In summary, sophistic legends could have influenced the tradition of Apollonius in several ways, either because the timeframe of the composition of the *VA* and *VS* overlapped somewhat or because the oral and written traditions about the sophists, on which Philostratus would later base the *VS*, would have predated the composition of these two books.

Assuming, then, that some sort of relationship between Apollonius and the sophists exists in Philostratus's writings, a historian should then weigh whether it is more likely that details from the life of the historical Apollonius influenced his portrayal of the historical sophists or that a few choice ornaments were borrowed from the trove of sophistic biographies to adorn his picture Apollonius. Philostratus may hint at the answer to this question; the histories of many Second Sophistic figures were well-known in the day of Philostratus, whereas he confessed that there was great ignorance about the Tyanean (*VA* 1.2–3). On balance, it seems less likely that Philostratus could have manipulated the traditions of famous sophists without being caught out than that he could have adorned the lesser-known legend of Apollonius with a few choice gems borrowed from the treasury of sophistic lore. This example of Apollonius's resemblance to the sophists in the *VS* is but one illustration of how useful the larger Philostratean corpus can be in asking historical questions about the *VA*.

Heroicus

Heroicus is a fictional dialogue about the appearance and continued worship of Homeric heroes near Troy centuries after the Trojan War.[94]

---

was while Philostratus was there with Julia Domna (c. AD 215). If this scenario is accurate, their discussion about the sophists would have been around the time Julia commissioned the *VA*. This information would indicate that before the composition of either book, Philostratus already possessed both interest in and copious knowledge of the sophists. See Hemelrijk, *Matrona Docta*, 303, n. 111. The date of AD 215 mentioned above would be further supported if Philostratus referred to a conversation with Gordian I (Marcus Antonius Gordian), for he may have been a legionary legate in Syria prior to 216 or may have been governor of Syria early in Alexander Severas's reign; Birley, *The Roman Government*, 340.

94. The "dramatic date" of the dialogue is uncertain, but it may have been set in the time of Philostratus himself. Ssee Rutherford, "Black sails to Achilles," 230. An

The primary character in the exchange is a vinedresser who leads the idyllic life of a farmer among his vines and arbors near Elaious, a site just opposite the Troad. The second character is a visiting Phoenician sailor who has come ashore seeking an omen for a good voyage before resuming his journey. Their conversation finds traction when the vinedresser claims that the ancient hero Protesilaus, who was interred nearby, still appears and converses with him. The farmer offers several lines of evidence to his skeptical visitor for the existence of enormous heroes in both the past and the present.[95] Although the Phoenician never lays eyes on Protesilaus himself, as the vinedresser claimed to have done, he is gradually moved from skepticism to belief during their conversation because of the farmer's convicting eyewitness testimony.

A major feature of this dialogue is the re-writing of history, which consists of correcting various details of the Homeric account of the Trojan War.[96] The farmer's friendship with Protesilaus, who was the first Greek hero to have died in the ancient conflict, gave him access to eyewitness information about the war. The Phoenician—and the reader of *Heroicus*—are confronted with a dilemma: is the testimony of Protesilaus, transmitted by the farmer, true or not? On the one hand, these corrections to the *Iliad* appear to be well-founded since they come from a hero who had lived at the time of the war. On the other hand, the dialogist has allowed his vinedresser to make several mistakes in his argument, errors "which are unlikely to be the author's or the result of textual corruption."[97] Miles notes that these "small slips of the tongue . . . are enough to give

---

argument for this date is supported the claim that Helix asked Protesilaus a question before his wrestling victories in AD 213 and AD 217 (*Her.* 15.8).

95. As a proof of the existence of past heroes, the farmer lists the skeletal remains of gigantic humans found around the world. As evidence of the current existence of heroes, the vintner offered his eyewitness testimony that Protesilaus, Palamedes, Ajax, and Hector still appeared at this site to perform miracles and give prophecies.

96. Miles, *Philostratus*, 51. For instance, Protesilaus informed the vintner that Odysseus was a villain rather than a hero during the campaign. Although Protesilaus credits Odysseus with the masterstroke of creating the wooden horse, he indicates that the Ithacan had poor character, was overrated as a warrior and tactician, and was an admirer of wickedness (*Her.* 34). After Homer sailed to Ithaca to summoned Odysseus's shade from the dead and learn from it the tales of Troy, Odysseus agreed to divulge this information to the blind poet if he would expunge the story of Odysseus's plot to murder Palamedes from the account (*Her.* 43.11–16; 33.31–33). Homer agreed to write the *Iliad* as if Palamedes had never gone to Troy. Therefore, Homer suppressed the stories of Protesilaus and Palamedes in the *Iliad* even though they were major figures in the conflict (Anderson, *Philostratus*, 244).

97. Philostratus, *Heroicus*, 37.

readers pause, to remind them to keep a critical distance ... in both cases, the dialogue steers a course between authority and disbelief."[98] Thus, the author of *Heroicus* seems to have intentionally introduced an aura of uncertainty into the dialogue. Did he genuinely want his readers to believe the vinedresser's account—like the Phoenician did—or not? Was the author motivated by a genuine religious purpose (e.g., the revitalizing hero cult; religious propaganda), was the dialogue composed to entertain, or is this tale just a venue for showcasing the writer's talent and knowledge of Homeric literature?[99] However one chooses to answer these questions, the author has demonstrated his sophistic erudition (e.g., his mastery of Homeric lore), creativity in generating alternative histories, and ability to write realistic fiction that could pass for true history. Although these skills would certainly be consistent with Philostratus II, was he the author of this piece of literature?

Unlike the case with the *VA*, the identity of the author of *Heroicus* cannot be established with absolute certainty. Classical scholars often attribute the dialogue to Philostratus II,[100] or they are at least satisfied with the likelihood that it was written by him.[101] However, a few have attributed it to another of the Philostrati[102] or have preferred to remain uncommitted on the issue of authorship.[103] The basic facts available for determining the authorship of this work are few and often inconclusive.[104] Yet, other details favor authorship by Philostratus II: (1) the *Suda* unambiguously attributed *Heroicus* to Philostratus II; (2) the shared wording, themes, and nearly identical stories in *Heroicus* and the *VA*[105] and the

---

98. Miles, *Philostratus*, 50–51.

99. For a discussion of the purpose of *Heroicus*, see Miles, *Philostratus* 5–6, 54; Anderson, *Philostratus*, 247–48.

100. Hadas, *Greek Lit*erature, 278; Philostratus, *Heroicus*, 7; Miles, *Philostratus*, 5.

101. Elsner, "Protean corpus," 4.

102. Philostratus and Eunapius, *The Lives of the Sophists*, ix.

103. Anderson, *Philostratus*, 241.

104. Some evidence is inconclusive because (1) The Greek text of *Heroicus* is anonymous; (2) Several of the manuscripts and sources attribute the work to Philostratus, but do not indicate which one of the Philostrati was intended (Philostratus, *Heroicus*, 5); and (3) the earliest external evidence to authorship, provided by Menander Rhetor, is ambiguous and debated. For the discussion of problems of authorship as they relate to Menander, consult Anderson, *Philostratus*, 295; Benner and Fobes, *Letters*, 388; Phillimore, *In Honour*, xxxv–xxxvii.

105. The *VA* and *Heroicus* share (1) a general concern for the renewal of traditional Greek religion, whether it be in the form of the traditional cults (*VA*) or the cult of heroes (*Heroicus*); (2) a claim that Homer and Odysseus conspired to eliminate

VS,[106] two works verified to be from Philostratus II, strongly suggest a common author;[107] and (3) the mention of the Olympic champion Helix by both *Heroicus* (*Her.* 15:8) and *Gymnasticus*, another work generally thought to have been authored by Philostratus II, suggest common authorship[108] and might place the date too late for it to have been composed by Philostratus I.[109] The evidence for the authorship of *Heroicus* strongly

---

Palamedes from the story of the Trojan War (*VA* 3.21.2; 4.15.6; *Her.* 43.11–16; 33.31–33); (3) the claim that Palamedes invented writing (*Her.* 33; *VA* 4.33); (4) a Hellenistic protagonist (Protesilaus; Apollonius) who serves as an expert interpreter for a non-Greek (the Phoenician; Damis); (5) a claim to authoritative, eyewitness sources for the accounts, whether these be from a Homeric hero or one of Apollonius's disciples (*Her* 17.9; *VA* 1.3); (6) the rapid conversion of a doubter to belief (*Her.* 17.1–18:1; *VA* 8.31; Philostratus, *Heroicus*, 42); (7) a stress on master-disciple relationships (Miles, *Philostratus*, 54–55); (8) the theme that the body impedes the function of the soul and that liberation from bodily constraints brings clarity, whether such freedom is achieved through asceticism (Apollonius), embracing a simple lifestyle (the vintner), or through death (Protesilaus; see Miles, *Philostratus*,70–71); (9) an apologetic for the existence of giants (*VA* 5.14–17) or heroes (*Her.* 7.8–8.8) based on skeletal remains; (10) accounts of dream interpretation (*VA* 1.23; *Her* 6.3; Miles, *Philostratus*, 28, 37); (11) trees near the graves of ancient figures whose characteristics indicate something about the sufferings of the occupant (dripping blood, *VA* 5.5; shedding leaves on the side facing Troy, *Her.* 9.1–4; Miles, *Philostratus*, 44–45); (12) the same noun ψυχοστασία used to refer to the Homeric *Nekuia* (*Her.* 51.7; *VA* 8.7.48; Miles, *Philostratus*, 50); (13) accounts of prophecies issuing from Orpheus's severed head (*Her.* 28.8–13; *VA* 4.14); (14) an interest in the hero Palamedes (*Her.* 33; *VA* 3.22.2; 4.33.9); (15) the talking colossus of Memnon (*VA* 6.4.1–3; *Her.* 26.16); and (16) an encounter with and questions asked to the shade of a Homeric hero near Troy (*VA* 4.16; *Her.* 24.2; 25.10–11; 33.36, 49; 51.3–7).

106. The *VS* and *Heroicus* share an interest in biographical vignettes. The bulk of *Heroicus* (*Her.* 27.17–57.17) consists of the vinedresser relating the biography of various heroes (*Her.* 25–51) and of Homer himself (*Her.* 43–44). Rusten notes that this section of *Heroicus* "constitutes a work not dissimilar to that undertaken in the *Lives of the Sophists*" (Philostratus, *Heroicus*, 51). Indeed, the *VS* and *Heroicus* list standard elements in the treatment of each sophist or hero and, like the *VS*, the entries for each figure are of unequal length so that "Philostratus' favorite heroes receive special treatment" (Philostratus, *Heroicus*, 51).

107. Koskenniemi, *Der philostrateische Apollonios*, 5. See also Miles, *Philostratus*, 22.

108. Bowie, "Philostratus: the life of a sophist," 31. Another potential connection between *Heroicus* and *Gymnasticus* is an interest in the Olympic games. For instance, Anderson noted that the miracles of Protesilaus that are mentioned in *Heroicus* are often associated with the Olympic games, *Philostratus*, 243.

109. There are also a few pieces of evidence that may help to narrow down a date for *Heroicus*. The most important indicator of date is that the work mentions the wrestler Helix's double victories at Olympia in AD 213 and AD 217 (*Her.* 15.8). The mention of these accomplishments and the failure to mention the athlete's double victory in the pankration at the Capitoline games in AD 219 (Dio Cassius, *Hist. rom.* 79.10.2–3) may indicate that the work should be placed between AD 217 and AD 219. See Philostratus,

suggests that the work is from one of the Philostrati and favors the view of Philostratus II as the author.

Perhaps the best way to illustrate how *Heroicus* helps in evaluating the historicity of the *VA* is by exploring the relationship between the nearly identical stories that the works share. Both accounts mention the talking statue of Memnon in Egypt[110] and record an encounter with the shade of a Homeric hero near Troy.[111] In the case of Memnon's colossus, the vinedresser in *Heroicus* merely relates a story that the image spoke, whereas, in the *VA*, Apollonius's party bears witness to the statue speaking at sunrise.[112] In the case of the meeting with the ghosts of Homeric heroes—Achilles in the *VA* and Protesilaus in *Heroicus*—the same five questions were asked to the warriors by a visitor. The basic details of the account of Memnon's statue and the events at Troy are the same so there is almost certainly a literary relationship between the two works. However, the chronological relationship between the *VA* and *Heroicus* is uncertain; the question of which work recycled the other's story remains unclear.

Whichever work was penned first, *Heroicus* still elicits some intriguing questions about the historicity of the *VA*. If the *VA* borrowed these two stories from *Heroicus* and attributed them to Apollonius, then how likely are they to be real historical events from the life of the sage? Alternately, if the *VA* were written first, why would Philostratus borrow two historical events from the travels of Apollonius and give them a new, fictional setting in *Heroicus* (and yet another setting, in the case of Memnon's colossus, in *Imagines I*)?[113] Could it be that Philostratus is

---

Heroicus, 151, n. 60). Some, however, would argue for a date in the 220s. See Philostratus, *Apollonius of Tyana*, 1:2; Philostratus, *Heroicus*, 10. A second clue to dating is a passage that reports that the Thessalians were producing illegal dye. This datum could indicate that the work was written sometime after the imperial edict on purple dye issued under Alexander Severus (AD 222–35). Yet, caution must be exercised here, for this ban on dye-making could also refer to an earlier decree; such regulations may have been in force as early as the reign of Nero (Suet., *Ner.* 32; Philostratus, *Heroicus*, 306, n. 201). The mention of Helix is the most certain clue to date while the issue of the prohibition of making dye is less certain. A date after 217 or later would fit well with the other evidence presented above that suggests Philostratus II as the author.

110. *VA* 6.4.1–3; *Her.* 26.16.

111. *VA* 4.16; *Her.* 24.2; 25.10–11; 33.36, 49; 51.3–7.

112. As will be shown in a future chapter, this eyewitness account in the *VA* is problematic tale from a historical perspective since the statue of Memnon—which was really an image of Amenhotep—had been damaged since the time of Strabo and, in the time of Apollonius, had no mouth with which to speak.

113. A third version of the tale of Memnon's speaking statue appears in *Imag. I* 1.7.19–25.

simply recycling what he regarded as a good tale in various works? A more shocking alternative may be that Philostratus borrowed the story of Memnon[114] and the encounter at Troy[115] from the earlier stories by the second-century author Lucian, thereby challenging the eyewitness testimony in the *VA* for both these events. Both the case of Memnon's colossus and the interrogation of the heroes near Troy will be pursued in more detail in a later chapter, but the problems they create are broached here to show how *Heroicus* can be used to formulate questions that may help in evaluating the veracity of the *VA*.

A careful reading of *Heroicus* also generates other important questions. One such query concerns how much weight should be placed on the eyewitness testimony in Damis's memoir, the primary source of the *VA*. Philostratus's eyewitnesses for biographical material are sometimes real and sometimes fictional. In the *VS*, the biographical vignettes of the sophists were presumably based on genuine oral or written tradition. But, in *Heroicus*, Philostratus's biographical sources for Homeric heroes derive from the fictional eyewitness, Protesilaus,[116] and the biographical data for Protesilaus himself comes from the fictional vintner. So then, when reading the *VA*, should the researcher regard Damis, the eyewitness, as a real person (as were the figures providing the sources in the *VS*) or as a fictional figure (as were Protesilaus and the farmer in *Heroicus*)? Another question has to do with Philostratus's practice of writing revisionist history: if Philostratus employed the fictional vintner's eyewitness testimony to negate Homeric tradition and rewrite the history of the Trojan War, what would prevent him from employing the fictional testimony of Damis to counter Moiragenes's earlier biography about Apollonius, a book with which he disagreed because it described the Tyanean as a magician (*VA* 1.3.2)?[117] Although an attempt will be made to address some aspects of these issues in future chapters, these matters are broached here as illustrations of the role *Heroicus* plays in critiquing the historical claims of the *VA* about Apollonius.

---

114. Lucian, *Philops.* 33.8–14. For a discussion of how Lucian may have influenced this passage, see Peter Grossardt, "How to Become a Poet?," 80–81.

115. Lucian, *Ver. Hist.* 2.20.

116. Most modern readers would regard these biographies of Homeric heroes as fictional as well. However, one cannot assume that such material would have been regarded as fiction by ancient people or by Philostratus.

117. *VA* 1.3.2.

THE LESSONS LEARNED FROM EXPLORING THE PHILOSTRATEAN CORPUS

One of the primary points gleaned from the material in this chapter is that Philostratus was a skilled author with wide interests that included biography (*VS*), fictional dialogue (*Heroicus, Nero*), art interpretation (*Imagines I*), athletics (*Gymnasticus*), fictional letter-writing (*Erotic Letters*), and rhetoric (*VS; Dialexis II*). Elements of these genres and themes that appear throughout the Philostratean corpus are also woven into the fabric of the *VA* itself. These very themes treated in the broader corpus help to formulate several historical questions about the *VA*.

One question is whether Philostratus employed fiction to a large degree in the *VA*. The above information has at least alerted the reader to the possibility of fictional elements in the *VA*. Philostratus was a gifted writer who was capable of writing fiction, history, and sometimes combined elements of the two genres within a single work (e.g., the *VA, Heroicus,* and *Erotic Letters*). Most Apollonius scholars will concede that Philostratus inserted some fictional material into the *VA*, but opinions range from the view that nearly all of the *VA* is a work of fiction to the position that much of it was historical.

Assuming for the moment that fictional elements have been inserted into the *VA*, another query concerns where exactly these additions might most likely be made. This study of the entire corpus would suggest, based on Philostratus's techniques elsewhere, that these insertions would likely appear where he has (1) created a fictive eyewitness (i.e., Damis) just as he created Protesilaus and the farmer in *Heroicus*; (2) rewritten the history of Apollonius as he rewrote the history of the Trojan War in *Heroicus*; (3) attributed sophistic characteristics, like those found in the *VS*, to Apollonius, just as he attributed the characteristics of philosophers, heroes, and gods to Apollonius elsewhere in the *VA*; (4) composed letters in the name of Apollonius for use in the *VA*, just as he wrote a fictional correspondence in the *Erotic Letters*; (5) attributed esoteric interests to Apollonius, as attested by the sage's vast knowledge of athletic training in *Gymnasticus*[118] or art theory and history in *Imagines I*,[119] that he may not have possessed in reality; or (6) recycled stories in the *VA* either from his other works[120] or from other authors, like Lucian.

---

118. *VA* 2.27.2; 5.43.2; 8.18.3.

119. *VA* 1.19; 2.20.2–3; 2.22.

120. A few examples of these shared stories in the Philostratean corpus are that

While none of these possibilities have been proven, one should be open to the possibility that they might be true. If they were proven to be true or likely, they would challenge the historicity of the *VA*. One should also remember that without some awareness of the contents of the entire *Corpus Philostrateum*, such questions would never have been formulated in the first place. A reading of the *VA* in isolation from the broader corpus could have never brought such possibilities to light.

---

(1) the tale of Memnon's talking statue appears in the *VA*, *Heroicus*, and *Imagines I* (1.19–25), (2) the questioning of long-dead Homeric heroes occurs in the *VA* and *Heroicus*; (3) the tale of a drunken satyr appears in the *VA* and *Imagines I*; and (4) the story of Musonius's role in helping dig the Corinthian canal appears in the *VA* and *Nero*.

6

An Introduction to the *VA*

THE *VA* IS A unique piece of literature in several respects. It was the longest biography of any philosopher to have been written in ancient times, assuming that it has been correctly classified as a "life" (βίος).[1] It was also the longest biography of any person to have survived from antiquity.[2] It stands out as the longest work within the Philostratean corpus.[3] Yet, what is perhaps most significant about the *VA* for this study is that it constitutes the largest repository of lore about Apollonius of Tyana. For this reason alone, the *VA* should rightly be given priority of place in any study of Apollonius.

The *VA* has been the chief source employed in the discussions of Apollonius since the time of Hierocles (AD 302) and even now it exerts tremendous influence over many researchers as they grapple with the question of the historical Apollonius. As the second chapter of this book demonstrated, some contemporary biblical studies researchers were unaware of the pitfalls associated with the *VA*, and many of them based historical claims about Apollonius on what Philostratus wrote, assuming

---

1. Taggart, "Apollonius," 1. For instance, Porphyry's *Vita Pythagorae* is only thirty-six pages long in the Teubner text (Taggart, "Apollonius," 29). Iamblicus's *Vita Pythagorae* was the longest biography of this philosopher. See Taggart, "Apollonius," 29. Iamblicus's work also fall well short of the *VA* in length; it is only about sixty-five pages long. See Guthrie, *The Pythagorean Sourcebook*, 57–122.

2. Philostratus, *Apollonius of Tyana*, 1:3; Elsner, "Protean corpus, 5.

3. Taggart, "Apollonius," 1; Miles, *Philostratus*, 3.

153

that he was essentially correct in the details. Consequently, it is important for those who are interested in researching Apollonius to learn more about the origin and content of this important work.

THE ORIGIN OF THE *VA*

The impetus for a book detailing Apollonius's life came from Empress Julia Domna herself. Given Julia's religious and philosophical proclivities, her interest in the Pythagorean holy man is understandable. Julia had a rich religious heritage as the daughter of the high priest of Baal, and her religious background may have predisposed her to an interest in Apollonius. Both Philostratus and Dio Cassius indicated that she was interested in philosophy, the former author calling her "the philosopher, Julia."[4] It seems that her pursuit of philosophy in earnest came around AD 200 when she withdrew from her tormentor Plautianus[5] and created her "circle" of philosophers and orators. Consequently, when Julia sought out an expert from within this coterie to transcribe and improve upon the barbaric style of Damis's memoirs of Apollonius, Philostratus was the obvious choice for the project.[6]

Ancient sources do not state when Julia first became acquainted with and interested in Apollonius, although several plausible scenarios have been proposed. Perhaps Julia first became interested in Apollonius in her youth while she still lived in Emesa. This is possible for, as both Dzielska and Jones suggest, Apollonius was likely to have been well-known in several of the cities near her childhood home: Aegae, Mopsuestia, Samosata, Tarsus, and Tyana.[7] Another possibility is that Julia's visit to Tyana with Septimius Severus in AD 202 brought her into contact with traditions about Apollonius for the first time or if she were already acquainted with him, may have spurred on her interest in the philosopher.[8] At least by the time of her second visit to Tyana in AD 215, both

---

4. Caracalla is called "the son of the philosopher Julia" (ὁ τῆς φιλοσόφου παῖς ʼΙουλίας VS 622). Dio Cassius notes that Julia was interested in philosophy both the lifetimes of Severus (*Rom. hist.* 76.15.7) and Caracalla (*Rom. hist.* 78.18.3). See Dzielska, 189; Taggart, "Apollonius," 51.

5. Taggart, "Apollonius," 49.

6. *VA* 1.3.

7. Dzielska, *Apollonius*, 188. Philostratus, *Apollonius of Tyana*, 3:17–18.

8. Phillimore writes of the royal visit to Tyana in 202, "Probably it was in the latter year that Plautian's dangerous attack of illness caused the army a long delay; and

she and the emperor Caracalla, her eldest son,[9] were well acquainted with Apollonius. Dio Cassius recorded that Caracalla was fascinated by the sorcerer and magician (γόης καὶ μάγος) Apollonius of Cappadocia, whom he honored and praised.[10] He even erected a structure for Apollonius during his visit to Tyana.[11] Some believe that this final visit to Tyana was the occasion upon which Julia received the memoirs of Damis that sparked the idea for the VA.[12]

THE DATE OF THE VA

Regrettably, evidence for a precise date of the publication of the VA does not exist. However, there are a few details worth keeping in mind while exploring the date of its composition. Since Philostratus did not dedicate the VA to Julia Domna, most scholars treat this as evidence that he published it after her death.[13] If this supposition is correct, Philostratus would have been charged with writing the VA sometime before Julia's suicide in AD 217[14] and it would have been published between 217 and the time of the publication of the VS, which referenced it (VS 2.5). Most

---

thereby (as has generally been supposed), gave Julia occasion to employ her curiosity with the local devotion" (Phillimore, *In Honour*, lxvi). Birley is also favorable to this view: "Julia's interest in the legendary sage may have been awakened during the course of this journey" (Birley, *Septimius Severus*, 141). Réville writes that "[t]he emperor had stayed some time in Tyana; he had been ill there, and his recovery possibly may have been attributed to the healing deity of the locality" (Réville, *Apollonius of Tyana*, 17). Although this theory cannot be proven, if the recovery of the emperor was attributed to Apollonius, this could have helped to capture the attention of Julia. For the sickness of Septimius Severus at Tyana, see Dio Cassius, *Hist. rom.* 76.15.4.

9. Bowersock, Introduction to *Life of Apollonius*, 12.

10. Dio Cassius, *Hist. rom.* 78.18.4.

11. This building was called both a hero sanctuary (ἡρῷον) by Dio Cassius (*Hist. rom.* 78.18.4) and a temple (ἱερόν) by Philostratus (VA 8.29; 8.31.3).

12. Jones suggests that "It was probably about this time that Julia commissioned a biography of this ascetic miracle worker, putting into Philostratus's hands the unpublished memoirs of a disciple named Damis and instructing him to rework them into a full biography" (Philostratus, *Heroicus*, 1:8). See also, Phillimore, *In Honour*, lxviii. As an additional argument in favor of this view, Bowie notes that Philostratus refers to the empress by verbs in the imperfect tense. See Bowie, "Philostratus: the life of a sophist," 29.

13. Phillimore, *In Honour*, lxxxiv; Bowersock, Introduction to *Life of Apollonius*, 9; Anderson, *Philostratus*, 121; Philostratus, *Apollonius of Tyana*, 3:10; Flinterman, "Pythagoras and Pythagoreanism," 164 n. 62.

14. Anderson, *Philostratus*, 5. Phillimore thought the work on it began in AD 215. See Phillimore, *In Honour*, lxxxiii.

scholars tend to date the *VA*'s publication around AD 220,[15] although some favor a date as late as the 220s or 230s.[16] Since the *VS* was written after the *VA*, the *terminus ad quem* for the *VA* would have been AD 238 if written under Gordian I or AD 242–43 if written under Gordian III.[17]

THE GENRE OF THE *VA*

Ancient literature normally displayed features that assisted a reader in identifying its genre. Unfortunately, the *VA* has successfully resisted academic attempts to pigeonhole it with respect to genre.[18] B. P. Reardon aptly described the work as "a veritable potpourri of literary forms" ("un véritable pot-pourri des forms littéraires.").[19] Experts have variously

---

15. Votaw dates the *VA* to around 217 (*The Gospels*, 18), Cartlidge and Dungan to about AD 218 (*Documents*, 205), Meier between AD 217–20 (*Mentor*, 577), and Koskenniemi between AD 217–22 (*Apollonius*, 170).

16. Philostratus, *Apollonius of Tyana*, 1:3. Swain believes the *VA* belongs to the time of Alexander (AD 223–235); Swain, "Culture and nature," 37.

17. As noted in the previous chapter, the *VS* was written to one of two men named Gordian: Gordian I (c. AD 159–238) or Gordian III (AD 223–244). Assuming for the sake of argument that the latter figure was intended, the *VA* would have been completed prior to this date and the completion of the *VS*. See Bowie, "Philostratus: the life of a sophist," 29. However, as was also noted in the previous chapter, the *VA* and *VS* may have been worked on simultaneously, so that, in theory, their dates of completion may not have been too far apart.

18. Petzke, *Die Traditionen*, 59; Burridge, *What Are the Gospels?*, 160.

19. Reardon, *Courants littéraires grecs*, 266.

classified it as biography,[20] romance,[21] novel,[22] aretalogy,[23] hagiography,[24] or some mixture of these types.[25] Anderson, however, warns that "[i]t is futile to 'explain' *Apollonius* in terms of any single genre" because the sophists often freely experimented with combining literary categories.[26] Likewise, Miles argues concerning the *VA* that "[i]t is better simply to acknowledge the generic hybridity of the text, especially its biographical and novelistic elements, than to assign it to one genre."[27] Nevertheless, scholars more often than not classify the *VA* as biography because it shares most of the key features of that genre, despite a few clear

20. Votaw, The *Gospels*, 6, 8–9, 15, 18; *Philostratus*, Apollonius of Tyana, 1:3; Burridge deems it a "philosophical biography" (Burridge, *What Are the Gospels?*, 75, 151). Petzke regards the work as romance and aretalogy. See Petzke, *Die Traditionen*, 51 and 60. Holzberg classifies the *VA* as "fictional biography" (Holzberg, "The Genre: Novels Proper," 18, 24). Anderson gives an extensive discussion of options concerning the genre of the *VA*. See Anderson, *Philostratus*, 227–37.

21. Phillimore, *In Honour*, xviii–xix, lxix; Kee, *Miracle*, 264. Cazemier writes, "Het geschrift hield het midden tussen een biografie en een roman en zou kunnen worden aangeduid als een *vie romancée*," (Cazemier, "Apollonius in magie," 52). Anderson regards Xenophon's *Cyropaedia* as providing the closest parallel to the *VA* in that it focuses on the career of a single figure, reports of encounters with exotic animals (e.g., a centaur) and magi, and possesses a high moral tone. Further, the protagonists are laconic, reserved sexually, reject homosexual advances, are careful with wealth, and are guided by a strict moral code. See Anderson, *Philostratus*, 231–33, 236.

22. Anderson compares the *VA*'s eight books to that of the Xenophon's *Cyropaedia*. See Anderson, "Philostratus on Apollonius of Tyana," 615. Anderson notes other similarities of it to Heliodorus' *Aethiopica*: adventures set in exotic places, interest in travelling holy men, sun-worship, the gymnosophists, and a conclusion with a trial scene. For this information, consult Anderson, *Philostratus*, 231. Petzke holds that the *VA* resists categorization and that it has no clear parallel. However, he believes that it stands closest to Iamblicus's *Life of Pythagoras*. For this evaluation, see Petzke, *Die Traditionen*, 60.

23. Hadas and Smith, *Heroes and Gods*, 101.

24. Dzielska, *Apollonius*, 12.

25. Although Beck describes the *VA* as a "biography of the god-man or holy man," he also refers to it as "fictional biography" and a "hagiographic account" (Beck, "Mystery Religions," 140–41). Anderson also detects hagiographic elements within the *VA* (*Philostratus*, 124, 236), but appears to prefer the designation "sophistic biography" (*Philostratus*, 235). Burridge regards the *VA* as biography but sees it as on the moving in the direction of the novel, hagiography, and travelogue. See his comments in Burridge, *What Are the Gospels?*, 184, 259, 324. Elsner deems it a biography, "virtually a prose epic or a hagiographic novel" ("Protean corpus," 5).

26. Anderson, *Philostratus*, 235. Anderson appears to settle on the designation "sophistic biography" (*Philostratus*, 235), which apparently includes an element of "hagiography" (*Philostratus*, 124, 236).

27. Miles, *Philostratus*, 3.

departures from it.[28] Thus, in making such a decision, it will be helpful to explore how well some of the features that customarily signal the genre of biography conform to the *VA*.[29]

Burridge observes that "The first feature to signal genre is often the title itself."[30] Regrettably, the word "life" (βίος), does not appear in the title of the *VA*—as the word does in the Greek title of Philostratus's other historical work, the *VS* (Βίοι Σοφιστῶν)—so that the matter of genre could quickly be put to rest. Rather, the significance of the title, Τὰ ἐς τὸν Τυανέα Ἀπολλώνιον[31] (or, as Boter would have it, Εἰς τὸν Τυανέα Ἀπολλώνιον)[32] is uncertain and is still debated. Some scholars have argued that the title should be translated as "In Honor of Apollonius of Tyana"[33] or "A Monument to Apollonius"[34] rather than as "The Life of Apollonius," and that by this title Philostratus was signaling that he was writing a "romance" or an "encomium" in the form of a biography.[35]

Yet, there are several reasons why the Greek title of the *VA*, however it is translated, does not preclude it from referring to a biography. First, Jones argues that "There is no need to assume that the preposition *es* implies a favorable account, 'in honor of': cf. e.g., I 3.2, where *es Apollonion* surely means no more than 'about Apollonius.'"[36] Second, several ancient sources identified the genre of the *VA* as βίος or *vita*.[37] As Adams astutely

---

28. Perhaps some scholars hesitate to identify the *VA* as biography because they view it more as a work of fiction than history. If so, this is not a valid reason to shy away from a biographical designation, for biography at times leaned more toward the historical end of the spectrum and at other times toward encomiastic or fictional end. See Richard A. Burridge, *What Are the Gospels?*, 2004), 62.

29. Burridge, *What Are the Gospels?*, 161, 162, 167, 168, 170.

30. Burridge, *What Are the Gospels?*, 108; see also Adams, *The Genre of Acts*, 117.

31. This title is known from manuscript headings and is confirmed by the words of Philostratus at *VS* 570 (εἴρηται σαφῶς ἐν τοῖς ἐς Ἀπολλωνίου). See Phillimore, *Philostratus*, xvi, n. 1.

32. Boter, "The Title," 1–7.

33. Phillimore, *Philostratus*, xvi; Philostratus and Eunapius, *The Lives of the Sophists*, xi; Cartledge and Dungan, *Documents*, 205.

34. Anderson, *Philostratus*, 235.

35. Anderson, *Philostratus*, 235. Cartledge and Dungan regard it as encomium: "for the entire account from beginning to end consists of a carefully constructed praise, using every device known to this well-trained writer" (*Documents*, 205).

36. See Jones's comments in Philostratus, *Apollonius of Tyana*, 1:3; see also Flinterman, who notes that "the preposition ἐς does not necessarily imply an encomiastic slant" (Flinterman, "Pythagoras and Pythagoreanism," 155, n. 1).

37. These sources are Photius (τὸν Ἀπολλωνίου τοῦ Τυανέως βίον, *Bibliotheca* 44), the *Suda* (Ἀπολλωνίου βίον τοῦ Τυανέως), Eunapius (βίον . . . Ἀπολλωνίου, *Lives of the*

observes, "Titles, even if not original, provide useful information about how works were received and indicate how ancient readers ... understood their contents and purposes."[38] Third, although the titles of ancient biographies named their subjects, they did not always include the words βίος or vita[39] so the lack of that feature alone should not count against identifying the VA with that genre. Fourth, Philostratus expressly stated that his purpose for writing the VA was biographical; Flinterman points out that Philostratus indicates that his objective was to "recount the life of Apollonius" (παραδοῦναι τὸν Ἀπολλωνίου βίον) to those who did not know it.[40] The Greek title Τὰ ἐς τὸν Τυανέα Ἀπολλώνιον, then, seems to be suitable for a biography and it certainly does not exclude the VA from this category.

Several additional features suggest that the VA is a biography. The prologue and introductory material in the VA are fairly consistent with those of other ancient biographies.[41] Like these other works, Philostratus provides a list of his sources.[42] The structure of the VA also fits within the parameters set by other biographies from antiquity;[43] "Philostratus provides a seemingly chronological account of his hero's travels, but there is

---

Philosophers and Sophists 2.1.4), and Sidonius (Apollonii Pythagorici vitam, Letters 8.3.1). For the Greek texts used here, see, Boter, "The Title," 3. Even if Boter is correct that "Life" was not in the original title, the point that some authors regarded the VA as a biography is still significant.

38. Adams, The Genre of Acts, 117. Burridge explains that the titles of many ancient works were supplied by librarians or grammarians: "However, this need not mean that they are worthless as generic indicators, since they still tell us, in our literary milieu, how literary people in the ancient world saw these works, in their literary milieu" (What Are the Gospels, 109). So then, although the VA differs from untitled works because Philostratus recorded a title, these other ancient sources are valuable indicators of how later figures classified this work in terms of genre.

39. Burridge, What Are the Gospels?, 157.

40. VA 5.39. Flinterman, "Pythagoras and Pythagoreanism," 155, n. 1.

41. Burridge, What Are the Gospels?, 109. Unlike many biographies and historical works whose first line announced the theme of the work, the VA unexpectedly begins with several paragraphs describing the renowned philosopher Pythagoras (VA 1.1.1–3). Philostratus explained that Apollonius was like Pythagoras but was superior to the former in many respects even though he was not as well known (VA 1.2.1). Philostratus indicated that his work was an attempt to set the record straight concerning Apollonius (VA 1.2.3), thereby situating himself as a biographer in the prologue.

42. VA 1:2–3.

43. Jones contends that this work is a biography with respect to its form and structure, whatever its title might convey. See his comments in Philostratus, Apollonius of Tyana, 1:3.

little dating: any story of a set of journeys will appear chronological."[44] In these respects, then, the VA qualifies as a biography.

Even so, the VA displays two main features that do not conform to the expectations of the genre of biography. The first of these abnormalities is its great length, for the length of an ancient work is often a clue to its genre.[45] Ancient biographies display a variety of lengths with the "medium length" being between "about 5,000 to 25,000 words at the very extremes."[46] Although works might fall outside this range, the VA with its 87,068 words[47] is well beyond the upper limit of the category. The VA is also an oddity within the *Corpus Philostrateum*, for none of the other works of Philostratus were nearly so long. Even the VS, Philostratus's other major biographical work, falls well short of it with a mere 29,905 words.[48] As noted earlier, this makes the VA the longest biography to have been written up until its time.[49] After an analysis of the size of several ancient biographies, Burridge comments that "The odd one out here is clearly Philostratus, who has given his *Apollonius of Tyana* a length beyond the medium range; significantly, it falls within the range of both longer philosophical works (e.g., Plato's *Republic*, 89,358) and also pseudo-historical / fictional works, like Xenophon's *Cyropaedia* (80,684). Once again, there is a problem describing the *Apollonius of Tyana* as a βίος."[50] So then, the VA is a biographical work with the length of an epic or historical work. Indeed, its eight-book structure has attracted

---

44. Burridge, *What Are the Gospels?*, 109. Burridge's research indicates that later Greco–Roman biographers (AD 100 and beyond) ranged from being rigidly chronological (e.g., Tacitus, *Agricola*; Plutarch, *Cato Minor*) to having very little (e.g., Suetonius, *Lives of the Caesars*) or no interest in sequence (e.g., Lucian, *Demonax*). Philostratus's VA nestles nicely between these two extremes. For a more detailed discussion of this material, see Burridge, *What are the Gospels?*, 151–68.

45. Adams explains that in the ancient world, "There appear to be three genres that are typically large in size: epic, history, and philosophical treatise" and that "Medium-range genres include some philosophical treatises, novels, and individual biographies" (Adams, *The Genre of Acts*, 138–39).

46. Burridge, *What Are the Gospels?*, 164.

47. Adams, *The Genre of Acts*, 139. In this same passage, Adams notes that Lucian's *Demonax* falls outside this range at the lower end with a word count of 3,179. Burridge gives a less specific word count for *Demonax* (just over 3,000 words) at the lower end of the spectrum, while he places the VA at the far end with its 82,000 words. See Burridge, *What Are the Gospels?*, 164.

48. Adams, *The Genre of Acts*, 139.

49. Taggart, "Apollonius," 1.

50. Burridge, *What Are the Gospels?*, 165.

comparisons to novels such as Chariton's *Chaereas and Callirhoe* and Xenophon's *Cyropaedia*.[51]

The colossal scale or breadth of the *VA*—the "canvas the author feels free to paint on"[52]—is the second deviation from the biographical genre. Burridge explains that in the case of Greco-Roman biographies "scale is limited to the subject's life, deeds, and character," and that the scale remains focused on the life of a single individual.[53] Yet, he notes a substantial departure from this norm when it comes to the *VA*: it did not adhere closely to the topic at hand but outstripped traditional βίοι both in scale and its inclusion of peripheral content.[54]

Because both the length and scale of the *VA* do not fit well with the genre of biography, they beg for some explanation. Votaw attributed the *VA*'s length to the amount of source material that was available and its "extraordinary attractiveness."[55] This is a plausible interpretation if, like Votaw, one assumes that the Damis memoir provided the bulk of the story.[56] But, if one assumes that much of the *VA* came from the imagination of Philostratus, then another explanation becomes more likely. Addressing the issues of size and scope, Anderson believes that, as the title of the work suggested, Philostratus wanted to create a monument for Apollonius, for "Apollonius is the ultimate sage, and this is the ultimate sophistic celebration. Comprehensiveness is more important than form."[57] Perhaps, then, Philostratus required a world-sized canvas upon which to paint his picture of Apollonius who had traveled farther than Odysseus, Alexander, Pythagoras, and Septimius Severus, who had completed Herculean labors, and who had endured a Socratic trial.[58] Philostratus, in a desire to portray his hero as the sophist of sophists, packed his narratives with sophistic themes related to art, literature, ethnography, geography, history, and mythology that celebrated the glories of Greek accomplishments. Most likely, Philostratus's desire to incorporate these

---

51. Anderson, "Philostratus," 615. Praet, "Pythagoreanism," 285 n. 7; Ewen Bowie, "Apollonius of Tyana, Tradition and Reality," *ANRW* 16.2:1664–65.

52. Burridge, *What Are the Gospels?*, 116.

53. Burridge, *What Are the Gospels?*, 137.

54. Burridge, *What Are the Gospels?*, 167, 172.

55. Votaw, *The Gospels*, 18.

56. Votaw, *The Gospels*, 18, 20.

57. Anderson, *Philostratus*, 235–36. For a similar assessment, see Elsner, "Protean corpus," 7–8.

58. Anderson, *Philostratus*, 235.

sophistic elements into his celebration of Apollonius's life best accounts for the abnormalities in the *VA*'s length and scope.

The above survey of characteristics that identify genre seems to confirm that the *VA* should be classified as biography, but with the qualification that it is a biography heading in the direction of the novel or hagiography. One must also remember the important point that the identification of the *VA* as a biography does not guarantee its historical accuracy.[59] Ancient biographers selected, edited, omitted, interpreted, suppressed, and even invented information.[60] Thus, to classify the *VA* as a biography does not answer questions of its veracity. An exploration of these issues—historicity, chronology, and general veracity of the *VA*—awaits the reader in future chapters of this book.

THE INTENDED AUDIENCE OF THE *VA*

Philostratus left few concrete clues concerning the intended audience of the *VA*, but a few suggestions that have been proposed by scholars will be briefly surveyed here for those who are interested in this aspect of the *VA*. Burridge notes the most obvious indication of its audience: "If Philostratus' claim to have been commissioned by the Empress Julia Domna, as a member of her circle, is true, this too sets us firmly in an upper social setting. However, Philostratus adds that he wants to correct widespread ignorance about Apollonius, so a wider audience is intended (1.2–3)."[61] Yet, one might make a case for two audiences based on timeframe: the one intended by Julia when the *VA* was commissioned (e.g., Julia and her salon) and the one that received the completed work at some point after her death. Unfortunately, information concerning the early reception of the *VA* is lacking; there is no clear indication of its popularity in the historical record until Hierocles employed it for an attack upon Jesus in AD 302. Other scholars, such as Bowie and Flinterman, find some hints that Philostratus was also writing for an Athenian audience.[62] Yet, these suppositions, even if correct, do not shed much light on the *VA*'s recipients.

---

59. Anderson recognized that biography may not always coincide with historical accuracy: "The material itself is biographical in nature, however much Philostratus may have interfered with it" (Anderson, *Philostratus*, 227).

60. Burridge, *What Are the Gospels?*, 138–39, 168–70.

61. Burridge, *What Are the Gospels?*, 180.

62. Bowie, "Apollonius of Tyana," 1679, n. 100. Also see Flinterman, "Pythagoras and Pythagoreanism," 164, n. 60.

Others have suggested that the *VA* was intended for the instruction[63] or entertainment[64] of Severan rulers. This latter proposal is possible but speculative. Philostratus does speak a lot about politics and he critiques the rulers of the past and perhaps those of his time (*Letters, VS*) in all of his works including the *VA*,[65] but who the intended recipients of this political message were—current or future readers—remains a task for a new generation of researchers to discover.

63. Göttsching, *Apollonius*, 80–89.

64. Phillimore believed that some of the contents of the work may have been included for the entertainment of Caracalla: "The enthusiasm for Apollonius, which induced him [Caracalla] to build the temple at Tyana, was doubtless inspired by Julia; but probably Julia employed Philostratus to put the new craze in such a literary light as might most favorably appeal to Caracalla's fancy; this is why we have so much of Asclepius, of Achilles, of Telephus, and so much theosophical stuff in the book" (Phillimore, *In Honour*, lxiv).

65. Koskenniemi, *Die philostrateishe Apollonios*, 37–40.

7

A Summary of the Contents of the *VA*

THE FOLLOWING CHAPTER IS a summary of the *VA* intended for those who are altogether unfamiliar with it or for those who might need a refresher on its contents.[1] Those already familiar with the work may choose to skip ahead to the next chapter. The synopsis below will adhere closely to Philostratus's storyline of the *VA*, but, for those serious about investigating the claims of Philostratus about Apollonius, there is no substitute for reading the *VA* itself.

BOOK ONE

Prologue (VA 1.1–3)

Philostratus framed the opening section of his work to counter the charge that Apollonius was a magician. He compared the highly regarded philosopher Pythagoras to the lesser-known Apollonius, who, he asserted, surpassed Pythagoras in many ways. Both philosophers had associated with magicians without being tainted by their practices, yet only Apollonius had been unjustly accused of being a sorcerer. Philostratus announced his desire to set the record straight about Apollonius by giving an accurate account of his life and defending him against the false

---

1. Readers may also wish to consult other summaries of the *VA* (e.g., Flinterman, *Power*, 54–59; Gildersleave, *Essays*, 257–92).

charges of being a magician and sham philosopher. The introduction concludes with a discussion of the various sources Philostratus utilized in the composition of the *VA*, including his justification for disparaging Moiragenes's biography of Apollonius because it was inaccurate.

Apollonius's Birth and Youth (*VA* 1.4–17)

The biography begins by relating details about Apollonius's family background, birth, and youth. Apollonius was born in Tyana of Cappadocia. His father was also named Apollonius; his mother's name was not recorded although her role in the story is more significant than that of his father. Apollonius's story began when the god Proteus appeared in a vision to Apollonius's mother during her pregnancy. When she inquired of the deity who this child would be, he replied "myself." When the child's birth drew nigh, she was instructed in a dream to gather flowers in a meadow. Once in the field, she fell asleep only to be awakened and sent into labor by a bevy of honking swans that had encircled her. At the very moment Apollonius was being born, a bolt of lightning descended, paused, and returned to the heavens. This prodigy indicated Apollonius's elevation above earthly things and his nearness to the gods.

The narrative fast-forwards to Apollonius's adolescence when his formal philosophical education began. In his fourteenth year, he began studies under Euthydemus at Tarsus. However, when that city was found to be corrupt and inimical to the study of philosophy, he and his teacher moved to nearby Aegae. There, at the temple of Asclepius, he had the option of joining several philosophical schools but settled upon the Pythagoreans. He studied Pythagoreanism under Euxenus of Heracleia, who knew the doctrines well enough but did not practice what he preached. At age fifteen, Apollonius left Euxenus and adopted the Pythagorean lifestyle in earnest by renouncing meat, wine, and the wearing of clothing made from living creatures. He resided in the sanctuary of Asclepius, where people in the surrounding area consulted him for medical advice and listened to his instructions about cultic matters. When Apollonius's father died, he gave away most of his inheritance.[2] He also decided to abstain from marriage and other sexual activity, thereby

---

2. Apollonius's father left behind a substantial estate that was divided between the Tyanean and his older brother. When Apollonius became an adult, he gave half of his own inheritance to his brother and most of the other half to some of his poorer relatives, keeping only a small amount for himself (*VA* 1.13.1–2).

surpassing the monogamous Pythagoras. He spent five years in total silence[3] while traveling about in Pamphylia and Cilicia, communicating with others through gestures or writing. Once this period of silence had ended, Apollonius visited Antioch of Syria, where he viewed the shrine of Apollo at Daphne, and corrected the behavior and traditions at that site. Thereafter, he lived and lectured in various regional sanctuaries.

The Journey to Mesopotamia (VA 1.18–41)

Prompted by his guardian spirit, Apollonius set out with two servants–a shorthand writer and calligrapher–to visit the Wise Men of India and to meet with the Magi of Babylon and Susa along the way. Old Ninos (Syrian Hierapolis)[4] was the starting point of this journey. Here the sage first met Damis the Assyrian, the man who would become his most faithful disciple and lifelong traveling companion. Damis was astonished that Apollonius's knowledge about the image of Io surpassed that of the local priests, that he knew all human languages without studying them, and that he even knew unspoken things. The Assyrian regarded him as a divine figure (δαίμονα) and became his disciple. From this point onward, Damis recorded Apollonius's words in minute detail in his diary entitled *Scraps from the Manger*. The travelers set out toward the east and, as they approached Babylon, Apollonius received several omens and dreams about their coming residence in the ancient city.[5] In Babylon, Apollonius visited with the Magi and found them to be wise, but not in every respect. He also met King Vardanes, who was so pleased by the sage that he allowed Apollonius to request ten gifts.[6] When their time in Babylon was

---

3. Several sources indicated that Pythagoreans observed a five-year vow of silence (Iamblicus, *Vit. Pyth.* 17; Diog. Laertius, *Vit. Pyth.* 8).

4. The Io statue at Old Ninos (1.19) and the Aphrodite statue at Paphos (3.58) form a ring structure around Apollonius's journeys to the east: "Both are liminal figures, on the border between Hellenic and non-Hellenic, thus neatly providing a frame for Apollonius' journey outside the Greek world." Miles, *Philostratus*, 44.

5. The travelers came upon a slain lioness whose belly contained eight cubs. Apollonius correctly interpreted as a sign that the length of their stay with the king of Babylon would be a year and eight months. As they entered Cissia, Apollonius had a dream-vision of fish stranded on land crying out with human voices to be returned to the sea. Apollonius explained to Damis that the dream concerned the Eretrians, a group of Greeks who had been exiled to Cissia by the Persian king Darius half a millennium earlier.

6. Apollonius told the king that he desired one gift above all others which was that the Eretrians be given the land originally granted to them by Darius. When the allotted

completed, the king sent the pilgrims on their way, supplying them with a guide, camels, and water for the journey to India.

BOOK TWO

The Journey over the Caucasus Mountains and across the Indus River (*VA* 2.1–19)

As Apollonius and his party continued their journey toward India, they passed near the Caucasus Mountain range, where Damis viewed the cave of Titan Prometheus and the chains that once bound him. Other wonders awaited them on the far side of the Caucasus: pygmies, a vampire (which Apollonius rebuked), and elephants. This trip also allowed the travelers to engage in several philosophical conversations.[7]

The Visit with King Phraotes at the City of Taxila (*VA* 2.20–43)

The journeyers finally approached the city of Taxila, which was near the home of the Wise Men. Their guide revealed to them that King Vardanes of Babylon had entrusted him with a letter for the Indian king, Phraotes, entreating him to care for Apollonius and his company. After crossing the Indus, the travelers were taken to the king's palace in Taxila. Apollonius was delighted to discover that Phraotes was a peace-loving, philosopher king; he was nonmaterialistic, moderate in drinking wine, and practiced vegetarianism. The king was likewise impressed by Apollonius, and he sought his council on a particularly difficult court case.[8] As the three-day visit was ending, the king supplied Apollonius's group with fresh camels,

---

time of Apollonius's visit had passed, he requested a second gift, which was that the king show kindness to the Magi.

7. While on the highest peak of the range, Apollonius asked Damis whether one could gain knowledge of the gods by mere proximity to the heavens. Once across the mountains, Apollonius also explained to Damis why, as a philosopher, he shunned wine even when it was made from dates; drunkenness, after all, comes not only from grapes. After crossing the river Cophen, the sight of a tiny boy governing an enormous elephant led to a discussion of whether the driver was a more important factor in this human-pachyderm relationship than the animal's governance of its own nature.

8. This case was about determining the rightful owner of a hidden treasure. Was the rightful owner of a treasure the seller of the property, who did not know about the trove, or its recent purchaser, who had discovered the jar of gold? Apollonius favored the latter, for he reasoned that the gods must have deprived the evil landowner of this prize and given it to the better person.

a guide, supplies, and a letter introducing Apollonius to Iarchas, the chief of the Wise Men and Phraotes's former teacher. Within two days, the party came upon the site of a battle between Alexander the Great and the Indian king Porus. Then, about thirty stades after crossing the Hydraotes River, they came upon inscribed altars and a bronze tablet that marked the terminus of Alexander's journey eastward and the limit of his empire.

BOOK THREE

The Hyphasis River and the City of Paraka (*VA* 3.1–9)

Book Three opens with a description of the exotic creatures and human inhabitants in and around the Hyphasis River[9] followed by a detailed description of the flora and fauna that lay between the river and the city of Paraka.[10] During their descent from a mountain, the explorers happened upon a snake hunt, from which account Philostratus digressed to catalog the varieties of snakes found in the marshes, plains, and mountainous regions. Some of these serpents he described were large enough to drag off an elephant, while others had magical stones in their heads which, when extracted by hunters, granted their possessors powers like the ring of Gyges.[11] At the base of the mountain was the city of Paraka, where many of the snake hunters lived. Its inhabitants had allegedly acquired the ability to understand the speech of animals by consuming the hearts or livers of snakes.

---

9. Its most notable inhabitants were the peacock fish, the unicorn, and a white worm that could be rendered to produce oil which fueled an inextinguishable flame. The group also encountered a woman who was black from head to breasts and white from her breasts to her feet. Although some members of the party fled from her, Apollonius received her because he realized that women born with such markings were sacred to Aphrodite.

10. The group passed an arm of the Caucasus on whose slopes the party saw spice-bearing shrubs, frankincense trees, and pepper trees, which the Indians used monkeys to harvest. As the travelers descended this mountain, they spotted a well-irrigated, fertile plain growing various grains.

11. Apparently, the gem extracted from the serpent's head granted invisibility to its owner, much like the fabled ring of Gyges (Plato, *Resp.* 359–60).

A SUMMARY OF THE CONTENTS OF THE *VA*

Apollonius's Visit with the Wise Men (*VA* 3.10–49)

The bulk of Book Three details Apollonius's sojourn with the Wise Men in their mountain city. After a four-day journey from Paraka, the travelers arrived at a village near the citadel of sages. There a Greek-speaking messenger invited Apollonius to a special meeting with these philosophers. Their citadel of the Wise Men was situated on a hill of the same height as the Acropolis of Athens. On its slopes, Apollonius noticed that the hoofmarks of an army of Pans were etched in the stone from when they, in the service of Dionysus and Hercules, had made a failed assault on the city in ancient times. Once atop the hill, Apollonius and Damis viewed the jar of rain and the jar of winds, whose contents the Indian philosophers released at designated times for the benefit of the land. The inhabitants of the city slept on the ground, wore their hair long like the Spartans, and dressed in simple cotton clothing. These Wise Men worshipped the sun and, in their adoration of this deity, levitated two cubits above the earth. The leader of these Indian philosophers was the sage Iarchas.

Iarchas invited Apollonius to ask the Wise Men any question that he desired, for he claimed that they knew all things. Their initial discussion concerned the nature and transmigration of the soul, past lives, and the history of the expulsion of the Ethiopians from India. As they conversed, a local king arrived at the city. The Wise Men had prepared an elaborate vegetarian feast for this monarch at which those present were served by four tripods that moved of their own accord[12] and by bronze statues that bore the likeness of Ganymede and Pelops served the guests. During the feast, Apollonius engaged in conversation with Iarchas and the king. That night, after the king had returned to the village, Apollonius and Damis took part in a further discussion with Iarchas about the number of elements of the universe, whether the cosmos was a living thing, the gender of the universe, the roles of the creator and lesser gods, and whether the land or the sea was greater in quantity. This conversation was interrupted by the report that several Indians had come for healing. The Wise Men promised to deliver a demoniac, cured a lion hunter's dislocated hip with massage, restored a blind man's sight, healed a man's withered arm, prescribed a cure for a woman who had experienced seven miscarriages,

---

12. Jones notes that these tripods (*VA* 3.27.2) are reminiscent of those fashioned by Hephaestus for the Olympian gods like in Homer's *Iliad*. See Philostratus, *Apollonius of Tyana*, 1:279, n. 23.

and gave a remedy for another man so that no more of his sons would die from drinking wine.

Apollonius and Damis were astonished at the wisdom of their hosts and, in the following days, gleaned from their wisdom on the topics of astral prophecy, foreknowledge, and prophecy. Even Damis had an opportunity to inquire about the truth of rumors about the existence of the fabulous animals, springs, and inhabitants of India. The sages confirmed that the reports of magnetic stones, pygmies, gold-quarrying griffins, and the phoenix were true, whereas they had never heard of the martichorus (i.e., manticore),[13] Shadow Feet,[14] or fountains of liquid gold.

Apollonius's Return from the East (*VA* 3.50–58)

After a four-month residence with the Wise Men, Apollonius began his return to the West. He left the citadel of the sages and reached the sea within ten days. Traveling by ship, the adventurers visited several sites between India and the mouth of the Euphrates River. The wayfarers sailed up the Euphrates River and visited Vardanes once more at Babylon. From there they journeyed overland to Old Ninos, where their eastern journey had begun, and passed on to Seleuceia Piria, the port of Antioch. From there they sailed to Paphos on Cyprus where they paused to admire the idol of Aphrodite before their voyage to Ionia.

BOOK FOUR

Apollonius in Ionia (*VA* 4.1–10)

Apollonius toured several Ionian cities. In Ephesus, many people followed him because of his lifestyle and wisdom. The local oracles praised him, referring the sick to him for healing. There, he lectured from the steps of the temple of Artemis encouraging the city to turn from their

---

13. The martichorus (i.e., manticore) was a mythical creature with a human head, leonine body, and a tail armed with quills that could be shot like arrows (*VA* 3.45).

14. Shadow Feet or monopods were a mythical race located in India, each of whom possessed a single, large foot that was used as a parasol during the heat of the day. According to Pliny the Elder (*Natural History* 7.2), these creatures were mentioned by Ctesias (fifth century BC) in his *Indika*. At *VA* 3.47, Iarchus attributed this false report to Skylax Caryanda (fifth century BC), who seems to have written about this race in his *Periplus*.

idleness and arrogance to the study of philosophy.[15] After a trip to Smyrna to unify that city, the Ephesians sent an embassy to fetch Apollonius in hopes that he might put an end to a grievous plague. Near the theater, Apollonius spotted an old beggar and commanded the Ephesians to stone him, for he perceived that the man was a demon that embodied the plague. After the execution, the citizens removed the mound of stones and found the dead body of a lion-sized dog where the beggar had once been. Thus did Apollonius avert the Ephesian plague.

The Journey to Greece and the Visit to Achilles's Mound (*VA* 4.11–16)

Departing Ionia, Apollonius set out for Greece, stopping at several sites along the way. He paused at Pergamum to visit the sanctuary of Asclepius and perform a few healings. Then he proceeded to Ilium (Troy), where he visited the tombs of the long-dead Achaean warriors and spent the night alone on the burial mound of Achilles, despite the protestations of his companions. He then sailed opposite Methymna to set up a fallen statue at the tomb of Palamedes of which the shade of Achilles had recently informed him and, on Lesbos, visited the shrine of Orpheus's prophesying head. Damis, vexed that Apollonius had never shared the details of his encounter with the ghost of Achilles, finally demanded that the details of that story of his night alone at Troy be told. Apollonius obliged, relating that, after an earthquake, Achilles emerged from his mound and grew from the height of five to twelve cubits. Achilles then charged Apollonius with telling the Thessalians that he was angry with them for neglecting their sacrifices to him and that, unless they changed their ways, they would face destruction. Achilles also allowed Apollonius to ask five questions about the events of the Trojan War and additionally charged him with re-erecting the buried statue of Palamedes. His conversation with the hero ended at cockcrow when Achilles disappeared in a flash of light.

15. During one such discourse, a chirping sparrow arrived and led away a flock of his companions. The activity of the birds so distracted the audience that Apollonius paused to explain the cause of the disturbance; the first sparrow had informed his companions that a slave had spilled a tray of grain and had come to invite his friends to share in the feast. Apollonius turned this event into an object lesson illustrating how the people of Ephesus should also share with each other. Several of his listeners followed the birds, confirming that grain had indeed been spilled just as Apollonius had said.

PART 2: PHILOSTRATUS II AND HIS LITERARY CORPUS

Arrival in Greece and Visit to Crete (*VA* 4.17–34)

In Greece, Apollonius visited several major cities on a whirlwind tour and participated in several religious and cultural events. Apollonius's ship arrived at Piraeus just in time for the Eleusinian mysteries, at which event he had hoped to be initiated. However, the hierophant refused Apollonius because he thought he was a magician and impure in spiritual matters. When Apollonius protested and asserted that he knew more about the ritual than the priest, the officiant backtracked and agreed to initiate the holy man. Apollonius declined this offer, informing the man that he would wait to be inducted at another time by another person—this prediction came true four years later.

During one of the sage's many lectures in Athens, he was interrupted by a demon-possessed youth. Apollonius cast out the demon and commanded it to give proof of its departure, which it did by toppling a statue in the colonnade. After the exorcism, the youth returned to his former self and even pursued philosophy. Apollonius also rebuked the effeminacy of the activities during the Dionysia and denounced the violence of the gladiatorial games that occurred at the base of the Acropolis.

At Thermopylae, the site of the last stand of the Spartans against the invading Persians, the Tyanean fulfilled his promise to Achilles to warn the Thessalians to recommence the rites at the hero's tomb. While some present there were disputing which was the highest peak in Greece, he, standing on the mound where the Spartan dead were interred, opined that this tumulus was the highest spot because it represented courage and the desire for liberty. Thereafter, he visited the sanctuaries at Dodonna, Delphi, and Abae, making various religious improvements at those sites.

At the Isthmus of Corinth, Apollonius cryptically predicted that it would be cut or not be cut. This inscrutable prophecy was fulfilled seven years later when Nero attempted to dig the Corinthian canal but failed. While at Corinth, Apollonius delivered one of his pupils from the designs of his fiancée, who was a flesh-eating *empusa* in the form of a beautiful woman.

On his way to Olympia, Apollonius met several beardless, Spartan ambassadors, who had smooth legs, oiled hair, and soft clothing. Apollonius wrote a letter of concern to the ephors of Sparta, thus leading to reforms there so that the city was restored to its former standards, complete with the reopening of wrestling halls and the expulsions of depilators. Apollonius later visited the Olympic games and Sparta.

Apollonius had intended to sail to Rome from Malea, but he had a vision that indicated he should first visit Crete. While he was lecturing on the island, there was an earthquake and the sea retreated. After witnessing this occurrence, he informed the people that the sea had given birth to land. The meaning of his enigmatic statement was revealed several days later when travelers reported the emergence of a new island between Thera and Crete.

Nero and Rome (*VA* 4.35–47)

A problematic situation awaited Apollonius in Rome: Nero had become hostile to philosophy because he believed that it had become a screen for the practice of divination. The emperor began to oppress philosophers, imprisoning the Stoic philosopher Musonius and so frightened Philolaus of Citium that, as he left Rome, he warned all philosophers to avoid the city lest they be arrested.[16] The consul Telesinus recognized Apollonius as he entered Rome and wrote letters to the priests of the city ordering them to allow the philosopher access to their temples and to accept any cultic improvements he suggested. Thus, Apollonius lived in the temples of the city and lectured openly, welcoming all the people.

However, several factors drew the attention of Nero's spies to Apollonius. The philosopher Demetrius, who had appeared in Rome, reverenced Apollonius. Demetrius had publicly criticized Nero's extravagance and, since Apollonius was believed to have instigated this denunciation, Tigellinus, prefect of the Praetorian Guard, expelled Demetrius from the city and sent spies to watch Apollonius. The Tyanean officially became a suspect when he made a cryptic comment about a clap of thunder that accompanied a solar eclipse; he predicted that this signified that something great was going to happen and not happen. Three days later, a thunderbolt split a cup that Nero was holding near his lips, yet the emperor was unharmed. Upon receiving a report of the fulfillment of this prophecy, Tigellinus began to fear Apollonius, yet he kept him under surveillance. Eventually, Apollonius was summoned to court to answer a charge of impiety towards Nero. A famous attorney brandished a scroll at Apollonius that contained the charges written against him but when Tigellinus unrolled the document, it was blank. Tigellinus thereafter suspected the

---

16. Philolaus's words so frightened the young philosophers in Apollonius's entourage that in a trice their number dwindled from thirty-four to eight.

philosopher to be a demon. The prefect further interrogated Apollonius in private, asking him about his prediction and attitude toward Nero, but in the end, he allowed Apollonius to go free because he feared his power.

Philostratus recorded two other significant events concerning Apollonius's visit to Rome. First, Apollonius stopped the funeral procession of a betrothed maiden and raised her from the dead. Second, Apollonius offered to liberate the philosopher Musonius from Nero's prison, but the noble Musonius refused. As Nero left for his tour of Greece, he issued an edict that forbade the teaching of philosophy in Rome. Apollonius also departed at this time, planning to visit the western portion of the world where wisdom was more highly regarded.

BOOK FIVE

Spain (*VA* 5.1–10)

Book Five opens with a description of the Pillars of Hercules, a location that marked the limit of the Western world. At Gadeira (Cádiz), the company visited the various altars, the bleeding trees that grew upon the grave of the monster Geryon,[17] and the temple of Hercules. At this temple, Apollonius discussed what would occur during Nero's Olympic adventures, predicting the tyrant's failure to complete the digging of the Corinthian canal and his panicked flight from Greece. Apollonius also met privately with the governor of Baetica for three days.[18]

From Spain to Egypt (*VA* 5.11–23)

After departing Spain, Apollonius traveled to various regions of the western Mediterranean (e.g., Africa, Etruria, and Sicily). While he was in Messina, a report came that Nero was in exile, Vindex had been killed, and many powerful men were vying for the throne. This triggered another of the sage's predictions that the throne would fall to many Thebans (i.e., the emperors Galba, Otho, and Vitellius). A bit later while in

---

17. Geryon was a giant that Hercules slew during his tenth labor, the task in which he stole the cattle of Geryon. Geryon lived on the island of Erytheia, off the coast of Spain and near the Pillars of Hercules.

18. Damis surmised that these men conspired against Nero and that Apollonius attempted to unite this official with the rebellious cause of Vindex in the western provinces. This supposition was confirmed by Apollonius later in the chapter (*VA* 5.35.4).

Syracuse, the travelers heard a tale of a woman who had given birth to a three-headed baby, which Apollonius interpreted as a sign of the coming of the three Thebans; this prediction was fulfilled within a year. At Mount Etna (Catania), Apollonius displayed his knowledge of volcanology.[19]

Apollonius left the western Mediterranean and visited several locations on its eastern shores. Apollonius changed ships at Leucas because he knew that the vessel on which he had been sailing would sink. At Athens, he was initiated into the mysteries—just as he had predicted earlier. He wintered in Greek temples and set out for Egypt in the spring. At Piraeus, he rebuked a ship captain for trafficking in the statues of the gods while hypocritically preventing philosophers from boarding his vessel for fear that they would defile the images. At Rhodes, Damis asked his teacher if anything was greater than the Colossus to which Apollonius replied, "a true man pursuing philosophy soundly and without guile."[20] This theme sets the stage for two final episodes before leaving Rhodes: Apollonius's rebuke of a wealthy man for valuing his mansion rather than his education and his astonishment at a glutton for prizing his ability to consume more food than anyone else.

Egypt (*VA* 5.24–43)

Apollonius received a hearty welcome in Alexandria: some citizens welcomed him as a celebrity, and some revered him as a god. He attracted large crowds, performed various feats of supernatural knowledge,[21] and, as his custom was, critiqued the religious practices and the actions of its citizens.[22]

---

19. Apollonius evaluated various theories as to the source of the mountain's smoldering fire. This discourse digressed into speculation about whether poetry or fable was more philosophic before returning once more to the original topic. In the end, Apollonius rejected the theory that the phenomenon was caused by imprisoned giants or by Hephaestus's forge underneath the mountain and proposed a naturalistic solution.

20. *VA* 5.21.1 (Conybeare, LCL).

21. As twelve men were being led away for execution, Apollonius told the executioners to stall the proceedings because the last man was innocent. Shortly after this, a rider arrived with the message to spare this very man. In the final story set in Alexandria, Apollonius encountered a man who owned a tame lion. This beast begged for food from city to city and was led about like a dog on a leash. When the beast nuzzled Apollonius, he informed those present that this lion had the soul of Amasis, a former king of Egypt. Apollonius advised them to send the animal to Leontopolis and dedicate it to the sanctuary, for a king should not have to beg.

22. Apollonius visited the Serapeum and reproved the blood sacrifices of the

Furthermore, he met with and advised General Vespasian, who happened to be in the city at the time of his visit. Vespasian requested that Apollonius make him king, for Vitellius was proving to be no better a ruler than Nero. Apollonius said that he had already granted that request through his prior prayers for a just ruler. Hoping to take advantage of the wisdom of the philosophers that were in Alexandria at that time, Vespasian called a meeting of Apollonius, Dio, and Euphrates to discuss his political options and to ask for their advice. Although Euphrates and Dio counseled him to replace the monarchy with democracy or to let the people decide the form of government, Apollonius encouraged Vespasian to become emperor. Vespasian's acceptance of Apollonius's advice marked the beginning of the bad blood between Apollonius and Euphrates, who became jealous of Apollonius's influence because his own reputation had been damaged. This was the last time Apollonius saw Vespasian.[23] After this encounter, Apollonius sailed up the Nile to visit the gymnosophists of Ethiopia.

BOOK SIX

The Naked Ones of Ethiopia (*VA* 6.1–28)

The first portion of Book Six deals with Apollonius's visit to the Naked Ones of Ethiopia. After a brief comparison of Ethiopia as the limit of the west with India as the limit of the east, the account of the journey up the Nile continued. Apollonius, with the help of a young guide named Timasion, reached the sanctuary and statue of Memnon, a hero from the Homeric era. At this site, the party was amazed that when the morning sun touched the lips of the colossus the image spoke and seemed to rise in honor of the sun.

Sailing south on the Nile, the group eventually arrived at the hill of the Naked Ones. Philostratus explained that the Ethiopian philosophers were wiser than the Egyptians, but not as wise as the Indians. The Naked Ones wore minimal clothing and lived outside. Euphrates attempted to

---

Egyptians. At the hippodrome, he criticized the human slaughter that took place there, noting that no one died at the Olympic events of wrestling, boxing, or pankration. He criticized their passion for the violent races by observing that the Trojans had been destroyed by one foreign horse, but that the Alexandrians were in danger from their many local ones.

23. Apollonius did, however, write to Vespasian condemning him for his mistreatment of Greece, but was pleased by how this emperor ruled thereafter (*VA* 5.41).

sabotage Apollonius's visit by sending Thrasybulus, his disciple, fifty days in advance of the sage's arrival to slander him to the Ethiopians. This emissary informed the Ethiopians that Apollonius wished to compare Indian to Ethiopian wisdom and that he had devised many difficult tests for them. Thus, when Apollonius arrived, the sages impolitely delayed meeting with Apollonius, pretending to be engaged in more important business.

Eventually, Thespesion, the oldest member of the Naked Ones, led the travelers to a grove for their first conversation. Defensive about the inferiority of Ethiopian wisdom to that of the Indians, the elder launched an attack upon the philosophy of the Indian Wise Ones. First, he demonstrated his power to do a miracle, like the Indian philosophers had done, by commanding an elm tree to speak to Apollonius. Second, employing the story of Hercules's choice,[24] he compared the luxurious lifestyle of the Indians to vice,[25] the austere Ethiopian lifestyle and wisdom to virtue, and Apollonius's situation to Hercules, who had to choose which of the two options was superior.

In response to Thespesion's speech, Apollonius showed the invalidity of the elder's analogy: Hercules was young when he made his choice between vice and virtue, but Apollonius was an old man and knew well how to determine that Pythagoreanism was the best philosophy. Apollonius also defended the adornments of the Indians by averring that even the gods called for the decoration of their temples and delivered their oracles in carefully crafted meter rather than in unvarnished words. He defended Wise Ones's use of mechanical, three-legged tables as waiters during their feast, for even the Olympian gods had Hephaestus fashion such devices for their meals. He also pointed out that the minimal dress of the Naked Ones was an affectation and prideful, for anyone could go naked in a temperate climate.[26] He concluded his speech by pointing out that those who want to please the Sun must rise above the earth (on which the Naked Ones slept) and join the god, and that only the Indians

---

24. Xenophon, *Mem.* 2.1.21–34.

25. Thespesion had contempt for the luxuries that the Indians shared with Apollonius: the luxurious bedding of flower petals, the magnificent food and drink, the golden chairs used for drinking, the three-legged tables that served the banqueters, and dream visions that lift one from the earth (*VA* 6.10.6). The final element appears to be a reference to the levitation practiced by the Wise Ones of India.

26. The Wise Ones had offered special lodgings for visitors. Apollonius refused to accept this offer because the climate was so temperate that any person could have lived as the Wise Ones did.

could do this by using levitation. Apollonius's rejoinder astonished the Ethiopians and even caused Thespesion to blush, black though he was. After this admonishment, Thespesion then confessed to Apollonius that Euphrates had sent an agent to slander him. Thereafter, the two holy men were reconciled, and Apollonius shared with the Gymnosophists the tales of his Indian journeys.

In a second conversation at the grove, Apollonius had an opportunity to learn about the wisdom of Ethiopia. Apollonius inquired about their theriomorphic depictions of the gods and about why some sites worshipped animals rather than the gods. While Thespesion argued that such portrayals were symbolic and venerable, Apollonius countered that the Ethiopians would have done better to have had no cult image at all and to have merely set up temples and altars, for the mind portrays the image of a god better than does a representation based on created beings. However, the two philosophers finally found common ground on one topic: what it takes to make a just man.

Apollonius eventually left the Naked Ones for other adventures in Ethiopia. Apollonius desired to visit the source of the Nile, but after exploring three of its cataracts, decided to turn back. Apollonius assisted some local villagers in stopping a satyr that had been terrorizing the village. Following this encounter, Apollonius left Ethiopia for good.

Encounter with Titus (*VA* 6.29–34)

Philostratus dedicated a small passage to Apollonius's interaction with Titus. Apollonius wrote a letter to Titus, praising him for his modesty after the capture of Jerusalem. Titus had refused crowns sent to him from the provinces, deeming himself unworthy of them. Instead, Titus attributed his martial success in Judea to the gods, regarding himself as their instrument, and, consequently, he did not consider the capture of Zion as his victory. When Titus became emperor, he invited Apollonius to Tarsus to serve as a counselor to him, since he was merely thirty years old and inexperienced as a ruler. Refusing this request, Apollonius recommended Demetrius to Titus as a teacher. In private, Titus asked Apollonius who he should be on guard against as emperor. Apollonius informed him that after Vespasian's death, he must fear those closest to him, revealing to him that he would die like Odysseus, from the sea. The nature of this prediction became clear two years later when Domitian poisoned Titus with the deadly secretions of a sea hare.

A Summary of Apollonius's Travels and Deeds (*VA* 6.35–43)

Book six concludes with a summary of Apollonius's career to this point in the narrative.[27] It reports that Apollonius made fewer journeys in his later years but did stay on in the coastal region of Egypt after his Ethiopian visit, and he once again visited Phoenicia, Cilicia, Ionia, Achaea, and Italy. Although Apollonius had visited many different places during his travels, his nature remained the same throughout his entire life.

A series of somewhat unrelated stories caps off the hero's adventures prior to his trial before Emperor Domitian. Apollonius convinced a wealthy young man, who was intent upon teaching his pet birds to speak, that he should take on teachers who would train him to speak in his defense against those who would sponge off his generosity. Apollonius also helped a poor man acquire much-needed wealth for feeding his family and providing dowries for his four daughters.[28] At Cnidus, the sage rebuked a man who was in love with a statue of Aphrodite and planned to marry it. When the Hellespont was experiencing earthquakes, Apollonius drove off the Egyptian and Chaldean charlatans who were charging the locals outrageous prices to sacrifice to Gaia and Poseidon, and he made inexpensive sacrifices for the inhabitants that appeased the gods. At Tarsus, a rabid cur bit a young man causing him to act like a dog. Apollonius located the diseased animal with his powers and had the beast lick the boy so that the "biter" would become the healer. Both the boy and the dog were cured.

---

27. The two most extensive summaries of Apollonius's career appear at *VA* 6.35 and 43, which seem to signal the end of the book (Petzke, *Die Traditionen*,77) or at least to indicate a division between Books 1–6 and Books 7–8. See Cazemier, "Apollonius in Magie," 69.

28. Apollonius convinced a man who had acquired some land dishonestly for 15,000 drachmas to sell it to the poor man for 20,000. Initially, the poor man though this was a bad idea, but once he purchased the property, he found a jar with 3,000 gold darics on the property and his olive grove had a yield that surpassed other crops in the region.

BOOK SEVEN

Preparation for the Trial with Domitian (*VA* 7.1–10.1)

The entirety of Book Seven dealt with Apollonius's encounter with the emperor Domitian. In preparation for Apollonius's climatic trial against Domitian, Philostratus recounted the confrontations of earlier philosophers with tyrants,[29] for, according to the author, the test of a philosopher was in how well one dealt with tyranny. Although all these philosophers were honorable, they also had flaws. Yet, the deeds of Apollonius surpassed them all, for he stood alone against the ruler of the whole world, not merely against a single, regional tyrant. Not only did Apollonius publicly speak out against the murderous deeds of Domitian, but he also successfully turned some senators and provincial governors against Domitian and shamed a cowardly governor of Asia during a theatrical performance for failing to stand against the emperor's tyranny.

In further preparation for the climactic showdown with the emperor, Philostratus related the backstory to the conflict between Apollonius and Domitian. The tyrant, suspecting that Nerva, Orfitus, and Rufus had plotted against him, had the latter two men exiled to islands and kept Nerva in Tarentum. Far away in Ephesus, Apollonius publicly informed a bronze statue of Domitian, as if he were addressing the emperor himself, that he could not defy fate, for even if he killed the person who would rule after him, that person (i.e., Nerva) would live again. When Domitian heard of this statement, he wrote a letter to the governor of Asia commanding him to arrest Apollonius. But, unbeknownst to Domitian, Apollonius was already on his way to meet him, for had already left Asia and had made his way to Dicaearchia, which was about a hundred and fifty miles from Rome.

The Meeting with Demetrius (*VA* 7.10.2–15.3)

At Dicaearchia, Apollonius found Demetrius, a once courageous philosopher, cowering in fear of Domitian. Demetrius informed Apollonius that Domitian was accusing the sage of plotting against him, sacrificing a boy to predict the future by examining his entrails, having unusual dress and diet, and receiving worship from some people as if he were a god.

---

29. Philostratus mentioned Zeno, Plato, Phyton, Heraclydes, Python, Callisthenes, Diogenes of Sinope, and Crates of Thebes.

Demetrius counseled Apollonius to flee to a foreign land, but he refused. Apollonius was willing to die for his beliefs for he had an obligation to the other men Domitian had accused and also would not betray himself before the tyrant. Should he forsake this contest with Domitian, he would be ashamed to face his friends—Phraotes, Vardanes, Iarchas, and Thespasion—or to ask them to shelter him from the wrath of the emperor. Then Apollonius departed for Rome with Damis, who was re-emboldened to share in his master's fate.

Apollonius's Arrest and First Encounter with Domitian (*VA* 7.16–42)

As Apollonius entered Rome, Aelianus, the praetorian prefect, arrested him and spoke with him privately intending to help him. He informed him that the emperor intended to use him as an excuse to execute men of consular rank with the appearance of legality and informed him of the charges against him, the most serious of which was that of sacrificing an Arcadian boy. Apollonius was then imprisoned while he awaited his trial. While in custody, he encouraged other prisoners who were awaiting trial to face their charges with fortitude.

Apollonius appeared before Domitian in private for the preliminaries to his defense. The emperor was focused on a sacrifice when Aelianus brought the philosopher into the chamber; when he turned, he claimed that he thought Apollonius was a demon. When Domitian asked Apollonius about Nerva, Rufus, and Orfitus, the alleged conspirators against him, Apollonius spoke well of them and asserted their innocence. Domitian, becoming angry at not receiving the response he desired, had Apollonius shorn of his hair and beard before having him shackled with the worst criminals in prison. Domitian slipped a spy into the prison in an unsuccessful attempt to catch Apollonius slandering the emperor. By this point, Damis was in deep despair. So, to lift the disciple's spirits, Apollonius took his leg out of the shackle and slipped it back into his restraints. Damis for the first time realized his master's divine nature.[30] Apollonius was eventually returned to the free prison. Before his trial, Apollonius sent Damis to Dicaearchia by land, for he knew a ship-sinking storm

---

30. Philostratus was careful to inform the reader at this point that no magical manipulation—e.g., a sacrifice, prayer, or word—was employed in this act.

was coming, and he promised to appear to him there soon as if he had returned from the dead.

BOOK EIGHT

Apollonius's Trial (*VA* 8.1–5)

The account of Apollonius's trial was rather brief. Domitian forbade Apollonius to bring any potentially magical item into the courtroom: no amulet, no document, no cane. A freedman of Apollonius's old enemy Euphrates was present to give evidence concerning Apollonius's Ionian address to Domitian's statue. Apollonius was questioned about four issues: his exotic clothing, why people called him a god, his foreknowledge of the Ephesian plague, and the sacrifice of the Arcadian boy. After the defense, Domitian acquitted him of the charges but when he asked to speak to Apollonius in private, the philosopher refused and stated that the emperor could not kill him for he was not mortal. He then disappeared from the emperor's presence.

Apollonius's Undelivered Speech (*VA* 8.6–8)

Although the account of the trial was brief, Philostratus included a lengthy speech in the *VA* that Apollonius supposedly wrote but did not deliver. The speech included items not addressed in the narrative[31] and a more fulsome response to the charges mentioned previously. Apollonius gave a thorough defense of his Pythagorean lifestyle (i.e., clothing, vegetarianism, long, and unkempt hair). He responded to the charge that he encouraged people to worship him as a god by saying that he never promoted such ideas and did not tell people to pray or sacrifice to him. He explained that he had been able to predict the plague at Ephesus—much like other men had done before him, yet without them being accused of employing magic—because his light diet allowed him to detect subtle clues to its arrival in the earth and air. Furthermore, he attributed the averting of the plague to a prayer he had directed to Hercules, not to his own powers. As to sacrificing a boy to gain insight to help conspirators, he responded that he did not commit the deed. Apollonius argued that he did not need to

---

31. E.g., the speech mentions Vespasian's favorable opinion of Apollonius and why he did not think that he was a sorcerer.

A SUMMARY OF THE CONTENTS OF THE *VA*

sacrifice to learn of future events, as his foreknowledge of the Ephesian plague demonstrated. He added that such a sacrifice was unnecessary because Nerva had no aspirations for the throne and Apollonius had no aspirations for wealth or power. Furthermore, this charge was unlikely because Pythagoreans did not perform blood sacrifices and because he had a strong alibi for the time when this deed supposedly took place, backed up by several credible witnesses. As to the events in Ionia, when he had addressed the statue of the emperor, he was speaking of the inevitability of Nerva one day taking Domitian's place, but that this statement should not be construed as a plot to overthrow the current ruler.

Apollonius's Final Days (*VA* 8.10–31)

Apollonius disappeared from Domitian's court in Rome before noon and, impossibly, arrived in Dicaearchia in the evening of the same day.[32] He surprised Damis and Demetrius in the grotto of the Nymphs, encouraging them to touch him and confirm that he was not a ghost. When Damis inquired about how he was able to travel so rapidly from Rome to Dicaearchia, Apollonius attributed the deed to a god.

After saying farewell to Demetrius, Apollonius and Damis sailed for Greece for a whirlwind tour of cities. At Olympia, travelers from various Greek cities came to visit the Tyanean.[33] Apollonius also visited the cave of Trophonius at Lebadea. When local priests refused his request to consult the oracle because he was a sorcerer, he slipped into the site in the evening and descended without their assistance. He tarried underground for seven days, longer than anyone ever had before, and emerged with a book of Pythagoras's teachings; this tome was construed as the divine response of the oracle to Apollonius's question about which philosophy was the best.

After two years in Greece, the sage moved on to Smyrna and Ephesus. Back in Rome, Domitian had just murdered Flavius Clemens and was seeking to kill the consul's wife Flavia Domitilla, as well. Her freedman Stephanus assassinated Domitian. At the very moment of the murder in Rome, Apollonius, now in Ephesus, paused amid his lecture to supernaturally view the tyrant's end and encourage the enemies of tyranny to strike.

---

32. Dicaearchia (Pozzuoli) is about 150 miles from Rome.
33. I.e., Sparta, Elea, Corinth, Megara, Boetia, and Argos.

About this time, Apollonius realized that his death was imminent and even predicted it. Thirty days after the assassination of Domitian, Nerva wrote a letter requesting that Apollonius come to him in Rome to serve as his advisor. Apollonius responded with a letter containing the cryptic message that the two of them would soon be together for a long time after they no longer ruled or were ruled by others. By this remark, he intimated that he would soon die and that Nerva would expire after a rule of only a year and four months. Before his death, Apollonius sent a second letter to Nerva by Damis, in part so that his disciple would not observe his end, for the sage believed that it was best to depart life unobserved. Philostratus indicated that Damis's account ended here. However, Philostratus recorded three traditions about how Apollonius may have died. One claimed that he died in Ephesus in the care of two maidservants, while the second had him enter the sanctuary of Athena at Lindos and vanish. The third view, which Philostratus seems to have preferred, is that Apollonius disappeared on Crete while visiting the sanctuary of Dictynna. The guards there had bound Apollonius as a sorcerer and robber because they thought he had bewitched and tamed the fierce guard dogs, but he slipped his chains and ran to the temple. The sanctuary doors opened for him, and he entered the temple to the accompaniment of female singers bidding him to ascend to heaven. Philostratus also included a postmortem appearance of the sage. A young skeptic at Tyana doubted Apollonius's teachings about immortality, so the sage appeared to him in a dream as confirmation of their veracity. The work concludes by noting that, although there is a temple of Apollonius in Tyana, Philostratus had never seen a tomb of Apollonius in all his travels.

Part 3

Investigating the Apollonian Decalogue

8

Items 1–2

Pre-Philostratean Sources and Sources Contemporaneous with Philostratus Not Used or Mentioned in the *VA*

THIS CHAPTER INITIATES THE analysis of the Apollonian Decalogue, the list that was formulated in the second chapter. This chapter investigates the earliest sources that speak of Apollonius and evaluates how well they cohere with the picture of the sage presented in the *VA*. These two are closely related:

> Item 1—Apollonius is mentioned by a few sources that are earlier than (i.e., Lucian) or contemporary with (i.e., Dio Cassius) Philostratus's *VA*. These sources were not mentioned by Philostratus.
>
> Item 2—Some of these sources disagreed with Philostratus's positive portrayal of Apollonius (e.g., both Lucian and Dio Cassius disparaged Apollonius as a magician and charlatan).

These two points emphasize that the *VA* was not the first source to speak of Apollonius and that sources earlier and contemporary with the *VA* sometimes disagree with it concerning important details about Apollonius. Taken together, these points make the case for an earlier, separate tradition that regarded Apollonius as a magician or a charlatan, the view against which Philostratus later sought to defend the sage. Those

PART 3: INVESTIGATING THE APOLLONIAN DECALOGUE

interested in investigating the historical Apollonius should also give heed to these alternative voices because, as was noted in chapter 2, many New Testament scholars present only the Philostratean version of the man from Tyana.

Pressing the case for the inclusion of these earlier and contemporary sources should not be interpreted as an anti-Philostratean agenda. The argument promoted here is not that earlier sources necessarily provide more accurate accounts of Apollonius than the *VA*. Rather, the point to be stressed is that a solid research methodology would attempt to incorporate or explain the existence of contradictory traditions. Indeed, these other sources sometimes agree with the traditions in the *VA*. When such alignments occur, this helps to make the case that Philostratus accurately transmitted those Apollonian traditions. Agreements between several ancient texts function somewhat like the "criterion of multiple attestation" that has been used in the study of the historical Jesus; the more independent witnesses there are to a tradition, the more plausible that tradition may be. Although there are certain disagreements between the earlier ancient traditions presented in this chapter and the traditions in the *VA*, there are also significant agreements between them.

This chapter will also examine a few other pre-Philostratean texts that were not mentioned in the original formulation of the Apollonian Decalogue. The most significant of these is a fragment from a work entitled *On Sacrifices* that was attributed to Apollonius in antiquity. Whether authentic or not, this piece differs significantly from the portrayal of Apollonius by Philostratus. It does not fit neatly into this chapter or the next, for it was mentioned by Philostratus in the *VA*, but was not employed as a source in that work, so it is included here for the sake of convenience. Philostratus's own *VS*, which was written after the *VA*, recorded a few statements about Apollonius that might be significant. This chapter will also briefly touch on two additional texts that are rarely mentioned in contemporary research that may refer to Apollonius—one of these was composed by Dio Chrysostom and the other by Apuleius.

Thus, the sources treated in the chapter are (1) earlier than (Lucian; *On Sacrifices*; Dio Chrysostom; Apuleius) or contemporaneous with Philostratus (Dio Cassius; Philostratus, *VS*), and (2) either not mentioned by Philostratus at all (Lucian, Dio Cassius, Dio Chrysostom, and Apuleius) or mentioned by him, but not utilized in composition of the *VA* (*On Sacrifices*).

ITEMS 1–2

THE ABSENCE OF APOLLONIUS IN FIRST-CENTURY AND EARLY-SECOND-CENTURY SOURCES

Except for the Damis diary, the existence of which will be treated in a later chapter, no first-century AD source mentioned Apollonius of Tyana. Not only is this lack of information unfortunate for historians, but its absence is difficult to explain. As far back as 1832, F. C. Baur called attention to this problem by noting that Apollonius, who, according to Philostratus, interacted with major historical figures and was afforded celebrity status throughout the Greek world, should have been mentioned by at least some source from that era:

> But, we find just the opposite of this. The man, who had already caused a sensation in Rome under Nero, and who had important contacts, who had such an important influence on Vespasian and Titus, that was decisive for the well-being of the Empire, their trusted friend and political advisor, so to speak, who was the soul of their governments, who had to pass a judicial examination under Domitian, the success of which constituted the most striking contrast with the usual manner of the tyrant, and for that very reason, when the news of it came to Greece, astonished all Greece, who finally contributed to the elevation of Nerva to the Roman imperial throne, this very man, who, because of his other celebrity, should scarcely have been ignored by a writer of that time, is so completely unknown to Tacitus and Suetonius and to all contemporary writers that they do not even tell us his name, which is all the more noticeable, since Philostratus, agrees with the those historians even in a few incidental circumstances as far as the historical events of that time are concerned. Among the historians, it is only the late Dio Cassius, who mentions Apollonius . . . However, there is not the slightest trace of the great political significance that Apollonius is said to have had under Vespasian and Titus, and the expression with which Dio Cassius designates him (Ἀπολλώνιός τις Τυανεύς) does not even permit one to infer such. Not even among other writers is there any mention of the man, who is said to have filled the whole Roman world with the reputation of his name in the first century, before the middle of the second century. Only Lucian and Apuleius, who are already quite close to Philostratus, mention an Apollonius from Tyana, who made himself known by magic.[1]

---

1. Baur, *Apollonius von Tyana*, 110–11. The translation above is the author's own.

PART 3: INVESTIGATING THE APOLLONIAN DECALOGUE

Baur is not alone in noting the first-century silence about Apollonius.

Similarly, Phillimore (1912) concluded that the Tyanean "was certainly a person of little importance, since he never so much as once comes into the horizon of any contemporary author, although the supposed scene of his alleged activities was now Rome, now Athens, now Alexandria, centres of resort and publicity. We have very abundant literary testimonies of the later first-century period surviving: Apollonius of Tyana is unknown to them all."[2] Phillimore points out that, although one might well expect that several of the first-century figures would have had reason to mention him, there is an absolute "want of any contemporary literary evidence for his reputation, or his very existence, in the works of any Greek or Latin writer. Just as he was ignored by Dio of Prusa, Seneca, Pliny the Elder, Josephus, and Tacitus, so is he ignored by Pliny the Younger, by Suetonius, by Plutarch."[3] He further noted that Pliny the Younger knew Euphrates, the supposed opponent of Apollonius in the VA and the Letters, and Plutarch was well studied in various subjects mentioned in the VA, such as Pythagoreanism, the grotto of Trophonius at Lebadea, and the Gymnosophists. Yet, neither figure mentioned Apollonius, with the result that "[a] terrible deal of explaining away and supposing is required if any room is to be made for the Tyanean to bulk at all large in the history of the first century."[4]

A long list of first-century Christian writers that do not mention Apollonius can be appended to the long roll of classical writers mentioned above. New Testament authors frequently referenced magicians like the famous Simon Magus (Acts 8:9–24), the lesser known Elymas or Bar-Jesus (Acts 13:6, 18), and even Jannes and Jambres (2 Tim 3:8), the Egyptian magicians who opposed Moses. Oddly, they never so much as hinted at the existence of the Tyanean.[5] The same is true of Christian writers of the second century. The third-century writer Origen was the first Christian author to mention Apollonius (ca. AD 248).

Most bewildering of all, the Pythagoreans and those who wrote about them do not mention Apollonius, even though according to

2. Phillimore, *In Honour*, xiii.

3. Phillimore, *In Honour*, xlvii–xlviii.

4. Phillimore, *In Honour*, xlix.

5. In church history, a few claimed that the book of Revelation alluded to Apollonius. Piotr Skarga held that Apollonius vilified John before Roman officials, leading to the apostle's exile on Patmos. A. Godeau identified Apollonius with Apollyon (Rev 9:11), whose minions had long hair like the Tyanean (Rev 9:8); for a discussion of these unsubstantiated views, see Dzielska, *Apollonius*, 200–201.

Philostratus he surpassed Pythagoras himself in the rigor of philosophical practice and extent of travel. Seneca (ca. 4 BC–AD 65), who was interested in Pythagoreanism and Neo-Pythagoreanism, curiously did not mention him.[6] Between the first and third centuries AD, no key figure who wrote on Pythagoreanism referred to Apollonius. Iamblicus (ca. AD 24–ca. 325) did not list him among the two-hundred and eighteen most celebrated Pythagoreans in his *Life of Pythagoras*. Neither Diogenes Laetius (third century AD)[7] nor Porphyry (ca. AD 234–ca. 305) cite him in their biographies of Pythagoras, although Porphyry may have cited Apollonius once.[8] If Apollonius had been a major Pythagorean philosopher as Philostratus claimed, surely someone of his own philosophical tribe would have taken note of him.

Plutarch (AD 45–120) never mentioned Apollonius even though he was his contemporary for at least 50 years. Van der Stockt argued that if Apollonius was well known for stopping earthquakes, descending twice into the Trophonium, and his rigorous practice of Pythagoreanism, Plutarch certainly would have known of and mentioned him. After all, Vand der Stockt points out, Plutarch had interests in these same three topics: he wrote extensively on Pythagoreanism, composed an essay *On earthquakes*, and wrote another essay *On the descent into the cave of Trophonius*. Plutarch was also in an excellent position to know of Apollonius's conversations with the priests at Delphi (*VA* 4.24)—where Plutarch himself served as a priest—and the sage's visits to the Trophonium in Lebedia (*VA* 4.24; 8.19)—where Plutarch's brother was a priest.[9] In the end, Van der Stock concludes, "in the information that is available to us, there is no conclusive material evidence that Plutarch actually ever heard of Apollonius. One might suspect that the historical Apollonius was less relevant to his own times than the *VA* intended to make him for posterity."[10] The absence of Apollonius's name from the works of

---

6. Phillimore, *In Honour*, xlviii; Seneca *Ep.* 108.17.

7. Phillimore, *In Honour*, lxxxvii.

8. Phillimore, *In Honour*, lxxxvii.

9. Van der Stockt, "Never the Twain," 188–89. Phillimore confirms that Plutarch was interested in Pythagoreanism, the cave of Lebadea, and the Gymnosophists, yet he did not mention Apollonius in connection with these topics. See Phillimore, *In Honour*, xlviii.

10. Van der Stockt, "Never the Twain," 190. After a discussion of Plutarch's rationalism and his skepticism about superstition, Van der Stock concludes that Plutarch would have rejected the supernatural stories about Apollonius, had he known him, just as he had done with the fabulous legends about Pythagoras and Numa. See Van der

PART 3: INVESTIGATING THE APOLLONIAN DECALOGUE

Plutarch, who was favorably disposed to Pythagoreanism, is difficult to explain; it should also be difficult for scholars to ignore.

The *VA* itself presents researchers with yet another conundrum; it mentions several famous characters, who were close associates of Apollonius, yet the man from Tyana does not appear in any of their extant writings. Musonius Rufus (ca. AD 30–ca. 100), a Stoic philosopher, appeared several times in the *VA*[11] and was the main character in Philostratus's dialogue *Nero*. Although the surviving lectures and sayings of Musonius are few,[12] one would not have been surprised had he mentioned Apollonius in the context of his lectures on the length of hair, exile, sexual behavior, food, or whether marriage hinders the study of philosophy.[13] Dio Chrysostom (ca. AD 40–ca. 115), the student of Musonius Rufus, is mentioned in both the *VA*[14] and the *VS*.[15] Interestingly, Apollonius comes off as the superior figure in the *VA* and Dio in the *VS*,[16] so it is difficult to determine which opinion Philostratus endorsed. Given Philostratus's accounts of close and amiable interaction between the two figures, it comes as a bit of a surprise that Apollonius of Tyana is never explicitly mentioned in the writings of Dio Chrysostom.[17]

Yet, perhaps Dio made an oblique reference to Apollonius when referring to the philosophers of his day. At least Phillimore believed so, for he claimed to have spotted a likely allusion to Apollonius in one passage in Dio's writings:

> I do seem to detect a probable allusion to Apollonius is in *Orat*. xxxv *ad Celaenenses* 3, 4: The allusion is not complimentary. He talks with ironical humour about strolling sages, who know everything, who grow long hair and wear outlandish costumes;

Stockt, "Never the Twain," 208.

11. According to Philostratus, the imprisoned Musonius corresponded with Apollonius (*VA* 4.46), was forced to help dig the Corinthian canal (*VA* 5.19), and was said to have been exiled to Gyara (*VA* 7.16).

12. For most of the extant lectures and sayings of Musonius, see King, *Musonius Rufus*, 21–92.

13. E.g., Musonius cites Pythagoras in a discussion of marriage; King, *Musonius Rufus*, 59.

14. *VA* 5.27–38; 8.7.7.

15. *VS* 487–88.

16. Anderson, *Philostratus*, 100.

17. Phillimore wrote, "It is surprising, no doubt, to find that Dio never mentions him by name–surprising, if we took Philostratus for history . . . When Dio speaks of Indian and the Brahmins, there is no hint of Apollonius," (*In Honour*, xlix).

and some 'who have been thought a great deal of, just from their silence.' Calaenae is not found on Philostratus' itinerary; but, from its communications with Tyana, Apollonius must surely have been well known there if anywhere.[18]

At first glance, it may seem that Phillimore has indeed located a hidden reference to Apollonius, for the philosophers in this passage do seem to resemble Apollonius in their practice of silence, sporting of shaggy hair, wearing of unusual clothing, and possessing a know-it-all attitude. Yet, a reference here to Apollonius is far from certain for elsewhere Dio also mentions that philosophers at times wore odd clothing and had long hair.[19] Dio himself wore his hair long, so it is unlikely that he intended to single out Apollonius with these comments, but rather he was probably emphasizing that a shaggy mane alone did not make one a philosopher.[20] Further, Dio referred to multiple philosophers in this passage, which indicates that he did not have a particular person like Apollonius in mind. Thus, this passage is not a clear reference to Apollonius.

Another potential reference to Apollonius appears in the *Apologia* of Apuleius. The *Apologia*, written around AD 160, was Apuleius's defense against the charge that he had used magic to persuade a wealthy woman named Pudentilla to marry him. Apuleius wrote, "if a single reason can be found, however slight, why I should have tried to marry Pudentilla for some advantage to myself, then call me the famous Carmendas or Damogeron, or their predecessors Moses, Iohannes, Apollobex, Dardanus himself, or any other celebrated magician since Zoroaster and Ostanes."[21] The names cited in this passage refer to famous magicians from the past from which Apuleius sought to disassociate himself. In some translations of this passage, the name Apollonius replaced the name Apollobex. If the reading "Apollonius" were correct, Apuleius's *Apologia* would have been the earliest reference to the Cappadocian wonderworker.

Alas, Apollonius does not appear to be the correct reading for a few reasons. First, the textual tradition contains several variations of this name (i.e., Apollohei, Apollo, Apollobec), but none of them were Apollonius—Hildebrand was responsible for correcting these variations to

---

18. Phillimore, *In Honour*, xlix. The passage to which Phillimore referred is Dio Chrysostom, *Cel. Phryg.* 35.

19. Dio Chrysostom, *Hab.*

20. Dio Chrysostom, *Dei cogn.*, 2 *Serv. Lib.*, *Cel. Phryg.*, *Hab.*

21. Apuleius, *Apologia*, 90.

"Apollonius."[22] The original reading was probably Apollobec.[23] Second, Pliny the Elder, writing between AD 77 and 79, gave a nearly identical list of magicians (Apollobex, Dardanus, Moses, and Jannes[24]); Apuleius may have been reliant on this passage, thus ruling out Apollonius as a candidate here.[25] Third, Apollobex was the name of a famous Egyptian magician (*PGM* 12.121) from before the time of the philosopher Democritus (ca. 460–370 BC).[26] Most likely, Apollonius's name was confused with Apollobex in some later texts, for Arnobius and Jerome had a similar list of magicians almost matching that of Apuleius that did contain the name Apollonius, perhaps in the place of Apollobex.[27] Yet, even though Apollonius has likely been confused with Apollobex in this passage, Petzke observes that Apollonius could not have entered into this tradition by mistake unless he had been regarded as a renowned magician.[28]

The silence of the first and second-century writers about the Tyanean is deafening. As Phillimore put it, "[a] little longer silence would give colour to the modernistic notion that Apollonius really never lived at all: but in the later Antonine Period, evidences at last begin to appear."[29] The "evidences" to which he refers begin with the very first mention of Apollonius in the historical record by Lucian of Samosata.

---

22. Taggart, "Apollonius," 43.

23. Butler and Owen, *Apulei Apologia*, 163.

24. Jannes (in Pliny) and Iohannes (in Apuleius) appear to refer to the same figure, the Egyptian magician who withstood Moses in Pharaoh's court. See Butler and Owen, *Apulei Apologia*, 162–63. This is unlikely to have been John the Baptist or John the Evangelist, as Taggart suggests. See Taggart, "Apollonius," 44.

25. Costantini, *Magic*, 244.

26. Pliny referred to Apollobex as "the Copt" (Pliny the Elder, *Nat.* 30.9–11). For a further discussion of Apollobex, see LiDonnici, "According to the Jews," 98.

27. Arnobius (c. AD 300) lists Zoroaster, Apollonius, Damigero, and Dardanus (*Against the Gentiles* 1.52). Jerome mentions the Egyptian magi that competed with Moses (i.e., Jannes and Jambres), Apollonius, and Apuleius (*Homily on Psalm* 81). Interestingly, Jerome and Augustine regarded Apollonius and Apuleius as magicians who had duped women into giving them money (Augustine, *Letters* 102.31; Jerome *Homily on Psalm* 81). This latter accusation is unconvincing for there is no example in the *VA* of Apollonius deceiving women with magic for financial gain. Rather, he is portrayed there as uninterested in both wealth and marriage. This could indicate that, as in the case of Apollobex, Apollonius had been confused with another figure.

28. Taggart, "Apollonius," 44; Petzke, *Die Traditionen*, 20.

29. Phillimore, *In Honour*, l.

LUCIAN OF SAMOSATA

Lucian (AD 125–190) was one of the more prolific writers in antiquity, publishing over eighty works in a variety of genres. He is perhaps best known for his satires, in which he often ridiculed Christians, new religious movements, religious charlatans, miracle workers, and traditional Greek religion and philosophy.[30] Most importantly for this study, Lucian has the distinction of being the first author in antiquity to mention Apollonius of Tyana.[31] Indeed, he may have mentioned him in more than one of his works.

The first potential reference to Apollonius of Tyana is found in Lucian's *Demonax*,[32] which was written ca. AD 174–177.[33] Lucian reports that the philosopher Demonax, "When he saw Apollonius the philosopher leaving the city with a multitude of disciples (he was called away to be tutor to the emperor) . . . remarked: 'There goes Apollonius and his Argonauts!'"[34] In this passage, Demonax was comparing a person named Apollonius, his contemporary, to the much earlier Apollonius of Rhodes (third century BC), who had written about the voyage of Jason and his crew to find the Golden Fleece in his work *Argonauts*. Moeser is open to the possibility that Demonax was referring here to Apollonius of Tyana[35] while Petzke is more hesitant in this identification.[36] If this passage proved to be a genuine reference to the Tyanean, it would support Philostratus's claims that Apollonius was a philosopher and had a group of disciples. Yet, if genuine, it would also contradict the *VA*, for the emperors that would have reigned during the period of overlap between the careers of Demonax and Apollonius could not have had the Tyanean as a tutor.[37] More likely, Demonax referred to Apollonius of Chalcedon, a Sto-

---

30. Kee, *Miracle*, 265.

31. Phillimore, *Philostratus*, lii; Taggart, "Apollonius," 33.

32. Lucian, *Demon.* 31. The work entitled *Demonax* was about a cynic philosopher. Although some scholars have questioned the historicity of Demonax, several sayings of Demonax that are not recorded by Lucian appear elsewhere lend some credence to the view that he did exist.

33. Moeser, *Anecdote*, 89.

34. Lucian, *Demon.*, 31.

35. Moeser, *Anecdote*, 100, n. 138.

36. Petzke, *Die Traditionen*, 20.

37. If Demonax was a historical figure, he appears to have lived to be one hundred and to have died about AD 170 (*Demon.* 62, 65). If Demonax referred to Apollonius of Tyana in this passage, the event described would have occurred during the reign of an emperor that would have overlapped with both of their timeframes (i.e., Vespasian,

ic philosopher, who was summoned to Rome by Antonius Pius to serve as tutor of Marcus Aurelius[38] and Verus.[39] Unlike the Philostratean version of Apollonius, Apollonius of Chalcedon was known for his greed,[40] a negative quality that Lucian seems to hint at in this passage.[41] Even if *Demonax* had referred to Apollonius of Tyana, this passage would have yielded the minimal information that Apollonius existed, had an imperial appointment (contradicting the *VA*), and had numerous disciples.

Fortunately, a second passage found in Lucian's *Alexander the False Prophet* makes a clear reference to Apollonius of Tyana. Lucian composed this work at the instigation of a person named Celsus,[42] who had written a book on magic and was interested in the activities of the prophet Alexander of Abonoteichus. Lucian's work chronicled the career of Alexander, who had begun life as a charlatan and eventually founded the popular oracle of a human-headed serpent god Glycon by which he duped elites and commoners alike. *Alexander* was written around AD 180,[43] placing its composition at least fifteen years after the events it

---

Titus, Domitian, and Nerva). The first three emperors are unlikely to have had Apollonius as a tutor, for Demonax might not have started his career as a philosopher by this point and is not likely to have been in a position to opine on the faults of a royal tutor. Even if Demonax had been a philosopher by this time, it is unlikely that Apollonius served as a tutor to any of these emperors, at least according to Philostratus. Apollonius only knew these emperors as adults, so he would not have been their tutors. His interaction with them as mature rulers was also limited, and he did not serve them much even in an advisory capacity. According to the *VA*, Apollonius and Vespasian met at Alexandria, and he never saw that emperor again in person (*VA* 41). Apollonius met and advised Titus once in Tarsus and promised to meet with him at a future time, but he recommended that the philosopher Demetrius serve him as an advisor (*VA* 6.31.1-2). Apollonius would not have served as a tutor to Domitian either, for at the preliminaries of the trial, Domitian was eager to see what sort of man Apollonius was (*VA* 7.29); this would have been an odd way to refer to a former instructor. Apollonius turned down Nerva's request to serve as his advisor because he realized that his death was quickly approaching (*VA* 8.27).

38. *Hist. Aug.*, Marc. Aur. 2.7; 3.1; Marcus Aurelius, *Meditations*, 8.

39. *Hist Aug.*, Marc. Aur. 2.5.

40. *Hist. Aug.*, Ant. Pius 10.

41. The allusion to the "golden fleece" in this context probably refers to Apollonius of Chalcedon's hopes of making a fortune as a tutor in the service of royal house.

42. Some believe that this Celsus was the same figure against whom Origen wrote his work *Contra Celsum* (*Cels.* 1.8). For this view, see Tooke, *Lucian of Samosata*, 630; Dzielska, *Apollonius*, 87; Phillimore, *In Honour*, xxvi.

43. Dzielska, *Apollonius*, 87.

describes,[44] about eighty years after the death of Apollonius of Tyana,[45] and about four decades before the earliest possible date for the *VA* of Philostratus.

Lucian records that before Alexander founded his new cult, he had studied under a teacher called Cocconas,[46] who had in turn been a follower of Apollonius of Tyana.

> This teacher [Cocconas] and admirer of his was a man of Tyana by birth, one of those who had been followers of the notorious Apollonius, and who knew his whole bag of tricks (καὶ τὴν πᾶσαν αὐτοῦ τραγῳδίαν εἰδότων). You see what sort of school the man that I am describing comes from! Alexander was just getting his beard when the death of the Tyanean put him in a bad way, since it coincided with the passing of his beauty, by which he might have supported himself. So he abandoned petty projects for ever. He formed a partnership with a Byzantine writer of choral songs, one of those who enter the public competitions, far more abominable than himself by nature—Cocconas, I think, was his nickname,—and they went about the country practising quackery and sorcery (γοητεύοντες καὶ μαγγανεύοντες), and "trimming the fatheads"—for so they style the public in the traditional patter of magicians (τῶν μάγων).[47]

As Raynor observes about this passage, Lucian "treats Apollonius as a charlatan, a trickster, and immoral to boot,"[48] and his evaluation of Apollonius's disciples was equally harsh. Taggart explains Lucian's strategy in this pericope of linking the character of teacher and pupil: since Apollonius was a wicked *goes* who preyed on the "superstitious credulity of the masses," it followed that his disciple Alexander was a charlatan as well.[49] The data about Apollonius that can be extracted from Lucian's account is that he was famous and had at least one disciple, Cocconas, who in turn made a disciple of Alexander. Thus, the earliest verifiable account of Apollonius is negative. But what is to be made of the veracity of Lucian's account?

---

44. Casson, *Selected Satires of Lucian*, 267; Robinson, *Lucian and his Influence*, 59.
45. Anderson, *Philostratus*, 123.
46. This odd moniker meant "pine kernel."
47. Lucian, *Alexander the False Prophet*, 183 (Harmon, LCL). The insertion of the Greek text into this English quotation was the current author's modification.
48. Raynor, "Moeragenes," 223.
49. Taggart, "Apollonius," 34.

On the one hand, the basic facts that Lucian presents about the existence of Alexander and the cult of the serpent god Glycon can be confirmed. Inscriptional and numismatic evidence bear witness to the existence of the cult of Glycon and to Alexander himself.[50] Furthermore, Publius Mummius Sisenna Rutilianus, who is mentioned in Lucian's account, is a verifiable historical figure.[51] Lucian's dates for Alexander are also plausible. Lucian met Alexander in AD 164, Alexander lived less than seventy years, thus placing the false prophet's birth about AD 100.[52] Lucian also claims to have been an eyewitness to some of this material that he recorded and wrote his account about Alexander just fifteen years after these events supposedly transpired. The historicity of this account may be further supported by the detail that this is one of two polemical texts in which Lucian openly names the person he attacks.[53]

On the other hand, Lucian's overly negative portrayal of Apollonius and Alexander has caused some to question the veracity of his account to varying degrees. For instance, Allison regards the account as essentially accurate once personal animosity against Alexander is factored in,[54] while others regard Alexander's attempted murder of Lucian and the other villainous deeds of Alexander with skepticism, arguing that Lucian may have exaggerated the evil character of Alexander.[55] Taggart even goes so far as to suggest that Lucian was employing stock literary themes used to describe quack philosophers to denigrate Alexander[56] and that "Lucian's purely invective statements have no historical value whatever."[57] Although Lucian may have drawn on conventional literary descriptions

50. Taggart, "Apollonius," 35; Casson, *Satires*, 268; Robinson, *Lucian*, 59.
51. Robinson, *Lucian*, 59.
52. Phillimore, *In Honour*, li; Dzielska, *Apollonius*, 38.
53. Allinson, *Lucian, Satirist and Artist*, 108.
54. Allinson, *Lucian, Satirist and Artist*, 109.
55. Réville quips that "[t]he picture may possibly be overdrawn, as all Lucian's pictures were" (Réville, *Apollonius of Tyana*, 84). Yet, in the same discussion, he mentions Anaxilaus of Larissa, another Pythagorean miracle worker, who was expelled from Italy by imperial decree, and he concludes with "[h]ence all these wonder–working Pythagoreans have a suspicious mark on their very face" (Réville, *Apollonius of Tyana*, 85). Casson also believes that Lucian has exaggerated in order to spin a better yarn, "The dramatic tale of a face-to-face encounter with Alexander, the bitter vignette of the Epicurean barely saved from stoning, the exciting story of the attempted murder—this is Lucian the master of narrative at work; they may or may not be true" (Casson, *Satires*, 267–68). On this matter, also see Robinson, *Lucian*, 60–61.
56. Taggart, 36–42; see also Casson, *Satires*, 267.
57. Taggart, 40–41. E.g., Alexander had a golden thigh like Pythagoras's and Alexander stood in the lineage of Apollonius.

of scoundrels to some extent and may have exaggerated certain aspects of his portrayal of the historical Alexander, his selection of Apollonius as a stock example of such a figure strongly suggests that the Tyanean had a prior reputation as an infamous magician and mountebank. In short, Apollonius's well-known reputation as a magician was used to smear Alexander's reputation rather than the other way around.

How well, then, do the few claims Lucian made about Apollonius match the assertions of Philostratus? In terms of agreement, both authors note that Apollonius had a reputation as a magician, even though Philostratus wanted to defend the wonderworker against this accusation. They also agree that Apollonius had a disciple (according to Lucian) or disciples (according to Philostratus). A major disagreement is that Lucian regarded Apollonius and his disciples as swindlers, whereas Philostratus goes to great lengths to show that Apollonius was not interested in wealth in any way. A further potential disagreement is that Lucian referred to the death of Apollonius, an event that upset Alexander, whereas Philostratus seems to favor the tradition that Apollonius ascended into heaven.

There are also several tantalizing correspondences between Lucian's depiction of Alexander and Philostratus's portrayal of Apollonius, which might suggest that the Tyanean left an imprint on his disciples that endured for several generations. One similarity is that Cocconas and Alexander, Apollonius's ideological son and grandson respectively, are described as dabbling in sorcery and magic, which is the exact accusation that Philostratus defended Apollonius against in the VA. A second resemblance is that, although Apollonius himself is not explicitly called a Pythagorean by Lucian as he was by Philostratus,[58] his great grand disciple Alexander appears to have cultivated Pythagorean attributes.[59] A third similarity is that Alexander even resembled Philostratus's Apollonius in appearance,

---

58. Taggart argued that Lucian connected Alexander to Pythagoras through Apollonius. See Taggart, "Apollonius," 41–42. However, Lucian himself never directly connected Apollonius to the Pythagoreans. Lucian connected Alexander directly to Pythagoras (Lucian, *Alex.* 4, 40), perhaps implying, but not directly stating, that Apollonius was the missing link in this Pythagorean lineage.

59. Alexander resembled Pythagaras in that he strapped on a golden thigh, (*Alex.* 40; cf. Aelian, *Var. Hist.* 2,26), claimed to be like Pythagoras (*Alex.* 4), and taught the doctrine of reincarnation or transmigration of souls (*Alex.* 40, 43). Alexander also encouraged the son of Rutilianus to study Pythagorean material (*Alex.* 33). Despite these similarities between Alexander and Pythagoras, Lucian dismissed the claim that Alexander in any way compared to this ancient philosopher, who was a σοφὸς ἀνὴρ καὶ τὴν γνώμην θεσπέσιος (*Alex.* 4). See Tiede, *The Charismatic Figure*, 67, 68.

abilities, and behavior.[60] One must be cautious about drawing too much from the similarities between Apollonius and his grandchild in the faith, but these three points may suggest that Alexander had inherited a few Apollonius attributes through the mediation of Cocconas. A few differences can also be spotted between Philostratus's Apollonius and Lucian's description of Apollonius's students, for Alexander, unlike the Apollonius of the *VA*, accepted money for his services (*Alex*. 23) and had sexual relations with women and boys (*Alex*. 39, 41, 42). Thus, the Lucianic description of Alexander both conforms to and contradicts aspects of his master, Apollonius, as he was presented in the *VA*.

Lucian's comments about Apollonius are significant despite their brevity. This earliest description of Apollonius in the historical record preserves the legend of an infamous magician, whose legacy consisted of two generations of huckster disciples that walked in his immoral footsteps. However, as several scholars have pointed out, Lucian's comments do not necessarily support the view that Apollonius founded a school or movement[61] and provide no evidence that he had nearly the number and quality of students that Philostratus claimed.[62] Finally, Apollonius's followers as described by Lucian resemble Philostratus's depiction of Apollonius in many ways, even though Lucian did not make this connection himself. Lucian's negative portrayal of Apollonius as a magician and cozener of the people is at odds with the much later view of him presented by Philostratus.

DIO CASSIUS

Dio Cassius (AD 155–235) was a Roman historian and statesman, who had served under several of the Severan rulers,[63] and he was a contem-

---

60. Alexander, like Philostratus's Apollonius, had long hair (*Alex*. 3, 13), delivered oracles (*Alex*. 9, 19), prescribed medical treatments and diets (*Alex*. 22), healed the sick (*Alex*. 24), raised the dead (*Alex*. 24), located buried treasures (*Alex*. 24), and was associated with the god Asclepius (*Alex*. 10, 14, 43, 58).

61. Taggart wrote "that Apollonius founded a religious school or movement cannot be inferred from Lucian's text" (Taggart, "Apollonius," 42).

62. From this passage we may deduce that Apollonius had later followers, although they do not appear to be of the number and quality of those presented by Philostratus. For the lack of evidence of a school of Apollonius, see Koskenniemi, *Der philostrateische Apollonios*, 17–18.

63. Dio entered "the senate under Commodus, became praetor (A.D. 194), *consul suffectus* (about 205), and consul for the second time with Alexander Severus in 229"

porary of Philostratus. His eighty-volume *Roman History* is thought to have been written between AD 201 and 222.[64] He discussed Apollonius twice in this work.

The first of these passages recounts a demonstration of Apollonius's gift of extra-sensory perception. In AD 96, the Tyanean was in Ephesus (or another city), when he supernaturally observed the assassination of Emperor Domitian in Rome:

> The matter of which I spoke, saying that it surprises me more than anything else, is this. A certain Apollonius of Tyana on that very day and at that very hour when Domitian was being murdered (as was afterwards accurately determined by events that happened in both places) mounted a lofty rock at Ephesus (or possibly it was somewhere else) and having called together the populace, uttered these words: "Good, Stephanus! Bravo, Stephanus! Smite the bloodthirsty wretch! You have struck, you have wounded, you have slain." This is what actually happened, though one should doubt it ten thousand times over.[65]

A strikingly similar and perhaps independent version of this account is found in the *VA* of Philostratus:

> Although this deed was done in Rome, Apollonius was a spectator of it in Ephesus. For about midday he was delivering an address, in the groves of the colonnade, just at the moment when it all happened in the palace at Rome; and first he dropped his voice, as if he were terrified, and then, though with less vigour than was usual with him, he continued Ephesus his exposition, like one who between his words caught glimpses of something foreign to his subject, and at last he lapsed into silence, like one who has been interrupted in his discourse. And with an awful glance at the ground, and stepping forward three or four paces from his pulpit, he cried: " Smite the tyrant, smite him,'—not like one who derives from some looking-glass a faint image of the truth, but as one who sees things with his own eyes, and is taking part in a tragedy. All Ephesus, for all Ephesus was at his lecture, was struck dumb with astonishment; but he, pausing like those who are trying to see and wait until their doubts are ended, said: "Take heart, gentlemen, for the tyrant has been slain this day; and why do I say to-day? Now it is, by Athene,

---

(McDonald, "Dio Cassius," 345).

64. Phillimore, *In Honour*, liv.
65. Dio Cassius, *Hist. rom.* 67.18.1 (Carey, LCL).

PART 3: INVESTIGATING THE APOLLONIAN DECALOGUE

even now at the moment I uttered my words, and then lapsed into silence." The inhabitants of Ephesus thought that this was a fit of madness on his part; and although they were anxious that it should be true, yet they were anxious about the risk they ran in giving ear to his words, whereupon he added: "I am not surprised at those who do not yet accept my story, for not even all Rome as yet is cognizant of it. But behold, Rome begins to know it: for the rumour runs this way and that, and, thousands now are convinced of it; and they begin to leap for joy, twice as many as before, and twice as many as they, and four times as many, yea the whole of the populace there. And this news will travel hither also; and although I would have you defer your sacrifices in honour thereof to the fitting season, when you will receive this news, I shall proceed at once to pray to the gods for what I have seen." They were still sceptical, when swift runners arrived with the good news, and bore testimony to the sage's wisdom; for the tyrant's murder, and the day which brought the event to birth, the hour of mid-day and the murderers to whom he addressed his exhortation, everything agreed with the revelation which the gods had made to Apollonius in the midst of his harangue.[66]

Both accounts agree that Apollonius displayed clairvoyant abilities by remotely viewing the death of Domitian in Rome from another city.

The similarities and differences found in these two accounts are worth noting. In many cases, the details of the tale are the same or similar: (1) Apollonius performed the miracle; (2) many people witnessed the phenomena; (3) the event took place in Ephesus, although Dio's account is less certain of this detail; (4) the supernatural display took place at the same time as Domitian's assassination in Rome; (5) Apollonius encouraged the assassin to "strike" (παῖε) Domitian; and, (6) the assassination of Domitian was later verified. Yet, Anderson and Phillimore note a few minor discrepancies between the two accounts: (1) Philostratus places the event in Ephesus, whereas Dio is not as certain of the location; (2) Philostratus is certain about the event, whereas Dio anticipates or has already encountered skepticism concerning the tale; and (3) the miracle in the VA is spontaneous, whereas it appears "arranged" in Dio's account.[67]

---

66. VA 8.26–27 (Conybeare, LCL).

67. Anderson, *Philostratus*, 123. Phillimore mentions only the first two items in this list (*In Honour*, liv). Anderson's latter point appears to be aimed at explaining away the miraculous component in Dio's story, suggesting that Apollonius had gained his alleged supernatural knowledge by some other means. Anderson would not be alone

Notwithstanding these differences, the core of the account is largely the same in both sources.

Several theories have been advanced to explain the similarities between the accounts of Dio and Philostratus. Most assume that there was a common source behind the accounts, with some experts favoring that Dio borrowed from Philostratus,[68] Phillimore thinking that Philostratus borrowed from Dio,[69] and Bowersock suggesting that both writers drew on a common account.[70] Regrettably, neither ancient author illuminated this situation by citing a source.[71]

A surprising feature of this passage is that Dio neither denied the miracle nor gave an overtly negative evaluation of Apollonius's public display of supernatural abilities, for he customarily frowned upon the use of magic in his writings[72] and disparaged Apollonius as a sorcerer in another passage that will be examined below. Perhaps this passage is not dismissed in this context because Dio interpreted the phenomenon as a

---

in such a supposition. Steven Jackson assumes that, if this event occurred, Apollonius knew of it in advance because he was a co-conspirator in the murder of Domitian. See Jackson, "Apollonius and the emperors," 29–30.

68. Bowersock, noting that the language in the two accounts is very close at some points, suggested that Dio had access to Philostratus's manuscript. See Bowersock, Introduction to *Life of Apollonius*, 19. Galimberti also believed Dio quoted Philostratus in this passage. See Galimberti, "La Vita," 134.

69. Phillimore writes of Dio's account that there is no "mention of Philostratus: which makes it probable that his book was not published when this was written—at least it might have been expected that Dio, instead of a mere emphatic assertion, would cite some testimony, if testimony had been to hand" (Phillimore, *In Honour*, liv). Phillimore also noted that Philostratus may have made use of other passages from Dio in the VA. See Phillimore, *In Honour*, cxii. Further, if the VA could be shown to be written late, then it could have been influenced by the account of Domitian's death in Dio's writings.

70. Bowersock entertained the possibility that both authors drew on a common source, but that this was not the Damis memoir. See Bowersock, Introduction to *Life of Apollonius*, 19. However, the view that Dio borrowed from Philostratus is unlikely, for then Dio would not have been uncertain about locating the event in Ephesus as Philostratus had done. Further, if the Damis account served as the source for both authors, the minor differences would probably have been absent as well.

71. Philostratus did not indicate whether this account was taken from the Damis memoirs; Damis is not mentioned in the account. Dzielska suggests that Philostratus "heard about it either in his youth or, more probably, when he was gathering materials for his romance" (Dzielska, *Apollonius*, 41). Philostratus indicates that he gathered materials from cities that were devoted to Apollonius (VA 1.3.2). Ephesus would likely be one of these locations, for several key episodes in Apollonius's life were set there.

72. Dio took an extremely negative view of sorcerers in *Hist. rom.* 7.39 (Phillimore, *In Honour*, lv).

benign supernatural act rather than a malevolent magical one. Alternately, Dio may have regarded this instance of remote viewing as magic but was so overwhelmed by the undeniability of the miracle that he did not think to evaluate or condemn it. Then again, perhaps Dio could not bring himself to let the Tyanean off so easily in this passage, for his phrase "*a certain* Apollonius of Tyana" (Ἀπολλώνιός τις Τυανεύς) may have had a derisive connotation.[73]

Yet, in a later passage in *Roman History*, Dio adopted an overtly negative stance towards Apollonius in the context of criticizing Caracalla for "his devotion to "magicians and imposters" and states that Caracalla's "delight in magicians and jugglers (τοῖς δὲ μάγοις καὶ γόησιν) was so great that he commended and honoured Apollonius of Cappadocia, who had flourished under Domitian and was a thorough juggler and magician (ὅστις καὶ γόης καὶ μάγος ἀκριβὴς ἐγένετο), and erected a shrine (ἡρῷον) to him."[74] In this passage, Dio describes Apollonius as a sorcerer, using essentially the same wording that Lucian had used of Apollonius's two disciples Alexander and Cocconas. In addition, the term used for the structure dedicated to Apollonius, a "shrine of a hero" (ἡρῷον), may indicate that Caracalla wanted to honor the Tyanean as a hero,[75] a term that Philostratus never used to describe the holy man.[76] Dio preserved two perspectives on Apollonius in this passage; his own view was of Apollonius as a magician and charlatan while the opinion of Caracalla was that the Tyanean was a miracle worker and hero.

Dio's two accounts alternately support and challenge aspects of Philostratus's vision of Apollonius. Dio agrees with Philostratatus that Apollonius visited Ephesus, considered Domitian a tyrant, was gifted with clairvoyance, and had been honored with an imperial monument. However, Dio's disapproving opinion about Apollonius as a sorcerer clashes with the view of Philostratus, for whom Apollonius was not a magician, and differs with the perspective of the emperor Caracalla for whom Apollonius's reputation as a magician was acceptable. Further, Dio's observation that Apollonius had achieved hero status in the eyes of

---

73. Phillimore may be correct that Dio's phrase "a certain Apollonius, a Tyanean" differs from the glowing terms by which followers of Apollonius refer to him. See Phillimore, *In Honour*, liv.

74. Dio Cassius, *Hist. rom.* 78.18.4.

75. This appears to be the same sanctuary (ἱερὰ) mentioned in *VA* 8.31.3, which, although not called a hero shrine, is distinguished from a tomb or cenotaph (τάφῳ ... ἢ ψευδοταφίῳ) mentioned earlier in this very passage.

76. C. P. Jones, "Apollonius of Tyana, Hero," 81, 83.

the emperor, a view never explicitly promoted in the *VA*, also contrasts with the portrayal of Philostratus's holy man.[77]

PHILOSTRATUS'S *VS*

The *VS* preserves three brief statements about Apollonius: his association with Dio Chrysostom (*VS* 488), his admiration of Scopelian (*VS* 521), and the rumor of an affair (*VS* 570). The claim that he had relationships with Dio (*VA* 5.33, 37) and Scopelian (*VA* 1.23.3; 1.24.3) is consistent with the accounts in the *VA*.

However, certain details of these two relationships are questionable. The claim in the *VA* that Apollonius wrote Scopelian from Cissia must be questioned since Scopelian would have still been a child at that time (*VA* 1.23.3); however, this mistake does not necessarily rule out a relationship between the two men once Scopelian was grown.[78] Furthermore, the *VA* and *VS* seem to differ concerning the status of Apollonius and Dio; the *VA* depicts Apollonius as Dio's superior, whereas in the *VS* Dio comes off as the better philosopher. The *VA* records a political discussion that involved Apollonius, Dio Chrysostom, and Euphrates (*VA* 5.32–40). When the Tyanian's viewpoint prevailed, Dio was ashamed of having taken Euphrates's side and needed to be reconciled with his teacher, Apollonius (*VA* 5.38.2). However, in the later version of this account given by the *VS*, Dio Chrysostom alone appears to have conducted himself well, while Apollonius and Euphrates did not behave in a philosophic manner (VS 488). This discrepancy seems to indicate a shift in Philostratus's opinion concerning Apollonius, at least as he viewed him in the context of this episode.

A FRAGMENT FROM *ON SACRIFICES*

The final text to be treated in this chapter is a fragment from a work called *On Sacrifices* (Περὶ Θυσιῶν). Three features of this text are noteworthy. One is that this fragment may have come from a document written by Apollonius himself. A work by the title *On Sacrifices* (Περὶ Θυσιῶν) is attributed to Apollonius by Philostratus (*VA* 3.41.2) and by the titles *Mystic Rites or On Sacrifices* (Τελεταὶ ἢ Περὶ Θυσιῶν) by the *Suda* under the entry

---

77. C. P. Jones, "Apollonius of Tyana, Hero," 81–83.

78. The disparity between the ages of Scopelian and Apollonius will be treated in chapter 11 under the section treating *VA* 1.24.3.

PART 3: INVESTIGATING THE APOLLONIAN DECALOGUE

for "Apollonius." The authenticity of the fragment is, of course, debated,[79] with views ranging from it possibly being a genuine work of Apollonius,[80] to it at least reflecting the thoughts of the historical figure,[81] to it being an outright forgery.[82] Unfortunately, the brevity of the fragment and the lack of other genuine writings of Apollonius with which to compare it hinder efforts to determine its authenticity. Yet, if at some point scholarship proves that it came from the pen of Apollonius, this would then be the earliest text to provide evidence of his existence and insight into his thinking. A second significant aspect of this work is that *On Sacrifices* appears to be a pre-Philostratean treatise. Philostratus claims that this work could be found in temples, cities, and the homes of many wise men (*VA* 3.41.2). A fragment from this work was also preserved by both Porphyry and Eusebius. Even some of the academics who question Apollonius's authorship of the fragment still regard it as pre-Philostratean.[83] A final point is that, although Philostratus mentioned this document in the *VA* (3.41.2; 4:19), he did not use it as one of his sources. Indeed, from his description of its contents, it could be that Philostratus did not know much about this work or that he simply chose to ignore it.

Two versions of this fragment have survived. The first passage below, from Porphyry (Porphyry, *Abst.* 2.34.2.), does not specifically identify Apollonius as the author but ascribes it to "a certain wise man."

> Let us therefore also sacrifice, but let us sacrifice in such a manner as is fit, offering different sacrifices to different powers; to the God indeed who is above all things, as a certain wise man said, neither sacrificing with incense, nor consecrating any thing sensible. For there is nothing material, which is not immediately impure to an immaterial nature. Hence, neither is vocal language, nor internal speech, adapted to the highest God, when it is defiled by any passion of the soul; but we should venerate him in profound silence with a pure soul, and with pure conceptions about him.[84]

---

79. Meier, *Mentor*, 602.

80. Koskenniemi believes that the authenticity of the fragments cannot be ruled out. See Koskenniemi, *Der philostrateische Apollonios*, 19; Koskenniemi, *Apollonios von Tyana*, 3, 176. Miles regards this document the "only possible surviving fragment of his writings" (Miles, *Philostratus*, 47).

81. Dzielska, *Apollonius*, 149.

82. Bowie, "Apollonius of Tyana," 1689–70.

83. See the discussion in Dzielska, *Apollonius*, 145–46.

84. Taylor, *Select Works of Porphyry*, 69–70.

ITEMS 1–2

The second fragment was preserved by Eusebius and derives from Porphyry (Eusebius, *Praep. ev.* 4.12–13), but here it is explicitly attributed to Apollonius:

> So speaks this author; and statements closely related and akin to his concerning the First and Great God are said to be written by the famous Apollonius of Tyana, so celebrated among the multitude, in his work Concerning Sacrifices, as follows: 'In this way, then, I think, one would best show the proper regard for the deity, and thereby beyond all other men secure His favour and good will, if to Him whom we called the First God, and who is One and separate from all others, and to whom the rest must be acknowledged inferior, he should sacrifice nothing at all, neither kindle fire, nor dedicate anything whatever that is an object of sense—for He needs nothing even from beings who are greater than we are: nor is there any plant at all which the earth sends up, nor any animal which it, or the air, sustains, to which there is not some defilement attached—but should ever employ towards Him only that better speech, I mean the speech which passes not through the lips, and should ask good things from the noblest of beings by what is noblest in ourselves, and this is the mind, which needs no instrument. According to this therefore we ought by no means to offer sacrifice to the great God who is over all.'[85]

These two texts envision a supreme, immaterial God, who requires nothing; he does not seek sacrifices but rather is to be worshipped by the mind in silence.

The sacrificial theology of these fragments coheres with two of the letters that are attributed to Apollonius.[86] In one epistle, Apollonius informed the priests at Olympia that the gods did not need sacrifices, but rather they desired humans to acquire wisdom and to do good to people who deserve it (*Ep.* 26). In another letter, Apollonius condemned the priests at Delphi for offering blood sacrifices because blood guilt could not be removed by more blood (*Ep.* 27). The material in *On Sacrifices* and these two letters appears to contradict Apollonius's perspective on sacrifice in the *VA*, for although Apollonius opposed blood sacrifice according to them, he did practice some forms of material sacrifice like the offering of incense. This evidence in these letters and *On Sacrifices* may

---

85. Eusebius, *Preparation for the Gospel*, 163–64.
86. The *Letters of Apollonius* will be treated in detail in the next chapter.

reveal a tradition about Apollonius that is independent of Philostratus,[87] perhaps one unknown to or rejected by him.

Significantly, Philostratus's description of the content of *On Sacrifices* in the *VA* does not match the content of the extant fragment either.[88] Philostratus claimed that *On Sacrifices* detailed how sacrifices were to be made to the gods (*VA* 3.41), the sorts of sacrifices appropriate to each god (e.g., sacrifices, prayers, and libations), and the correct times of day or night to conduct these rituals (*VA* 4.19). Yet, the extant fragment from Eusebius *On Sacrifices* mentions none of these things but was concerned only with spiritual sacrifice offered by the human mind to the supreme god, while the fragment from Porphyry mentions only that sacrifices to different gods differ in nature. These differences might suggest that Philostratus only knew of this alleged work of Apollonius by its title and had guessed at its content. Indeed, Dzielska chastised Bowie for naively following Philostratus's claim that *On Sacrifices* was about offering sacrifices when in reality the document was entirely against offering material sacrifices to the deity.[89]

Further, the contents of the two fragments do not cohere well with the sacrificial practices and instructions of Apollonius preserved in the *VA*. Dzielska also catalogs the differences between the *VA* and the fragment *On Sacrifices*: (1) The Apollonius of the *VA* indicates that pure material sacrifices (e.g., incense, libations, honey cakes, and traditional sacrifices) may be presented to the deity, whereas the Apollonius of *On Sacrifices* claims that the deity needs no sacrifices at all; and (2) the Apollonius of the *VA* presents prayer as the highest form of sacrifice, whereas the Apollonius of *On Sacrifices* forbids even the sacrifice of oral prayer.[90] Dzielska concludes from these discrepancies that Philostratus either did not know the contents of *On Sacrifices* at all, had reinterpreted the work, or may have known of it but that it was inaccessible to him because it was written in Apollonius's native Syriac or a Semitic style (*VA* 4.19).[91] Others suggest that Philostratus may have known the contents of the work, but rejected it in favor of his own agenda.[92]

---

87. Koskenniemi also notes that the fragment is from a tradition that differs from Philostratus. See Koskenniemi, *Der philostrateische Apollonios*, 19; *Apollonios*, 3.

88. Taggart, "Apollonius," 91; Dzielska, *Apollonius*, 141; Flinterman, *Power*, 76–77.

89. Dzielska, *Apollonius*, 147, 149.

90. Dzielska, *Apollonius*, 147.

91. Dzielska, *Apollonius*, 141, 149–50.

92. Taggart allows that Philostratus may have suppressed the contents of this

ITEMS 1-2

The discrepancies in Apollonius's sacrificial ideology found in *On Sacrifices* and the *VA* have resulted in three theories: (1) the fragment preserves the essence of a larger document and contradicts the *VA* (e.g., Taggart, Flinterman, Dzielska, as seen above); (2) the *VA* and fragment can be reconciled (e.g., Petzke[93]): the *VA* accurately preserves what Apollonius taught about sacrifices to the lower gods, whereas the fragment preserves his teaching about the worship of the supreme deity; and (3) Porphyry's version of the fragment hints at two forms of sacrifice, but the fragments of Porphyry and Eusebius only preserved a detailed discussion about offerings to the supreme god: the section about how to sacrifice to the lesser gods was missing. Option three, while possible, is largely an argument from silence; there is no clear indication that a lost section of *On Sacrifices* gave the specifics of sacrifice to the other gods. Option two is problematic as well, for Apollonius's worship of the traditional gods in the *VA* appears to be identical to that of his worship of the Sun god,[94] perhaps also known as Zeus,[95] who appears to be the most likely candidate for the role of the high god in the *VA*.[96] In the *VA*, the Sun is worshipped

---

fragment, if he had known of it. See Taggart, "Apollonius," 98. Dzielska also suggested that Philostratus may have thought that the content of *On Sacrifices* differed from what he thought Apollonius should taught. See Dzielska, *Apollonius*, 147.

93. Petzke, *Die Traditionen*, 210. Petzke believes the fragment upholds a polytheistic viewpoint, with one supreme god presiding over the pantheon. See Petzke, *Die Traditionen*, 199. This perspective resembles the view expressed in *VA* 3.35, where the creator of the universe is compared to the captain of a ship and the lesser gods who govern parts of it are likened unto the sailors.

94. In the *VA*, Apollonius's teaching is consistent throughout. He teaches others how they should pray and sacrifice to the gods (*VA* 4.40.2; 8.39; e.g., Heracles accepted only an offering of a honey cake and frankincense; *VA* 8.29). He seems to have followed the advice that he gave to others, praying to the gods and sacrificing incense to them. Apollonius prayed to all the gods at once (*VA* 4.40.2), to Heracles (*VA* 8.7.28-29), to Apollo (*VA* 8.13.2), but he also prayed to his favored Sun god as well (*VA* 1.31; 7.31; 8.13.2). Just as he instructed others to offer incense to the gods, he offered incense to the Sun (*VA* 1.31).

95. In the *VA*, Apollonius prayed aloud to Zeus (*VA* 5.30; 8.19) and did not object to pouring out a libation to him (*VA* 2.7), as long as wine was not involved. In similar fashion, Empedocles offered an ox made of pastry to the god (*VA* 1.1).

96. It is unclear whether Apollonius regarded the Sun or Zeus as the high god of the *VA*. Perhaps he viewed them as one and the same deity. Kosenniemi notes that Philostratus's Apollonius revered Helios above all and was almost exclusively dedicated to him, although he did not advocate for sun worship. His daily worship of a deity was unusual in the ancient world. See Koskenniemi, *Die philostraetische Apollonios*, 71, 74. Apollonius prayed to the Sun at daybreak (*VA* 2.38; 7.31) and evening (*VA* 8.13.2), along with performing regular rituals in honor of the Sun (*VA* 6.10; 7.10). The Wise Ones of India, the most enlightened characters in the book, also prayed to the Sun, perhaps giving another indication that this is the supreme deity of the *VA* (*VA* 3.15.2).

with audible prayer (*VA* 1.31) rather than by silence and with incense (*VA* 1.31) rather than with immaterial sacrifice. Thus, the *VA* contradicts what the fragment *On Sacrifices* directs concerning the proper method of worshipping the high god. Further, there is no other god in the *VA* to whom Apollonius was said to offer non-material, rational, or silent sacrifice. On balance, then, option one seems to be the best alternative. The *Letters of Apollonius* complicate this matter even further, for they claim that multiple deities (Zeus of Olympia and Apollo of Delphi) did not need sacrifices, particularly not bloody ones, whereas the fragment *On Sacrifices* seems to only address the preferences of the one high god. This suggests that there are two or three traditions about what Apollonius taught and practiced concerning sacrifices: multiple gods rejected material sacrifices (*Letters of Apollonius*), the supreme god alone rejected material sacrifices (fragment *On Sacrifice*), and all the gods accepted non-bloody, material sacrifices (*VA*).

CONCLUSION

The pre-Philostratean texts surveyed in this chapter were texts either not mentioned by Philostratus (Lucian; Dio Cassius; Philostatus, *VS*) or were mentioned but not employed as a source in the *VA* (*On Sacrifices*). The aspects of Apollonius found in these documents that support Philostratus's narrative are that Apollonius performed supernatural deeds (Dio Cassius), had disciples (Lucian), may have been a Pythagorean philosopher (Lucian), and may have had a relationship with various characters—Scopelian and Dio Chrysostom—mentioned in the *VA* (Philostratus, *VS*). The differences from the *VA* were that Apollonius was regarded as a disreputable magician and sorcerer (Lucian; Dio Cassius) in the earliest texts—a view that Philostratus knew of but fought against—and that he allowed for non-bloody material sacrifices to the gods (contra *Epp. Apoll.* 26, 27 and *On Sacrifice*). In addition to these examples, Philostratus himself seems to have modified his views on Apollonius a bit (*VS*). These tensions are significant, for they may indicate that Philostratus modified the earlier tradition about Apollonius or that he had received alternate traditions.

Yet, a good case could be made for Zeus as the supreme god of the *VA*, for he is the architect of the universe who holds the seasons winds, stars in his power (*VA* 4.30). When Domitian commanded Apollonius to look at the god of all mankind, referring to himself, Apollonius stared heavenward toward Zeus (*VA* 8.4).

9

Items 3–4

Pre-Philostratean Sources Used or Mentioned in the *VA*

THIS CHAPTER WILL INVESTIGATE the pre-Philostratean sources that were used by Philostratus in the composition of the *VA* or that were mentioned by him. This chapter will focus on items three and four of the Apollonian Decalogue. As a reminder, these points are:

> Item 3—Philostratus relied upon several earlier sources in the composition of his biography of Apollonius (e.g., the biographical materials of Maximus of Aegae and Moiragenes).
>
> Item 4—Philostratus differed strongly from Moiragenes's perspective on Apollonius, which resulted in his disparagement of that source.

These two points are important because they indicate that Philostratus used or interacted with previously existing sources in his composition of the *VA*. Item 3 reinforces the point of the previous chapter that Philostratus was not the first author to write about Apollonius. Altogether, six identifiable sources predate Philostratus's *VA*. Three that were not mentioned by him were treated in the previous chapter (Lucian, Dio Cassius, *On Sacrifices*). The three that will be covered in this chapter pre-existed the *VA* and were used by Philostratus in its composition: the biography of Moiragenes, the accounts of Maximus of Aegae, and a collection of the

PART 3: INVESTIGATING THE APOLLONIAN DECALOGUE

Letters of Apollonius.[1] Item 4 of the Apollonian Decalogue strengthens the findings of the previous chapter by demonstrating that the earlier picture of Apollonius did not always match the picture that Philostratus gave in the *VA*.

THE SOURCES FOR THE *VA*

Philostratus listed six sources he used to compose his work in a rather lengthy passage at the beginning of the *VA* (1.2–3). These sources were (1) materials that he collected from the many cities that were devoted to Apollonius, from shrines he had reformed, and from the reports of other people. Philostratus does not indicate whether these sources were written, oral, or a mixture of both;[2] (2) a collection of Apollonius's letters; (3) the notebooks preserving the memoirs of Damis, a disciple of Apollonius, which provided the framework for the *VA*; (4) a book by Maximus of Aegeae; (5) the will of Apollonius, which is no longer extant; and (6) a four-volume biography of Apollonius by Moiragenes, that Philostratus dismissed as unworthy. Of these six sources, the collection of the letters has survived along with some evidence concerning the existence and contents of the works of Moiragenes, Maximus, and Damis. This chapter will treat the first three of these surviving works while reserving the examination of the controversial memoir of Damis for the next chapter.

Moiragenes

Biographical information about Moiragenes (or Moeragenes) is sparse. All that can be known of him derives from a few brief passages in the writings of Origen and Philostratus. Origen contributed a few details about him and his writing in his *Contra Celsum* (c. AD 248):

---

1. The *Letters of Apollonius* were not included in the Apollonian Decalogue because they were not uniformly mentioned by Apollonius scholars. Since, however, they were used by Philostratus in the *VA* and pre-dated him they will be included in the examination of sources conducted in this chapter.

2. Koskenniemi surmised that these materials were used to flesh out some of the fourth book of the *VA* because it is organized by Apollonius's visits to various cities and places. Yet, he did not believe that these legends and stories about Apollonius contributed much to understanding the real Apollonius for they seem to drink of the same spirit of the second and third centuries as did the apocryphal Acts of the apostles. For more detail on this topic, see Koskenniemi, *Apollonios*, 177.

> If, now, it had been our purpose to treat of magic, we could have added a few remarks in addition to what we have already said on this topic; but since it is only the more important matters which we have to notice in answer to Celsus, we shall say of magic, that any one who chooses to inquire whether philosophers were ever led captive by it or not, can read what has been written by Moiragenes regarding the memoirs of the magician and philosopher Apollonius of Tyana, in which this individual, who is not a Christian, but a philosopher, asserts that some philosophers of no mean note were won over by the magic power possessed by Apollonius, and resorted to him as a sorcerer; and among these, I think, he especially mentioned Euphrates and a certain Epicurean.[3]

The yield of information from this passage is meager: Moiragenes was a philosopher, a non-Christian, and had written a work entitled *Memoirs of Apollonius of Tyana, Magician and Philosopher* (Τὰ Ἀπολλωνίου τοῦ Τυανέως μάγου καὶ φιλοσόφου ἀπομνημονεύματα). Philostratus's comments about Moiragenes contribute nothing to the information about the author himself except for the biased comment that he was inaccurate in his assessment of Apollonius (*VA* 1.3.2). Neither of these authors contributes to a better understanding of Moiragenes's identity, his dates, or the date of his biography about Apollonius. Some historians have pondered whether this author was the same Moiragenes who was a contemporary of Plutarch,[4] an Athenian, and an initiate of the Perfect Mysteries.[5] Such an identification would help to narrow down a date for the author.[6] Although this possibility is intriguing, especially given the rarity of the name Moiragenes, there is insufficient evidence to make this

---

3. Origen, *Cels.* 6.41 (*ANF* 4:591).

4. For overviews of this discussion in the older literature see, Phillimore, *In Honour*, xxvi–xxx; Bowie, "Apollonius of Tyana," 1678.

5. Plutarch, *Quaest. conv.*, 4.6.

6. Phillimore notes that if this author is the same as Plutarch's Moiragenes, then "we can hardly suppose him to have written later than the reign of Pius, perhaps as early as Hadrian" (Phillimore, *In Honour*, xxvii). Phillimore further suggests that the work of Moiragenes could have been the source from which Lucian gained his opinion of Apollonius that was expressed in *Alexander*, since there is no earlier attested account of Apollonius. See Phillimore, *In Honour*, xxvi. Bowie writes, "Several scholars have supposed that he might be the Moiragenes of Plutarch's 'Quaestiones convivales', a work parts of which postdate 99 A.D. and which was dedicated before 116" (Bowie, "Apollonius of Tyana," 1678). If Bowie's supposition that this figure was Moiragenes Dromocleous is correct, then the date could be further narrowed down, for this figure would have been born around AD 75. See Bowie, "Apollonius of Tyana," 1679.

identification.[7] Bowie also suggests that if Moiragenes were an Athenian, that portion of Philostratus's polemic against his biography may have been due to domestic rivalry between professional writers.[8] This clutch of facts and speculations about the author can be supplemented by a few more details about the work itself.

Moiragenes's biography of Apollonius is no longer extant. But because this text was attested by both Philostratus and Origen, its existence is beyond doubt.[9] A few details about its contents can be determined for these two authors agreed that Moiragenes regarded Apollonius as a magician. Origen indicates this both by the title of the work, which identifies Apollonius as a sorcerer, and by his citing of a specific episode from it in which Apollonius used his powers to get the better of a group of philosophers that included Euphrates the Stoic and an unnamed Epicurean.[10] Philostratus also relates that Moiragenes's biography was four volumes long and inaccurate (VA 1.3.2). Another detail, presumably taken from Moiragene's book by Philostratus, is that Apollonius had authored a book on planetary prophecy (περὶ μαντείας ἀστέρων, VA 3.41). However, Philostratus does not dwell on this subject,[11] perhaps because astrology and prophecy might undermine his carefully argued case that Apollonius was not a magician.[12] Apart from these details, nothing else is known about this astrological work ascribed to Apollonius.

Most modern research on this lost biography has focused on whether Moiragenes was sympathetic toward Apollonius. Several scholars

---

7. Van der Stockt remarks that it would be marvelous if this was the Moeragenes of the VA and the Moeragenes of Plutarch's *Quaestiones Convivales* IV 6 were one and the same person—the latter knew a good deal about the Jewish faith—but there is not enough information to make a positive identification. See Van der Stockt, "Never the Twain," 190.

8. Bowie, "Apollonius of Tyana," 1679.

9. Koskenniemi, *Apollonios*, 175–76.

10. Philostratus may allude to the same event in VA 5.39, where Euphrates attempted to strike Apollonius, but somehow missed his target. Philostratus claims that "many" (perhaps including Moiragenes) attributed the failed attack to Apollonius's cunning. Several scholars have identified this event mentioned by Origen (*Cels.* 6.41) with the one recorded in the VA. See Bowie, "Philostratus: Writer of Fiction," 194; Bowersock, Introduction to *Life of Apollonius*, 11; Philostratus, *Apollonius of Tyana, Philostratus*, 3:91, n. 9.

11. Praet writes, "[a]s has been observed by Flinterman, Anderson, and others, Philostratus seems to distance himself from this work, even from its very existence" (Praet, "Pythagoreanism," 310).

12. Praet, "Pythagoreanism," 310.

have argued that Moiragenes portrayed Apollonius in a negative light.[13] For instance, Bowersock remarked on Origen's account that, "from his comment it appears that the account was hostile, perhaps incorporating the views of Apollonius's greatest enemy, the long-bearded philosopher Euphrates."[14] Yet, Bowie, swimming against the prevailing scholarly opinion of his day, argued that Moiragenes approved of Apollonius.[15] Raynor advanced Bowie's position by offering a compelling explanation for why Philostratus might have taken issue with Moiragenes's portrayal.[16] Because the word "magician" (μάγος) could be understood in either a pejorative or complementary sense, he postulated that Moiragenes had seen Apollonius as both a magician, in the positive sense of the word, and as a philosopher. However, Raynor argued, Philostratus was embarrassed by the term "magician" and was "accordingly concerned that his subject should be recognized to be no common thaumaturge, but an ascetic Pythagorean philosopher; he stresses that all the wonders with which the sage is associated derive from his particular wisdom and the high spiritual state which he attained . . . In short, it was no hostility on the part of Moiragenes which turned Philostratus against him, but rather misplaced enthusiasm."[17] Raynor believed that, whereas Philostratus emphasized only the philosophical dimension of the sage in the *VA*, Moiragenes had blended the magical and the philosophical aspects of Apollonius in his biography. It appears that the interpretation of Bowie and Raynor is currently adopted by most scholars.[18]

The ramifications of Raynor's view are important in sorting out the various traditions about Apollonius. If Raynor is correct that Moiragenes regarded Apollonius as a white magician—a Gandalf rather than a Saruman—this view may represent a missing link between the earliest

13. Harris, "Apollonius of Tyana," 191–92. For instance, Phillimore argued that this Moiragenes view was skeptical of Apollonius and for this reason Philostratus and his patroness, Julia, dismissed it: "It is a case of *odium philosophicum*. Moeragenes' point of view was not pious towards Julia's candidate for apotheosis, but skeptical, Lucianic, Epicurean" (Phillimore, *In Honour*, xxv).

14. Bowersock, Introduction to *Life of Apollonius*, 11.

15. Bowie pointed out that the scale of Moiragenes's four-volume biography suggests a positive view of Apollonius. He also pointed out that the word μάγος, used in the title of Moiragenes's work, was not necessarily negative, as is shown by two letters of Apollonius that use it in a positive sense. See Bowie, "Apollonius of Tyana," 1674.

16. Raynor, "Moeragenes and Philostratus, 222–26.

17. Raynor, "Moeragenes and Philostratus," 224.

18. C. P. Jones, "Apollonius of Tyana, Hero," 77; Flinterman, *Power*, 70; Koskenniemi, *Apollonios*, 175.

level of tradition (Lucian) and the final one (Philostratus). Flinterman convincingly distinguished three layers of Apollonian tradition.[19] The first stratum of tradition was that of Lucian and Dio Cassius in which Apollonius was thought of as a magician and charlatan; this first view is entirely negative concerning Apollonius. The second layer of tradition was the sympathetic view of Moiragenes; this perspective considered Apollonius to be both a benevolent magician and a philosopher. The third was Philostratus's view that recast Apollonius solely as a philosopher, whose supernatural powers were attributed to his ascetic lifestyle and close communion with the gods rather than to magic. However, if Raynor is incorrect, then all the sources before Philostratus viewed Apollonius as a black magician, including that of Moiragenes. In either case, Philostratus appears to have been an innovator by stressing Apollonius as a philosopher to the exclusion of his role as a sorcerer.

Maximus of Aegae

Practically nothing is known about Maximus of Aegae except for the few details that Philostratus preserves: he oversaw imperial correspondence and was a native of Aegae in Cilicia (*VA* 1.12.2). Years later, Hierocles quipped that Maximus was a highly educated man, yet he may have simply deduced this fact from reading the description of this author in Philostratus's text.[20] About a hundred years ago, Meyer wrote off Maximus's account as a fiction that was created by Philostratus and he questioned its authenticity because of several chronological errors in the section treating Apollonius's stay in Aegae.[21] Later scholars, however, have tended to accept the authenticity of the work because (1) the chronological issues that the Maximus material produced in the *VA* are likely to have been caused by Philostratus's failure to successfully incorporate a real source into his biography; had he manufactured these stories himself, he could have easily fit them into his storyline;[22] and, (2) the reality of Maximus is difficult to deny for, even though the name of the emperor he served

---

19. Flinterman, *Power*, 70.

20. Phillimore, pulling no punches, noted that in Hierocles's writing, "the same complement includes the idiotic Damis" (Phillimore, *In Honour*, xxiii).

21. Meyer, "Apollonios von Tyana," 401–5. Bowersock writes, "This source and its author, a Maximus of Aegae, have been called into question by modern scholars" (Bowersock, Introduction to *Life of Apollonius*, 11).

22. Flinterman, *Power*, 68–69.

is unknown,[23] his high post in the Roman government would have been difficult for Philostratus to fake.[24] Although the reality of this work is widely accepted today there is unfortunately not enough evidence to postulate dates for either Maximus or his work.

The content of Maximus's work is indicated by its presumed title: *All the Things that Apollonius did in Aegae* (τὰ ἐν Αἰγαῖς Ἀπολλωνίου πάντα).[25] Because this description suggests a collection of local traditions about Apollonius, most scholars believe that the accounts in the *VA* recounting his youth in Aegae were based on this source (*VA* 1.7–12).[26] As partial confirmation of this view, the story of a Roman governor's attempt to seduce the young Apollonius is directly linked to the material attributed to Maximus (*VA* 1.12). Perhaps Maximus's book also served as the basis for Apollonius's visits to nearby Aspendus and Antioch (*VA* 1.7–16).[27] Based on the assumption that these early portions of the *VA* are taken from Maximus's account, academics have attempted to tease out various agendas from Maximus's book. These include the suggestion that the work sought the rehabilitation of Apollonius's reputation[28] or that it was a propagandist tract promoting Aegae over its rival Tarsus in the context of their second-century AD rivalry.[29] So then, the historical errors

---

23. Phillimore suggested that Maximus served the reigning emperor at the time of the *VA*'s composition (i.e., Septimius, Caracalla, Elagabalus, or Alexander). For this perspective, see Phillimore, *In Honour*, xxiii. Others have suggested that he could have served sometime between the reigns of Trajan and Caracalla. For this position, see Graf, "Maximos von Aigai," 72; Flinterman, *Power*, 69.

24. C. P. Jones, "Apollonius of Tyana, Hero," 77. As Bowersock convincingly argues that Maximus was a real figure, who had been placed in charge of the emperor's Greek correspondence. He comments, "that post could not have had a fictitious incumbent" (Bowersock, Introduction to *Life of Apollonius*, 11).

25. *VA* 1.3.2. For scholars who see this as a title, see Phillimore, *Philostratus*, xxii–xxiii; Graf, "Maximos von Aigai," 65.

26. Phillimore, *Philostratus*, xxii; Flinterman, *Power*, 68; Koskenniemi, *Apollonios*, 175.

27. Bowie, *Apollonius of Tyana*, 1684.

28. Phillimore, *In Honour*, xxiii.

29. Flinterman suggests that Maximus's book was propaganda intended to increase the status of Aegae against its rival city of Tarsus (*VA* 1.7). The status of Aegae increased in the second century. Perhaps Maximus thought that linking Apollonius to Aegae's temple of Asclepius was a means of increasing the city's reputation. See Flinterman, *Power*, 69. As perhaps another piece of evidence of such a purpose, Graf notes that Tarsus was slighted in *VA* 1.7, perhaps because of the jealousy that other cities had due to Tarsus's reputation for philosophy, one that challenged Athens and Alexandria. See Graf, "Maximos von Aigai," 70–71. Since, Philostratus had strong associations with Athens, the rivalry suggested by this text may been due to tensions between Athens

PART 3: INVESTIGATING THE APOLLONIAN DECALOGUE

within *VA* 1.7–12, such as its apologetic slant and supernatural content,[30] raise serious questions about the historical trustworthiness of Maximus's account, unless Philostratus was responsible for adding these emphases while editing it.

Despite its dubitable historical merit, Maximus's account may provide yet another wrinkle to the traditions about Apollonius, for scholars are not entirely in agreement about which version of Apollonius is depicted in this text. Although Maximus's Apollonius is a Pythagorean philosopher (*VA* 1.7–8), one scholar also spies a magician in these tales,[31] while another believes that all traces of a magician are absent from them.[32] Within Maximus's account, Apollonius cured a drunkard by altering his diet (*VA* 1.9), knew the intimate details of the immoral lifestyle of a petitioner (*VA* 1.11), and accurately predicted the death of a governor (*VA* 1.12). The first of these items does not necessarily constitute a supernatural act, but at the same time, it resembles cures performed by the Wise Ones of India, who were called magicians by some.[33] The second and third deeds, which displayed Apollonius's ability to know a person's past actions and to predict the future, are supernatural, but the text does not indicate whether this information derived from magic, his ascetic training, his divine nature (*VA* 1.4),[34] or the god Asclepius (*VA* 1.9; 1.10.2), who had told the priest of Aegae that he would heal people with Apollonius serving as his witness (*VA* 1.8). So then, is unclear whether Maximus intended to portray Apollonius as a sorcerer, a healer, or merely the favorite of Asclepius.

---

and Tarsus in his own day rather than to a rivalry between Tarsus and Aegae in the time of Apollonius.

30. Anderson calls Maximus's work "miraculous drivel" (Anderson, *Philostratus*, 124).

31. Bowie, *Apollonius*, 1684. Graf describes Apollonius as a combination of ascetic philosopher, critic of religion, and magical miracle man ("magischem Wundermann"). See Graf, *Maximos von Aigai*, 73.

32. Koskenniemi, *Apollonios*, 175.

33. The Wise Ones cast out a demon with a letter (*VA* 3.38), restored a lame man's hip by massage (*VA* 3.39), proscribed a cure for miscarriage by releasing a hare during a woman's labor (*VA* 3.39), and instructed a father to give a boiled owl's eggs to his sons to prevent them from desiring wine (*VA* 3.40).

34. The account of Apollonius's supernatural birth (*VA* 1.4) is probably not based on Maximus's account. Yet, in this very passage, Apollonius is said to have been the incarnation of the god Proteus, and notes that he possessed all knowledge and foreknowledge, skills that are somewhat analogous to those displayed in the section of the *VA* that is probably based on Maximus's account.

Although Maximus's account is favorable to Apollonius, it seems unlikely that he had depicted Apollonius as both a praiseworthy magician and a philosopher as Moiragenes had done. If he had, it would be difficult to explain why Philostratus did not censure him as he did Moiragenes. More likely, Philostratus at least thought Maximus agreed with his position that Apollonius was a philosopher and a worker of mighty deeds, but that his powers did not derive from magic. In support of this interpretation, the material that seems to derive from Maximus (*VA* 1.7–12) does not contain miracles like the ones appearing later in the book that ran the risk of being associated with magic.[35] In the end, Maximus's Apollonius comes off looking more like a Pythagorean philosopher (*VA* 1.7–8), a healer (*VA* 1.8–10), and an expert in sacrifices (*VA* 1.10–11) than a magician.

Letters of Apollonius

The *Letters of Apollonius* constitute the second largest source of Apollonius material, being surpassed in length only by the *VA*. This material, or at least some of it, may have been written by Apollonius of Tyana. If some of the letters in this collection are authentic, they would be among the earliest sources available for the study of Apollonius and would predate the *VA* by over a century.[36] Whether or not some of them belong to Apollonius, they, along with the fragment *On Sacrifices*, are the only extant documents to have been attributed to the Tyanean. The following section will discuss the authenticity of this collection of letters and their relationship to the *VA* with which it overlaps some in content.

The collection of letters attributed to Apollonius survives in three bodies of literature: the *VA* (14 letters),[37] the collection of John Stobaeus (22 or 23 letters),[38] and two groups of medieval manuscripts that differ

---

35. These miracles that appear later in the *VA* include exorcisms, resurrections, speaking with dead heroes, preventing earthquakes, warding off plagues, disappearances, and travel over great distances in a short time.

36. Horsley, review of *Philostratus*, 162–63.

37. In the current collection of Apollonius's letters, the letters from the *VA* are numbered 42a–h and 77a–f.

38. The letters preserved by Stobaeus are numbered 78 [or 79]–100. Penella lists twenty-two letters by Stobaeus. See Penella, *Letters*, 3. However, Jones counts twenty-three letters. See Philostratus, *Apollonius of Tyana*, 3:6.

PART 3: INVESTIGATING THE APOLLONIAN DECALOGUE

somewhat concerning date and content.[39] The current editions of Apollonius's letters now contain a hundred epistles written to, from, or about Apollonius, along with a few fragments attributed to him that are more like "snappy comments" than actual letters.[40]

The epistolary collection's content is diverse, and its arrangement is haphazard. The letters do not appear to be arranged chronologically, although a handful of them give the impression of having been written around the same time (*Epp. Apoll.* 42b–42e).[41] There appears to have been an attempt to group a few of the letters,[42] which may suggest that they were published or arranged by an editor or, if they derive from multiple sources, by multiple editors.[43] Some letters appear to be grouped based on their addressees[44] or by similarity of theme.[45] Still, others appear to be placed more randomly, sometimes in clusters and sometimes not, such as those written to his relatives and friends from Tyana.[46] A few letters seem out of place in this collection in that they are written to Apollonius (*Epp. Apoll.* 62, 77f). Even more oddly, some are written "neither by nor to Apollonius,"[47] but rather spoke of him (*Epp. Apoll.* 53, 77b), or discussed a dispute between foreign kings without a mention of the Tyanean at all (*Epp. Apoll.* 59). Horsley notes that the inclusion of such epistolary outliers "points to what we may with due reserve term a 'hagiographical' motive in their being assembled—or perhaps even in some instances devised."[48]

For all the lack of a recognizable organization in the collection, a surprisingly coherent picture of Apollonius and his world still emerges

---

39. Penella, *Letters*, 4–18; Philostratus, *Apollonius of Tyana*, 3:4–6.
40. Horsley, review of *Philostratus*, 162.
41. Horsley, review of *Philostratus*, 162.
42. Philostratus, *Apollonius of Tyana* 3:4.
43. Horsley, review of *Philostratus*, 162.
44. E.g., letters to the philosophers Euphrates (*Epp. Apoll.* 1–8, 14–18, 50–52, but 60, 82, 94), Dio of Prusa (*Epp. Apoll.* 9–10, but 90), and letters to and from Musonius Rufus (*Epp. Apoll.* 42b–42e) are grouped together, as are letters to magistrates in Palestine (*Epp. Apoll.* 11), officials in Syria (*Epp. Apoll.* 12–13), the emperor Vespasian (*Epp. Apoll.* 42f–42h), and the emperor Domitian (*Epp. Apoll.* 20–21).
45. Penella, *Letters*, 19–20. In this same entry, Penella noted grouping of letters under the themes of praise and gratitude to addressees (11–12), the Olympic games (24–25), sacrifice (26–27), and criticism of the use of Roman names by Greeks (77d–e).
46. *Epp. Apoll.* 35, 44–45, 55, 72–73, 95.
47. See Jones's comments in Philostratus, *Apollonius of Tyana*, 3:5.
48. Horsley, review of *Philostratus*, 162.

from these epistles. The collection of letters reveals a man actively engaged in politics,[49] religion,[50] philosophy,[51] and various other activities of everyday life.[52] Much like the epistles of the apostle Paul, the impression of Apollonius that materializes is of a man who employed his letters to communicate with disciples and friends, extend his influence, exercise authority, correct religious errors, and grapple with opponents. While this depiction of Apollonius that emerges from the epistles is fascinating, are any of these letters really from the pen of the man from Tyana?

The survival of a collection of Apollonian letters that pre-date Philostratus is certainly within the realm of possibility. As it happens, several ancient authors mentioned such collections of the Tyanean's correspondence. Philostratus quoted fourteen letters of Apollonius in the *VA*,[53] rejected a fabricated letter of Apollonius (*VA* 7.35) that may have belonged to yet another epistolary collection,[54] and claimed that Hadrian housed a collection of Apollonius's letters at Antium (*VA* 8.20).[55] Phi-

---

49. In addition to writing Roman emperors, Apollonius wrote political bodies and cities (*Epp. Apoll.* 25, 33, 38–40, 42a, 47, 56, 63–65, 70, 71, 75–76), a consul (*Epp. Apoll.* 58), a proconsul (*Epp. Apoll.* 67a), procurators (*Epp. Apoll.* 31, 51), a magistrate (*Epp. Apoll.* 32), a lawgiver (*Epp. Apoll.* 29), and foreign kings (*Epp. Apoll.* 28, 59, 61, 77c).

50. Apollonius communicated with priests (*Epp. Apoll.* 27) and cult personnel at various sanctuaries (*Epp. Apoll.* 26, 65–67).

51. Apollonius addressed philosophers of several schools (*Epp. Apoll.* 42, 43, 74, 77e), in addition to addressing the key figures of Euphrates, Dio, and Musonius mentioned above.

52. Apollonius wrote to authors (*Epp. Apoll.* 57), a physician (*Epp. Apoll.* 23), Olympic judges (*Epp. Apoll.* 24), grain merchants (*Epp. Apoll.* 77a), disciples (*Epp. Apoll.* 77, 85, 92–93), and Brahmans (*Epp. Apoll.* 78).

53. Philostratus himself quotes fourteen letters in full that also appear in this collection, appears to quote an opening sentence from another letter (*Epp. Apoll.* 9) and alludes to two others (*Epp. Apoll.* 63 and 71). Philostratus may have also based two of his quotations in the *VA* on the letters, even though he does not indicate this in the text (*VA* 5.4, *Epp. Apoll.* 9; *VA* 6.29, *Epp. Apoll.* 77d). He also mentioned letters written by Apollonius to the Delphians and Egyptians (*VA* 1.2), to Bassus and Dio (*VA* 4.26, 5.40), and to numerous letters to Euphrates (*VA* 5.39), beyond the one to him that he quotes.

54. However, Dzielska believes that this letter "was probably written by Philostratus himself in order to magnify the seriousness of Apollonius' trial and the way he was beset by slanderers and informers" (Dzielska, *Apollonius*, 39).

55. Although Phillimore believed the *Letters of Apollonius* are largely apocryphal, he did argue that there was a collection of authentic letters at Antium, "for imposture so early as the time of Hadrian is surely incredible" (Phillimore, *In Honour*, xiii). However, Philostratus merely states his opinion that the letters came into the emperor's possession at the same time as a book containing the doctrines of Pythagoras, which was given to Apollonius by a mysterious figure in the cave of Trophonius (*VA* 8.19–20). Although there may have been letters at Antium, there is no guarantee apart from Philostratus's

lostratus of Lemnos (first half of the third century), who remarked on the superior quality of Apollonius's epistolary style, must have had access to some such collection of letters.[56] Porphyry quoted a portion of one of Apollonius's letters,[57] and Stobaeus (early fifth century?) included twenty-two or twenty-three letters in his anthology under the name of Apollonius (*Epp. Apoll.* 79–100).[58] So then, there is ample evidence for collections of Apollonius's epistles in ancient times and some are even willing to concede that the historical Apollonius wrote letters to important figures of his age.[59] In theory, then, authentic letters could have survived. Yet, it is an entirely different matter to determine whether any of this century of epistles preserved in this collection were penned by the historical Apollonius or whether they were all forgeries. Although an occasional supporter of the authenticity of the entire collection of letters can be found (e.g., Morton Smith),[60] most scholars are skeptical about the genuineness of some of the letters,[61] and others believe that they are mostly apocryphal.[62]

Assessing the authenticity of these letters is difficult for several reasons. One challenge to their authentication is that there are no known writings of Apollonius with which to compare the letters apart from the brief and contested fragment *On Sacrifices*.[63] Another is that the letters in this anthology possibly derive from several authors, perhaps including Apollonius himself, thus leaving investigators with the nearly impossible task of separating these various layers of tradition.[64] As Jones opines,

---

statement that they were deposited there in the time of Hadrian or that they were any more authentic than the (likely fictional) document retrieved from Trophonius's cave.

56. Penella, *Letters*, 2; Philostratus, *Apollonius of Tyana* 3:91.

57. *Epp. Apoll.*, 78 is quoted in Porphyry, *De styge*. See Penella, *Letters*, 3, 133; C. P. Jones, "Some Letters of Apollonius," 249; Philostratus, *Apollonius of Tyana* 3:95.

58. Penella, *Letters*, 3.

59. C. P. Jones, "Some Letters of Apollonius," 249. Cf. Philostratus lengthy list of those who received letters from Apollonius (*VA* 1.2.3).

60. Koskenniemi wrote that Smith's wholesale acceptance of the letters shows that he did not subject them to source critical principles. See Koskenniemi, *Apollonios*, 150.

61. Phillimore, *In Honour*, ci; Penella, *Letters*, 25; Bowersock, *Introduction to Life of Apollonius*, 11. Koskenniemi, who sees this collection, along with the *VA*, as the most important source concerning Apollonius, believes some letters were written by Philostratus (who quotes them in the *VA*) but that others were independent of it (e.g., *Epp. Apoll.* 53). See Koskenniemi, *Apollonios*, 1.

62. Phillimore, *In Honour*, xiii; Dzielska, *Apollonius*, 39, 43, 190.

63. Penella, *Letters*, 24.

64. For instance, a transitional passage connecting two letters suggests that they

"[t]here will probably never be agreement on criteria for judging which of the letters are authentic."[65] Rather than making the case for authenticity for the entire collection, the current trend seems to be to study each letter in isolation and let it stand or fall on its own merit.[66]

A few promising advances have been made in confirming and rejecting the authenticity of some of these letters. For instance, the discovery of an inscription in Sardis confirmed several details mentioned in a group of Apollonius's letters, proving that their author was aware of early local traditions. *Epp. Apoll.* 56, 75, and 75a claimed that Sardis was a cult center for Demeter and spoke of the earth "bringing crops" (ἡ γῆ φέρει καρπὸν ὑμῖν; *Epp. Apoll.* 56). These two statements were unverified until inscriptional evidence on an altar was discovered in 1984 (but this discovery was only published in 1998).[67] The details in these letters suggest an early date for their composition and would certainly allow for the possibility of belonging to the era of Apollonius. Unfortunately, this evidence does not altogether exclude the possibility of pseudepigraphy, for an early forger might also have had access to accurate information about local cults.[68]

---

were extracted from a biography. This transition appears between *Epp. Apoll.* 62 and 63. Bowie favors the view that these letters and the segue were extracted from the biography of Moiragenes for inclusion in the letter anthology. For this perspective, see Bowie, "Apollonius of Tyana," 1677–78. So, in this case, it is difficult to determine whether these letters be regarded as forgeries of the biographer, forgeries unknowingly incorporated into a work by the biographer from an earlier collection of letters, or genuine letters of Apollonius.

65. C. P. Jones, "Some Letters of Apollonius," 249.

66. Koskenniemi opines, "It is therefore by no means out of the question that part of this collection contains real letters, so that the question of authenticity must be considered separately for each letter, although the answer is usually less certain" (Koskenniemi, *Apollonios*, 4). The previous quotation is the author's own translation from German.

67. For the phrase "Bringer of Crops" (Καρποφόρος), see Philostratus, *Apollonius of Tyana*, 3:6; C. P. Jones, "Some Letters of Apollonius," 254–55.

68. *Epp. Apoll.* 26 refers to the cult personnel at Olympia as *theêkoloi* (τοῖς ἐν Ὀλυμπίᾳ θεηκόλοις). This title correctly used the plural form, referring to the three functionaries serving at the site at a given time, and matches several inscriptions discovered at Olympia that date from 36 BC to AD 265; C. P. Jones, "Some Letters of Apollonius," 250–251. Jones also notes the connection between the "feast givers," "dinner guests" (*Epp. Apoll.* 65), and the worship of Artemis: "This very precise detail surely comes from Apollonius himself, and not a forger" ("Some Letters of Apollonius," 253). Yet, Jones's claim does not necessarily follow, since Pausanias, a later author (AD 110–180), makes a similar observation about functionaries at a shrine of Artemis near Arcadian Orchomenos ("Some Letters of Apollonius," 253). This last example demonstrates the possibility that the information given in *Epp. Apoll.* 26 might have been

Other letters have been dismissed as spurious on historical grounds, for Apollonius would have died before the time of an addressee or because some action of his was deemed historically implausible.[69] For example, Valerius, the recipient of one of the letters, creates a dilemma (*Epp. Apoll.* 58.1). If the epistle were written to Valerius Asiaticus Saturninus, it would have been written after the death of Apollonius, at least according to Philostratus's reckoning.[70] If Valerius Festus was the intended recipient, who was a figure well within the timeframe of Apollonius, this identification is likewise problematic for he was not attested as a proconsul of Asia, as the letter indicates.[71] Further, Penella gave a host of reasons why some of these letters are suspect as products of the historical Apollonius. For instance, he noted that (1) because Apollonius's friendship with several famous philosophers is uncertain, the letters he wrote to those individuals are also questionable, (2) many doubt that Apollonius wrote and received letters from Roman emperors, and (3) the letters related to Apollonius's journey to the East are as doubtful as the account written in the *VA*.[72] So then, beyond culling out a few pseudepigraphical letters or identifying a handful of very early ones, there is not at present a way to determine which of the remaining letters are fictitious and which might be genuine.

The most headway in rooting out Apollonian forgeries has been made by comparing the collection of letters with their duplicates in the *VA*. The letters that are duplicated in the *VA* appear in the anthology of letters in two groups (*Epp. Apoll.* 42a–h and 77a–f). Penella thinks that these clusters of material "suggest that the *VA* itself and not, say, some ancient epistolographical anthology was the ultimate source from which these fourteen letters passed into the Byzantine epistolographical tradition."[73] Although these groupings of epistles appear to have been

---

available to a forger living as late as the second century AD.

69. Penella rejected as spurious Apollonius's letters that rebuked Vespasian for revoking the free status of Greece (*Epp. Apoll.* 42f–h; *VA* 5.41). For a discussion of these letters see Penella, *Letters*, 112.

70. Penella, *Letters*, 119; Philostratus, *Apollonius of Tyana*, 3:51, n. 66.

71. Philostratus, *Apollonius of Tyana*, 3:51, n. 66.

72. For these points, see Penella, *Letters* 25. With respect to philosophers, Penella doubted Apollonius's friendship with Musonius Rufus, Demetrius the Cynic, and Dio Chrysostom. Similarly, Dzielska questioned the authenticity of the letters to the philosophers Musonius Rufus and Demetrius, as well as the *VA*'s account of their friendship with Apollonius. See Dzielska, *Apollonius*, 41.

73. Penella, *Letters*, 20.

extracted from the *VA* for inclusion in the later anthology of Apollonius's letters, this does not answer the question of how they came to be in the *VA* in the first place. Two theories of their origin seem most likely: either Philostratus took them from some earlier collection of epistles, as he claims, or he composed them himself.[74]

Several points have been put forward for and against Philostratus's authorship of these letters. If one believes Philostratus invented the figure of Damis, wrote Apollonius's undelivered speech (*VA* 8.7),[75] and invented the fictional *Erotic Letters* of the Philostratean corpus, it would not be much of a stretch to imagine that he could have also composed the letters of Apollonius found in the *VA*. Philostratus might have had strong motives for composing some of these letters.

While it is certainly possible that Philostratus penned these letters, possibilities alone do not constitute strong arguments. Indeed, Penella, playing devil's advocate to his own skeptical position, marshaled several arguments showing that Philostratus could have been working from a previously existing source.[76] For instance, Philostratus sometimes seemed to struggle to insert some of the letters into his narrative. The insertion of a letter to Scopelian into the narrative (*VA* 1.21–22), which created the chronological error of having Apollonius write the epistle in AD 4 when the recipient was a mere child, suggests that Philostratus did not manufacture this letter but was attempting to incorporate an earlier source into his narrative and that he did not spot the mistake.[77] In another instance, the correspondence between Apollonius and Musonius (*Epp. Apoll.* 42 b–e; *VA* 4.46.2–5) is not likely to be the creation of Philostratus, because the latter came off as the more noble philosopher in the exchange. Unfortunately, the arguments on both sides of this issue are inconclusive and, at the end of the day, it is difficult to decide whether the material shared

---

74. Penella, *Letters*, 25.

75. Penella, *Letters*, 25.

76. Penella, *Letters*, 25–26, 138. Petzke also argued that there was evidence for pre-philostratean letters in the anthology and the *VA*. He believed that the negative view of Vespasian in the collection of letters contradicted the depiction of a solid relationship between Apollonius and Vespasian in the *VA*. See Petzke, *Die Traditionen*, 122. However, Penella pointed out that the letters did not reject that emperor wholesale, but merely disagreed with him over his treatment of Greece—a view that was entirely consistent with that of the *VA*. See Penella, *Letters*, 26.

77. Dzielska, however, regards this letter as a Philostratean invention "and, not without reason, he presented Apollonius as Scopelianus' acquaintance" (Dzielska, *Apollonius*, 42).

by the *VA* and the letters stem from Apollonius, Philostratus, or an early forger.[78]

Perhaps the most important issues for the beginner in Apollonian studies to note are the similarities and differences between the *Letters of Apollonius* and the *VA* in their respective portrayals of Apollonius. After reading the letters and the *VA*, one can agree with Penella's assessment that, "[f]or the most part, the Apollonius of the letters and the Philostratean Apollonius are concordant personalities."[79] The details of Apollonius's family are consistent with the *VA*.[80] The sage's appearance,[81] lifestyle,[82] and views on wealth[83] are the same. In both the *Letters* and the *VA*, Apollonius had been accused of being a *magos*, yet he accepted this designation in the non-derogatory definition of the term since it was also used to refer to Pythagoras and the Wise Ones.[84] His supernatural abilities and divine nature are mentioned in the letters.[85] Some of the friends of Apollonius in the *VA* are also mentioned in the letters (e.g., Scopelian),[86] as are his enemies Euphrates and Bassus.[87] His advice to

---

78. Bowie argues that Apollonius's frequent attacks upon his Greek contemporaries for falling below the standards of their "classical ancestors" in the letters is probably authentic, for Philostratus minimizes this aspect of Apollonius's career and does not emphasize it elsewhere. See Bowie, "Apollonius of Tyana," 1680. However, Philostratus does emphasize the return to earlier Greek standards in several works within the corpus (*Gymnasticus*; *Heroicus*), thus leaving open the possibility that this theme was Philostratus's own invention.

79. Penella, *Letters*, 28.

80. Apollonius had a father, who was also named Apollonius (*Epp. Apoll.* 72; *VA* 1.4), and brothers (*Epp. Apoll.* 35, 44, 45, 72, 73; *VA* 1.13; 8.7.3).

81. Apollonius had long hair (*Epp. Apoll.* 8; *VA* 1.8, 32, 8,7.6) and wore linen (*Epp. Apoll.* 8; *VA* 1.8, 32; 2.40; 6.11).

82. The sage followed a strictly vegetarian diet (*Epp. Apoll.* 8, 43; *VA* 1.8, 21, 32, 6.11) and stayed in temples (*Epp. Apoll.* 8?, 66; *VA* 1.8, 16; 4.40; 5.20; 8.15).

83. Apollonius warned the dangers wealth posed for its possessors (*Epp. Apoll.* 6, 14; *VA* 5.22), travelled to gain wisdom not money (*Epp. Apoll.* 35; *VA* 1.18), did not take fees for teaching philosophy, and was critical of instructors who did so (*Epp. Apoll.* 2, 42, 51; *VA* 1.13.3).

84. Penella, *Letters*, 100. *Epp. Apoll.* 16, 17; *VA* 7.39; cf. *VS* 523, 590.

85. Apollonius predicted earthquakes (*Epp. Apoll.* 68; *VA* 4.6) and is described as "godlike" (*Epp. Apoll.* 44.1; *VA* 1.5, 19; 3.50; 4.44; 5.24; 7.21; 8.5). See Penella, *Letters*, 113.

86. *Epp. Apoll.* 19; *VA* 1.24.3.

87. The picture of Euphrates matches that of the *VA* on several points. Apollonius (1) has an ongoing conflict with Euphrates (*Epp. Apoll.* 1–8, 14–18, 50–52; *VA* 1.13.3; 5.38.3; 6.7; 6.9.1; 6.28; 7.9.2; 8.7.11); (2) critiques Euphrates's philosophy (*Epp. Apoll.*18, 50; *VA* 2.26, 5.39, 6.7); (3) condemns Euphrates's interest in money (*Epp. Apoll.* 2, 3, 7;

Domitian about attempting to rule over barbarians was similar to the recommendation given in the *VA* (*Epp. Apoll.* 21; *VA* 8.7.25). Several events are identical in the letters and the *VA*;[88] other events are merely similar to those in the *VA*.[89] The *Letters* also appear to support the *VA*'s claim that Apollonius traveled to Babylon and India,[90] and they seem to confirm that he interacted (in person or through correspondence) with Indian kings and philosophers.[91] If these details were all that the letters contained, they would match the *VA*'s portrayal quite nicely.

However, the picture of Apollonius in the *Letters* does not always align with that of the *VA*. Penella lists several potentially problematic passages:

> *Epp. Apoll.* 8.1 and 43 disagree with the *VA* on Apollonius's bathing habits. *Epp. Apoll.* 10 and 34 differ from the *VA* on the question of Apollonius's attitude towards the usefulness of speaking before large audiences. *Epp. Apoll.* 26 is discordant with both the *VA* and with *Epp. Apoll.* 27 on Apollonius's view of religious sacrifice. *Epp. Apoll.* 53 does not fit with the chronology of the *VA*. *Epp. Apoll.* 58 fails to present the doctrine of metempsychosis, attributed to the Pythagorean Apollonius in the *VA*. *Epp. Apoll.* 14 and 64 may contradict the *VA* on the question of invitations of Apollonius to Italy and Sparta respectively, and *Epp. Apoll.* 24 may do so on the question of Apollonius's attendance at the Olympic Games.[92]

VA 1.13; 8.7.11); (4) accused him of selling wisdom (*Epp. Apoll.* 1; *VA* 1.13.3) and of taking imperial gifts (*Epp. Apoll.* 51; cf. *VA* 5.38 where he petitions for them); and, (5) rebukes him for vilifying the Pythagoreans (*Epp. Apoll.* 50; *VA* 5:37). For the matter of Bassus, see *Epp. Apoll.* 36, 37; *VA* 4.26; Penella, *Letters of Apollonius*, 90.

88. Apollonius attempted a reform at Sparta (*Epp. Apoll.* 63; *VA* 4.27) and issued a complaint against the Ionians (*Epp. Apoll.* 71; *VA* 4.5).

89. Apollonius had connections to Rhodes (*Epp. Apoll.* 45; *VA* 5.21–23; 8.30) and was honored by the Spartans (*Epp. Apoll.* 62; *VA* 4.31). See Penella, *Letters of Apollonius*, 114, 122.

90. *Epp. Apoll.* 59 was sent from Garmus, king of Babylonia, to Neogyndes, king of the Indians. The *VA* does not mention these monarchs, but a Garmus is mentioned in Iamblicus's novel *Babyloniaca* (Philostratus, *Apollonius of Tyana*, 3:57, n. 73). Also see *Epp. Apoll.* 77b–c; *VA* 3.51.

91. *Epp. Apoll.* 77b is quoted in *VA* 2.41.

92. Penella, *Letters*, 27. Dzielska would agree with several of the contradictions between the *VA* and the letters that Penella's mentioned. For instance, she questioned Apollonius's visit to Italy and his involvement in public discourse. See Dzielska, *Apollonius*, 39–43.

PART 3: INVESTIGATING THE APOLLONIAN DECALOGUE

A few more differences could be appended to this list. Rather than discovering Philostratus's orthodox, Pythagorean philosopher in the epistles, Apollonius may be cast as an eclectic philosopher.[93] Whereas Apollonius disdained sophists in the letters (*Epp. Apoll.* 1, 2), Philostratus's Apollonius is at times portrayed as a sophist, as was discussed in an earlier chapter of the current book. The anti-Roman sentiment in several letters may be at odds with Philostratus's pro-Roman Apollonius.[94] Koskenniemi notes that, unlike the *VA*, "the letters contain very little material concerning the miracles or other 'divine man' topics,"[95] but this claim is challenged by the letters that mention Apollonius's knowledge of the future (*Epp. Apoll.* 8.1), prediction of earthquakes (*Epp. Apoll.* 68), and his claim that the gods thought him godlike (*Epp. Apoll.* 48.3) and men thought him to be close to a god (ἰσόθεον) or to be a god (θεόν; *Epp. Apoll.* 44.1; 48.1). Penella wisely cautions that "[i]f we had fuller information on Apollonius, at least some of these differences between the *Vita Apollonii* and separately transmitted letters might prove to be reconcilable and only apparent."[96] Yet, as it stands, the Apollonius of the letters does not perfectly match the version of the sage in the *VA*.

93. See *Epp. Apoll.* 58; Penella, *Letters*, 28. Penella's interpretation conflicts with Bowie's view that even in the *VA* Apollonius represents a blending of Socratic, cynic, and Pythagorean philosophies. See Bowie, "Philostratus: Writer of Fiction," 188.

94. Bowie, "Apollonius of Tyana," 1682. One letter (*Epp. Apoll.* 67a) may challenge the view that all the letters are anti-Roman, for one of them seems to indicate that Apollonius was a Roman citizen because of his *tria nomina*, Lucius Pompeius Apollonius. Perhaps an anti-Roman tendency of the letters is mistaken or perhaps the letters, deriving from different sources, reflect more than one perspective. Jones points out that Apollonius's rebuke of his brother (*Epp. Apoll.* 72) and of members of the Ionian league for using Latin names (*VA* 4.5) may not be a condemnation of their Roman citizenship but rather a rebuke for "abandoning their traditional style of nomenclature" in official documents. For this suggestion, see C. P. Jones, "Some Letters of Apollonius," 259–60.

95. Koskenniemi, "Apollonius of Tyana," 460.

96. Penella, *Letters*, 27. Perhaps the discrepancies between some of these letters and the *VA* could be reconciled if more information was available. For instance, *Epp. Apoll.* 14 states that Apollonius had never had an invitation to Italy or to the emperor's court (according to the *VA*, he rejected invitations by Vespasian, Nerva, and Titus prior to his accession; *VA* 5.37, 41; 6.31; 8.27; Penella, *Letters*, 99; Dzielska, *Apollonius*, 40–41) but perhaps this refers to an invitation from Domitian instead of from the emperors who are said to have offered invitations in the *VA* (Penella, *Letters of Apollonius*, 99). Another example of reconciliation might be possible in the case of *Epp. Apoll.* 53. If the epistle is from Claudius the emperor, then the letter is a forgery: Apollonius's tour of Greece during the reign of Claudius (AD 41–54) is impossibly early and contradicts the claims of the *VA* that Apollonius first visited Greece in the time of Nero (*VA* 4). See Penella, *Letters*, 117. However, Jones suggests that this may have been a magistrate named Claudius rather than the Roman emperor (Philostratus, *Apollonius of Tyana*,

In summary, the *Letters of Apollonius* are significant for several reasons. This collection preserves a unique picture of Apollonius, thereby demonstrating that scholars should not rely entirely upon the *VA* for their reconstructions of the historical Apollonius. Further, some of these letters likely pre-date the *VA* and, assuming Philostratus did not write them himself, preserve an impression of the sage from an earlier era.[97] Perhaps these letters derive from different sources and contain multiple pre-Philostratean traditions about Apollonius. So, whether written by Apollonius or not, these epistles preserve an alternative view of the Tyanean.

CONCLUSIONS FOR ALL PRE-PHILOSTRATEAN SOURCES

The first four items of the Apollonian Decalogue dealt with pre-Philostreatan sources, so the concluding section of this chapter will attempt to sum up the evidence for all these materials from this chapter and the previous one to see how well they match with the portrayal of Apollonius in the *VA*. In all, six sources have been compared to the *VA*. Two of these documents were never mentioned by Philostratus (Lucian, Dio Cassius); one was mentioned but not employed (*On Sacrifices*); three of them were mentioned or used as sources for the *VA* (Moiragenes, Maximus, *Letters of Apollonius*).

These sources strongly support Philostratus's claim that Apollonius was a philosopher. Bowie argues that "[t]here are several grounds for thinking that Apollonius had already been cast into the mould of a philosopher in the second century."[98] He presented three arguments in support of his claim, only one of which was based on a pre-Philostratean source: (1) Apollonius's dispute with Euphrates the Stoic, mentioned in several of the *Letters*, is philosophical rather than personal;[99] (2) Philostratus did not feature neo-Pythagoreanism elsewhere in his corpus, thus making it likely that Apollonius was already associated with that philosophical group and that this was not his invention; and, (3) Philostratus claimed that Apollonius received a tome of Pythagorean

---

47, n. 60).

97. Petzke, *Die Traditionen*, 41. Penella, *Letters*, 27.

98. Bowie, "Apollonius of Tyana," 1671–73. In this section, Bowie develops his three arguments.

99. Bowie, "Apollonius of Tyana," 1671–72.

doctrines at the cave of Trophonius at Lebadeia and that this book was deposited in Hadrian's library at Antium so that "whether the story is true or false a date between 117 A.D. (Hadrian's accession) and ca. 160 A.D. is probable as a terminus ante quem for association of Apollonius with Pythagoreanism."[100] Bowie's argument can be supplemented by evidence culled from the pre-Philostratean materials investigated in the last two chapters. Lucian, while not explicitly calling Apollonius a Pythagorean, portrayed his follower Alexander as a Pythagorean philosopher. Also, Apollonius was described as a philosopher, or he was associated with philosophical themes in at least three other sources (fragment *On Sacrifices*; *Moiragenes*; *Letters of Apollonius*), even though it is unclear from these texts whether he was supposed to be a Pythagorean or an eclectic philosopher. Nevertheless, the evidence suggests that Apollonius was a philosopher of some stripe and that it is likely that Philostratus simply built upon a previously existing tradition rather than creating a philosophical pedigree for him out of thin air.

However, in some instances, the Apollonius of the earlier sources and the Apollonius of the *VA* differ. Although several texts agreed that Apollonius opposed blood sacrifice (*Fragment*, Maximus, *Letters*, *VA*), some claimed that he allowed other forms of material sacrifice, such as incense (Maximus, Philostratus), and others forbad anything other than spiritual sacrifice (*Fragment*). Apollonius's reputation as a world traveler, as a god, and as one who rubbed elbows with the elite of the world is also not widely attested, for these claims found support only in the *VA* and possibly in the *Letters*.[101] Likewise, only two texts portrayed him as a healer (Maximus, *VA*).[102] Although two texts indicate that he either despised Domitian (Dio Cassius) or wrote to him (*Letters*), neither confirms the *VA*'s claim that he stood trial before that emperor or that he ever met with him in person. The *Letters* disagree with the *VA* over Apollonius's belief in the transmigration of souls, willingness to attend the Olympic games, and habits of bathing. These tensions between and contradictions with the *VA* may well represent different strands of Apollonian tradition.

---

100. Bowie, "Apollonius of Tyana," 1673.

101. Two letters hint at the eastern travels of Apollonius (*Epp. Apoll.* 77b–c). However, the correspondence between a Babylon and an Indian king (*Epp. Apoll.* 59), "has no apparent connection with the sage or the story of his eastern travels" (Penella, *Letters*, 121).

102. Lucian did not call Apollonius a physician, but the Tyanean's later follower Alexander did sometimes function in that capacity.

The most notable contradiction between Philostratus and the traditions before his time was his assertion that Apollonius was not a magician. Yet, Apollonius is explicitly called a magician in three of the earlier traditions (Lucian, Dio Chrysostom, Moiragenes, *Letters*) and in four of them displayed supernatural powers as well (Dio Chrysostom, Moiragenes, *Letters*, Maximus). However, the ability to perform powerful deeds does not necessarily count as proof that Apollonius was a magician. Supernatural power was not the sole domain of the magician; ancients believed that there were several sources of power or knowledge, which could have included the direct assistance of the gods (e.g., *VA* 8.7.28–29), the aid of a guardian spirit (e.g., *VA* 1.18; 8.7.30), or Apollonius's innate power as a divine figure (e.g., *VA* 7.38). Furthermore, such deeds of power might be interpreted differently by the followers of Apollonius and his opponents; as in the case of Jesus of Nazareth, one person's messiah (Matt 12:23; Origen, *Cels*.1.38, 68) might be another person's magician (Matt 12:24; Origen, *Cels*.1.6). Still, evidence for Apollonius being a magician in the earliest strata of tradition is substantial and the term is used of him by both his enemies (Lucian, Dio Chrysostom) and by texts that were favorable toward him (Moiragenes and the *Letters*). Except for Maximus (who may have merely noted Apollonius's powers without a reference to magic) and *On Sacrifices*, Apollonius was viewed as a magician, which is a position with which Philostratus differed and from which he sought to distance his hero.

The main takeaway from this and the previous chapter is that Philostratus's protagonist differed in many respects from those of his predecessors. Sometimes the differences between the earlier traditions are slight, and sometimes they constitute outright contradictions to *VA*. The most significant difference by far is that the tradition uniformly claims that Apollonius was a magician and that Philostratus dedicated so much of his work to countering it.[103] This gives some credence to Flinterman's argument that the tradition moved from Apollonius as a sorcerer, to both a white magician and philosopher, and was finally transformed by Philostratus into a philosopher alone. Although Philostratus's version of Apollonius's life eventually won the day, it does not appear to be an accurate version of the real Apollonius of Tyana in some respects.

---

103. Taggart, "Apollonius," 58.

10

Item 5

Damis and His Memoirs

MANY OF THE WORLD'S most famous teachers wrote nothing themselves[1] and others wrote little,[2] so that it fell to their disciples to preserve a record of their words and deeds. Without Plato and Xenophon, little would have been known of Socrates. Without Arrian, the lectures of Epictetus would have been lost. Without the authors of the canonical Gospels, little would be known about the historical Jesus.[3] Likewise, Apollonius's disciple Damis was instrumental in the preservation of the majority of what his master had said and done if what Philostratus reports is true.[4]

Yet, there is no consensus about the truth of Philostratus's claims about Damis among Apollonius scholars, as item 5 of the Apollonian Decalogue asserts: "Scholars disagree concerning the veracity of Philostratus's claim that he had access to the memoirs of a first-century eyewitness and disciple of Apollonius named Damis." Therefore, this chapter

---

1. E.g., Socrates, Buddha, Epictetus, Jesus, and Muhammad.

2. E.g., Apollonius of Tyana (*VA* 1.14; 3.41.2). See also Koskenniemi, *Der philostrateische Apollonios*, 18–20.

3. This claim is true whether one holds the view that the Gospels were written by the actual disciples of Jesus (e.g., Matthew, John) or that the Gospels were compiled by others but nevertheless preserve traditions concerning Jesus's life.

4. Although Apollonius supposedly wrote several works, none of them have survived, with the possible exceptions of the fragment *On Sacrifices* and a few letters.

will be dedicated to an examination of the Damis source for much of the historicity of the VA depends upon its existence and veracity.

PHILOSTRATUS'S DESCRIPTION OF THE MEMOIRS OF DAMIS

Philostratus provided a generous amount of information concerning Damis and his memoirs. Within one passage, he discussed the identity of Damis, the contents of his book, and related how the source first came into the hands of the empress Julia Domna:

> And the precise details I have collected are as follows. There was a man, Damis, by no means stupid, who formerly dwelt in the ancient city of Nineveh. He resorted to Apollonius in order to study wisdom, and having shared, by his own account, his wanderings abroad, wrote an account of them. And he records his opinions and discourses and all his prophecies. And a certain kinsman of Damis drew the attention of the empress Julia to the documents containing these memoirs hitherto unknown (VA 1.3).

Regrettably, Philostratus did not indicate when and where the documents were delivered to the empress, but, if this event transpired, it likely took place during her visit to Tyana in AD 202 with Severus or in AD 215 when she visited the city again with Caracalla.

Philostratus also discussed the state of this manuscript when it was handed over to him for editing. First, he indicated that the document was extremely detailed. Not only did it contain Apollonius's travels, sayings, speeches, and predictions as he indicated earlier (VA 1.3), but it even preserved minutiae about Damis's master:

> At any rate the volume which he calls his scrap-book, was intended to serve such a purpose by Damis, who was determined that nothing about Apollonius should be passed over in silence, nay, that his most casual and negligent utterances should also be written down. And I may mention the answer which he made to one who cavilled and found fault with this journal. It was a lazy fellow and malignant who tried to pick holes in him, and remarked that he had recorded well enough a lot of things, for example, the opinions and ideas of his hero, but that in collecting such trifles as these he a reminded him of dogs who pick up and eat the fragments which fall from a feast. Damis replied thus: "If banquets there be of gods, and gods take food, surely

PART 3: INVESTIGATING THE APOLLONIAN DECALOGUE

they must have attendants whose business it is that not even the parcels of ambrosia that fall to the ground should be lost." Such was the companion and admirer that he had met with, and in common with him most of his travels and life were passed. (*VA* 1.19.2–3)

Second, Philostratus related that Damis, while accurate and detailed in what he recorded, was deficient concerning style: "This Assyrian's language, however, was of a mediocre quality, for he had not the gift of expressing himself, having been educated among the barbarians; but he kept a journal of their intercourse, and recorded in it whatever he heard or saw, and he was very well able to put together a memoir of such matters and managed this better than anyone else." (*VA* 1.19.2). Since Julia Domna wanted these documents to be edited, Philostratus explains that he was the obvious talent for this task: "Now I belonged to the circle of the empress, for she was a devoted admirer of all rhetorical exercises; and she commanded me to recast and edit these essays, at the same time paying more attention to the style and diction of them; for the man of Nineveh had told his story clearly enough, yet somewhat awkwardly." (*VA* 1.3). In addition to style, Philostratus appears to claim that he edited the memoir extensively in terms of content.[5] If these claims are true, this blending of Damis's content with Philostratus's content and style would make it impossible to reconstruct the original form and exact wording of the disciple's memoirs.

Damis's text is variously described by Philostratus. He refers to it as a "journal" (διατριβὴν *VA* 1.19.2), "notes" (ὑπομνήματα *VA* 1.3.1; 19.2), "memoirs" (ἀναγεγραμμένα *VA* 8.29), and "tablets" (δέλτοι *VA* 1.3.1). Its official title seems to have been either *Scrap Book* or *Scraps from the Manger* (Ἡ . . . δέλτος ἡ τῶν ἐκφατνισμάτων; *VA* 1.19.3).[6] This curious title for the work refers to Damis's practice of collecting even the most insignificant bits of Apollonian lore (*VA* 1.19.2). However, the word δέλτοι is most helpful in terms of the physical description of the documents, for this term appears to refer to "wooden tablets (Greek *deltoi*; Latin *tabulae*, *tabellae*), often coated with a layer of wax and written on

---

5. Thomas Schirren's analysis of the language of *VA* 1.3 indicates that Philostratus not only claimed to have edited the Damis material extensively but that he sometimes altogether modified it. See Schirren, "Irony," 165.

6. The latter term comes from Phillimore, *In Honour*, 25. Bowie provides "tit-bits" a third translation of the title. See Bowie, "Philostratus: Writer of Fiction," 188.

with a stylus."[7] If Philostratus is truthful about the physical description of these documents, one can only imagine a rather large collection of such tablets, given the volume of material that Philostratus attributed to Damis in the *VA*.

As with the use of other sources in the *VA*, Philostratus is notoriously unclear about which portions of the work were reliant on the *Scrapbook* or about delineating where Damis's comments end and Philostratus's begin. The narrative itself suggests that the Damis material was bracketed by the accounts in which the disciple first met Apollonius (*VA* 1.19) and with their parting in the last book of the biography (*VA* 8.29). Although Philostratus does not indicate that all the material at the core of his work relies upon Damis, he does frequently cite the Assyrian or indicate that he was a participant in encounters within this section. Since Philostratus often mingles his thoughts and other sources with what is allegedly based on Damis material, getting a clear sense of the document's original content and wording is impossible.

In summation, Philostratus made the following claims about Damis and his *Scrapbook*. Damis was a disciple of Apollonius during most of his master's mission. At some point, Damis wrote down his memoirs of Apollonius's travels, words, deeds, and predictions, along with other minutiae about his teacher. These materials were written on wooden tablets and preserved by Damis's family. Over a century after the departure of Apollonius, one of Damis's relatives presented these documents to the empress Julia Domna, who in turn put Philostratus in charge of editing them. The revised material taken from the diary was incorporated into and served as the substratum for Philostratus's *VA*. As will probably come as no surprise, almost every aspect of these claims has been challenged by modern scholarship.

THE MODERN CONTROVERSY ABOUT DAMIS AND HIS MEMOIRS

According to Koskenniemi, three main schools of thought concerning the existence of Damis and the authenticity of this account have existed side by side for several decades.[8] The first is that Damis and his memoirs were genuine. This view has the double privilege of being both the

---

7. Oleson, *Handbook of Engineering*, 719.
8. Koskenniemi, *Der philostrateische Apollonios*, 9.

most ancient and longest-held view. It appears that the reality of Damis and his memoirs was taken for granted by many from antiquity[9] up until the nineteenth century. However, now this is the minority view. In recent times, none have argued for this position with as much passion as Fulvio Grosso (1954).[10] Although his argument attracted a few followers (e.g., Ferdinando Lo Cascio), his views that the Damis memoirs are genuine and historically accurate have been rejected for the most part.[11] Still, several reputable older and more recent scholars have argued that both Damis and his *Scrapbook* were real (e.g., Phillimore, Taggart, and Petzke[12]), including a few New Testament scholars (e.g., Votaw and Boring[13]). The second view, which many believe was first proposed by F. C. Baur in 1832,[14] is that Damis and his memoirs never existed, but were the creations of Philostratus. This position appears to be the majority view of Apollonius scholars currently.[15] The third view, introduced by Meyer in 1917,[16] is that the memoirs were a forgery written in the second or third centuries.[17] This view is held by a few notable classical[18] and New Testament[19] scholars. In the following sections, the stronger arguments for each of the three positions will be presented along with counterarguments to them.

---

9. E.g., Eusebius, *Hier.* 2.2–3; 3; 43.4.

10. Grosso, "La 'Vita di Apollonio," 33–532.

11. Dzielska, *Apollonius*, 25; Flinterman, *Power*, 80.

12. Phillimore, *In Honour*, xxi–xxii; Taggart, "Apollonius," 68–76; Petzke, *Die Traditionen*, 67–72.

13. Votaw, *The Gospels*, 17–29; Boring, *Introduction*, 468.

14. Baur, *Apollonius von Tyana*, 112–13. Interestingly, as early as 1681, Samuel Parker pondered whether there ever was a Damis document. See Parker, *Demonstration*, 294.

15. For an excellent overview of the arguments by key scholars against the existence of Damis and his memoirs see Koskenniemi, *Der philostrateische Apollonios*, 9–15.

16. Meyer, *Apollonios von Tyana*, 371–424.

17. Samuel Parker suggested that the person that delivered the Damis memoir to Julia Domna "might probably have forged (as is common in Courts) to pick her pocket" (Parker, *Demonstration*, 293).

18. Speyer, "Zum Bild des Apollonios," 48–63; Flinterman, *Power*, 79–88. Anderson while arguing for the historical Damis is open to the possibility that the memoirs were a forgery. See Anderson, *Philostratus*, 169.

19. Smith, *Jesus the Magician*, 86; Although he does not specify a date, Keener holds to the view that the Damis document was a forgery. See Keener, *Christobiography*, 47.

ITEM 5

The Case for the Existence of Damis and His Memoirs

Philostratus's Use of Other Genuine Sources

In his thesis on Apollonius, Taggart made the case that the Damis memoir was likely to be genuine because Philostratus had used two other genuine sources elsewhere in the *VA* (i.e., the writings of Maximus of Aegae and Moiragenes). He argued that "[b]ecause the historical existence of these two writers whom Philostratus claims as writers of Apollonica is established, the historical existence of Damis, whom Philostratus also claims as a writer of Apollonica is, therefore, more than probable."[20] Flinterman, who believes that Damis's diary was a forgery, countered this sort of argument by pointing out that nothing prevents the use of authentic and fictional materials side-by-side, such as was done in the *Historia Augusta*.[21] Flinterman's point could also be applied to the theory that the Damis memoir was a Philostratean fabrication, for nothing would have prevented Philostratus from weaving fictional material from his imagination into a document that also contained genuine historical sources. Thus, Philostratus's use of a few genuine historical sources in the *VA* cannot guarantee that the Damis account itself was genuine.

The Practice of Preserving Pythagorean Memoirs

Taggert also argued that the emergence of memoirs that had been kept within a family would not have been an unusual occurrence because the Pythagoreans also kept such "character sketches" (ὑπομνήματα) and passed them down from father to son.[22] Indeed, Philostratus employed this very phrase—"memoirs" (τῶν ὑπομνημάτων)—to describe the notebook of Damis (*VA* 1.3.1). Unfortunately, this argument is not entirely persuasive because the neo-Pythagoreans were notorious for their production of forgeries.

---

20. Taggart, "Apollonius," 71–72.

21. Flinterman, *Power*, 84.

22. Taggart, "Apollonius," 74. Here cites *Iamblicus, VP* 35.253 as an example of this practice.

PART 3: INVESTIGATING THE APOLLONIAN DECALOGUE

Damis's *Scrapbook* Fits the First-Century Historical Context Well

Grosso argued that the Damis material had been vindicated as a first-century source because it matched the historical data from that era.[23] Taking an extreme position, Grosso attempted to defend the historical accuracy of Philostratus (and the Damis text on which it was based) at almost every turn. Pointing out the flaw in Grosso's line of reasoning, Bowie observed that,

> The coherence of Philostratus's picture only requires him to know the history of the period well enough to insert the activities of Apollonius without contradictions of the existing tradition. It does not demonstrate that the part given to Apollonius is historical. Since Philostratus must have had at his disposal a wider range of literary sources than are available to us we should not be surprised if he avoids contradicting our tradition.[24]

This procedure is the same as the goal of an author of modern historical fiction; the life of fictional character can be easily set against a real historical background. Further, Bowie followed this comment with a list of several egregious historical errors in the *VA* as a means of challenging the claims that Damis was an eyewitness to events of the first century. Although much of what Philostratus wrote about well-known events in the first century is confirmed by other ancient sources, when it came to inserting Apollonius into this broader historical framework, he still made many mistakes, inserted implausible details, and related events that cannot be independently confirmed in the historical record.[25]

Narrative Gaps and Chronological Errors in the *VA* Suggest a Source

At times, Philostratus's narrative seems to have gaps, and he struggles with problems of chronology.[26] These factors might suggest that the Philostratus was working from a source rather than simply inventing an

---

23. Grosso, "La 'Vita di Apollonio," 33–532.

24. Bowie, *Apollonius of Tyana*, 1655.

25. Koskenniemi, *Der philostrateische Apollonios*, 11. Dzieska called the Damis material "a falsification compiled with a chronicler's precision" because they generally conform to the history and chronology of the first century, yet none of the other first century sources confirm that Apollonius was the great figure that Philostratus claims him to be. See Dzielska, *Apollonius*, 25.

26. Flinterman, *Power*, 85.

itinerary for Apollonius.[27] Long ago, Phillimore (1912) suggested that Philostratus had followed the outline of Damis's book in shaping the VA. According to VA 1.3, the *Scrapbook* consisted of Apollonius's journeys (ἀποδημίας), sayings (γνώμας), speeches (λόγους), and predictions (ὁπόσα ἐς πρόγνωσιν εἶπε).[28] Phillimore suggested that, if Philostratus had followed Damis's account of the journeys as a blueprint, this might account for why in the VA the journeys in Books 1–6 were in some sort of chronological order (i.e., Mesopotamia, India, and Ethiopia). Likewise, Philostratus's reliance on Apollonius's speeches, sayings, and predictions might explain (1) why sections of Books 4–5 do not have the appearance of a continuous narrative,[29] but give the impression of being organized around various locations or literary forms (e.g., lectures at Athens)[30] and (2) the chronological mistakes in this section.[31] Phillimore's theory that

---

27. Noting Philostratus's "shabby treatment" of the period between Apollonius's stay at Aegae and his arrival Nineveh, Taggart postulated that this was because neither Maximus nor Damis had provided the biographer material for this section. See Taggart, "Apollonius," 72–73.

28. Phillimore, *In Honour*, cxvii. Similarly, Anderson thought the material that is attributed to Damis "is best accounted for as an itinerary with miraculous elements and a martyrology" (Anderson, *Philostratus*, 159).

29. Petzke's observations on chronology seem to match with Phillimore's, even though the former did not speculate that this section belonging to the Damis account. Petzke notes that the itinerary for the journey east was mostly complete (e.g., the journey to Mesopotamia and India), but that other travel descriptions were vaguer (e.g., Spain; Rome) or gave practically no information at all (the journey from Babylon to Ionia; VA 3.15 to 4.1; 4.23–34. After the return from the Nile (VA 6.27), Apollonius's travels are not mentioned again until the general summary of his journeys in VA 6.35. Within the section comprising VA 6.36–43, a group of traditions occur that are not brought into a temporal or spatial context. Some of these, in fact, do not indicate a location at all (VA 6.36, 39); Petzke, *Die Traditionen*, 87–89.

30. Phillimore lists these speeches and events along with their locations: discourses at Ephesus (VA 4.2–3), lectures at Athens (VA 4.19), cultic corrections made at Athens (VA 4.22), events at Olympia (VA 4.27), lectures at Olympia (VA 4.31), an incident in Sparta (VA 4.33), lectures and events in Crete (VA 4.34.3–4) activities at Rome (VA 4.34.4), an account of things in Corinth (VA 4.42), a miracle performed at Rome (VA 4.45.1) discourses in Spain (VA 5.7), events in Rhodes (VA 5.23), events in Alexandria (VA 5.24), and a miracle done in Egypt (VA 5.42). For this list, see Phillimore, *In Honour*, cxviii.

31. Phillimore, *In Honour*, cxix–cxxi. Phillimore also pointed out chronological problems in this section. The journey from Crete (VA 4.34.4; AD 46) to Rome (4.34.4; AD 66) is brief, although twenty years would have transpired between these two episodes. Another chronological error is that in AD 60 Apollonius was in Corinth (VA 4.24), seven years before Nero attempted to dig the Corinthian canal, whereas the visit to Crete (AD 46) that follows it is out of sequence. These matters will be treated in more detail in the next chapter.

the *VA* follows the outline of the Damis book is plausible, however, it does not appear to have been taken up by later scholars.

Like Phillimore, Petzke postulated that the gaps and breaks in the *VA*'s narrative showed that Philostratus was trying to cope with sources available to him rather than resorting to outright invention,[32] and like Phillimore, he sometimes suspected that a travelogue was being used as a template (e.g., a now lost travelogue of Alexander the Great's travels or the Damis account). Yet, Petzke admitted that his suspicions of Philostratus's reliance on Damis as a source could not be proven and the diary may have been a fiction.[33] He also noted that it was difficult to isolate the Damis material in the *VA* from other local traditions to prove that a companion of Apollonius supplied the first model for the work.[34] At this point in scholarship, it is impossible to demonstrate the existence of a Damis source by arguing from what appear to be gaps within the narrative of the *VA*. Even if the perceived problems with the gaps in the narrative are genuine, their value for determining the nature of a source would still be ambiguous. Still, these oddities could support the existence of a forgery attributed to Damis just as well as a genuine diary of Damis.

Philostratus's Treatment of Magical Material in the Damis Memoir Suggests a Source

On several occasions, Philostratus appears to disagree with Damis's opinion or to be embarrassed by it, especially in instances involving magic.[35] Because Philostratus disparaged the use of magic in both the *VA* and the *VS*, the viewpoints expressed in these documents probably represent his true opinion as an author.[36] Therefore, it seems unlikely that Philostratus would invent episodes in the *VA* that challenge his own viewpoint. More likely, Philostratus felt compelled to include them because they were found in a source or because these stories were too well known to omit.

Philostratus's discomfort seems particularly evident in the Damis material that treats magical themes. Several writers have noted passages in which Philostratus attempts to counter's a deed related to a Damis

32. Petzke, *Die Traditionen*, 72.
33. Petzke, *Die Traditionen*, 83, 85, 93, 99.
34. Petzke, *Die Traditionen*, 149–50.
35. Petzke, *Die Traditionen*, 75, n. 4. Also see Tiede, *The Charismatic Figure*, 27.
36. Flinterman observes that a source fabricated by Philostratus that deals with magic can be expected to reflect his own opinions about it. See Flinterman, *Power*, 85.

account that could have been construed as magical, such as when (1) Apollonius raised a girl from the dead, Philostratus offered the alternative, naturalistic explanation that Apollonius had merely revived a still-living person (*VA* 4.45);[37] (2) Apollonius cured a dog of rabies by praying to the river and having the animal swim across it, Philostratus attributes the cure to the hound's drinking of the water, a known cure for the disease, rather than to Apollonius's powers (*VA* 6.43);[38] (3) Apollonius freed his leg from a shackle in prison and Damis first realized his master was divine, Philostratus launched into a detailed polemic against magic to defend Apollonius against this seemingly magical escape (*VA* 7.38–39);[39] (4) Philostratus explained that Apollonius's prognostications derived from wisdom and not sorcery (*VA* 5.12; cf. 4.44);[40] (5) Philostratus felt obliged to include the story of Apollonius's unmasking of the vampire at Corinth because this story was well known and it had been told by Damis (*VA* 4.25);[41] and (6) Damis mentioned Apollonius's book on planetary prophecy and Philostratus circumvented the topic (*VA* 3.41).[42] Anderson observed that problematic stories like these do not help Philostratus's case that Apollonius is not a magician and, "suggest that Philostratus really is content to use what is in front of him, and take a superstitious source at face value."[43] An issue with Anderson's argument could be that two of the above accounts do not explicitly mention Damis (*VA* 4.45; 5.12), but otherwise his observations about Philostratus's discomfort with certain traditions are persuasive.

The Case for Damis and His Memoirs as the Creation of Philostratus

Damis Is Unattested as a Historical Figure

Apart from the writings of Philostratus, there is currently no evidence that Damis existed. No source before the time of Philostratus knew of

---

37. Petzke, *Die Traditionen*, 148.
38. Petzke, *Die Traditionen*, 148.
39. Tiede, *The Charismatic Figure*, 27; Petzke, *Die Traditionen*, 148; Anderson, *Philostratus*, 158, 170; Flinterman, *Power*, 85.
40. Tiede, *The Charismatic Figure*, 28; Flinterman, *Power*, 85.
41. Anderson, *Philostratus*, 163.
42. Flinterman, *Power*, 85.
43. Anderson, *Philostratus*, 163.

PART 3: INVESTIGATING THE APOLLONIAN DECALOGUE

him,[44] and the writers after his era appear to accept Damis's existence because of the claims of the VA (e.g., Hierocles and Eusebius).[45] Although a Sanskrit text does mention Damis and several other characters from the VA (e.g., Apollonius, Iarchus, and Phraotes), it postdates Philostratus's work and appears to be reliant upon it.[46] Anderson made a noble but unconvincing effort to demonstrate the reality of Damis by linking three similar names and stories: an Epicurean named Damis in Lucian's *Juppiter trageodeus*, Damis the disciple of Apollonius in VA 2.4–5, and a Dini in the medieval Persian work called *Marzuban-nameh*.[47] The spiritualist medium J. M. Roberts thought that Damis was the same man as Demas mentioned by the apostle Paul (Phlm 24; Col 4:14; 2 Tim 4:10).[48] So unless one is inclined to entertain highly speculative (Anderson) or fringe theories (Roberts), the curious reader must await further evidence for proof of Apollonius's faithful follower.

With the lack of hard evidence for the historical Damis, a few academics have explored the possibility that the Assyrian companion of Apollonius was the product of the fertile imagination of Philostratus. Some of these researchers dismissed Damis on literary grounds, noting that (1) Damis resembles other fictive witnesses that are attested in Second Sophistic literature[49] (e.g., the diaries of Dictys of Crete, the tale

44. Koskenniemi, *Apollonios von Tyana*, 174.

45. Dzielska, *Apollonius*, 28–29.

46. Dzielska, *Apollonius*, 29; Anderson, *Philostratus*, 173.

47. Anderson, *Philostratus*, 166–67. For Flinterman's assessment of the argument, see his *Power*, 80, n. 113. Although Anderson is correct that there are few similarities between the three stories, the finer details differ with respect to (1) the occasions (the gods wanted to silence an Epicurean philosoopher [*Jupp. trag.*]; a random encounter with a vampire during night journey [*VA*]; demons summon a sage to debate their efficacy [*Marzuban-nameh*]); (2) the opponents (the Greek gods [*Jupp. trag.*], an *empusa* [*VA*], and a demon [*Marzuban-nameh*]); (3) the results (the gods are confounded by Damis [*Jupp. trag.*], Apollonius rebukes the *empusa* [*VA*], the demons are confounded [*Marzuban-nameh*]); and (4) the locations (the gods in heaven watch Damis debate an opponent on earth [*Jupp. trag.*]; between the Caucasus and the Indus River [*VA*]; the top of a mountain [*Marzuban-nameh*]). Even if one grants the remote possibility that the story in the *VA* is related to the *Marzuban-nameh*, this could be a case of the earlier work of Philostratus influencing the latter. Indeed, the *Marzuban-nameh* has much more in common with *Juppiter Tragoedus* than either tale does to the story in the *VA*. A final problem is that the Epicurean Damis of Lucian's tale would not fit well with the Damis of the *VA*, who, in anti-epicurean fashion, endorses the Greek gods and Pythagorean philosophy. If Lucian's Damis represents the historical figure, then the Damis of the *VA* is a fiction.

48. Roberts, *Antiquity Unveiled*, 38.

49. Ferguson, *Religions*, 183.

of Deinias in *The Wonders Beyond Thule*,[50] and perhaps the diaries of Dares of *Acta diurnal belli Troiani*[51]); (2) Philostratus signaled the literary elite of the fictionality of Damis because the name begins with the letter *delta* like those of other fictional eyewitnesses (e.g., Dictys, Deinias, and Dares);[52] (3) Philostratus himself created at least one other fictional witnesses, the vinedresser in *Heroicus* was an eyewitness of Protesilaus,[53] whose role corresponds to that of Damis, the eyewitness to Apollonius in the *VA*;[54] (4) Philostratus probably created Damophyle, a fictional poet and companion of the historical Sappho, that resembles Damis in his role as a disciple for the historical Apollonius (*VA* 1.30);[55] (5) the contradictory and sometimes negative critique of Damis makes his existence unlikely, for no author would disparage himself in his own memoirs;[56] and (6) his invention of Damis was a signal to his more sophisticated readers that he was writing fiction.[57] These are but a few of the arguments dismissing the reality of the Assyrian disciple from a literary perspective.

Apollonius scholars have also found historical reasons for dismissing Damis as a real figure. Bowie rejected his existence because no eyewitness would have made such horrendous historical errors about

---

50. Bowie, "Apollonius of Tyana," 1663–64.

51. Kim suspects that an original Greek version of this tale pre-dates Philostratus yet acknowledges that there is no hard data to support this position. See Kim, *Homer*, 179–80.

52. Gyselinck and Demoen, noted that "[i]t is a curious and perhaps no coincidence that authors of pseudo-documentary fiction show a preference for names beginning with a *delta*" (Gyselink and Demoen, "Author and Narrator," 100, n. 18).

53. Kim, *Homer*, 181; Koskenniemi, *Apollonios von Tyana*, 174.

54. Bowie, "Apollonius of Tyana," 1663; C. P. Jones, "Passage to India," 197–98.

55. C. P. Jones, "Passage to India," 197–98; Bowie, "Philostratus: Writer of Fiction," 188.

56. Koskenniemi notes that Damis is sometimes said to be "not without wisdom" (*VA* 1.3) but that at other times he is somewhat foolish (*VA* 3.43) and guilty of cowardice (*VA* 7.13). See Koskenniemi, *Apollonios von Tyana*, 174. As a critique of these statements, there are two points that need to be made: (1) the statement in *VA* 1.3 is Philostratus's own positive assessment of Damis's wisdom, whereas the other examples would have been Damis's self-description. The views of Philostratus and Damis, whether the Assyrian is a real or fictional character, need not agree and do not necessarily contradict; and (2) inconsistency in the description or portrayal of a character need not be a sign of fictionality. Both real and fictional characters can be complex, displaying development over time or contradictory attributes. For instance, Damis's cowardice in one episode (*VA* 7.13) was overcome by courage in the end (*VA* 7.15).

57. Bowie wrote, "Damis in an invention of Philostratus, who will not have expected his readers to take him seriously"; Bowie, "Apollonius of Tyana," 1653.

the Neronian and Flavian periods.[58] Yet, rather than suggesting Damis emerged entirely from Philostratus's imagination, Bowie suggested that Flavius Damianus of Ephesus was the inspiration for the character Damis. Damianus was a protector of sophists in the court of the Severi and, since Philostratus had interviewed Damianus thrice (VS 606), Bowie suggested that he had been a possible source of information about Apollonius in western Asia Minor, especially in Ephesus where Apollonius may have visited.[59] Several scholars have even questioned the existence of Damis on archaeological grounds because his alleged *patria*, Nineveh, had been a ghost town for centuries before his time. However, as we shall see in the next chapter of this book, Old Ninus did not refer to the biblical city but to Syrian Hierapolis, so this argument falls flat.

All the above reasons attempt to demonstrate that Damis did not exist. But if Damis did not exist and was just a fictional character, why would Philostratus have felt the need to create him? Several responses have been given to this query. Some think that Philostratus required Damis as a "fictive witness"[60] to give the impression of eyewitness testimony and lend credibility to the narrative.[61] Damis plays the role of a mediator between the story of Apollonius and the reader, much like the realistic—yet fictional—Doctor Watson does in the Sherlock Holmes stories.[62] The illusion that Damis provided eyewitness testimony also helps to "persuade the reader that Apollonius played a significant role at the time,"[63] while distracting the reader from the fact that none of the stories about the sage's encounters with high-profile figures of the first century AD were attested by independent sources. Meyer more particularly argued that Philostratus fabricated Damis out of a need for an authoritative source to counter Moiragenes's claim that Apollonius was a magician.[64]

---

58. Bowie, "Apollonius of Tyana," 1655–62

59. Bowie, "Apollonius of Tyana," 1670. Dzielska seems to have favored this suggestion, *Apollonius*, 28, 191.

60. Bird, *Gospel of the Lord*, 49.

61. Bowersock, Introduction to *Life of Apollonius*, 10, 17. Martin Hengel writes that Damis "was the authority for the entire tradition about Apollonius and is most likely an invention of the author" (Hengel, *Charismatic Leader*, 27). Francis noted that Damis's testimony "forms the authoritative basis" for Philostratus's own work. See Francis, "Truthful Fiction," 420, 432.

62. Francis, "Truthful Fiction," 434, n. 51.

63. Dzielska, *Apollonius*, 20.

64. Meyer, "Apollonios von Tyana," 392.

Others believe that Philostratus needed Damis as an interlocutor[65] (like Glaucon in several of the Platonic dialogues) or a foil for Apollonius (like Sancho Panza in *Don Quixote*[66]) to help drive the narrative forward, much as Menecrates did in Philostratus's *Nero* and the Phoenician sailor did in his work *Heroicus*. In support of this opinion, Damis's foolish questions, inadequate responses to Apollonius's questions, and sometimes disappointing behavior provide Apollonius an opportunity to lecture the reader on various sophistic themes and allow Philostratus, under the guise of Apollonius, to exhibit his intellect and talent.[67] Finally, there is Bowie's view that Philostratus was not attempting to write history at all, but that Damis's functioned as a sort of inside joke to literati of his day that signaled he was writing fiction.[68] Yet, does this vast array of literary and historical argumentation best account for why Damis was such a central figure in the *VA*?

Anderson, while conceding the possibility of explanations like those presented above, noted that "an equally cogent reason for Philostratus' use of Damis would have been the latter's actual existence."[69] He also pointed out that, "an *ex silentio* argument carries little weight,"[70] for many other figures in antiquity were mentioned by a single author in a single document, yet they most certainly existed.[71] Anderson also pushed back against the view that Damis was a fictional disciple with several arguments. First, he noted that Damis did not function merely as an interlocutor or "errand boy," but rather that "most of the conversations with

---

65. Koskenniemi, *Apollonios von Tyana*, 174.

66. Gildersleave, *Essays*, 261.

67. Gyselinck and Demoen write that Damis does "not just function as a 'credibility device'; at the same time it enables Philostratus to highlight his literary art in a subtle way" (Gyselink and Demoen, "Author and Narrator," 99).

68. Bowie, "Apollonius of Tyana," 1665. Bowie also believes that Philostratus may have left some ambiguity regarding his purpose for employing Damis since "[t]he sober and skeptical reader who wants a good but credible story will welcome the apparently reliable source that Philostratus claims Damis to be; the more sophisticated connoisseur of literary technique will interpret the 'notebooks' of Damis as a covert admission of fictionality" (Bowie, "Philostratus: Writer of Fiction," 196).

69. Anderson, *Philostratus*, 156.

70. Anderson, *Philostratus*, 156.

71. For instance, only Philostratus mentioned the sophist Secundus (*VS* 544–45, 564) and Lucian was the only contemporary figure to mention Alexander of Abonouteichos (Anderson, *Philostratus*, 156). Even Koskenniemi, who argues that Damis was a fictional character, admits that Damis's absence from independent sources does not necessarily weigh against his existence. See, Koskenniemi, *Der philostrateische Apollonios*, 10.

Damis are no more than extensions of his role as a faithful disciple."[72] Second, Anderson pointed out the Damis material supposedly supplied much of the itinerary for the *VA*, thereby showing that the role Philostratus assigned him was much broader than a mere interlocutor.[73] Third, he challenged Meyer's theory that Damis was needed to combat Moiragenes's portrayal of Apollonius as a magician, for he was never used to refute Moiragenes and he even sometimes introduced material that could have undermined Philostratus's case that Apollonius was not a magician.[74]

The jury is still out on the historical Damis. On the one hand, there is still no solid evidence for Damis's existence. On the other hand, although the arguments against Damis's existence are significant and interesting, Anderson has demonstrated that few of them were conclusive. Furthermore, even if Damis himself never existed, that does not mean that Philostratus did not possess a pseudepigraphical document supposedly written by Damis or that Philostratus himself did not believe in the reality of that disciple.

Damis's Memoirs Are Unattested Elsewhere

Damis's memoirs were unknown before Philostratus's time[75] and are unattested thereafter as a source independent of the *VA*.[76] What accounts for these two facts? One version of events is that a relative of Damis brought these unknown documents to light, these were incorporated into the *VA*, and then they disappeared forever. Yet, to some scholars, these circumstances are suspicious and suggest that the document never existed.[77] Instead, they propose another version in which Philostratus referenced the diary whenever he was expressing his views about Apollonius.[78] For academics that suspect Philostratus of creating fictional characters (e.g., Damis and Damophyle in the *VA*), fictional eyewitnesses (e.g., Damis in the *VA* and the vinedresser in *Heroicus*), and fictitious documents even

---

72. Anderson, *Philostratus*, 159.
73. Anderson, *Philostratus*, 159.
74. Anderson, *Philostratus*, 163.
75. Jones, *Apollonius*, 77; Koskenniemi, *Apollonios von Tyana*, 174.
76. Bowersock, Introduction to *Life of Apollonius*, 19; Flinterman, *Power*, 79.
77. Meyer, "Apollonios von Tyana," 371
78. Taggart, "Apollonius," 69.

within the *VA*,⁷⁹ his creation of the tale of ancient diary about Apollonius would not seem farfetched.

However, just because Philostratus was the master of fiction does not mean that he was not reliant on documentary sources in the *VA*. As Taggart pointed out in an earlier section of this chapter, Philostratus sometimes used verifiable sources in his writings. In the *VS* he also used sources when writing about the sophists, and he claims to have employed them in the *VA* (e.g., Moiragenes and Maximus of Aegae). Furthermore, the story that Julia received a document from the purported relatives of Damis is not necessarily unlikely, whether the work itself was authentic or a forgery. It is not altogether implausible that a collection of writings may have been kept privately by the family of Damis or that such documents were later forged by someone only to be brought forward perhaps during one of Julia's visits to Tyana. Finally, the notebooks may have disappeared after being edited and incorporated into the *VA*.⁸⁰ Much like advocates of Q⁸¹ would argue that no evidence of no independent evidence for that document survived because it had been subsumed by Matthew and Luke, the incorporation of Damis's memoir into the *VA* would have likewise rendered it obsolete.⁸²

Fictional Documents Abound in the Literature of the Second Sophistic

The rediscovery of long-lost documents is a *topos* in ancient fiction, thereby raising the possibility that the rediscovery of Damis's diary might

---

79. Dzielska lists and evaluates seven documents that were attributed to Apollonius by Philostratus in the *VA*. For a more detailed discussion, see Dzielska, *Apollonius*, 130–36.

80. Koskenniemi, *Der philostrateische Apollonios*, 11. In a different scenario, the five-volume work of Jason of Cyrene appears to have perished, whereas its abridgement, 2 Maccabees, has survived (2 Macc 2:23–32). Ptolemy's account of Alexander's life, which serves as a major source for Arrian's *Anabasis*, is so poorly attested in other literature that it is difficult to tell how much Arrian omitted from it. See Brunt's comments in Arrian, *Anabasis*, 1:xxxi.

81. The field of biblical studies entertains several theories about hypothetical documents that became obsolete once they had been incorporated into other documents. The Documentary Hypothesis postulates the incorporation of J, E, P, and D into the Torah. Such theories also abound in the study of the Synoptics Gospels (e.g., Q, M, and L), John (e.g., the "signs Gospel," the "discourse source"), and Acts (the "we" passages).

82. Votaw suggested, "The journal has not come down to us intact, but the extensive Life by Philostratus is made up chiefly from Damis' material. Presumably it was because the journal was so fully taken up into the Life that the journal itself was allowed to disappear" (Votaw, *The Gospels*, 17).

also belong to such tales. Antonius Diogenes's romance entitled *The Wonders Beyond Thule* (Τὰ ὑπὲρ Θούλην ἄπιστα) opens with just such a discovery. After the capture of Tyre, the work relates that a soldier informed Alexander the Great of an underground chamber containing several sarcophagi. While exploring this hypogeum, Alexander found small, cypress chests that contained the adventures of Deinias and Derkyllis written on cypress tablets.[83] Another fictional work of the era, *Dictys of Crete: Chronicle of the Trojan War* (*Dictys Cretensis Ephemeris belli Trojani*), follows this traditional theme in reporting the discovery of wooden tablets preserving the diary of Dictys that told the story of the bygone conflict. This tale of discovery is set in the time of Nero and begins with an earthquake breaking open the tomb of Dictys on Crete. Within this riven crypt, shepherds found a coffer containing documents written in Phoenician characters on linden tablets. Praxis, the owner of the property on which the discovery was made, had the document transliterated into the Attic alphabet. Later, Lucius Septimius translated the tale into Latin and abridged some portions of it in the third or fourth century AD. Both fictional tales come from the era of the Second Sophistic, the same era in which Philostratus wrote the *VA*.

A few modern academics suggest that Philostratus utilized this common literary theme of the recovery of a lost document to set the stage for the *VA*. In support of this hypothesis, the Damis memoir shares several features with *The Wonders Beyond Thule* and *Dictys of Crete*. All three fictional documents (1) related tales from an earlier era; (2) were rediscovered under unusual circumstances; (3) were written on wooden tablets; (4) were delivered to a person of high status;[84] and (5) were edited to some extent before final publication.[85] Philostratus may have introduced the fictional diary to lend credibility to his account or he may have used this *topos*, especially the use of *deltoi*, as "a covert admission of fictionality."[86] Another point that buttresses this interpretation is that

---

83. This work was composed by Antonius Diogenes (second century AD). Although the text is no longer extant, Photius preserved a synopsis of at least a portion of it. Lucian appears to parody elements of *The Wonders Beyond Thule* in his famous satire *Vera Historia*. See Morgan, "Lucian's *True Histories*, 475–90.

84. Gyselinck and Demoen, "Author and Narrator," 100.

85. Balagros transcribed *The Wonders Beyond Thule* account of Dictys (Photius, *Bibliotheca*, 66), Lucius Septimius translated the work of Dictys into Latin, abridging the material after chapter five, and Philostratus supposedly improved upon the style of Damis.

86. Bowie, "Philostratus: Writer of Fiction," 196; Francis, "Truthful Fiction," 420, n. 5, 432.

Philostratus employed this theme in the VA when he had Apollonius discover a lost work of Pythagoras in the cave of Trophonius (VA 8.19.2).[87] Like the other works just discussed, Apollonius's tome contained material from an earlier era (i.e., Pythagoras's doctrines), was found in an unusual place (i.e., a grotto), and given to a person of high status (i.e., Apollonius; Hadrian). These facts suggest that the Damis document was a piece of fiction like these other works.

However, history is replete with examples of genuine, re-discovered documents that were found in manners akin to those told in these fictional accounts. Some lost documents were recovered in antiquity like Origen's biblical scroll that was found in a jar at Jericho (*Hist. Eccl.* 6.16.3) and the trove of books, written in Hebrew script, that was discovered in a cave dwelling near Jericho in the days of Patriarch Timothy I (the forty-seventh letter of Timothy[88]). Further, there are accounts of the discovery of documents in tombs in ancient times that do not appear to be fictional.[89] Other lost documents had to await discovery until recent times, but these examples at least demonstrate that the potential for finding such documents had always been present.[90] Thus, claims about the discovery of lost documents in ancient times should not always be written off as fiction. Further, the circumstances of such finds should also be weighed carefully before dismissing them as fabrication, even though they mirror fictional themes. Much like the fictional discoveries of two works *Dictys of Crete* and *The Wonders Beyond Thule*, the *Apocalypse of Peter* was discovered in 1887 within the tomb of an eighth- or ninth-century

---

87. Speyer, an advocate of a forged Damis source, notes this. See Speyer, "Zum Bild des Apollonios," 53.

88. Jenkins, *Lost History of Christianity*, 7–8; Brock, *A brief outline*, 63.

89. Pliny the Elder reports that Democritus entered the tomb of Dardanus the Phoenician to obtain his works (*Nat.* 30.9). However, this should be balanced by another of his stories in which female relatives found a letter in the tomb of the geometrician Dionysodorus; this tale claimed that Dionysodorus had passed from the tomb to the bottom of the earth (*Nat.* 2.248).

90. Sometimes entire collections of texts have been discovered, such as the library of Ashurbanipal at Nineveh (1849), the Amarna letters (1887), the Nag Hammadi codices (1945), Dead Sea Scrolls (1946–47), the archives of Ugarit (1928–29), and the Hittite archives at Bogazköy (1906). The Oxyrynchus papyri, discovered between 1887–1907, revealed a few works that were thought lost (e.g., Aristotle's *Constitution of the Athenians*; an epitome of seven lost books of Livy's *History of Rome*) and some that were previously unknown (e.g., *Hellenica Oxyrhynchia*). The Codex Tchacos, discovered in the 1970s, contained two previously unknown texts: the *Gospel of Judas* and *The Temptation of Allogenes* (this work should be distinguished from the Nag Hammadi text *Allogenes*).

monk at Akhmim, Egypt.[91] Much like the fictional account of finding the works of Dictys, shepherds allegedly discovered some of the Dead Sea Scrolls. Examples of real discoveries like these demonstrate that it takes more than a few references to fictional documents to dismiss the possibility that Empress Julia did indeed receive a previously unknown and privately preserved document of some sort that dates to the first or second century AD.

Finally, the differences between the Damis memoir and *Dictys of Crete* and *The Wonders Beyond Thule* are perhaps worth pondering. The status of the Damis documents differs from these in that it was not said to be lost, but rather that it was simply unknown. The location of the discovery of the Damis document also differs from these other works, for the work of Damis was not discovered in a tomb, but rather it was supposedly in the possession of a relative of Damis. The manner of its discovery differs as well; the work of Damis was supposedly presented to Empress Julia, whereas the other works were found by exploration or accident. Although these differences may be slight, they may suggest that Philostratus was not employing a *topos* after all.

Eyewitness Testimony vs. the Errors and Implausible Events in the VA

One of the strongest arguments against the reality of an authentic account written by a first-century eyewitness is that such a witness would not have made the number and sort of errors found in the VA.[92] This is not the place for cataloging such errors—this will be the task of the next chapter—but it will be helpful to discuss the general nature of these errors here. First, there are the numerous historical (e.g., the existence of the "ghost town" Babylon as a thriving city VA 1.25), geographical (e.g., the location of the Eretrians VA 1.24.1–2), chronological (e.g., the age of Scopelian VA 1.24.3) and zoological errors (e.g., hippopotami in the Indus River) that appear all eight books of the VA. Second, the VA

---

91. Van Minnen, "Greek Apocalypse of Peter," 17. In addition to this find, other discoveries have been found in similar locations. Although there are disputes about the exact location of the Nag Hammadi discovery, the accounts seems to at least indicate that the cache of documents was found in a cave or a tomb. Likewise, there are reports of documents (e.g., the Chester Beatty biblical papyri; a Coptic version of the Gospel of John; a Coptic version of Deuteronomy, Jonah, and Acts) that were found in tombs or in the vicinity of tombs, although the evidence for these finds has been questioned. For a discussion of these materials, see Nongbri, "Finding Early Christian Books," 11–19.

92. Taggart, "Apollonius," 70.

is filled with many magical supernatural details that are implausible. Although some researchers, particularly those who are believing Christians, will not *a priori* rule out the possibility of the supernatural, some of the tales in the *VA* are rather outrageous, such as those of a talking statue (*VA* 6:4.2–3), a talking elm (*VA* 4.10.3), and the bleeding trees at Geryon's tomb (*VA* 5.5). The *VA* also mentions fictional creatures and animals, such as *empusai* (or vampires; *VA* 2.4; 4.25), unicorns (*VA* 3.2), a phoenix (*VA* 3.48), a griffin (*VA* 3.48), and enormous serpents capable of dragging off elephants (*VA* 3.7.2). Some of these beings appear to be based on descriptions found in earlier Greek historical and geographical writings (e.g., Ctesias's *Indika*) and are far more likely to have been the additions of the sophist Philostratus than to have come from a genuine eyewitness account. Third, the text is filled with wonders performed by Apollonius (e.g., predictions, exorcisms, a resurrection of a dead girl, and a disappearance during his trial) and by other characters (e.g., levitation performed by the Wise Ones of India in *VA* 3.15). This small sampling of materials from the *VA* should be sufficient to illustrate why many have questioned the genuineness of the eyewitness testimony of the Damis account and its existence.

Yet, the sorts of material just presented do not necessarily rule out the possibility that a source was employed in the composition of the *VA*. Several scenarios are possible. One option is that Philostratus may have used an eyewitness source or a forgery as the foundation of his tale, while most of the errors in it are due to his elaborations of that source. If he meant to write history, he may have simply been careless; if he intended to write fiction, he may have inserted materials drawn from exotic travel narratives and mythological themes. A second possibility is that Philostratus embellished a forgery that was already filled with inaccuracies and that both that source and its editor, Philostratus, share responsibility for the errors found therein. On balance, the former option seems the more likely of the two if a source was involved, especially since (1) some of the encounters in the *VA* appear in Philostratus's other writings (e.g., the statue of Memnon *VA* 6.4.1–3; *Her.* 26.16; *Imag. I* 1.7.19–25) and (2) the bizarre creatures in the narrative seem to derive from Greek literature (e.g., Herodotus) are not likely to have been known to the uneducated Assyrian disciple of Apollonius. Yet, either option shows that it is difficult to exclude Philostratus's use of a source simply because of the numerous errors or supernatural elements in the narrative.

PART 3: INVESTIGATING THE APOLLONIAN DECALOGUE

Assuming for the moment that Philostratus employed some sort of source as the framework for the *VA*, the mistakes in the *VA* cannot all be blamed on the Damis material for errors also appear in sections attributed to Philostratus his other unnamed sources. Further, the Damis material is difficult to identify resulting in Damis or pseudo-Damis sometimes being blamed for the mistakes of another contributor to the *VA*. This is partly because Philostratus was notoriously unclear about what sources he was quoting, thereby making the alleged Damis material difficult to isolate in the *VA*. Although Philostratus sometimes distinguished between his own opinion (e.g., *VA* 1.25; 4.22) and that of Damis (e.g., *VA* 3.41; 8.28), he often employed the ambiguous formula "they say" (e.g., *VA* 5.2-3, 5-6), which concealed the identity of his source. Bowie believed by using this vague reference Philostratus seemed to block any attempts to determine his sources. Bowie also argued that Philostratus's use of "they say" was merely an ethnographic formula that he thought was suitable to the genre of the *VA*.[93] Yet, this interpretation is challenged by Philostratus's use of this formula numerous times in his other historical work, the *VS*,[94] where he also failed to indicate the specific written or oral source from which he was quoting. This formula also appears in *Heroicus*,[95] where Philostratus sometimes identified travelers,[96] poets,[97] or the fictional Protesilaus[98] as the source. Again, the "they say" and "some say" introductions appear in the non-fictional *Gymnasticus*.[99] This formula's use in several books within his corpus suggests that Philostratus was not intentionally hiding his source, but rather that this was his preferred method of citation whether he was writing biography (*VS*) or fiction (*Heroicus*). He employed this formula whether quoting real figures or fictional ones, like Protesilaus, which raises the question of which of these categories Damis belonged to himself. Yet, the takeaway from his use of the "they say" formula is that critics of the Damis source should

---

93. Bowie, "Philostratus: Writer of Fiction," 195.

94. E.g., *VS* 482, 494, 497, 498, 514–15, 522, 524, 530, 543, 553, 559, 570, 576, 581, 582, 583, 595, 597, 612.

95. E.g., *Her.* 1.5; 2.10; 7.2, 8.5, 14–11; 9.5; 17.4; 33.8, 14, 16, 28, 40, 42; 43.7; 53.21; 55.5; 57.1.

96. E.g., *Her.* 55.2.

97. E.g., *Her.* 7.1, 56.11.

98. E.g., *Her.* 28.3; 29.1; 31.1.

99. E.g., *Gymn.* 13, 16, 18.

not too hastily charge Damis with an error when this figure cannot be identified as the speaker or participant in the story.

Assuming for the moment that the Damis source existed, a proper methodology for extracting it from the VA should be employed. Even Bowie, who is skeptical of a Damis source, writes that researchers must resist "wholesome foisting upon Damis of material not explicitly attributed to him by Philostratus."[100] Anderson formulates a sensible approach: if Philostratus said that "Damis says" or the equivalent in the VA, then Damis must be held accountable for that material. However, if Philostratus wrote "it is said" or some other formula in which the subject is not identified, Damis cannot be held responsible for the material in these accounts.[101] Although this seems fair and the approach is promising in theory, applying it to and extracting data from the VA is often difficult. Nevertheless, this at least points the way toward the sort of method that should be implemented for this task.

Anderson's use of this methodology to isolate the Damis source produced some interesting results. First, he noted that many of the excursuses in the VA are from Philostratus himself; the contents of these cannot be attributed to Damis.[102] Second, he observed that most of the "incredible and anachronistic material" in the VA was not attributed to Damis, but to an ambiguous "they said" source.[103] Third, Damis's contributions were often modest and credible.[104] Fourth, he noted that Damis was often absent from the narrative.[105] The disciple appeared largely in the journeys to India and Rome, appeared little in the Ethiopian and Athenian accounts, and played a limited role in the seventh and eighth books of the VA.[106] Damis was absent from the introductory material (i.e., birth and education of Apollonius), some of the meetings with Indian sages, the last phase of the visit to the cataract of the Nile, Apollonius's discussion

---

100. Bowie, "Philostratus: Writer of Fiction," 198, n. 28.

101. Anderson, *Philostratus*, 157.

102. Anderson, *Philostratus*, 157–58.

103. Anderson, *Philostratus*, 162. However, Flinterman makes a strong case that the "they said" material can only plausibly be attributed to Damis, Apollonius, and other travelling companions. This is clearly the case in some episodes (e.g., VA 3.2; cf. 2.20). See Flinterman, *Power*, 82.

104. Anderson, *Philostratus*, 161.

105. Anderson, *Philostratus*, 161–62. Koskenniemi also notes that Damis is absent from some episodes. See Koskenniemi, *Der philostrateische Apollonios*, 11.

106. Anderson, *Philostratus*, 163. Flinterman notes that a similar distribution of Damis episodes appear between VA 1.19 and VA 8.28. See Flinterman, *Power*, 81–82.

with the Governor of Baetica, the meeting with Vespasian, and the end of the narrative (i.e. Apollonius's trial and disappearance at Rome, the second sight episode predicting Domitian's death, the descent into the cave at Lebadea, and Apollonius's departure).[107] This uneven use of Damis as a character in the *VA* may suggest that Philostratus was reliant on some sort of source.[108] Otherwise, if Philostratus were freely inventing material, he could have pulled Damis into many other episodes as a witness.[109] An approach like Anderson's takes seriously the possibility of a source; he was careful to isolate genuine Damis material while at the same time holding the Damis source accountable for its errors.

The Damis Material Coincides with Philostratus's Interests

Long ago, Meyer argued that several features of the Damis material suspiciously coincided with the interests of Philostratus. He listed numerous topics that would have been implausible for the uneducated Assyrian, Damis, to have known about. Rather, as he put it, all of these were examples of pure sophistic work deriving from the pen of Philostratus.[110] The topics that he identified could not creditably stem from Damis were: (1) historical details that are dependent on literary sources such as Herodotus, Xenophon, and Ctesias;[111] (2) art history;[112] and (3) geography that was based on Nearchus's *Indike*.[113] Consequently, Meyer concluded that Damis and his source never existed, but that both were the creations of Philostratus.

Meyer is likely correct that most of these details came from Philostratus, but this does not necessarily indicate that the sophist was not working from a source. Most scholars who adhere to the forgery

---

107. Anderson, *Philostratus*, 161–64.

108. Anderson, *Philostratus*, 164.

109. Flinterman, however, points out several instances in which Philostratus may have introduced Damis into a narrative to dramatize a traditional element and that, in such cases, this material should not be regarded as part of the Damis source. See Flinterman, *Power*, 82.

110. He writes, "Das alles ist echte Sophistenarbeit." See Meyer, "Apollonios von Tyana," 378.

111. Meyer, "Apollonios von Tyana," 375.

112. Meyer, "Apollonios von Tyana," 378.

113. Meyer, "Apollonios von Tyana," 379.

hypothesis[114] and those who endorse an eyewitness account[115] point out that Philostratus thoroughly worked over his source material so that the topics, style, and wording were remade in his own image. Thus, much of the similarity between the Damis sections and Philostratus may be due to the sophist's enrichment of those passages.

Meyers's thesis can be further challenged by the aspects of the Damis material that do not align well with Philostratus's viewpoint. For instance, Philostratus appears to disagree with or be embarrassed by some of the Damis material.[116] If the Damis material was indeed fictional, this raises the question of why Philostratus would introduce it only to disagree with it or allow it to contradict or challenge his agenda. Additionally, several emphases found in the Damis sections are not found elsewhere in the Philostratean corpus (e.g., theosophy,[117] Pythagoreanism, and the religions and philosophies of India or Africa[118]). Although miraculous events are sometimes featured in *Heroicus* and the *VS*,[119] these examples do not verge on magic—a practice Philostratus uniformly opposed in his writings—as they sometimes do in the *VA*. These dissimilarities from the Philostratean corpus tend to blunt the force of the argument for the similarities that were proposed by Meyer.

---

114. Hadas and Smith write concerning Philostratus's use of the Damis material and other sources, "Material from these sources he supplemented from his general literary knowledge and his own imagination. Appealing to the interests of his time, he inserted large sections of fanciful geography and anthropology, much of it from sources of what was already classical antiquity" (Hadas and Smith, *Heroes and Gods*, 197). Anderson similarly suspects that many of such passages "were very probably elaborated by Philostratus, as he claims" at *VA* 1.3.1. See Anderson, *Philostratus*, 157. Flinterman wrote, "The fact that Philostratus appeals to Damis to credit Apollonius with his own interests may be a matter of embroidering on the information derived from the Damis source. It is not itself evidence for the claim that the author of the *VA* made this source up himself" (Flinterman, *Power*, 84–85).

115. Taggart assumed that Philostratus re-worked the Damis material so much that "it is really impossible to detect in the *Vita* anything which could be identified with certainty as taken from the pen of Damis" (Taggart, "Apollonius," 76).

116. Anderson, *Philostratus*, 158; Flinterman, *Power*, 85.

117. Hadas and Smith, *Heroes and Gods*, 196.

118. Hadas and Smith, *Heroes and Gods*, 196. While some of these themes are occasionally touched upon elsewhere in the corpus, they are not developed and may have been influenced by the materials used earlier in composing the *VA*. Philostratus mentions that the sophist Alexander ("Clay Plato"), whom some claimed to be the illegitimate child of Apollonius of Tyana, once visited the Naked Ones of Ethiopia (*VS* 571). He also briefly mentions the Chaldean and Indian philosophers in that work (*VS* 481).

119. Philostratus, *Her.* 14,17; *VS* 554.

PART 3: INVESTIGATING THE APOLLONIAN DECALOGUE

The Unwieldiness of the Vast Number of Tablets
Required for Damis's Memoir

As noted earlier in this chapter, the Damis memoirs were said to have been written on wooden tablets. The logistics of transporting such writing materials while Damis traveled with Apollonius creates doubts about the reality of such documents. Such problems, perhaps raised in jest by Schirren, still offer a good reason for rejecting the claims of a diary inscribed on tablets. He writes, "But how many of these *deltoi* did Damis need? I imagine that quite a retinue was required to transport hundreds of wooden tablets during the journeys of the sage, like the outside broadcast trucks today when a soccer game takes place or a pop star goes on stage in a concert."[120] Wooden tablets were bulkier, heavier, and more limited in the number of characters that could be written on them than on a roll of papyrus or parchment. So, Schirren is correct to draw attention to the logistical problem posed by transporting these tablets while on a journey from one end of the known world to the other.

Assuming for the moment the existence of an authentic Damis source, how many tablets would this disciple have needed to complete his *Scrapbook*? The *VA* is a massive work that contains 87,068 words.[121] Not even those who believe in the existence of Damis's memoir would claim that the entire *VA* was once written on tablets; Philostratus did not attribute all of it to Damis and he certainly made his unique contributions while editing it. Therefore, no attempt will be made here to estimate how many tablets the alleged Damis documents would have filled.

Yet, a few samples of passages attributed to Damis will illustrate the problems posed by choosing tablets as a form of record keeping. A baseline for these examples is needed for estimating how many characters could be written on a tablet. The senatorial decree that recorded the judicial proceedings against Piso at the time of Tiberius will serve this purpose and indicates that about 892 characters could be written on the front and back of a single wax tablet.[122] By using this number and by

120. Schirren, "Irony," 165.

121. Adams, *The Genre of Acts*, 139; Burridge, *What Are the Gospels?*, 164.

122. Oleson comments, "Undoubtedly, these tablets took up much more space than papyrus documents. The approximately 12,500 characters of the senatorial decree recording the judicial proceedings against Piso under Tiberius discovered on bronzes ... were copied by the emperor's quaestor on fourteen tablets (*tabulae*), probably written on both sides and undoubtedly bundled up into one booklet" (Oleson, *Handbook of Engineering*, 730).

counting the number of Greek characters in a few Damis passages, one can get a sense of the number of tablets needed to account for the material in the *VA*. Approximately 22.5 wooden tablets would have been needed to record the material found in only three brief Damis passages.[123] Thus, Damis would have needed hundreds of tablets to record the contents of the numerous Damis sections in the *VA*. How would these tablets have been transported and protected from the elements while on journeys to India, Spain, Ethiopia, and Rome? How would this ever-growing number of tablets have been transported when traveling by camel, by ship, and on foot? How did the relative of Damis later transport the entire collection to Empress Julia Domna when she was at Tyana (or Rome)? How did Philostratus cart these documents around before or after Julia's death as he labored to complete the *VA*? Questions like these about such an unwieldy collection of documents make the possibility of real memoirs unlikely.

Still, it is possible that such a document was originally composed on *deltoi*. Perhaps the Damis document originally delivered to Julia was brief. The text may have been as brief as Lucian's *Demonax* (3000 words),[124] Xenophon's *Agesilaus* (5,000)[125] the Gospel of Mark (11,242),[126] or Suetonius's *Augustus* (16,000 words),[127] or even Iamblichus's *Life of Pythagoras*. If the Damis memoir was about the same length as these texts, it would have required far fewer tablets. The *VA* may create the illusion that the diary was enormous, while this impression might be because Philostratus expanded Damis's account and supplemented it with other materials.[128] Other solutions that would help solve this problem are also at hand. Assuming Damis was the real author, he could have composed

---

123. The passage in *VA* 1.22.2–24.3 contains approximately 5744 Greek characters [and 928 words] and would have required 6.4 tablets to record its contents. The story in *VA* 8.10–17 is approximately 9287 characters in length [1511 words]) and would have required 10.4 tablets. Another tale in *VA* 8.38, 40–42.5, containing approximately 5093 Greek characters [and 830 words] would have needed 5.7 tablets to write.

124. Anderson, *Philostratus*, 165. For this word count, see Burridge, *What are the Gospels?*, 164.

125. Burridge, *What are the Gospels?*, 134.

126. Burridge, *What are the Gospels?*, 194.

127. Burridge, *What are the Gospels?*, 164.

128. Flinterman is helpful at getting a sense of how little material supposedly belonged to the Damis account. He counted thirty-eight chapters of the *VA* in which Damis is cited as a source: sixteen while travelling in Mesopotamia and India, four while in Spain, six while in Ethiopia, and seven during the encounter with Domitian in Rome. Beyond these episodes, he lists a few other brief passages that attribute material to Damis (*VA* 4.19; 4.25; 5.26; 6.32; 8.28). See Flinterman, *Power*, 81, n. 121.

a document later in life from memory or brief notes after his journeys with Apollonius had ended and left the problem of delivering hundreds of tablets to Julia Domna for his relative to solve. Assuming the document to be a forgery, transporting these tablets would not have been a problem at all since the journey itself was fiction, although their later transport to the empress would remain an issue. In either of the above scenarios, Damis's alleged relative could have delivered the diary to Julia in the form of a scroll. In either scenario above, Philostratus, who would have needed to consult these texts while writing the VA, could have had their contents transferred from *deltoi* to papyrus or parchment for ease of transport if they were not already in a portable format. Although all these suggestions are hypothetical, they do demonstrate that Philostratus could have possessed a document that had at one time been preserved on wooden tablets.

The Case for a Forged Document

Previously-employed Arguments That also Support a Forged Document

The case for a Philostratus's use of a pseudepigraphical document, although a minority position, is still relatively strong, and is the position favored by this study. Many of the points that have already been addressed in this chapter in support of a genuine Damis document could also be used to support a forgery. These arguments will not be rehashed in detail here, but a quick review of the more substantial arguments that could be harvested from the above discussion and repurposed for the support of the theory of a forgery are that (1) the material in the VA and particularly in the Damis material that does not align with the interests of Philostratus (e.g., Pythagoreanism) may suggest that he relied on input from a source rather than from his own imagination; (2) several chronological errors and the presence of narratives gaps may have been caused by Philostratus's inability to incorporate successfully some of the Damis material into his storyline; (3) Philostratus's discomfort with Damis material that associated Apollonius with magic, which went against the VA's agenda, may suggest that he was obliged to incorporate a contrary source; (4) the circumstances of the preservation and discovery of a forged journal attributed to Damis do not necessarily signal a fictional theme,¹²⁹ for genuine documents were preserved and discovered in similar ways; (5) the lack of attestation of pseudo-Damis's journals can be accounted for by their incorporation into the *VA*, much like in the case of other known documents (2 Macc 2:23) and theoretical ones (e.g., Q or JEDP); (6) the transportation of numerous tablets on Damis's travels is not a problem if the documents were forgeries written at a later time; and (7) the transport of the alleged Damis document by a relative of the Assyrian to the empress or the later transport of the document by Philostratus as he was writing the *VA* need not weigh against its existence, for the document may have been transferred to papyrus or parchment at some point.

However, one argument from the discussion above that may tip the scale in favor of a forgery is that there are numerous historical inaccuracies in the *VA*. These would not be likely to have come from a genuine eyewitness. For this reason, this investigation favors the position that there was a genuine document from which Philostratus worked, but that it was a forgery. Apart from these points, there is one more argument left to explore that favors a pseudepigraphical source.

The Empress Julia as a Deterrent to Forgery or Philostratean Invention

Speyer, a forgery theorist, argued that Philostratus must have received some sort of text from the empress, Julia Domna, for the sophist would not have dared to add his own material to a document written under the royal name.¹³⁰ More recently, Keener acknowledged this view. While allowing for the possibility that the Damis notebook was a Philostratean fiction or a pseudepigraph, he explained that "I tend to think that Philostratus would not have dared claim that the empress brought this source to his attention unless he believed that she thought it to be authentically from Damis, however much Philostratus may have adapted it for literary purposes."¹³¹

This view has been criticized by advocates of a fictional document and supporters of a forged document alike. Bowie, who believed that the diaries of Damis were a Philostratean fiction, responded to Speyer

---

129. Speyer believed that the forged Damis memoirs were influenced by the story of Dictys. He suggested the Philostratus may have seen through this fiction and used them anyway because they were useful in challenging the view of Moiragenes that Apollonius was a magician. See Speyer, "Zum Bild des Apollonios," 49–50.

130. Speyer, "Zum Bild des Apollonios," 49.

131. Keener, *Christobiography*, 47.

that "Philostratus . . . could himself be responsible for the invention of Damis in conscious evocation of a novelistic tone and setting. No abuse of Julia Domna's name is involved if the technique and its implications were as patent to every Greek reader as is suggested by consideration of the motif's ramifications in novelistic productions."[132] Flinterman, who endorsed the forgery hypothesis, offered up two points: (1) the VA was completed after the death of Julia and (2) the assumption that attributing his forged material to a source given to him by Julia Domna would have given offense is unproven.[133] So then, this argument does not have much force, for either the living empress might have endorsed the VA as a work intended for entertainment or the deceased empress would not have had a say in what Philostratus did in her name.

CONCLUSION

Making a final decision on the existence of Damis and whether his *Scrapbook* was written by Damis, a forger, or Philostratus is difficult. Currently, there does not appear to be a way to arrive at absolute certainty on these issues. However, a few words can be said about this issue with certainty. Most of the arguments above both for and against a forged document were inconclusive, while many others were even implausible and were dismissed. Others seemed to have some merit. For instance, Philostratus's inclusion of materials that ran counter to his agenda strongly suggests he was reliant on a real source. Yet, one of the strongest arguments above concerning the alleged Damis source, whether it is forgery or fiction, is that it does not reflect accurate eyewitness testimony in numerous places, as demonstrated by several historical errors and his inclusion of rather unlikely supernatural details (e.g. a talking elm or levitation). This latter point appears to eliminate the option of a genuine Damis account but still leaves the options of the diary being a forgery—the view favored by this study—or a piece of fiction. The investigation of these historical problems is the topic of the next chapter.

---

132. Bowie, *Apollonius*, 1663.
133. Flinterman, *Power*, 84.

11

Item 6
Historical and Geographical Errors in the *VA*

MOST SCHOLARS WOULD AGREE with the claim of the sixth item of the Apollonian decalogue that "numerous verifiable historical and geographical errors appear in the *VA*." This chapter will examine such problems in the *VA* and ask to what extent they compromise the historical value of the work. Most of the problems that will be investigated are historical, geographical, or chronological in nature. Occasionally attention will also be given to reports of mythical beings and unusual flora and fauna when data allow for historical or literary analysis.[1] In examining these issues,

---

1. This study will not evaluate the historicity of the supernatural powers of Apollonius or other figures mentioned in the *VA*. The reason for this decision is that: (1) some scholars will rule out such events *a priori* while others may deem them possible based on their prior philosophical and theological commitments, and (2) most of the accounts dealing with the supernatural do not normally lend themselves to historical investigation (e.g., there are usually no historical accounts that confirm or deny these phenomena). However, a representative list of the supernatural feats performed by Apollonius is included here for those who might want to pursue such matters. Apollonius's supernatural abilities include (1) a knowledge of all languages without study (*VA* 1.19.1); (2) a knowledge of things not said by people (*VA* 1.19.2; 7.22); (3) an understanding of animal languages (*VA* 1.20; 4.3; 5.42); (4) the subjugation of fierce animals (*VA* 6.43; 8.30.2); (5) the interpretation of signs and events (*VA* 1.22; 4.34, 43; 5.13; 8.23); (6) the interpretation of dreams (*VA* 1.23; 4.55); (7) second sight (*VA* 4.3; 5.30; 8.26); (8) foreknowledge and prognostication (*VA* 1.2, 34, 37; 4.4, 18; 5.18, 19, 37.1–3; 8.20.1); (9) the control of storms (*VA* 4.15; cf. 4.13.1); (10) rapid travel (*VA* 4.10; 8.12.2); (11) the destruction of plague demons (*VA* 4.10); (12) the exorcism of demons (*VA* 3.38; 4.20); (13) exposing and repelling vampiric spirits (*VA* 2.4; 5.25); (14) detecting lost treasures (*VA* 6.39); (15) deliverance of cities from earthquakes (6.41);

the investigation will make the effort to identify mistakes that appear within Damis's accounts, since these are valuable in weighing claims of reliability or existence of Damis as an eyewitness and of his diary.

The topics discussed in this section are treated in the order in which they appear in the VA rather than arranging them by topic (e.g., chronological errors, mythological fauna).[2] This choice of organization may make the subject matter a bit difficult to understand for those who are unfamiliar with the storyline of the VA. Although an effort has been made to make this chapter as comprehensible as possible, some readers may wish to consult the summary of the VA presented earlier in this book or they may merely wish to sample sections of this chapter rather than reading it straight through.

SELECT ERRORS WITHIN THE VA

Philostratus Commits a "Capito" Offense by Confusing Two Men of That Name (VA 1.12)

While Apollonius was still a youth living in Aegae, a lecherous, Roman governor of Cilicia attempted to seduce him. When Apollonius rebuffed his advances, the official threatened to have him beheaded. Apollonius laughed at this threat and then predicted that the governor would be executed on a particular day. This prophecy was fulfilled on the designated day; the governor was executed along with Archelaus, the king of Cappadocia, for conspiring against Rome.

Philostratus's information concerning this event is not entirely correct. Even though Archelaus was executed in AD 17 in Rome by Emperor Tiberius, there is no record of an execution of the governor of Cilicia at this time. However, Dio Cassius did mention the execution of Archelaus

---

(16) healing rabies (6.43); (17) raising the dead (VA 4.45); (18) making an indictment against him disappear from an official's manuscript (VA 4.44); and, (19) escaping from chains (VA 7.38.2; cf. 30.3). The Wise Ones of India also performed miracles in the VA that include (1) levitation (VA 3.15; 17.2); (2) clairvoyance (VA 3.16); (3) healings of a lame man, a blind man, a man with a withered hand, and a woman experiencing miscarriages (VA 3.39); and (4) exorcising a demon by means of a letter (VA 3.38). For a more thorough listing of the miracles in the VA and a comparison to those performed by Jesus, see Petzke, *Die Traditionen*, 125–34.

2. Since most of the errors treated in this chapter would be classified as historical or geographical, there was not much benefit in employing a topical format for their examination.

in the same passage as a man named Aetius Capito, but this Capito was neither the governor of Cilicia nor was he executed (*Hist. rom.* 57.17.2–7). The most likely explanation for this error is that Philostratus was using Dio Cassius as his source for this episode[3] and confused Aetius Capito with Cossutianus Capito, a governor of Cilicia, who was indeed executed by Nero in AD 57 (Tacitus, *Annals*, 13.33).[4] This relatively minor error should probably be chalked up to an honest mistake. Still, this blunder could have serious ramifications for the chronology of the historical Apollonius,[5] for it raises the question of whether Philostratus thought Apollonius was a youth in AD 17, when Archelaus was killed, or a youth in AD 57 when Cossutianus Capito was executed.

The Existence of Nineveh (*VA* 1.3; 1.18–20)

A commonly cited example of Philostratus inaccuracy is his assertion that the old Assyrian city of Nineveh still existed in the first century.[6] This claim is problematic for the historicity of the *VA* for several reasons. The first of these is that biblical Nineveh had been abandoned since the fourth century BC.[7] A second problem is that Philostratus appears to have been confused about the geography of Mesopotamia. His omissions from Apollonius's travels there are curious; for instance, he failed to mention crossing the Tigris River on the way to Nineveh.[8] Furthermore, Apollonius's Mesopotamian itinerary is nonsensical in several ways. Philostratus made the absurd claim that Apollonius, traveling from west to east, visited Nineveh before crossing the Euphrates River (*VA* 1.20). He also claimed that between Apollonius's visits to Antioch (*VA* 1.18) and Zeugma (*VA* 1.20.2), he stopped at Nineveh (*VA* 1.19); this would be much like visiting New York on the way from Richmond to Washington DC.[9] A third matter concerns the existence of Damis since he suppos-

---

3. This mistake could have been made by Maximus of Aegae for he was presumably Philostratus's source for this section of the *VA* (*VA* 1.12.2).

4. Phillimore, *In Honour*, cxi–cxii; Harris, "Apollonius of Tyana," 192.

5. Phillimore, *In Honour*, cxii–cxiii.

6. Gildersleave wrote concerning the inaccuracy, "What if he builds up Nineveh and Babylon from their ruins?" (Gildersleave, *Essays*, 259).

7. Habermas, "Did Jesus Perform Miracles?," 122; Kee, *Miracle*, 256; David K. Clark, "Miracles in the World Religions," 211.

8. C. P. Jones, "Passage to India," 187; Miles, *Philostratus*, 55, n. 5.

9. Gildersleave, *Essays*, 259.

edly came from "the nonexistent city of Nineveh"[10] (*VA* 1.3). A fourth problem is that all these inaccuracies and oddities occur in what appear to be a Damis account, thereby calling its claim of eyewitness testimony into question. Thus, Apollonius's visit to Jonah's Nineveh appears to be one whale of a tale.

Despite repeated references to the alleged inaccuracy concerning the existence of Nineveh, it appears that Philostratus was correct after all in his statements about Old Ninos, for ἀρχαῖα Νίνος ("ancient Nineveh" or "old Ninos") does not refer to the ancient Assyrian capital of biblical fame, but rather to Syrian Hierapolis (i.e., Mabog or Bambyce). Jones adduced several arguments in favor of this identification. To begin with, he demonstrated that Ammianus Marcellinus referred to Hierapolis as Old Ninos ("Hierapoli, vetere Nino"; *Res Gest*.14.8.7) and that the name "Old Ninos" was used to distinguish Hierapolis from *Nineve* or *Ninos*, the Assyrian Nineveh (*Res Gest*. 18.7.1, 23.6.22).[11] Another clue that identifies Old Ninos with Hierapolis is that it was the home of the cult of Atargatis (called Io by Philostratus), the Syrian Goddess, whose horned image was visited there by Apollonius (*VA* 1.19).[12] A final piece of evidence is that Hierapolis makes more sense of the itinerary of the *VA*, for Old Ninos is situated between Antioch (*VA* 1.18) and Zeugma (*VA* 1.20).[13] This also explains how Apollonius could have visited this city before crossing the Euphrates River and why no mention of the crossing of the Tigris appears in the account. In this case, at least, Philostratus and Damis appear to be vindicated.

---

10. Habermas, "Did Jesus Perform Miracles?," 123.

11. C. P. Jones, "Passage to India," 188. Jones notes in this entry that the adjective ἀρχαῖα used with reference to a city often indicated the existence of a more recently built city that bore that same name. He explains that the use of the title "old Ninos" for Hierapolis implies that it was regarded as the more ancient of two sites, although the reasons for this assertion are unknown.

12. C. P. Jones, "Passage to India," 189. Philostratus referred to little "horns" projecting from the image's head (καὶ κέρατα τῶν κροτάφων ἐκκρούει μικρά), whereas Lucian described the image as bearing "rays" on her head (καὶ ἐπὶ τῇ κεφαλῇ ἀκτῖνάς τε φορέει; *Syr. d.* 32). This confusion of horns and light rays resembles the situation in which the rays of glory that issued from Moses's face after his encounter with God were later interpreted as horns in later Christian literature (the Vulgate translates the wording of Exod 34:29 as *cornuta*) and art (e.g., Michelangelo's statue of Moses).

13. C. P. Jones, "Passage to India," 187–88.

ITEM 6

King Vardanes: His Existence and His Capital (*VA* 1.21.1–2)

Philostratus related that Apollonius visited the Parthian king Vardanes II in his capital city Babylon. The plausibility of this visit is supported by Philostratus's claims that (1) Vardanes I, son of Atrabanus II, was a historical figure who reigned from AD 40–45,[14] (2) he was a contemporary of Apollonius, and (3) he had lost and reconquered his kingdom (*VA* 1.12.2).

Yet, Philostratus did make a few minor blunders in this passage. He was mistaken in his claim that Babylon served as Vardanes's capital. Perhaps most problematic for this claim is that Greek and Roman sources were practically unanimous in portraying Babylon as nearly desolate during this time.[15] Furthermore, there is good evidence that Ctesiphon was Vardanes's capital at the time rather than Babylon. Some commentators, attempting to vindicate Philostratus's claim of a Babylonian capital, suggest that with the revolt in the city of Seleucia just across the Tigris River from Ctesiphon, Vardanes may have made Babylon his temporary residence. Yet, numismatic data from Seleucia controverts this theory by showing that Vardanes had recovered Ctesiphon soon after his reign began.[16] A final problem is that Ctesiphon was almost certainly not the border of the empire in the time of Tiberius when this episode is set,[17] thereby challenging the eyewitness account of Damis.[18] Thus, in reporting Apollonius's visit with Vardanes, Philostratus was correct about the broader aspects of the story but he falters when reporting some of its finer details.[19]

---

14. C. P. Jones, "Passage to India," 192; Bowersock, *Introduction to Life of Apollonius*, 16.

15. Babylon's existence will be discussed in an upcoming section of this chapter.

16. C. P. Jones, "Passage to India," 193.

17. Kee, *Miracle*, 256–57.

18. Kee appears to attribute this mistake to Damis. See Kee, *Miracle*, 256. This attribution appears to be fair, for Damis is mentioned just prior to this account (*VA* 1.20.3) and after it (*VA* 1.22.2). Apollonius's companions are also mentioned within this account, thereby making Kee's claim that this is a Damis account plausible (*VA* 1.21.1).

19. A minor point worth mentioning is that Vardanes's brother Megabates is usually thought to be fictional (*VA* 1.31). See C. P. Jones, "Passage to India," 192.

PART 3: INVESTIGATING THE APOLLONIAN DECALOGUE

The Location of the Eretrians: Near Babylon, Susa, or Ecbatana? (*VA* 1.24.1–2)

In what can be identified as a Damis account,[20] the *VA* indicates that the Persians had relocated exiles from the Greek city of Eretria to the city of Ardericca in the district of Cissia,[21] which was said to be a four-day journey from Babylon (*VA* 1.24.1). Yet, Cissia is neither north of Babylon nor is it even near that city, for it is located far away in western Iran.[22] Further, Philostratus's description of Ardericca is also inaccurate. The most likely explanation for both of these errors is that Philostratus misread Herodotus, his presumed source here, and mistakenly combined characteristics of two cities that shared the name Ardericca; one was located near Babylon and the other near Susa.[23] Jones comments that the conflation of these two locations "is not favorable to the idea that Damis was an eye-witness companion of Apollonius; this is an error resulting from the misunderstanding of Herodotus, either on Philostratus' part or on that of an earlier writer equally dependent on classical literature."[24]

A related oddity occurs in the following section of the *VA*. The travelers—presumably Damis included—encounter an inscription carved on an Eretrian tomb that states, "here now we lie on Ecbatana's plain" (*VA* 1.24.2).[25] This message inaccurately located the exiles living at Ardericca about 300 kilometers north of Susa, rather than near it, as if Susa and Ecbatana were near each other. This alleged Damis account is inaccurate,[26]

---

20. Damis is mentioned twice in this account: his memoir is referenced in *VA* 1.24.1 and "Damis said" that Apollonius restored some of the Eretrian tombs in *VA* 1.24.3. The context also suggests that the report that "they" heard reports about the Eretrians refers to Apollonius and Damis as well (*VA* 1.24.2).

21. In 490 BC, Persian forces besieged and captured the Greek city of Eretria. After their defeat at Marathon, the Persians retreated with the captive Eretrians and resettled them at Ardericca in Cissia (Herodotus, *Hist*. 6.116).

22. C. P. Jones, "Passage to India," 195.

23. One of these cities named Ardericca, the one with canals, was upstream from Babylon (*Hist* 1.185; *VA* 1.24.1), while the other was in Iran, 40 kilometers from Susa; the latter was 40 stades from a well of bitumen, salt, and oil (*Hist*. 6.119; *VA* 1.24.1).

24. C. P. Jones, "Passage to India," 195.

25. This epigram is attributed to Plato in some traditions. See C. P. Jones, "Passage to India," 196. If this attribution is correct, it would raise the issue of how this passage had ended up in Mesopotamia (or Persia) before Plato existed (428–348 BC).

26. As noted earlier, this mistake seems to be due to a misreading of Herodotus. One must wonder whether Philostratus, the uneducated Damis, or a forger (pseudo-Damis) would have been more likely to be familiar with this passage from Herodotus.

The Age of Scopelian (*VA* 1.24.3)

In the Eretrian episode, Philostratus quoted from a letter that Apollonius wrote to the sophist Scopelian about the Greek exiles.[28] In the epistle (*VA* 1.24.3), Apollonius claimed that he "was still young" (νέος ὢν ἔτι) when he assisted the Eretrians, yet Apollonius's visit to Cissia would have been around AD 45 and the letter itself would have been written shortly thereafter (*VA* 1.23.3). This date creates two chronological problems. The first is that when the letter was written "Scopelianius was a young child at best, not the full-fledged sophist that Philostratus' remarks imply."[29] At that time, Scopelian would have been about five years old.[30] The second issue is that Apollonius described himself as young during the Eretrian

---

27. Priaulx raised two further objections to the veracity of this account. See Priaulx, *Indian Travels*, 3. First, he found it unlikely that these exiled Greeks would have been able to retain their language and culture for so many years while in exile. The Eretrians, numbering only 400 men and perhaps 10 women when the first arrived in Persia (*VA* 1.24.2), would have been forced to intermarry with the native population to survive. He reasoned that with 10 families speaking Greek and 390 speaking Persian, assimilation to the new culture would have occurred within a few generations. Second, Priaulx asked, "how is it that from the age of Herodotus to that of Apollonius we never hear the voice of these Eretrians save in these pages? And how is it that though so near to Babylon they escaped the notice of Alexander and his historians, who, the one so signally punished, and the other so carefully recorded the punishment of the perfidious and self-exiled Branchidae?—Strabo, B. xi, xii, c. 49." These two intriguing points may support the fictional nature of this episode.

28. The origin of the letter itself is unclear. It does not appear in the larger collection of Apollonius's letters, so this may have been (1) an unknown letter, (2) a part of the Damis memoir, or (3) an original composition of Philostratus. In favor of option two, in the lines prior to quoting the letter, Damis reported that Apollonius repaired the ancestral tombs of the Eretrians. This matches some of the content of the letter written to Scopelian. Penella, supporting the third option, argues that this letter is a fabrication, and that Philostratus created it to back up the fictional account of Damis concerning the Eretrians. Philostratus's reason for citing the letter appears to have been to confirm that Apollonius had been to Cissia (*VA* 1.23.4) and acted on behalf of the Eretrians (*VA* 1.23.3). Penella argues that Philostratus admired Scopelianus (*VS* 1.21) and notes that the sophist was praised for his declamations on Persian themes. Thus, he posits that Philostratus might have been aware of a declamation composed by the sophist concerning the Eretrians on which he based the current episode in the *VA*. See Penella, "Scopelianus," 299–300.

29. Penella, "Scopelianus," 297–98.

30. Phillimore places Scopelian's birth c. AD 40. See Phillimore, *In Honour*, cvii.

PART 3: INVESTIGATING THE APOLLONIAN DECALOGUE

visit when he would have been nearly forty-five years old at that time.[31] Therefore, the chronology of the letter and the narrative do not match.

The Existence of Babylon (VA 1.25)

Philostratus gave a detailed description of the city of Babylon where Apollonius resided for several months. In this account, Babylon had enormous walls (VA 1.25.1), palaces with domed bronze roofs (VA 1.25.2; 1.25.3), and decorated chambers, whose walls of pure gold portrayed subjects from Greek mythology and Xerxes's Greek campaign (VA 1.25.2). Jones notes that much of Philostratus's description of Babylon (VA 1.25) closely resembles, and may have been based on, that of Herodotus *Hist.* 1.179–86.[32] Assuming that Philostratus was influenced by this earlier account, how closely did the city described in Herodotus's *Histories* (c. 425 BC) correspond to Babylon of the first century AD?

Unfortunately for the historicity of Philostratus's account, the city of Babylon had been in ruins since the third century BC[33] and was a "ghost town" at the time of the historical Apollonius.[34] Strabo (64 BC–AD 24) wrote,

> ... and even what was left of the city was neglected and thrown into ruins, partly by the Persians and partly by time and by the indifference of the Macedonians to things of this kind, and in particular after Seleucus Nicator had fortified Seleuceia on the Tigris near Babylon, at a distance of about three hundred stadia therefrom. For not only he, but also all his successors, were strongly interested in Seleuceia and transferred the royal residence to it. What is more, Seleuceia at the present time has become larger than Babylon, whereas the greater part of Babylon is so deserted that one would not hesitate to say what one

---

31. Priaulx also notes this discrepancy. See Priaulx, *The Indian Travels*, 2, n. 2.

32. See Jones's comments in Philostratus, *Apollonius of Tyana*, 1:97, n. 45. Jones's proposal seems to be borne out by the evidence: both accounts mention the height and width of the walls (*Hist.* 1.178; VA 1.25), the use of bitumen in construction projects (*Hist.* 1.179; VA 1.25), the division of the city in half by the Euphrates River (*Hist.* 1.178, 180; VA 1.25), and a woman or queen of the Medes (*Hist.* 1.185; VA 1.25), who diverted the river so that she could construct a bridge to span its flow (*Hist* 1.186; VA 1.25).

33. Kee, *Miracle*, 256; Hadas and Smith, *Heroes and Gods*, 197; Habermas, "Did Jesus Perform Miracles?," 122; Newman, *Life of Apollonius*, 355, n. 85; Clark, "Miracles," 211.

34. Révelle, *Apollonius of Tyana*, 81; Philostratus, *Apollonius of Tyana*, 1:73, n. 25.

ITEM 6

of the comic poets said in reference to the Megalopolitans in Arcadia: "The Great City is a great desert."[35]

When Trajan visited the site in AD 116, "he saw nothing but mounds of stones and ruins."[36] The thriving city of Philostratus's tale and the ruins of the historical Babylon of Apollonius's day do not match at all, likely because Philostratus was reliant upon earlier literary sources for his description of the city rather than on the testimony of the first-century Damis. That Babylon did not exist, at least not in its Philostratean grandeur, and that Damis is presented as a visitor to that city[37] justify the rejection of this passage as an eyewitness account.

The Length of Darius II Ochus's Reign (*VA* 1.28)

Philostratus made a relatively insignificant error in calculating the number of years that Darius II Ochus ruled. Philostratus claimed that the monarch reigned for sixty years when he was in power for only twenty.[38]

The Walls of Ecbatana (*VA* 1.39)

According to this passage, the king of Babylon showed his guest Apollonius the famed walls of Ecbatana to impress him. At first glance, this story seems credible, especially given Herodotus's claim that Ecbatana was encircled by seven concentric and multicolored walls in his own time.[39] Yet, some scholars have questioned whether these walls existed at all.[40] Absolute certainty about this supposition must await the findings of the archaeologist's spade. But, since literary evidence claims that the

   35. Strabo, *Geogr.* 16.1.6.
   36. Dio Cassius, *Hist. rom.* 68.30.1.
   37. Although Philostratus did not specify that the description of Babylon was from Damis, Apollonius's companion did visit the palace with its long forecourt (*VA* 1.30–31), "they" visited the elaborate men's quarters with its elaborately decorated domed roof (*VA* 1.25.3), and Damis was also mentioned several times during the overall narrative about Babylon (*VA* 1.26, 32–35, 37, 40). The Assyrian eyewitness cannot easily be excused from being the source of this account.
   38. Philostratus, *Apollonius of Tyana*, 1:103, n. 49.
   39. Herodotus, *Hist.* 1.98.
   40. Summers suggests that Herodotus's description of the walls of Ecbatana were not literal. See Summers, "Ecbatana," 99. Rawlinson proposed that Herodotus had described a seven-tiered ziggurat rather than a city wall. For a summary and critique of Rawlinson's views, see James and van der Sluijs, "Ziggurats," 57–79.

city was unwalled sometime after the day of Herodotus, some researchers have more modestly questioned whether Ecbatana had walls when Apollonius supposedly visited the region.[41]

Assuming for the sake of argument that these walls did still exist in Apollonius's time, the sage's viewing of these fortifications in this episode is still somewhat suspicious because Ecbatana is about 280 miles from Babylon as the crow flies. Although Philostratus failed to report a round-trip visit of the king and Apollonius to this faraway site, a more likely interpretation is at hand. Since Philostratus incorrectly thought that the Eretrians lived just a short distance from Babylon (*VA* 1.24.1) and dwelt on Ecbatana's plains (*VA* 1.24.2), he likely imagined that these two sites were near each other.

The Location of the Caucasus Mountains (*VA* 2.1–4)

Seemingly, Philostratus was confused about the location of the Caucasus Mountains[42] and of the cave in this range where the Prometheus had been bound. Rather than situating these two locations between the Black Sea and the Caspian Sea as some ancient authors did,[43] he positioned them instead between Mesopotamia and India (*VA* 2.2, 4). Kee seized upon this as one of his chief points for rejecting the historicity of Philostratus's account.[44] But, in Philostratus's defense, he was neither the first Greek writer to refer to the Hindu Kush[45] as the Caucasus[46] nor the first author

---

41. Aelian claimed that Alexander tore down Ecbatana's wall (*Var. hist.* 7.8). Polybius (c. 200–c. 118 BC) claimed that at his time it had a citadel, but no wall (Polybius, *Hist.* 10.27.6). Ezra 6:2 mentioned the citadel of the city of Ecbatana but did not mention its walls; this omission, however, may not be significant.

42. Kee, *Miracle*, 257.

43. Aeschylus locates Prometheus's incarceration in the Scythian region (Aeschylus, *Prom.* 1; Pseudo-Apollodorus, *Bibliotheca*, 1.15).

44. Kee writes, "[i]n part, the account offered is apparently dependent on older sources, going back to Herodotus, and cannot be considered eyewitness testimony. The Damis diary reportedly includes description of the Caucasus as (1) providing the divide between Babylon and India, and (2) as the location of the sources of the Indus" (Kee, *Miracle*, 257). See also the similar critique of Wilson, "Miracles," 21.

45. Philostratus, *Apollonius of Tyana*, 1:14; Flinterman, *Power*, 54.

46. Arrian distinguished the traditional Caucasus (between the Caspian Sea and the Black Sea) from the Caucasus associated with the Hindu Kush. Arrian indicates that the Macedonians called this area the Caucasus but distinguished it from the Scythian Caucasus (Arrian, *Ind.* 2.4).

to relocate the cave of Prometheus to this area.[47] Most likely, Philostratus was simply following the lead of such writers as Arrian for his geography and had appended to these earlier tales the "eyewitness" testimony of Damis which claims that the disciple saw the cave of Prometheus and the chains forged from an undeterminable metal attached to rocks (*VA* 2.3).[48]

The Cleft of the Rock: A Tale about the Forecourt of the Parthenon (*VA* 2.10)

This account made a historical blunder in describing a feature of the Athenian Parthenon. As Apollonius's party passed near the Indian fortress of Aornos, the narrator noted that this site received its name "birdless" (Ἄορνος) from a cleft at its summit that inhaled birds that flew over it. The chronicler further interjected that one can observe the same phenomenon at the forecourt of the Parthenon in Athens. To this latter claim, Jones responds, "Untrue: there was however a cleft under the Erechtheion and also a legend that Athena had banned crows from the Acropolis."[49] So, although the Parthenon may have indeed been "birdless," this was not because of a mysterious opening that inhaled any unsuspecting avians that were unfortunate enough to fly near it.

The Location of the Headwaters of the Indus (*VA* 2.18)

The *VA* appears to place the source of the Indus River in the Caucasus Mountains (*VA* 2.18) rather than in the Tibetan Plateau. Kee included

---

47. Arrian relates that the Macedonians visited the cave of Prometheus (*Anab.* 5.2) and "that the Macedonians in their account transferred Mount Caucasus from the Pontus to the eastern parts of the world and the country of Parapamisadae as far as India, and called Mount Parapamisus Mount Caucasus, all for the glory of Alexander, suggesting that he had truly crossed Mount Caucasus" (*Anab.* 5.3 [Brunt, LCL]).

48. The account in *VA* 2.3 reports that Damis witnessed chains fashioned from an unknown metal. This was a reference to the adamantine, unbreakable chains that Hephaistos fashioned to bind Prometheus (Aeschylus, *Prom.* 1–6, 155). One must wonder whether the uneducated Damis would have shown an interest in the material from which the chains were made or whether this detail more likely came from the pen of the sophist Philostratus.

49. See Jones's quote in Philostratus, *Apollonius of Tyana*, 1:151, n. 11. The cleft to which Jones refers appears to refer to a fissure in the floor under the north porch of the Erechtheion that was supposedly caused by Poseidon's trident (Pseudo-Apollodorus, *Bibliotheke*, 3.14; Pausanias, *Descr.* 1.26).

PART 3: INVESTIGATING THE APOLLONIAN DECALOGUE

this point in his list of errors that question the accuracy of the Damis account.[50] Yet, once again, the *VA* is neither the first nor only account to make such an assertion. For instance, Arrian places the headwaters of the Indus in Mount Taurus (i.e., the Himalayas[51]), which is in the Caucasus mountains that were associated with the Hindu Kush (*Ind.* 2.1—3.2). Thus, the worst that can be said of Philostratus was that he was mistaken because he relied upon earlier Greeks who wrote about India[52] and followed their information about rivers, regions, and mountains.

A "Hippo" in the Wrong "Potamos"[53] (*VA* 2.19.1; 6.1.1)

Unlike the mythological creatures mentioned in the *VA*,[54] hippopotami ("river horses") are quite real. However, Philostratus's reports of sighting hippos in the Indus River verges on the mythical. Indeed, this claim is made twice in the *VA*, first in a description attributed to the travelers[55] (*VA* 2.19) and later in what appears to be the narrator's comparison of India and Ethiopia (*VA* 6.1). Unfortunately for the veracity of both passages, hippos are not native to India. Still, Philostratus was not alone in claiming that hippos lived in the Indus; Arrian before him noted that Onesicritus had also asserted that Hippos were in the Indus, although Arrian dismissed that claim.[56] The significance of the blunder is that it

50. Kee, *Miracle*, 257. Whether this is a Damis account can be debated for it never explicitly mentions Damis. Damis is mentioned a bit prior to the account (*VA* 2.15.2; 2.17) and after it (*VA* 2.22). However, *VA* 2.18 does say that "they" crossed the Indus, a statement that presumably includes Damis in Apollonius's entourage.

51. Brunt, *Arrian*, 1:524.

52. Philostratus acknowledges the works by Nearchus and Orthagoras in *VA* 2.17, as well as that of Skylax in *VA* 3.37.

53. For those who do not dabble in Greek etymology, this section heading may require a brief explanation. The English word hippopotamus (ἱπποπόταμος; ὁ ἵππος ὁ ποτάμιος) derives from the Greek words meaning "horse" (*hippos*) and "river" (*potamos*). This heading is a play on the word hippopotamus: a "hippo" in the wrong "river" (i.e., the Indus River). Nothing ruins a pun like explaining it.

54. For instance, the existence of gryphons and phoenixes is confirmed by the Indian Wise Ones (*VA* 3.48–49). However, there are no reports that Damis or Apollonius saw these creatures themselves.

55. The account says that "they say" that they chanced upon many hippopotami while crossing the Indus (κομιζόμενοι δὲ διὰ τοῦ Ἰνδοῦ πολλοῖς μὲν ποταμίοις ἵπποις ἐντυχεῖν φασι). This account does not appear to be a "they say" account that might be attributed to a source that is being quoted by Philostratus (e.g., Ctesias) and appears to be a passage attributed to Damis or someone else in Apollonius's entourage.

56. Arrian, *Indica*, 6.8.

seriously challenges the eyewitness character of the Damis source and favors the view that this error was due to a pseudepigraphical source, the use of a travel guide, or the imagination of Philostratus.

The Location and Description of Taxila and Jandial (*VA* 2.20–23)

The accuracy of Philostratus's description of the Indian city of Taxila and its environs, including Jandial, is a controversial portion of Apollonius's journey to India.[57] Although earlier archaeological discoveries seemed to confirm several of the *VA*'s claims about Taxila,[58] some of these were later disputed and were even proven to be incorrect.

Philostratus's description of the temple at Jandial (700 meters north of Taxila) appears to have been inaccurate. The material used to construct this temple—limestone with "embedded shells or shell fragments" (λίθου κογχυλιάτου; *VA* 2.20.2)—was not found at the temple Jandail[59] (or at Taxila).[60] Another variety of limestone was used to construct the walls of the temple, but it would have been hidden from view by a thick layer of stucco at the time of Damis's visit in the first century AD so that he could not have seen or reported on it.[61] Additionally, the temple at Jandial lacks the architectural features that Philostratus described; it had no real peristyle and showed no evidence of metal decorations on its walls. Rather, Philostratus's description is suspiciously reminiscent of the temple of Athena on the Athenian Acropolis.[62]

Philostratus's description of Taxila does not fit perfectly with the archaeology of the site either. The *VA*'s description of the city fits the

---

57. For a discussion of the literature on this subject, see Bernard, "L'Aornos bactrien," 505–6.

58. For instance, Petzke claims that the excavations of Taxila have largely confirmed the report of Philostratus. See Petzke, *Die Traditionen*, 85.

59. Marshall attempted to salvage the accuracy of the *VA*'s claim by arguing that the temple was made of a stucco made of crushed stone (in his view, a diminutive of κογχή). Bernard, however, demonstrated that the Greek word κογχυλιάτης unambiguously refers to a type of shell limestone. For these competing views, see Marshall, *Taxila*, 223, 227; Bernard, "L'Aornos bactrien," 509.

60. Philostratus, *Apollonius of Tyana*, 1:177, n. 21.

61. Bernard, "L'Aornos bactrien," 510.

62. Bernard, "L'Aornos bactrien," 510. Perhaps the shell limestone of the temple was also an allusion to the materials used for the Athenian Acropolis, for some of the limestone used in the construction of its buildings have embedded bivalve fossils.

archaeology of the era of Alexander the Great (at Bhir Mound)—perhaps suggesting reliance on earlier travelogues—but this was not the site that would have been inhabited in Apollonius's day (at Sirkap).[63] Even the name of the ruler of the city presents a problem for the veracity of the account, for no Indian king named Phraotes is known to have ruled Taxila.[64]

Since the description of Taxila and its surroundings appears to be within a Damis account,[65] any minor agreements between the *VA* and archaeological remains that might suggest an eyewitness account are offset by a host of errors that suggest otherwise. Barring future discoveries, the information in this passage appears to be mostly incorrect. However, should future findings prove some details to be correct, these discoveries would still need to be examined carefully, for some details might be explained by Philostratus's reliance on earlier texts that recount Alexander's travels through this region and still might not be due to eyewitness testimony.[66]

63. The description of Taxila's irregular streets may evoke the layout of Athens (*VA* 2.23). Some manuscripts indicate that the houses were laid out orderly, while others have that they are irregular. See Philostratus, *Apollonius of Tyana*, 1:187, n. 28. The Taxila of Apollonius's era (at Sirkap) did have a grid-like plan, but the earlier city of Taxila (at Bhir Mound) from the time of Alexander the Great had meandering streets. Bernard suggests that Philostratus may have had access to a report from the time of Alexander, thus indicating that Apollonius was not an eyewitness. See Bernard, "L'Aornos bactrien," 513–14. If one instead chooses to go with the manuscripts that claim that Taxila's streets ran on a checkerboard design at the time of Apollonius—thus vindicating Philostratus's account—then there is the oddity that the city plan does not mimic the maze of streets in Athens at the time of Apollonius as Philostratus claims.

64. Puri identified Phraotes with Gondophares I, who ruled from AD 19–46. See Puri, "The Sakas and Indo-Parthians," 2:190. Jones, however, is open to the possibility that he was a fictional character. See his comments in Philostratus, *Apollonius of Tyana*, 1:191, n. 30.

65. Although this account is not directly attributed to Damis and is a "they say" account (*VA* 2.20.1, 2), it follows the statement that "they" (i.e., the travelers) had crossed the river, by a statement by Apollonius, and by a comparison of Damis's hometown of Ninos to Taxila. The context seems to attribute the information to Damis.

66. The Taxila of Alexander's era (Bhir Mound) and the Taxila of Apollonius's time (Sirkap) were totally different sites. Should the *VA* match a description of the site at Bhir Mound, it would most certainly not be a text from the time of Damis. Likewise, one cannot assume that details matching Taxila of Damis's day at Sirkap are based on his own experiences, since they could have been based on more contemporary information from Philostratus's time.

ITEM 6

An Indian Bestiary (*VA* 3.2.1, 3.6–8)

The mention of mythological creatures in Apollonius's journey to India has been cited as a reason to question the veracity of Philostratus's narrative.[67] Some of this talk about fantastic beasts is probably due to Philostratus's reliance on works of earlier writers (e.g., Ctesias),[68] who shared an interest in reports of bizarre creatures, but it could also be due to the claims of the Wise Ones of India.[69] Yet, the *VA* does not claim that Apollonius and Damis saw such creatures themselves, so the two travelers cannot be held accountable for claims of the existence of these beasts. However, there are two instances in which bizarre animals were seen by Apollonius and his companions. These will be the focus of this section.

In the first of these encounters, Apollonius saw a "wild onager" (*VA* 3.2.1). This creature was not an equine, as the word donkey in the original text might suggest (τοὺς ὄνους δὲ τοὺς ἀγρίους) but rather an animal with a single horn on its forehead. Perhaps it was an Indian antelope or, more likely, a rhinoceros.[70] Legend had it that a magical drinking cup could be formed from this horn that would protect one who drank from it from wounds, fire, and poison (*VA* 3.2.1). The description of this beast and the cup made from its horn closely resembles the accounts of

---

67. Gildersleave, displaying skepticism concerning Philostratus's account, asks, "What if he introduces us to a menagerie of marvelous monsters, the griffins of India, the original phoenix, the colossal dragons, thirty cubits long, with flaming crest, golden beard and jeweled eyes?" (Gildersleave, *Essays*, 259).

68. This "they say" account (λέγουσιν) mentions the peacock fish and the white worm, whose essence was used to fuel an inextinguishable fire (*VA* 3.1.2). The description of these and other bizarre creatures in this account were probably derived from Ctesias. See Gyselinck and Demoen, "Author and Narrator," 111.

69. At this point in the narrative, Damis inquired about the existence of several strange beasts. The Indian philosophers denied the existence of the martichas (*VA* 3.45.2) but did allow that the gryphon (*VA* 3.48) and the phoenix (*VA* 3.49) existed. The account indicates that strange things had been reported about India (*VA* 3.45.1). This list of topics, along with questions about the existence of pygmies (3.46.2; Photius 21) and "shadow feet" people, probably came from a reading of Ctesias (Photius on Ctesias, *Indica*, 15, 21) or Skylax (*VA* 3.47). See Gyselinck and Demoen, "Author and Narrator," 111–12.

70. Nichols, "Complete Fragments of Ctesias," 215. Also, Genghis Khan's biographer, Chuchai, relates the encounter of the conqueror with a unicorn-like beast in India (Humble, "The Biography of Yelü Chucai," para. 5).

the unicorn mentioned by Ctesias,[71] Aristotle,[72] and Aelian.[73] Although the exact details of the quote do appear to derive from Ctesias, there is nothing improbable about Apollonius having observed a rhinoceros in northern India.[74]

In the second instance, Philostratus claimed that he would report about a snake hunt that Apollonius and his companions witnessed as they were descending from a mountain (*VA* 3.6–8). Yet, instead of relating an account of the hunt that the travelers observed, the narrator—either Damis or Philostratus[75]—gave a general lecture about the varieties of gigantic snakes in India[76] and of serpents whose heads contained magical

---

71. Photius, in summarizing Ctesias, writes that "[t]here are wild asses in India the size of horses and even bigger. They have a white body, crimson head, and deep blue eyes. They have a horn in the middle of their brow one and a half cubits in length. The bottom part of the horn for as much as two palms towards the brow is bright white. The tip of the horn is sharp and crimson in color while the rest in the middle is black. They say that whoever drinks from the horn (which they fashion into cups) is immune to seizures and the holy sickness and suffers no effects from poison, whether they drink wine, water, or anything else from the cup either before or after ingesting the drug." This translation is taken from Nichols, "Fragments of Ctesias," 115.

72. Aristotle described one-horned animals: the Oryx and the so-called "Indian Ass" (ὁ Ἰνδικὸς καλούμενος ὄνος)" (Aristotle *Part. An.* 3.2).

73. Aelian wrote of Indian horses and asses with one horn. These horns were used to make drinking-vessels which were able to neutralize poison (Aelian, *Nat. An.* 3.41).

74. For a more skeptical perspective, Gyselinck and Demoen asked, after reviewing the list of mythical animals in this passage, "[a]re we to suspend our disbelief, to believe or to smile about the canniness of our sophisticated author?" (Gyselinck and Demoen, "Author and Narrator," 111–12).

75. In favor of Damis as the narrator in this passage, *VA* 2.17.1 indicated that Damis would describe a fabulous snake hunt; the events in *VA* 3.6–8 were probably intended to include that promised tale even though it is difficult to identify it for certain. Perhaps Philostratus recast the tale or created a new one, for he seems a more likely candidate than the Assyrian disciple for referencing snake lore from Homer (*VA* 3.6.2) and the story of Gyges's ring mentioned within the context of this adventure (*VA* 3.8.2).

76. Philostratus's description of gigantic serpents may go back to books relating the travels of Alexander in India, like that of Aelian or Ctesias. Aelian mentioned two snakes kept by Abisares the Indian; one measured one hundred and forty cubits and the other a mere eighty cubits (*Nat. an.* 16.39). Aelian also recorded that Cleitarchus's book on India claimed that there were snakes in that country that reached sixteen cubits in length (*Nat. an.* 17.2). Ctesias, according to Photius, spoke of a "worm" (e.g., serpent or crocodile?) that was seven cubits long that lived in the Indus; it could drag oxen and camels into the river (Photius, *Bibliotheca*, 46). See Nichols, "Fragments of Ctesias," 115. The largest of Philostratus's serpents were thirty or more cubits in length (*VA* 3.6.2; 3.7) and capable of dragging off an adult human being (*VA* 3.8.2) or an elephant (*VA* 3.7.2).

gems.⁷⁷ Oddly, the narrator appears to have forgotten to indicate which part, if any, of this herpetological discourse was related to Apollonius's hunt, unless this is related in *VA* 3.8.2. In the end, the passage does not inform the reader about the sort of serpents Apollonius supposedly saw or provide any details of the hunt he witnessed.

Therefore, charges of historical inaccuracy based on Philostratus's treatment of mythical animals in this section cannot be substantiated.⁷⁸ It is possible that Apollonius saw a unicorn (i.e., a rhinoceros) in India, and he may have observed a snake hunt, even though the account of it appears to have been forgotten in the storyteller's exhaustive discourse on herpetological trivia. Still, Apollonius cannot be held responsible for the claims that the Wise Ones or Philostratus made about fantastic creatures, but that he is not reported to have seen himself. These observations, however, do not rule out the possibility that Philostratus shaped these stories from the reports about the strange animal of India or that he may have included allusions to Ctesias's account of India to entertain sophisticated readers and hint to them that he was writing fiction.⁷⁹

Jars of Rain and Wind (*VA* 3.14.2)

In what is presumably a Damis account,⁸⁰ Apollonius and his companions reported seeing the jar of rains and the jar of winds, which the Indian sages used to control the weather. Philostratus explained that the jar of winds operated much like Aeolus's bag of wind that is mentioned in the Odyssey (*Od.* 10.19–27). These mythological devices have been cited

---

77. Some serpents were hunted for the gems in their heads that possessed the powers of invisibility, much like the powers attributed to the famed ring of Gyges (*VA* 3.8.2).

78. Kee is incorrect in claiming that "[t]here were straightforward accounts of encounters with dragons whose eyes bore mystic gems" (Kee, *Miracle*, 257). Such creatures were discussed, but there are no accounts of encounters with such creatures in the *VA*.

79. Gyselinck and Demoen notes that Lucian referenced Ctesias in his *True Stories* as an example of the writers he would parody in that book. They suggest that Philostratus's allusions to Ctesias may have had a similar function in that they indicating to his sophistical audience that he was writing fiction. See Gyselinck and Demoen, "Author and Narrator," 111.

80. This account is introduced by "they said that they saw" (*VA* 3.14.2) and, in context, appears to report eyewitness testimony. It does not seem likely that it was taken from an earlier Greek travelogue. For a similar argument in support of this view, see Hamilton, "Storm-making Springs," 215, n. 11.

by ancient writers as proof of sorcery[81] or fiction.[82] Some modern writers have attempted to demythologize this account by noting that Greek tradition regarded the Indians as masters of meteorological prediction.[83] Although the Indians were no doubt skilled in predicting the weather, the character of this passage in the *VA* is supernatural, not scientific. The report of these magical urns might cast doubt on the prospect of a true eyewitness account behind this tale. However, there is no evidence in the tale that the travelers saw these devices in operation, so perhaps they were merely shown two jars that were reported to have these abilities.

Levitation (*VA* 3.15, 17)

In this eyewitness account (*VA* 3.15.1), Damis reports that he (or perhaps Apollonius) observed the sages of India levitating two cubits off the ground while they performed sacred rites for the sun. One of their rituals is described in more detail in a later passage. When the holy men struck the ground with their staves, the earth bounced them two cubits in the air. After they had sung a hymn, they returned to earth (*VA* 3.17.2).[84] Perhaps Apollonius witnessed the famous levitation trick, employed by yogis, in which a holy man is supported by a camouflaged platform held up by his staff, which is actually an iron rod driven into the ground.[85] Perhaps Philostratus misinterpreted the concept of spiritual or mental flight as literal levitation.[86] These views, however, do not match the phenomenon described by Damis that involved the physical body (unlike mere spiritual levitation) and a dynamic movement (rather than a static levitation trick) in which the earth bent like a wave and propelled these

---

81. Eusebius, *Hier.* 24; 42.2.

82. Photius, *Myrobiblion* 44.5.

83. After citing several Greek sources that speak of the ability of Indian sages to predict weather, McVane writes that these passages are "certainly not so different from the power of Philostratus' Wise Men to control the rains and winds through their two magic jars" (McVane, "The Bare Necessities," 59).

84. The Gymnosophists of Ethiopia also referred to this miracle of the Indians being suspended in air (*VA* 4.10.2).

85. Livingston, *Rising Force*, 4, 12.

86. Anderson, *Philostratus*, 211. Anālayo argues that most forms of early Buddhist levitation (e.g., departure, celestial travel, and travels on earth) were by means of a mind-made body that later led to the idea of levitation with the physical body. See Anālayo, "Levitation," 11–26.

sages upward.[87] Given the unlikelihood of the phenomenon of levitation, this is probably not a genuine eyewitness account and might be best attributed to Philostratus, a Greek guidebook to India that he used as a source, or to pseudo-Damis.

Automata as Servants (VA 3.27.2)

During a feast thrown by the Wise Ones, the travelers witnessed a meal that was served by automata. As the meal began, self-propelled urns like the wheeled tripods of Hephaestus rolled out to serve wine and water to the guests (VA 3.27.2).[88] These were immediately followed by bronze cupbearers that were fashioned to look like Pelops and Ganymede, the cupbearers of the Olympian gods.[89] The two waiters were not merely painted human beings, for a later passage confirms that both the tripods and the servers were mechanisms that had been designed to move of their own accord (VA 5.12). Later writers have described this episode as sorcery,[90] "a fairy banquet,"[91] or a "fantastic banquet."[92] Although this episode could be written off as sheer fantasy or as a misunderstanding of Buddhist teaching,[93] numerous automata like the devices described above had been invented by Apollonius's time.[94] While such technology cannot be dismissed as fantasy and while it is certain that Philostratus was aware of such mechanical devices (VS 550), it is impossible to demonstrate that Apollonius saw such devices in India. Although this report, or at least part of it, comes from a Damis account (VA 3.27.3), it may be

---

87. Anderson writes, "Whatever might be the authenticity of the practice, there can be no doubt at all about its practicality: Philostratus is describing nothing more remarkable than the trampoline effect of a sprung floor" (Anderson, "Folklore," 216–17).

88. Hephaestus created robotic tripods for service in the hall of the gods (Homer, Il. 18.375–79). See VA 5.12 for a reference connecting these tripods to Homer and VA 6.9.18 for a connection to Hephaestus.

89. First Pelops (Pindar, Ol. 1.40–45) and later Ganymede (Homer, Il. 20.232) had been taken from earth by Zeus to serve as cupbearers for him in the hall of immortals.

90. Eusebius, Hier. 24; 25.1; 42.2.

91. Gildersleave, Essays, 268.

92. Anderson, Philostratus, 211.

93. Anderson, Philostratus, 211.

94. Bur lists several humanoid automata, such as the libation-pouring statue of Nysa, the dancing figurines at the shrine of Dionysus, and figurines that poured libations at an altar. She also notes devices that resemble Philostratus's self-propelled tripods, such as the Panathenaic ship of Herodes Atticus, an automated wagon, and self-rotating wheels. See Bur, "Mechanical Miracles," 72–80, 99–118, 133–42.

PART 3: INVESTIGATING THE APOLLONIAN DECALOGUE

more likely that Philostratus himself invented these robotic tripods and android cupbearers for this part of the story because he wished to depict the sages of India as being on par with the Olympian "gods" themselves (*VA* 3.18; 8.5.1).[95]

The Hyphasis River (*VA* 3.50, 52)

Once again, the geographical accuracy of the *VA* is called into question. On his return from India, Apollonius made his way to the sea with the Ganges on his right and the Hyphasis on his left, thereby generating one of the great geographical howlers of the *VA*.[96] The narrative goes on to claim that the party sailed down the Hyphasis River to the sea. As Kee pointed out, this journey was impossible because the Hyphasis "is a tributary of the Indus and joins it far inland."[97] Furthermore, the description of the mouth of the Hyphasis (or Indus) was most likely based on a description of the Ganges River.[98]

Questions Asked to the Ghost of Achilles (*VA* 4.16)

The report of Apollonius's encounter with the shade of Achilles promises to have ramifications for the historicity of the Damis account. This episode calls for investigation, not because it contradicts historical sources or because it is a supernatural encounter, but because this presumably historical event nearly parallels an account in Philostratus's fictional *Heroicus*. The literary dependence of these accounts could call into question the accuracy of what Damis reported.

The major points of correspondence between the accounts in the *VA* and *Heroicus* have been meticulously analyzed by Philostratean scholars.[99] The most important correspondences are that both episodes (1)

---

95. References to nectar (*VA* 6.10.6) and the "banquets of the gods" (*VA* 6.11.18) appear in later descriptions of this scene. Gyselinck and Demoen note that there is a comparison between the dwelling place of the Wise Ones and the home of the Olympic gods. See Gyselinck and Demoen in their "Author and Narrator," 109.

96. Anderson, *Philostratus*, 207.

97. Kee, *Miracle*, 257. Here, Kee mistakenly lists the reference to this episode as *VA* 2.52 rather than 3.52. In this passage, Arrian was correct in his description of this river (Arrian, *Indica*, 6.14.5).

98. Anderson, *Philostratus*, 207.

99. Huhn and Bethe, "Philostrats Heroikos und Diktys," 613–24; Solmsen, "Some

happened near Troy,[100] (2) involved conversations with Homeric heroes (i.e., Achilles and Protesilaus), (3) discussed the appearance of these heroes in detail,[101] especially their great height,[102] (4) allowed a visitor (i.e. Apollonius or the vinedresser) to ask five nearly identical questions about Homeric literature to the shade of a hero,[103] (5) mentioned Achilles's disapproval that the Thessalians had neglected his rites (VA 4.15.3; Her. 52–57),[104] and (6) employed intermediate figures (i.e., Damis and the vinedresser), who relate the account of the querists Apollonius and the vinedresser.[105] In light of these correspondences, it is no surprise that scholars are in general agreement that these two stories are related. These correspondences also suggest that the two accounts were written by the same person.[106]

There is no certainty as to which of these two accounts was written first,[107] but knowing the correct order might help to identify whether the tale in the VA has any historical validity. Until this matter can be settled, researchers will have to be content with thinking through the ramifications that each possibility might have for the validity of the Damis story. If the tale in Heroicus was written first, the historicity of Damis's report is irreparably undermined, for neither the first-century Apollonius nor Damis could have borrowed from the third-century work Heroicus. In this scenario, the encounter in the VA would surely be a Philostratean

---

Works," 556–72; Grossardt, "How to Become a Poet?," 75–94.

100. Apollonius's encounter with Achilles was at his burial mound on the plains of Troy (VA 4.11), while the vinedresser's encounter with Protesilaus occurred near Elaious, a site just opposite the Troad (Her. 9; 23.1).

101. Solmsen, "Some Works," 559, 562, 565.

102. Achilles grew from five to twelve cubits in height (VA 4.16.2), whereas Protesilaus was about ten cubits tall (Her. 10.5).

103. Solmsen, "Some Works," 560–61; Philostratus, Heroicus, 9; Grossardt, "How to Become a Poet?," 82. The five Homeric questions asked were whether (1) the Muses or Nereids attended or sang at the burial of Achilles (VA 4.16.4; Her. 51.7); (2) Polyxena was sacrificed by the Achaeans or had killed herself with a sword out of love for her dead Achilles (VA 4.16.4; Her. 51.3-6); (3) Helen had really been at Troy (VA 4.16.5; Her. 25.10–11); (4) Greece was able to produce as many heroes as Homer claimed (VA 4.16.5; Her. 36.3), and (5) Palamedes was excised from the Homeric account (VA 4.16.6; Her. 24.2).

104. Huhn and Bethe, "Philostrats Heroikos und Diktys," 620–21.

105. C. P. Jones, "Passage to India," 197.

106. Grossardt, "How to Become a Poet?," 90.

107. Miles explains that "the shorter text may just as plausibly be the summary as the longer text may be the elaboration" and that "[t]he chronological relationship between the two is harder to pin down with certainty" (Miles, Philostratus, 22).

creation. If, however, *Heroicus* was an expansion of the earlier tale in the *VA*, as several believe,[108] one must weigh whether it is more likely that the simple-minded Assyrian disciple,[109] a magician like Apollonius,[110] or the sophist Philostratus would have been interested in (or capable of generating) such questions about Homeric minutiae.[111] Of these three options, Philostratus remains the most likely candidate for the creation of this story for he, as a sophist and pro-Hellene, unquestionably had a deep knowledge of and interest in Homeric trivia[112] and also wrote an entire work that questioned aspects of the blind poet's work (*Heroicus*).

Fortunately, a more convincing explanation than the options above may provide a way around this impasse. Grossardt believes that Philostratus's two stories about the shades of Homeric heroes were influenced by three factors: (1) Caracalla's (and probably Philostratus's) visit to Achilles's tomb at Troy in AD 214/215;[113] (2) several pre-Philostratean texts mentioned that Homer, like Apollonius, visited the burial mound of Achilles, offered a meatless sacrifice (libations) to the hero,[114] beheld the glorious aspect of the warrior, and received arcane knowledge there;[115] and (3) Lucian, who in his satirical *Vera Historia* visited the Homer at the Island of the Blest and asked him five questions (like Apollonius in the *VA*) about his life and his two works, the *Iliad* and the *Odyssey* (*Ver*.

---

108. Solmsen, "Some Works," 571–72; Anderson, "Folklore," 218. Grossardt, "How to Become a Poet?," 91. Philostratus, *Heroicus*, 7. Rutherford leans in the direction of the *VA* having been written first. See Rutherford, "Black Sails," 237.

109. Diehard advocates of Damis existence might respond that (1) the disciple merely recorded what Apollonius reported about his solo visit to the tumulus of Achilles (*VA* 1.19.3; 4.11.3) and that Damis should not be held accountable for what he did not see himself, or (2) Damis himself may have had a personal interest in relating this story since he aspired to absorb Greek culture (*VA* 3.43), and he had a rudimentary knowledge of Homer (*VA* 1.2).

110. The historical Apollonius himself may have possessed a deep knowledge of Homeric lore (e.g., *VA* 1.2; 4.11.3; 5.26; 6.11.18, 32.2; 7.14.8, 11; 22.2. 32.2, 36.2; 8.5.3, 7.48), like other figures of his era (e.g., Dio of Prusa, Bardesanes) who were competent in aspects of philosophy, religion, and sophism (Anderson, *Philostratus*, 147–48).

111. Solmsen, "Some Works," 571.

112. E.g., *VA* 3.13, 27.2; 4.15; 5.4; *VS* 489, 568, 577; cf. *VS* 521.

113. Grossardt, "How to Become a Poet?," 75–76. Other scholars have also argued this point. See Solmsen, "Some Works," 559; Rutherford, "Black Sails," 237–38.

114. In addition to contrasting Apollonius's actions to those of Caracalla and connecting the Tyanean's act to that of his hero Achilles, a bloodless sacrifice may have also served the purpose of distancing Apollonius from the charge of being a sorcerer or necromancer. See Hadas and Smith, *Heroes and Gods*, 198.

115. Grossardt, "How to Become a Poet?," 76–80.

Hist. 2.20).[116] These three items suggest that Philostratus borrowed his idea about communing with and questioning dead warriors from earlier sources and his visit to Troy. The *VA*'s similarity to Homer's meeting with Achilles to ask five questions and Lucian's meeting with Homer to ask five questions seems to be more than a coincidence. If Grossardt is correct, then both of these Philostratean accounts set at Troy are best understood as fiction. Further, if Lucian's tale or Caracalla's visits were influences on these tales, as they seem to be, they both postdate the time of the historical Damis, thus making an event from the disciple's timeframe impossible.[117]

The Corinthian *Empusa* (*VA* 4.25)

An *empusa* (Ἔμπουσα) was a shape-shifting phantom that often assumed the appearance of an attractive female to seduce and feed upon young men.[118] Apollonius encountered this sort of creature twice in the *VA*,[119] but only one of these lends itself to historical investigation.

The tale in question was set in the city of Corinth and involved Menippus of Lycia, a new disciple of Apollonius. Menippus, a handsome and well-built twenty-five-year-old (*VA* 4.25.1), intended to marry a beautiful, wealthy Phoenician woman who had proclaimed her love for him (*VA* 4.25.2–3). Apollonius immediately deduced the true nature of

---

116. Grossardt, "How to Become a Poet?," 80–82. Schirren also noted a connection between the *VA* and *Vera Historia* on these questions. See Schirren, "Irony," 173. The five questions that Lucian asked Homer were: (1) where he came from; (2) whether the bracketed lines had been written by him; (3) why he began the *Iliad* with the theme of the wrath of Achilles; (4) whether he wrote the *Odyssey* before the *Iliad*; and (5) whether he was blind—this final question was one that Lucian intended to ask, but did not because he could discern for himself that Homer was not blind.

117. Another possibility might be that Lucian had access to Damis's account. This option seems to be ruled out because, according to Philostratus, the Damis document was unknown until the time it was delivered to Julia Domna (*VA* 1.3.1). Of course, if the document were a Philostratean fiction, there would have been nothing for Lucian to have plagiarize in the first place.

118. Scholars sometimes employ the terms vampire, lamia, or hobgoblin to describe this creature. However, the term vampire is a bit misleading for, as Stannish and Doran point out, "ancient vampires are specters, while modern ones are the risen corpse of the lost" (Stannish and Doran, "Magic and Vampirism," 129–30). Here, these authors point out that the mythologies of ancient and modern vampires have a few similarities such as that they are most often portrayed as female, sexually aggressive, marginalized, and involved in sorcery (e.g., they are shapeshifters and require blood).

119. *VA* 2.4; 4.25.

this female and, at the wedding feast, demonstrated to the youth that his bride-to-be was a vampire. The holy man forced her to admit that she was an *empusa* who was fattening the boy to feed on his body because his blood was fresh and that she had only created the illusion of wealth and beauty to deceive him.

Since most readers probably do not believe *empusai* really exist, what accounts for the report of this creature in an eyewitness account given by Damis?[120] Anderson is open to there being a historical core to the tale: Apollonius's may have accused a wealthy young woman was guilty of demonic activity at her wedding feast, thereby setting this legend in motion.[121] Yet, Schirren seems to hint at a possible case of Philostratus's dependence on and reversal of earlier *topoi*. In Menander's fragmentary play *Phasma*, a young man encountered a beautiful spirit only to discover in time that the apparition was a beautiful girl, a woman he eventually wed. Here, Philostratus has turned the wedding story around so that the girl is really a demon.[122] Since *empusai* do not exist and since this account may well riff on Menander's idea, this tale of a phantom is probably best classified as Philostratean fiction or the work of a forger rather than as the account of an eyewitness.

The Great Omission—A Journey from Crete to Rome in One Sentence (*VA* 4.34)

A temporal aporia occurs between Apollonius's visit to Crete and his visit to Rome. Fortunately, both events are datable. The first, Apollonius's visit to Crete, took place around AD 46/47 when an earthquake struck the island, and a new isle was formed between Thera and Crete (*VA* 4.34). The emergence of this new island was also mentioned by three other ancient authors, who tend to date the event in the 40s.[123] The second event,

---

120. Philostratus explicitly attributed the Corinthian tale to Damis (*VA* 4.25.6). The encounter with the Indian *empusa* is a bit more difficult to assign to Damis with certainty (*VA* 2.3–5). However, Philostratus appears to place this within Damis travel narrative. The account in *VA* 2.4 involves Apollonius and some unnamed travel companions (e.g., "they were going" and "those around him"), while the previous passage mentions Damis (*VA* 2.3). The passage that follows records that "they" (i.e., Apollonius and his companions) were traveling on foot and mentions that Damis was in the group (*VA* 2.5).

121. Anderson, "Folklore," 221.

122. Schirren, "Irony," 166.

123. Forsyth places the date in AD 46/47. See Forsyth, "After the Big Bang,"

Apollonius's visit to Rome, occurred during the consulship of Telesinus, which would have been in AD 66 (*VA* 4.40). Philostratus appears to be correct in his statements about these two facts.

Yet, how this data fits with the broader narrative of the *VA* creates two puzzles. The first conundrum is that the journey from Crete to Rome is reported within the space of one sentence without any indication that a score of years elapsed between the visits to these locations (AD 47–66).[124] The second oddity is that Apollonius's visits to Lechaeum, Crete, and Rome in the *VA* are out of chronological order. The event related in *VA* 4.24 happened in AD 60 at Lechaeum, seven years before Nero attempted to cut the canal near Corinth (AD 67). So then, in the order set forth by the *VA*, Philostratus first relates the events of Lechaeum (AD 60), then those in Crete (AD 46), and finally the events in Rome (AD 67).[125] In proper sequence, the visits would have been to Crete, Lechaeum, and Rome. Although these issues do not constitute historical errors, they certainly raise questions about the value of the *VA* for understanding the timeframe and chronology of the historical Apollonius.

The Manner of Agrippina's Death (*VA* 4.38.4)

The details of the death of Nero's mother Agrippina in *VA* do not cohere well with other historical accounts. In this passage, Apollonius cautioned his disciples about Nero, who had murdered his mother by means of arranging a shipwreck in which she died close to land. Other ancient sources agree that Nero had designed a boat that would collapse and sink with his mother aboard. Yet, Apollonius is incorrect in claiming that this plot was successful, for Agrippina survived and was killed ashore later

---

198–202. Seneca dates the appearance of the island in AD 46 (*Nat* 2.26.4) and Dio Cassius in AD 47 (*Hist. rom.* 61.29.7), while Pliny the Elder appears to contradict himself by dating it in both AD 43 (*Nat* 2.202; 4.70) and AD 19.

124. Phillimore rather passionately inquired, "does any biographer, any man of letters, however flibberty-gibbet, take a leap of twenty years between one sentence and another, with no more by-your-leave and with-your-leave than 'let us have done with a long story'?" (Phillimore, *Philostratus*, cxx).

125. Petzke notes that the *VA* appears to place the events at Crete around AD 60. He argues that there is no reason for rejecting Philostratus's date for this event because Pliny and Seneca give different dates for it and they may not be reliable. See Petzke, *Die Traditionen*, 152–53. However, Petzke appears to have overlooked that three writers—Pliny, Seneca, and Dio Cassius—agree that the event occurred in the AD 40s or, in one case, perhaps earlier. A threefold cord is not quickly broken.

that very night.[126] Flinterman, attempting to account for the differences between the *VA* and other classical sources, suggested that Philostratus "simply preferred a more colorful version of the incident to the historical one for his hero's tirade against the tyrant."[127] Although this detail could be written off as a minor error, it does not inspire confidence in Philostratus when he is dealing with well-known events; he may be ignorant of the facts, blindly following an unknown faulty source, reliant upon on an inaccurate Damis account,[128] or, worse, creating details out of thin air for the sake of a telling a more interesting tale.

The Chronology of Demetrius's Banishment (*VA* 4.40, 42)

On the surface, the story of Nero's banishment of the philosopher Demetrius from Rome has the appearance of historical plausibility. According to the *VA*, Demetrius had spoken out against the construction of Nero's new gymnasium, incurred the wrath of Tigellinus, and was expelled from Rome (*VA* 4.40). In favor of the accuracy of this report, Apollonius interacted with three historically verifiable figures: the Cynic philosopher Demetrius, Tigellinus, the prefect of the Praetorian Guard from AD 62–68, and Gaius Luccius Telesinus, the consul of Rome in AD 66 (*CIL* XI, 395).

A closer inspection of this story reveals that it is shot through with chronological problems. According to the *VA*, Demetrius's banishment would have taken place during the consulship of Telesinus in AD 66, when Apollonius first visited Rome (*VA* 4.40). Yet, the gymnasium that Demetrius condemned had been built in AD 60–62[129] before Tigeliunus became prefect in AD 62 and before Apollonius would have visited the city in AD 66. Another chronological problem concerns the timing of Demetrius's banishment. Bowersock writes,

> . . . in Philostratus's own narrative, when Apollonius comes to Rome in the year A.D. 66 (a date guaranteed by references to the consul Telesinius, a real person known to have been consul

---

126. Philostratus, *Apollonius of Tyana*, 1:403, n. 63; Suetonius, *Nero*, 34; Tacitus, *Ann.* 14.1–8.

127. Flinterman, *Power*, 132.

128. Although the text does not explicitly state that Apollonius speech was recorded by Damis, the Assyrian is said to have been present at this speech (*VA* 4.37.1; 4.38.1).

129. Bowersock, Introduction to *Life of Apollonius*, 17; Flinterman places this event between AD 60 and 61. See Flinterman, *Power*, 133.

in 66), Demetrius is then in Rome. Back so soon from an exile which is dated by a chronological impossibility? In the next year Apollonius finds Demetrius in Athens, in exile and, we are told, precisely because of that speech of at least five years earlier against the gymnasium.[130]

Koskenniemi notes that such a minor mistake concerning the life of a philosopher would not normally reflect much on the question of the reliability of the *VA*, but since Demetrius was alleged to have been one of Apollonius's best friends and his life story is closely intertwined with that of Apollonius the severity of this mistake is magnified.[131] The sequential problems encountered in this episode question the accuracy of the passage.

The one who bears the responsibility for the errors in this passage is unclear. Bowersock argues that the author is not the historical Damis, despite what the VA implies, and that the historical errors in this passage damage the claim that he was an eyewitness. Bowersock claims that the stories in books 4 and 5 about Demetrius are "expressly connected with the testimony of Damis" and "cannot be reconciled with the facts of Roman history."[132] He further wrote of this episode, "[i]t takes a mighty faith (some scholars have it) to think that an eyewitness, such as Damis, could have made chronological blunders of the most elementary kind."[133] However, the evidence for this being a Damis account is questionable since the disciple does not appear in these episodes.[134] This leaves the possibility that the mistakes in the account were due to Philostratus or to one of his other sources. Whoever the source of this material was, the *VA* is not historically accurate in this episode.

Nero's Close Call (*VA* 4.43)

One of Apollonius's miracles in Rome converges with two historical accounts of that time, thereby allowing for an assessment of its plausibility. Philostratus reported that there was an eclipse of the sun that occurred simultaneously with a thunderclap—a phenomenon that was thought to

---

130. Bowersock, Introduction to *Life of Apollonius*, 18.
131. Koskenniemi, *Apollonios*, 182.
132. Bowersock, Introduction to *Life of Apollonius*, 17.
133. Bowersock, Introduction to *Life of Apollonius*, 18.
134. Damis appears before these episodes in 4.38 and is perhaps implied by the "they" in 4.39. He appears again in 4.46.1.

be unusual during an eclipse. After this event, Apollonius looked at the heavens and stated that "something great will occur, but not occur" (*VA* 4.43.1). The meaning of his enigmatic prediction was revealed three days later when it was reported that lightning had struck Nero's banquet table and split the cup that he held in his hands close to his lips. Nero had nearly been struck dead by lightning but had survived.

The historicity of this event in the *VA* is a mixed bag.[135] On the one hand, the report of the lightning strike is verified by both Tacitus (Tac. *Ann.* 14.22.2) and Dio Cassius (*Hist. rom.* 61.16.5). On the other, the chronology of the event is problematic, for Tacitus and Dio date the event to around AD 59 or 60[136] and not to AD 66 when, according to Philostratus, Apollonius was in Rome.[137] The historicity of the lightning bolt from above is verified, but Apollonius's presence in Rome at that time is not, thereby rendering this event unlikely.

Geryon's Bleeding Trees (*VA* 5.5)

At Gadeira (modern Cádiz), Apollonius's party saw two trees, unlike any others on Earth. These trees, partaking of the nature of both pine and fir, grew from the grave of the slain giant Geryon and dripped blood.[138] The blood shed by these trees was associated with the slaughter of Geryon during the tenth labor of Hercules.[139] What then should historians make of the claims of unusual flora?

There are several reasons to suspect that Philostratus was playing with a mythological or literary theme in relating this tale. Twice more in the Philostratean corpus, trees on tombs are associated with their occupants. The first reference is in this very passage (*VA* 5.5.1), where Philostratus compares these bleeding trees to the Heliad poplar that bled gold.[140] The second is in his own *Heroicus*, in which he mentioned trees

135. This account does not appear to be attributed to Damis; the last reference to the disciple was in *VA* 4.38, while the next one was in *VA* 4.46.1.

136. Dio Cassius situated the omens of the eclipse and thunderbolt within the context of ceremonies performed shortly after the death of Agrippa in AD 59 (*VA* 61.16.4).

137. Flinterman, *Power*, 133. As mentioned in the previous section, Telesinus, with whom Apollonius interacts while in Rome, was consul for the year AD 66.

138. Pausanius mentioned trees that had different shapes at Gadeira but argued that Geryon's tomb was not there (*Descr.* 1.35.7–8).

139. Praet, "Pythagoreanism," 297.

140. After the death of Phaethon, his sisters were turned into amber-weeping poplars. Diodorus of Sicily, *Library of History* 5.23.2; Ovid, *Metam.* 2.340–366. Interestingly,

at the tumulus of Protesilaus. Miles notes the foliage in both passages signifies something about the sufferings of the tombs' occupants: the trees on Protesilaus's mound drop their leaves on the side facing Troy (Her. 9:1–4) while the fir and pine trees on Geryon's tomb—symbols of destruction—drip blood in remembrance of the giant's death by the poisoned arrow of Hercules.[141] In addition to this recurrent Philostratean theme of trees on tombs reflecting something about the story of their inhabitants, Philostratus also reports mythical flora elsewhere in his writings.[142] Thus, the story of Geryon's trees is best attributed to the sophist's imagination or his borrowing from earlier literature.[143] Interestingly, though, no modern scholar appears to have attempted to demythologize this story, even though trees from regions near Gadeira bleed sap that closely resembles blood (e.g., *Dracaena draco* of Morocco and Macaronesia).[144] If the case were made for a connection of the text to this local flora, this account might reflect an eyewitness account. If so, there is no evidence that this account came from Damis, for he is not mentioned.[145] More likely, it would have come from Philostratus, who may have visited this region earlier in his travels (*VA* 5.1.1).

The Revolt of Julius Vindex (*VA* 5.10)

Philostratus[146] claimed that Apollonius met with Julius Vindex and several other politicians from the western provinces at Gadeira to encourage

---

Ovid associates these trees with a sepulcher too.

141. Miles, *Philostratus*, 44.

142. The talking elm that Apollonius encountered in Ethiopia may fall under the rubric of Philostratean mythical flora (*VA* 6.10.3).

143. A few correspondences to Lucian's *Vera Historia* might further suggest that Philostratus is exploring a mythical theme here. Both stories reference (1) the Pillars of Hercules (*Ver. Hist.* 1.5; *VA* 5.1, 3); (2) inscriptions related to Hercules (*Ver. hist.*1.7; *VA* 5.5); (3) sites that marked the limits of Hercules's journey to the west (*Ver. hist.*1.7; *VA* 5.4); and (4) mythical flora (*Ver. hist.* 1.8; *VA* 5.5).

144. Trees from other parts of the world also bleed sap that closely resembles blood (e.g., the bloodwood tree of southern Africa; *pterocarpus angolensis*).

145. Both *VA* 5.5.1 and 5.5.2 constitute "they say" accounts. Although no source is given for this episode, Damis is a likely source for he commented on the golden belt of Telamonian found within the temple to Hercules (*VA* 5.5.2).

146. Bowersock argued that account concerning Vindex was a Damis account (Bowersock, Introduction to *Life of Apollonius*, 18), while Flinterman warns against such a hasty assumption. Flinterman correctly points out that Philostratus did not mention his source here but simply mentions that "it is said" (λέγεται). See Flinterman,

their revolt against Nero while he was absent on his singing tour of Greece. Bowersock contends that this conclave would have been impossible, for the revolt of Vindex took place in AD 68 after Nero was already back in Italy from his tour.[147] However, Flinterman points out that this may not have been a historical blunder after all, for it is "extremely plausible" that the event described may have been a planning session for the revolt that was held while Nero was still abroad.[148] In this case, it is uncertain whether Philostratus made a historical error.[149]

The Timing of Vespasian's Arrival in Alexandria (*VA* 5.27–30)

Bowie and Flinterman have noted that, although many classical sources agree that Vespasian visited Alexandria,[150] there was a chronological contradiction between Philostratus and other classical sources with respect to the exact time of Vespasian's arrival in Alexandria Egypt.[151] The *VA* indicates that Vespasian met with Apollonius in Alexandria one day after the destruction of the temple of Jupiter Capitolinus in Rome (*VA* 5.30), thus placing this meeting on December 20 of AD 69 (Tacitus, *Hist.* 3.67–74). However, Flinterman writes, "This is difficult to reconcile with the historiographical data, which point to a date in the second half of November."[152] That said, Flinterman does note that several other items in Philostratus's account do match well with what the historical sources say about Vespasian's visit.[153]

Power, 135. Once again, Philostratus's gift for obscuring the nature of his sources raises its ugly head.

147. Bowersock, Introduction to *Life of Apollonius*, 18. The date of Nero's arrival in Rome may even have been just prior to December 31 of AD 67. See Bradley, "Chronology," 72.

148. Flinterman, *Power*, 135.

149. Gasco la Calle finds the historical details of Apollonius's visit to Spain to be accurate. A few philosophers were in this area (*VA* 4.47) as were the barbarians that Philostratus mentioned (*VA* 5.9). Likewise, he found the report of a visit to the Heracleon (*VA* 5.5) and the political situation plausible (*VA* 5.10). At the same time, he admitted that there was no conclusive evidence that the historical Apollonius visited Spain. See Gasco la Calle, "El viaje de Apolonio," 17–22.

150. Tacitus, *Hist.* 3.48.3; Suetonius *Vesp.*, 7.1; Dio Cassius, *Hist. rom.* 65.9.2; Josephus, *B.J.* 4.605–616.

151. Bowie, "Apollonius," 1660.

152. Flinterman, *Power*, 137–38.

153. Flinterman, *Power*, 138.

ITEM 6

Galba Adopts Otho (*VA* 5.32)

Although many of Philostratus's comments on the Year of the Four Emperors (AD 69) are supported by other ancient authors,[154] he made a minor error concerning the adoption of Otho. At *VA* 5.32, Philostratus reported that Vespasian rehearsed to his companions how Galba, after adopting Otho and Piso, was slain in the middle of the forum. However, Philostratus is incorrect; Galba did not adopt Otho but rather passed him over in favor of Piso.[155] One could argue that this mistake was made by Vespasian, who was the speaker in this passage of the *VA*, and that Philostratus merely recorded the inaccuracy. Yet, it is unlikely that the emperor would have been unaware of the events that transpired just a year before his visit to Egypt.[156] More likely, the mistake was due to Philostratus himself.

Philosophical Advice to Vespasian on Government (*VA* 5.32–36)

While still in Alexandria, Philostratus reported that Vespasian summoned the philosophers Apollonius, Euphrates,[157] and Dio so that they might give him counsel on the proper use of power. Bowie detects a possible "broadly-based intertextuality" between *VA* 5.32–36 and a story in Herodotus (*Hist.* 3.80–83.1) in which three conspirators—Otanes, Megabyzus and Dareius—discuss the form of government that should be used to rule over Persia.[158] Pursuing Bowie's observation a bit fur-

---

154. Flinterman, *Power*, 136.

155. Flinterman, *Power*, 142; Philostratus, *Apollonius of Tyana*, 2:59, n. 47.

156. Flinterman, *Power*, 143.

157. The negative evaluation of the philosopher Euphrates creates a historical problem for the *VA*. Philostratus depicted him as an evil opponent of Apollonius who slandered him and even hired a false witness against him (*VA* 1.13; 5:28–39; 7.9; 8.3). This contrasts the with the opinions of several other ancient writers (i.e., Pliny, Epictetus, and Fronto), who all spoke well of Euphrates. See Penella, *Letters*, 89; Anderson, *Philostratus*, 135. Although this difference of opinion could be a significant historical issue, it is also possible that the historical Apollonius did indeed differ with Euphrates for reasons of his own. The *Letters*, if authentic, also bear witness to poor relationship between Euphrates and Apollonius (*Epp. Apoll.*1–8.1, 14–18, 50–52, 60, 94). Further, Moiragenes's account indicates that Apollonius had gotten the better of Euphrates by his magic (Origen, *Cels.* 6.41), thus giving another reason for the bad blood between these two philosophers.

158. Bowie, "Quotation of Earlier Texts," 62. Anderson also notes a similar debate

ther, several more similarities between these accounts can be teased out making Philostratus's dependence on Herodotus even more likely.[159] Although such similarities do not demand that the entire account in the *VA* is fictional, at the same time they do not strengthen the case for its historicity. Perhaps it is also significant to note here that over half of Philostratus's allusions derive from four classical sources, one of which was the writings of Herodotus.[160] Flinterman also regards this episode as fictional and makes several pertinent points. First, there is no mention of Vespasian's meeting with these three philosophers by the chief historians of the day (i.e., Tacitus, Suetonius, or Dio Cassius).[161] Second, the only sources referenced in this section are epistles of Apollonius that were written to Dio and Euphrates, perhaps suggesting that Philostratus had invented this episode based on this epistolary material.[162] Third, the position held by Euphrates is remarkably similar to that held by a Stoic senator, Helvidius Priscus (Dio Cassius, *Hist. rom.* 66.12.2f.).[163] All things considered, this account bears the marks of invention.

The Description of the Nile River and Its Sites (*VA* 6.1–27)

Much of what Philostratus had to say about the Apollonius's extensive exploration of the Nile Valley is incorrect, particularly concerning the direction in which certain sites were situated and the distances between them:

---

on kingship in Xenophon, *Cyr.* 8.1.1–5, 8.5.24–26. See Anderson, *Philostratus*, 231, 238.

159. The accounts in the *VA* and in Herodotus possess several similarities. In the *VA*, Euphrates promoted overthrow of monarchy and the restoration of democracy (*VA* 5.33.5). Dio preferred democracy but counselled Vespasian to let the Roman people make their decision between democracy and monarchy (*VA* 5.34), and Apollonius preferred monarchy (*VA* 5.35). The latter view was adopted by Vespasian (*VA* 5.36). Similarly, in Herodotus's debate, Otanes counselled democracy (*Hist.* 3.80), Megabyzos argued for oligarchy (*Hist.* 3.81), and Darius, partly agreeing and partly disagreeing with Megabyzos, argued for monarchy (*Hist.* 3.82). Darius's position was the one adopted (*Hist.* 3.83). Two additional similarities between the *VA* and the account in Herodotus are that there is a discussion of selecting various officials by lot and that the two figures arguing for democracy delivered a parting shot (*VA* 5.37) before withdrawing with their respective entourages (*VA* 5.37; *Hist.* 3.83).

160. Bowie, "Quotation of Earlier Texts," 60.
161. Flinterman, "Power," 137.
162. Flinterman, "Power," 144.
163. Flinterman, "Power," 139, 144.

Here his travels bear even less relation to actuality than in India, even when he is inside Roman Egypt. The excursus that opens Book Six alleges that Ethiopia joins Egypt at Meroe (1.1: north of modern Khartoum); just below, however, Philostratus puts the boundary at "Sykaminos" (2.1), which must be the site usually called Hierasykaminos, the modern Muharraka some eighty miles north of Assouan. Apollonius then proceeds towards "Memnon," the celebrated statue of Amenhotep III at Thebes, to which he is guided by a youth who plies a boat out of Memphis (3.1). This is doubly impossible, since Thebes is some two hundred and fifty miles north of Sykaminos, and Memphis some three hundred miles north of Thebes. Philostratus appears to place the Naked Ones close to Memnon (6.1), and after leaving them Apollonius proceeds up the Nile, eventually reaching 'the last [cataract] for those descending the river', which in reality is just above Assouan (26.1).[164]

Two solutions to these geographical oddities have been proposed: either Philostratus was confused about these locations, or he intentionally rearranged the account for some other purpose. Manolaraki argues for the latter view:

> Evidently, this itinerary makes no pretensions to realism. Why does Philostratus strain geography to its breaking point? Certainly not because of ignorance, since his Nilotic landmarks are geographical and literary topoi. Moreover, Septimius Severus' trip to Egypt with Julia Domna in 199 must have renewed these locations in collective memory, or at least for those as close to the empress as Philostratus presents himself. Even if we were to assume his unfamiliarity with Egyptian landmarks, Philostratus could have easily avoided rather than accented the details of Apollonius' itinerary from Alexandria to the no man's land that is the sources of the Nile.[165]

In the end, Manolaraki attributes the odd itinerary to Philostratus's "educative agenda," which was to track Apollonius's spiritual progress.[166] But it is perhaps more likely that, as was the case relating Apollonius's eastern journeys to Mesopotamia and India, Philostratus was misled by

---

164. See Jones's comments in Philostratus, *Apollonius of Tyana*, 1:16–17.
165. Manolaraki, *Noscendi Nilum Cupido*, 274.
166. Manolaraki, *Noscendi Nilum Cupido*, 275.

his sources or was creating his own material. In either case, this account does not represent the genuine itinerary of the historical Apollonius.[167]

The Talking Statue of Memnon (*VA* 6.4)

Apollonius's visit to the statue of Memnon presents one of the more difficult obstacles to the view that Damis was an eyewitness to the travels of Apollonius. A bit of background history will be necessary for those unfamiliar with the history of this colossus to understand the problematic nature of this episode. The colossi of Amenhotep III (1386–1353 BC) are located west of Luxor, Egypt. Beginning with Manetho (first century BC), these statues were incorrectly associated with the Ethiopian king and Homeric hero Memnon.[168] As early as Strabo's time, reports began to circulate that each day at dawn a strange sound would emanate from the northernmost image.[169] Visitors to the site attested to the continuation of this phenomenon throughout the first and second centuries.[170] Pilgrims visited this image from the first until the third century AD and some left inscriptions on the statue as their testimony to hearing the sound.[171] According to some scholars, the image's voice was silenced when Septimius Severus allegedly attempt to repair the image in AD 199.[172] Bowersock, however, suggests that the legend of this repair and the muted statue is not based on any ancient evidence–the latest inscription that attests to the voice is superimposed on one dating from AD 205, thus debunking the theory that an attempted repair by Septimius in AD 199 silenced its voice. Instead, Bowersock attributes the origin of this false theory to J.

---

167. Damis and his account are frequently referenced throughout this section (*VA* 6.3.1, 4; 6.4.1; 6.5.1; 6.7; 6.9; 6.12.1; 6.22.1; 6.26.2). However, it is unclear whether the geographical errors in the itinerary are due to the Damis source or to Philostratus himself.

168. Manetho, *Aeg.* Fg. 52.8, Fg. 53.7. *Heroicus* made the same association with Memnon (*Her* 26.16). An additional piece of incorrect lore about the colossus was that it had been damaged by Cambyses (e.g., Pausanius, *Desc.* 1.42.3). Perhaps it had been damaged by the earthquake of 26 BC, just two years before Strabo's visit. See Bowersock, "Memnon," 25.

169. Strabo, *Geogr.* 17.46. Also see Pliny the Elder, *Nat.* 36.58.

170. Some of the more notable visitors include Germanicus (AD 19; Tacitus *Ann.* 2.54.1, 59–61), Hadrian (AD 130), and Septimius Severus (AD 199; *HA* Sept. Sev. 17.4). See Bowersock, "Memnon," 26–27.

171. Bowersock, "Memnon," 22. For the texts themselves, see Rosenmeyer, *Language of Ruins*, 26, 28–33, 43–44.

172. Platt, "Virtual Visions," 136.

A. Letronne, whose argument has been repeated by scholars ever since its publication in 1833.[173] Whatever the exact cause, the image fell silent sometime between AD 205 and the time of the composition of Jerome's *Chronicle* c. AD 380.[174]

Philostratus appended Damis's testimony (*VA* 6.4.1) to that of this great cloud of witnesses who asserted that a sound issued forth from the statue. Damis described in detail both the image of Memnon and its miraculous transformation at dawn:

> Now this statue, says Damis, was turned towards the sunrise, and was that of a youth still unbearded; and it was made of a black stone, and the two feet were joined together after the style in which statues were made in the time of Daedalus; and the hands were thrust down supporting the body upright upon its seat, for though the figure was still sitting it was represented in the very act and impulse of rising up. We hear much of this attitude of the statue, and of the expression of its eyes, and of how the lips seem about to speak; but they say that they had no opportunity of admiring these effects until they saw them realised; for when the sun's rays fell upon the statue, and this happened exactly at dawn, they could not restrain their admiration; for the lips spoke immediately the sun's ray touched them, and the eyes seemed to stand out and gleam against the light as do those of men who love to bask in the sun. Then they say they understood that the figure was of one in the act of rising and making obeisance to the sun, in the way those do who worship the powers above standing erect. (*VA* 6.4.2–3)

The astounding detail of this eyewitness account is only surpassed by its inaccuracies. Rosenmeyer summarizes the most pertinent of these mistakes in the description of the statue:

> But there are serious problems with much of the rest of Damis's report: the color of the stone (black, not light quartzite), the position of its arms (straight instead of bent), and the existence of eyes and lips are all incorrectly represented. Most important, as we noted earlier, and as Verity Platt reminds us, "there never was a time at which the statue both uttered a cry at dawn *and* had a visible torso and head." Memnon only spoke after being partially destroyed; once the statue was repaired, it ceased speaking altogether. So whether Philostratus imagines the statue in

---

173. Bowersock, "Memnon," 24, 30.
174. Bowersock, "Memnon," 24, n. 10.

its original undamaged state, in its later repaired format, or in Apollonius's lifetime, when the cry emerged miraculously from a headless trunk, the narrative is as untrustworthy as Lucian's earlier version.[175]

Bowersock also noted that Lucian (AD 120–180) was the first author to mention that the sound issued from the mouth of the image in his work *The Lover of Lies* (*Philops.* 33.8–14). He suggests that Lucian intended this mistake as "high humor,"[176] since ancient texts had described the statue as broken off from the waist up since the time of Strabo. Although Philostratus never indicated he knew Lucian's writings, he must have known of him and may have been misled by him on this very detail.[177] Verity Platt, however, thinks that Philostratus was intentionally "highlighting the fictional nature of his text" to contrast Damis's failed attempt to describe and interpret the image with that of the authoritative interpreter, Apollonius.[178] Whether this inaccurate description was the invention of Philostratus,[179] inspired by Lucian, or came from Damis's diary, as he claims, it is particularly damning for those who see the *VA* as a work of history rather than fiction.[180] If Philostratus did employ an account from

---

175. Rosenmeyer, *Language of Ruins*, 95. For the reference within the quote, see Platt, *Facing the Gods*, 304. For a similar catalogues of the errors of Damis, see Platt, "Virtual Visions," 139–40; Bowersock, "Memnon," 27–28.

176. Bowersock, "Memnon," 29.

177. Bowersock, "Memnon," 29. For other similarities to themes in Lucian, see Anderson, *Philostratus*, 126, 130.

178. Platt, who believes the Damis papers to be the invention of Philostratus, notes that Damis is explicitly mentioned as the narrator and that Philostratus "seems to deliberately problematize the unreliability of his source" by stating that one should not believe or disbelieve everything when in India (*VA* 3.45). See Platt, *Facing the Gods*, 140–41. However, assuming Philostratus II to be the author of *Imag.* 1.7.19–25 and *Her.* 26.16, where many of the same details are mentioned and Damis is absent, the three versions of the tale might best be attributed to Philostratus.

179. The description of the statue is much more reserved in *Heroicus* and *Imagines* but has many of the same details mentioned in the *VA*: the image was of the Ethiopian Memnon, and it spoke when the sunlight appeared (*Imag.* 1.7). However, the passage in *Heroicus* made no explicit reference to the mouth of the statue like there is in the *VA* 6.4.3 and *Imag.* 1.7.22, and there is no mention of the statue being constructed from black stone, as is stated in *VA* 6.4.2 and *Imag.* 1.7.20.

180. Réville scathingly comments on Apollonius's adventures in Egypt in general, "It is more than evident that when people invent, as Philostratus has invented when he speaks of a country to which he thinks none of his readers will follow him, it is very easy to give the reins to one's own imagination in a description of events which occurred a century ago" (Réville, *Apollonius of Tyana*, 81).

Damis, this episode strongly suggests that it was a pseudepigraph and not an eyewitness account.[181]

The Existence of Gymnosophists in Ethiopia (*VA* 6.5–23)

According to Philostratus, a thriving community of gymnosophists existed in Ethiopia. He also claimed that these naked philosophers were originally of Indian descent and had resettled in Ethiopia in ancient times (*VA* 6.13). In many ways, this group is a pale reflection of the Wise Ones of India in that they failed to match their wisdom, supernatural powers, and ability to impress Apollonius with their displays of austerity.

Did such a group of gymnosophists reside in Ethiopia? Some researchers argue that they did exist,[182] while others doubt this claim. One reason for skepticism about their existence is that only Heliodorus (*Aethiopica*) and Philostratus (in the *VA* and *VS*)[183] mentioned them, except for a handful of later Christian writers who knew about the group from reading the *VA*.[184] A second and related point is that either Heliodorus or Philostratus likely borrowed the idea of Ethiopian philosophers from the other author. Despite Robiano's claim that there are no connections between the writings of Philostratus and Heliodorus, the evidence for borrowing between the two works is substantial.[185] If there was borrowing between these

---

181. Bowersock concludes that "this account of Memnon is so erroneous as to provide another good reason for doubting the authenticity of Damis as a source" (Bowersock, "Memnon," 27–28).

182. Robiano, "Les gymnosophistes," 413–27.

183. Morgan, "The Emesan Connection," 273. Bowie mentions the possibility that the Ethiopian journey was mentioned in the biography of Moiragenes. See Bowie, "Philostratus: Writer of Fiction," 195. The gymnosophists of Ethiopia are also mentioned briefly in the Philostratus's *VS* (484).

184. Robiano is correct to caution that this same sort of argument was used against the existence of Philo's Therapeutae. As was seen earlier in the current study, this argument was also used against Damis, who was known only through Philostratus. Robiano further points out that Jerome and other Christian authors mentioned the Gymnosophists, although their knowledge of them was admittedly based on a reading of the *VA*, and they never disputed their existence. See Robiano, "Les gymnosophistes," 413, n. 1. However, one must wonder whether these authors had the literary resources, opportunity for travel to Ethiopia, or the desire to challenge this claim. More likely, they simply took Philostratus at his word. In the case of Cyril of Alexandria, it was to his advantage that these philosophers existed because he used them to demonstrate that Apollonius was a sorcerer (*Against Julian* 3).

185. Hilton noted numerous similarities between the portrayal of this group in the writings of these two authors, suggesting that there is literary reliance of Heliodorus on

two works, as seems likely, then Heliodorus, who wrote in the second half of the third century (or the first half of the fourth),[186] borrowed this idea from Philostratus. This data could also suggest that Philostratus was the originator of the tale of the gymnosophists. A third reason for doubting the existence of this group is that all attempts to identify the gymnosophists with similar groups mentioned in ancient literature have failed.[187] As Morgan pointed out, "Although there was a long-standing tradition in classical literature of Ethiopian piety and wisdom, Philostratus and Heliodorus are the only Greek authors we know of to have a community of naked sages in Ethiopia."[188] In the end, Robiano's evidence for Ethiopian philosophers is unconvincing. A fourth reason is that Philostratus implausibly situates the gymnosophists between Egypt and Ethiopia (*VA* 6.4),[189] a point that even Robiano concedes is incorrect.[190] Therefore, the case against the existence of the Naked Ones is strong, and no solid evidence has been produced so far in favor of their reality.

If the gymnosophists were fictional, Philostratus may have had good reasons for inventing them. Anderson suggests that Egypt was a much more important location for a miracle worker to visit than even India; even Pythagoras supposedly visited there.[191] Philostratus may have

---

Philostratus. See Hilton, "Speaking Truth to Power," 203. Morgan cites twelve parallels between *Aethiopica* and the *VA*. See Morgan, "The Emesan Connection," 270–73. For the view that there is no substantial connection between Philostratus and Heliodorus, see Robiano, "Les gymnosophistes," 413–27.

186. Morgan, "The Emesan Connection," 280; Miles, *Philostratus*, 12. Bowie, however, entertained the notion that Heliodorus wrote *Aethiopica* before the time of Philostratus and that Philostratus may have stressed the inferiority of the Ethiopian sages to the Indian philosophers to devalue the world that Heliodorus had created. See his "Philostratus: Writer of Fiction," 194–95. Bowie does, however, acknowledge that this dating of Heliodorus is problematic; "Philostratus: Writer of Fiction," 198, n. 26. Should Heliodorus prove to have been written first, then it is highly likely that Philostratus borrowed the idea of the gymnosophists from him.

187. Anderson rehearsed a series of unsatisfactory attempts by scholars to identify the Gymnosophists with various groups in Egypt. In response to various proposed groups, he noted that Cynics were unlikely to have formed communities, adherents of Serapis would have been organized around a temple rather than in a scattered group, and Philo's Therapeutae were a sect of Jews that wore clothing, did not worship the Greek gods, and lived well north of Ethiopia, at Lake Mareotis. See Anderson, *Philostratus*, 216.

188. Morgan, "The Emesan Connection," 273.

189. Anderson writes, "no serious author places his gymnosophists between Egypt and Ethiopia" (Anderson, *Philostratus*, 216).

190. Robiano, "Les gymnosophistes," 416.

191. Anderson, *Philostratus*, 216. See Dzielska for a similar view, *Apollonius*, 94. As

even wanted Apollonius to journey as far south as Ethiopia so that he could surpass the journeys of his master, Pythagoras.[192] A second reason for creating the Ethiopian sages might have been to use them as a vehicle for rehabilitating Apollonius's image. The introduction to the *VA* (1.2.1) states that Apollonius was not a magician or sham philosopher even though he associated with Babylonian, Indian, and Ethiopian sages. Other philosophers (e.g., Pythagoras, Empedocles, Democritus, and Plato) had also visited with magicians yet were not vilified as magicians themselves. Perhaps the encounter with the Ethiopian sages was created to provide an opportunity for Apollonius to make his case that he was a holy man and philosopher while refuting the charges of sorcery.[193] A third possibility is that the Ethiopians were created to improve the status of a Pythagorean hero, Apollonius, in the pro-Cynic environment of the second century AD. By imbuing the Ethiopians with negative Cynic characteristics and the Indian sages with positive Pythagorean characteristics, Philostratus may have hoped to pave the way for a better reception of Apollonius's philosophical perspective in his own time.[194] So then, although the Naked Ones probably existed only in the stories of Philostratus, they seem to have played an important role in supporting the agenda of the *VA*.

---

a bit of support for this idea that Apollonius's trip to Ethiopia was related to Pythagoras, the Samian's name is invoked in the Ethiopian section several times (*VA* 6.5.3; 6.11.3, 5, 7, 12, 13; 6.15, 6.20.6). In additional to Pythagoras, the philosophers Solon, Thales, Plato, and Eudoxus supposedly visited Egypt; Plutarch, *Is. Os.* 10.1.

192. Pythagoras had only travelled as far east as Babylon and Persia and as far south as Egypt (Diogenes Laertius, *Lives* 8.1.3; Iamblicus. *Vit. Pythag.* 2-4; Porphyry, *Vit. Pythag.* 6, 11, 12). Apollonius surpassed Pythagoras by going further east to India (but see Clem. Alex. *Strom.* 1.15; Apuleius, *Flor.* 15) and further south into Ethiopia.

193. McVane argues that Apollonius's encounter with these Ethiopian sage's functions to rehabilitate his image. This was done, in part, by portraying the Ethiopian sages with the negative characteristics of Cynics—all the while stressing that they were not magicians (*VA* 6.10.3)—and endowing the Indian philosophers with the positive characteristics of Pythagoreans, while also defending them against charges of magic (*VA* 6.10.2). See McVane, "The Bare Necessities," 74–82. McVane, however, does not discuss whether the Ethiopian gymnosophists really existed.

194. Flinterman, building off an older theory of Reitzenstein, argues that the Indians were depicted as Pythagoreans and the Ethiopians as Cynics; Flinterman, *Power*, 87.

The Cataracts of the Nile (*VA* 6.26)

The *VA*'s description of the first three cataracts of the Nile is faulty on several counts. Philostratus recorded that about 15 stades (about 1.7 miles) after the first cataract the party heard the noise of the second cataract (*VA* 7.26.1). Unfortunately for this account, the distance from the first to the second cataract is over 190 miles if one hugs the banks of the Nile; hearing the falls from that distance would have been impossible. In an exaggerated account, the waterfall of the second cataract was said to fall from the mountains that were 8 stades (over 4000 feet) in height and to produce a roar that could damage human hearing. Although the second cataract is now underneath Lake Nasser due to the building of the Aswan High Dam, descriptions and pictures[195] of the falls from an earlier era demonstrate that the rapids made their way through giant boulders but that they did not fall from the lofty heights of the mythical mountain mentioned in the *VA*.[196] Further, there are no reports from modern visitors to the cataract before it was submerged that indicate its roar was damaging to human hearing. Therefore, this Damis account does not appear to have been written by a person who had traveled the Nile and seen the second cataract in person.

An Encounter with a Satyr (*VA* 6.27)

While visiting an Ethiopian village, Apollonius had an opportunity to rescue its inhabitants from the savage attacks of a satyr. This satyr had harassed the villagers for months and driven by its lust for women had already killed two females. Apollonius directed the villagers to pour four gallons of wine into a cattle trough and then he summoned the creature to drink. Once the satyr had drained the trough, it settled down and withdrew to a nearby cave to sleep. Apollonius told the villagers to leave it alone in the future since it had ceased its mischief.

Anderson attempted to salvage the historicity of this account by offering several suggestions. While he allowed that Philostratus may have

---

195. Lord Lindsey described the rapids as being ten miles in length, two miles in breadth, and hundreds of collateral streams making their way through little black islets. See Manley and Abdel-Hakim, eds., *Travelling through Egypt*, 194.

196. Even the impressive Rock of Abusir that towers above the Nile at the second cataract cannot rival the heights of Philostratus's imaginary peak. The deafening noise of an unidentified Nilotic cataract is, however, mentioned by Seneca (*Ep.* 56.3; *Nat.* 4.2.5), but it was certainly not the second waterfall travelling south on the Nile River.

created this story, also notes that this technique was used in antiquity to capture monkeys, and that Apollonius may have tried it on this occasion.[197] However, the evidence seems stronger for the view that this is a mythological story. It is difficult to believe that the native Ethiopians would be so unfamiliar with local fauna as to confuse a monkey with a satyr. Even Apollonius, who had allegedly observed apes (*VA* 3.4.2, 3.50.2), would have been unlikely to have misidentified the creature. Further, this satyr consumed an unbelievable 100 liters of wine, something that a whole troop of monkeys would not have been able to do.[198] In a later essay, Anderson suggests that the satyr may have been a "rustic rapist" in a faun skin.[199] Again, it is unlikely that a man could not be distinguished from a mythological creature or that a single man could consume so vast a quantity of wine.

A more likely explanation is that Philostratus is drawing on literary traditions about satyrs. Perhaps he used his own work *Imagines* as a source for this tale. At *VA* 6.27.2, Apollonius employed a technique of King Midas to capture a satyr with wine who is later found asleep in a cave, while *Imagines* 1.22 describes a painting of a sleeping satyr that Midas had captured by using a spring full of wine. Quite possibly, then, this satyr story in the *VA* is another of Philostratus's twice-told tales. Alternately, both Philostratean stories may have been inspired by a type of statue that depicts a satyr asleep in a grotto[200] or by earlier tales of the capture of Silenus, the drunken satyr, by King Midas's servants (Herodotus, *Hist.* 8.138.1; Ovid, *Metam.* 11.89–99; Pausanius, *Descr.* 1.4.5).

Titus and the Crown (*VA* 6.29)

The story of Titus's rejection of a crown stands in tension with the account found in Josephus's *Jewish Wars*. According to the *VA*, Titus attributed his capture of Jerusalem to a god and therefore refused to be crowned by neighboring peoples (*VA* 6.29.1). Soon after the victory, Apollonius

---

197. Anderson, *Philostratus*, 218. Claudius Aelianus (c. AD 175–235), a contemporary of Philostratus and Second Sophistic author mentions creatures resembling satyrs in the Kolounda region of India (*De Natura Animalium* 16.21). See Parker, *Roman India*, 79.

198. In Philostratus's *Imagines* 1.29, a satyr drank an entire spring dry. For an estimation of how much wine the satyr drank, see Schirren, "Irony," 168.

199. Anderson, "Folklore," 223.

200. See Schirren, "Irony," 170.

wrote Titus a letter (identical to *Epp. Apoll.* 77b) praising his actions and presenting him with a metaphorical crown of modesty (*VA* 6.29.2). Yet, according to Josephus, Titus refused a crown that was brought to him by a delegation from the king of Parthia (*B.J.* 7.5.2). These two ancient authors appear to disagree on this major detail.

Researchers differ over whether these accounts contradict or whether they can be reconciled. For instance, Grosso reconciled Philostratus with other historical accounts by arguing that the passage in the *VA* referred not to the crown sent by Vologases, but to the act of Titus's soldiers hailing him as imperator (*B.J.* 6.6.1).[201] However, Penella pointed out that these Roman soldiers could not be identified as the neighboring peoples mentioned in the *VA*,[202] thus leaving the tension between the claims of the *VA* and Josephus. The letter of Apollonius that Philostratus quoted in the *VA*, if it is a genuine source and not one manufactured by Philostratus, may help explain the contradiction, for it does not mention Titus's refusal of a literal crown, but only a metaphorical crown of modesty presented to Titus by Apollonius. Perhaps Philostratus reasoned that the figurative crown of modesty mentioned in the letter needed a material counterpart and so manufactured the story of Titus's rejection of a crown for the sake of improving the narrative. In favor of the truth of Josephus's account, Suetonius confirms that Titus had no aversion to accepting crowns offered to him by foreigners,[203] for shortly after the fall of Jerusalem he wore a diadem at the consecration of the Apis bull in Memphis (Suet. *Tit.* 5).[204] So then, the contradiction between Josephus and Philostratus is likely due to the sophist's addition to the story and does not coincide with other passages that indicate that Titus had no compunction about wearing royal symbols.

---

201. Grosso, "La 'Vita di Apollonio,'" 431.

202. Penella, *Letters*, 132.

203. Perhaps there is a difference in how Vespasian, his father, would have regarded the report of Titus receiving a crown from the Parthians and the Egyptians. Since Parthia was not a part of the Roman Empire, the action of the former group might be considered harmless. But, because it was a part of the Roman Empire, the offering of a crown by the Egyptians was initially perceived as an act of rebellion by which Titus had proclaimed himself to be the emperor of the east.

204. Speculations about the significance of this headgear suggest that it represented the crown of Upper and Lower Egypt, a Hellenistic diadem, or the golden diadem worn by the high priests of Ptah. For this discussion see Marković, "Titus," 103–16.

ITEM 6

The Two Edicts of Domitian (*VA* 6.42)

Philostratus is correct in his assertion that Domitian issued two edicts: a prohibition of castration and a prohibition of planting vines and cutting down those that had been planted.[205] The vine edict, at least, is attested in pagan[206] and perhaps even in Christian texts.[207]

Nevertheless, several historical aporias appear in this passage. One of these is that the two edicts were not issued "about the same time," as Philostratus claims (*VA* 6.42), but rather were delivered about a decade apart.[208] Another issue is that, in *VS* 520, the report of Scopelian's success in convincing the emperor to rescind this edict is questionable because it was implemented in various places and times, not just on this occasion. Possibly, Philostratus conflated two separate policies in this passage for the sake of brevity.[209] Finally, there is no independent evidence to verify the role of Apollonius in challenging this legislation.[210] Most likely, Philostratus has collapsed the timeframe between the edict on castration and the edict on vines so that he could have Apollonius deliver a memorable epigram that contains elements of both texts.[211]

The Exile of Nerva (*VA* 7.8)

The *VA*'s claim that Domitian exiled Nerva to the town of Tarentum appears to be incorrect. This is because neither Suetonius nor Dio Cassius mentions this exile and because there is no other evidence suggesting that Nerva was exiled to Tarentum.[212] Flinterman convincingly argues that the

205. Bowersock, Introduction to *Life of Apollonius*, 16.

206. Suetonius, *Dom.* 7.2; 14.2; Statius, *Silvae* 4.3.11–12.

207. Rev 6:6 (?); Jerome, *Chron.* 3.160; *Chronicon Paschale* 1.466; Aune, *Revelation 6–16*, 2:399; Flinterman, *Power*, 151.

208. Jones writes, "[i]n fact, Domitian's law against castration appears to date from 82, and his edict on growing vines to 92" (Philostratus, *Apollonius of Tyana*, 2:207, n. 55).

209. Aune, *Revelation*, 399; Levick, "Domitian," 72–73.

210. Bowersock remarks, "[b]ut then, is the role of Apollonius in the response to the vine edict also historical?" (Bowersock, Introduction to *Life of Apollonius*, 16).

211. Apollonius remarked, "These rescripts do not concern me, for I, alone perhaps of mankind, require neither to beget my kind nor to drink wine; but our egregious sovereign seems not aware that he is sparing mankind, while he eunuchises the earth." (*VA* 6.42 [Conybeare, LCL]).

212. Bowersock, Introduction to *Life of Apollonius*, 18; Philostratus, *Apollonius of Tyana*, 2:223, n. 13.

chronology of the *VA*—which appears to place the alleged exile of Nerva around or slightly before AD 93[213]—is impossible. Martial published epigrams to Nerva (AD 93 and 94) and Pliny wrote letters to him that indicate that he was a part of Domitian's inner circle even toward the end of that emperor's reign.[214] Some scholars graciously suggest that Philostratus was confused and thinking of the exile of Calpurnius Crassus by Nerva to Tarentum.[215] Although others have attributed this mistake to the Damis account, there does not appear to be any solid reason for doing so.[216] Whatever the reason for mentioning Nerva's exile, most scholars believe that Philostratus was mistaken about it.

Apollonius's Disappearance from Domitian's Court (*VA* 8.5)

Apollonius's supernatural disappearance from his trial is one of the few miracles that offers a possibility of historical verification. Phillimore, although writing scathingly and emotionally, raises several interesting points against its believability.

> That this should happen at Rome, in the Emperor's own court, in the presence of all the Notables (ἐλλόγιμοι) of the capital— and yet, everywhere else but in Philostratus, dead silence about it! And then, considered in itself, what a fiasco! What could be more incredible than Domitian's behaviour? And, again, the very miraculous disappearance, how shyly, shamefacedly, does Philostratus shrink from asserting it with the proper emphasis of conviction! He has the candor to admit that Damis was not in Rome during the trial; and this allows him to arrange his Emmaus meeting, which is prettily told, but at what expense of plausibility to the trial-narrative![217]

Phillimore's case against the plausibility of this miracle is sound. However, the unlikelihood of Apollonius vanishing from the court does not prove that Apollonius did not stand trial before Domitian, as some suggest.[218] Apollonius's trial plausibly fits within the context of Domitian's

213. Flinterman, *Power*, 153, n. 143.
214. Flinterman, *Power*, 153–54.
215. Bowersock, Introduction to *Life of Apollonius*, 18; Flinterman, *Power*, 154, n. 145.
216. Flinterman, *Power*, 160.
217. Phillimore, *In Honour*, xviii.
218. Dzielska, *Apollonius*, 41.

banishment of philosophers from Italy[219] and this was the only emperor with whom Apollonius can be associated in some way in multiple, extra-Philostratean sources.[220]

Apollonius's Implausible Speech to Domitian (*VA* 8.7)

According to Philostratus, Apollonius wrote a speech for his trial that he did not get to deliver because he had been constrained from answering Domitian's questions (*VA* 8.7). The origin of this lengthy speech is uncertain; it may have derived from an unnamed source or may have been created by Philostratus himself to flesh out Apollonius's defense.[221] Whatever the case, most modern scholars are skeptical about the authenticity of the speech.[222]

Several components of the speech challenge its genuineness because it contradicts the *VA* itself. For example, when Apollonius was charged with sacrificing a boy in the presence of Nerva (*VA* 7.20.1), who then resided in Italy, he defended himself by indicating that he had been elsewhere in the city of Rome on the night of the alleged crime and that he had numerous witnesses (*VA* 8.7.41–42). Unfortunately, this contradicted Philostratus's claim that Apollonius was arrested when he first appeared in Italy (*VA* 7.16.1) and was kept under guard until his trial (*VA* 7.20.4). These circumstances suggest that Apollonius would not have been allowed freedom of movement within the city after his incarceration. Against those who might claim that Apollonius referred to an earlier visit to the city, Philostratus claimed that Apollonius had not been to Italy between the days of Nero until the trial before Domitian (*VA*

---

219. Domitian banished philosophers around AD 89 and 95. See Reasoner, "Emperor, Emperor Cult," 322; B. W. Jones, *The Emperor Domitian*, 189.

220. *VA* 8.26; Dio Cassius, *Hist. rom.* 67.18.1. Although the letters of Apollonius are often addressed to various emperors (e.g., Vespasian, Titus, Domitian), the jury is still out as to whether these documents were authentic, forgeries, or the compositions of Philostratus himself.

221. Anderson, *Philostratus*, 145. The source could not have been Damis, for Apollonius had sent him to Dicaearchia while he stood trial (*VA* 7.41; 8.10).

222. Baur, *Apollonius von Tyana*, 11; Bowersock, Introduction to *Life of Apollonius*, 15; Flinterman, 156. Dungan and Cartlidge believe that the speech was "[a]ctually written by none other than Philostratus" (Dungan and Cartlidge, *Documents* 206). For similar opinions, see Koskenniemi, "Philostratean," 329; Anderson, *Philostratus*, 228. Indeed, Anderson spotted a historical implausibility within the speech: "the imputation that Vespasian interrupted the Jewish War to come to Egypt to see Apollonius is nonsense, in view of the strategic importance of the province" (Anderson, *Philostratus*, 181–82).

8.7.33).[223] Another oddity in the speech is that the charge that Apollonius used magic to predict the Ephesian plague implies that this was a recent event (VA 8.5; 8.7.9), while the narrative places this event long before or at the time of Nero (VA 4.4 and 10).[224] Yet another contradiction in this defense is that Apollonius supposedly had an aversion to long speeches (VA 1.17), yet Philostratus would have the reader believe that Apollonius had intended to deliver this protracted speech at his defense. Further, Philostratus's claim that Apollonius chose to go to his trial unprepared (VA 7.30) is controverted by the assertion that Apollonius wrote a speech in advance of the proceedings (VA 8.7).[225] Such contradictions seem to lead to two possibilities: either Philostratus was using a source for the speech that contradicted his narrative or the speech was the creation of Philostratus, who was careless in matching its claims with the rest of the biography.

Assuming for the moment that this speech was the sophist's creation, one might wonder why he would have included it. Perhaps he was embarrassed by the lack of source material for this part of the narrative and decided to write a speech that was suitable for this occasion.[226] Perhaps he wanted to give Apollonius a chance to present a powerful closing argument rather than simply have him disappear from the courtroom.[227] Perhaps Philostratus hoped that the extensive argumentation in the undelivered speech would put the finishing touches on transforming Apollonius from a magician into a philosopher,[228] a trick that the brief narrative account of the trial was unable to accomplish.

The Execution of Flavius Clemens and Flavia Domitilla (VA 8.25)

Although the accounts of Philostratus, Suetonius, and Dio Cassius coincide on several key details concerning Domitian's treatment of the consul Flavius Clemens and his wife Flavia Domitilla, there are still a

---

223. Flinterman, *Power*, 154–55.
224. Flinterman, *Power*, 154–55.
225. Petzke, *Die Traditionen*, 104.
226. Anderson, *Philostratus*, 145.
227. Anderson, *Philostratus*, 228.
228. Hadas and Smith, *Heroes and Gods*, 198.

few contradictions between the account of the *VA* and other classical writers.[229] According to the *VA*, Domitian's execution of Clemens was followed two or three days later by the order for the execution of his wife (*VA* 8.25), but Dio Cassius claimed that Domitilla was exiled to Pandateria (*Hist. rom.* 67.14). The *VA* also insinuates a brief period between the execution of Flavius Clemens and the assassination of Domitian, whereas according to Suetonius these events were separated by about 18 months (Suetonius, *Dom.* 17.2).[230] Anderson lays the blame for these mistakes at the feet of an unknown source, rather than accusing Philostratus or Damis.[231]

CONCLUSION

As this chapter has demonstrated, the historical, chronological, and geographical errors in the *VA* exist but they vary in importance. In some cases, Philostratus has been proven correct and his critics wrong.[232] In others, his errors are relatively minor.[233] However, some of his mistakes are more serious when they concern the details of rivers,[234] specific cities,[235] and chronology.[236] Most damaging to the veracity of the *VA* are

---

229. Flinterman, *Power*, 152; Anderson, Philostratus, 180.

230. Flinterman, *Power*, 152; Anderson, *Philostratus*, 180.

231. Anderson, *Philostratus*, 181.

232. E.g., the existence of Old Ninus (*VA* 1.3, 19), the location of the Caucasus Mountains (*VA* 2.1–4), and the headwaters of the Indus (*VA* 2.18).

233. E.g., the length of Darius II Ochus's reign (*VA* 1.28), the manner of Agrippina's death (*VA* 4.38.4), the time of Vespasian's arrival in Alexandria (*VA* 5.27–30), Galba's adoption of Otho (*VA* 5.32), the exile of Nerva (*VA* 7.8), and the time of the executions of Flavius Clemens and Flavia Domitilla (*VA* 8.25).

234. E.g., the geography of the Hyphasis River (*VA* 3.50, 52), the geography of the Nile River (*VA* 6.1–27), and incorrect description of the cataracts of the Nile River (*VA* 6.26).

235. E.g., the location of the Eretrians near Babylon, (*VA* 1.24.1–2), the non-existence of Babylon (*VA* 1.25), the distance from Babylon to Ecbatana (*VA* 1.39), the absence of a bird-devouring cleft at the Acropolis (*VA* 2.10), and problems related to the archaeology of Taxila (*VA* 2.20–23).

236. E.g., the unreconcilable ages of Scopelian and Apollonius (*VA* 1.24), the timing of Demetrius's exile (*VA* 4.40, 42), the omission of twenty years between Apollonius's journey from Crete to Rome (*VA* 4.34), the chronological problem related to Demetrius's banishment (*VA* 4.43), and the conflation of the two edicts of Domitian that were issued a decade apart (*VA* 6.42).

his references to non-existent human communities,[237] mythical flora,[238] non-mythical fauna (in the wrong location),[239] paranormal activities,[240] and mythical creatures.[241] Many of these errors occur in Damis's material, making it almost certain that this memoir was not the work of an eyewitness, but rather was a pseudepigraph or the product of Philostratus's imagination. The mistakes related to Apollonius's travels to Babylon, India, and Egypt[242] do not stem from an eyewitness account but are fiction,[243] and some scholars have questioned whether he traveled to some of these locations at all.[244] Perhaps Philostratus was most accurate when dealing with the emperors, as he was obliged to be because that information was so well-known,[245] but still, there is no confirmation by ancient sources that Apollonius was involved in any of the events he describes. So then, although Philostratus was not always incorrect, errors are frequent enough to demonstrate that he was not always a careful historian. Perhaps this is because history was not his agenda, but rather fiction or hagiography, as many scholars have suggested.

237. E.g., the Eretrians (*VA* 1.24) and the gymnosophists of Ethiopia (*VA* 6.5–23).

238. E.g., the bleeding trees of Geryon (*VA* 5.5) and the talking elm of the Gymnosophists (*VA* 6.10.3).

239. E.g., the existence of hippopotami in the Indus River (*VA* 2.19; 6.1.1).

240. E.g., levitation (*VA* 3.15, 17), the talking statue of Memnon (*VA* 6.4), the ghost of Achilles (*VA* 4.16), and the disappearance of Apollonius from his trial (*VA* 8.5).

241. E.g., the *empusai* (*VA* 2.4; 4.25) and the satyr (*VA* 6.27).

242. E.g., *VA* 1.24.1–2, 25; 2.20–23; 3.15, 17; 4.16, 25; 6.4, 26.

243. A few ancient writers appear to be skeptical of the supernatural elements of the Indian trip (e.g., Eusebius, *Hierocles*; Photius, *Myriobiblos*). Photius wrote, "All that he says about the Indians is a tissue of absurd and incredible statements. He asserts that they have certain jars full of rains and winds, with which in time of drought they are able to water the country, and again to deprive it of moisture, after the rain has fallen, since in these casks they have the means of controlling the alternate supply of wind and rain. He tells similar stories, equally foolish and preposterous, and these eight books are so much study and labor lost." See Freese, *The Library of Photius*, 38.

244. C. P. Jones, "Passage to India" 185–99. Bowie believes that the Indian journey is fiction but argues that such a tradition of Apollonius's visit there might have already been in the account of Moiragenes. See Bowie, "Philostratus: Writer of Fiction," 194–95. While not attributing an Indian account to Moiragenes, Flinterman similarly thinks that there may have been pre-Philostratean legends of Apollonius travelling to India. See Flinterman, *Power*, 86–87. However, Dzielska is even skeptical of Apollonius's journeys to Spain, Italy, and Athens. See Dzielska, *Apollonius*, 83.

245. Phillimore, *In Honour*, cxxii.

12

Item 7

Potential Political, Philosophical, Pagan Religious, and Literary Agendas of the *VA*

AN AUTHOR'S MOTIVE FOR writing a biography could influence how his subject is portrayed. For instance, a biography written about president of the United States of America by a Democratic author would differ substantially from one written about the same figure by a Republican biographer. Even a biographer with the purest of intentions would struggle to keep personal agendas and biases at bay. Surely Philostratus, who had his own agenda and wanted to achieve the purposes of the empress that commissioned him to write, must have faced such challenges in producing his work on Apollonius.

As item 7 of the Apollonian Decalogue indicates, "Researchers debate whether the religious, philosophical, political, or literary agendas of Philostratus or the Empress Julia Domna, his patroness, may have influenced the portrayal of Apollonius in the *VA*." Put another way, scholars aim to discern such things as whether Philostratus's agenda for Apollonius's biography was predominately antiquarian, motivated by a desire to create an accurate account of an important person, or whether he consciously shaped the story of Apollonius to promote some other agenda. This chapter will explore several of the more commonly proposed agendas (i.e., religious, philosophical, political, apologetic, and encomiastic) and inquire into what ways these agendas might have modified the tradition about Apollonius. The reader should keep in mind that these agendas overlap at times,[1] so the neat compartmentalization of these topics is not always possible.

A PAGAN RELIGIOUS AGENDA[2]

There are several variations on the proposal that Julia Domna's worship of the Syrian Sun god influenced the depiction of Apollonius in the VA. This agenda, in its simplest form, is that Julia wanted Apollonius portrayed as a Pythagorean saint who worshipped the same deity that her father had served as a priest.[3] Other proposals go further in claiming that the VA was commissioned by Julia as propaganda for a syncretistic campaign to combine the best components of Greek religion with the other religions of the eastern and western halves of the Roman Empire.[4] A much more extreme variation of this agenda was endorsed by Réville, who suggested that Julia sought to reform the paganism of her day to establish "the supremacy of the Eastern deity," the Sun god.[5] These proposed agendas have not fared particularly well in recent times.

One good reason to question all varieties of the agenda proposed above is that the Sun god is not singled out for special honors in the VA. Although Helios was worshipped by Apollonius according to the VA,[6]

---

1. For instance, a philosophical agenda could also have a religious component (e.g., Apollonius's Pythagoreanism) or a philosophical agenda might involve a critique of political viewpoints (e.g., Apollonius's advisement and critique of political leaders).

2. The exploration of an anti-Christian, religious motive will be reserved for the following chapter.

3. Solmsen, "Some Works," 568.

4. Harris writes, "Julia, having obtained Damis's memoirs, commissioned the sophist 'to transcribe them and also to improve their style', for she had a definite goal—to employ the historical figure of Apollonius, who embodied the best of Greek religion, as she thought, with the wisdom also of the East and Egypt, in order to create a new ideal of syncretism. This masterful woman wanted the waters of the Orontes to flow in full flood into the Tiber, and Philostratus was brought into a programme in which literature was to serve the interests of philosophy and religion" (Harris, "Apollonius of Tyana," 192–93). Bidez argued for a similar syncretistic scenario, but also saw the VA as propaganda against the Christian Gospels. See Bidez, "Literature and Philosophy," 12:613–14.

5. Réville argued that Julia was not hostile to Christianity, but rather jealous of it. See Réville, *Apollonius of Tyana*, 68. Therefore, Apollonius would have to "be like Christ, but it was also necessary that he should be different from, and superior to him" (Réville, *Apollonius of Tyana*, 69).

6. VA 1.31; 7.31; 8.13.2.

the holy man neither advocated for the Sun cult[7] nor limited his prayers and offerings to Helios,[8] as one would have expected if the text's goal was to promote the Sun as either the sole or the supreme deity. Rather, Apollonius traveled throughout the Roman world giving religious advice and correcting the practices at sites dedicated to the traditional Greek gods, while never once attempting to establish a cult to Helios or convert others to his way of worship. Indeed, one could make a good case Philostratus regarded Zeus, rather than Helios, as the supreme god of the *VA*.[9] So then, if Julia intended to use the *VA* to promote the elevation of one deity, this book did a poor job of proclaiming that gospel. Since the Sun god is not given priority in the *VA*, perhaps it is better to suggest that Helios is featured as Apollonius's god either because this was historically true[10] (or at least earlier traditions claimed this about him), rather than that Philostratus made the sage into a Sun worshipper merely out of "a desire to please Julia Domna."[11]

Several other reasons seem to undermine the hypothesis that the *VA* was propaganda for the Sun god. In response to the claim that the *VA*'s goal was to promote exclusive worship of the solar god, historical evidence suggests that Julia honored several deities during her lifetime, not Helios alone.[12] Likewise, Philostratus himself is unlikely to have promoted the exclusive worship of Helios. Although he had an interest in the supernatural and mythology, neither Helios nor traditional religion are

---

7. Koskenniemi, *Der philostrateische Apollonios*, 74.

8. Koskenniemi claims that Apollonius only prayed to one god other than the Sun, namely Apollo (*VA* 8.13.2; *Der philostrateische Apollonios*, 71, n. 8). However, Apollonius also prayed to Heracles (*VA* 8.7.28–29), poured a libation to Zeus (*VA* 2.7), prayed to Zeus (*VA* 5.30), and prayed to all the gods at once (*VA* 4.40.2).

9. Apollonius described Zeus as the architect of the universe and the father of gods and men (*VA* 4.30.1). When during Apollonius's trial Domitian commanded the sage to look at the god of all mankind—a reference to himself as emperor—Apollonius stared heavenward toward Zeus (*VA* 8.4).

10. Koskenniemi notes that in the fragment *On Sacrifice* Apollonius is monotheistic, but that the specific name of the deity he worshipped was never mentioned. He also notes that the first mention of Sol Invictus is in AD 158. Because of this date, Apollonius's probably never encountered this deity unless, perhaps, he had really travelled to the East, *Der philostrateische Apollonios*, 78. Knoles essentially makes these same points, in his "Literary Technique," 244–45.

11. Knoles, "Literary Technique," 243.

12. If numismatic evidence is an indication of the deities that Julia worshipped, she had a fondness for several traditional female deities with whom she was associated. The reverse sides of many of her coins depict deities such as Roma, Venus, Vesta, Cybele, Ceres, Isis, Diana, Fortuna, Hilaritas, and Luna. See Bertolazzi, "Julia Domna," 464–86.

major features of the rest of his literary corpus.[13] Therefore, at present, there is no strong evidence that either Philostratus or his royal patron promoted the worship of Helios to any great degree.

Likewise, the argument that Julia used the *VA* to promote a syncretistic agenda that would combine the best of Eastern and Western religions also appears to be built on sand. The chief problem with this proposal is that there is no textual or archaeological evidence to support the claim that Julia promoted such an agenda. This claim may be due to a misguided, scholarly retrojection of Elagabalus's much later religious reforms into the earlier years of Julia's life. Another reason to question this part of the above agenda is that Apollonius's rejection of the widespread practice of blood sacrifice (*VA* 5.25.1; 8.7.30, 39), and his harsh critique of the therianthropic Egyptian gods is out of place in a book that supposedly sought to promote religious syncretism (*VA* 6.10.10–14). Yet, the unlikelihood of a syncretistic motive for the *VA* does not necessarily rule out other religious options.

Another type of religious agenda that is plausible suggests that the *VA* sought to revive traditional Greek religion. The Second Sophistic was a Hellenist project concerned with the goal of reviving and celebrating all aspects of Greek culture, including the worship of the Greek gods. Swain theorized that Philostratus was aware of rapid changes in his world caused by the Roman and Christian worldviews that threatened the traditions of Hellenism.[14] Philostratus's response to these emerging threats was "to bring forward a more exclusive model of Hellenic culture than had been accepted before and to present this as the natural culture of his elite peers."[15] Philostratus's used his writings to advance this Hellenic agenda in several areas, including Greek religion.[16] Swain believes that the religious agenda of the *VA* has often been overlooked because "the apparent triviality of so much of the work, including its very 'sophistic' parade of knowledge, has made it difficult to see the serious purpose behind it."[17]

---

13. Koskenniemi, *Der philostrateische Apollonios*, 75, 77. A possible exception to this claim is that Philostratus did show interest in the revival of the hero cult in *Heroicus*.

14. Swain, "Culture and nature," 33–34.

15. Swain, "Culture and nature," 34.

16. For instance, *Heriocus* spoke to the revival of hero cults in Philostratus's own time, *Gymnasticus* advocated for the return to the physical and educational standards of an earlier age, and *Imagines* made the case for the continued value of Greek mythology and culture. See Swain, "Culture and nature," 38–40.

17. Swain, "Culture and nature," 36–37.

According to Swain, Philostratus invented the story that Apollonius was a successful religious reformer of degenerated Greek culture in the first century to convince his third-century peers that such a reformation of Hellenic culture was also possible in their day.[18] The suggestion that Philostratus has exaggerated the role of the historical Apollonius as a successful, religious reformer is plausible for it contrasts with the sage's description in the *Letters of Apollonius*, in which he appears to be "a marginal if perhaps embarrassing" critic of first-century culture and by no means a consistent and religious reformer.[19] Thus, Swain concludes that Apollonius's "reinvention as a central reformer of Greek culture has nothing to do with his own time and everything to do with that of Philostratus."[20] Perhaps, then, this is one place where Philostratus has altered the tradition for the sake of his Hellenic agenda.

So then, this final religious theory has the appearance of plausibility.[21] The agenda of the Second Sophistic can be seen throughout the work, not only in its interest in renovating Greek cults, but in its celebration of Greek literature, philosophy, art, and history. Yet, for this very reason the *VA*'s *raison d'être* was not primarily to push a religious agenda, for religion was only a small part of the whole package of Hellenistic cultural ideas that Philostratus wanted to promote.

A PHILOSOPHICAL AGENDA

Another agenda that has been proposed for the *VA* is that it sought to emphasize Apollonius's connections to Pythagoreanism for the furtherance of that philosophical movement. Most scholars would probably not object to Solmsen's assertion that Julia wanted her hero to be depicted as a Pythagorean saint and that Philostratus sought to please his patroness by proving that the sage was not a mere sorcerer.[22] However, did

18. See Swain, "Culture and nature," 36–37.

19. Koskenniemi, *Der philostrateische Apollonios*, 73. Only four letters in the collection were written to the cult personnel at two sites: the sanctuary of Zeus at Olympia (*Epp. Apoll.* 26) and the sanctuary of Artemis at Ephesus (*Epp. Apoll.* 65–67).

20. Swain, "Culture and nature," 36–37.

21. Swain's dates the *VA* to the reign of Severus Alexander (and assumes Philostratus was still a courtier of the Severans) when Christianity had already begun to attract several members of the royal household (e.g., Julia Mamaea and Alexander). See Swain, "Culture and nature," 36–37. Although this setting is possible, there is no solid evidence that Philostratus was still a part of the royal household after the death of Julia.

22. Solmsen, "Some Works," 567–68.

Philostratus or Julia plan a more substantial philosophical mission for Apollonius than this in the *VA*? Kee thinks so: "[t]he cause for which the *Life of Apollonius* serves as propaganda is not a cult in the ordinary sense of the term, but the religious and personal values of the Pythagorean tradition as it was understood in the late second and early third centuries."[23] Kee also points out that by the end of the second century, pagans and Christians were exploiting the genre of romance not merely for entertainment but because "it served as a vehicle for conveying religious truth or as an apology for a philosophical view."[24] Additional points that might favor this line of argumentation are that Julia was interested in philosophy,[25] that she may have had Pythagorean philosophers in her salon,[26] and that the *VA* had a lot to say about Apollonius's Pythagorean practices, Pythagoras, and philosophy in general.

There are, however, even better reasons to suggest that the *VA* is not a piece of Pythagorean propaganda. The Pythagoreanism of the *VA* is rather superficial; the work does not address the key tenets of Pythagorean belief in any detail (e.g., mathematics, music, and astronomy).[27] Moreover, Apollonius does not take the opportunity to malign his philosophical rivals in the *VA*, as one might expect in a work advocating for Pythagoreanism. Rather than rejecting other philosophers because of their incorrect philosophical affiliations, Apollonius's negative critique of philosophers of other schools was because of their immorality,[28] style

---

23. Kee, *Miracle*, 264.

24. Kee, *Miracle*, 252, 254. In this entry, Kee cites the example of Lucian's *Alexander*, Apuleius's *Metamorphoses*, the second century redaction of Xenophon's *Ephesiaca*, Philostratus's *VA*, and the Acts of Paul.

25. Dio Cassius, *Hist. rom.* 76.15.7.

26. At the very least, Julia had both "mathematicians" (γεωμέτραις) and philosophers in her circle (*VS* 622). The former term refers either to astrologers or Pythagorean/Platonic mathematicians; Maclean and Bradshaw, *Flavius Philostratus*, xlvi; Philostratus and Eunapius, *The Lives of the Sophists*, 301, n. 4.

27. Knoles writes, "[i]t is an odd circumstance then that the *VA*, which seems to show a strong interest in the subject, actually contains a relatively small amount of material on Pythagoreanism. Furthermore, it is curious that of the Pythagorean material present in the work, the emphasis is strongly upon the trappings of the system, rather than upon its philosophical principles: the greatest interest is in the dress and eating habits of the Pythagorean sage, and not on the comprehensive set of theories which Pythagoras had devised" (Knoles, "Literary Technique," 248–49).

28. E.g., Euphrates the Stoic (*VA* 1.13.3; 5.37.2 6.7).

of instruction,[29] faulty reasoning,[30] or inadequacy in the face of tyranny.[31] At times, Apollonius even associated with or praised philosophers from other sects.[32] In addition to these points, Philostratus himself does not seem to have been deeply interested in Pythagoreanism for he rarely mentions it in the rest of his writings,[33] and he does not mention Apollonius's affiliation with this group elsewhere in his corpus.[34] For these reasons, the VA does not have the earmarks of a Pythagorean manifesto.

More likely, Apollonius's Pythagorean pedigree was stressed in the VA not because it would help champion the Pythagorean cause, but because Apollonius was already affiliated with this group in the pre-Philostratean tradition.[35] Because Philostratus's audience was likely aware of this traditional affiliation, he was obliged to interact with it, even if the treatment was superficial.[36] To slightly modify Knoles's summary of the VA, it is not a deep (Pythagorean) philosophical work about a man, but a work about a man who happened to be a (Pythagorean) philosopher.[37]

A POLITICAL AGENDA

Was the VA driven in part by a political agenda of some sort, as several researchers have suggested? Apollonius sometimes advised leaders on the proper way to rule[38] and criticized officials who governed poorly.[39]

---

29. E.g., Dio Chysostom (VA 5.40).

30. E.g., Euphrates the Stoic and Dio Chrysostom, an eclectic philosopher (VA 5.35–37).

31. E.g., Demetrius the Cynic (VA 7.10.2–7.15.1), Zeno of Elea (pre-socratic), Diogenes of Sinope (Cynic), and Plato (VA 7.2–3).

32. E.g., Demetrius the Cynic (VA 4.25) and Musonius Rufus the Stoic (VA 4.46).

33. Bowie, *Apollonius of Tyana*, 1671; Knoles, "Literary Technique," 250. Solmsen warns, however, that Philostratus may have been interested in Pythagoreanism while a part of Julia's literary circle, but that his passion for it may have waned later in his career. See Solmsen, "Some Works," 568, n. 41.

34. VS 521; 570.

35. Knoles lists several lines of evidence that strongly suggest that the historical Apollonius was a Pythagorean or at least that he had Pythagorean interests. See Knoles, "Literary Technique," 250–51.

36. Knoles, "Literary Technique," 249–53.

37. Knoles, "Literary Technique," 254.

38. E.g., Vardanes (VA 1.37), Vespasian (VA 5.28–36), Titus (VA 6.29), and Nerva (VA 7.8).

39. E.g., Nero and Domitian.

Because of the sage's occasional involvement in the political sphere, some have suggested that one of the *VA*'s real agendas was to instruct or warn the Severan emperors of Philostratus's age. As was discussed in chapter 4, some scholars have even proposed that several of the first-century Flavian emperors in the *VA* (e.g., Vespasian, Titus, and Domitian) were carefully modeled after the Severan rulers or other members of their court (e.g., Severus, Geta, and Caracalla). Johannes Göttsching (1889) proposed that the educative agenda for the *VA* was intended for the instruction of Severus Alexander, for it implicitly compared the best and worst emperors from Apollonius's time to the best and worst rulers from the Severan family.[40] In a similar argument, Calderini (1940/1) argued that Julia Domna had Philostratus's fashion the *VA* as a tool to warn Septimius Severus about the dangers of bad counselors like Plautinius.[41] Did the *VA*, like Xenophon's biography entitled *Cyropaedia*, belong to the genre of "mirrors for princes" (*specula principum*) and have the instruction of contemporary Severan rulers as its primary aim?[42]

Flinterman has pushed back against both scenarios. In response to Göttsching, Flinterman claims that most of the alleged parallels between the Flavians and Severans are unconvincing, noting that "[i]n most cases, correspondences between the *VA* and situations in the Severan period can be satisfactorily accounted for by historically verified parallels between the two periods; there is no need to assume that the writer deliberately created these parallels in order to hold a mirror up to the faces of his contemporaries, including Severus Alexander."[43] Flinterman also found fault with Calderini's theory since went against the consensus in requiring an exceedingly early date for the *VA*. Further, if the agenda of the *VA* was to warn Alexander Severus against wicked advisors, it was poorly planned for it ran the risk of sending a mixed message; Aelianus, a prefect like the wicked Plautianus, is presented in a favorable light in the *VA*.[44] Although modern scholars are willing to concede that there are al-

---

40. Göttsching, *Apollonius*, 80–89.

41. Calderini, "Teoria e pratica," 213–41.

42. The *VA* and the *Cyropaidia* are similar in that both are exceedingly long biographies with eight books. However, they differ in that Xenophon's protagonist was a monarch and the contents of the work focused on training the prince for his position, whereas Philostratus's main character was a philosopher who was only tangentially concerned with politics.

43. Flinterman, *Power*, 218.

44. Flinterman, *Power*, 219.

lusions to Severan rulers in the *VA*,[45] still "[there] are therefore absolutely inadequate grounds for the supposition that Philostratus intended to advise one of the Severan emperors by means of the portraits of rulers in the *VA* and the counsels of the protagonist."[46] So then, the *VA* neither appears to present a substantial educative agenda for monarchs in general nor to have the instruction of a particular ruler in mind.

In truth, the political instruction found in the *VA* is rather bland. Knowles noted that political advice in the *VA* consists of general counsel: be moderate, be just.[47] However, he does allow that its instruction may have been intended to have a "modestly edifying effect on its imperial readers."[48] So, although the *VA* promotes good rule and condemns tyranny, the work does not read like an instruction manual for monarchs, senators, or other political leaders.

Although the *VA* does not have a strong political agenda, Philostratus may have invented the role of Apollonius as an advisor to kings to advance the plot of the *VA*. Apart from the *Letters*, there is no solid evidence that the historical Apollonius interacted with any Roman rulers, with the possible exception of Domitian.[49] The *Letters* contain several epistles to and from emperors; these are also found in the *VA*.[50] If these letters are authentic, perhaps Philostratus used them to exaggerate the role of Apollonius as an imperial advisor. If instead these letters were Philostratean creations that were later included in the collection of *Letters*, then they would provide no proof at all of Apollonius's political interactions with

---

45. Even Flinterman finds allusions to Caracalla, Geta, and Elagabalus within the *VA*. See Flinterman, *Power*, 220–221. Koskenniemi finds allusions to Severus and Caracalla but does not believe that there is any evidence of allusion to Elagabulus or his reforms (*Der philostrateische Apollonios*, 41, 81).

46. Flinterman, *Power*, 221.

47. Knoles, "Literary Technique," 231–32.

48. Knoles, "Literary Technique," 237.

49. Knoles, "Literary Technique," 234–36. *Epp. Apoll.* 21 and 22 were addressed to Domitian, but not were not cited in the *VA*, which might indicate that these epistles were pre-Philostratean and that the historical Apollonius wrote to the emperor. Yet, Dio Cassius's account that Apollonius predicted the assassination of Domitian from afar did not indicate that Apollonius and Domitian had ever met and, therefore, cannot be used as evidence that Apollonius and Domitian knew each other.

50. E.g., Apollonius to Vespasian (*VA* 5.41; *Epp. Apoll.* 42f, 42g, 42h); Apollonius to Vespasian again (*VA* 8.7; *Epp. Apoll.* 77–78); Titus to Apollonius (*VA* 6.29; *Epp. Apoll.* 77d); Apollonius to Nerva (*VA* 7.8; *Epp. Apoll.* 11); Apollonius to Nerva and Nerva to Apollonius (*VA* 8.27; *Epp. Apoll.* 15); Apollonius to Domitian (*VA* 7.35; *Epp. Apoll.* 15). See Knoles, "Literary Technique," 284, n. 13 and 14.

emperors. A further point to ponder is that Pythagoreans did not have a strong tradition of counseling rulers. However, philosophers from various groups often took on this role[51] as did some sophists. So, the depiction of Apollonius as a political advisor may well have been an invention of Philostratus that was based on the model of sophists and philosophers rather than on pre-Philostratean traditions about the Tyanean.

A few writers have proposed that Philostratus may have had a selfish political agenda of embellishing this account; he may have sought political advancement or financial gain. This argument goes back at least as far as Newman (1826), who stated that the credibility of miracles is impugned "[i]f desire of *gain, power*, or other *temporal advantage* may be imputed to them. This would detract materially from the authority of Philostratus, even supposing him to have been in a *situation* for ascertaining the truth of his narrative; as he professes to write his account of Apollonius at the instance of his patroness, the Empress Julia, who is known to have favoured the Eclectic cause."[52] More recently, Eddy and Boyd implied that Philostratus stood to gain wealth and power from writing the VA. They wrote that Philostratus had been commissioned to rehabilitate the reputation of Apollonius, but that the Gospel writers "had no such clear financial and/or political motives."[53] Did Philostratus shape Apollonius in such a way as to advance his political career or to benefit financially?

Most scholars would probably concede that Philostratus received some benefit from Julia in exchange for his work and that he most likely fashioned Apollonius to suit her tastes. Yet, one must balance these facts with the likelihood that the VA was completed after Julia's death. After her departure, Philostratus may not have been obligated to finish the work or to remain true to Julia's agenda. Unfortunately, not enough can be known about Philostratus's career after the empress's death to determine whether he ever gained anything politically or financially from the publication of the VA. While the Severan interest in Apollonius that continued during the reign of Alexander may have been due to Philostratus's presence in the court or to the influence of the VA in royal circles, there is no certain proof that the sophist benefitted from its publication beyond the enhancement of his reputation as a literary master for having written it.

---

51. Knoles, "Literary Technique," 231–32.

52. Newman, *Life of Apollonius*, 289.

53. Eddy and Boyd, *The Jesus Legend*, 151–52. Boyd makes a similar statement in Lee Strobel, *The Case for Christ*, 160.

ITEM 7

APOLOGETIC AND ENCOMIASTIC AGENDAS

The task of sorting out Philostratus's agenda for the *VA* can be exasperating. After all, many of the proposed options that were already explored in this chapter could arguably be a part of his literary agenda (e.g., politics, religion, philosophy, and the promotion of Hellenic culture), including his desire to show off his sophistic talents.[54] Yet, these subthemes appear to be in the service of his primary agenda:[55] the improvement of Apollonius's reputation.

To this very end, the *VA* combines both encomiastic (the praise of Apollonius) and apologetic agendas (a defense of Apollonius). These approaches are not at odds with one another but rather are two sides of the same coin. On the obverse of the coin, Philostratus defended Apollonius from the charges of being a magician.[56] On the reverse of the coin, he embellished the reputation of Apollonius so that he surpassed all philosophical, sophistic, and heroic rivals. Both approaches gave Philostratus

---

54. Some experts have even suggested that Philostratus's real agenda "was most plausibly that of a professional writer, to produce a well-rounded and entertaining piece of literature, rather than to further a propogandist interpretation of Apollonius" (Bowie, "Apollonius," 1666). See the similar views of Flinterman, "Pythagoras," 157.

55. Meier points out that although Philostratus's main purpose was to defend Apollonius against the charge of magic, this agenda did not preclude him featuring his skill as a writer; Meier, *Mentor*, 578. Likewise, Knoles notes that motifs such as "how one should rule, Hellenism, worship of Helios, Pythagoreanism" only serve the main purpose of the *VA* in constructing the narrative of a holy man. See Knoles, "Literary Technique," iii.

56. A subtheme of the apology of Apollonius in the *VA* is the defense of Apollonius against the claim that he had an illicit affair in Scythia (*VA* 1.13.3). Interestingly, a separate but similar accusation in Philostratus's *VS* claimed that Apollonius had an affair with a married woman in Cilicia, by whom he sired Alexander (or Clay Plato; *VS* 570). Philostratus rejected such tales of the sage's misbehavior in Cilicia, asserting that what he had written about Apollonius in the *VA*—presumably a reference to several generic accounts of Apollonius's reputation for chastity (*VA* 1.12–13.3; 6.42)—demonstrated the absurdity of such accusations. A much better case for Apollonius's innocence in the Cilician incident could have been made on chronological grounds, an issue that does not appear to have dawned on Philostratus. In this very passage, Philostratus claims that Alexander, when he had reached manhood, pleaded the case of Seleucia before the emperor Antonius Pius. Phillimore explained the problem well: "As Pius only became Emperor in 138, Terracotta Plato's birth, at the very earliest, does not fall before A.D. 110–15. Suppose his mother even to have been born in AD 70 or 75. The result is that, according to the received chronology for Apollonius, he inspired a lady *at least 80 years younger than himself* with a passion as monstrous as ridiculous. It would indeed be the greatest of his miracles" (Phillimore, *In Honour*, cviii). This serves as another example of why one must be cautious in trusting the chronological information that Philostratus provides in the *VA* or the *VS*.

a chance to display his sophistic skills, especially in the areas of epideictic rhetoric (the praise of Apollonius), forensic rhetoric (the defense of Apollonius), and invention.[57]

An Apologetic Agenda

The most obvious and all-pervading of Philostratus's agendas in the *VA* is his defense of the Tyanean against the charge of being a magician and a fraud.[58] This apologetic agenda is introduced at the onset of the work (*VA* 1.1-3),[59] revisited in several passages,[60] examined in minute detail

---

57. For the importance of invention in Philostratus's *VS*, see Brunt, "The Bubble," 30-31.

58. For an extensive treatment of Philostratus's defense of Apollonius against the charge of magic, see the entire thesis of Cazemier, "Apollonius en magie." For other scholars who identify the major purpose of the *VA* as an apologia against claims of Apollonius's opponents that he was a magician and a sorcerer, see Martin Hengel, *The Charismatic Leader*, 27; Harris, "Apollonius of Tyana," 190. Koskenniemi, while admitting that Philostratus had to distance Apollonius from a pre-existing view that he was a magician, does not regard this defense as the main agenda of the *VA*. See Koskenniemi, *Der philostrateische Apollonios*, 59. Meier argued that Philostratus was correcting the view of the educated class, which had perhaps been influenced by the polemics of Lucian, Euphrates, and Moeragenes. See Meier, *Mentor*, 577-78. Concurring with the essence of that assessment, Lesky wrote that Philostratus "seeks to raise him from a of a lower order γόης to the level of a Neopythagorean ascète and prodigy, a true θεῖος ἀνήρ," (Lesky, *Greek Literature*, 837).

59. Two charges are countered in this opening passage. The first charge was that Apollonius was guilty because of his association with the magicians of Babylon, the Brahmins of India, and the Gymnosophists of Egypt. Philostratus's response to this claim is that other great philosophers of the past (e.g., Pythagoras, Empedocles, Democritus, and Plato) had also interacted with such magicians, but had not been labelled magicians. The second charge was that Apollonius's prophetic abilities smacked of magic. Mirroring his first response, Philostratus argued that earlier philosophers like Socrates and Anaxagoras had performed such supernatural feats but were not charged with being magicians.

60. Philostratus employed a new strategy in a few passages in which he distanced Apollonius from magic and magicians. He pointed out that Apollonius's behavior was unlike that of magicians: he did not demand money for his services or scam people (*VA* 7.39.2) and he did not attempt to influence the future with his skills, consult ghosts, use spells, or sacrifice to alter events (*VA* 5.12). Further, Philostratus attempted to distanced Apollonius to some degree from the Wise Men of India, whose practices might have been associated with magic (e.g., sympathetic magic, levitation, and meal-serving automata; *VA* 5.12). Yet, Philostratus is inconsistent in his employment of this line of argument, for he sometimes defended the Wise Ones against their critics. For a full discussion of this line of argumentation, see Cazemier, "Apollonius en magie," 56-68.

during Apollonius's trial before Domitian (*VA* 8.5),[61] and reexamined in the sage's undelivered speech (*VA* 8.7.1–50). This speech is the capstone of the apology; it answered all the charges that could have been leveled against the sage, many of which were never addressed during his abbreviated hearing in the main narrative.[62] From the opening of the *VA* until its end, Philostratus's tale is infused with a defense of Apollonius against the accusation of being a magician.

Oddly, Philostratus did not spell out the exact reason that he felt that such an extensive and unrelenting defense was necessary. Most likely the apology was a reaction to the four-volume work on Apollonius by Moiragenes (*VA* 1.3.2), which probably portrayed Apollonius as a magician and philosopher.[63] If so, Philostratus probably sought to drive a

61. During his defense before Domitian, Apollonius restated many of the arguments employed earlier in the *VA*, yet he also introduced several new ones. On this, see Cazemier, "Apollonius en magie," 68–91. A new argument was that Domitian's own father, Vespasian, would have never had anything to do with Apollonius if he had considered him a magician (*VA* 8.7.6–12). Unlike Domitian, Vespasian had not been put off by Apollonius's hairstyle and manner of dress. Vespasian conversed with Apollonius publicly in a temple, not in private and at night as magicians were wont to do. Further, this conversation was held in the company of the philosophers Dion and Euphrates, respectively Apollonius's best friend and greatest enemy, thus making any talk about magic impossible. Finally, a letter written by Vespasian was introduced as evidence that Apollonius had not sought money but had chosen a life of voluntary poverty.

62. In this undelivered speech, Apollonius attempted to allay any suspicions about his strange clothing and vegetarian diet (*VA* 8.7.13) by explaining that these were consistent with Pythagorean lifestyle. Likewise, he defended his long, disheveled hair as a Spartan practice that symbolized courage. In response to the rumor that certain people had honored him as a god (*VA* 8.7.19), he replied that he had never promoted such an idea and that he know of no city that sacrificed to him. To the accusation that he had predicted the plague at Ephesus (*VA* 8.7.24–29), he pointed out that Thales and Anaxagoras had done similar feats without being accused of sorcery (cf. *VA* 1.2). He explained that, at Ephesus, he had been able to detect the coming plague because his light diet had sharpened his senses and that, at that time, he had prayed to Hercules, a god that no magician would have invoked. Philostratus distanced Apollonius from the behavior of magicians, for a charlatan would not have attributed a supernatural feat to a god rather than taking credit for it himself (*VA* 8.7.29). Finally, against the charge that he had sacrificed of a boy for Nerva (*VA* 8.7.30), Apollonius stated that he was opposed to blood sacrifice and that money could not have been a motive for the boy's murder since the sage lived a life of poverty. His alibi for the night on which that grisly deed supposedly took place was that he had spent the evening at the house of a dying friend, Philiscus of Melos.

63. Philostratus maligned Moiragenes because he considered him to be very "ignorant" about the man, Apollonius (πολλὰ δὲ τῶν περὶ τὸν ἄνδρα ἀγνοήσαντι; *VA* 1.3.2.). Philostratus probably alluded to a story from Moiragenes's book about Apollonius—probably the same one mentioned by Origen (Origen, *Cels.* 6.41)—when he tells the tale in *VA* 5.39. In Moiragene's version of the story, Apollonius used magic to ward off

wedge between those two roles by dismissing the former and enhancing the latter. Perhaps this defense was deemed necessary as a response to the views of Philostratus's contemporaries (e.g., Dio Cassius), authors from an earlier era (e.g., Lucian), or popular opinion that viewed Apollonius as a magician. In truth, there is nothing implausible about Philostratus simultaneously defending against both Moiragenes and these other traditions.

Either of these scenarios could have called for Philostratus to alter his depiction of the historical Apollonius; magical components would need to be deemphasized or eliminated, while philosophical details might need to be magnified or invented.[64] Yet, historical constraints prevented Philostratus from shaping the Apollonian tradition in any way that he pleased. Since the reports of Apollonius's miracles were too deeply embedded in the tradition to alter (e.g., Lucian, Dio Cassius, and the *Letters of Apollonius*), Philostratus wisely chose not to deny these feats. Instead of attributing these wonders to magic, he attributed them to Apollonius's asceticism and arcane, Pythagorean wisdom.[65]

For all the space dedicated to Apollonius's defense, Philostratus's case is not altogether convincing. Cazemier enumerated several flaws in his argument. Philostratus's comparison of Apollonius to the philosophers Pythagoras and Empedocles—and to a lesser extent Democritus— was risky, since these figures had sometimes been accused of dabbling in magic.[66] Further, Philostratus's argument is undercut by a rather long list

---

a blow from Euphrates, but Philostratus states there that he wanted to relate the life of Apollonius for those who "do not know it" (παραδοῦναι τὸν Ἀπολλωνίου βίον τοῖς μήπω εἰδόσι). This charge of Moiragene's ignorance is reminiscent of Philostratus claim that *VA* aims to remedy such general "ignorance" about Apollonius (τὴν τῶν πολλῶν ἄγνοιαν; *VA* 1.3.1). Koskenniemi notes that although the scholarly consensus is that the *VA* served as a corrective to Moiragenes's negative portrayal of Apollonius has been challenged, most agree that Philostratus was attempting to exonerate Apollonius from his reputation as a magician. See Koskenniemi, *Die philostrateishe Apollonios*, 58, 66.

64. Apollonius's speech presented before Domitian, which most scholars believe was a Philostratean creation, is likely to be the place where Philostratus's concerns and modifications to the tradition are to be found, if they exist.

65. Dzeilska, *Apollonius*, 92. As Van der Stockt correctly observes, "the facts are not denied, but the conclusions from it are rejected" (Van der Stockt, "Never the Twain," 196–97).

66. Cazemier, "Apollonius en magie," 58, 94; Flinterman, "Pythagoras and Pythagoreanism," 155. For a more detailed discussion the tension between traditions that portray Pythagoras and Empedocles as magicians, philosophers, and gods see Tiede, *The Charismatic Figure*, 14–29. This same tension appears to have existed in traditions about Apollonius, where earlier sources portrayed him as a magician, but from the

of contradictory statements: (1) at times Apollonius distanced himself from the magical practices of the Wise Men of India, but at other times he defended them (*VA* 6.11);[67] (2) Apollonius spoke out against magic, but then performed deeds that involved a magical component as is suggested either by details the immediate context in the *VA* or by similar practices in contemporary literature;[68] (3) Philostratus claimed that sages, unlike magicians, only predicted events but did not manipulate them (*VA* 5.12), but then portrayed Apollonius as influencing future events;[69] (4) Apollonius claimed that he could not raise the dead (*VA* 8.41), yet he raised a girl from the dead (*VA* 4.45);[70] (5) Apollonius asserted he was not a magician, for a magician could not be shackled (*VA* 7.34), but then freed himself from his shackles twice (*VA* 7.38; 8.30.3). Another of Cazemier's points is that, on occasion, when Apollonius was associated with magic,

---

time of the *VA* onward sources stress his role as a philosopher. Interestingly, Tiede points out that it was reported that Empedocles had the power "to bewitch" (γοητεύειν), which resembles the charge against Apollonius. See Tiede, *The Charismatic Figure*, 21. In Porphyry's *VP*, both Empedocles and Pythagoras are associated with magic, yet Porphyry did not attempt to defend them against this charge. Diogenes Laertius records that Timon spoke of Pythagoras who tended toward sorcery (Πυθαγόρην τε γόητας ἀποκλίναντ' ἐπὶ δόξας), *Lives* 8.1.36. See Tiede, *The Charismatic Figure*, 29, 33. Thus, Philostratus's comparison of Apollonius to Empedocles and Pythagoras was potentially damaging to the case that the Tyanean was not a magician.

67. Cazemier, "Apollonius en magie," 95.

68. Cazemier lists several categories of such deeds: (1) control over other entities: contact with the shade of Achilles while alone and at night (cf. *Cels.* 1.68 sorcerers invoking the souls of heroes), driving away an *empusa* (plural?), the expulsion of demons, employing a "secret threat" against a Satyr (plague demon apparently smacked of magic; torture and coercion *VA* 4.20, 4.25), healing a dog bite (spell), and raising the dead by saying something incomprehensible (spell); (2) control over nature and the environment: prevention of plague and earthquake; (3) control over his own body: liberation from chains (*VA* 7.38; 8.30.3, spell), rapid movement (*VA* 7.41), and disappearance (*VA* 8.5.4); (4) a good memory (spell) and facility in all languages including those of animals; (5) finding lost treasure (Lucian); and (6) making the charges written against him on a scroll disappear. For a more detailed discussion of these points, see Cazemier, "Apollonius en magie," 107–32.

69. For instance, Apollonius manipulated future catastrophes by commanding an impending plague not to approach Ephesus (*VA* 4.4), praying to the gods that disaster not come on the Ionians (*VA* 4.6), and preventing earthquakes near the Hellespont by sacrificing (*VA* 6.41). See Cazemier, "Apollonius en magie," 118–27.

70. Yet, in this instance, Philostratus offers an alternative, naturalistic explanation of this event. Perhaps this explanation was to distance the resurrection of the maiden from any magical associations.

Philostratus mounted little[71] or no defense of the sage at all.[72] Finally, Cazemier observed that, while Philostratus made it clear that Apollonius was not a magician, the biographer never proposed a clear alternative role for him.[73] At the end of the day, Philostratus's effort to weaken the charge of sorcery is nullified by his introduction of data supporting the verdict that the holy man was in truth a magician.[74] Why Philostratus did not do a better job of tying up these loose ends is an unsolved puzzle.[75]

Another unresolved matter is whether this apologetic agenda originated with Julia Domna or Philostratus. Julia Domna probably commissioned Philostratus to exonerate Apollonius from this negative accusation; some have explicitly attributed this motive to her.[76] Yet, even if the impetus to defend the Tyanean originated with Julia, Philostratus may have chosen to defend Apollonius for reasons of his own. If the consensus of scholarship is correct that the *VA* was written after the death of Julia Domna, Philostratus would have had an opportunity to revise the *VA*'s defense of Apollonius if he had strongly disagreed with her perspective. Since the apologetic agenda was retained, he was likely sympathetic to it.[77]

---

71. *VA* 6.11.

72. Apollonius did not defend himself when refused access to shrines because he was a magician (*VA* 8.19.2; 8.30.3). He gave no explanation of his rapid movement between distant locales (*VA* 8.12.2). Philostratus did not explain the significance of a four-volume work on planetary prophecy that Moiragenes claimed Apollonius had written (*VA*, 3.41.1.). See Cazemier, "Apollonius en magie," 92.

73. Cazemier proposes that Philostratus probably intends Apollonius to be understood as a divinely inspired Pythagorean sage, although there are also hints that he was divine. See Cazemier, "Apollonius en magie," 96– 97. Harris believes that Philostratus's agenda was to rehabilitate and raise the reputation of Apollonius from sorcerer to that of a true *theios anēr* and philosopher. See Harris, "Apollonius of Tyana," 190.

74. Cazemier, "Apollonius en magie," 137.

75. Conceivably, Philostratus may have felt that he was so constrained by the tradition that he could not convincingly eliminate some of these obstacles to his case. Alternately, he may have felt confident that his anti-magical apology did not need to address all these issues. Possibly, Philostratus did not regard these issues as problematic in the first place. However inconsistent Philostratus may appear to modern readers in presenting his case that Apollonius was not a magician, his argument largely succeeds in the end.

76. Schirren opines, "The narrator tells us that it was the Empress Julia Domna who commissioned him to write the biography, obviously intending to liberate Apollonius' image from prejudices concerning his sophistry and wizardry" (Schirren, "Irony," 164).

77. The Severin court was not unified in its viewpoint about Apollonius. Figures like Julia and Dio may have wanted to distance the sage from magic, but apparently Caracalla did not have a problem with Apollonius as a practitioner (Dio Cassius, *Hist.*

Philostratus's disdain for magic probably played a part in his campaign to clear his protagonist of the charge of being a magician. In the VS, a later work not written for Julia Domna and one that is more likely to reflect his perspective, Philostratus defended two sophists against charges of using magic,[78] much like he had done for Apollonius in the VA.[79] He may also have indicated a negative view of the use of magic in *Imagines* 1.6.6–7, where he mentioned that a hare was part of a ritual to coerce love.[80] *Heroicus* may prove to be the exception in the corpus, for several figures within this text employ magic—or at least what could be understood as magic—without the censure of Philostratus.[81] Yet, even the potentially magical examples in *Heroicus* work may harmonize with the negative stance found in the rest of his writings, for they are merely reported without a positive or negative evaluation,[82] and they do not employ the magical nomenclature found in the VA and VS to describe these actions (e.g., μάγος, γόης).[83] It appears that Philostratus is consistent, or nearly so, in his disapproval of magic throughout his writings. Thus, it is likely that the defense of Apollonius against magic was consistent with his views elsewhere and that, even if he did not originate this apologetic, he was personally in agreement with it. Philostratus's rejection of magic

---

rom. 78.18.4.).

78. Two passages in the VS give insight into Philostratus's own view of magic. In the first, he defended Dionysius of Miletus against the charge that he had taught his students the art of memory by means of the Chaldean arts. Philostratus explained that the art of memory taught by this sophist came from training and was not related to magic, for a wise man would not risk his reputation by teaching his students the magical arts (γοητεύων; VS 523). In a second passage, Philostratus dismissed the belief that a well-educated man like Adrian the Phoenician was a magician (γόης) simply because he had lived to the advanced age of eighty; he would not have been deceived by the magic arts (γοήτων ὑπαχθείη τέχνας) or the practices of the magicians (τὰ τῶν μάγων ἤθη; VS 590). For a discussion of these passages, see Cazemier, "Apollonius en magie," 34–35.

79. Anderson noted that not even the sophists were exempt from the charge of magic. See Anderson, *Philostratus*, 126. Also see Schmitz, "Narrator and audience," 50.

80. Cazemier notes that the hare may simply be a lover's gift, but also notes that animal parts are used in magical ritual in Books 2 and 3 of the VA. She also observes that a hare was specifically used in VA 3.39 by the Indians in a sympathetic magical context. See Cazemier, "Apollonius en magie," 36, 47.

81. Cazemier, "Apollonius en magie," 44, 47. She notes in this passage that Protesilaus is depicted as curing petitioners and used love spells, Circe is skilled in magic, and several other figures could be regarded as dabbling in magic: Helen, Sophocles, and Orpheus.

82. Philostratus merely reports that Circe was well-versed in magic potions, but no positive or negative evaluation of this skill is given (*Her.* 25.13).

83. Cazemier, "Apollonius en magie," 45–46.

may have been, in part, because he regarded it as a practice of the common folk but not of the wise and highly educated.[84] Given Philostratus's bias against magic, one wonders whether he labored to free Apollonius from association with it because he thought that the charge was false or because of his prejudices against the dark arts. If the latter is the case, the VA probably does not give an accurate picture of Apollonius's relationship with magic.

An Encomiastic Agenda: Apollonius as Quintessential Hero and Sage

Philostratus promoted an encomiastic agenda by portraying Apollonius as a superman of sorts,[85] an ideal and omnicompetent figure who outstripped or at least rivaled the philosophical, political, religious, and globe-trekking accomplishments of the greatest figures of the past. Several scholars have noted this motif in the VA. Platt explains,

> In its encyclopedic range, the text manages to penetrate the geographical limits of the known world, to cover radically different approaches to religious practice, philosophical inquiry and systems of government, and even to traverse time and rewrite Greek literary history. It is a text that absorbs, appropriates and represents virtually every aspect of the intellectual culture of its time, all to further Philostratus' promotion of Apollonius as the Hellene *extraordinaire*, demonstrating his all-encompassing wisdom, his ability to embrace and master the familiar and the foreign, the practical and the intellectual, the human and the divine. Working toward this end, the narrative repeatedly plays with the *topoi* of Greek literary tradition, allowing Apollonius to subvert and surpass his models in terms of paideia, Sophia, and piety, while demonstrating Philostratus' own skills at outstripping the literary achievements of his predecessors.[86]

In like fashion, Anderson explained how Philostratus associated Apollonius with all the great figures of the past, "Apollonius performs the labors of Hercules, the voyages of Odysseus, the conquests of Alexander, the

---

84. Cazemier, "Apollonius en magie," 34. She notes that Apollonius makes the same point during his trial (VA 8.7.2) that wise men have no truck with magic; "Apollonius en magie," 35.

85. Francis believed the agenda of the book was to show how Apollonius came to be considered a divine man. See Francis, "Truthful Fiction," 437.

86. Platt, "Virtual Visions," in *Philostratus*, 131.

trial of Socrates and the transmigrations of Pythagoras, all in one ... And of course, he bypasses his predecessors in every department: he goes further than Alexander, Pythagoras or Septimius Severus."[87] The following section will examine the *VA*'s comparison of Apollonius to select figures in the areas of philosophy, history, and mythology. Three representative areas will be explored below: Apollonius as the new Pythagoras, Apollonius as a world traveler, and Apollonius as the greatest philosopher.[88]

The first of these themes that will be explored is Philostratus's portrayal of Apollonius as the new Pythagoras, the philosophical luminary that the sage most closely resembles in the *VA*.[89] In part, such a resemblance is to be expected since Apollonius is portrayed as a rigorous adherent of Pythagoreanism.[90] As a member of this philosophical sect, Apollonius observed five years of silence,[91] abstained from wine,[92] ate a

87. Anderson, *Philostratus*, 235. Scholarly examples of this sort could be multiplied. Phillimore's comment also deserves a quote: "Pythagoras had learned from Brahmins: so must Apollonius the new avatar of Pythagoras. Democritus had been the great traveler of his day, and visited Babylonia and Egypt: Apollonius must outdo him. Zeno and Plato and Diogenes and many more had boldly confronted tyrants and endured persecution: Apollonius must be brought before Nero and Nero's *portio de crudelitate*, Domitian" (Phillimore, *In Honour*, lxxiii).

88. One could add to this list the theme of Apollonius as the greatest sophists, but this topic was introduced earlier in this study. The focus on Apollonius as the greatest sophist also differs a bit from these other three topics, in that this comparison can only be detected by comparing the numerous similarities between Apollonius in the *VA* and the sophist in the *VS*. The three themes to be treated in this chapter only appear in the *VA*.

89. Lardner, *The Works*, 4:263, 269. To my knowledge, Réville is the only scholar to express the belief that Iamblicus and Porphyry had modeled their biographies of Pythagoras on that of Philostratus. See Réville, *Apollonius of Tyana*, 90.

90. Philostratus claimed that Apollonius received instruction in Pythagoreanism at Aegae while he was a young man; although his instructor was immoral, Apollonius recognized the value of this philosophical system and accepted it as his own (*VA* 1.7.2–3). Flinterman notes that Apollonius twice called Pythagoras called the "ancestor" of Apollonius's wisdom in the *VA* (4.16.1; 8.7.14). See Flinterman, "Pythagoras and Pythagoreanism," 155, n. 2. Even in his old age, Apollonius saw that he had chosen his path well, for he still deemed the teachings of Pythagoras the best of the philosophies (*VA* 6.11.3, 5). In answer to Apollonius's question to the oracle of Trophonius about which philosophy was the best and purest, he was given a book containing the teachings of Pythagoras (*VA* 8.19.19). Another telling feature of the *VA* that shows the importance of Pythagoras is that, rather than beginning with a family history, Philostratus began Apollonius's tale with a "philosophical pedigree" (Flinterman, *Power*, 155).

91. Pythagoras is said to have observed five years of silence (Diogenes Laertius, *Lives* 8.1.10; Iamblichus, *Vit. Pythag.* 17), as did Apollonius (*VA* 1.14.1–16.1). Apollonius only revealed certain rites to those who had observed silence for four years (*VA* 1.16.3).

92. *VA* 4.11.5; 6.11.5; Iamblicus *Vit. Pythag.* 3, 16, 21. For a detailed discussion of

PART 3: INVESTIGATING THE APOLLONIAN DECALOGUE

vegetarian diet,[93] eschewed blood sacrifice,[94] wore his hair long,[95] dressed in linen instead of animal hide or hair,[96] and endorsed the doctrine of the transmigration of the soul.[97] Apollonius is depicted as going the second mile as a member of the Pythagorean school.

Yet, the resemblance of Apollonius to Pythagoras goes much deeper than that of a dedicated practitioner of Pythagoreanism, for his life and deeds mirror those of Pythagoras himself in many respects.[98] The two sages possessed similar abilities: prognostication,[99] prediction or prevention of earthquakes,[100] warding off pestilence,[101] bilocation or rapid travel from place to place,[102] communication with animals,[103] a heightened awareness of events aided by ascetic practices,[104] capacious memories,[105] and awareness of their previous incarnations and those of others.[106] Their biographies even display a similar pattern: their births were predicted by the gods;[107] they frequented temples throughout

---

these comparisons, see Flinterman, "Pythagoras and Pythagoreanism," 159–60.

93. VA 1.32.1-2; 4.11.5; 6.11.5; 8.7.3-14; Diogenes Laertius, *Lives* 8.1.13, 38, 44; Poryphyry *Vit. Pythag.* 7; Iamblichus *Vit. Pythag.* 6, 16, 24, 31.

94. VA 1.31.2; Diogenes Laertius, *Lives* 8.1.13, 20, 22; Poryphyry, *Vit. Pythag.* 7, 36; Iamblichus *Vit. Pythag.* 11, 21, 24. Both figures used frankincense in worship to the gods (VA 1:31; Diogenes Laertius, *Lives* 8.1.20; Porphyry, *Vit. Pythag.* 11).

95. VA 1.32.2. At other times, Apollonius's hairstyle is said to have been modelled on the Spartans (VA 3.15.4; 8.7.17).

96. VA 1.32.2; 4.11.5; 6.11.5; 8.7.14, 16. Pythagoras wore white wool, for linen had not yet come into his part of the world (Diogenes Laertius, *Lives* 8.1.19). Iamblichus indicates that Pythagoras wore pure, white garments and his sheets were white, not made of wool. Pythagoras also encouraged his disciples to follow this example (Iamblichus *Vit. Pythag.* 21, 28).

97. VA 5.42.1; 8.7.14. Iamblichus, *Vit. Pythag.* 18, Porphyry, *Vit. Pythag.* 19, 26, 45.

98. Flinterman notes that Apollonius "is credited with a number of miraculous feats which are strongly reminiscent of elements of the Pythagoras legend" (Flinterman, "Pythagoras and Pythagoreanism," 172).

99. VA 4.34; 8.5.1; Iamblichus *Vit. Pythag.* 28; Porphyry *Vit. Pythag.* 25.

100. VA 4.41; Iamblichus, *Vit. Pythag.* 28; Porphyry *Vit. Pythag.* 29.

101. VA 4.10; Porphyry *Vit. Pythag.* 29.

102. VA 4.10.1 explicitly compares Apollonius's gift of bilocation with that of Pythagoras; see Iamblichus, *Vit. Pythag.* 28; Porphyry *Vit. Pythag.* 27, 29.

103. VA 1.20; 4.3; 5.42; Iamblichus *Vit. Pythag.*13; Porphyry *Vit. Pythag.* 23-24.

104. VA 8.5.1; Iamblichus *Vit. Pythag.* 15-16.

105. VA 1.14.1; Diogenes Laertius, *Lives* 8.1.4.

106. VA 3.24, 5.42, 8.7.20; Diogenes Laertius, *Lives* 8.1.4, 14-15, 36; Iamblichus *Vit. Pythag.* 14.

107. VA 1.4; Iamblicus *Vit. Pythag.* 2.

their lives;[108] both were initiated into various mysteries;[109] they took on disciples[110] (some of whom regarded them as divine);[111] they descended into the underworld;[112] both visited the Idaean cave on Crete;[113] they referenced the same Homeric passage while standing trial before their respective tyrants (*Il.* 22:13);[114] they both lived about eighty or ninety years.[115] Their biographers record several traditions about their deaths, some of which placed this final event within a temple.[116] Not deeming it enough for the disciple to be like his teacher, Philostratus's Apollonius surpassed Pythagoras in the extent of world travel,[117] the rigor of

---

108. *VA* 1.2–11; 2.22; 4.4, 31; 4.40.4; Diogenes Laertius, *Lives* 8.1.3, 7.7; Porphyry *Vit. Pythag.* 32; disciples, Iamblichus, *Vit. Pythag.* 21.

109. *VA* 4.18; 5.19.1; Diogenes Laertius, *Lives* 8.1.3; Iamblichus *Vit. Pythag.* 3.

110. *VA* 1.16.3–4, 18; 4.36–38; 5.43.3; 6.9, 27.2; 8.19.2, 24; Diogenes Laertius, *Lives* 8.1.3; 8.1.11, 41; Iamblichus *Vit. Pythag.* 6, 19, 27.

111. *VA* 7.38; Diogenes Laertius, *Lives* 8.1.41; Iamblichus *Vit. Pythag.* 6, 35.

112. *VA* 8.19.2; Diogenes Laertius, *Lives* 8.1.41; Porphyry, *Vit. Pythag.* 17.

113. *VA* 4.34.2–3; Diogenes Laertius, *Lives* 8.1.3.

114. Flinterman notes these examples in "Pythagoras and Pythagoreanism," 172–73.

115. Philostratus mentions the opinions that Apollonius lived to be eighty, over ninety, or over a hundred (*VA* 8.29). In like fashion, Diogenes Laertius records tradition that Pythagoras was eighty or ninety at the time of his death (*Lives* 8.1.44).

116. Philostratus recorded three traditions concerning Apollonius's end: the sage either died in Ephesus, vanished from the temple of Athena in Lindos, or vanished from the sanctuary of Dictynna in Crete (*VA* 8.30). Similarly, Diogenes Laertius also provides three versions of Pythagoras's death: either his pursuers captured him at the edge of a bean field and cut his throat, he died of self-starvation in the temple of the Muses at Metapontum, or he was slain in battle by the Syracusans (*Lives*, 8.1.39–40).

117. Although Pythagoras travelled abroad for study with the Arabians (Porphyry, *VP* 11), priests in Egypt, and the Magi of Babylon and Persia (Diogenes Laertius, *Lives* 8.1.3; Iamblicus. *Vit. Pythag.* 2–4; Porphyry, *Vit. Pythag.* 6, 11, 12), Apollonius travelled to these places and beyond them to the extremities of the known world, gleaning wisdom from the Brahmins of India in the east and debated the Gymnosophists in Ethiopia in the south (*VA* 1.2). Perhaps Philostratus's Apollonius was merely travelling in the footsteps of his master, who, according to a few later sources, may have visited India (Clem. Alex. *Strom.* 1.15; Apuleius, *Flor.* 15). However, at least as far as the *VA* indicates, Pythagoras had acquired Indian teaching from the Egyptians (*VA* 8.7.14). Later traditions also indicate that Pythagoras visited Iberia (Iamblicus, *Vit. Pythag.* 28); although Apollonius journeyed to Gadeira in the *VA*, where people are said to have been rather religious (*VA* 5.4), Philostratus does not indicate that he was retracing the journey of Pythagoras in this episode.

asceticism,[118] the number of miracles,[119] and "approached wisdom and overcame tyrannies in a more inspired way than Pythagoras."[120] These similarities do not seem to be motived by a desire to promote Pythagorean doctrine, as Kee proposed, but by the agenda of showing that the pupil had surpassed his master and earned an incomparable reputation as a philosopher.

The second theme to explore in this section is that of Apollonius as a world traveler. As a wayfarer and seafarer, Apollonius not only outdistanced Pythagoras, but also matched or surpassed other famous explorers by visiting the limits of three of the four corners of the known world: India in the east, Gades in the west, and Ethiopia in the south.[121] Apollonius left only Scythia, the northernmost region of the earth, unexplored, perhaps because of accusations of sexual misconduct there[122] Such broad-ranging travels allowed Philostratus to develop and elevate the status of his hero by associating and comparing him with gods and cultural heroes from the Greek past.

Apollonius's pilgrimage to India in the east is peppered with references to the travels of Dionysus, Hercules, and Alexander the Great, who were renowned for their exploration of this region in earlier centuries.[123] According to Greek literature, Dionysius was a great cultural hero whose invasion of India marked its transition from a nomadic to an urban society. Dionysus allegedly also traveled to Persia, Media, and Arabia, much like Apollonius.[124] Hercules, another ancient globetrotter, had surveyed

118. Although Pythagoras taught that sexual intercourse should be restricted to one's own wife (Diogenes Laertius, *Lives* 8.1.9), Apollonius went further than this by practicing celibacy (*VA* 1.13.3).

119. Apollonius predicted the sinking of a ship not once, as did Pythagoras, but twice (*VA* 5.18; 7.41). See Flinterman, "Pythagoras and Pythagoreanism," 173.

120. *VA* 1.2.

121. The consensus of ancient writers seems to be that India in the east, Gades in the west (and the nearby Pillars of Hercules), Scythia in the north, and Ethiopia in the south marked the limits of the earth (Strabo *Geogr*.1.2.28; Pliny in *Nat*. 2.67).

122. Anderson, *Philostratus*, 129. For references to this scandal, see *VA* 1.13.3; *VS* 570.

123. The mention of these three figures may be due to Philostratus's reliance on Arrian as a source for this section of the *VA* because the Nicomedian frequently referenced them. Furthermore, in Plutarch, Alexander is sometimes portrayed as the successor of Hercules. See Tiede, *The Charismatic Figure*, 95, 97. Although not mentioned in the *VA*, Pyrrho of Elis was a philosopher who, like Apollonius, had visited the Magi and Indian Gymnosophists (Diogenes Laertius, *Lives* 9.11.61; see Parker, *Roman India*, 264).

124. For Dionysus's travels in these regions, see Euripides, *Bacch*. 14–16; Arrian *Ind*.

the entire world to its boundaries (*VA* 5.4). Not to be outdone by that mighty son of Zeus, Apollonius retraced the demigod's footsteps. In doing so, he visited the cave where Hercules shot the bird that ate the entrails of Prometheus (*VA* 2.3) and the site where Hercules and Dionysus, during their invasion of India, had failed to capture the citadel of the Wise Men (*VA* 3.13; 2.9; 2.33.2).[125] Apollonius's eastern itinerary most closely followed the campaign of Alexander, who had also traveled as far as the Indus Valley, the border of the known world, before he and his troops turned back.[126] As a conqueror and explorer, Alexander sought to outdo Hercules and Dionysus.[127] In like manner, Apollonius proved himself superior to Alexander, who had failed to enter India or meet the Wise Ones,[128] and to Dionysus and Hercules, who had failed to capture the city of the Wise Men (*VA* 33.1–2); his welcome into the citadel of the Gymnosophists certified him as the greatest of these eastern expeditioners. Indeed, he was the greatest of all Hellenistic travelers, for no one from Greece had ever visited the Wise Men before him (*VA* 3.16.2).

In his travels to the limits of the West, Philostratus continued to associate Apollonius with the great explorers of an earlier age. Apollonius

---

7.4—8.1. Parker notes that Euripides was the first Greek author to connect Dionysus to India and that the theme of Dionysus's triumphal return from India was mentioned in the Augustine era but had become a favorite by Antonine and Severan times; Parker, *Roman India*, 81, 84, 125. This theme is mentioned in *Daphnis and Chloe* 4.3 (second century AD) and in the later Nonnus's *Dionysiaca*. See Parker, *Roman India*, 84.

125. Miles, *Philostratus*, 19.

126. Parker, *Roman India*, 2. As evidence of Alexander's presence in the region, the *VA* notes several of the stops along his Indian campaign (*VA* 2.9.2; 2.10), bronze panels commemorating his exploits (*VA* 2.2–3), statues of Alexander (*VA* 2.24), and an aged elephant that had supposedly fought against Alexander over 350 years before (*VA* 2.12.2).

127. Quintus Curtius (first century AD), frequently noted how Alexander imitated or excelled the exploits of Hercules and Father Liber (i.e., Dionysus) in *Hist. Alex.* 3.10.5, 12.18; 9.2.29, 4.21. See Arrian for similar passages (*Anab.* 4.28.1, 30.4; 5.1.5, 26.2, 5; 7.10.6; *Indica* 9.9–12).

128. Alexander had interviewed Indian naked sophists near Taxila (Arrian, *Ind.* 7.1–2), although he did not meet Philostratus's Wise Ones. Later authors like Philostratus and Plutarch shaped the conqueror into a sage. Parker argues that this portrayal as a sage set the stage for the tradition of Alexander as a pilgrim in the Alexander literature of the Middle Ages. See Parker, *Roman India*, 2, 316. The attempt to portray Alexander as a great philosopher can be found in even Plutarch where the Macedonian conqueror is praised for civilizing a savage world, credited with carrying out the project that Zeno only spoke about, and compared to Socrates, Plato, Zeno, and Pythagoras; Plutarch, (εἰκότως ἂν φιλοσοφώτατος νομίζοιτο, Plutarch, *Alex. fort.* 5; also see *Alex. fort.* 6, 9, 11–12). See Tiede, *The Charismatic Figure*, 95.

PART 3: INVESTIGATING THE APOLLONIAN DECALOGUE

visits Gadiera in Spain where Hercules had bound the elements of sea and land (cf. *VA* 2.33.2).[129] Pythagoras had also journeyed there,[130] although he is not explicitly mentioned in connection with Iberia in the *VA*. Van Dijk points out that, in Apollonius's journeys within the Mediterranean,[131] Philostratus sometimes touches on the itinerary of Odysseus.[132] Retracing Odysseus's travels, Apollonius visited the island of Aeolus twice (*VA* 3.14; 7.14),[133] drew near Charybdis as he passed through the Strait of Messina (*VA* 5.11), visited the island of Calypso (*VA* 7:10, 41; 8.11), and finally arrived at the cave of the Nymphs with its ever-flowing spring (*VA* 8.11–14; 1:14). Perhaps there is even an allusion to Scylla, when a three-head baby was born in Sicily—near Scylla's home—that foreshadowed the fateful Year of the Four Emperors (*VA* 5.13).[134] Apollonius also likened his brush with the tyrants Nero and Domitian to entrance into the Cyclops's cave (*VA* 4.36; 7.28) and referenced Leucothea's veil—which had protected Odysseus from drowning—just before his near-fatal encounter with Domitian (*VA* 7.22).[135] Thus, Apollonius's odyssey was as wide-ranging and fraught with peril as that of the famous son of Laertes.

129. Miles suggests that the golden olive and the girdle of Teucer found in the temple of Hercules at Gadeira were really the golden apple of the Hesperides and the girdle of Hippolyta, trophies from the journeys of Hercules, misinterpreted by the barbarian Damis. He writes, "These associations would reiterate the theme of the edges of the earth and the role of Heracles as a forerunner of Apollonius" (Miles, *Philostratus*, 46).

130. Iamblicus, *Vit. Pythag.* 28.

131. Philostratus may have even alluded to the journeys of Odysseus in relating Apollonius's eastern journeys. First, Apollonius conversed with the shade of Achilles as did Odysseus (*VA* 6.32). Yet, it is unclear whether Philostratus intended to compare Apollonius to Odysseus on this occasion, who visited the shade of Achilles at the city of the Cimmerians (*Od.* 11.465–504), or Alexander the Great, who visited the tomb of Achilles at Troy (Arrian, *Anab.* 1.12). Second, the Tyanean appealed to the story of the Lotus-eaters when he thought his companions had stayed too long in Babylon (*VA* 1.40).

132. Van Dijk believes that Philostratus modelled the travels of Apollonius after those of Odysseus and that the Tyanean either matched him or surpassed him in these key episodes; See van Dijk, "The Odyssey of Apollonius," 176–202.

133. This event does not transpire in the western Mediterranean.

134. According to Philostratus, some had interpreted the birth of this multi-headed child to mean that many-headed Typho intended something catastrophic for Sicily. Although Typho is the more likely referent here, he was the father of both multi-headed children Scylla and the Lernaean Hydra (Hyginus, *Fab. praef.* 151). Thus, this passage may still associate Apollonius's travels with Odysseus, if Scylla was hinted at, or Hercules, if the hydra was intended.

135. Apollonius also alludes to the Sirens in *VA* 6:11, but this is within the context of describing the ornamentation of the temple at Delphi and was not an episode in the

ITEM 7

Apollonius's visit to the south, including both Egypt and Ethiopia, may have also been in imitation of other great men who had journeyed there in search of wisdom. Several great philosophers (Thales,[136] Pythagoras,[137] and Plato,[138]) and lawgivers (Lycurgus[139] and Solon[140]) had visited Egypt before Apollonius's time. Perhaps Philostratus hinted at a connection between his hero and these figures, for Apollonius cites the examples of Plato, Lycurgus, and Solon with approval while visiting the Gymnosophists in the south (*VA* 6.11,8; 6.20.1, 3; 6.21). Like these earlier Greek pilgrims, Apollonius sought wisdom in the south (*VA* 6.7); unlike them, he ended up imparting wisdom to its inhabitants (*VA* 6.11–23).

The final theme to be explored in this section is that of Apollonius as the greatest philosopher. For Philostratus, the sign of a true philosopher was how he dealt with tyranny, and, in his opinion, the philosopher who handled this trial the best was Apollonius of Tyana:

> I am aware that the conduct of philosophers under despotism is the truest touchstone of their character, and am in favour of inquiring in what way one man displays more courage than another ... so I must first of all enumerate all the feats of wise men in the presence of tyrants, which I have found—worthy of commemoration, and contrast them with the conduct of Apollonius. For this I think is the best way of finding out the truth.[141]

As proof of this assertion, Philostratus evaluated the accomplishments of other renowned philosophers–Zeno of Elea (*VA* 7.2.1), Plato and Dion (7.2.1; 7.3.1), Phyton (7.2.2), Diogenes of Sinope (7.2.3), Crates of Thebes (7.2.3)—and found them wanting. Pythagoras, Apollonius's

---

life Apollonius.

136. Plutarch, *Is. Os.* 10. Thales is referenced elsewhere in the *VA* as one who predicted events and yet was not a sorcerer (e.g., *VA* 8.7.28).

137. Plutarch, *Is. Os.* 10; *VA* 8.7.14.

138. Plutarch, *Is. Os.* 1; *VA* 1.2.

139. Parker, *Roman India*, 263; Herodotus, *Hist.* 1.30; Plutarch, *Sol.* 26. Plutarch, *Is. Os.* 10.

140. Parker, *Roman India*, 263. Plato, *Tim.* 21E; Plutarch, *Lyc.* 4.5. Plutarch, *Is. Os.* 10.

141. *VA* 7.1. Apollonius regarded the willingness to face fear and death at the hands of a tyrant as a way of distinguishing his true disciples from those who were philosophers in name only (*VA* 4.37.1, 5). The twenty-six followers that forsook Apollonius in Rome had fled both from Nero and from philosophy (*VA* 4.37.2). Later, Apollonius reminded the philosophers Dio and Euphrates that true philosophers had toppled numerous tyrants in the past (*VA* 5.35.4).

master, could not compare to his student in resisting tyranny.[142] Even Socrates, who is referenced frequently with approval in the VA and during Apollonius's trial scene,[143] who was skilled in silence,[144] and who—like Apollonius—was advised by a "guardian spirit,"[145] did not compare to the Tyanean, for the accusations against Socrates were more modest.[146] In the end, Philostratus awarded the prize of opposition to tyranny to Apollonius: "Many more examples of this kind could be adduced, but my treatise does not allow me to prolong them. It is indeed incumbent upon me to criticise these examples, not in order to show that they were not as remarkable as they are universally famous, but only to show that they fall short of the exploits of Apollonius, in spite of their being the best of their kind." (VA 7.2.3)

If the best of humankind could not compare to Apollonius as opponents of tyranny, at least the gods Hercules and Dionysus proved worthy rivals.[147] Hercules provided philosophers with a model for confronting rulers through his decisive triumphs over tyranny: he successfully endured the twelve labors imposed on him by King Eurystheus[148]

---

142. Unlike Apollonius, Pythagoras sometimes simply moved away from regional tyrants (Porphyry, *Vit. Pythag.* 9; Iamblichus, *Vit. Pythag.* 2). Pythagoras, however, did persuade the tyrant Simicus to abdicate his rule (Porphyry, *Vit. Pythag.* 21) and stood trial before Cylon (Porphyry, *Vit. Pythag.* 54). Even in the opening of the VA, Philostratus wrote, "For quite akin to theirs was the ideal which Apollonius pursued, and more divinely than Pythagoras he wooed wisdom and soared above tyrants" (*VA* 1.2 [Conybeare, LCL]).

143. *VA* 1.2.1; 4.4; 4.5; 6.19.5; 7.11.2; 8.7.26.

144. *VA* 8.2. Within this passage, Philostratus may suggest another similarity to Socrates: Apollonius claims that Socrates did not die, as the Athenians assumed (*VA* 8.2). Furthermore, before disappearing from Domitian's courtroom, Apollonius told the emperor that he could not be killed because he was not mortal (*VA* 8.5.3). The later statement is from *Il.* 22.13 rather than an ancient source about Socrates, but still constitutes a similarity.

145. For the reference to "guardian spirit" of Socrates, see *VA* 1.2.1; 8.7.26. For the guardian of Apollonius, consult *VA* 1.18; 8.7.31.

146. *VA* 8.7.1.

147. The numerous parallels between the travels of Apollonius and these two gods were catalogued earlier in this chapter. A significant connection between Apollonius and Hercules in the VA is that his choice of the virtuous life and his philosophical sect, Pythagoreanism, is likened to the story "The Choice of Hercules," where the hero wisely chose virtue over vice (*VA* 6.10.5–11.2). Xenophon related the myth of "The Choice of Hercules" in *Mem.* 2.1.21–34. Tiede gives several other examples of the use of this motif in his book (E.g., Lucian, *Gall.* 7; Dio Chrysostom, *1 Regn.* 1.66). See Tiede, *The Charismatic Figure*, 72.

148. McNiven writes, "Eurystheus' capricious abuse of power makes him akin to a

and slew Lycus, the tyrant and usurper of Thebes.[149] The strong man's twelve labors were a favorite theme of several philosophical schools.[150] It comes as no surprise, then, that aspects of Apollonius's mission recall the labors of Hercules.[151] During Apollonius's first encounter with tyranny, he described the tyrant Nero as Cerberus, the multi-headed and jagged-toothed guardian of Hades, who was defeated by Hercules during his last labor.[152] Soon after this episode, Apollonius offered to rescue the philosopher Musonius from Nero's prison, much like Hercules had once delivered Theseus from the underworld when he subdued Cerberus.[153] As Apollonius's second major contest with tyranny drew nigh, the trial before Domitian, the timid philosopher Demetrius called Damis "the Iolaos of Apollonius's labors," after the name of Hercules's faithful assistant.[154]

---

tyrant, though technically a legitimate ruler, and he is explicitly described as such in Euripides' Herakleidai . . ." (McNiven, "Behaving Like an Other," 91). For Eurystheus described as a "the violent lord of Argos's city" (Argivae impotens dominator urbis), see Seneca, Herc. fur. 1180-81.

149. Euripides provides the most famous rendition of Hercules's encounter with Lycus (Euripides, Herc. fur.). Seneca, in his own version of the tragedy, used the Hercules myth to explore the evils of tyranny during the Imperial era. See Shelton, Seneca's Hercules Furens, 32-33, 33 n. 28.

150. Tiede writes that for various philosophical schools, Hercules "and his labors had been transformed into paradigmatic moral actions" (Tiede, The Charismatic Figure, 67). Tiede also cites several examples of this theme in the writings of Plato, the Stoics, the Cynics, the Epicureans, and Lucian. For these examples, see his The Charismatic Figure, 44, 51, 67, 71-100.

151. Apollonius visited an altar at Gaideira that depicted all twelve labors of Hercules. The visit to this site recalled the labor of capturing Geryon's cattle (VA 5.5.1). Thespasion, the Ethiopian elder, argued that Apollonius could wander the earth with a will like Hercules and claim the capture of lions, Hydra, Geryon, Nessus, and the other labors, but that he had still chosen poorly if he rejected the wisdom of Ethiopia (VA 6.10.5-6). As a partial answer to Domitian's inquiry concerning averting the plague at Ephesus, Apollonius claimed that he prayed to Hercules to cleanse the city just as the god had once cleansed the Augean stables (VA 8.7.28-29).

152. VA 4.38.3. Anderson believes that Nero was being compared to a manticore, a creature that had already been introduced in VA 3.45 (Anderson, Philostratus, 130). However, the beast that is compared to Nero had an unknown number of heads, while the manticore in the VA had only one head. The is image is more likely of Cerberus who had multiple heads and "jagged teeth" (χαραχαρόδουν; VA 4.38.3) a description that resembles the description of Cerberus as "jagged-toothed" (καρχαρόδοντα) in Bacchylides, Odes, 60.

153. VA 4.46.2-3. Apollonius raised a girl from the dead in a deed resembling Hercules's act of returning Alcestis from the underworld (VA 4.45). On the Heracles and Theseus theme in VA 4.46, see Miles, Philostratus, 19.

154. VA 7.10.

PART 3: INVESTIGATING THE APOLLONIAN DECALOGUE

Apollonius's herculean labors against Nero and Domitian help build the case for him being the most courageous opponent of tyranny.

Likewise, Dionysus served as a model for Apollonius's battle against tyranny. The god Dionysus, missing in the VA since the early Indian adventures of Apollonius, returned just in time to form part of the backdrop for the Tyanean's trial before Domitian (VA 7.32–34).[155] Apollonius's trial has several obvious connections to Dionysus's showdown with the tyrant, Pentheus. Both Apollonius and Dionysus were (1) accused of being wizards (γόης),[156] (2) accused of being gods,[157] (3) in possession of the gifts of prophecy and foresight,[158] (4) shaved by their captors,[159] (5) secured by chains,[160] (6) interrogated by a king,[161] and (7) seen again by their followers after harrowing encounters with a tyrant.[162] In the persons of Hercules and Dionysus, Philostratus had finally found adversaries of despots worthy of comparison to the Tyanean.

These three examples demonstrate that Philostratus has developed the historical figure of Apollonius by building on the pattern of earlier gods and men unless one wants to argue that the historical Apollonius is accurately preserved in the VA. After all, it would be exceedingly improbable that the best-traveled man in the ancient world, who fearlessly faced down Nero and Domitian, and surpassed the accomplishments of the great Pythagoras, was not mentioned by any of his contemporaries or by later writers until the time of Lucian. All things considered, Philostratus's imagination has been at work here to inflate the importance and competence of his main character.

---

155. Flinterman correctly argues that Apollonius's trial before Domitian was based in part on the showdown between Pentheus and Dionysus. He notes that Philostratus casts Domitian in the role of king Pentheus and Apollonius as the god Dionysus, who is thrown into prison for being a magician and shorn; see Flinterman, "Ascension," 231–32.

156. Euripides, *Bacch.* 234; VA 7.17.1; 7.33.2; 7.34; 8.3
157. Euripides, *Bacch.* 242; VA 7.21.1.
158. Euripides, *Bacch.* 298–300; VA 7.20.1.
159. Euripides, *Bacch.* 240–241, 493; VA 7.35, 36.2.
160. Euripides, *Bacch.* 355; VA 7.36, 38.
161. Euripides, *Bacch.* 460–518; VA 7.32–35; 8.4–5.
162. Euripides, *Bacch.* 608–41; VA 8.12.

CONCLUSION

This chapter has argued that the primary agenda of Philostratus was the rehabilitation of the reputation of Apollonius of Tyana. This agenda does not preclude lesser goals but regards them as subordinate to this apologetic agenda. In defending Apollonius against his accusers, Philostratus transformed his hero from a magician into a holy man. In describing his travels and his trials, he has shown him to be superior to most men—even Pythagoras and Alexander the Great—and to be the rival of the gods.

Did this apologetic agenda radically impact how Apollonius was portrayed in the *VA*? Philostratus's defense and enhancement of his hero raises questions about the historicity of portions of the account. He also appears to have created Apollonius's role as a religious reformer, which does not match with the *Letters of Apollonius*, and his role as a political advisor, since the historical sources are silent on this issue, apart from the *Letters of Apollonius*. To Philostratus's credit, he appears to have been faithful to the tradition that Apollonius was a philosopher. Yet, he seems to have gone too far in transforming Apollonius from a relatively insignificant figure into a character who rivaled the best of humans and gods. To his credit, he did not attempt to eliminate the tradition of Apollonius's mighty deeds from the account, but he attempted, with some difficulty, to shift the source of his supernatural powers and feats from the sphere of magic into that of philosophy. This alteration in the depiction of Apollonius was not likely historical and can probably be attributed both to Julia's desire to see him depicted as a holy man and to Philostratus's contempt for magic. This alteration is perhaps the most significant of all. Before the *VA*, tradition held that Apollonius was a magician; after the *VA*, most writers would regard him as a sage. In the end, Philostratus pulled off the rehabilitation of Apollonius's reputation by transforming him from a magician into a philosopher or a god.

Philostratus's idealized portrayal of Apollonius is difficult to accept as historical. One reason for this is that Philostratus overplayed his hand in developing his protagonist. In the terminology of modern fiction, Philostratus's Apollonius is a "Mary Sue" (or rather a "Marty Stu") character: Apollonius possessed no major flaws, was never caught off guard in debate, knew the appropriate solution to all difficult situations, and never panicked in a crisis. Apollonius's only faults are that he is unable to shake off entirely the charges that he was a magician and the suspicion that he was involved in a sexual scandal in Scythia. Another reason for suspecting that this portrayal is not historical is that, as this chapter argues, Apollonius appears to be a composite character. Just as Philostratus seems to have mined the stories of the sophists (e.g., Scopelian) for raw material to flesh out the image of Apollonius, he also appears to have borrowed material from other figures (e.g., Pythagoras, Odysseus, Hercules, and Dionysus) to construct the story of Apollonius. If the attributes and deeds of such figures have been transferred to Apollonius, did the historical sage really do and say all that Philostratus claims? Or did Philostratus merely weave a semi-fictional hero into the history of the first century AD, much like an ancient version of Forrest Gump, to give the appearance that Apollonius participated in the major events of the time and met all the luminaries of his age?[163] Did Apollonius truly walk in the footsteps of gods and heroes? Unfortunately, the literature of Apollonius's contemporaries is silent concerning these details.

---

163. I would like to credit Marshall McDaniel, one of my PhD students, for drawing attention to the similarities between Apollonius and the fictional character Forrest Gump, whose life—according to the novel—intersected with several major figures (e.g., Bear Bryant, Bob Dylan, President Lyndon B. Johnson, and President Richard Nixon) and historical events (e.g., the Vietnam War) in the twentieth century.

13

Items 8–9

Potential Anti-Christian Agendas and Borrowing of Christian Texts or Ideas

THIS CHAPTER WILL EXPLORE the relationship that the *VA* may have had with Christianity. Items 8 and 9 in the Apollonian Decalogue deal with two aspects of this issue: "Scholars disagree over whether the *VA* was intended as a counterblast to the Gospels or Christianity" and "experts disagree over whether the Philostratus was consciously or unconsciously influenced by the Gospels or later Christian sources." The topics addressed in this chapter are related to the previous chapter in that they address the agendas of the *VA*, yet they differ from it in that their focus is on whether it was intended as anti-Christian propaganda or borrowed ideas from the Gospels.

DOES THE *VA* HAVE AN ANTI-CHRISTIAN AGENDA?

Several theories have been proposed to account for the numerous commonalities between the stories of Apollonius recorded in the *VA* and Jesus preserved in the canonical Gospels. One common view is that Philostratus or Empress Julia intended the *VA* as a counterblast to Christianity.[1] Some researchers, who do not fully endorse this view, are open

---

1. At least as early as Cudworth (1617–1688), Philostratus was charged with molding Apollonius into the likeness of Jesus so that he would attract followers. See

to the possibility of such influences.² Another view is that these similarities to the story of Jesus are due to the influence of Christian literature on the *VA*, but that these borrowings were not intended as an attack on Christianity.³ A third view, which appears to be the majority position, is that Philostratus did not intend the *VA* as an attack at all and that the similarities between Apollonius and Jesus can be accounted for in other ways.⁴ Although it is important to be aware of these various theories in case new data emerges, most of them are theoretical except for the final view, which possesses the most historical support at the moment.

The current study supports the view that the *VA* was not intended as a direct attack upon Christianity. Several lines of evidence converge in favor of this interpretation: (1) The *VA* never mentions Christianity or Christ;⁵ if the *VA* were intended as an attack upon the Christians, it

---

Cudworth, *True Intellectual System*, 437. Newman also held this view in his *Life of Apollonius Tyanaeus*, 341. Ferguson claims that Julia Domna had the agenda: "It was she who encouraged Philostratus to put together a life of Apollonius of Tyana as a counterblast to Jesus" and that this was "no doubt to counterweigh the increasingly insistent propaganda of the Christians" (Ferguson, *Religions*, 51, 181–82). See also David K. Clark, "Miracles," 211; Habermas, "Did Jesus Perform Miracles?," 124. Hoffmann writes, "The biography of Apollonius was composed deliberately to emphasize its similarities with the gospels" (Hoffmann, *Porphyry's Against the Christians*, 39, n. 14). A good portion of Réville's book is dedicated to this theory that the *VA* imitates the Gospels. See Réville, *Apollonius*, 63–79. Bidez believed that Empress Julia realized "the need of finding a historical figure fitted to counter the propaganda of subversive gospels, she sought particularly to revive the memory of a hero of pagan hagiography, Apollonius of Tyana, who lived under the first two Flavians" (Bidez, "Literature and Philosophy," 613).

2. Kee, "There are some details which might indicate that the author commissioned by a vigorous opponent of Christianity to do this work was writing consciously a pagan gospel, as Eusebius of Caesarea maintains" (Kee, *Miracle*, 264). Also see Swain, "Culture and nature," 38, 45.

3. Meier was open to the notion that the *VA* borrowed from the Gospels. He noted that such mining of the story of Jesus cannot be proven but would explain some of these correspondences. Meier noted that, if the *VA* did recycle Gospel stories, they would not have been intended as a counterblast to Christianity, but rather would have been used to flesh out the portrait of Apollonius. See Meier, *Marginal Jew*, 2:580.

4. Lardner, *Works*, 4:261–64; Votaw, while allowing for the possible influence of Christian ideas, argues that "Neither Philostratus nor the empress seems to have had a specific intent or interest against the Christians and the Gospels" (Votaw, *The Gospels and Contemporary Biographies*, 29). Parker rejected this idea as well in his *Demonstration*, 296–97; Bowersock also dismissed this agenda: "For Philostratus, Apollonius was not an anti-Christ, but in his biography he provided the stories which made him one" (Bowersock, Introduction to *Life of Apollonius*, 9).

5. Lardner wrote, "Philostratus has never once mentioned our Saviour, or the Christians his followers, neither in this long work, nor in the Lives of the Sophists, if it

certainly does not give a clear indication that this group was its target;[6] (2) The *VA* never directly quotes the Gospels or other portions of the Bible;[7] (3) resemblances between aspects of Apollonius's biography and miracles and those of Jesus related in the Gospels may be coincidental, for Apollonius's exploits and miracles also resemble supernatural deeds recorded in tales of the Greek gods, biographies of Greek philosophers (e.g., Pythagoras), Jewish writings, and Christian literature from after the time of the composition of the New Testament; (4) no early Christian authors expressed the opinion that the *VA* was written against Christians;[8] and (5) Koskenniemi argues that Philostratus speaks very little about religion in general in the *VA*; Philostratus does not appear to promote any particular trend, even the oft proposed Helios cult.[9] He also noted that Philostratus's "religious superficiality" (die religiöse Oberflächligkeit) is

---

be his, as several learned men of the best judgment suppose" (Lardner, *Works*, 4:263). Also see Koskenniemi for a more recent statement of this point in *Der philostrateische Apollonios*, 75, 77.

6. Lardner cites with approval a statement of Michael de la Roche, "that Philostratus said nothing more in the Life of Apollonius, than he would have said if there had been no Christians in the world." He himself opines, "At first it appeared strange to me; but upon further consideration, and upon reading Philostratus again, I have embraced the same opinion, and am not confirmed in it. Hierocles made used of the work of Philostratus in forming his comparison of Christ and Apollonius; and many heathen people afterwards were willing enough to set up Apollonius against our Saviour: but it does not appear that Philostratus had any such thing in view . . . nor is there any hint, that Apollonius any where in his wide travels met with any followers of Jesus. There is not so much as an obscure or general description of any men met with him, whom any can suspect to be Christians of any denomination, either catholics or heretics" (Lardner, *Works*, 4:261–63). Koskenniemi also writes that "Es fehlt in der *VA* jede kritische Stimme gegen das Christentum wie überhaupt in der Production des Philostratos" (Koskenniemi, *Die philostrateische Apollonios*, 79).

7. Lardner stated that, "Upon the whole, I do not see any reason to believe, that Philostratus had read any of our gospels, or any other of the books of the New Testament, or that he any where makes any reference to the history of our Lord and Saviour Jesus Christ" (Lardner, *Works*, 4:264). Some argue that the *VA* borrowed a few words from the Gospels. See Parker, *Demonstration*, 296–97; Schaff, *Ante-Nicene Christianity*, 2:99–100, n. 1.

8. Kee incorrectly asserts that Eusebius regarded the *VA* as a "pagan gospel" (Kee, *Miracle*, 264). Rather, Eusebius claimed that Hierocles was the first writer to produce a formal comparison of Apollonius to Christ (*Hier.* 1.2). As Votaw remarks, "Eusebius did not take the view that the Life of Apollonius had been produced by Philostratus as a pagan counterwork to the Gospels," a statement which he follows with a quote from Eusebius himself: "Hierocles, of all the writers who ever attacked us, stands alone in selecting Apollonius . . ." (Votaw, *The Gospels*, 28–29). Phillimore's opinion closely resembles that of Votaw; see Phillimore, *In Honour*, lxxvi.

9. Koskenniemi, *Der philostrateische Apollonios*, 75.

PART 3: INVESTIGATING THE APOLLONIAN DECALOGUE

evident throughout the work.[10] These pieces of evidence strongly suggest that Philostratus had no interest in writing about or against Christianity at all.

Another obstacle to seeing the *VA* as anti-Christian propaganda is that there is no evidence to suggest that the Severan rulers (AD 193–235) displayed hostility toward Christianity or mounted a religiopolitical campaign to compete with them. Although historians are agreed that Christian persecutions occurred during the reign of Septimius Severus,[11] many no longer think that Severus played an active role in them as a persecutor. While it is true that some ancient sources describe Severus as an aggressor,[12] many modern scholars now question the claim that he pursued Christians at all and suggest that these persecutions were carried out by local rulers without imperial sponsorship.[13] Even early Christian authors were divided in their view of Severus: Eusebius regarded him as a persecutor,[14] while Tertullian did not.[15] At any rate, anti-Christian attacks under this regime had died down by AD 212[16] long before Phi-

10. Koskenniemi, *Der philostrateische Apollonios*, 81.

11. Frend writes, "Between 195 and 212, there were sporadic persecutions of varying degrees of violence in many parts of the empire" (Frend, *Rise of Christianity*, 293). He lists the execution Leonides, Origen's father, in Alexandria under the prefect of Egypt Q. Maecius Laetus (c. AD 201–3), the martyrdoms of Perpetua and Felicitas in Carthage (AD 203), persecutions under the prefect Ti. Claudius Subatianus Aquila (AD 206–10), and Hippolytus's report of mob violence against Christians in Rome. See Frend, *Rise of Christianity*, 293–94. Other persecutions took place in Antioch and Corinth. For further discussion of these persecutions, see Grant, *Augustus to Constantine*, 100.

12. Some of this evidence is based on the historically questionable *Historia Augusta* (71.17), which relates that Septimius Severus issued a decree around AD 202 threatening a death penalty for those who converted to Judaism and Christianity. Although some have doubted the existence of the decree (Grant, *Augustus to Constantine*, 100), most tend to believe the report is legitimate (Frend, *Rise of Christianity*, 294).

13. Grant, *Augustus to Constantine*, 99–100. For a discussion of several scholars who reject the view that Septimius Severus was a persecutor (e.g., Molthagen, Sordi, and Durst), see Koskenniemi, *Die philostrateische Apollonios*, 76–77.

14. Eusebius speaks explicitly of Severus "stirring up persecution against the churches," and cites the persecutions at Alexandria around AD 202 as an example (Eusebius, *Hist. eccl.* 6.1.1).

15. Around AD 212, Tertullian gave several indications that that the Severans were not anti-Christian. He recorded that a Christian healer and miracle worker named Proculus was kept within the Severan court, that prince Caracalla had a Christian wet nurse, and that Severus had rescued numerous Christians of the highest rank from a rowdy mob (Tertullian *Ad Scapulam*, 4).

16. Frend, *Rise of Christianity*, 294.

lostratus penned the *VA*. Furthermore, there is no reason to think that Julia Domna had a personal desire to fight against Christianity, although, as Koskenniemi points out, this myth is slowly dying.[17] Thus, evidence is rather thin for the argument that the *VA* was produced as an imperially sponsored counter-Gospel at the direction of Severus and Julia Domna.

The odds of an anti-Christian agenda by the monarchy decrease even more if the composition date of the *VA* is pushed later in the third century, for Severan attitudes toward Christians softened with time and these rulers would have been less likely to launch such a literary attack on that faith. For instance, Julia Avita Mamaea, (AD 180–235), mother of Alexander Severus and niece of Julia Domna, expressed some interest in Christianity, interacted with renowned Christian teachers (e.g., Origen[18] and Hippolytus[19]), and was described by Eusebius as "a most pious woman."[20] Her son, the emperor Alexander Severus (AD 222–35), was also sympathetic to Christianity: he supposedly had images of several holy men within his chapel (among whom were Apollonius and Jesus[21]), was lenient toward the Christians,[22] and "charged the Christian intellectual Julius Africanus (a celebrated correspondent of Origen) with the establishment of a library in the Pantheon (of all places)."[23] Even the non-Severan ruler Philip the Arab (AD 244–49), in whose time Philostratus died, was pro-Christian. The sole exception to this open attitude toward Christianity would have been during the reign of the Severan ruler Elagabalus (AD 218–22), who may have decreed that only one God could be worshipped in Rome and that Jews, Samaritans, and Christians transfer

---

17. Koskenniemi, *Die philostrateische Apollonios*, 77. Also see Votaw, *The Gospels*, 29.

18. Mamaea sent a military escort to accompany the Christian scholar Origen to Antioch, where he stayed for some time while teaching her (Eusebius, *Hist. eccl.* 6.21). Several modern scholars place Origen's encounter with Julia Mamaea in Alexandria rather than at Antioch (Gonzalez, *The Early Church*, 84; Lightman and Lightman, *A to Z*, 167. It also appears that Oden has confused the many Julias of the Severan dynasty, for he incorrectly indicates that Julia Domna rather than Julia Mamaea had visited with Origen. See Oden, *Early Libyan Christianity*, 115.

19. Perhaps about the same time as her meeting with Origen, Hippolytus appears to have preached a sermon to Julia Mamaea on the topic of the resurrection of the flesh. See Cerrato, "Hippolytus," *DMBI*, 526; Chadwick, *The Early Church*, 110, n. 1; Allen Brent, *Hippolytus*, 84.

20. *Hist. eccl.* 6.21.3–4; Swain, "Culture and nature," 37.

21. *Hist. Aug.*, Alex. Sev. 29.1.

22. *Hist. Aug.*, Alex. Sev. 22.4; Swain, "Culture and nature," 37.

23. Swain, "Culture and nature," 37.

their rites to his temple so that it "might include the mysteries of every form of worship."[24] But, if the *VA* had been intended as a propaganda tool of his regime, one would have expected to have seen an aggressive promotion of the Sun cult to the exclusion of all other forms of worship in the *VA*. Yet, there is no evidence for this view. For these reasons, it is unlikely that the *VA* was intended as an imperial weapon wielded against the Christians.

However, these points are not proof that Philostratus knew nothing about Christianity or that he did not regard it as a genuine threat.[25] As several researchers have argued, he may have promoted Hellenic religious revival as a way of addressing Christianity's challenge to the Hellenic worldview.[26] While this is certainly a possibility, the *VA* never directly addressed the Christian problem so the validity of this suggestion cannot be confirmed. Just why Christianity is not mentioned in *VA* is difficult to explain, especially since Philostratus would have known something of Christians from their presence in the royal court and because of the persecutions of previous years. Various explanations have been proposed for why Christianity is absent from the *VA*: jealousy of its growing influence on society,[27] contempt for or suspicion of it,[28] or a lack of interest in Christianity or religion in general.[29] Perhaps it is not mentioned because the *VA* was a passive-aggressive attack on that foreign faith.[30] Although

---

24. *Hist. Aug., Ant. Hel.* 3.5

25. Swain argues that one should not mistake Philostratus's silence about Christianity for his ignorance of that religion. He further notes that Greek culture was stable at the time of Philostratus, but that Christianity was gradually growing in influence and exposing the weaknesses of pagan culture. Thus, Philostratus's heavy emphasis on the value of Greek culture was intentional; Swain, "Culture and nature," 46.

26. Elsner believes that the *VA* did have an agenda of religious revival in the Severan court but does not claim that this program was anti-Christian. See Elsner, "Hagiographic Geography," 35. Swain believes that the work was intended to counter the threat of rising Christian popularity. See Swain, "Culture and nature," 38, 45.

27. Réville observed that the *VA* "contains no evidences of indifference or hostility to Christianity, but rather of jealousy." See his *Apollonius*, 68.

28. Phillimore, *In Honour*, lxxvii–lxxix.

29. Koskenniemi notes that Philostratus was religiously passive and was proud of his own Greek culture so much so that a Semitic novelty like Christianity did not interest him. See Koskenniemi, *Der philostrateische Apollonios*, 77.

30. Rather than meeting his cultural rival head on, Philostratus may have preferred to deal with the Christian threat to Hellenic culture simply by displaying the riches of his traditions and trusting in the superiority of Greek culture to win the day. Perhaps this strategy involved pitting the sophists (the *VS*) against saints and Apollonius (the *VA*) against Jesus. Such tactics would have also exposed certain weaknesses in

these theories are interesting and well may represent Philostratus's viewpoint, they are also still speculative at this point in Philostratean studies.

DOES THE *VA* BORROW CHRISTIAN TEXTS OR IDEAS?

Because Philostratus was aware of Christianity, he may have consciously or unconsciously absorbed material from some of its teachings and literature, including the story of Jesus found in the Gospels.[31] However, one should not too hastily equate the possibility of Christian influences on the *VA* with the probability of such an influence.

The similarities between the *VA* and the Gospels are most likely explained either through coincidence or borrowing. Yet, if appropriation took place, such borrowing could only have taken place in only one direction because the Gospels pre-date the *VA*.[32] In such a case, the story of Apollonius would have drawn on that of Jesus, not the other way around. Indeed, several scholars have expressed the possibility that the *VA* did borrow ideas from the Gospels.[33] Others more hesitantly allow for some Gospel influence on the *VA*.[34] Then, some believe that there was no bor-

---

Christianity: the Nazarenes had no athletics (*Gymnasticus*) and their art (*Imagines I*) was limited to religious themes or was derivative of Greco-Roman models. If Swain is correct in dating to the work to the time of Alexander Severus (Swain, "Culture and nature," 37), Philostratus may have looked back upon the reign of Elagabalus (AD 218–22) as another threat posed to Hellenism by an eastern religion.

31. Phillimore wisely counsels, "We must steer between two absurdities. It is absurd in the face of the evidence to deny that he had knowledge of Christian documents . . . But on the other hand it would be a great mistake to impute any positive or particular anti-Christian bias to Philostratus" (Phillimore, *In Honour*, lxxix–lxxx).

32. Some might object that the Damis diaries were available in the first century and might have been borrowed upon. However, the existence of this document is debated and, if it existed, it appears to have been a forgery. One might also wonder how this document would have become available to the Gospel writers in the first place.

33. Ehrman, *How Jesus Became God*, 373, n. 3. Votaw, holding a similar view, writes that Philostratus may have been familiar with the Gospels and interested in the similarities between Jesus and Apollonius. He also holds that some of the supernatural aspects of Jesus's story may have influenced Philostratus's presentation of Apollonius. See Votaw, *The Gospels*, 29.

34. Copleston writes, "There are indications that Philostratus knew and utilized the Gospels, Acts of the Apostles, and Lives of the Saints, but it remains uncertain how far it was his conscious intention to substitute the ideal of the 'Hellenistic Christ' for the Christian Christ: resemblances have been greatly exaggerated" (Copleston, *Greece and Rome*, 449). Bell stated, "the written account of his life is later than the Gospels and Acts, so we cannot be sure how much the picture of Apollonius is influenced by stories

rowing at all.³⁵ The following section will attempt to determine which of these views is most likely to be correct by examining a few of the most likely parallels between the *VA* and the New Testament.

LOCATING THE MOST LIKELY BORROWINGS FROM THE GOSPELS

Where should the search begin for potential examples of borrowing between the *VA* and the Gospels? Because the *VA* never directly quotes the Gospels³⁶ and does not mention Jesus or Christianity, researchers often default to building a case for reliance on the similarity of themes that in literature about the Tyanean and the Nazarene. Unfortunately, this methodology is imprecise because the criteria for detecting similarities can be subjective. For instance, can a methodology based merely on seeking parallels determine whether the miracles of Apollonius were based on the deeds of Jesus in the Gospels or based on the similar miracles of

---

about Jesus and Paul, which were relatively well known by A.D. 200" (*Exploring*, 176). Koskenniemi found no proof of direct or indirect evidence for the *VA*'s dependence on the Gospels but remains open to an indirect literary dependency that would explain these striking similarities. See Koskenniemi, *Apollonios*, 201–3, 230–31.

35. Bowie, writes, "[a] Christian reader can of course see many similarities with the Gospels, but these are not so close as to require the supposition that Philostratus knew of and drew upon them" (Bowie, "Philostratus: Writer of Fiction," 193). Likewise, Petzke, in summing up the similarities between the Gospels and the *VA* writes, "Damit kann und soll keine literarische Abhängigkeit der VA von den Evangelien behauptet warden" (Petzke, *Die Traditionen*, 62). Even several older scholars rejected the idea that the *VA* drew the Gospels. See Parker, *Demonstration*, 296–300.

36. Parker reported that Philostratus may have taken one word from Luke, although he admits that this could also have been due to coincidence. See Parker, *Demonstration*, 296–97. Schaff does, however, regard Philostratus's use of this word as an allusion to the Gospel of Luke. See Schaff, *Ante-Nicene Christianity*, 2:99–100, n. 1. The alleged quote referred to by Parker and Schaff appears in *VA* 4.25, where an *empusa* wept and begged Apollonius not to force her (μὴ βασανίζειν) to reveal her true nature. Similarly, in Luke 8:28, the Geresene demonic made the request of Jesus, "do not torment me" (μή με βασανίσῃς). Yet, the wording, the type of entity (vampire vs. demon), and the situations (a disclosure vs. an exorcism) differ. One might also be tempted to suggest borrowing in the instance in which both Apollonius and Jesus tell their listeners to "take courage" (θαρσεῖτε) when the sea seemed threatening. However, the context of Apollonius's statement was during an earthquake that was just prior to the emergence of a new Island (*VA* 4.34), whereas Jesus's statement was on a contrary sea when the disciples saw him walking on the water (Matt 14:34, 26). Furthermore, both Jesus (Matt 9:2, 22; John 16:33) and Apollonius (θάρρει *VA* 7:23.4; 7.38.2) often used such encouragements in different contexts, thereby illustrating the difficulty of making a solid case that Philostratus mined the Gospels for quotations like these.

Pythagoras? Can it sort out whether the reference to finding a treasure in a field (*VA* 2.39) was borrowed from Jesus's parable (Matt 13:44),[37] mirrored a skill in the repertoire of various Pythagorean philosophers,[38] or was merely due to coincidence?[39] Several examples from the *VS*, another work of Philostratus—statements about laying up treasures[40] or a physician healing himself[41]—almost certainly do not borrow from the Gospels.[42] Examples like these in the *VS* should caution researchers against too hastily assuming that a *VA*-Gospel parallel has been located. Such cases point to the need for more methodological precision in this quest.

In this investigation, two criteria will be utilized to determine whether a theme in the *VA* was based on a Gospel text. The first is the criterion of dissimilarity, which will seek out details about Apollonius recorded in the *VA* that cannot be derived from (or at least do not fit neatly within) the realm of Hellenism but details that do smack of Christianity or Judaism. Since Philostratus was a thoroughgoing pro-Greek sophist, a good way to sniff out borrowings from the story of Jesus would be to identify themes in the *VA* that are foreign to the sophist's worldview yet at the same time are present in the Gospels. This approach is helpful, for it culls out oft-suggested parallels of Jesus to Apollonius that were common fare in Greco-Roman texts,[43] such as healings,[44] the ability to control the wind

---

37. This episode in *VA* 2.39 resembles the Parable of the Hidden Treasure (Matt 13:44; Gos. Thom. 109) in a few ways (e.g., a treasure was found in a field; a buyer acquired the field and the treasure). However, they differ in several other details: (1) in Matthew, the protagonist finds the treasure first and then purchases the field, whereas in the *VA* (and Gos. Thom. 109) the treasure was discovered only after the land was purchased; (2) the treasure's exact location is not disclosed by Matthew but in the *VA* it is described as being in a fissure that opened in the earth (in Gos. Thom. 109, the treasure was discovered in the field by plowing); (3) the *VA* presents this as an actual event, whereas it is a parable in Matthew; and (4) the *VA* examines the rights that the previous and current owner of the land had, whereas Matthew does not.

38. Alexander of Abonoteichus, a follower of Apollonius and Pythagoras, supposedly had this skill (Lucian, *Alex.* 5).

39. Stories of treasure buried in fields appear in many ancient texts. For a list of Jewish texts about buried treasures, see Anderson, "Folklore," 219, n. 12.

40. *VS* 547; Matt 6:20.

41. *VS* 500; Luke 4:23.

42. The musical illustration in *VS* 502 that resembles idea in 1 Cor 13:1 is more likely based on a passage from Aeschines (*Ctes.* 229). Also, see Philostratus and Eunapius, *The Lives of the Sophists*, 48, n. 2.

43. Various miracles and supernatural skills, Blackburn claims, "are easily paralleled in the relevant literature" (Blackburn, "ΘΕΙΟΙ ΑΝΔΡΕΣ," 192).

44. Keener writes, "Of all ancient stories about miracle workers, those about

and waves,[45] an ascension into heaven,[46] a posthumous appearance to a skeptic,[47] and knowledge of the future.[48] Although future research might prove that stories like these about Apollonius's supernatural abilities were borrowed from the Gospels, they are not the best place to begin the quest for parallels and borrowings. The second criterion employed in this study, a criterion of textual similarity, argues that any passage from the VA that is proposed as a parallel should closely resemble the Gospel narrative that it was potentially derived from in both the broad strokes of the passage and its specific details. These two criteria should considerably narrow the field for indicating borrowings in the VA.

At least three ideas in the VA seem to meet the standard for the criterion of dissimilarity. The first of these notions is that of bodily resurrection from the dead. One the one hand, bodily resurrection from the dead as a permanent form of afterlife is altogether unknown in Greco-Roman religion. On the other, even stories of resurrections from the dead for the continuation of normal human existence—along the lines of Lazarus's resurrection or the resurrection of Jairus's daughter—are rare in pagan literature[49] but are common in the Gospels and Acts. Whether all ancient

---

Apollonius come closest to the stories about Jesus in the Gospels. Only these two figures stand out as immanent bearers of numinous power of whom multiple healing narratives are reported" (Keener, *Miracles*, 1:53).

45. Blackburn notes that several figures were said to have been able to control the sea, such as Orpheus, Abaris, Epimenides, Pythagoras, Empedocles, and Apollonius. See Blackburn, "ΘΕΙΟΙ ΑΝΔΡΕΣ," 192.

46. The ascensions of various pagan figures were reported: Romulus (Ovid, *Metam.* 14.806; Livy 1.16; Plutarch, *Rom.* 27.6–7), Julius Caesar (Suetonius, *Jul.* 88), Augustus Caesar (Suetonius, *Aug.* 100), Aeneas (Vergil, *Aen.* 1.289), Peregrinus (Lucian, *Peregr.* 39), and Mithra (*PGM* 4.475–834). For a discussion of most of these texts see Ehrman, *How Jesus Became God*, 25–38.

47. The posthumous appearance of Apollonius to a skeptic in a dream (*VA* 8.31) is only slightly reminiscent of Jesus's appearance to Saul of Tarsus near Damascus (Acts 9:3–7; 22:6–11; 26:12–19). Not only is this account not a resurrection story in the *VA*, but the other details of the two stories do not suggest the Philostratus had borrowed on Acts here. Rather than reliance on the New Testament, Schirren suggests that Apollonius's postmortem visit with a doubting disciple is based on an episode in Lucian's *Peregrinus*. These stories in the *VA* and *Peregrinus* contain similar wording, suggesting intertextuality See Schirren, "Irony," 171–72.

48. Diogenes Laertius, *Lives*, 2.3; Iamblichus, *Vit. Pythag.* 28.

49. Examples of the temporary resurrection of the dead in bodily form in Greco-Roman literature would include two accounts in Apuleius (*Metam.*1.11–14; 17–19; 2:21–30), one in Heliodorus (*Aeth.* 6.14–15), and a magical spell for reanimating the dead (*PGM* IV.2006–2125). Examples of resurrections of the dead for a prolonged period are also in evidence: Alcestis (Euripides, *Alcestis*), Protesilaus (Philostratus,

people viewed stories about bodily resurrection as mythical or fictional might be debated,[50] but, as modern folk would classify them, the resurrection story in the *VA* is virtually unique in Greco-Roman literature in that it appears to describe a historical event.[51] Naturally, then, a story about Apollonius raising the dead would be a fruitful place to investigate an intersection of Gospel narratives with the *VA*.[52]

A second idea that was not in vogue in the pagan world was that of a previously existing deity being born as a human being. Although there are numerous stories of gods fathering children by humans, humans becoming gods, or gods posing as humans in Greco-Roman mythology, the notion of a previously existing god becoming incarnate through childbirth only appears in the instances of Apollonius (*VA* 1.4) and Jesus (e.g., John 1:1, 14; Phil. 2:5; 1 Cor 8:6). Ehrman explains apart from the case of these two figures, Jesus and Apollonius, "I don't know of any other cases in ancient Greek or Roman thought of this kind of 'god-man,' where an already existing divine being is said to be born of a mortal woman."[53]

The third theme to qualify as an oddity for this study is the phenomenon of exorcism, for, as Blackburn explains, "[e]xorcisms, which are relatively prominent among Jesus' miracles, would be completely absent from the repertoire of our pagan wonder workers if it were not for Philostratus, who in his early third century *Vita Apollonii* relates one executed by Apollonius (4.20) and one by the Indian sage, Iarchas (3.38)."[54] These three themes appear to meet the criterion of dissimilarity and now must clear the hurdle of the second criterion.

As to the second criterion of textual similarity, several scholars have noted close resemblances between *VA* and Gospel texts that roughly

---

Heroicus; Chariton, *Chaer.*5.10.1), and Zamolxis (Photius, *Biblioth.* 166). Yet, in the examples of Zamolxis and Protesilaus, even Celsus doubted that they had returned with the same body as they possessed before (Origen, *Cels.* 2.55). The power to raise the dead was attributed to Asclepius, Empedocles, and Alexander Abonoteichos. See Blackburn, "ΘΕΙΟΙ ΑΝΔΡΕΣ," 192. However, Diogenes Laertius's (third century AD) account of Empedocles, who revived of a woman who had no pulse or respiration for thirty days (Empedocles, 60–61, 67), could be classified as either a resurrection or the revival of a comatose person. For an excellent overview of potential resurrections in the ancient world, see Bowersock, *Fiction*, 99–119.

50. Origen, *Cels.* 2.55.
51. Bowersock, *Fiction*, 111.
52. Koskenniemi, *Apollonios*, 36, 203–4.
53. Ehrman, *How Jesus Became God*, 18.
54. Blackburn, "ΘΕΙΟΙ ΑΝΔΡΕΣ," 192.

coincide with the three ideas identified in the first criterion:[55] aspects of the birth narratives (or incarnation), an exorcism, and the theme of resurrection—the resurrection of a girl from the dead and the appearance of the sage to his disciples after being dead or being thought dead.[56] Having identified these three ideas as the likely candidates for borrowing from the Gospels, each of them will be examined in detail for additional clues.

Birth Accounts

The birth narratives of Jesus and Apollonius are similar in a few respects: (1) both children were products of non-sexual, divine-human unions; (2) in both cases, a previously existing deity was born as a human being through a human mother; and (3) the announcement of the children's births took place while the recipient of the message was in an altered state of consciousness: Apollonius's mother received a vision (φάσμα), while Joseph's encounter was in a dream (κατ' ὄναρ, Matt 1:20);[57] (4) both births were accompanied by unusual heavenly phenomena: a moving star (Matt 2:2, 7–10) or bolt of lightning that stopped midway to earth and then retreated into the sky (VA 1.5). The second point provides the best reason for suggesting that the VA borrowed on Christian themes because Jesus and Apollonius were the only ancient god-men to share this common trait. Yet, these few similarities do not provide conclusive evidence that Philostratus borrowed from the Gospel accounts.

The differences between the births of Apollonius and Jesus also aid in evaluating the issue of borrowing. For instance, Jesus had one human parent, a divine father, and a stepfather[58] while Apollonius had two hu-

---

55. Of the five chief points of resemblance between Jesus and Apollonius, Schaff lists these three in *Ante-Nicene Christianity*, 2:100. Blackburn singles out two stories from the VA that formally resemble the Gospels, one of which was the resurrection of a girl and the other of the healing of a lame man. See Blackburn, "ΘΕΙΟΙ ΑΝΔΡΕΣ," 201–2. Koskenniemi singled out the birth stories (VA 1.4–6; Matt 1:18–25; Lk 1:28—2:20), the resurrection of the dead (VA 4.45; Mark 5:22–24, 35–43; Luke 7.11–17), and the resurrection appearances (VA 8.12: Luke 24:36–49; John 20: 24–29) as potentially parallels in his study. For more on these accounts, see Koskenniemi, *Apollonios*, 36.

56. Gildersleave, *Essays*, 276; Keener, *Miracles*, 1:55.

57. There is no indication in the text that the angel's appearance to Mary was a visionary experience (Luke 1:26–38). However, the parallel account of the angel's appearance to Zachariah is described as a vision (Luke 1:22).

58. Petzke overstates the similarity between Apollonius and Jesus with respect to their origins. He argues that that both figures had human fathers, while noting that the Gospels tend to eliminate the paternity of Joseph (Matt 1:16, 25). See Petzke, *Die*

man parents[59] and a divine parent. In the *VA*, the god Proteus announced his own birth as Apollonius, whereas an angel announced Jesus's birth to his parents (Luke 1:25–38; Matt 1:20–23). Another difference is that the annunciation to Jesus's mother took place before conception (Luke 1:34–35), whereas Apollonius's mother was already with child when she received word of the divine birth to come (*VA* 1.4).[60] Further, Mary was a virgin when she conceived (Matt 1:23, 25; Luke 1:27, 34), but Apollonius's mother had already given birth to another son two years earlier (*VA* 1.13.1). Moreover, Mary gave birth at the end of a normal gestational period (Luke 2:6), whereas Apollonius's mother went into premature labor. Jesus was a firstborn son (Luke 2:7), while Apollonius was not (*VA* 1.12.2). Jesus's delivery took place in a town (Luke 2:4), but Apollonius was born in a meadow. These differences, however slight, might indicate that Philostratus was not reliant on Gospel texts. If Philostratus had mined the infancy narratives of the Gospels for ideas, he certainly did not take full advantage of the spectacular material found there; he did not include a full genealogy of Apollonius, a moving star, angelic hosts, a manger, foreign and local visitors, ancient prophecies predicting this birth, and royal rivals who posed a threat to the newborn child. These differences and absences could suggest that borrowing from the Gospels did not take place in the case of the birth narratives of Apollonius and that another source should be sought for them.

Fortunately, the traditions about Pythagoras provide offer several promising parallels to the birth narrative of Apollonius in the *VA*.[61] Both Pythagoras and Apollonius were related to Zeus.[62] Both Pythagoras and Apollonius were the product of a divine-human union. The union of

---

Traditionen, 163. Yet, to be fair to the Gospel accounts, Joseph is not portrayed as the biological father of Jesus (although he was assumed to be such by others; e.g., Luke 3:23; 4:22); no other option for his paternity is suggested, except for perhaps the late Pandera and Stara legend (b. Šab 104b; b Sanh 67a). Although John 8:41 might be indicate that some believed Jesus was an illegitimate child—and the offspring of some unidentified human male—there are other interpretations of this passage. For a discussion of this passage, see Keener, *Gospel of John*, 1:759–60.

59. The name of the human father of the Tyanean was also Apollonius (*VA* 1.4, 6). The name of his mother was not given in the *VA*.

60. One might suggest that the announcement to Apollonius's pregnant mother parallels the announcement to Joseph (Matt 2:18–25).

61. The details of Pythagoras's birth given in this paragraph come from Iamblicus (*Vit. Pythag.* 2) and Porphyry (*Vit. Pythag.* 2).

62. Both of Pythagoras's earthly parents were descendants of Zeus (Iamblicus, *Vit. Pythag.* 2). Apollonius was called the "son of Zeus" by the Tyaneans (*VA* 1.6).

Parthenis ("the Virgin") and Apollo produced Pythagoras,[63] just as Apollonius resulted from the union of an unnamed deity (probably Zeus) and an unnamed human mother.[64] The births of both men were announced by supernatural means: the Delphic oracle predicted that of Pythagoras, while a vision predicted the birth of Apollonius.[65] So then, these correspondences between Pythagorean legends and the VA may be the source of Philostratus's account of Apollonius's divine birth rather than the Gospel accounts.

Other aspects of the story of Apollonius's birth can probably also be accounted for by parallels from Philostratus's own writings or other Greek literature. For instance, the unusual brontological phenomena at Apollonius's birth may borrow from the experiences of the sophist Scopelian in the VS,[66] since Philostratus appears to have utilized details of that sophist's life to flesh out the story of the Tyanean elsewhere.[67] Just as a lightning bolt that was about to strike the earth stopped and retreated skyward at Apollonius's birth (VA 1.5), the five-day-old Scopelian was also spared when lightning hit his cradle—unfortunately, his twin who lay next to him was struck dead and several bystanders were killed or severely injured (VS 515).[68] Another possibility is that the addition of lightning

63. Mnesarchus and Parthenis were the human parents of Pythagoras. Parthenis had shown no signs of pregnancy prior to her husband's journey to Delphi. While there, an oracle informed Mnesarchus of his wife's pregnancy and that this child would surpass all others in wisdom and beauty. Thereafter, he changed Parthenis's name to Pythais and named his son Pythagoras ("altar of Pythia") to commemorate this divine gift from Pythian Apollo.

64. Petzke claims that there were several traditions about Apollonius's divine paternity. Some traditions held that he was the "son of Zeus" (VA 1.6), while others claimed that Proteus was his father. E.g., "Die bereits schwangere Mutter ercheint Proteus und kündet sich als Vater an (I,4)" (Petzke, *Die Traditionen*, 162). Yet, Proteus never claimed to be the father of Apollonius in the VA; rather Proteus claimed that he was the child that would be born, thereby identifying himself with Apollonius (VA 1.4). This interpretation makes better sense of the VA for it relieves the tension of Apollonius having two divine fathers: Zeus and Proteus. Yet, it also creates another problem for, in traditional mythology, Proteus was the son of Poseidon, not Zeus—how then is Apollonius, as the incarnation of Proteus, a son of Zeus? In the case of Jesus, reconciling the two human genealogies has always been a challenge but reconciling the divine genealogies of Apollonius is the real puzzlement.

65. The Pythia told Pythagoras's father of the upcoming birth of this child of Apollo (Iamblicus, *Vit. Pythag.* 2), while Proteus heralded the birth to Apollonius's mother (VA 1.4).

66. Koskenniemi, *Apollonios*, 192.

67. Anderson, *Philostratus*, 124.

68. This theme was especially common in contexts related to children, sometimes twins: lightning apparently spared the babes Apollonius and Scopelian, while

to the tale helped Philostratus in aligning Apollonius's nativity with the fulminological elements in the birth accounts of Dionysus and Alexander the Great, who were also the offspring of Zeus and a human mother, just as he had compared these two heroes to the Tyanean in other contexts.[69] Yet another possibility is that Philostratus came up with this detail on his own, for one of his recurrent themes is of divine intervention by a bolt of lightning.[70] These three possibilities involving lightning certainly come closer to the storyline of the *VA* than does the moving star of Bethlehem.[71] Another portion of Apollonius's birth narrative may betray reliance on a story about Apollo in which swans circled Delos seven times and sang during his birth (Callimachus *Hymn. Del.* 4.249).[72] Similarly, near the time of Apollonius's birth, his sleeping mother was surrounded by a bevy of swans while she slept—their honking caused her to go into premature labor (*VA* 1.5). This tale of birds at Apollo's birth is closer to the account of Apollonius's birth than any portion of the Gospel infancy narratives unless one wants to argue for the unlikely possibility that the appearance of the angelic host (Luke 2:13) was the inspiration for Philostratus's flock of swans.

In the end, the hypothesis that the *VA* drew inspiration from the infancy narratives of Jesus is unproven and unlikely. Most of the suggested parallels are rather generic, while the parallels between the *VA* and non-Christian materials are persuasive and account for most of the details found therein. Apart from the notion of the birth of a previously

---

Scopelian's twin and the twin girls who were in the service of Herodes were killed by heavenly bolts (*VS* 560). Later, on the Island of Lemnos, Scopelian escaped a second thunderbolt that killed eight robust harvesters, thereby demonstrating that he was under the protection of the gods (*VS* 516).

69. Semele, the mortal mother of Dionysus, wishing to see her lover Zeus, was slain by the lightning of his divine presence (Euripides, *Bacch.* 3, 8, 88–95). In the case of Alexander, Olympias—on the night prior to consummating her marriage to Philip—dreamt that a thunderbolt struck her womb which kindled a wide spreading fire (Plutarch, *Alex.* 2). After seeing Olympias sleeping with a serpent at her side, Philip's attraction for his wife waned, possibly because he thought she had been the consort of a superior being (Plutarch, *Alex.* 2). Koskenniemi notes this latter example, *Apollonios*, 192. At the shrine of Zeus-Ammon, Alexander was called the son of Zeus (Plutarch, *Alex.* 27). Apollonius was also said to be the son of Zeus in *VA* 1.6.

70. *VA* 1.5, 4.43; *VS* 515, 560. In *VA* 2.33.1, the Indian Wise Men did not fight against invaders but were protected by divine thunder and lightning because they were beloved by the gods.

71. Bart Ehrman, writing of the lightning at the birth of Apollonius, stated that "[t]his sign is obviously different from a star that led a group of wise men to a child, but it is in the same celestial ballpark" (Ehrman, *How Jesus Became*, 14).

72. Baur, *Apollonius von Tyana*, 97; Koskenniemi, *Apollonios*, 192.

existing god in human form, the other details in the *VA*'s birth stories have parallels in Greco-Roman material, especially the lore of Pythagoras, Alexander, Dionysus, and Scopelian. Therefore, it appears that the *VA* most likely did not borrow from the birth narratives of Jesus.

Resurrection Accounts

By far, the most promising area for discovering instances in which the *VA* borrows from the Gospels are found in its stories of the bodily resurrection of the dead. This is because accounts of resurrection were rare in Greco-Roman literature (the criterion of dissimilarity) and because these episodes closely resemble several specific resurrections attributed to Jesus (the criterion of textual similarity). Two texts from the *VA* will be probed to determine whether they have borrowed from Gospel texts: Apollonius's apparent resurrection of a young girl (*VA* 4.45) and his unexpected appearance to his disciples after he was presumed dead (*VA* 8.11–13).

Apollonius's resurrection of a maiden in *VA* 4.45 resembles two Gospel stories in particular: the resurrection of Jairus's daughter and the resurrection of the widow of Nain's son. Several authors have noted the striking similarities.[73] Even Koskenniemi, who does not believe Philostratus was under the sway of the Gospels, seems open to a potential borrowing here.[74]

Looking first at the account of Jairus's daughter (Matt 9:18–26; Mark 5:21–43; Luke 8:40–56), several similarities between it and the *VA* 4.45 are noteworthy: (1) a girl had recently died;[75] (2) the girl was young;[76] (3) the girl's death caused lamentation;[77] (4) bystanders were present at the

---

73. Vincent Taylor remarked concerning Apollonius's resurrection of a girl, "No one, I think, can read this story without being reminded of the Young Man at Nain" (Taylor, *Formation*, 127). Réville, however, notes the story's similarity to another Gospel account: "immediately remind us of the return to life of the daughter of Jairus" (Réville, *Apollonius of Tyana*, 62). Newman believed *VA* 4.45 was based on the language and detail of both Mark 5:39 and Luke 7:11. See Newman, *Life of Apollonius*, 350. See also Gildersleave, *Essays*, 276–77.

74. Koskenniemi, *Apollonios*, 197. However, Koskenniemi notes that there are no direct quotes from the Gospel stories and notes several deviations from them. He claims that if borrowing took place, Philostratus did not lift details directly from the Gospels, but probably took material from a Jesus tradition in which elements from the two stories were already merged (Koskenniemi, *Apollonios*, 198).

75. Matt 9:18; Mark 5:35; Luke 8:49; *VA* 4.45.1.

76. Matt 9:25 (τὸ κοράσιον); Mark 5:23 (τὸ θυγάτριόν μου), 41–42 (τὸ κοράσιον); Luke 8:42 states she was "twelve years old." *VA* 4.45.1 indicates that the girl (κόρη), also called a "child" (ἡ παῖς), had died right at the time of her wedding. Her exact age is not given.

77. Matt 9:23; Mark 5:39; Luke 8:52. *VA* 4.45.1.

resurrection including the maiden's family members;[78] (5) the deceased girl belonged to an important family;[79] (6) the imagery of sleep was used to describe the girl's death;[80] (7) the holy man raised the dead by touching[81] and speaking to the corpse;[82] (8) the raised girl gave evidence that she had resumed normal life.[83]

The next passage, the story of the resurrection of the widow of Nain's son (Luke 7:1–17), also exhibits potential points of contact with *VA* 4.45: (1) a funeral bier was used to carry the corpse;[84] (2) the holy man stopped the procession;[85] (3) bystanders witnessed the miracle;[86] (4) the holy man addressed the "crying" of the crowd;[87] (5) the holy man raised the dead by speaking to the deceased;[88] (6) the resurrected person spoke;[89] (7) the resurrected person returned to his or her parent;[90] and (8) the bystanders were astonished.[91]

At first glance, these numerous textual similarities suggest that the *VA* has borrowed from these two Gospel stories. But are these texts

78. Matt 9:25 (ἐξεβλήθη ὁ ὄχλος); Mark 5:40 (αὐτὸς δὲ ἐκβαλὼν πάντας). *VA* 4.45.1.

79. Matt 9:25 indicates that the girl was the daughter of a "ruler," Mark 5:22 of Jairus "one of the rulers of the synagogue," and Luke 8:40 says that she was the child of Jairus "a ruler of the synagogue." The girl in *VA* 4.45.1 belonged to a consular family. For a discussion of these elements, see Koskemmiemi, *Apollonios*, 194.

80. Matt 9:24; Mark 5:39; Luke 8:52. Although *VA* 4.45.1 seems to indicate that the girl was dead and that Apollonius "woke" (ἀφύνισε) the girl from apparent death, Philostratus allows for the possibility that she may not have been in fact dead (*VA* 4.45.2).

81. Matt 9:25; Mark 5:41; Luke 8:54; *VA* 4.45.1. See Koskenniemi, *Apollonios*, 195.

82. Mark 5:41 (λέγει αὐτῇ· ταλιθα κουμ, ὅ ἐστιν μεθερμηνευόμενον· τὸ κοράσιον, σοὶ λέγω, ἔγειρε); Luke 8:54 (ἐφώνησεν λέγων· ἡ παῖς, ἔγειρε). *VA* 4.45.1 says that Apollonius said something secretly after touching the girl (τι ἀφανῶς ἐπειπών). Koskenniemi, *Apollonios*, 195.

83. Mark 5:41 ("she got up and walked"); Luke 8:55 ("and he [Jesus] directed that something should be given her to eat"). Philostratus states that the girl spoke (*VA* 4.45.1).

84. Luke 7:14 (τῆς σοροῦ); *VA* 4.45.1 (τῇ κλίνῃ).

85. Luke 7:13 (καὶ προσελθὼν ἥψατο τῆς σοροῦ, οἱ δὲ βαστάζοντες ἔστησαν); *VA* 4.45.1 ("κατάθεσθε" ἐφη "τὴν κλίνην").

86. Luke 7:12 (ὄχλος τῆς πόλεως ἱκανὸς ἦν σὺν αὐτῇ); *VA* 4.45.1.

87. Luke 7:13 (μὴ κλαῖε); *VA* 4.45.1 (ἐγὼ γὰρ ὑμᾶς τῶν ἐπὶ τῇ κόρῃ δακρύων παύσω).

88. Luke 7:14; *VA* 4.45.1. See Petzke, *Die Traditionen*, 130.

89. Luke 7:15; *VA* 4.45.1. See Petzke, *Die Traditionen*, 130.

90. Luke 7:15 (ἔδωκεν αὐτὸν τῇ μητρὶ αὐτοῦ); *VA* 4.45.1 (ἐπανῆλθέ τε ἐς τὴν οἰκίαν τοῦ πατρός). Koskenniemi, *Apollonios*, 194. This phrase in Luke appears to echo Elijah's resurrection of a boy (1 Kgs 17:23), whereas that in the *VA* mentions that the return to her father's house was like the case of Alcestis after Hercules raised her.

91. Luke 7:16; *VA* 4.45.2. See Koskenniemi, *Apollonios*, 195.

similar because of the reliance of the *VA* on the Gospels or are these similarities merely coincidental? This question is important because these stories in the *VA* and the Gospels also resemble other ancient accounts of resurrection and *Scheintod* ("apparent death").[92] The category of *Scheintod* is worth exploring in this discussion because Philostratus himself was uncertain whether Apollonius had raised the maiden from the dead or had merely recognized some subtle sign that indicated she was still alive (*VA* 4.45.2).

Although the many features in the resurrection accounts in the *VA* might suggest that it borrowed from the Gospels, this may be because readers are unfamiliar with other resurrection and *Scheintod* accounts from the ancient world. Such accounts often report similar details. For instance, the two Gospel stories examined above from the first century AD compare surprisingly well to two stories told by Apuleius in his second-century AD works *Florida* and *Metamorphoses*. In *Flor.* 19, Apuleius recorded that the physician Asclepiades saved a comatose man, thought to be dead, from being accidentally burned alive on a funeral pyre. This account has several similarities to the two Gospel resurrection stories mentioned above.[93] In *Metam.* 2.21–30, Apuleius relates the story of an Egyptian prophet and priest named Zatchlas, who raised a dead man just long enough for the deceased to relate the manner of his death to a crowd. This account also resembles the passages in Luke in many details.[94] These

---

92. Meier writes that the story in *VA* 4.45 looks like a conflation of Mark 5:21–43 and Luke 7:11–17, many of these motifs are also found in other ancient miracle accounts. See Meier, *Mentor*, 580. Anderson points out that in three cases (Apuleius, *Flor.*19, *VA* 4.45, and Mark 5:35–43), a holy man (or physician), raised the dead, the client was socially prominent, the holy man intervened when others had lost hope, and, in the cases of Mark and the *VA*, the intervention was something whispered. See Anderson, "Folklore," 214. However, the story that Anderson cites from Apuleius (i.e., Apuleius, *Flor.*19) is more likely a case of *Scheintod* ("apparent death") than true resurrection.

93. In *Flor.* 19, Asclepiades interrupted a funeral procession just outside of a city (cf. Luke 7:12) that was attended by a crowd (cf. Luke 7:12), went up to the body the man laid out on a bier (cf. Luke 7:14), and touched it (cf. Luke 8:54). Although some in the crowd mocked the physician for claiming that the man was still alive (cf. Luke 8:53), Asclepiades took the body to his home and, in a private setting (cf. Luke 8:51), restored him to life as one who had returned from the underworld.

94. In *Metam.* 2, the deceased was a leading citizen (*Metam.* 2.27; cf. Luke 8:41), mourners attended the funeral (*Metam.* 2.23–24, 27; cf. Luke 8:52), a crowd was present to witness the miracle (*Metam.* 2.28–29; cf. Luke 7:12), a man touched the holy man's knees or feet to encourage him to act (*Metam.* 2:28; cf. Luke 8:41), the funeral procession was stopped by someone touching the bier (*Metam.* 2.27; Luke 7:14), the prophet raised the dead (*Metam.* 2.29; cf. Luke 7:15–16; 8:55), and the resurrected

comparisons show that the few ancient reports of resurrections or the restoration of comatose people to normal life tend to contain similar details and that such details may not necessarily indicate borrowing. Thus, Philostratus may not have borrowed from the Gospels any more than Apuleius borrowed from the Gospels in these two cases. Unless there are good reasons to suspect borrowing, the similarity between the account in the VA and the Gospels should probably be chalked up to coincidence.

Yet, thankfully, Philostratus did indicate that he based his story on a particular Greek tale, for he invited comparison of this episode of resurrection to the Greek tragedy *Alcestis* (*VA* 4.45). This story closely resembles the key elements of the resurrection account concerning Apollonius's resurrection of the maiden.[95] In the Euripidean version of this tale, Hercules wrested Alcestis, the recently-deceased wife of King Admetus, from Thanatos, who had come to take her to the underworld in the place of her husband.[96] Although Koskenniemi argues that this story of Alcestis had little,[97] if anything, in common with the resurrection story in the *VA* and the Gospels, the story of Alcestis and the resurrection account in the *VA* do have a good deal in common, as this list of similarities demonstrates: (1) a young woman had recently died;[98] (2) the deceased woman was of high rank;[99] (3) the marital status of the deceased was noted;[100]

---

person spoke (*Metam.* 2.29–30; cf. Luke 7:15).

95. Gildersleave, "The resemblance to the Gospel story of the young man of Nain is striking, but Philostratus seems rather to have had in his mind the pagan story of Alcestis" (Gildersleave, *Essays*, 276–77). Petzke also believes that Alcestis was the basis for this account. See Petzke, *Die Traditionen*, 130.

96. *VA* 4.45.1. The myth of Alcestis appears multiple versions. The version to which Philostratus alludes here is most likely the one represented by Euripides's tragedy *Alcestis*. Pseudo-Apollodorus relates two versions of the Alcestis story. In one, Persephone sent Alcestis back to the land of the living and in the other Hercules fought with Hades and brought her up from the underworld as he did in Euripides's play (Pseudo-Apollodorus, *Bibliotheca* 1.9.15).

97. Koskenniemi, *Apollonios*, 195.

98. The girl's youthfulness is stressed throughout the narrative in that (1) Death counted Aclestis among his young victims (νέων; Euripides, *Alc.* 55); (2) she did not spare her own young life (οὐδ' ἐφεισάμην ἥβης; Euripides, *Alc.* 288–89); (3) the text states of her she died in her prime as a young bride (σὺ δ' ἐν ἥβᾳ νέα νέουπροθανοῦσα φωτὸς οἴχῃ; Eurpides, *Alc.* 471–72); (4) she, a young person, died instead of Admetus's old father (παρεὶς ἄλλῳ θανεῖν νέῳ; Euripides, *Alc.* 634–35); (5) the resurrected Alcestis's youth is indicated by her clothing (Eurpides, *Alc.* 1046–47); and (6) Admetus is again described as being young (Euripides, *Alc.* 697; cf. *VA* 4.45.1).

99. Alcestis was the wife of king Admetus of Pherae (*Alc.* 130). Cf. *VA*. 4.45.1.

100. Alcestis was a wife who had voluntarily died in the place of her husband

(4) the hero inquired about name of the deceased;[101] (5) the husband or betrothed was mentioned in the narrative;[102] (6) the entire city or region mourned the woman's death;[103] (7) the corpse had been or was being carried to the place of burial;[104] (8) the hero brought an end to the crying or grieving of those present;[105] (9) the rescued woman spoke;[106] (10) the resurrected woman returned to her house;[107] and (11) the theme of dowry or wedding preparations is assumed in both accounts.[108] Even if the *VA* is not identical to Euripides's tragedy in all its details, it does follow the basic contours of the story. That this Greek story is the basis of the *VA*'s account is a simpler and more likely explanation than that Philostratus had combined the details of two resurrection miracles from Gospel texts to create this his own story. Also, there are no strong verbal connections between Philostratus's tale and the two Gospel stories mentioned above; if Philostratus drew on the Gospels, he has carefully erased his tracks.

There are other reasons for positing the primary background for this story about Apollonius was based on the story of Alcestis rather than on

---

(Euripides, *Alc.* 17–18, 34–37, 152–55, 176–78, 433–34, 524, 996). The girl in the *VA* was a bride-to-be who had died at the time of her wedding (*VA* 4.45.1).

101. Heracles asked the name of the deceased from Admetus, who evaded the question (Euripides, *Alc.* 530) but later asked and received an answer from a household servant (Euripides, *Alc.* 819–20). Apollonius asked the name of the deceased (*VA* 4.45.1).

102. Admetus played a major role in Euripides's tragedy, whereas in the *VA*, the betrothed is unnamed and is simply said to have followed the bier (ὁ νυμφίος ἠκολούθει τῇ κλίνῃ; *VA* 4.45.1).

103. Admetus commanded all the Thessalians of his realm to mourn (Euripides, *Alc.* 425–31; cf. 540, 542, 550, 762). All of Rome mourned the death of the young bride in *VA* 4.45.1.

104. According to Euripides, the body of Alcestis is carried on the shoulders of his servants (Euripides, *Alc.* 606–8). In the *VA*, she is carried on a "bed," (τῇ κλίνῃ; *VA* 4.45.1).

105. Hercules tells Admetus to stop his grieving (λύπης δ' εὐτυχῶν μεθίστασο; Euripides, *Alc.* 1122). Apollonius tells the mourners he will end their crying about the girl (ἐγὼ γὰρ ὑμᾶς τῶν ἐπὶ τῇ κόρῃ δακρύων παύσω; *VA* 4.45.1).

106. Alcestis was not permitted to speak for three days after her resurrection for she first had to become purified with respect to the gods of the underworld, but presumably she would do so after the designated time had passed (Euripides, *Alc.* 1143–46). The woman that Apollonius raised appears to have spoken immediately (*VA* 4.45.1).

107. Hercules brought Alcestis back to Admetus's house (Euripides, *Alc.* 1024, 1097, 1110). After Apollonius raised the girl, she returned to her father's house (*VA* 4.45.2).

108. Praet explains that *Alcestis* begins when Admetus offended Artemis by failing to make the proper wedding sacrifice to her. In the *VA*, Apollonius was offered 150,000 drachmas by her father for raising the girl, but he gave it to her as an extra dowry. See Praet, "Pythagoreanism," 292.

the Gospels. Although resurrection stories in the Greco-Roman world are rare, thus justifying the widespread scholarly suspicion that Philostratus borrowed here from the Gospel resurrection accounts, the tale of Alcestis is one of the few pagan tales of a genuine, bodily resurrection from the dead. N. T. Wright, who has written extensively on the topic of resurrection, agrees that "Alcestis does indeed return from the dead to bodily life. She will presumably die again, like Lazarus in John's gospel, but even so her return is remarkable enough, being the only such tale we have from the entire ancient world."[109] Wright is correct that this is a tale about bodily resurrection, for, in the Euripidean tragedy, Hercules made it clear that the woman he had snatched from Thanatos was no mere ghost or spirit, but was the actual flesh-and-blood wife of Admetus.[110] Philostratus's allusion to this rare pagan story of bodily resurrection in this story makes theories of his borrowing from the Gospels unnecessary and unlikely.

Another reason for regarding Alcestis as the backdrop of Apollonius's resurrection story is that a Hercules motif runs throughout book 4 of the *VA*,[111] the section in which the story of the maiden's resurrection by the holy man appears. At the beginning of Book Four, Hercules is given credit for assisting Apollonius in averting a plague at Ephesus (*VA* 4.10); toward its end, two episodes compare the deeds of Apollonius to Hercules (*VA* 4.45–46), and the final passage anticipates a journey to the "pillars" of Hercules (*VA* 4.47). Further, the resurrection of the girl (*VA* 4.45) and the episode following it (*VA* 4.46) are both related to the labors of Hercules. The Alcestis story, alluded to in *VA* 4.45.1, was set in classical texts just prior to Hercules's eighth labor of capturing the horses of Diomedes,[112] while Apollonius's reference to Hercules's rescue of Theseus from the underworld, alluded to in *VA* 4.46.2 during his attempt to rescue Musonius from prison, occurred during the strongman's twelfth and

---

109. Wright, *The Resurrection of the Son of God*, 67. In this same context, Wright notes that Hercules's rescue of Alcestis appears in the Via Latina Catacomb in Rome alongside other biblical themes, and he asks whether this story might have served as "the model for the subsequent regular iconographic tradition of depicting Jesus leading Adam and Eve out of the underworld" (Wright, *Resurrection*, 66, n. 198).

110. Euripides, *Alc.* 1127–28.

111. Praet has argued that each book of the 8 books of the *VA* based on a ring structure that takes a Greek god (and a corresponding planet) as its theme in his "Pythagoreanism," 283–320. Praet acknowledges several Hercules stories in this section of the *VA* but believes that book 8 is related to the goddess Artemis. See Praet, "Pythagoreanism," 292–96.

112. Euripides, *Alc.* 482–83, 1149–50.

final labor of capturing Cerberus.[113] The two Hercules myths alluded to in these back-to-back episodes in the *VA* share the motif of Hercules rescuing the dead from the underworld (i.e., Alcestis and Theseus), thereby suggesting that their placement in book four of the *VA* is thematic. Apollonius, the new Hercules, rescued a girl from death and attempted to rescue the philosopher Musonius from prison and impending death at the hand of Nero. Thus, the evidence seems to lean strongly in favor of this tale of Apollonius raising the dead being based on a Herculean (or Euripidean) legend, with which it matches closely in theme and context, rather than of a Gospel account.[114]

The final text to compare to the Gospels is one in which Apollonius appeared to his disciples giving them many infallible proofs that he was alive although they presumed that he had died. Kee noted the similarities of Apollonius's unexpected return to the resurrection appearances in the Gospels and hints that Philostratus borrowed from them. Kee notes that both Jesus and Apollonius invite their disciples to touch them as proof that they were alive and that elements of the post-ascension accounts about Apollonius bear a resemblance to the post-resurrection accounts of Jesus.[115] Kee is correct, for there are several more places where the *VA* and the Gospel accounts are similar, especially if one allows for comparison of data from the entire passion narrative: (1) the master predicts that he will appear to his disciples as if risen from the dead;[116] (2) the master faced humiliation at the hands of his captors;[117] (3) the master

---

113. Diodorus of Sicily, *Library of History* 26.1; Euripides, *Herc. fur.* 1170; Seneca, *Herc. fur.* 645–51.

114. Several lesser considerations make the theory of Philostratus's borrowing this story from the Gospels unlikely. It is difficult to see how he would have imagined such a story undermining or challenging Christianity. Further, why would Philostratus want to demonstrate that Apollonius had power over physical death in a pagan culture that did not believe in bodily resurrection in the first place? Why would he run the risk of relating such an act that might associate Apollonius with magic? More likely, this was a traditional tale about Apollonius, which did not cohere with Philostratus's own viewpoint but that he felt that he had to include in the narrative. Given that Philostratus seems uncomfortable with the idea of resurrection (he offers a naturalistic explanation of the event at *VA* 4.45.2) and later has Apollonius deny the ability to raise the dead (*VA* 8.7.42), the suggestion that Philostratus would have borrowed it from the Gospels seems unlikely.

115. Kee, *Miracle*, 264. Others have also noted the similarities between this passage and the resurrection appearance of Jesus to his disciples. See Réville *Apollonius*, 63 and Koskenniemi, *Apollonios*, 36, 199–203.

116. *VA* 7.41; cf. Luke 18:33; 24:6.

117. *VA* 7.34; Luke 22:63–65; 23:11.

faced the prospect of death at a Roman trial;[118] (4) the dejected disciples gather together;[119] (5) the master suddenly appears to the disciples;[120] (6) the disciples doubt the reality of their master's return;[121] (7) the master invites the disciples to touch him to confirm his physicality and that he is not a ghost;[122] and (8) the disciples finally believed that the master had returned.[123] With such a list of many convincing parallels, it might seem that there is no reason to doubt that Philostratus lifted key elements from the Gospels.

Yet, as one might expect, there are also differences between the *VA* and Gospel resurrection accounts that challenge the theory of borrowing. Most significantly, the Gospels related a resurrection of Jesus from the dead whereas the *VA* merely reported that Apollonius escaped execution.[124] In short, this episode in the *VA* is not a resurrection account at all. Although Apollonius, like Jesus, stretched out his hand to his disciples, beckoning them to touch him as proof that he was not a spirit (*VA* 8.12.1; Luke 24:39),[125] he did not present his hands to display his wounds, as in the case of Jesus (John 20:20, 25, 27). Yet, these points alone are not enough to disprove the possibility that Philostratus borrowed from a Gospel account.

Philostratus hints to his readers once again that he was telling an event from the life of Apollonius against the backdrop of a Greek story, this time an episode from the *Odyssey*. The location of Apollonius's appearance to his disciples in the cave of the Nymphs suggests that Philostratus had the later portion of the *Odyssey* in mind. The tale of Odysseus's return to Ithaca and reunion with his family after he was presumed dead, offers

---

118. *VA* 7.34–38.5.4; John 18:28—19:16; Luke 23:1–4, 18–25.
119. *VA* 8.11; John 20:19.
120. *VA* 8.12; John 20:19; Luke 24:36.
121. *VA* 8.12.1; Luke 24:38.
122. *VA* 8.12.1; John 20:20, 27; Luke 24:39–43.
123. *VA* 8.12.2; John 20:27–29.

124. Blackburn, who suspected a Gospel borrowing in this case, correctly notes this difference: "The links with Luke 24:36ff. and John 20:19ff. are obvious, but there is the difference that while Apollonius proves that he has not been killed, Jesus proves his bodily life after death" (Blackburn, "ΘΕΙΟΙ ΑΝΔΡΕΣ," 193).

125. In the Odyssey, Odysseus was unable to hold the spirit of his mother with his hands because of her immateriality (Homer, *Od.* 11.204–8). Later, Telemachus believed that his father was a spirit (*Od.* 16.194). If *VA* 8.12.1 alludes to the Odyssey and Philostratus has cast Apollonius as Odysseus, episodes like these might explain why Philostratus chose to use physical touch as a proof that Apollonius was not a spirit.

several striking similarities to Apollonius's appearance to his disciples in the *VA*: (1) omens were given in response to libations that foreshadowed the return of the hero;[126] (2) the hero was conveyed speedily from a distant location to the cave of the Nymphs;[127] (3) the cave of the Nymphs was the setting for at least part of the story;[128] (4) prior to the hero's appearance to his loved ones, a storm arose at sea that sank a ship;[129] (5) after the journey the hero required sleep and laid down to rest;[130] (6) the hero's identity was doubted even after he revealed himself to those closest to him;[131] (7) the hero was initially mistaken for an intangible spirit;[132] (8) the hero re-

---

126. In the Odyssey, the libations of Menelaus (Homer, *Od.* 15.145–50) and of Theoclymenus (*Od.* 15.256–59) are followed by omens that predict the return coming and defeat of the suiters: an eagle is spotted with a goose in its talons (*Od.* 15.160–78) and a hawk grasping a dove (*Od.* 15.525–34). The vision of Telesinus in the *VA*, likewise associated with a libation (*VA* 12.3), predicted that Apollonius would survive his encounter with Domitian. Telesinus's dream of a fire that overtook other people but that parted for Apollonius to swim through is reminiscent of the Odyssey as well; Zeus's lightning destroyed Odysseus's ship and crew, but Odysseus floated to safety (Homer, *Od.* 12.415–50).

127. Odysseus was transported from Phaeacia to Ithaca by a ship so swift that it could outpace a falcon (Homer, *Od.* 13.81–92). Apollonius's means of transportation is not revealed, but he travelled a two-day's journey (*VA* 7.41) in half a day (*VA* 8.12.2).

128. The Phaeacians deposited the sleeping Odysseus near this cave in Ithaca (Homer, *Od.* 13.96–112, 345–51). Apollonius made his appearance to his friends, who were in this cave (*VA* 8.11). Although the name and the description of the contents of the cave with its spring and stone jars are the same in both accounts, Philostratus has located the grotto in Dicaearchia (near Naples, Italy) rather than on Ithaca.

129. In the Odyssey, Zeus raised a storm, at Poseidon's request, that sank the Phaeacian vessel that had brought Odysseus home (Homer, *Od.* 142–90). In the *VA*, Apollonius instructed Damis to walk to his destination because he foresaw that a storm would arise that would sink several ships heading toward Dicaearchia (*VA* 7.41).

130. Odysseus slept in route to Ithaca (Homer, *Od.* 13.75), while Apollonius slept only after his arrival (*VA* 8.13.2), perhaps suggesting that his stamina exceeded that of the Ithacan hero.

131. Odysseus's initial appearance is rejected by his son (Homer, *Od.* 16.193), his wife (*Od.* 23.27–232), and his father (*Od.* 24.365–83), while Apollonius's return is doubted by his two disciples (*VA* 8.12).

132. Telemachus first imagined that his father was a god (Homer, *Od.* 16.179, 183, 197) or a spirit (δαίμων *Od.* 16.194), while Apollonius protested that he was alive and not a ghost (*VA* 8.12). This story in the *VA* may also recall an earlier story in the Odyssey when the hero visited the underworld. Apollonius's encouragement to his disciples to touch him to see if he would elude them like a ghost (εἴδωλον) from the realm of Persephone (Φερσεφάττης) to cause grief; this sort of creature recalls Odysseus's visit to the house of Hades. There, Odysseus attempted but failed to grasp his mother's shade three times, wondering if she were a phantom (εἴδωλον) sent by Persephone (Περσεφόνεια) to cause him sorrow (*Od* 11.204–14).

sponded to doubts that he was alive by providing proofs;[133] (9) the hero and his loved ones embraced;[134] and, (10) the hero was asked about his means of arrival.[135] These similarities suggest that the return of Apollonius to his followers has been crafted after Odysseus's return rather than after a resurrection appearances of Jesus.

Neither of the stories in the *VA* that resemble the resurrection Gospel accounts were shown to be reliant on them. The first story, which was either the restoration of a comatose girl or a resurrection, appears to have been based on *Alcestis*. The second story, which was not a resurrection tale at all, seems to have been based on a story from the *Odyssey*. Both stories in *VA* appear to have been shaped by Greco-Roman tales.

Exorcism Accounts

The topics of exorcisms and exorcists in the *VA* easily meet the criterion of dissimilarity. Indeed, exorcism is a rarity in ancient texts. The names of very few exorcists in antiquity have survived. A few Jewish and Christian exorcists are mentioned in ancient sources,[136] but Apollonius was the sole pagan exorcist to be called by name. Further, although a few accounts of exorcisms appear in Christian and Jewish texts,[137] they are less common in Greco-Roman materials.[138] In the Gospels, many of Jesus's miracles

---

133. Apollonius offered to let his disciples touch him as proof of his reality and to demonstrate that he was not a ghost (*VA* 8.12.1). Odysseus's evidence concerning his reality was that his loved ones could touch his body (*Od.* 16.215, 244–45).

134. Odysseus was embraced by Telemachus (*Od.*16.214), Penelope (*Od.*23.205–9), and Laertes (*Od.*24.345–50), while Apollonius was embraced by Damis and Demetrius (*VA* 8.12.2).

135. *Od.* 16.222–24; *VA* 8.12.2.

136. Twelftree, *Jesus the Exorcist*, 48.

137. There are several examples of Jewish and Christian exorcisms apart from the numerous references to Jesus casting out demons in the Gospels (E.g., 11QPs^a 27.10; T. Sol. 1.5–7; Josephus, *Ant.* 6.166–69; 8.46–49; Num. Rab. 19.8; Matt 12:27; Mark 9:38–39; Acts 19:13–19).

138. Celsus refers to sorcerers and others, trained by Egyptians, who performed miracles and drove demons out of men (Origen, *Cels.* 1.68). Plutarch's description of a man feigning demon possession suggests that there were cases deemed real by ancient authors (*Marc.* 20.5). Lucian's satire about the gullibility of religious folk gives details of a "Syrian from Palestine" who casts out demons (*Philops.*16). Some believe that this mysterious Syrian was Christ, but others believe that the context favors the view that he was a contemporary of Lucian (Ferguson, *Demonology*, 56–57). This reference is not a reference to Jesus, for this exorcist charged a hefty fee whereas Jesus offered his services for free in the Gospels.

PART 3: INVESTIGATING THE APOLLONIAN DECALOGUE

of healing were exorcisms;[139] in the *VA*, Apollonius only performed one exorcism himself (another was performed by an Indian wise man). Thus, the rarity of exorcists and accounts of exorcisms in Greco-Roman literature builds a solid case this meeting the standard for the case for dissimilarity.

However, the criterion of textual similarity is more difficult to assess. Some elements within the *VA*'s exorcism accounts are admittedly like those performed by Jesus, but they do not resemble specific Gospel stories. Some writers believe that the accounts in the *VA* are dependent on Gospel stories,[140] while others are content to note the similarities between these passages without weighing in on the issue of borrowing.[141]

The first order of business is to cull through the passages in the *VA* that supposedly deal with exorcism. The *VA* contains numerous stories of Apollonius's encounters with demons and spirits, yet the classification of some of these accounts as exorcisms is questionable.[142] The two stories in which Apollonius drives away ἔμπουσαι (female vampires) will not be treated in this study[143] because these encounters do not qualify as exorcisms—although some have regarded them as such.[144] They are excluded as exorcisms here because (1) demons and vampires are not the same spiritual entities, and (2) *empusai* did not possess human beings; in the *VA* demons possess their hosts, while vampires seek to devour or frighten their victims. Likewise, the account in which Apollonius prevents a plague at Ephesus by inciting a crowd to stone an old beggar disguised as a demon does not qualify as an exorcism (*VA* 4.10).[145] This story will not be included in this analysis because the demon involved (*VA* 4.10.2) was not cast out of its host; in truth, there was no host at all

---

139. Twelftree points out that four of the thirteen healing miracles in Mark were exorcisms, *Jesus the Exorcist*, 3.

140. Réville, *Apollonius*, 63. Regarding Gospel influence on *VA* 4.20, see Keener, *Miracles*, 2:782, n. 153.

141. Gildersleave writes, "But especially famous is his adventure with the young man possessed of a devil, a scene which is supposed to be modelled after the Gospel narrative ... We will leave our reader to decide whether the resemblance of this story to any of the similar Gospel narratives is due to the elements which are necessarily common, or to a direct appropriation of material" (Gildersleave, *Essays*, 272–73).

142. Ferguson identifies several such accounts (*VA* 2.4, 3.38, 4.10, 20, 25, 44). See Ferguson, *Demonology*, 67, n. 97.

143. Apollonius encounters an ἔμπουσα in India (*VA* 2.4; also called a φάσμα) and an ἔμπουσα in Corinth (*VA* 4.25.4–5). This same entity is called a λάμια in *VA* 8.7.29.

144. Ferguson, *Demonology*, 67, n. 97.

145. Contra Ferguson, *Demonology*, 67, n. 97.

(*VA* 8.7.28). This event of stoning the plague demon is better classified as an expulsion of a *pharmakos*, which is an act somewhat akin to the OT scapegoat ritual.[146] After the eliminations of these passages, only two exorcism accounts remain to be explored in the *VA*.

The first story, indisputably a case of exorcism, occurred in Athens while Apollonius was lecturing on the topic of libations (*VA* 4.20). As the sage was speaking, a young man who had a bad reputation laughed at Apollonius's instructions. Apollonius, realizing that the boy was demon-possessed, stared directly at the spirit thereby causing it to utter sounds as if it were being burned or tortured. After the spirit promised to keep away from this boy and other humans, Apollonius demanded that it give proof of its departure from the boy. The demon agreed to this, telling Apollonius that it would knock over one of the statues in the Royal Stoa, which it did to the amazement of the onlookers. After the spirit's departure, the boy came to himself and returned to his pre-possessed state, with the exception that he began to dress in simple clothing like Apollonius.

This exorcism account does not resemble a particular exorcism story in the Gospels, but some of its contents resemble details found in exorcism accounts found in Christian, Jewish, and pagan literature. The similarities are that (1) the holy man held a conversation with the demon;[147] (2) the demon was expelled by an authoritative command rather than by magical spells or paraphernalia;[148] (3) the demon was commanded to give proof to the spectators of its departure, much like in an account of Josephus in which a demon overturned a basin of water[149] or like in later Christian texts in which a spirit knocked over a statue;[150] (4) the host is returned to his normal state after the demon's departure;[151] and, (5) the demon was commanded not to return to the host.[152] The differences between this passage in the *VA* are also significant. For instance, the misbehavior of the demon in this episode—rude laughter and bawdy

---

146. Walter Burkert cites this and other passages as examples of expelling the *pharmakos*. See Burkert, *Greek Religion*, 82–84. For an example of the practice of stoning human beings to remove *miasma* from the community, see Aeschylus, *Ag.* 1117–18, 1615–16.

147. Mark 1:24–26; 5:7–9, 12–13; cf. b. Pesaḥ. 112b.

148. Mark 1:27; 5:12–13; 9:25; b. Meʿil. 17b; Lucian, *Philops.* 16.

149. Josephus, *Ant.* 8.48.

150. Acts of Pet. 2.4.11. This work dates prior to AD 190 according to Hennecke, *Writings*, 2.275.

151. Mark 5:15; Josephus, *Ant.* 8.49; Lucian, *Philops.*, 16.

152. Mark 9:25; Josephus, *Ant.* 8.45, 47.

behavior—is benign in comparison to the more malevolent actions of demons in the New Testament toward their hosts (Mark 5:5; 9:18, 20–21, 25–26) or bystanders (Acts 19:16). Furthermore, Jesus never demanded that demons give proof of their departure from a host.[153] Such differences may suggest that Philostratus did not harvest the components of his tale from Gospel accounts. However, his accounts parallel details from Jewish, pagan, and later Christian literature, so he may have been familiar with some of these sources.

Perhaps Philostratus once again borrowed a story from the *Odyssey* to flesh out his exorcism account. Two details of his story hint at this possibility: the young man who interrupted Apollonius's lecture was explicitly said to have been a descendant of Alcinous, Odysseus's host on Phaeacia, and the youth's home was Corcyra, which is probably the same place as Phaeacia in the *Odyssey*.[154] Book 8 of the *Odyssey*, which details Odysseus's visit with the Phaeacians, may provide a few parallels with this exorcism story in the *VA*. The two accounts mention a cup with handles that was used for pouring libations to the gods[155] and tell of a disrespectful youth, who challenged a visitor, was defeated by him, and later changed his perspective about him.[156] As intriguing as these commonalities are, there is unfortunately no indication of demonic activity in the Homeric passage. Still, the impertinent youth of the *Odyssey* may have served as a prototype for the demoniac Philostratus described in the *VA*.

---

153. Anderson sees similarity between *VA* 4.20 and Mark 5:1–17 (and other NT exorcisms), in that the exorcist directly addressed the demon and commanded it to leave its host. Further, the accounts give proof of the demon's departure by either knocking of a statue or stampeding a herd of pigs. See Anderson, "Folklore," 215. However, a difference here is that Apollonius commanded the demon to give proof of its departure, whereas the Gerasene demons entered the herd of swine after their expulsion on their own initiative, for Jesus had not commanded them to give proof of their exit (Mark 5:12, 13, 16). Likewise, Lucian's demons appeared as black smoke after leaving their host but did not become visible in this way because they were commanded to give proof of their exit (Lucian, *Philops.* 16).

154. Thucydides, *P.W.* 1.25.4.

155. Apollonius explains how to pour libations to the gods using a cup with handles (*VA* 4.20), while Odysseus used a "two-handled cup" (ἀμφικύπελλον; *VA* 8.89) to pour libations to the gods (ἑλὼν σπείσασκε θεοῖσιν ; *VA* 8.89).

156. In the *VA*, the demoniac laughed at and interrupted Apollonius's lecture (*VA* 4.20.1–2) but took up philosophy after the demon was expelled (*VA* 4.20.3). In the *Odyssey*, the youth Euryalus insulted the social status of the visiting Odysseus (*Od.* 8.158–64) but later made amends by giving him an incomparable sword (*Od.* 396–415).

ITEMS 8–9

The second exorcism in the *VA* (*VA* 3.38) was performed by an Indian Wise Man, not by Apollonius himself.[157] In this episode, a woman approached the healer asking his assistance with her sixteen-year-old son who had been possessed by a demon for two years. The boy's symptoms were that he was irrational, his voice was deeper than normal, and his eyes were not his own. The demon would lead the youth away into desert places so that he could not attend school and practice archery. A year before, the demon had informed the mother that he was the ghost of a man whose wife had left him. Thereafter, he hated women and decided to pursue her son instead.[158] When the Wise Man inquired if the boy was nearby, she told him that the spirit forbade the boy to accompany her and had threatened to kill her son if she went to see the holy man. The Wise Man gave the woman a letter filled with threats and rebuke to deliver to the spirit, telling her that the demon would not kill her son after he read it. This account, then, is not technically an exorcism, for neither the expulsion of the spirit nor the letter's efficacy was reported.[159]

Once again, no single Gospel account suggests itself as the source of this exorcism. A few of its features resemble fragments of Gospels stories: (1) the act was performed at a distance;[160] (2) the length of time the boy had been possessed is mentioned;[161] (3) the demon forced its host into desert regions;[162] (4) the demon threatened to do or did harm to its host;[163] (5) this account appears in the context of other healings, much like the Gospel accounts;[164] and (6) although the word "cliff" is

157. Strangely, both Twelftree (*Jesus the Exorcist*, 26) and Keener (*Miracles*, 2:782) mistakenly identified the Wise Man in this episode with Apollonius. Rather, this exorcist is one of the Indian sages that Apollonius was visiting. The mother of the demoniac claimed that she had been warned a year earlier by the demon not to come to this healer (*VA* 3.38.2); this person could not have been Apollonius since he had only just arrived at the city of the Wise Men (*VA* 34). However, other scholars correctly attribute this healing to an Indian healer. See Petzke, *Die Traditionen*, 125; Blackburn, "ΘΕΙΟΙ ΑΝΔΡΕΣ," 192.

158. Keener lists a few magical papyri that make a correlation between possession and male homosexuality. See Keener, *Miracles*, 2:782, n. 155.

159. Parker, *Demonstration*, 298; Twelftree, *Jesus the Exorcist*, 26. Petzke, however, takes for granted that the exorcism was a success. See Petzke, *Die Traditionen*, 125.

160. *VA* 3.38.3. In Mark 7:29–30, Jesus casts out a demon from a distance.

161. *VA* 3.38.1. See Mark 9:21.

162. *VA* 3.38.1. See Mark 5:2 and Matt 12:43.

163. Mark 5:5; 9:18.

164. Much like people came to Jesus for exorcisms in the company of others seeking healing from various sicknesses (Mark 1:32–34), so people came to the Indian Wise

mentioned in *VA* and the Gospels, this is probably a coincidence, for the contexts differ greatly.[165] None of these examples definitively point to reliance on the Gospels.

Two points, however, suggest that this exorcism did not derive from the Gospels. The first is that the Gospels do not speculate about the origin or nature of demons, whereas *VA* 3.38 identified this demon as the soul of a dead man. This sort of speculation could derive from certain Greco-Roman or Jewish accounts for some of them regarded possessing demons as the spirits of the human dead[166] or as the souls of the hybrid offspring of humans and angels that died in the flood.[167] A second point is that the Wise Man's method of expelling the demon with the written word contrasts with Jesus's and Apollonius's method (*VA* 4.20) of exorcising evil spirits employing the spoken word alone. In the end, nothing suggests that the story in the *VA* is based on an exorcism account in the Gospels.

Before wrapping up this section, it is worthwhile to note a few general differences between the Gospels and the two exorcism accounts in the *VA*. Jesus is reported to have cast out numerous demons, while Apollonius could only boast of expelling one. Jesus's disciples also cast out demons,[168] whereas Apollonius's followers did not. Finally, Jesus's exorcisms were at the core of his ministry for they were evidence of the coming of the Kingdom of God and the dismantling of the dominion of Beelzebub,[169] while Apollonius's expulsion had no such agenda. The number of Jesus's exorcisms and the centrality of these acts of deliverance to his mission in bringing the Kingdom of God stand in stark contrast to their near absence in the life of Apollonius.

Ones for an exorcism, the healing of a damaged hip, the preventing of miscarriage, and the preventing of death due to the consumption of wine (*VA* 3.38–40).

165. In the Gospels, the possessed swine run down a cliff (κατὰ τοῦ κρημνοῦ) into the sea (Matt 8:32; Mark 5:13; Luke 8:33). In *VA* 3.38, the demon threatened demoniac's mother with "cliffs and chasms" (κρημνοὺς καὶ βάραθρα).

166. Both Josephus and Philo expressed the opinion that demons could be the ghosts of human beings. See Ferguson, *Demonology*, 82–83, 85. Various Greek writers (e.g., Hesiod, Euripides, Plutarch, and Pausanias) also held this view. See Ferguson, *Demonology*, 35, 41–42.

167. A few Jewish works understood Gen 6:1–4 to refer the marriage of angels and human females. The offspring of this hybrid union were the giants. When these giants were drowned in the flood, their souls became evil spirits on the earth (e.g., 1 En. 15:7—16:1; Jub. 10:1–13).

168. E.g., Mark 6:7, 13; Luke 10:17–20; Acts 5:16; 8:7; 19:12.

169. Twelftree, *Jesus the Exorcist*, 218.

ITEMS 8–9

It seems, then, that two exorcisms of the *VA* were not modeled on the Gospel accounts. Perhaps the story drew on accounts taken from pagan, Jewish, or extrabiblical Christian reports of exorcism. Perhaps Philostratus drew ideas from some of the sources he used in composing the *VA* (e.g., Moiragenes) that may have mentioned Apollonius's exorcisms, but there is no extant evidence to support that suggestion. At any rate, it seems unlikely that Philostratus drew directly from the Gospels or that he sought to set Apollonius against Jesus. Had Philostratus wanted to portray Apollonius as a rival to Jesus as an exorcist the number of the Tyanean's exorcisms would likely have been more numerous.

CONCLUSION

This chapter has attempted to answer two of the issues raised in the Apollonian Decalogue: did the *VA* have an anti-Christian agenda and did the *VA* borrow Gospel materials? No clear evidence was found to support the views that the *VA* had an anti-Christian agenda or that it was reliant, either consciously or unconsciously, on the Gospels.

14

Item 10

The Temporal "Gap" between Apollonius and the Composition of the *VA*

THE ONE-HUNDRED-TWENTY-YEAR GAP BETWEEN the time of Apollonius and the writing of the *VA* is an important issue to address in the investigation of this ancient holy man. As item 10 of the Apollonian Decalogue states, "Philostratus (third century AD) may have been too far removed from the time of Apollonius (first century AD) to ensure his access to accurate information." This brief chapter will address the question of whether Philostratus could have spanned this temporal gap.

THE EXTENT OF THE GAP

The length of the historical gap between the days of Apollonius and the composition of the *VA* can be measured in several ways. Most often, this gap is measured from around the time of Apollonius's death around the year AD 100[1] and sometime after AD 217, the earliest accepted date for the composition of the *VA*. In this case, the gap would have been a bit over a hundred years long.[2] However, should the starting point

---

1. According to the *VA*, Apollonius and Nerva died about the same time. This date would have been around AD 98 (*VA* 8.27).

2. Boring, *Introduction*, 149; Votaw, *The Gospels*, 3; Meier, *Mentor*, 578–79; Boyd and Eddy, *Lord or Legend*, 57; Eddy and Boyd, *The Jesus Legend*, 151; Koskenniemi, *Apollonios*, 170.

be placed in the first half of the first century—at Apollonius's birth near the beginning of the first century AD[3] or early in his travels[4]—and should the *terminus ad quem* for the *VA* be set in the 230s or 240s, as some scholars suggest, the gap could be well over two hundred years in length. However one chooses to measure the gap, the historical distance is tremendous.

THE SIGNIFICANCE OF HISTORICAL DISTANCE

This gap is one of the more significant challenges to the historicity of the *VA*. One of the chief questions is whether Philostratus could have had access to accurate information about events that transpired a century or more before his time. This issue needs to be raised because, although some of the materials Philostratus used might have been early, they may have accumulated legendary features over this vast length of time.[5] Normally, the closer a text was written to the event it describes, the better the chances are of avoiding the pollution of the tradition. As Bart Ehrman explains, "The logic of this principle, especially when dealing with ancient sources, is that as an event gets discussed and reports about it circulate, there are greater and greater opportunities for it to be changed—until just about everyone gets it wrong. The less time that has elapsed, the less time there is for alteration and exaggeration."[6] With these two challenges in mind, it is time to consider how Philostratus might have addressed them.

HOW TO CLOSE THE GAP

Would it have been possible for Philostratus to have overcome the gap and avoid the possible intrusion of legendary materials into the sources available to him? Challenges such as these could be overcome in some

---

3. Philostratus recorded that some said Apollonius lived eighty, ninety, or over a hundred years (*VA* 8.29), thus placing his birth early in the first century.

4. The tales told by Damis allegedly began early in the first century AD (*VA* 1.19), shortly before Apollonius's encounter with Vardanes (*VA* 1.21.1–2). This is the first event by in the *VA* that is datable by extra-Philostratean sources. So then, assuming for the moment that the Damis memoir is authentic, then the gap could be measured from such an earlier encounter.

5. Keener, *Christobiography*, 241.

6. Ehrman, *The New Testament*, 242.

PART 3: INVESTIGATING THE APOLLONIAN DECALOGUE

circumstances, for several ancient biographers were able to bridge the gap between remote historical events and their own time. In a few instances, these writers were separated from the events they described by distances even greater than those faced by Philostratus, yet they were still able to produce authoritative works on their topics.

In large part, these ancient authors wrote successful biographies because they had access to sources that were written close to the time of the events they described. In some cases, these sources were from eyewitnesses, which added heft to their credibility.[7] Despite being written nearly five-hundred years after the time of Alexander's conquests, Arrian's seven-volume *Anabasis of Alexander* is regarded as one of the most reliable sources on the Macedonian conqueror because it employed a wide variety of contemporary materials.[8] Among these sources were the eyewitness accounts of Alexander's general Ptolemy, his engineer Aristobulus, and his fleet commander Nearchus.[9] In addition to these sources, Arrian used the *Royal Journals* (the *Ephemerides*) which were attributed to Eumenes, the royal secretary.[10] Although the accuracy of the *Royal Journals* has been challenged by a few modern scholars,[11] most of the objections raised against them have been addressed and the evidence seems to indicate that they were in reality daily logs of Alexander's activities (or at least extracts from them).[12] Plutarch, who also wrote a biography of Alexander the Great, was reliant on some of these same sources in his research, such as the *Royal Journals* (23.3; 77.1) and writings of Aristobulus (15.1; 16.7; 18.2; 21.9; 22.5; 46.1; 75.4).[13] Yet, most of all Plutarch took his information from the letters of Alexander (e.g., 7.1,

---

7. This is not to say that all claims of eyewitness testimony are equal or that an eyewitness cannot be mistaken, lie, or exaggerate. However, in most of the cases given here for Arrian, Plutarch, and Diogenes Laertius the sources were written by eyewitnesses and, therefore, indisputably early.

8. Keener, *Christobiography*, 246, 250.

9. Keener, *Christobiography*, 250. See Brunt's comments in Arrian, *Anabasis*, 1.xxx.

10. Keener, *Christobiography*, 250. See Brunt's comments in Arrian, *Anabasis*, 1.xiv–xxvi.

11. Both Pearson and Bosworth regard the Royal Journals as a forgery or propaganda; Pearson, "Diary," 429–39; Bosworth, "Death of Alexander," 117–21.

12. Anson, "The 'Ephemerides' of Alexander," 501–5. Here, Anson appears to answer most of the objections to the historicity of the Royal Journals that were raised by Pearson and Bosworth.

13. Plutarch employed around twenty-four sources in his treatment of Alexander. See Powell, "The Sources," 229.

4; 20.5; 22.1, 3; 23.4; 27.5; 39.3; 42.1; 55.3; 60.1, 6; 77.1).[14] Likewise, "the earliest extant, fairly full biography of Aristotle comes from Diogenes Laertius, more than half a millennium after the philosopher's death."[15] Yet, this study of the philosopher is valuable because Diogenes had access to early writings like those of Hermippas of Smyrna (third century BC) and Theocratus of Chios (310–250 BC).[16]

Ancient biographers sometimes indicated an awareness that their sources might have been compromised and unreliable. For instance, Plutarch was aware that some of his sources for figures from the distant past, like those about Theseus or Romulus, were likely shaped by poets and the makers of fables. In such cases, he claims, these sources had to be purified (Plutarch, *Thes.* 1) or, as modern scholars might put it, "demythologized." However, temporal distance was not the only cause of inaccurate sources, for ancient biographers also indicated that even eyewitness sources could sometimes be unreliable. As an illustration of this claim, both Plutarch and Arrian employed the work of Onesicritus, who was a naval pilot in Alexander's fleet, even though they were aware that this source was a mixture of true history, falsehood, and fantasy.[17] Ancient authors who were alert to untrustworthy sources would have been more likely to have written accurate biographies.

So then, under the best conditions, ancient biographers could be considered credible despite living long after the historical figures about which they wrote. In part, this was because they employed materials written close to the period being examined.[18] Furthermore, when they

14. Pearson notes that this collection of Alexander's correspondence must be treated with caution because fictitious letters certainly existed in ancient times and were sometimes mingled with authentic ones. Since students of rhetoric sometimes composed letters to or from Alexander as exercises (e.g., P. Oxy. 1.13), some of these may have been confused with authentic documents. See Pearson, "Diary," 449. Pearson regards the collection of letters used by Plutarch with suspicion but allows that the letters cited by Arrian may have been authentic. See Pearson, "Diary," 449.

15. Keener, *Christobiography*, 249.

16. Anton-Hermann, in analyzing the technique of Diogenes Laertius, notes that this ancient author probably included favorable and unfavorable accounts concerning Aristotle to appear unbiased. See Anton-Hermann, "A Brief Analysis," 97–129. As Keener notes, Hermippas still wrote about a century after Aristotle's death. See Keener, *Christobiography*, 249, n. 82. Thus, the temporal gap in this case remains about as great as that faced by Philostratus.

17. E.g., Plutarch, *Alex.* 46.1; Arrian, *Anab.* 6.2.3; *Indica* 3.6.

18. In addition to the writings of Arrian and Diogenes Laertes, Keener lists Plutarch's work *Agesilaus*, which was written long after the death of that Spartan king. See Keener, *Christobiography*, 249. However, most of Plutarch's biography of Agesilaus

were aware of the possibilities of legend, exaggeration, or falsehood in certain accounts, they were in a better position to produce a reliable biography. When it comes to Philostratus's sources, were these materials close enough to the time of Apollonius to close this gap and were they early enough to have been free of legendary development?

PHILOSTRATUS'S SOURCES AND HISTORICAL DISTANCE

Most of Philostratus's sources are of uncertain date, as the earlier chapters that treated these documents have already demonstrated. Even Philostratus did not claim or imply that these sources were early, except for Damis's diary. Perhaps a brief recap of the date of Philostratus's sources is in order.

One of Philostratus's sources consisted of oral traditions about Apollonius that he gathered from various shrines, individuals, and cities. On the one hand, some of these stories might have been ancient (VA 1.2.3). Even so, there is no guarantee that they had not accrued a patina of myth over the years. Anderson, speaking on the matter of legendary development, believes that these traditions "had had about a century in which to get completely out of hand."[19] Keener agrees that these accounts were well over a century old, "hence, beyond living memory."[20] On the other hand, there is no evidence that these tales were early; they may have even been roughly contemporary with Philostratus. These oral sources are also nearly impossible to evaluate because Philostratus did not indicate exactly where in the narrative he was drawing upon them, what they contained, or where they originated.

Another of Philostratus's sources was a book written by Maximus of Aegeae. Scholars are not certain of the date of this work; some date it to the second century[21] and some to the third.[22] As noted earlier in the book,

---

was based on Xenophon's works *Hellenica* and *Agesilaus*, with other sources playing a supplementary role. See Shipley, "Plutarch's Life of Agelsilaos," 1. Indeed, much of what Xenophon has to say about Agesilaus was probably based on his personal experiences of serving under him in 396–94 BC to which he allotted about 37 percent of his biography. See Burridge, *What are the Gospels?*, 132, 138.

19. Anderson, *Philostratus*, 124.
20. Keener, *Christobiography*, 46–47.
21. Philostratus, *Apollonius of Tyana*, 1:39, n. 7.
22. Phillimore, *In Honour*, xxiii.

Flinterman suggests that clues to the second-century rivalry between Aegeae and Tarsus run through Maximus's material. If he is correct, this would help to date the work in the second century.[23] In addition to its late date, this source contains at least one historically inaccurate statement[24] and Anderson describes several of its tales as "miraculous drivel."[25] This source is not useful in closing the gap because it is not likely to be early and its historical content is of questionable value. At any rate, Maximus's work was only employed for a short section that described the youth of Apollonius (*VA* 1.7–12) and does not play a major role in the biography.

Moiragenes's material was also difficult to date. If Moiragenes was Plutarch's contemporary,[26] then his work could be dated to the second century, but this identification is uncertain. The date of this work probably does not matter a great deal for this study, for Moiragenes probably did not serve as a major source for the *VA*. Philostratus did not regard this work as accurate and seemed more interested in correcting it than in employing it as a source (*VA* 1.3.2).

Although some of the *Letters* of Apollonius might be authentic or at least early,[27] there is a good possibility that the fourteen letters used in the *VA* were Philostratus's compositions. Yet, even if the letters he incorporated into the biography happened to be original, they merely support the narrative; they do not shape it to a great degree.

So then, the meager evidence available for dating and evaluating the reliability of these sources suggests that most of the ones mentioned above would not have been written close to the time of Apollonius (except perhaps some of the *Letters of Apollonius*) and that some of them may have been vulnerable to development. In the end, only the Damis memoir holds the promise of providing a window into the real Apollonius for it claims to have been the work of his first-century contemporary.[28]

---

23. Flinterman, *Power*, 69.

24. Philostratus, apparently drawing on Maxiumus as a source here, incorrectly mentions the execution of the governor of Cilicia (*VA* 1.12).

25. Anderson, *Philostratus*, 124.

26. Plutarch, *Quaest. Conv.* 4.6.

27. Keener, *Christobiography*, 47.

28. Perhaps the works of Moiragenes and Maximus could have been shown to draw on earlier sources had they survived.

PART 3: INVESTIGATING THE APOLLONIAN DECALOGUE

ATTEMPTS TO BRIDGE THE HISTORICAL GAP WITH THE DAMIS MEMOIR

Several researchers contend that the gap between the historical Apollonius and the composition date of the *VA* is easily bridged because Philostratus had access to a first-century document: the Damis memoir.[29] Philostratus certainly claimed that Julia had given him a document that was written by a close disciple of Apollonius. If Philostratus in truth had a reliable, eyewitness account in hand, such an account would certainly help to close the distance between the first and third centuries provided it was accurate.

However, even if one accepts the claim that Damis's *Scrapbook* is authentic, this does not guarantee the historical accuracy of a document. This is because, as Keener points out, even an eyewitness might be biased, limited in vantage point, incompetent, or disagree with the reports of other eyewitnesses.[30] An eyewitness account might increase the odds of having access to reliable information, but even eyewitness testimony does not ensure accuracy. If, for the sake of argument, this diary existed, how well would it have fared in each of these areas?

Assuming for the moment that the Damis source existed and that the essence of its content was unaltered by Philostratus's editing, the material it presents does not appear to have been particularly biased. Although Damis's fawning admiration for his master could be interpreted as a sort of bias, this is not necessarily a fair conclusion. Many ancient biographers admired the figures about which they wrote and sought to honor them.[31] Damis is portrayed as preserving the words of his master because he believed that they were important (*VA* 1.19.3). However, there is no evidence of bias or external pressure that might have influenced his

---

29. Votaw, *The Gospels*, 21; Petzke, *Die Traditionen*, 234.

30. Keener, *Christobiography*, 244. As examples some of these categories from this entry, Keener gives several sources. As an example of contradictory early witnesses, he points out that after just forty years of Galba's assassination, writers were not agreed upon who had killed him. He also notes examples of incompetence (Strabo, *Geogr.* 2.5.10) and suspected dishonesty (Lucian, *Hist. cons.*, 25, 29). In addition to Keener's examples in this latter category, one could add Onesicritus is an example of an inaccurate eyewitness source when it came to relating certain events from the campaign of Alexander the Great. Both Plutarch and Arrian cited him, but with the awareness that he was not always reliable.

31. Several examples of biographers that admired the figures about which they wrote can be cited, including the Gospel writers (e.g., Xenophon, *Memorabilia* and *Agesilaus*; Philo, *Life of Moses*; Lucian, *Demonax*).

document. Philostratus does not mention that Damis had a patron who might have pressured him to depict Apollonius in a particular manner; instead, Damis supposedly created his notebook on his own initiative. Further, there is no strong indication in the *VA* that Damis intended for his *Scrap Book* to be published, although his aim of preserving information about Apollonius might hint at that objective (*VA* 1.19.3). If publication was Damis's goal, apparently this did not occur, for Philostratus claimed that his journal was unknown until the time of Julia Domna (*VA* 1.3.1). Overall, Philostratus's description would suggest that the work was free of bias.

Perhaps Damis's vantage point was limited to some degree, as might be suggested by several gaps in the story of Apollonius. For example, Damis did not relate information concerning Apollonius's youth; Maximus of Aegeae appears to have been Philostratus's source for most of that period. Damis was also absent from several episodes during the adult life of his master. Further, his narrative ended before the death of Apollonius. Yet, surely Damis could be forgiven such omissions when he served as the source of "nineteen-twentieths of Philostratus's biography."[32] In most episodes within the narrative, Damis was at Apollonius's side for nearly five decades, recording his every word (*VA* 1.19.3).

Was Damis competent as an eyewitness? Perhaps Damis could be described as incompetent in that his literary style was poor, yet Philostratus called Damis's account "clear" and detailed (*VA* 1.3.1; 1.19.3). Perhaps Damis could be deemed incompetent because he was gullible or misinterpreted events. After all, Philostratus sometimes seemed hesitant to relate some of Damis's tales (*VA* 1.25.6) or to offer an alternative explanation to that offered by Damis (*VA* 4.45.2). But, for the most part, Philostratus appears to endorse Damis's version of events and does not appear to find his account to be in tension with other sources about Apollonius.[33] If Philostratus had not regarded this account as authoritative, he probably would not have made it the foundation of the biography.

The memoir, as Philostratus would have his readers believe, does quite well in most respects, for he depicts it as the word of an eyewitness, free of bias, and as an accurate version of events from the life of Apollonius. If these facts are correct, then the Damis diary just might be the

---

32. Votaw, *The Gospels*, 21.

33. Philostratus did note discrepancies concerning the circumstances of Apollonius's death, but this was not a part of the Damis account.

means of spanning the temporal gap between Apollonius's time and the date of the *VA*'s composition.

Unfortunately, the document fails in that several details in the Damis material make it nearly impossible to accept as an eyewitness account unless the witness was incompetent or a liar. The greatest challenge to an eyewitness claim was presented earlier in the exploration of item 6 of the Apollonian Decalogue, where several Damis accounts were shown to be inaccurate in terms of history and geography; basic accuracy would have been expected in the case of an eyewitness. In his journey to the east, Damis did not view Babylon in its grandeur (*VA* 1.25, 30), for that city was in ruins in the first century. He did not spot a hippopotamus in the Indus River, for that was not the habitat for that creature (*VA* 2.19.1; cf. 6.1.1). Unless one allows for paranormal entities or events, he did not witness genuine levitation of Indian sages (*VA* 3.15, 17), and he did not encounter an *empusa* at Corinth (*VA* 4.25). On his Egyptian and Ethiopian journey, he did not view the still-intact colossus of Memnon—for it was broken from the waist up in the first century—and he certainly did not hear it speak or see it rise to greet the sun (*VA* 6.4.2–3). Damis was also confused about the geography of the Nile (*VA* 6.26) and, most likely, wrong about the existence of the Gymnosophists who lived along its banks in Ethiopia (*VA* 6.5–23). Therefore, the Damis memoir is unlikely to have been the report of an eyewitness.

As noted earlier in this study, two options appear most likely: either the *Scrap Book* was a Philostrataen fiction or Philoastratus possessed a forged document. In neither of these cases is the document useful in bridging the gap. In terms of date, neither scenario seems hopeful. If Philostratus pretended that there was a document, then the contents attributed to it would date to his time in the third century; if the document was a pseudepigraph, although one of uncertain date, it only came to light in the third century under suspicious circumstances. The alleged source fails the test in terms of bias. If the Damis document were composed by Philostratus, it would not likely be entirely free from his biases or those of his patron, as was discussed in an earlier chapter of the book. If the document were a forgery by a relative of Damis or someone else, although it was unlikely to have been written under pressure from a patron, its author might have written it for Empress Julia assuming he knew of her impending visit to Tyana and her interest in Apollonius. As to the matter of the accuracy of the material recorded in the memoir, several major issues remain, whether one believes the diary to be fiction or a pseudepigraph. The so-called Damis material is the only source to present Apollonius as a philosopher rather than a magician or a magician-philosopher before the time of Philostratus; this strongly suggests that Philostratus was involved here in revisionist history. Another nagging issue is that no extra-Philostratean materials from the first century or early second century confirm most of the claims about Apollonius recorded in the *VA* and the memoir allegedly behind it. This leaves several questions unanswered, such as whether Apollonius truly visited India and Ethiopia or ever met Vespasian and Titus. In the end, the Damis document is unable to bridge the chronological gap between the Tyanean and his biography.

15

Summary and Concluding Remarks Concerning the Apollonian Decalogue

THE APOLLONIAN DECALOGUE

THE RESULTS OF THE study of the Apollonius Decalogue are now complete. While the conclusions drawn from this investigation will not satisfy all Apollonius scholars, hopefully, most will agree that this study identified the key issues that needed to be discussed in approaching the historical Apollonius, pointed the reader to useful resources for further investigation of this figure, and treated the various viewpoints of scholars charitably.

In treating the first two items of the Decalogue, three pre-Philostratean texts that referred to Apollonius and were not used as sources in the *VA* were examined (Lucian, Dio Cassius, and *On Sacrifices*). Aspects of the data from these sources cohered with the claims of the *VA*; Apollonius performed at least one miracle (Dio Cassius), had a disciple (Lucian), and appeared to be a philosopher of some sort (Lucian; fragment *On Sacrifices*). However, there were also departures from the *VA*. Two authors regarded Apollonius as a disreputable magician or charlatan (Lucian and Dio Cassius), a view that is opposed to Philostratus's claim that Apollonius was only a philosopher. Further, the fragment *On Sacrifices* claimed that Apollonius only allowed spiritual offerings to the supreme deity, whereas the *VA* allowed for non-bloody offerings.

Items 3 and 4 of the Decalogue dealt with the pre-Philostratean sources, excluding the Damis document, that were used in the composition of the *VA*. Several of these sources supported the view of the *VA* that Apollonius was a philosopher of some sort (Moiragenes, *Letters of Apollonius*) and that he had supernatural powers (Dio Chrysostom, Moiragenes, *Letters of Apollonius*, Maximus). Yet, the *Letters of Apollonius* disagreed with the *VA* over Apollonius's practice of bathing, attendance at the Olympic games, and his belief in the transmigration of souls. Most significantly, he was called a magician in two of these sources, although these writers still seemed to have had a favorable opinion of him (Moiragenes and *Letters of Apollonius*).

Item 5 of the Decalogue examined whether the evidence for the existence of Damis and his memoir were plausible. The investigation yielded no solid evidence for the existence of Damis but also noted that this lacuna in the historical record might not be overly problematic because many ancient figures were mentioned only once. Likewise, many of the arguments for and against the possibility of Damis's memoir were inconclusive. This chapter left open the possibility that the memoir may have been written by Damis himself, a forger, or Philostratus. Whatever the case, Philostratus's hand was evident in the document's incorporation into the *VA*: he was either its editor or its creator.

However, the exploration of the historical and geographical errors in the *VA* (item 6) helped to narrow the options just mentioned. The document was filled with historical and geographical errors. While some of these mistakes can be attributed to Philostratus, some of these were found in accounts attributed to Damis. The most damaging material to the Damis theory dealt with paranormal activities, mythical flora and fauna, non-existent cities and peoples, and the location of hippos in the Indus River. These mistakes suggest that Damis's "memoir" was either a forgery or the creation of Philostratus because it is implausible that a first-century eyewitness would have made too many errors.

Items 7 and 8 both dealt with the various agendas of the *VA*, while items 8 and 9 overlapped in addressing the relationship of the *VA* to Christianity. The investigation of item 7 concluded that the agenda of the *VA* was largely apologetic and encomiastic. The apologetic agenda attempted to shift Apollonius's reputation from that of a magician to that of a philosopher. The encomiastic agenda exaggerated the tale of the

PART 3: INVESTIGATING THE APOLLONIAN DECALOGUE

Tyanean so that he was the best philosopher of all times and the greatest world traveler. Neither of these agendas help the case that Philostratus aimed at an accurate historical portrayal of his protagonist. Little evidence was discovered for the promotion of a pagan religious, political, or philosophical agenda, although elements of these were not entirely ruled out. Likewise, the investigation discovered no clear evidence for either an anti-Christian agenda for the *VA* (item 8) or that it borrowed ideas from the Gospels (item 9).

The tenth item of the Apollonian Decalogue showed that while there was substantial evidence that a temporal gap could have been overcome by a genuine first-century document, the Damis document was unlikely to have come from an eyewitness of that period, largely because its historical accuracy was poor in many respects. None of Philostratus's other sources could be shown to have dated to the first century AD.

These findings have several ramifications for students of the New Testament. The assumption that the *VA* accurately portrays a first-century version of Apollonius is questionable. This is because (1) other early sources challenge or contradict aspects of the *VA*'s portrayal of Apollonius in the third century AD, (2) the portrayal of Apollonius in the *VA* is likely to be due to the apologetic and encomiastic agenda of Philostratus, and (3) the *VA*, while not entirely unreliable historically, contains many historical errors and it therefore unlikely to have been based on eye-witness testimony or to be an unquestionably reliable source for Apollonius or other first-century events.

For these reasons, the *VA* should be used with care by those exploring the topic of Apollonius. Both biblical and classical scholars should be aware that they are looking at this figure through the lens of Philostratus's agenda, an agenda which is not the only perspective about Apollonius that has survived from antiquity. Biblical scholars should also be aware that the Apollonius of the *VA*, who is often compared to the first-century Jesus, may be largely a third-century reimaging of the historical Apollonius. Researchers should be wary of studies that rely heavily on the Philostratean account of Apollonius because of the possibility that this depiction is inaccurate. This study suggests that the best way to address the topic of Apollonius is for authors and teachers to mention or discuss the items in the Apollonian Decalogue so that their readers and students will be up to speed, whatever their perspective. Hopefully, the day is passing in which New Testament scholars unquestioningly accept that the *VA* is historically reliable.

SUMMARY AND CONCLUDING REMARKS

APOLLONIUS AS A HISTORICAL FIGURE

This study concludes that Apollonius of Tyana did exist and was a contemporary of Jesus and his apostles. Many of the sources portray him as a magician of some sort and indicate that he had some association with philosophy, most likely Pythagoreanism. However, apart from the claims of Philostratus, there is no solid evidence that he interacted with major political, religious, and philosophical figures of his day, that he traveled beyond a few cities in Asia Minor and perhaps Greece, or that he was exceptionally well-known in his own era.[1] Apollonius's absence from the earliest historical records could have been because (1) he was not particularly famous, (2) authors felt the need to distance themselves from him for some reason (e.g. his reputation as a magician), or (3) the ancient historical records that would have spoken about him did not survive.

This study took the view that the Damis memoir was not an eyewitness source from the first century—because of its many inaccuracies—but was rather either a later forgery or the product of Philostratus's imagination. The internal evidence of the *VA* leaned slightly in favor view that Philostratus employed a real document because he appears to have differed with it in terms of viewpoint (e.g., magic) and seems to have struggled to incorporate some content into his narrative. If the forgery theory is correct, Philostratus may have believed that this document was genuine. Alternately, he may have realized that it was a pseudepigraphical source and used it anyway because Julia commissioned him to edit it.

The *VA* was not the first source to refer to Apollonius, but it was the first source to claim that Apollonius was a philosopher and defend him against the charge of being a magician. Philostratus's positive perspective on the sage forever changed how Apollonius would be remembered in history. Nevertheless, history left enough early fragmentary sources about Apollonius as a sorcerer to challenge Philostratus's more positive view and to allow those who are interested to reinvestigate Apollonius afresh. This book is written in hopes that the information found therein will aid a future generation of authors and researchers in being responsible about their claims concerning Apollonius and their comparisons of Apollonius to Jesus. Hopefully this work will also assist those who are approaching Apollonius for the first time.

1. As John Chrysostom summed up Apollonius's career, he was famous "In a tiny part of the world, and for a short time" (Hom. 4.8.198). Eusebius agreed with this assessment: "he is not remembered by certain of our contemporaries even as a philosopher, let alone as a holy, miraculous, and remarkable man" (*Hier.* 36)

Part 4

Apollonius and Jesus

16

The Sources for Apollonius and Jesus Compared

INTRODUCTION

MOST LIKELY, MANY READERS of this book were never truly interested in learning more about Apollonius as a historical figure but rather were interested in him only insofar as he compares to Jesus. Perhaps this chapter will reward the patience of such readers.

A few words should be said about what the objectives of this chapter are and are not. This chapter will not attempt to discover the truth about the supernatural claims made about these two figures in the extant traditions (e.g., Was Jesus divine? Did Jesus rise from the dead? Did Apollonius truly possess the gift of second sight?). Furthermore, this chapter will not attempt to prove the veracity of the historical claims made about both figures although the sources explored in this study could arguably lay the cornerstone for such historical investigations. Rather this chapter's goals are more modest. It will simply investigate the claims made by the traditions about both figures with respect to their (1) quantity (do sufficient sources exist so that traditions can be compared to one another?); (2) date (were the sources composed near to the time of the events they describe?); (3) independence (did the authors of these works collude with other sources?); (4) consistency with other traditions (do the sources contradict one another?); (5) internal consistency (does a source contradict itself?); and (6) biases (are the sources relatively free of bias?). Although sources that meet these standards are not necessarily true from a historical standpoint, they would at least tend to be more reliable in reconstructing past events.

The need for such a method of examining sources can be illustrated by the claim of some New Testament scholars that much more can be known about Apollonius than Jesus. At least two scholars, Votaw and Boring, have asserted that more can be known, biographically speaking, about figures like Epictetus and Apollonius than about Jesus.[1] This, they argue, is because of (1) the quality of the material available for these two figures; the method of verbatim note-taking that Arrian and Damis used to preserve the teachings of their masters was more accurate than the method employed by the anonymous tradents who passed down oral traditions about Jesus; and (2) the quantity of material available for these figures; Arrian and Damis respectively preserved material about their teachers that was about twice the length of all four canonical Gospels. According to this view, the quality and quantity of the material that attests to the words and deeds of Apollonius is far superior to that which is available for Jesus.

This argument for the superiority of the Apollonian material can be challenged in several ways. One potential flaw in this reasoning is the assumption that oral tradition cannot accurately preserve wording or traditions nearly as well as written records. In his book *Christobiography*, Keener dedicates several chapters to a discussion of the pros and cons of oral tradition as a vehicle for preserving information in antiquity. He demonstrates that in some cases oral tradition accurately preserved information and that it was certainly capable of doing so in the short interval between the time of Jesus and the composition of the Gospels.[2] In terms of quality, then, the oral materials that stand behind the Gospels were quite capable of preserving accurate traditions about Jesus. As an addendum to this point, written traditions have problems of their own. For instance, written traditions can accurately preserve inaccurate traditions. Furthermore, authors who were also eyewitnesses could be mistaken, biased, or liars. Both oral and written traditions need to be

---

1. Votaw, *The Gospels*, 14, 29; Boring, *Introduction*, 468–69.
2. Keener, *Christobiography*, 369–496.

evaluated with care; neither type of tradition should get a free pass when it comes to historical value.

Another flaw in this argument is that Boring and Votaw have placed the traditions preserved by Arrian and Damis on equal footing. While neither the fact nor the accuracy of Arrian's notes taken in Epictetus's lectures hall is disputed here, both Votaw and Boring have assumed too much in regarding Damis as a historical figure and as a first-rate notetaker for (1) neither the existence of Damis nor his notebook can currently be substantiated (both Arrian and his writings are well-attested);[3] (2) the many inaccuracies in material attributed to Damis in the *VA* do not inspire confidence that his alleged account preserves accurate biographical material about Apollonius; this point lends weight to the theories that either the notebook was a forgery that contained inaccuracies or that Philostratus wrote the Damis material himself and is himself responsible for these flaws; and (3) there is no solid proof that Damis practiced stenographic notetaking beyond the claim of the *VA* (1.19.3). With respect to the last point, evidence for differences in style is demonstrable between the writings of Arrian (the student) and Epictetus (his instructor),[4] whereas the style of Philostratus and Damis in the *VA* are virtually indistinguishable. Perhaps this is because Philostratus edited the Damis document as he claimed (*VA* 1.3.1), in which case all proof of his reworking the notebook has been erased. However, it is also possible that the style of Damis and Philostratus is indistinguishable because the sophist invented the material attributed to Damis.[5] Since there is no

---

3. Arrian is mentioned by several ancient authors (Lucian, *Alex* 2; Dio Cassius, H*ist. rom.* 15.1). Arrian's literary output was also substantial: *Alanica, Anabasis, Bithyniaca, Discourses of Epitetus, Enchiridion of Epictetus, Conversations with Epictetus, Cynegeticus, History of the Diadochi, Indica, Tactica, Parthica*, and *Periplus Maris Eyxini*.

4. Some of the differences between Arrian and Epictetus are that (1) Arrian composed his works in Attic Greek, whereas Epictetus's words are preserved in Koine Greek; and, (2) their use of prepositions and other features is markedly different; Oldfather, *Epictetus*, 1:xiii. However, the differences between Damis and Philostratus are more difficult to assess. It is true that Philostratus claimed Damis had a crude style that differed from his own and that Apollonius had a distinct idiom. Unfortunately, these differences in style are no longer possible to demonstrate because Philostratus would have erased any evidence of Damis's or Apollonius's *ipsissma verba* in his thorough revision of this notebook if it existed.

5. Interestingly, a kindred question could be raised about the similarities between the content of material attributed to Apollonius and Philostratus. In the *VA*, Apollonius and Philostratus (as narrator) quote the same authors and stories with about the same frequency, perhaps suggesting that Philostratus has placed his own words in Apollonius's mouth on several occasions. In books I–III of the *VA*, the narrator quoted

recourse to the actual words of Damis, there is no proof that he practiced stenographic notetaking, as these scholars have assumed above. The evidence for Damis as a careful notetaker is consequently speculative.

A final challenge to the claim that more can be known about Apollonius than Jesus is that Votaw and Boring scholars myopically focused on the *VA* as a source and did not interact with the full range of materials that are available for the study of these two figures. Had they done so, the discrepancies between the various accounts and the *VA* might have led them to question the quality of Philostratus's information.[6] Furthermore, a broader investigation of the evidence for Jesus, some of which is rather early and consistent, might have given them a more positive view of the material that was preserved about him. Although the massive *VA* easily makes Apollonius the clear winner over Jesus when it comes to the quantity of information, quantity does not matter as much as the quality of information when it comes to historical research.

What the remaining pages of this chapter seek to investigate is whether the historical (or biographical) material available for the study of the historical Jesus is inferior to, comparable to, or superior to the sources available for researching the historical Apollonius. This decision will be explored by examining the data in light of the six criteria mentioned above.

CRITERIA FOR COMPARING SOURCES ABOUT APOLLONIUS AND JESUS

The criteria that will be used to compare the available sources for these two figures will be based on methods normally used in historical research to determine which sources or traditions are most useful in reconstructing events. This investigation will adopt the six methodological principles suggested by Bart Ehrman for approaching historical sources:

---

or alluded to classical sources 26 times to Apollonius's 15 times. In books IV–VIII, 23 classical sources are used by the narrator and 61 by Apollonius. Both the narrator and Apollonius are aware of the history of the battle of Arginusae (4.32, which was probably based on Xenophon's *Hellenica*) and of the story of Phaedra and Hippolytus (4.3, probably based on Euripides's *Hippolytus stephanephoros*). For this information, see Bowie, "Quotation of Earlier Texts," 63.

6. The discrepancies within the text of the *VA* itself might also cause one to question the accuracy of this work. Several of these will be treated later in the chapter.

... historians would agree that for reconstructing a past event the ideal situation would be to have sources that (a) are numerous, so that they can be compared to one another; (b) derive from a time near the event itself, so that they are less likely to have been based on hearsay or legend; (c) were produced independently of one another, so that their authors were not in collusion; (d) do not contradict one another, so that one or more of them is not necessarily in error; (e) are internally consistent, suggesting a basic concern for reliability; and (f) are not biased toward the subject matter, so that their authors have not skewed their accounts to serve their own purposes.[7]

These principles will serve as guideposts for this investigation. They will also be used as section headings throughout the remainder of this chapter in which the materials for the Tyanean and the Nazarene are compared.

Sources Are Numerous, so That They Can Be Compared to One Another

The best scenario for reconstructing a historical event is one in which a researcher has numerous sources to examine. One reason for this is that multiple sources allow for the comparison of details. Although a single source could in theory preserve accurate information about the past, multiple sources often aid in confirming or rejecting historical claims.[8] So then, when multiple, independent sources agree on a particular detail, historians would consider this information stronger evidence for that detail than information supported by a single witness.[9]

Another benefit of having multiple sources is that they may provide varying perspectives on a historical figure or event. For instance, some accounts might be favorably disposed toward an ancient figure, while others might be disinterested or hostile. Some researchers have even suggested that neutral[10] or hostile sources constitute stronger evidence than a friendly source, for the issue of bias would be likely removed.[11] Admit-

---

7. Ehrman, *The New Testament*, 236.

8. Ehrman, *The New Testament*, 236.

9. Habermas writes that a claim "attested to by multiple independent witnesses is usually considered stronger than the testimony of one witness" (Habermas, *Case for the Resurrection*, 40).

10. Ehrman, *Did Jesus Exist?*, 41.

11. Habermas and Licona state, "Affirmation by a neutral or hostile source is usually considered stronger than affirmation from a friendly source, since bias in favor of the

tedly, hostile sources could provide insights that might be overlooked, ignored, or hidden by authors who were sympathetic toward their subject. However, a genuinely hostile source, while potentially useful, might not be free of bias itself for it might tend to exaggerate or demonize its subject.[12] Therefore, hostile sources should not necessarily be privileged over favorable ones, for an account from an admirer or follower of a historical figure, although perhaps biased in some ways, might preserve accurate information that was not available to outsiders. At the very least, both favorable and unfavorable reports may aid the historian in gaining a more accurate description of a historical figure.[13] The issues of multiple sources for Jesus and Apollonius and the biases of these sources will be revisited later in this chapter, but these are broached here simply to assure the reader that there are sufficient sources, both favorable and unfavorable, for conducting this study.

A quick review of the sources available for the study of Apollonius is probably in order even though these have already been discussed in detail in earlier chapters of this book. Some of these sources are rather brief, amounting to only a few lines of text (Lucian, *Alexander*; *On Sacrifices*; Dio Cassius, *Hist. rom.*). In other cases, the original documents have been lost (Moiragenes, Maximus), but have been referenced and described by later sources (Origen, *VA*). Still, other sources are substantial (*Letters*; *VA*). These sources will supply the rudiments for reconstructing a rough biography of Apollonius of Tyana.

Numerous sources are also available for the study of the historical Jesus. These include the New Testament corpus (especially the four Gospels[14] and the Pauline writings), Christian documents of the late first century (1 Clement), Christian works of the second century (Ignatius, the Epistle of Barnabas, Quadratus, and Hegesippus),[15] and extrabiblical materials

---

person or position is absent" (Habermas and Licona, *The Case for the Resurrection*, 40).

12. As was shown earlier in chapter 8 of this study, several modern scholars accused Lucian of exaggeration and of demonizing Alexander of Abonoteichus.

13. Sanders and Davies, *Synoptic Gospels*, 302.

14. Depending on one's view of the Synoptic Problem, further sources might be added to the list of canonical Gospels. Scholars who endorse the Two Source or Four Source Hypothesis could add Q (perhaps distinguishing Q^1 from Q^2), L, and M to this list. However, the case would be viewed differently by those holding to other hypotheses (e.g., the Griesbach and Farrer Hypotheses). Due to disagreements over the existence of this source, Q is not considered as a source in this study.

15. An explanation for why these Christian sources were included in this study and others were excluded will be provided a bit later in this chapter.

(Tacitus, Suetonius, Josephus, and Lucian). These sources should provide sufficient material for evaluating elements of the historical Jesus.

Sources Derive from a Time Near the Event Itself, so That They Are Less Likely to Have Been Based on Hearsay or Legend

Habermas and Licona explain the importance of this principle for historians: "early testimony from very close to the event in question is usually considered more reliable than one received years after the event."[16] The distance between the time of an event and its recording needs to be taken into consideration when conducting historical research because a tradition might become vulnerable to intentional or unintentional distortion during a long interval of time.

The alterations that might take place in a tradition over time could take many forms. Somewhat like the incremental growth of a snowball rolling downhill, a tradition might slowly accumulate additional, inaccurate details as it moved through time. In other instances, rather than a tradition growing in size, important details could be lost, suppressed, or modified by their tradents.[17] More to the point of the current study, some scholars believe that the earliest testimony is most useful in historical investigations because it tends to be free of theological development in the case of traditions about Jesus[18] or of character development in the case of Apollonian traditions (e.g., transforming Apollonius from a sorcerer into a sophist or a divinity).[19] As a rule, then, earlier sources are better than late ones when it comes to historical research.

---

16. Habermas and Licona, *The Case for the Resurrection*, 40.

17. Barr, notes that some traditions might be altered as they are "filtered through later concerns" of other authors. See Barr, *Introduction*, 465.

18. Ehrman regards some of the claims of the Gospel of John to be due to later theological reflection on the Jesus tradition. Examples of these would be that Jesus was a preexistent figure who came to live among men (John 1:1–14), he was equal to God (John 10:30), or that he who had seen Jesus had seen the Father (John 14:8). See Ehrman, *The New Testament*, 244–45. Other scholars see this differently, for other early sources said similar things about Jesus. Paul, the earliest source for Jesus, made similar statements about Jesus's equality to God, his preexistence and his taking the form of a servant (Phil 2:6–7). Sayings in the Synoptic Gospels—or perhaps Q—sometimes resemble sayings in the Gospel of John. For instance, both traditions claim that one knows the Father through Jesus (Matt 11:27; Luke 10:22).

19. Since Philostratus's presentation of Apollonius differed from the earlier views of him as a magician that had been given by Lucian, Moiragenes, and his contemporary Dio Cassius, he appears to be creating a different version of Apollonius.

PART 4: APOLLONIUS AND JESUS

How historians determine which traditions are early enough or too late for inclusion in historical research is subjective. After all, there is no clear standard that can be used by historians to determine the precise moment at which the distance between an event and the source reporting the event is too late to preserve credible information. Should the limit for accurate reporting be set at a decade, a century, or two centuries?[20] There are no definitive answers to these questions. For the sake of simplicity, this study will utilize two categories for sorting the available materials: first-tier and second-tier sources.

The term "first-tier" will refer to sources that appear within a century of the times of Jesus and Apollonius. This period of a century is adopted from Ehrman's discussion of historical materials.[21] His justification for selecting this length of time is that "[s]ources produced much later than this are almost certainly based on hearsay and legend rather than reliable historical memory."[22] In the case of Jesus, viable traditions would fall approximately between AD 30 and AD 130; for Apollonius, dates would range from about AD 100 to 200. In both cases, the countdown begins around the time of the respective deaths of these figures.

---

20. Biographers of Muhammad work with documents written centuries after his time. The Quran itself does not provide much personal information about Muhammad, so scholars are reliant on later sources for such information. Muhammad lived from AD 570–632, yet the first biography of Muhammad was written by Ibn Ishaq (d. AD 765). Regrettably, Ibn Ishaq's work survives only in an edited version produced by Ibn Hisham (d. AD 833). Another biographer of Muhammad was Al-Waqadi (AD 747–823), who was also separated by quite some time from his subject. The *ahadith*, which are regarded as the most authoritative sources for Muhammad according to most Muslims, were collected by figures like Al-Bukhari (d. AD 810–70) and Muslim ibn al-Hajjaj (d. AD 875). Al-Tabari also preserved a great deal of biographical information about Muhammad in his writings (d. AD 839–923). Thus, in the case of Muhammad where early sources are lacking, historians have been forced to deal with the material that is available even if it was written a century or more later than the subject it concerns.

21. Although setting the terminus for the likelihood of historical accuracy in traditions is subjective, at some point such a boundary must be set. Most scholars would probably agree that after a certain period the quest for early and independent traditions in centuries-old sources must be abandoned. In the case of Jesus, sources like the later church fathers and the Talmud are unlikely to contain independent, early traditions, although they may still be significant in some respects. Likewise, there is probably little new information to be learned about the historical Apollonius from later sources like Porphyry, Hierocles, the magical papyri, and Arabic traditions. Furthermore, sources like Hierocles and Porphyry are less valuable as historical source because they seem to have based their ideas on the *VA* itself.

22. Ehrman, *The New Testament*, 236. Keener also suggests that materials over a century old are beyond living memory. See Keener, *Christobiography*, 46–47.

However, some researchers may call foul on this study for limiting the timeframe for sources to a century because such a narrow range of dates would exclude two of the most important sources for the study of Apollonius: Philostratus's *VA* and the statements of Dio Cassius. As a concession to this viewpoint, this study will also examine a second tier of material: sources that were written within a century and a half of Apollonius and Jesus. This expanded timeframe will allow for the addition of Jesus sources dating up until AD 180 and for Apollonius AD 250 will be the terminus. This approach will allow for the inclusion of the *VA* and Dio Cassius in the study for Apollonius and will also allow for the inclusion of passages from Lucian[23] and Hegesippus for the historical Jesus. A distinction between the two tiers of material will be maintained in the following analysis.

In the remainder of this subsection, the reader will note a disparity between the amount of space dedicated to the discussion of the dates and contents of the Jesus material and the space allotted to the Apollonian sources. Numerous pages of this book have already been devoted to establishing the dates and content of the Apollonian materials, so only a brief refresher will be provided for the reader at the end of this section. However, the dates and content of the Jesus materials have not been discussed at all so far. Consequently, a thorough treatment of the sources about Jesus is necessary to balance out what has already been presented about the sources for Apollonius and to build a solid foundation for comparing the two bodies of material.

Several solid sources of information about Jesus fall within a century of his crucifixion, the earliest of which comes from the apostle Paul. Although many readers are familiar with the epistles of Paul, perhaps they have not noted that the apostle preserved a sizable cache of biographical information concerning Jesus. The search for sources about Jesus in the writings of Paul is complicated by the scholarly debate over which of the letters attributed to the apostle the NT are authentic,[24] yet, whatever view one prefers concerning the disputed works, all these works still date from

23. Lucian contains one of the latest references to Jesus that is used in this study, while Lucian also supplies the very first historical reference to Apollonius.

24. Although most contemporary scholars seem to think Paul did not compose all the letters attributed to him in the New Testament, some reputable academics hold that all thirteen letters are ultimately from the mind of Paul. For instance, Witherington points out that many of the objections raised against Pauline authorship could be explained by his use of amanuensis, by his ability to vary style and language to fit differing situations, and, in the case of the Pastorals, by his desire as an aging apostle to leave behind instruction to and provide structure for his churches. See Witherington, *Invitation*, 237–53. Similar views are expressed by Johnson, *The Writings*, 240–42.

PART 4: APOLLONIUS AND JESUS

the first century and, at the very least, stand within the Pauline tradition. To simplify the argument as it relates to authentic Pauline materials, most of the Jesus traditions below are taken from the universally accepted letters of Paul,[25] but these works may occasionally be supported by letters whose authenticity is disputed by some scholars.

Paul's writings contain a wide array of biographical details about Jesus. Some of these statements are quite early, for not only do his letters predate the four Gospels[26] but some of the traditions about Jesus embedded in them harken back to a time before Paul's conversion and perhaps, in some cases, to the ministry of Jesus.[27] A brief survey of these statements about Jesus reveals that some of them are generic in that they would have been true of many Jews of that era.[28] But other details that relate to Jesus's family,[29] ministry,[30] and passion[31] are particular to him.

25. I.e., Romans, 1 Corinthians, 2 Corinthians, Galatians, Philippians, 1 Thessalonians, and Philemon.

26. Much of the material in this paragraph concerning historical details about Jesus in Paul is indebted the material found in the following works: Eddy and Boyd, *Jesus Legend*, 209; Stout, *The "Man Jesus Christ,"* 189–91; Ehrman, *The New Testament*, 240, 424; Sanders and Davies, *Synoptic Gospels*, 323–30.

27. Paul claims to have received these traditions from others before him (1 Cor 11:23; 15:3). Some, like Riesner, contend that Paul passed down oral tradition that may date back before Easter. See Riesner's discussion in Porter and Dyer, *The Synoptic Problem*, 97–99. Others would also date these traditions to shortly after the crucifixion of Jesus in the early AD 30s. See Habermas, *Ancient Evidence*, 125.

28. Jesus was a male, a descendant of Abraham (Gal 3:17), an Israelite (Rom 9:5), "born of a woman" (Gal 4:4), and he was brought up under the Law (Gal 4:4).

29. The biographical details that Paul records about Jesus's family, which are also mentioned by later Gospels, are that he was of Davidic lineage (Rom 1:3; 15:12; 2 Tim 3:8; Matt 1:1–6; Luke 3:31) and had several brothers (1 Cor 9:5; John 7:3), one of whom was named James (Gal 1:5; Mark 6:3).

30. Paul mentions that Jesus was a servant to the Jewish people (Rom 15:8; Matt 10:6; 15:24) and that he had twelve disciples (1 Cor 15:7; Mark 3:13–19). One of these followers was named John (Gal 2:9; Mark 1:17); another was named Cephas (1 Cor 15:7; John 1:42). Paul also adds that Peter was married (1 Cor 9:5; Mark 1:30).

31. Paul records that Jesus instituted a supper (1 Cor 11:23–25; Matt 26:26–28), was delivered up that same night (1 Cor 11:23; Matt 26:25, 48), stood trial before Pontius Pilate (1 Tim 6:13; Matt 27:2), and was killed both by a group of Judean Jews (1 Thess 2:14–15; Matt 26:4; John 11:53) and by the rulers of this age (1 Cor 2:8; Acts 4:27). This execution consisted of Jesus being nailed (Col 2:14; John 20:25, 27) to a cross (Gal 6:14; Phil 2:8). After his death, Jesus was buried (1 Cor 15:4; Matt 27:59–60; John 19:38–42), raised on the third day (1 Cor 15:4; Matt 16:21; 17:23; 20:19, 27:64), appeared to his followers (1 Cor 9:1; 15:5–7), and ascended into heaven (Rom 8:34; Eph 1:10; 1 Tim 3:16). For a discussion of the difficulties raised by 1 Thess 2:14–15 and a defense of its authenticity, see Eddy and Boyd, *Jesus Legend*, 211–14; Stout, *The "Man Jesus Christ,"* 125. Somewhat surprisingly, Bart Ehrman also defends the authenticity of 1 Thess

Even the titles and designations for Jesus used by Paul seem to match those later recorded in the Gospels and other New Testament writings.[32] Pauline traditions about Jesus sometimes sound like the logia preserved in the Synoptic Gospels. For instance, Paul explicitly cites Jesus as source of teaching on the topics of divorce (1 Cor 7:10–11; Matt 5:32; 19:3–9), the payment of missionaries (1 Cor 9:14; 1 Tim 5:17–18; Matt 10:10), the institution of the Lord's Supper (1 Cor 11:23–25; Matt 26:26–28), and eschatology (1 Thess 4:15–17; Matt 16:27–28; 24:31).[33] On other occasions, the language of certain Pauline passages seem to echo the words of Jesus found in the Synoptic Gospels, even though the apostle did not explicitly cite Jesus as their source.[34] While some biblical scholars will dispute that these unattributed sayings came from Jesus,[35] Paul had access to several early dominical traditions, and some of these were directly ascribed to Jesus.[36]

2:14–16; *Did Jesus Exist?*, 122–25.

32. E.g., Paul referred to Jesus as Messiah and Son of God. Paul also called him the "cornerstone" (Eph 2:20; Rom 9:33), as did other writers of the NT (Matt 21:42; 1 Pet 2:7).

33. In favor of 1 Thess 4:15–17 being based on eschatological statements of Jesus, see Sanders and Davies, *Synoptic Gospels*, 329–30.

34. A few examples of such statements are concerned with making unclean foods clean (Rom 14:14; Mark 7:18–19), not judging others (Rom 14:13; Matt 7:1), loving others as fulfillment of the Law (Rom 13:8, 10; Gal 5:13; Matt 7:12; 22:39–40), blessing persecutors (Rom 12:14; Matt 5:44), returning good for evil (1 Thess 5:15; Matt 5:39–40), paying taxes (Rom 13:7; Matt 22:21), storing up treasures in heaven by means of generous giving (1 Tim 5:19; Matt 6:19–20; Luke 12:33–34), referring to God as Abba (Rom 8:15; Gal 4:6; Mark 14:36), the tendency of Jews to seek for signs (1 Cor 1:22; Luke 11:29–32), remaining alert for the Lord's return (Rom 13:11–14; Luke 21:28, 31, 34), and the Lord's coming being like a thief in the night (1 Thess 5:1–2; Matt 24:43–44).

35. Some will object to these traditions being sayings of Jesus because Paul does not quote Jesus as an authority. Yet, several scholars have defended these view that these are sayings of Jesus (Eddy and Boyd, *Jesus Legend*, 226–28) or at least allow that they may have been (Ehrman, *The New Testament*, 424). Stout suggests that Paul presumed "that his readers share with him a common pool of information about the life and teachings of Jesus, and that for the sake of brevity, he proceeds in his epistles on the assumption that his readers already know some basic facts about the historical Jesus" (Stout, *The "Man Jesus Christ,"* 140).

36. Historians variously assess the important of the Jesus traditions preserved by Paul. Ehrman is unimpressed with the biographical data presented by Paul and mentioned in this chapter because it only gives a basic outline of who Jesus was and what he taught. See Ehrman, *The New Testament*, 240, 242. However, others are satisfied that Paul provides a good deal of historical information about Jesus. See Stout, *The "Man Jesus Christ,"* 191. Whatever one's view on this matter, the conclusions for this comparative study should be clear: the Pauline corpus provides much more information about Jesus than do the extent sources about Apollonius, with the possible exceptions of the *VA* and the *Letters of Apollonius*.

PART 4: APOLLONIUS AND JESUS

The Gospels, while not quite as early as Paul's material, are still by far the best sources for studying the historical Jesus, and they easily fall within the confines of the century-long limit set for first-tier documents. The consensus of New Testament scholars is that the Synoptic Gospels were written within just a few decades of Jesus's lifetime,[37] although debate continues over their precise dates of composition and whether they were written by or based on the teachings of the apostles.[38] Even John's Gospel is normally considered to have been written in the first century and is still sometimes defended by credible scholars as having been written by or at least based on traditions coming from the apostle John.[39] In the case of the Synoptics and John, most scholars agree that portions of them are based on even more ancient traditions, whether oral or written. These four canonical Gospels are biographies of Jesus and contain the most comprehensive records of his words and deeds. Whether one believes that these works go back to the apostles, eyewitness accounts, or merely early oral or written traditions, the Gospels were still written relatively close to the time of Jesus.

The remaining material that is scattered throughout the New Testament also gives an impression of how Jesus was remembered by the earliest Christian communities and like the other works just studied, falls within the time limit for first-tier sources.[40] A remarkably consistent picture of who Jesus was, according to his followers, emerges from these sources.[41] In addition to these details, there are even quotations or echoes

37. As to the Gospel materials, Ehrman stresses that they were written "forty to sixty-five years after the events they narrate," *New Testament*, 241. Other scholars allow that Mark might have been written as early as twenty to thirty years after the time of Jesus. For the arguments for this earlier position, see Carson and Moo, *Introduction*, 182; Bernier, *Rethinking the Dates*, 67.

38. As an example of scholars that find probable the traditional authorship of the Gospels by apostles (Matthew; John) or "apostolic men" (Mark; Luke), see Carson and Moo, *Introduction*, 140–150, 172–77, 203–6, 229–53; Eddy and Boyd, *Jesus Legend*, 390–95. As an example of those who reject apostolic authorship altogether, see Ehrman, who finds it implausible that the Gospels were written by the earliest followers of Jesus or that later traditions about their authorship can be trusted, *New Testament*, 241.

39. Blomberg, *Historical Reliability*, 22–41; Keener, *Gospel of John*, 1:81–139.

40. The classification of Acts is a bit difficult. Acts could be treated along with the Gospels because of its close association with the Gospel of Luke, but it could also be treated apart from them based on its content. For the purposes of this part of the study, it is treated apart from Luke, much as the Johannine epistles are kept separated from the Gospel of John, despite their many commonalities. Yet, later in this chapter, Luke and Acts will be combined (i.e., Luke-Acts) when Luke's second volume serves as a representative of Jesus material.

41. With respect to Jesus, these texts collectively mention his descent from Judah

of Jesus's words in these texts. The book of Acts even preserves an otherwise unattested logion of the historical Jesus: "It is more blessed to give than to receive" (Acts 20:35).[42] Several passages in the book of James bear a strong resemblance to the wording of Jesus in the Synoptic Gospels, even though its author did not directly attribute them to him.[43] These snippets of traditions concerning Jesus found in the New Testament writings, while not as fulsome as the Gospel material, are important first-century indicators of what early Christians thought about Jesus.

The letter of 1 Clement is an early, Christian document that may contain extrabiblical traditions about Jesus.[44] This document was written sometime in the latter half of the first century AD.[45] The author relates one piece of biographical information about Jesus that is not explicitly stated in the New Testament: he was descended from the line of Jacob (1 Clem. 32.2).[46] The author goes on to confirm the claims of earlier traditions

---

(Rev 5:5: Heb 7:14), Davidic lineage (Rev 5:5; 22;16), home in Nazareth (Act 2:22), baptism (1 John 5:6) by John the Baptist (Acts 10:37), reception of the Holy Spirit (Acts 10:38), temptation (Heb 2:18), teaching (Acts 1:1), preaching in Galilee (Acts 10:37), work in Judea and Jerusalem (Acts 10:39), exorcisms (Acts 10:38), performance of signs and wonders (Acts 2:22), transfiguration (2 Pet 1:16–18), prayer for rescue from death (Heb 5:7), patient suffering without threatening his persecutors (1 Pet 2:22–24), crucifixion (Acts 2:23; Heb 6:6, 12:2; 1 Pet 2:24; Rev 11:8), death at Jerusalem (Rev 11:8), execution outside the city (Heb 13:12–13), resurrection (Acts 2:24; Heb 13:20; 1 Pet 1:3), resurrection appearances (Acts 1:3; 10:40–41), and ascension (Acts 1:9–11; 2:23; Rev 12:5). Jesus was associated with a kingdom (Acts 1:3–6; 2 Pet 1:11) and the bringing of a new covenant (Heb 8:6–13; 10:29). As in the Synoptics, Jesus instructed his followers about the law of love (James 2:8; Matt 22:39), not making oaths (James 5:12; Matt 5:33–37), asking God for what one needs (James 1:5; Matt 7:7), and the inclusion of the poor in the kingdom (James 2:5; Luke 6:20). For many of the examples in this paragraph, see Johnson, *Living Jesus*, 78–97.

42. The exact wording of this logion is not found in the Gospels, but, as Bruce comments, "its spirit is seen in Lk. vi.38; xi.9; Jn. xiii. 34" (Bruce, *Acts*, 383).

43. Johnson, *The Letter of James*, 55–57.

44. The author of 1 Clement is clearly aware of a few New Testament books like Philippians (47.1–2), Hebrews (17.5; 36), and 1 Peter (49.5). However, the Jesus traditions he cites may or may not come directly from the canonical Gospels.

45. Some scholars have dated 1 Clement as early as the reign of Nero (AD 54–68). For an argument for a pre-70 date, see Bernier, *Rethinking the Dates*, 239–50. Most, however, favor the view that it was written during the time of Domitian (AD 81–96) or Nerva (AD 96–98). The epistle was written during a time of persecution (1 Clem 1:1; 7:1), which would fit well with a time during the reign of Nero or Domitian. The epistle would have been written after the deaths of Peter and Paul in the 60s (1 Clem 5 and 6), but before the deaths of some of the bishops that had been appointed by the apostles (1 Clem 44.3–5).

46. This detail could have been deduced from a few NT passages (Matt 1:2; Luke 1:33; 3:34), but alternately it may have been rooted in the prophecy of Num 24:17 that

that Jesus was a teacher,[47] and he includes examples of Jesus's teachings that resemble, but do not perfectly match, the wording of the Gospels (1 Clem. 13:2; 24.1, 5).[48] These slight departures from the wording of the canonical Gospels could be due to the author's use of independent traditions.[49] The letter also claims that Jesus possessed a gospel (1 Clem. 42.1), had apostles (1 Clem. 42.1–4; 44.1), came in humility (1 Clem. 16.2, 17), and, perhaps, was adorned with good works (1 Clem. 33.7).[50] The crucifixion is not explicitly mentioned in 1 Clement, but Jesus is said to have suffered (1 Clem. 2.1) and shed his blood for his people (1 Clem. 7.4; 12.7; 21.6; 49.6). The author also claimed that Jesus was raised from the dead (1 Clem. 24.1; 42.3). In addition to these biographical details, several of the titles of Jesus also found in the New Testament are attested in this book.[51]

Non-Christian sources do not have much to say about Jesus in the first century. Ehrman states that "[n]othing written by any pagan author of the first century so much as mentions Jesus's name."[52] Other scholars think that the comments of pagan writers Thallus[53] and Mara bar-Sarap-

---

states a star shall come forth from Jacob.

47. The letter notes that Jesus gave commandments (49.1), instructed people (59.4), and taught the virtues of gentleness and patience (13.1).

48. Interestingly, a statement attributed to Jesus in Acts 20:35 is quoted in 1 Clement 2.1, but it is not attributed to Jesus in this passage.

49. Alternately, these differences might be due to paraphrase, an imperfect memory when quoting the Gospels, or the use of slightly different texts of the canonical Gospels.

50. Ehrman understands the phrase "adorned with good works" to refer to Jesus as Lord (33.7). See Ehrman, *Did Jesus Exist?*, 105. However, the referent may be to God the Father here. The statement that the Master and Creator of the universe "rejoiced" at his "works" (33.1) is followed by the claim that the Lord (33.7) "rejoiced" after adorning himself with good works. This suggests that God the Father was the one who rejoiced at the completion of the world's creation. Perhaps the author envisioned Jesus as creator here (as in John 1:3; Col 1:16; Heb 1:2) but still the "good works" would refer to his role in the creation and not to his good deeds in general (as in Acts 10:38).

51. Jesus is referred to in 1 Clement as high priest (36.1; 61.3, 64), guardian (36.1; 61.3; 64), helper of our weakness (36.1), servant/child (59.2, 4), Lord (16.2, 17; 20.11; 21.6; 32.2; 49.6; 50.7; 58.2), Christ (3.4; 16.1; 22.1; 46.6), son (36.4), and master (24.1).

52. Ehrman, *The New Testament*, 237. Ehrman's claim may be accurate, but the jury is still out on the exact content of Thallus's statement and the date of Mara bar-Sarapion. Perhaps time will tell wither these pagan sources will be shown to have mentioned Jesus in the first century.

53. Thallus was a pagan historian who probably wrote around AD 50. In a passage quoted by Julius Africanus, Thallus mentioned an eclipse of the sun. Africanus believed that this event corresponded to the darkness of Jesus's crucifixion that is reported in the Synoptic Gospels. However, it is unclear whether Thallus himself explicitly linked

ion[54] about Jesus also ought to be considered, but the dates and contents of these sources are somewhat problematic. Until the dispute over the date of these first-century pagan writers is settled, Josephus the Jew is the only non-Christian author from this period that can be said to have unquestionably mentioned Jesus.

Josephus's *Jewish Antiquities*, completed around AD 93, mentioned Jesus twice. Although scholars sometimes question the validity of the *Testimonium Flavianum* as it stands written (*Ant.* 18.3.3), most acknowledge that the core of the passage is essentially intact and that it preserves a valid account of what Josephus thought about Jesus.[55] This passage states that Jesus was a wonder worker, followed by both Jews and Greeks, accused by Jewish leaders, condemned to be crucified by Pilate, and seen alive again on the third day according to his disciples. In addition to this passage, many scholars accept Josephus's testimony later in the *Antiquities* that James was the brother of Jesus, who was called the Christ (*Ant.* 20.9.1).[56] Although Jesus was only mentioned for certain by one non-Christian source in the first century, there are still more non-Christian data to analyze from the first three decades of the second century.

By the early second century, several pagan authors had taken note of Jesus, although their writings just barely fall within the century-long limit set for this the first-tier sources in this investigation. These authors

---

the eclipse to the darkness in the time of Jesus or whether Thallus merely mentioned an eclipse and Africanus himself connected the eclipse to the crucifixion. See Van Voorst, *Jesus*, 20–23. For a defense of the inclusion of Thallus's account, see Boyd and Eddy, *Lord or Legend*, 122–23. Because it is uncertain which ancient author—Thallus or Africanus—connected the eclipse to the crucifixion, Thallus's account will be excluded from this study.

54. Some scholars would date Mara bar-Serapion's possible reference to Jesus in a letter within the first century. This passage will not be treated here because (1) Jesus is not explicitly mentioned by the passage, although he is most likely the intended referent of the "wise king" who was executed by the Jews; and (2) the date for this source is uncertain, with opinions on the composition date ranging from the first to the third centuries AD. See Habermas, *Ancient Evidence*, 101. Most researchers favor a view that this letter was written a bit after AD 73. See Van Voorst, *Jesus*, 53–56. Should this date prove accurate, Mara bar-Sarapion would be an example of a first-century pagan that referred to Jesus.

55. For statements indicating that most scholars accept some version of Josephus's statements about Jesus, see Ehrman, *The New Testament*, 239–40; Keener, *Christobiography*, 4. For a presentation of arguments for and against the authenticity of this passage, see Eddy and Boyd, *Jesus Legend*, 190–98.

56. Ehrman, *The New Testament*, 239. For a presentation of arguments for and against the authenticity of this passage, see Eddy and Boyd, *Jesus Legend*, 185–90.

PART 4: APOLLONIUS AND JESUS

were Pliny the Younger (AD 112),[57] Tacitus (c. AD 115),[58] and Suetonius (c. AD 122).[59] Tacitus, who provides the most useful historical information about Jesus of the three writers, confirmed that "Christus" began a movement in Judea and that he was later executed by Pontius Pilate during the time of Tiberius Caesar. Regrettably, at least with respect to the topic of this study, Pliny and Suetonius spoke more about the early Christians than they did about Jesus himself.[60] However, all three authors appear to have been aware of a figure called Christ.

A large batch of second-century Christian documents was composed before the cutoff for first- and second-tier sources, and these occasionally preserve early traditions concerning Jesus. Some of these sources have been excluded from this study because what they say about Jesus is derived from the writings of the New Testament and, consequently, cannot be counted as independent traditions (e.g., Didache and Infancy Gospel of Thomas[61]). Other sources have been excluded because their exact dates and their reliance on the Synoptic Gospels are disputed (e.g., Gospel of Thomas and the Gospel of Peter).[62] Others were not explored because their contribution was minimal: the writings of Justin Martyr are early and evince reliance on both the Gospels and free traditions, but the sayings

57. Pliny the Younger, *Ep. Tra.* 10.96–97.

58. Tacitus *Ann.* 15.44. For a discussion of writers that question the historicity of this passage, see Eddy and Boyd, *Jesus Legend*, 179–84.

59. Suetonius mentions the expulsion of Jews from Rome due to a disturbance over a person named "Chrestus" (*Claud.* 25). While many scholars agree is a reference to Christ and this episode to the events of Acts 18:2, some believe that another figure was intended. For a discussion of whether Suetonius's Chrestus refers to Christ or to some other figure, see the discussion by Eddy and Boyd, *Jesus Legend*, 176–78. Suetonius also mentions Nero's persecution of the newly emerging group called Christians (*Nero* 16).

60. Pliny's statement seems to indicate that Christians ate a communal meal (perhaps hinting at Jesus's institution of the supper) and that they worshipped on a certain day of the week (a possible allusion to the day of Jesus's resurrection). See Habermas, *Ancient Evidence*, 95.

61. The Infancy Gospel of Thomas may date as early as AD 125. It might be used to confirm that Joseph was a carpenter (13). However, this work is clearly conversant with the infancy traditions in the Gospel of Luke and, therefore, cannot be regarded as independent testimony.

62. Ehrman indicates that the Gospel of Peter or the Gospel of Thomas might occasionally contain historically accurate material. See Ehrman, *Did Jesus Exist?*, 76–77. Ehrman does, however, acknowledge the ongoing debate concerning the date of these two works and that some believe that the Gospel of Thomas is reliant on the Synoptics. Brown posited that the author of the Gospel of Peter had heard the Gospel of Matthew read several times and had likely heard rephrasing of Luke and John but likely had no Gospel text before him to copy. See Brown, *Death of the Messiah*, 2:1334–35.

from the latter category are relatively few and would not add much to a study of this nature.[63] However, four Christian documents hold more promise of preserving oral or written traditions about Jesus that are independent of the Gospels. Three documents made the cut for the first-tier category: the letters of Ignatius of Antioch, the Epistle of Barnabas, and a brief passage from Quadratus. The only second-tier Christian text to be included in this study is that of Hegesippus. Because the dates of these documents are relatively certain and the Jesus material that they include has some probability of being independent of the canonical Gospels, only these four Christian documents are included in this study.

The letters of Ignatius, written sometime during the rule of Trajan (AD 98–117), may contain traditions about Jesus that are independent of the four Gospels. These epistles contain a variety of statements about Jesus such as his Davidic pedigree (*Eph.* 18.2; *Trall.* 9.1; *Rom.* 7.3; *Smyrn.*1.1), birth heralded by a star (*Eph.* 19.2),[64] birth by the virgin Mary (*Eph.* 19.1; *Smyrn.* 1:1), baptism by John (*Eph.*18.2; *Smyrn.* 1.1), and his anointing (*Eph.* 17.1). The letters also refer to Jesus's suffering, crucifixion, and resurrection during the times of Pilate (*Trall.* 11:2; *Magn.* 11; *Smyrn.* 1.2) and Herod the tetrarch (*Smyrn.* 1.2).

The Epistle of Barnabas, which can be dated somewhere between the destruction of the temple in AD 70 and the rebuilding of Jerusalem in AD 132–35 (*Barn.* 16.3–5), contains two quotes of Jesus that differ somewhat in wording from the canonical Gospels (*Barn.* 4.14; 5.9). Interestingly, Barnabas seems to have used Old Testament passages rather than Gospel texts to demonstrate that Jesus (1) was of Davidic lineage (*Barn.* 12.10; Ps 110:1), (2) was scourged, pierced, suffered on a tree (*Barn.* 5.13–14; Ps 22:16, 20; 119:120; Isa 50:6–7), (3) was given gall and vinegar to drink (*Barn.* 7.3; Lev 23:29), and (4) had lots cast for his garments (*Barn.* 6.6; Ps 22:18). The quotes and biographical details in the letter may be independent of earlier Gospel traditions.

Quadratus's apology to Hadrian is yet another first-tier, Christian document. This address was probably delivered during that emperor's visit to Athens around AD 124.[65] Within this text, Quadratus claimed

---

63. Koester, *Ancient Christian Gospels*, 360–402.

64. Although this passage might derive from Matthew, a good case has been made for its independence. See Brown, "Gospel of Ignatius," 49.

65. Hadrian visited Athens three times during his reign (AD 124/5, 128/9 and 131/2). See Syme, "Journeys of Hadrian," 162, 163, 165. Quadratus appears to have delivered his apology to Hadrian in AD 124. See Hamell, *Handbook of Patrology*, 37; Goodspeed, *The Earliest Apologists*, 1.

PART 4: APOLLONIUS AND JESUS

that Jesus had healed the sick and raised the dead. While those two details could have been based on accounts from the canonical Gospels, Quadratus went on to claim that some of those who had experienced these miracles were still alive in his day.[66] This extrabiblical tradition affirms both the existence of Jesus and the tradition that he was a healer. This document is the last of the first-tier documents written within a century of Jesus's crucifixion.

The second tier of data used in this study, which expands the timeline fifty more years, allows for the inclusion of two further pieces of data: Lucian's *Passing of Peregrinus* and the fragments of Hegesippus. Lucian's work recounts the self-immolation of the cynic Peregrinus after the Olympic games of AD 165. Lucian claims to have witnessed this event and to have written this satire shortly thereafter. In the context of parodying Christians for their gullibility at being taken in by the charlatan Peregrinus, Lucian reported that Jesus (1) originated the Christian sect in Palestine (*Peregr.* 11), (2) introduced novel rites (*Peregr.* 11), (3) was a sage and a lawgiver, who taught his followers that they were brothers (*Peregr.* 13), (4) was crucified (*Peregr.* 11, 13), and (5) was worshipped as a god by his followers (*Peregr.* 11, 13). The second source in this category is that of the Christian chronicler Hegesippus (c. AD 110–c. 180). His work has been lost except for a few fragments that are preserved by Eusebius. Hegesippus provides two traditions about Jesus's relatives. He mentions details about the death of Jesus's brother James (*Hist. eccl.* 2.23.3–19) and the trial of Jude's two sons before the emperor Domitian because they were from the family of David (*Hist. eccl.* 3.19.1–20.7). These two sources, while contributing little new material, confirm the earlier traditions about Jesus.

In contrast to the early dates for the Jesus material, there are only three datable sources for the study of Apollonius. The first of these, Lucian's *Alexander*, is the only datable first-tier source. This document falls at the far end of the century limit set for first-tier materials; its date of composition is separated from Apollonius's death by eighty years. The next datable authors that mention Apollonius (Philostrastus and Dio Cassius) are second-tier writers who are about a hundred and twenty years distant from Apollonius's time.

The remaining sources that mention Apollonius are currently undatable. Moiragenes and Maximus of Aegeae predated Philostratus

---

66. Eusebius, *Hist. eccl.* 4.3.1–2.

(*VA* 1.3.2), but by how many years is unknown. Other texts, as we have seen, are potentially early, especially so if Apollonian authorship could be demonstrated (i.e., *On Sacrifices, Letters*), but as it stands, their dates and authorship cannot be determined. Finally, the existence and, consequently, the date of the Damis memoir is highly contested. While several New Testament scholars and a minority of classical scholars believe that this was a genuine account from the first century, most Apollonius researchers believe either that it was a Philostratean fiction (thus its alleged content was from his own time) or that it was a forgery of uncertain date (but at least not contemporary with Apollonius). There is not much to go on in terms of unquestionably early materials that mention Apollonius like there was in the case of Jesus.

Of the two ancient holy men, the date of the material available for the Nazarene is far earlier and more abundant, as the following chart illustrates:

First-tier Sources for Jesus (AD 30–130)	First-tier Sources for Apollonius (AD 100–200)
The Pauline Corpus (AD 40s–60s)—Romans, 1 Corinthians, 2 Corinthians, Galatians, Philippians, 1 Thessalonians, and Philemon	Lucian, *Alexander* (c. AD 180)
The Canonical Gospels (AD 60s–100)—Matthew, Mark, Luke, John	
Other New Testament Writings (first century)—Acts, Ephesians, Colossians, 2 Thessalonians, 1 Timothy, 2 Timothy, Titus, Hebrews, James, 1 Peter, 2 Peter, the Johannine epistles, Jude, and Revelation.	
1 Clement (mid- to late first century)	
Letters of Ignatius (early second century)	
Epistle of Barnabus (late first century or early second century)	
Quadratus (early second century, c. AD 124)	

Second-tier Sources for Jesus (AD 131–80)	Second-tier Sources for Apollonius (AD 201–50)
Lucian, *The Passing of Peregrinus* (c. AD 165)	Philostratus, *VA* and *VS* (early third century)
Hegesippus (mid- to late second century)	Dio Cassius, *Hist. rom.* (early third century)
	Undatable Sources for Apollonius Written Before Philostratus's Time
	Damis memoir
	Moiragenes
	Letters of Apollonius
	Maximus of Aegae
	On Sacrifices

Sources were Produced Independently of One Another so That Their Authors were not in Collusion

This principle seeks to ensure that the authors of sources (1) have not collaborated with like-minded companions or contemporaries to produce their accounts, and (2) have not merely copied earlier accounts.[67] Sources that have not colluded are much more valuable in historical research than those that have simply repeated earlier material. Therefore, it is important to review the sources for Apollonius and Jesus to detect any instances of collusion.

The inquiry into collusion within the Apollonian material will begin with Lucian. He appears to have been entirely independent of other literary sources. He also seems to indicate that he and Celsus, the recipient of this work, were aware of the sort of charlatan Apollonius had been, although he does not indicate by what means they had arrived at this conclusion (*Alex.* 5). Not only was Lucian the first author to mention Apollonius, but his negative view of Apollonius contrasts with the more

---

67. Ehrman gives an excellent illustration of why independent accounts are superior to copied accounts: "If four ancient authors mention Marcus Billius as a Roman aristocrat in Ephesus, but it turns out that three of these authors derived their information from the fourth, then you no longer have multiple sources, but only one. Their agreements do not represent corroborations but collaboration, and that is much less useful"; Ehrman, *Did Jesus Exist?*, 41–42).

positive portrayal of some other writers from a later period (e.g., Maximus of Aegae, Moiragenes, *Letters of Apollonius*, and Philostratus). No collusion seems to have taken place in the case of Lucian.

A case of collusion is possible in the nearly identical accounts of Apollonius's remote viewing of Domitian's assassination that were related by the second-tier sources of Dio Cassius and Philostratus.[68] The similarities between the two versions of this miracle could indicate that these authors drew from a common source—oral or written—or that one of these writers was aware of the other's account. If collaboration did take place between these two authors, it appears to have been limited to this episode. This is because Dio only spoke about Apollonius in this passage, where he concedes the reality of the miracle, and in one other entry in which his negative evaluation of Apollonius elsewhere as a sorcerer differed sharply from Philostratus's entirely favorable view. This suggests that if Dio borrowed here on the *VA*, he was certainly not under the sway of Philostratus in painting Apollonius as an upstanding figure. Of course, it is also possible that Philostratus borrowed from this one episode from Dio or that both men had access to a common oral or written tradition about Apollonius's miracle.

In other cases, collusion is well-nigh certain, at least from the perspective that Philostratus has been influenced by other writers.[69] Philostratus knew of and even sometimes incorporated the material from earlier writers, such as the works of Maximus of Aegeae and Moiragenes (*VA* 1.3.2). Philostratus seems to have incorporated the essence of the accounts of Maximus of Aegeae into the early portion of the *VA* that dealt with Apollonius's youth. Philostratus's claim that Moiragenes's biography of Apollonius was inaccurate probably indicates that he did not use it as a source, but in rebutting it he may have been influenced by Moiragenes much more than he let on or realized.[70] Thus, Philostratus borrowed heavily from the work of Maximus of Aegeae, and he was at least aware of the content of Moiragenes's work.

---

68. Dio Cassius, *Hist. rom.* 67.18; Philostratus, *VA* 8:26–27.

69. One might question whether Philostratus was truly guilty of collusion in instances when he named his sources. However, the charge of collusion might be justified when he cites an unidentified source.

70. Several works in antiquity appear to have been written to correct the claims of earlier works. For instance, Eusebius's corrected the *VA* of Philostratus (*Contra Hieroclem*), Origen responded to Celsus (*Contra Celsum*), and Josephus reacted to Apion (*Contra Apionem*).

PART 4: APOLLONIUS AND JESUS

Collusion on the part of Philostratus is difficult to assess in other instances because the authenticity of the sources he claims to have employed is difficult to determine. As discussed in earlier chapters, scholars still debate whether the *Letters of Apollonius* that appear in the *VA* and the Damis memoir were genuine sources or rather Philostratus's fabrications that were later extracted from the *VA* and appended to a collection of Apollonius's letters. If Philostratus did draw on a genuine, earlier collection of Apollonius's letters, these fourteen, brief letters would have contributed minimally to the overall shape of the *VA* but still he may have been influenced in this biography by other details in the letters collection even if he did not quote them. The enigmatic Damis memoir, if a pseudepigraph, would constitute a more serious case of collusion or outside influence since the *VA* claims to rely on it more than any other source (*VA* 1.3.1). However, if Philostratus concocted the diary, he would be guilty not of collusion but of deception.

The investigation of collusion in the case of the sources for Jesus comes with a definitional problem unlike that encountered in studying Apollonius. New Testament scholars could understand the term "collusion" in the sense of the material shared (1) by multiple Gospels (e.g., the Synoptics and John), (2) by multiple Gospel sources (e.g., Q, M, L, and Mark),[71] (3) by multiple form-critical genres (e.g., parables and controversy stories), or (4) by the Synoptic Gospels, John, Paul, and other literature, Christian or otherwise.[72] For the sake of clarity, this study defines "collusion" in the broadest sense of the term mentioned above (i.e., option four), and it will seek to determine whether collusion has taken place between the Synoptics (as a group), John, Paul, the other New Testament writings, later Christian literature, and extrabiblical Jewish and pagan material.

---

71. In determining whether collusion has taken place in Gospel sources and what sources might have been involved depends upon which view one takes in solving the Synoptic problem. While some scholars contend that Q is necessary for solving the Synoptic problem (Two-Source Hypothesis; Four-Source Hypothesis), others argue that Q did not exist (Farrer Hypothesis; Griesbach Hypothesis). These questions directly relate to whether or how collaboration took place. It is beyond the scope of this study to make the case for a particular solution to the Synoptic problem. Instead, for simplicity's sake, the Synoptics will be regarded as a unit to be compared to other documents in this section. For an excellent overview of the major theories concerning the Synoptic problem, see Porter and Dyer, *The Synoptic Problem*.

72. These four categories were taken and modified from Sanders and Davies, *Synoptic Gospels*, 323.

In most cases, there is little evidence of collusion among the sources that have been chosen for this study. Paul could not have borrowed from the Synoptics, since he wrote before they were composed, yet he may have sometimes drawn upon a similar vein of oral traditions later used by them.[73] In exploring collusion in the Gospels, there are a few possible points of contact between the Synoptics and John,[74] but these similarities might be explained in different ways. The author of John may have been unaware of the Synoptic writings yet shared some of their traditions. Yet, even if the author of the Gospel of John were familiar with the Synoptics, he does not appear to have slavishly copied them. The authors of other New Testament books (e.g., Acts) were or might have been able to have accessed Gospel texts (or to have heard them read or talked about), but it is also possible that some of the similarities between them and earlier materials are due to their access to similar traditions about Jesus, whether in oral or written form. Quadratus's claim that Jesus healed the sick and raised the dead could perhaps have been based on the Gospels, but his claim that some of these people had lived unto his own time appears to have been based on the claims of Christians from his own generation. The details preserved in Hegesippus align with the details of the Gospel that Jesus was from the family of David and had brothers named James and Judas, but the specific stories in which these claims are embedded (e.g., the murder of James; Domitian's trial of the sons of Jude) do not come from the Gospels. The writings of Josephus,[75] Tacitus, Suetonius, Pliny, and Lucian were independent of each other and do not appear to have been aware of the New Testament documents.[76] It is possible, of course, that these non-Christian writers gleaned information from Christians or

---

73. Choice examples of Paul material that resembles Synoptic traditions are 1 Cor 7:10–11 (Matt 5:32; 19:3–9), 1 Cor 9:14 ([1 Tim 5:17–18]; Matt 10:10), 1 Cor 11:23–25 (Matt 26:26–28), and perhaps 1 Thess 4:15 (Matt 16:27–28; 24:31).

74. For instance, one could ask whether a common source stood behind the Passion Narratives or, more specifically, behind the account of the feeding of the five thousand (Matt 14:13–21; Mark 6:30–34; Luke 9:10–17; John 6:1–14). For a good discussion of the similarities and differences between the passion narrative of John and that of other Gospels, see Koester, *Ancient Christian Gospels*, 253–55.

75. Ehrman regards Josephus as an independent source. See Ehrman, *The New Testament*, 243.

76. For the issue of whether Lucian's material was based on second-hand reports of early Christians, see the discussion by Eddy and Boyd, *Jesus Legend*, 178–79. As an indication that Lucian used independent sources, these authors point out that Lucian used the verb *anaskolopizein* to refer to the crucifixion of Jesus, a word not found in early Christian accounts to describe Jesus's execution.

Christian sources, but there is no way to know for certain. Overall, the earliest and most significant of these traditions do not appear to have been in collusion.

However, collusion is possible in two of the later Christian sources that were cited. Concerning the first of these, Ehrman notes, "[i]t is debated among scholars whether Ignatius had actually read any of our written Gospels (e.g., Matthew) or had simply heard some of the oral traditions about Jesus' life."[77] In favor of collusion in the letters of Ignatius, several passages resemble Matthean or Johannine language. If Ignatius copied, quoted (even incorrectly), or was influenced by Matthean or Johannine theology even without reading those works,[78] then his letters would not constitute independent sources for Jesus. An argument against collusion in Ignatius's writings is that the wording of these passages differs somewhat from the Gospels, thereby leaving open the possibility that Ignatius was working from an alternative oral or written source.[79] In such a case, Ignatius would represent an independent source, as some have suggested.[80] Perhaps Ignatius's reference to the star at Jesus's birth is additional proof that he had access to independent traditions (Ign. *Eph.* 19.2). Although this story might have been based on Matthew's account (Matt 2:2, 7, 9–10), there is little linguistic similarity between the two accounts apart from the word "star," and a moderate case can be made that this detail was based on the star mentioned in Num 24:17 instead of the story of the star of Bethlehem located in Matthew's Gospel.[81]

---

77. Bart Ehrman, *Other Early Christian Writings*, 325.

78. Brown believes that Ignatius certainly knew Paul's writings and possibly knew the Gospel of Matthew but that much of what Ignatius called "gospel" was oral in nature that was passed down/received through preaching. See Brown, "The Gospel of Ignatius," 53, 56, 186, 188, 306. Similarly, Burghardt, argues that Johannine language appears to have been used by Ignatius, but that this may be due to oral traditions not from direct access to the text of John. See Burghardt, "Saint Ignatius," 130–56. Although several passages in Ignatius resemble Matthean or Johannine language, the wording is often not an exact match, which might suggest that Ignatius was working from an alternative oral or written source.

79. E.g., see Ign. *Eph.* 14:2 (Matt 12:33); Ign. *Smyr.* 1.1 (Matt 3:15); Ign. *Pol.* 2.2 (Matt 10:16); Ign. *Magn.* 9:1 (Matt 23:8); Ign. *Trall.* 11.1, Ign. *Phil.* 3.1 (Matt 15:13); Ign. *Smyrn.* 3.2 (Luke 24:39); Ign. *Phil.* 7.1 (John 3:8); Ign. *Eph.* 5.2 (John 6:33); Ign. *Phil.* 9.1 (John 10:9).

80. Crossan believes that Ignatius was independent of the canonical Gospels. See Crossan, *The Historical Jesus*, 432.

81. Although this passage might derive from Matthew, a good case can be made for its independence. See Brown, *Gospel of Ignatius*, 49.

Academics also disagree when it comes to detecting collusion in the Epistle of Barnabas. Crossan asserts that Barnabas contains traditions that are independent of the canonical Gospels,[82] and Koester more cautiously claims that "[i]t cannot be shown that Barnabas used the Gospels of the New Testament."[83] Yet, Treat is at least open to the notion that the author of Barnabas quoted Matthew,[84] and Jacquier is adamant that the author did, for the introductory formula "it is written" at Barn. 4.14 confirms for him that this Gospel was his source.[85] The two passages that could be construed as quotes from the Gospel of Matthew (Barn. 4.14 and Matt 22:14; Barn. 5.9 and Matt 9:13) admittedly resemble the language of the Gospel but are not identical in wording. These slight departures from the Matthean text may suggest that the author was quoting a Gospel from memory (perhaps Matthew or some other work), copying from a different text of Matthew, or working from some other written tradition. If Barnabas knew of the Gospel of Matthew, this might explain why the two books chose to highlight some of the exact details of Jesus's life.[86] Yet, Matthew did not cite the Old Testament passages as prooftexts of these events like the Epistle of Barnabas did, so a firm connection to that Gospel is uncertain. Therefore, the possibility remains that the author of Barnabas either matched traditions about Jesus with OT passages on his own or that this pairing was based on an earlier, Christian catenae of Scriptures that had already linked these prooftexts and events.

Of all the Jesus traditions that date within a century of the crucifixion, only the Epistles of Ignatius and the Letter of Barnabas are somewhat questionable concerning the issue of collusion. Should future research discount them because they directly or indirectly borrowed from Gospel traditions, this will not radically affect the outcome of the sources for the historical Jesus for they are the last and least significant of the sources to be used in this inquiry. The earlier Christian, Jewish, and pagan materials alone provide a sufficient collection of traditions about Jesus from which to work, and these documents reveal clear evidence of collusion.

---

82. Crossan, *The Historical Jesus*, 431.

83. Helmut Koester, *Introduction*, 2:278.

84. Treat, "Barnabas, Epistle of," 1:614.

85. Jacquier, "Matthew," 10:57–58.

86. Barnabas and Matthew both mention Jesus's (1) Davidic lineage (Matt. 1:1; 20:33–31; Barn. 12.10), (2) scourging (Matt 27:26; Barn. 5.13–14), (3) reception of gall and vinegar on the cross (Matt 27:34; Barn. 7.3), and (4) garments being divided after the casting of lots (Matt 27:35; Barn. 6.6).

PART 4: APOLLONIUS AND JESUS

Sources Do not Contradict One Another, so That One or More of Them Is not Necessarily in Error

This section will catalog the data for the respective traditions about Jesus and Apollonius, noting where they align and differ. Agreements between friendly and hostile sources concerning the major details of an ancient figure are significant; such alignments often constitute good evidence for a particular historical claim. However, a singly attested tradition that differs from a tradition supported by multiple witnesses might be a clue to spotting an author's bias or help in detecting an ancient, revisionist historian at work.

The criterion of multiple attestation (independent attestation) will be the method used to establish a historical core for the two figures. When multiple, independent sources agree with each other on a particular detail, the likelihood that the tradition is authentic increases. This principle has been long used by New Testament scholars to determine which traditions are more likely to preserve the words and deeds of Jesus.[87] This method works equally well in the case of Apollonius and has already been used in this book toward this end by comparing the disparate sources about him. This criterion is not foolproof, for a singly reported tradition about a historical figure might also be trustworthy,[88] but it can serve as a helpful tool in historical investigation.

One of the most contentious disagreements in the sources about Apollonius concerns whether he was a magician and, if he were a magician, whether he was a benign or malevolent one. As we saw earlier in the study, there are several perspectives on this idea: (1) Lucian and Dio Cassius, representatives from first- and second-tier literature, regarded him as a magician in the negative sense of that term; (2) Moiragenes and the *Letters*, materials of uncertain date, took a positive view of him as a magician and coupled it with his role as a philosopher; and (3) Philostratus, a second-tier source, denied that Apollonius was a magician, but affirmed his role as a philosopher. The earliest and most prevalent notion is that Apollonius was a magician—whether that designation had

---

87. Two classic examples of the use of multiple attestation in confirming details about Jesus are that (1) he shared a meal with his disciples toward the end of his ministry (Mark 14:22–25; John 13:1–20; 1 Cor 11:23–26) and (2) he had brothers (Matt 13:55; Mark 6:3; John 7:3; Acts 1:14. 1 Cor. 9:5; Gal 1:5; Josephus, *Ant.* 20.9.1; Hegesippus in Eusebius, *Hist. eccl.* 2.23.3–19; 3.19–20.7).

88. Ehrman observes that this criterion is limited because a singly-reported tradition about a historical figure might be still be accurate. See Ehrman, *Did Jesus Exist?*, 187.

positive or negative connotations—and the latest view was that of Philostratus, who was the sole author to deny this claim and to claim he was only a philosopher. Philostratus's presentation of Apollonius marks an abrupt shift in Apollonian tradition and, consequently, appears to have been an innovation. Ironically, this late-coming tradition was the one that was most widely remembered in antiquity and the one that is still commonly accepted by many biblical scholars to this day since most of their information about Apollonius comes from the *VA*. This is a good example of how the criterion of multiple attestation helps to spot similarities in the tradition and to spot divergences that should raise a red flag for historians.

Apart from the question of Apollonius's association with magic, there are also a few lesser contradictions within the *VA*. Did Apollonius bathe (*VA* 1.16; 2.27; 8.13) or not (*Epp. Apoll.* 8.1; 43)? Did he offer non-bloody physical sacrifices (e.g., *VA* 1.1; 31–32; 4:19; 8.7, 12), or did he only promote spiritual sacrifice (*Epp. Apoll.* 26–27; fragment *On Sacrifices*)? Did he customarily speak briefly and infrequently, while preferring silence (*Epp. Apoll.* 8.2, 92–94), did he practice silence for only five years with difficulty (*VA* 1.14.2), or did he lecture often (*VA* 1:11, 16.4, 38.3; 4.2–3, 8–9, 19–20, 24.1, 31, 41; 5.7; 6.35.2; 7.38; 8.19, 23, 26) and discourse at great length (*VA* 2.22–23; 5.7.2–4, 14–17; 6.11; 7.14, 26.2–6)? Did Apollonius address large audiences throughout his career (*VA* 1.11; 4.2–3, 8–9, 31; 8.26.2) or abandon this practice at some point in his life (*Epp. Apoll.* 10, 34)? Had Apollonius received an imperial invitation to Italy (*VA* 5.39.3; 6.31.2; 8.27) or not (*Epp. Apoll.* 14)[89]? Did he receive an invitation from the umpires of the Olympic games (*Epp. Apoll.* 24) or not (*VA* 4.24.1)?[90] Although some of these tensions in the Apollonian traditions might be capable of reconciliation, many of them appear to constitute genuine contradictions in the tradition.

Of course, there are also several places where the Apollonian sources are multiply attested and align quite well. Slight variations aside, the near consensus of the traditions regarded Apollonius as a magician of some sort, except for the latecomer Philostratus. According to several sources, Apollonius appears to have had some philosophical leanings (fragment

---

89. Perhaps *Epp. Apoll.* 14 was written before Vespasian extended Apollonius an invitation to Rome, but Penella deems this unlikely, *Letters*, 99.

90. Apollonius did attend the games in AD 93 (*VA* 8.15–19), but this visit does not appear to have been at the invitation of the Eleans; such an invitation is unlikely due to the rumor that the sage had died after his encounter with Domitian.

PART 4: APOLLONIUS AND JESUS

On Sacrifices; Moiragenes; Epp. Apoll. 8.1, 42, 45, 68; *VA* 8.7.2, 11), and he is sometimes specifically associated with the Pythagoreans (*Epp. Apoll. Letters* 53, 55, 62.2; *VA* 1.2; 1.7.3; 6.6.3–7). In keeping with his role as a Pythagorean master, he had disciples (Lucian; *Epp. Apoll.* 43, 85, 92–93; *VA* 1.18; 4.2.14; 4.37.2; 5.43.3), wore his hair long (*Epp. Apoll.* 8.1; *VA* 1.32; 8.7.17), was a vegetarian (*Epp. Apoll.* 8; *VA* 1.8.1; 6.15; 8.7.15), and often lived in local temples (*Epp. Apoll.* 8; *VA* 1.8, 16; 4.40; 5.20; 8.15). The Tyanean had a father named Apollonius (*Epp. Apoll.* 72; *VA* 1.4, 6), a brother or brothers (*Epp. Apoll.* 55.1–2; 95; *VA* 1.13), a philosophical rival named Euphrates (*Moiragenes; Epp. Apoll.* 1–8.1; 14–18; 50–52, 82, 94; *VA* 1,13.3; 5.27–28, 31–35, 37–38; 8.7.7), a sophist friend named Scopelian (*Epp. Apoll.* 19; *VA* 1.23–24), and philosophical acquaintance called Dio (*Epp. Apoll.* 9, 10, 90; *VA* 5.27; 8.7.2). He is credited with one noteworthy miracle for certain—he remotely viewed the assassination of Domitian according to Dio Cassius and *VA*—and possibly another supernatural feat by predicting an earthquake in Miletus (*Epp. Apoll.* 68; *VA* 4.7). He may have traveled to Ephesus (Dio Cassius; *VA*) and Rhodes (*Epp. Apoll.* 45; *VA* 5.21–22). Some people of his generation regarded him as a god or at least as godlike (*Epp. Apoll.* 44.1; *VA* 1.2, 5, 19; 2.17, 40; 3.28; 7.31, 38; 8.7.19).

Yet, these details may not be as well-attested as they first appear, for a review of the evidence for these items will show that in many cases they are confirmed by only two sources: the *VA* and the *Letters of Apollonius*, the latter of which was purported to be a source for the former (*VA* 1.2). If Philostratus drew on the *Letters* for content or even inspiration, these details would be singly rather than doubly attested. Regrettably, these few agreements do not leave a very clear picture of the man and certainly do not do much to suggest that the *VA*'s account of worldwide travels[91] and encounters with world leaders have a footing in real events.

Shifting to the story of Jesus, several details of his life are confirmed by various sources. His descent from Judah[92] and David[93] are attested

---

91. Two letters suggest that Apollonius travelled to India (*Epp. Apoll.* 77b, 77c). Both epistles are quoted in the *VA* (*VA* 2.41; 3.51). If Philostratus found these letters in a previously existing collection, they might indicate that Apollonius visited India. In such a case, he may have gleaned his knowledge of Apollonius's Indian travels from this source, thus making this a singly-attested detail. However, if Philostratus composed these letters himself and they were extracted from the *VA* for later inclusion in a collection of other letters, this detail may still be singly-attested claim, but as a Philostraean creation.

92. Matt 1:2–3; Luke 3:33; Heb 7:14; Rev 5:5.

93. Jesus's Davidic lineage is attested by Paul (Rom 1:3; 15:20; 2 Tim 2:8), the

in several sources as are his birth in Bethlehem[94] and later residence in Nazareth.[95] He was immersed by John the Baptist[96] and the Holy Spirit came upon him in the context of that event.[97] Jesus had several brothers,[98] one named James[99] and another named Jude.[100] He also had a following of twelve disciples (or apostles),[101] two of whom were named in multiple traditions: Peter[102] (who was married[103]) and John.[104] Jesus's ministry, which took place in both Judea[105] and Galilee,[106] involved such activities as teaching,[107] exorcism,[108] and miracle-working.[109] At some point, Jesus

---

Synoptics (Matt 1:1; 22:45; Mark 10:47; Luke 1:32; 3:31), possibly John (7:42), several other New Testament writings (Acts 13:22–23; 34–37: Rev 3:7; 5:5; 22:16), and the post-NT Christian writings (Ign. *Eph.* 18.1.2; Ign. *Trall.* 9.1; Ign. *Rom.* 7.3; Ign. *Smyrn.* 1.1; Barn. 12.1; Hegesippus [Eusebius, *Hist. ecc.* 3.19–20.7]).

94. Matt 2:1, 5, 6, 8, 16; Luke 2:4–7; John 7:42 (?).

95. Matt 2:23; 21:11; Luke 2:39, 51; 4:16; John 1:45–46; Acts 2:22; 10:38; 26:39. See Ehrman's endorsement of Jesus's association with Nazareth in, *Did Jesus Exist?*, 189.

96. Mark 1:9–11; John 1:29–34; Acts 10:37; Ign. *Eph.* 18.2; Ign. *Smyrn.* 1.1. 1 John 5:6 may be an allusion to Jesus's baptism as well, although other interpretations of this passage have been suggested.

97. Luke 3:21–22; 4:1; John 1:32–33; Acts 10:38–39.

98. 1 Cor 9:5; Matt 13:55; John 7:3; Acts 1:14.

99. Gal 1:5; Mark 6:3; Josephus, *Ant.* 20.9.1; Hegesippus (Eusebius, *Hist. eccl.* 2.23.3–19).

100. Mark 6:3; Jude 1:1; Hegesippus (Eusebius, *Hist. eccl.* 3:19–20.7).

101. 1 Cor 15:7; Mark 3:13–19; John 6:67, 70–71; 20:24; Acts 6:2; Rev 21:14. Similarly, Jude (17) and Clement (1 Clem 42.1–4; 44.1) mention that Jesus had "apostles," but these passages did not indicate their exact number.

102. 1 Cor 15:7; John 1:42.

103. 1 Cor 9:5; Mark 1:30.

104. Gal 2:9; Mark 1:17; Acts 1:13.

105. Luke 23:5; John 3:22; 4:3; Acts 10:39.

106. Matt 4:23; John 1:43; 2:1; 4:3; Acts 10:37.

107. Matt 4:23; John 6:59; 18:20; Acts 1:1; 1 Clem. 13.1; 49.1; 59.4; Josephus, *Ant.* 18.3.3; Lucian, *Peregr.* 13. Jesus was also called "teacher" (Matt 8:19; 9:11) and "rabbi" (Matt 26:25, 49; John 1:38).

108. Matt 10:1; Mark 1:15; 9:18, 28; Luke 10:17–19; Acts 10:38. Although the Gospel of John contains no exorcism accounts, John 12:31 speaks of Jesus casting out the ruler of this world.

109. Matt 11:20–23; John 6:2; 11:47; Acts 2:22. Quadratus (*Hist. eccl.* 4.3.1–2), Josephus, *Ant.* 18.3.3.

PART 4: APOLLONIUS AND JESUS

experienced a transfiguration on a mountain.[110] Some of his followers regarded him as the Messiah[111] and as a divine figure.[112]

Because the events of the passion and resurrection narratives take up a good percentage of each Gospel text,[113] it should come as no surprise that its details are mentioned in the surviving traditions as well. Examples of these traditions from the passion narrative are that Jesus (1) ate a special meal with his disciples,[114] (2) prayed to be rescued from death,[115] (3) was turned over to authorities on the same night as this meal,[116] (4) was accused or killed by Jewish leaders,[117] (5) was tried or died during the governorship of Pontius Pilate,[118] (5) died during the rule of Herod (Antipas),[119] (6) died by crucifixion,[120] (7) was nailed to the cross[121] rather than being tied to it, (8) died around Passover,[122] (9) died at Jerusalem[123] or at least in Judea,[124] (10) was executed outside of the city of Jerusalem,[125] and (11) was buried.[126] After the crucifixion, his disciples claimed that Jesus (12) was raised from the dead,[127] (13) was raised on

110. Mark 9:2–8; 1 Pet 2:22–24.

111. Josephus, *Ant.* 18.3.3; *Ant.* 20.9.1.

112. John 1:1–3; 10:34–38; 20:28; Phil 2:5–8; Col 1:15–18; Heb 1:1–2, 8–12; 13:8; 1 John 5:20; Rev 22:13; Ign. *Eph.* 18.2; *Magn.* 6.1; Pliny the Younger, *Ep. Tra.* 10.96–97; Lucian, *Peregr.* 11, 13.

113. The passion and resurrection narratives take up about a third of Matthew (Matthew 21–28), a third of Mark (Mark 11–16), a quarter of Luke (Luke 19–24), and a half of John (John 12–20). As Martin Kähler quipped in his famous footnote, "one could call the Gospels passion narratives with extended introductions" (Kähler, *The So-Called Historical Jesus*, 80, n. 11).

114. 1 Cor 11:23–25; Matt 26:26–28; John 13:1–4.

115. Mark 14:32–42; Heb 5:7.

116. 1 Cor 11:23; Matt 26:25, 48.

117. 1 Thess 2:15; Matt 26:4; John 11:53; Acts 1:27–28; Josephus *Ant.* 18.3.3.

118. 1 Tim 6:13; Matt 26:26–28; Acts 4:27; 14:28; Josephus, *Ant.* 18.3.3; Tacitus, *Ann.* 15.44; Ign. *Magn.* 11; Ign. *Smyrn.* 1.2.

119. Luke 23:8–12; Acts 2:22; 4:27; Heb 6:6; 12:2; 1 Pet 2:24; Rev 11:8; Ign. *Smyrn.* 1.2.

120. Gal 6:14; Phil 2:8; Rev 11:8; Josephus, *Ant.* 18.3.3. Tacitus, *Ann.* 15.44; Ign. *Trall.* 11:2; Barn 5:13–14; Lucian, *Peregr.*11, 13.

121. Col 2:14; John 20:25, 27.

122. John 13:1; 18:28.

123. Luke 24:18–20; Acts 4:27; 10:39; Rev 11:8.

124. 1 Thess 2:14; Acts 2:14–24.

125. John 19:17–20; Heb 13:12–13.

126. 1 Cor 15:4; Matt 27:59–60; John 19:38–42.

127. Acts 2:24; Heb 13:20; 1 Pet 1:3; Rev 1:5, 8; 1 Clem 24.1; 42.3; Josephus *Ant.*

the third day,[128] (14) appeared to his followers,[129] and (15) ascended into heaven.[130] The rough contours of the last days of Jesus are recognizable in these multiply-attested traditions.

However, there are also several genuinely problematic areas with some traditions about Jesus. A few examples of these concern the different genealogies of Jesus,[131] the date of his birth,[132] the chronology of

---

18.3.3; Ign. *Smyrn.* 1; Ign. *Trall.* 11.2; Barn. 15.9.

128. 1 Cor 15:4; Matt 16:21; 17:23; 20:19; 27:64; Josephus, *Ant.* 18.3.3.

129. 1 Cor 9:1; 15:5-7; Acts 1:3; 10:40-41; Josephus, *Ant.* 18.3.3; Ign. *Smyrn.* 3.1.

130. Rom 8:34; Eph 1:10; 1 Tim 3:16; Acts 1:9-11; 2:23; Heb 9:24; 10:24; 1 Pet 3:22; Rev 12:5; Barn 15.9.

131. Ehrman flatly rejects any attempt to reconcile the genealogical lists of Matthew and Luke (*Did Jesus Exist?*, 183). Yet, for a concise listing of attempts to reconcile the different genealogies in Matt 1:2-17 and Luke 3:23-38, see Nettlehorst, "The Genealogy of Jesus," 169-72. In this brief article, Nettlehorst summarizes attempts to reconcile these lists by (1) Annius of Viterbo (c. 1490), who assigning one list to Mary and the other to Joseph–this view is not convincing since both lists in the Gospels are traced through Joseph, (2) Julius Africanus, who, by the custom of levirate marriage, argued that Matthan (Matt 1:15) and Matthat (Luke 3:24) were the same person; Matthan's (Matthat's) son Jacob died without offspring and his nephew Heli became his heir, (3) Hervey, who thought Matthew traced Jesus's royal (or legal) line and that Luke recorded Jesus's actual physical descendants although, as Nettlehorst indicates, this requires an odd usage of the word "begot" in Matthew's list, and (4) Nettlehorst, who believed that Matthew traced Joseph's matrilineal line (Matthew) and Luke though his patrilineal line (Luke)—in this model, Matthew traces from Jacob, Joseph's maternal grandfather (the mother is unlisted) directly to Joseph. Although these theories may not be satisfying to some skeptics, options 2 and 4 give plausible explanations for how both these lists could be genuine.

132. The problem with the birth of Jesus is that Matthew appears to place it prior to the death of Herod the Great (i.e., prior to 5 BC; Matt 2:1, 19), while Luke appears to place it during the taxation of Quirinius (AD 6; Luke 2:2). Therefore, the accounts in Matthew and Luke appear to contradict. However, some authors hold that (1) the word "first" may refer to an earlier census under Quirinius prior to the one in AD 6—this view holds that Quirinius was held command in the region during the time of Herod the Great and prior to his brief legateship in Syria (AD 6-7); or (2) the word πρώτη in Luke 2:2 should be translated "before" rather than "first," thus placing this taxation prior to the census at time of Quirinius, the latter of which would have been more famous due to the tax rebellion that accompanied it. For a defense of this position, see Garland, *Luke*, 117-19.

PART 4: APOLLONIUS AND JESUS

his youth,[133] the location of his first calling of the disciples,[134] the timing of the temple cleansing,[135] and the timing of the Last Supper and Jesus's crucifixion as they relate to Passover.[136] Despite these problems, the historian must also concede that the broader framework of the Jesus tradition remains intact. This can be illustrated by considering the events of Jesus's last week and the Passion Narrative; whatever one's view of the minute details, many scholars still believe that Jesus cleansed the temple at some point in his ministry, ate a special meal with his disciples before his death, was crucified around the time of the Passover feast, and that his disciples claimed that he rose from the dead. The minor snags in the tradition, whether real or merely apparent contradictions, do not impact the overall picture of his life story.

---

133. In the Lukan account, Jesus's birth is followed eight days later by his circumcision (Luke 2:21), his purification thirty-three days later (Luke 2:22; Lev 12:1–4), and his family's return to Nazareth from Bethlehem (Luke 2:39–40). At first glance, this does not appear to allow for Matthew's account of the flight to Egypt (Matt 2:13–20) prior to the family's return to Nazareth (Matt 2:22–23). However, it is possible that Luke omitted the sojourn in Egypt to condense his infancy narrative. Ehrman, while skeptical about such scenarios, admits that "certainly Matthew and Luke do not explicitly contradict each other"; Ehrman, *The New Testament*, 156.

134. According to John, the disciples of Jesus were called while he was in Judea (John 1:39–51) and while John the Baptist was still active (John 1:19–36). In the Synoptic Gospels, the call of the disciples appears to be in Galilee (Mark 1:16–20; 2:14) after the arrest of John (Mark 1:14). Although these traditions could be pitted against each other, it is also possible that Jesus initially associated with some of his disciples in Judea and later regathered them when he began his ministry in earnest in Galilee. The word "call" probably does not describe the exact moment in which a disciple decided to follow Jesus. After all, even in the Synoptics Jesus called the Twelve again later in his ministry (Mark 3:13–19) long after he had first summoned some of them by the Sea of Galilee (Mark 1:16–20, 13–14).

135. The cleansing of the temple occurs during the passion narrative in the Synoptic Gospels but is placed early in the Gospel of John. Several solutions for this oddity have been suggested by scholars. One common view is that John relocated the story for theological reasons. Another suggestion is that Jesus cleansed the temple twice, once at the beginning of his ministry and again at its end. For a good overview of attempts to reconcile John and the Synoptics with respect to the cleansing of the temple, see Blomberg, *Historical Reliability*, 87–91.

136. In the Synoptics, the Last Supper appears to have been a Passover meal, with the crucifixion occurring the day after Passover. Yet, John 18:28 appears to place the crucifixion on the Passover. Ehrman believes that these views are irreconcilable (*Did Jesus Exist?*, 183). However, Blomberg plausibly argues that the passage can be reconciled with the timing of the Synoptics and that "Passover" can refer more broadly to the events of the week after the feast. For a discussion of the timing of the Last Supper as it relates to John and the Synoptics, see Blomberg, *Historical Reliability*, 237–39.

The criterion of multiple attestation seems to indicate that the traditions about Jesus agree with each other on major biographical details far more than those about Apollonius. Although there is certainly more material about Apollonius than there is about Jesus, many of these traditions are unsupported by other sources. To be fair, some of the information in the *VA*'s vast store of tradition may eventually be proven accurate. However, without external confirmation, historians should continue to treat these unsupported claims about Apollonius with great caution until such evidence emerges.

Sources Are Internally Consistent, Suggesting a Basic Concern for Reliability

Boyd and Eddy explain the importance of the concept of the internal consistency of historical accounts: "Generally speaking, fabricated accounts tend to include more inconsistencies than truthful accounts. Hence, the absence of inner contradictions contributes to a positive estimation of the document's historical veracity."[137] Due to the constraints of space, an inquiry into inconsistencies cannot be carried out for each of the sources for Jesus and Apollonius. Therefore, this study will treat contradictions within a sizable, representative document from each group: Luke-Acts[138] will serve in the case of Jesus and the *VA* in the case of Apollonius.

The *VA* contains numerous internal contradictions. Many of these tensions have been known since ancient times. This is illustrated by *Against Hierocles*, in which Eusebius systematically worked through the *VA* and pointed out its many inconsistencies. In more recent centuries, researchers have added to this list of problems in the *VA*. In investigating a few examples of the tensions that exist within this massive work, one might ask how Philostratus reconciled (1) the living reincarnation of the Homeric hero Palamedes, who he met in India (*VA* 3.22), with the

---

137. Boyd and Eddy, *Lord or Legend*, 111.

138. A word of explanation may be needed for why Luke-Acts was chosen as the representative for the study of Jesus. Since Luke and Acts appears to have had a common author, who intended these works to be read together, this study will treat them as if they were a single document. Furthermore, Luke-Acts makes up about 27 percent of the New Testament. Even though more of the New Testament text may have been written by Paul, Luke-Acts is a better choice as a representative of Jesus materials for this study because (1) Luke deals directly with the story of Jesus; and (2) the issue of the authenticity of some of Paul's letters would require more space for argumentation than this study allows.

PART 4: APOLLONIUS AND JESUS

dead Palamedes to whom Apollonius offered up a prayer (*VA* 4.13.2),[139] (2) the vegetarian Apollonius's acquisition of the ability to understand the language of animals (*VA* 1.20) with the claim that he learned this skill "in the Arabian way," which involved the consumption the hearts or livers of snakes,[140] (3) the portrayal of Apollonius as a divine figure or an autodidact with statements that he had instructors,[141] (4) the claim that Apollonius knew all human languages without studying them (*VA* 1.19.2) with his occasional need for a translator (*VA* 2.26, 27.1; 3.31.2; Eusebius, *Hier.* 14), (5) Apollonius's ability to know the mind of others (*VA* 1.19.2) with his astonishment that a king could speak Greek (*VA* 2.27.1; Eusebius, *Hier.* 14), (6) Apollonius's endorsement of the transmigration of souls with the view that souls of Homeric heroes had not moved on to other bodies or from their tumuli at Troy,[142] (7) Apollonius's affirmation of the mythological traditions about the Titans (*VA* 3.14; 25) with his dismissal or demythologization of such stories (*VA* 5.13, 16),[143] (8) the claim that Apollonius did not prepare for his trial (*VA* 7.30) with the insertion a long and detailed manuscript of the speech that contained what Apollonius had intended to say in his defense before Domitian (*VA* 8.7), (9) Apollonius's frequent endorsement of the notion of leaving this life unobserved (*VA* 8.28) with his going to great lengths to be observed by his jailors when he departed the world (*VA* 8.30.3),[144] (10) Apollonius's preference for brief discourses (*VA* 1.17) with his use of several lengthy

139. Yet, as Solmsen notes, "Apollonius later discusses Palamedes with Achilles, and pays a visit to Palamede's tomb (IV.13, 16) but does not seem to remember that he has met him in India" (Solmsen, "Some Works," 566. n. 36). He writes, Philostratus "does not allow him to remember that he has met his soul before in a different body" (Solmsen, "Some Works," 567). On this point, also see Schirren, "Irony," 173.

140. Eusebius, *Hier.* 10.1. Pythagoras prohibited the eating of the hearts of animals (Diogenes Laertius, Lives 8.1.19.).

141. Schirren "Irony," 180–81. The Wise Ones of India surpassed the wisdom of Apollonius, correcting him (*VA* 3.18) and teaching him (*VA* 3.16.2, 4).

142. Solmsen discusses the tension between the Apollonius's Pythagorean views of transmigration of souls and the fact of Achilles's soul still residing at his tomb. See Solmsen, "Some Questions," 566–69. See also Gyselinck and Khristoffel, "Fiction and Metafiction," 117. Schirren, perhaps incorrectly, suggests that Apollonius adopted an Epicurean-like perspective in *VA* 8.31.3. See Schirren, "Irony," 172–73.

143. Anderson, "Folklore," 214. Perhaps, the rationalistic explanation in *VA* 5.13 and 16 is related to the theme of Apollonius displaying the superiority of his own view over local traditions (*VA* 1.19; 5.2).

144. Flinterman noted the contradiction between Apollonius gaining the attention of his jailors to be witness to his ascent and the claim in *VA* 8.28 that he desired to leave this life unobserved. See Flinterman, "Ascension," 226.

ones in the narrative (*VA* 2.22–23; 5.7.2–4, 14–17; 6.11; 7.14, 26.2–6), (11) the claim that Apollonius wore long hair because of his association with the Pythagoreans (*VA* 1.32) with his claim that he based the practice on his admiration for the Spartans (*VA* 8.7.17), (12) Apollonius's claim that he could not raise the dead (*VA* 8.7.41) with the account in which he raised a dead girl (*VA* 4.45),[145] and (13) the assertion that Apollonius only predicted events without influencing them (*VA* 5.12), yet influenced several future events (*VA* 4.4, 6; 6.41). These are but a few of the tensions in the *VA*. Unresolved issues like these tend to weaken the case for the historicity of the *VA*.

As for the Lukan writings, one might also point out a few internal inconsistencies. Much of the discordant material that has been scrutinized by scholars appears in Acts[146] but, while having a bearing on the overall historicity of that book and perhaps Luke as a historian, these tensions in Acts do not directly relate to traditions about Jesus in Luke-Acts. The tensions in materials about Jesus in the Gospel of Luke are not particularly problematic, for the apparent differences can potentially be resolved by viewing them in their respective contexts. For instance, did Jesus's coming effect peace (Luke 2:14; Acts 10:36) or not (Luke 12:51; 19:42)?[147] Was Jesus intended to be a light to the Gentiles (Luke 2:32) or was Paul identified as this light (Acts 13:47)?[148] Did Jesus know all things

---

145. In this passage, Philostratus seems to leave open the possibility that the girl was not actually dead, thereby making Apollonius's claim that he could not raise the dead potentially consistent with his claim that he did not raise the dead.

146. A few examples of alleged contradictions in Acts will suffice to illustrate the sorts of historical problems encountered there. In the various accounts of Paul's Damascus Road experience, did the men with him see anything during the encounter (Acts 22:9) or not (Acts 9:7)? Did his companions hear anything (Acts 9:7) or not (Acts 22:9)? Also, did the Holy Spirit fall on Cornelius and his family while Peter was speaking (Acts 10:44) or as Peter began to speak (Acts 11:15)? For an attempt to explain such anomalies, see Kurz, "Effects of Variant Narrators," 570–86.

147. Luke 2:14 promised peace to people of goodwill but not to all humans. Throughout Luke, Jesus offers peace to those who respond favorably to him (Luke 7:50; 8:48; 24:36), thus he did preach peace (Acts 10:36). However, Luke also recognized that Jesus's ministry would divide people, depriving them of peace (Luke 12:51); some would accept Jesus's missionaries and receive a blessing of peace (Luke 10:5), while others would reject them would and have that blessing of peace retracted (Luke 12:52). Further, the inhabitants of Jerusalem were blind to the things that would have made for peace, which would result in their destruction by the Romans (Luke 19:42). In summation, Jesus brought the offer of peace, but only those who accepted his message benefitted from it.

148. Jesus did indeed interact with Gentiles in the Gospel of Luke, but his mission to the nations was carried out by sending the apostles to them (Acts 1:8). Indeed, Paul

PART 4: APOLLONIUS AND JESUS

(Luke 5:22; 6:8; 9:47) or was he unaware of some matters (Luke 9:47)?[149] There are also occasional tensions between Luke and Acts. For instance, Jesus appears to ascend on the same day as his resurrection in the Gospel (Luke 24:36–53), but in Acts his ascension (Acts 1:9–11) is said to have been forty days later (Acts 1:3). Most likely, Luke himself did not consider this tension as a contradiction, but rather regarded it as a way of condensing of the ending of the Gospel without indicating an extended gap in time between Luke 24:43 and 44; he may have anticipated that the first chapter of Acts would eventually inform readers of his two-volume work of the forty-day gap.[150] So then, although there are a few difficulties with the Jesus traditions within Luke-Acts, most of which have plausible explanations, these two works are internally consistent.

It appears that the internal contradictions in the *VA* are more widespread and problematic than those in the Luke-Acts. Most of the internal contradictions in Luke-Acts have been addressed by biblical scholars and, in many cases, plausible explanations have been offered for them. With the *VA*, a few explanations for its tensions have been suggested but some internal issues have not yet been explained and others probably cannot be resolved.[151] In the end, the material concerning Apollonius seems to be less internally consistent than the sources sampled for Jesus.

---

was a vessel fashioned for that very purpose (Acts 9:15; 22:21; 26:17–18). In his mission to the Gentiles, Paul, like Jesus (Luke 2:32), was a light to the nations as he carried the gospel to them (Acts 13:47).

149. Fitzmyer believes that Luke 8:45 is an admission that Jesus did not know the identity of the person in the crowd that had touched him. See Fitzmyer, *Luke: I–IX*, 746. Other commentators believe that Jesus did know the identity of the woman, but that his question was asked to force her to come forward to acknowledge her faith. See Garland, *Luke*, 368. Geldenhuys also believed Jesus knew her identity but wanted to have her come forward publicly to remove the scorn that the community had for her. See Geldenhuys, *Luke*, 261.

150. Marshall writes, "[u]nless Luke altered his chronology between the composition of the Gospel and Acts (which is improbable in view of the unified character of Lk.-Acts), he has consciously telescoped his story at some point," (Marshall, *Commentary on Luke*, 904). Similarly, Garland conjectures that Luke "telescopes this event knowing that he will give further details in the opening of the second book" (Garland, *Luke*, 969).

151. Perhaps the vast number of internal contradictions in the *VA* are due to its great length. Philostratus may have struggled to keep the finer details of his narrative straight over the course of the eight-volume work.

Sources Are not Biased Toward the Subject Matter, so That Their Authors Have not Skewed Their Accounts to Serve Their Own Purposes

Scholars of all stripes have noted that bias is an important factor in evaluating the historicity of a tradition or text. In some ways, this is the easiest of the criteria to detect because all ancient authors have biases, just as do all modern scholars.[152] However, bias may also be the most difficult criterion to critique, because the historian must decide if or to what degree an ancient author's biases, agendas, or emotional involvement in the subject matter devalue a document's historical worth.

In some cases, biases do not hinder the extraction of historical data from such sources. For instance, even though the Epistle of Barnabas[153] and the Gospel of Peter[154] have strong anti-Jewish biases, this emphasis has little bearing the value of the Jesus traditions preserved in these documents.[155] Likewise, sources should not be discounted merely because of their author's admiration for a biographical subject or because they were written by a devout follower, for, as Ehrman puts it, "[t]o refuse to use them as sources is to sacrifice the most important avenues to the past we have, and on purely ideological, not historical, grounds."[156] Moreover, as Boyd and Eddy point out, if historians who object to such biases were consistent, they would have to dismiss all historical accounts stemming from people who were emotionally involved in or believed in what they were reporting, whether ancient or modern;[157] this would result in historians being able to say very little about the human past. An author's belief in Jesus or Apollonius as men worthy of emulation or even as divine

---

152. For an overview of the difficulties modern historians encounter in overcoming biases, see Licona, *Resurrection*, 58–62.

153. Ehrman, *Introduction*, 484–88.

154. Ehrman, *Introduction*, 226–28, 243.

155. An exploration of these traditions in the Epistle of Barnabas appeared earlier in this chapter. For such traditions in the Gospel of Peter, see Ehrman, *Introduction*, 228, 240.

156. Ehrman, *Did Jesus Exist?*, 74. Several scholars have given excellent examples to illustrate this point. Ehrman points out that historians would neither dismiss accounts of the Revolutionary War just because they were written from an American perspective nor reject accounts of George Washington written by some of his contemporary admirers. See Ehrman, *Did Jesus Exist?*, 74. Boyd and Eddy similarly point out that western leaders in 1942 had no reason to deny the eyewitness accounts of the atrocities of the Nazi concentration camps, even though the reporters were emotionally involved and believed in the things that they had witnessed. See Boyd and Eddy, *Lord or Legend*, 98.

157. Boyd and Eddy, *Lord or Legend*, 97.

figures should certainly be noted and scrutinized by historians, but such views do not necessarily negatively impact the historical value of all other traditions about them.

In what ways and to what extent are the reports about Apollonius biased? At one end of the spectrum, both Lucian and Dio Cassius despised magic in general; this opinion may have led these authors to depict Apollonius as a disreputable magician. Lucian also hated Alexander, the disciple of Apollonius, for personal reasons and this may have colored his opinions of Apollonius to some extent. At the other end of the spectrum, the bias of Philostratus may be detected in his portrayal of Apollonius in an entirely positive light; he too despised magic but rather than rejecting him because of his supernatural powers sought to transform Apollonius into a wonderworking philosopher. The *Letters of Apollonius* and the biography of Moiragenes seem to stand at the midpoint of these perspectives; both sources gave a favorable depiction of the sage while accepting him as both a magician and a philosopher, but since neither of these sources have survived, bias is difficult to assess in these two cases. Despite these disparate views, many aspects of the story of Apollonius remain the same, as was shown above in this chapter, thus suggesting that the broader strokes of his portrayal are largely unaffected by such biases.

However, the biases of Philostratus may be significant in a few cases and may even suggest that he was sometimes historically untrustworthy. Perhaps the clearest indication of a bias in the *VA* is when he goes against the grain of all the earlier and contemporary traditions that portrayed Apollonius as a magician and argued instead that he was merely a Pythagorean sage. Whether this agenda was Philostratus's, as one who frowned upon magic, or Julia Domna's is difficult to determine, but in the end, the tradition has markedly changed and should be regarded as suspect.

Historians should also carefully evaluate the agendas and biases of sources about Jesus. The Gospel writers had discernable agendas, just as the authors of extrabiblical sources about Jesus had theirs. One illustration of this can be seen in how the Gospel writers treated potentially self-damaging details about Jesus.[158] At times, these authors clarified or may have softened potentially embarrassing traditions.[159] However, rather than de-

---

158. For a list of potentially self-damaging statements in the Gospel of Mark, see Boyd and Eddy, *Lord or Legend*, 108.

159. Boyd and Eddy point out that Mark's claim (Mark 1:4–11) that John the Baptist immersed Jesus had two potentially damaging implications: (1) it might suggest that John was superior to Jesus because he baptized Jesus rather than the other way

leting these potentially dangerous details to sanitize the story of Jesus, they retained them. This suggests that the Gospel writers respected these earlier traditions.[160] Apart from the Gospels, the *Testimonium Flavianum*, in its slightly reconstructed form, appears to have been more-or-less neutral in its presentation of Jesus, while several of the pagan texts regarded Jesus as a criminal (e.g., Tacitus) and his disciples as criminals (e.g. Tacitus) or as gullible folk taken in by charlatans (e.g., Lucian). Despite various biases, the overall picture of Jesus as a teacher and miracle-worker (Josephus), who was crucified (e.g., Josephus, Tacitus, and Lucian) and whose disciples believed he was divine (e.g., Lucian) and had risen from the dead (e.g., Josephus), is consistent, although not always flattering.

CONCLUSION

Returning to the question asked at the beginning of this chapter, is it true that more can be known, biographically speaking, about Apollonius than can be known about Jesus? This query must be answered in the negative. This study has shown that Apollonius is the more shadowy of the two figures because the extant traditions about him are late in date (or undatable), contradictory at points, and many traditions about him are supported only by the assertions of the *VA*. The Jesus material, on the other hand, is quite early, consistent, and attested in multiple sources. There is no doubt that the ancient traditions give a more concrete picture of Jesus than they did of Apollonius, despite more material having been written about the latter. Therefore, unless more convincing arguments than those offered by Votaw or Boring can be presented, the historical (or biographical) evidence for Jesus appears to be far superior to that available for Apollonius. Again, the superiority of the Jesus material according to the criteria explored in this chapter do not demonstrate that the traditions about Jesus are historically true, but that the traditions are

---

round; and, (2) it might suggest that Jesus was a sinner because John practiced a baptism for the remission of sins. Therefore, according to Boyd and Eddy, the other Gospels attempted to soften this tradition by further explaining the details of the baptism (Matt. 3:13–17; Luke 3:19–22; John 1:29–34). See Boyd and Eddy, *Lord or Legend*, 107. Another example of softening a tradition about Jesus is that in Mark 6:5 Jesus "could not" (potentially implying his inability) perform miracles at Nazareth because of lack of faith—although he did heal a few sick people—but Matt 13:58 claims Jesus "did not" perform many miracles (implying choice on his part) because of lack of faith.

160. For a list of representative self-damaging traditions that were not excised from the Gospels, see Boyd and Eddy, *Lord or Legend*, 107–9.

earlier and more consistent than those for Apollonius and have at least passed the preliminary tests concerning historical veracity.

Hopefully, this chapter has also underscored the importance of interacting with all the ancient sources about Apollonius, not just with the VA. As chapter 2 of this book indicated, many New Testament scholars base their claims about Apollonius solely on Philostratus's version of the sage, despite its late date (a second-tier source), lack of independently attested traditions, and departure from earliest sources that claim Apollonius was a magician. Because the claims of the VA are often taken at face value and alternative voices about Apollonius often are excluded from the discussion, researchers frequently have a distorted sense of how much can be known about this ancient figure. Thus, the selection entitled *One Remarkable Life*, which was cited in full in chapter 1 of this book, would more accurately be entitled, *One Remarkable Life according to Philostratus*. Lucian and Dio Cassius would have agreed that Apollonius's life was remarkable but would have found it so because they thought Apollonius was a consummate fraud and magician.

Bibliography

Abraham, Roshan. "The Geography of Culture in Philostratus's *Life of Apollonius of Tyana*." *CJ* 109 (2014) 465–80.
Adams, Sean A. *The Genre of Acts and Collected Biography*. Society for New Testament Studies Monograph Series 156. New York: Cambridge University Press, 2013.
Allinson, Francis G. *Lucian, Satirist and Artist*. New York: Cooper Square, 1963.
Anālayo, Bhikkhu. "Levitation in Early Buddhist Discourse." *JOCBS* 5 (2016) 11–26.
Anderson, Graham. "Folklore Versus Fakelore: Some Problems in the *Life of Apollonius*." In *Theios Sophistes: Essays on Flavius Philostratus's Vita Apollonii*, edited by Kristoffel Demoen and Danny Praet, 211–24. Mnemosyne Supplements 305. Leiden: Brill, 2009.
———. *Philostratus: Biography and Belles Lettres in the Third Century A.D.* New York: Routledge, 1986.
Anson, Edward M. "The 'Ephemerides' of Alexander the Great." *Historia* 45.4 (1996) 501–5.
Anton-Hermann, Chroust. "A Brief Analysis of the Vita Aristotelis of Diogenes Laertius (DL V 1–16)." *L'antiquité Classique* 34 (1965) 97–129.
Arrian. *Anabasis of Alexander*. Translated by P. A. Brunt. 2 vols. LCL. Cambridge: Harvard University Press, 1975–1983.
Aslan, Reza. *Zealot: The Life and Times of Jesus of Nazareth*. New York: Random House, 2013.
Aune, David. *Revelation 6–16*. WBC 52B. Nashville: Nelson, 1998.
Baldelli, Franceso., trans. *Filostrato Lemnio Della uita di Apollonio Tianeo*. Florence: Appresso Lorenazo Torrentino, 1549.
Barber, Charles. *Contesting the Logic of Painting: Art and Understanding in Eleventh-century Byzantium*. Visualising the Middle Ages 2. Leiden: Brill, 2007.
Barnes, T. D. "Porphyry 'Against the Christians': Date and the Attribution of Fragments." *JTS* 24 (1973) 424–28.
———. "Scholarship or Propaganda? Porphyry *Against the Christians* in Its Historical Setting." *BICS* 34 (1994) 53–65.
———. "Sossianus Hierocles and the Antecedents of the "Great Persecution."" *HSCP* 80 (1976) 239–52.
Barrett, C. K., ed. *The New Testament Background: Selected Documents*. New York: Harper & Row, 1987.

Baur, F. C. *Apollonius von Tyana und Christus: Ein Beitrag zur Religionsgeschicte der ersten Jahrhunderte nach Christus.* 1876. Reprint, Hildesheim: Olms, 1966.

Beck, Roger. "Mystery Religions, Aretalogy and the Ancient Novel." In *The Novel in the Ancient World,* edited by Gareth L. Schmeling, 131–50. Mnemosyne Supplements 159. Leiden: Brill, 1996.

Beker, J. Christiaan. *Paul the Apostle: The Triumph of God in Life and Thought.* Philadelphia: Fortress, 1987.

Bell, Albert A. *Exploring the New Testament World: An Illustrated Guide to the World of Jesus and the First Christians.* Nashville: Nelson, 1998.

Benner, Allen Roger, and Francis H. Fobes. 1949. *The Letters of Alciphron, Aelian, and Philostratus: The Letters of Alciphron, Aelian, and Philostratus.* LCL. Cambridge: Harvard University Press.

Bernard, Paul. "L'Aornos Bactrien et l'Aornos Indien. Philostrate et Taxila: Géographie, Mythe et Réalité." *Topii* 6 (1996) 475–530.

Bernard, Raymond W. *Apollonius of Tyana: The Nazarene.* Woodland, CA: Ancient Wisdom, 2009.

———. *Apollonius the Nazarene: The Life and Teachings of the Unknown World Teacher of the First Century.* Lorida, FL: New Age Publications, 1945.

Bernier, Jonathan. *Rethinking the Dates of the New Testament: The Evidence for Early Composition.* Grand Rapids, Baker, 2022.

Bertolazzi, Ricardo. "Julia Domna and Her Divine Motherhood: A Re-examination of the Evidence from Imperial Coins." *CJ* 114.4 (2019) 464–86.

Betz, Otto. "The Concept of the So-Called 'Divine Man' in Mark's Christology." In *Studies in New Testament and Early Christian Literature: Essays in Honor of Allen Wikgren,* edited by David E. Aune, 229–40. Novum Testamentum Supplements 33. Leiden: Brill, 1972.

Bidez, J. "Literature and Philosophy in the Eastern Half of the Empire." In *The Cambridge Ancient History,* edited by S. A. Cook et al., 12:611–45. London: Cambridge University Press, 1971.

Bird, Michael F. *The Gospel of the Lord: How the Early Church Wrote the Story of Jesus.* Grand Rapids: Eerdmans, 2014.

Birley, Anthony R. *The Roman Government of Britain.* New York: Oxford University Press, 2005.

———. *Septimius Severus: The African Emperor.* Roman Imerial Biographies. 1971. Reprint, New York: Routledge, 1999.

Blackburn, B. L. "Divine Man/Theios Anēr." In *DJG,* 189–92. Downers Grove, IL: InterVarsity, 1992. 189–92.

———. "Miracle Working ΘΕΟΙ ΑΝΔΡΕΣ in Hellenism (and Hellenistic Judaism)." In *The Miracles of Jesus,* edited by David Wenham and Craig Blomberg, 185–218. Gospel Perspectives 6. 1986. Reprint, Eugene, OR: Wipf & Stock, 2003.

Blomberg, Craig L. *The Historical Reliability of John's Gospel: Issues and Commentary.* Downers Grove, IL: InterVarsity, 2001.

Blount, Charles. *The Two First Books of Philostratus, Concerning the Life of Apollonius Tyaneus: Written Originally in Greek, And Now Published in English: Together with Philological Notes Upon Each Chapter.* London: Nathaniel Thompson, 1680.

Boring, M. Eugene. *An Introduction to the New Testament: History, Literature, Theology.* Loiusville: Westminster John Knox, 2012.

Bosworth, A. B. "The Death of Alexander the Great: Rumour and Propoganda." *ClQ* 21 (1971) 112–36.

Boter, Gerard. "The Title of Philostratus' *Life of Apollonius of Tyana*." *JHS* 135 (2015) 1–7.

———. "Towards a New Critical Edition of Philostratus' Life of Apollonius: The Affiliation of the Manuscripts." In *Theios Sophistes: Essays on Flavius Philostratus's Vita Apolloni*, edited by Kristoffel Demoen and Danny Praet, 21–56. Mnemosyne Supplements 305. Leiden: Brill, 2009.

Boyd Gregory A., and Paul Rhodes Eddy. *Lord or Legend? Wrestling with the Jesus Dilemma*. Grand Rapids: Baker, 2007.

Bowersock, G. W. *Fiction as History: Nero to Julian*. Berkeley: University of California Press, 1994.

———. *Greek Sophists in the Roman Empire*. London: Oxford University Press, 1969.

———. Introduction to *Life of Apollonius*. Edited by G. W. Bowersock. Translated by C. P. Jones, 9– 22. Baltimore: Penguin, 1970.

———. "The Miracle of Memnon." *BASP* 21 (1984) 21–32.

Bowie, Ewen. "Apollonius of Tyana, Tradition and Reality." *ANRW* 16.2:1652–99. Part 2, Principat, 16.2. Edited by Wolfgang Haase. New York: de Gruyter, 1978.

———. "The geography of the Second Sophistic: Cultural Variations." In *Paideia: The World of the Second Sophistic*, edited by Barbara Borg, 65–86. Berlin: de Gruyter, 2004.

———. "The Importance of Sophists." *YCS* 27 (1982) 29–59.

———. "Philostratus: The Life of a Sophist." In *Philostratus*, edited by Ewen Bowie and Jaś Elsner, 19–32. GCRW. Cambridge: Cambridge University Press, 2009.

———. "Philostratus: Writer of Fiction." In *Greek Fiction: The Greek Novel in Context*, edited by J. R. Morgan and Richard Stoneman, 181–99. New York: Routledge, 1994.

———. "Quotation of Earlier Texts in the Τὰ ἐς τὸν Τυανέα Ἀπολλώνιον." In *Theios Sophistes: Essays on Flavius Philostratus's Vita Apolloni*, edited by Kristoffel Demoen and Danny Praet, 57–74. Mnemosyne Supplements 305. Leiden: Brill, 2009.

Bowie, Ewen and Jaś Elsner, eds. *Philostratus*. GCRW. Cambridge: Cambridge University Press, 2009.

Bradley, K. R. "The Chronology of Nero's Visit to Greece." *Latomus* 37 (1978) 61–72.

Brent, Allen. *Hippolytus and the Roman Church in the Third Century: Communities in Tension before the Emergence of a Monarch-Bishop*. Vigiliae Christianae Supplements 31. Leiden: Brill, 1995.

Brock, S. P. *A Brief Outline of Syriac Literature*. Baker Hill, India: SEERI, 1997.

Brown, Charles Thomas. "The Gospel of Ignatius of Antioch." PhD diss., Loyola University, 1997.

Brown, Colin. *Miracles and the Critical Mind*. Grand Rapids: Eerdmans, 1984.

Brown, Raymond E. *The Death of the Messiah*. 2 vols. New York: Doubleday, 1994.

Bruce, F. F. *The Acts of the Apostles: The Greek Text with Introduction and Commentary*. 2nd ed. Grand Rapids: Eerdmans, 1984.

———. *Paul: Apostle of the Heart Set Free*. Grand Rapids: Eerdmans, 2000.

Brunt, P. A. "The Bubble of the Second Sophistic." *BICS* 39 (1994) 25–52.

Buck, David F. "Eunapius of Sardis." PhD diss., Oxford University, 1977.

Bultmann, Rudolf. *The Gospel of John*. Translated by G. R. Beasley-Murray. Philadelphia: Westminster, 1971. Reprint, Johannine Monograph Series. Eugene, OR: Wipf & Stock, 2014.

Bur, Tatiana. "Mechanical Miracles: Automata in Ancient Greek Religion." MPhil thesis, University of Sydney, 2016.

Burckhardt, Jacob. *The Civilization of the Renaissance in Italy*. London: Phaidon, 1951.

Burghardt, Walter J. "Did Saint Ignatius of Antioch Know the Fourth Gospel?" *TS* 1 (1940) 130–56.

Burian P. and N. J. Richardson. "The Epigram on Apollonius of Tyana." *GRBS* 22 (1981) 283–85.

Burkert, Walter. *Greek Religion*. Translated by John Raffan. Cambridge: Harvard University Press, 1985.

Burridge, Richard A. *What Are the Gospels? A Comparison with Graeco-Roman Biography*. Grand Rapids: Eerdmans, 2004.

Butler, H. E., and A. S. Owen. *Apulei Apologia sive Pro se de Magia Liber*. 1914. Reprint, Hildesheim: Olms, 1967.

Calderini, A. "Teoria e pratica politica nella 'Vita di Apollonio di Tiana.'" *RIL* 74 (1940/1) 213–41.

Carson D. A., and Douglas J. Moo. *An Introduction to the New Testament*. Grand Rapids: Zondervan, 2005.

Cartlidge, David R., and David L. Duncan, eds. *Documents for the Study of the Gospels*. 2nd ed. Philadelphia: Fortress, 1994.

Casson, Lionel. *Selected Satires of Lucian*. Edited and translated by Lionel Casson. New York: Norton, 1962.

Cazemier, Annelies. "Apollonius en Magie in Philostratus' *Vita Apollonii*." MA thesis, Vrije Universiteit Amsterdam, 2002.

Cedrinus, Georgius, and Immanuel Bekker, eds. *Georgius Cedrenus, Ioannis Scylitzae ope*. Edited by Immanuel Bekker. CSHB 8. Bonn: Weber, 1838.

Cerrato, J. A. "Hippolytus." In *DMBI*, 526.

Chadwick, Henry. *The Early Church*. Rev. ed. New York: Penguin, 1993.

Chandler, Samuel. *A Vindication of the Christian Religion: In Two Parts. A Discourse of the Nature and Use of Miracles*. London: Cross-Keys, 1725.

Charpentier, J. "The Indian Travels of Apollonius of Tyana." In *Skrifter utgivna av. K. Humanistika Vetenskaps-Samfundet i Uppsala*, 29.3.1–66. Uppsala: Almqvist & Wiksells, 1934.

Chesterton, G. K. *The Everlasting Man*. 1925. Reprint, San Francisco: Ignatius, 1993.

Chrysostom, John. *Discourses Against Judaizing Christians*. Translated by Paul W. Harkins. Fathers of the Church 68. Washington, DC: Catholic University of America Press, 1979.

Clark, David K. "Miracles in the World Religions." In *In Defense of Miracles: A Comprehensive Case for God's Action in History*, edited by R. Douglas Geivett and Gary R. Habermas, 119–213. Downers Grove, IL: InterVarsity, 1997.

Clarke, Samuel. *A Discourse Concerning the Being and Attributes of God, the Obligations of Natural Religion, and the Truth and Certainty of the Christian Revelation*. London: Botham, 1782.

Cobb, Matthew Adam. "Apollonius in India: The *Vita Apolonii* and the Indographic Tradition." *CJ* (2023) 440–73.

Colavito, Jason. "Book of the Secret Creation." https://www.jasoncolavito.com/the-secret-of-creation.html.
Costantini, Leonardo. *Magic in Apuleius' 'Apologia': Understanding the charges and the forensic strategies in Apuleius' speech*. Berlin: de Gruyter, 2019.
Conzelmann, Hans. *Acts of the Apostles*. Translated by James Limburg et al. Hermeneia. Philadelphia: Fortress, 1987.
Copleston, Frederick. *Greece and Rome*. A History of Philosophy 1. New York: Doubleday, 1993.
Cotta, A. L. *Gewißheit der Beweise des Apollonismus oder Widerlegung der Prüfung und Vertheidigung der apollonischen Religion*. Frankfurt and Leipzig, 1787.
Crafer, T. W. *The Apocriticus of Macarius Magnes*. New York: Macmillan, 1919.
Cragg, Gerald R. *The Church and the Age of Reason, 1648–1789*. Grand Rapids: Eerdmans, 1962.
Crossan, John Dominic. *The Historical Jesus: The Life of a Mediterranean Jewish Peasant*. San Francisco: HarperSanFrancisco, 1991.
Cudworth, Ralph. *The True Intellectual System of the Universe*. London: Haddon, 1845.
D'Aussy, Pierre Jean-Baptiste Legrand. *Vie d'Apollonius de Tyane*. Paris: Collin, 1807.
De Lannoy, L. "Le problème des Philostrate (État de la question)." *ANRW* II 34.3:2363–449.
De Vigenère, Blaise. *Philostrate de la Vie d'Apollonius*. Paris: L'Angelier, 1596.
Delatte, A. "Le déclin de la Légendes des VII Sages et les Prophéties théosophiques." *Musée Belge* 27 (1923) 97–111.
Demoen, Kristoffel, and Danny Praet, eds. *Theios Sophistes: Essays on Flavius Philostratus's Vita Apollonii*. Mnemosyne Supplements 305. Leiden: Brill, 2009.
Didron, M. *Manuel D'Iconographie Chrétienne Grec et Latine*. Paris: Royal, 1845.
Dio Cassius. *Roman History*. Translated by Earnest Cary. 9 vol. New York: Macmillan, 1914–1927.
Dionysios (of Fourna). *Manuel D'Iconographie Chretienne*. St. Petersburg: Kirschbaum, 1909.
Dolce, Lodovico, trans. *La vita del gran philosopho Apollonio Tianeo, composta da Philostrato scrittor greco, et tradotta nella lingua volgare*. Venice: Gabriele Giolito de' Ferrari, 1549.
Dudley, Donald R. *The Civilization of Rome*. New York: Meridian, 1962.
Duliére, W. L. "Protection permanente contre des animaux nuisibles assurée par Apollonius de Tyane dans Byzance et Antioch: Evolution de son mythe." *ByzZ* 63 (1970) 247–77.
Dzielska, Maria. *Apollonius of Tyana in Legend and History*. Translated by Piotr Pieńkowski. Problemi e Ricerche di Storia Antica 10. Rome: Bretschneider, 1986.
Eddy, Paul Rhodes, and Gregory A. Boyd, *The Jesus Legend: A Case for the Historical Reliability of the Synoptic Jesus Tradition*. Grand Rapids: Baker Academic, 2007.
Ehrman, Bart. *A Brief Introduction to the New Testament*. New York: Oxford University Press, 2004.
———. *Did Jesus Exist? The Historical Argument for Jesus of Nazareth*. New York: HarperCollins, 2012.
———. "Ehrman vs. Craig: Evidence for Resurrection." YouTube, Aug 9, 2016. https://youtu.be/MW5_nJYSKyk?si=C8wDC-AIzBnRKZjw.
———. *How Jesus Became God: The Exaltation of a Jewish Preacher from Galilee*. New York: HarperOne, 2015.

———. *The New Testament: A Historical Introduction to the Early Christian Writings.* New York: Oxford University Press, 2016.
———. *The New Testament and Other Early Christian Writings: A Reader.* New York: Oxford University Press, 2004.
Elsner, Jaś. "A Protean Corpus." In *Philostratus,* edited by Edwin Bowie and Jaś Elsner, 3–18. GCRW. Cambridge: Cambridge University Press, 2009.
Elsner, John. "Hagiographic Geography: Travel and Allegory in the *Life of Apollonius of Tyana.*" *JHS* 117 (1997) 2–37.
Epictetus. *Discourses and Enchiridion.* Translated by W. A. Oldfather. 2 vols. LCL. Cambridge: Harvard University Press, 2000.
Evans, Craig A. *Jesus and His Contemporaries.* AGJU 25. Leiden: Brill, 2001.
Eusebius. *Church History.* In vol. 1 of *The Nicene and Post-Nicene Fathers.* Series 2. Edited by Philip Shaff and Henry Wace. 1890. 14 vols. Reprint, Peabody, MA: Hendrickson, 1999.
———. *Preparation for the Gospel.* Translated by Edwin Hamilton Gifford. Oxford: Clarendon, 1903.
Ferguson, Everett. *Backgrounds of Early Christianity.* Grand Rapids: Eerdmans, 2003.
———. *Demonology of the Early Christian World,* Symposium Series 12. Lewiston: Edwin Mellen, 1984.
Ferguson, John. *The Religions of the Roman Empire.* Ithaca: Cornell University Press, 1970.
Ficino, Marsilio. *Meditations on the Soul: Selected Letters of Marsilio Ficino.* Translated by members of the Language Department of the School of Economic Science, London. Rochester, VT: Inner Traditions International, 1997.
Fitzmyer, Joseph A. *The Gospel According to Luke: I–IX.* AB 28. Garden City, NY: Doubleday, 1981.
Fleury, Claude. *The Ecclesiastical History of M. L' abbé Fleury,* vol. 1. London: Wood, 1727.
Flinterman, Jaap-Jan. "'The ancestor of my wisdom': Pythagoras and Pythagoreanism in *Life of Apollonius.*" In *Philostratus,* edited by Ewen Bowie and Jaś Elsner, 155–75. GCRW. Cambridge: Cambridge University Press, 2009.
———. *Power, Paideia & Pythagoreanism: Greek Identity, Conceptions of the Relationship between Philosophers and Monarchs in Philostratus' Life of Apollonius.* Dutch Monographs on Ancient History and Archaeology 13. Amsterdam: Gieben, 1995.
Fontainelle, Earl. "Graeme Miles on Apollonius of Tyana." *The Secret History of Western Esotericism Podcast,* July 16, 2019. https://shwep.net/podcast/graeme-miles-on-apollonius-of-tyana/.
Forsyth, P. Y. "After the Big Bang: Eruptive Activity in the Caldera of Greco-Roman Thera." *GRBS* 33 (1992) 191–204.
Fox, Robin Lane. *Pagans and Christians.* New York: Knopf, 1987.
Francis, James A. *Subversive Virtue: Asceticism and Authority in the Second-Century Pagan World.* University Park: Pennsylvania State University Press, 1995.
———. "Truthful Fiction: New Questions to Old Answers on Philostratus's 'Life of Apollonius.'" 119 *AJP* (1998) 419–41.
Francis, James Allan. *The Real Jesus, and Other Sermons.* Philadelphia: Judson, 1926.
Freed, Edwin, D. *The New Testament: A Critical Introduction.* Belmont, CA: Wadsworth, 2000.

BIBLIOGRAPHY

Freese, J. H., *The Library of Photius*. Translated by J. H. Freese. Charleston: BiblioBazaar, 2009.

Frend, W. H. C. *The Rise of Christianity*. Philadelphia: Fortress, 1984.

Galimberti, Alessandro. "La Vita di Apollonio di Tiana e Caracalla: Chronologia e Contest Storico." *Aev* 88 (2014) 125–36.

Gardiner, Philip, dir. *Bible Conspiracies*. Gravitas Ventures, 2016.

Garland, David E. *Luke*. Zondervan Exegetical Commentary on the New Testament 3. Grand Rapids: Zondervan, 2011.

Gasco la Calle, Fernando. "El viaje de Apolonio a la Betica (Siglo I d.C.)." *Revista de Estudios Andaluces* 4 (1985) 13–22.

Geisler, Norman L. *The Big Book of Christian Apologetics: An A to Z Guide*. Grand Rapids: Baker, 2012.

Geivett, R. Douglas, and Gary R. Habermas. *In Defense of Miracles: A Comprehensive Case for God's Action in History*. Downers Grove, IL: InterVarsity, 1997.

Geldenhuys, Norval. *The Gospel of Luke*. NICNT. Grand Rapids: Eerdmans, 1983.

Georgi, Dieter. *The Opponents of Paul in Second Corinthians: A Study of Religious Propaganda in Late Antiquity*. Translated by Harold W. Attridge et al. Philadelphia: Fortress, 1986.

Gildersleeve, Basil Lanneau. *Essays and Studies: Educational and Literary*. Baltimore: Friedenwald, 1890.

Godeau, Antoine. *Histoire de l'Eglise*. Vol. 1. 5th ed. Paris: Covrbé, 1680.

Goldhill, Simon. "Constructed Identity in Philostratus' Love Letters." In *Philostratus*, edited by Edwin Bowie and Jaś Elsner, 287–305. GCRW. Cambridge: Cambridge University Press, 2009.

Gonzalez, Justo L. *The Early Church to the Dawn of the Reformation*. Vol 1. of *The Story of Christianity*. New York: HarperCollins, 1984.

Goodspeed Edgar J., ed. *The Earliest Apologists: Texts with Brief Introductions*. Göttingen: Vandenhoeck & Ruprecht, 1914. Reprint, Rochester, NY: Irenaeus Press, 2013.

Göttsching, Johannes. *Apollonius von Tyana*. Leipzig: Hoffmann, 1889.

Graf, Fritz. "Maximos von Aigai: ein Beitrag zur Überlieferung über Apollonios von Tyana." *JAC* 27/28 (1984) 65–73.

Grant, Robert M. *Augustus to Constantine: The Thrust of the Christian Movement into the Roman World*. New York: Harper & Row, 1970.

Green, Peter. *Alexander of Macedon, 356–23 B.C.: A Historical Biography*. Berkeley: University of California Press, 1991.

Grossardt, Peter. "How to Become a Poet? Homer and Apollonius Visit the Mound of Achilles." In *Theios Sophistes: Essays on Flavius Philostratus's Vita Apollonii*, edited by Kristoffel Demoen and Danny Praet, 75–94. Mnemosyne Supplements 305. Leiden: Brill, 2009.

Grosso, Fulvio. "La 'Vita di Apollonio di Tiana' come Fonte Storica." *ACME* 7 (1954) 33–532.

Gualandi, Giovambernardo. *Filostrato greco scrittore elegantissimo Della vita del mirabile Apollonio Tyaneo, tradotto in linga fiorentina*. Venice: Comin da Trino di Monferrato, 1549.

Guthrie, Kenneth Sylvan. *The Pythagorean Sourcebook and Library*. Edited by David Fideler. Grand Rapids: Phanes, 1988.

Gyselinck, Wannes, and Kristoffel Demoen. "Author and Narrator: Fiction and Metafiction in Philostratus' *Vita Apollonii*." In *Theios Sophistes: Essays on Flavius Philostratus's Vita Apollonii*, edited by Kristoffel Demoen and Danny Praet, 95–128. Mnemosyne Supplements 305. Leiden: Brill, 2009.

Habermas, Gary R. *Ancient Evidence for the Life of Jesus: Historical Records of His Death and Resurrection*. Nashville: Nelson, 1984.

———. "Did Jesus Perform Miracles?" In *Jesus Under Fire: Modern Scholarship Reinvents the Historical Jesus*, edited by Michael J. Wilkins and J. P. Moreland, 118–40. Grand Rapids: Zondervan, 1995.

Habermas, Gary R. and Michael R. Licona. *The Case for the Resurrection of Jesus*. Grand Rapids: Kregel, 2004.

Hadas, Moses. *A History of Greek Literature*. New York: Columbia University Press, 1950.

Hadas, Moses and Morton Smith. *Heroes and Gods: Spiritual Biographies in Antiquity*. London: Routledge & Kegan Paul, 1965.

Hägg, T. "Hierocles the Lover of Truth and Eusebius the Sophist." *Symbolae Osloenses* 67 (1992) 138–50.

Hamell, Patrick J. *Handbook of Patrology*. New York: Alba House, 1968.

Hamilton, J. L. "Storm-making Springs: Rings of Invisibility and Protection–Studies on the Sources of the Yvain of Chretien de Troies." *The Romanic Review* 5 (1914) 213–37.

Harris, B. F. "Apollonius of Tyana: Fact or Fiction." *JRH* 5 (1969) 189–99.

Hemelrijk, Emily Ann. *Matrona Docta: Educated Women in the Roman élite from Cornelia to Julia Domna*. New York: Routledge, 2004.

Hengel, Martin. *The Charismatic Leader and His Followers*. New York: Crossroad, 1981.

———. *The Son of God: The Origin of Christology and the History of Jewish Hellenistic Religion*. 1976. Reprint, Eugene, OR: Wipf & Stock, 2007.

Hennecke, Edgar. *Writings Relating to the Apostles Apocalypses and Related Subjects*. Vol. 2 of *New Testament Apocrypha*. Edited by Wilhelm Schneemelcher. Translated by R. McL. Wilson. Philadelphia: Westminster, 1965.

Herzog, M. Io. Christianus, *Philosophiam Practicam Apollonii Tyanei in Sciagraphia*. Leipzig: N.p., 1709.

Hilton, John. "Speaking Truth to Power: Julian, the Cynics, and the Ethiopian Gymnosophists of Heliodorus." In *Intellectual and Empire in Greco-Roman Antiquity*, edited by Philip R. Bosman, 202–15. London: Routledge, 2019.

Hoffmann, R. Joseph. *Porphyry's Against the Christians: The Literary Remains*. Translated by R. Joseph Hoffmann. Amherst: Prometheus, 1994.

Holladay, Carl H. *Theios Aner in Hellenistic Judaism: A Critique of the Use of this Category in New Testament Christology*. SBLDS 40. Missoula, MT: Scholars, 1977.

Holzberg, Niklas. "The Genre: Novels Proper and the Fringe." In *The Novel in the Ancient World*, edited by Gareth L. Schmeling, 11–28. Leiden: Brill, 1996.

Hooker, Morna D. *Paul: A Short Introduction*. Oxford: Oneworld, 2003.

Horn, Trent. "Bart Ehrman's Bad Arguments." YouTube, July 5, 2023. https://youtu.be/AVca4k27sHU

Horsley, G. H. R. Review of *Philostratus, III. Apollonius of Tyana. Letters of Apollonius, Ancient testimonias, Eusebius' Reply to Hierocles*, by C. P. Jones. *JRH* 37 (2013) 162–63.

Huhn, F., and E. Bethe. "Philostrats Heroikos und Diktys." *Hermes* 52 (1917) 613–24.

Humble, Geoff, trans. "The Biography of Yelü Chucai." https://www.academia.edu/38936635/Yelu_Chucai_Yuanshi_Biography.
Jacquier, E. "Matthew, Saint, Gospel of." In *The Catholic Encyclopedia* 10:57–58
James, Peter, and Marinus Anthony van der Sluijs. "Ziggurats, Colors, and Planets: Rawlinson Revisited." *JCS* 60 (2008) 57–79.
Jenkins, Philip. *The Lost History of Christianity: The Thousand Year Golden Age of the Church in the Middle East, Africa, and Asia—and How it Died*. New York: HarperCollins, 2008.
Johnson, Luke Timothy. *The Letter of James*. AB37A. New York: Doubleday, 1995.
———. *Living Jesus: Learning the Heart of the Gospel*. New York: HarperCollins, 1999.
———. *The Writings of the New Testament*. 3rd ed. Minneapolis: Fortress, 2010.
Jones, Brian W. *The Emperor Domitian*. New York: Routledge, 2002.
Jones, Christopher P. "Apollonius of Tyana in Late Antiquity." In *Greek Literature in Late Antiquity: Dynamism, Didacticism, Classicism*, edited by Scott Fitzgerald Johnson, 49–66. New York: Routledge, 2016.
———. "Apollonius of Tyana, Hero and Holy Man." In *Philostratus's Heroicus: Religion and Cultural Identity in the Third Century C.E.*, edited by Ellen Bradshaw Aitken and Jennifer K. Berenson, 75–84. Writings from the Greco-Roman World 6. Leiden: Brill, 2004.
———. "Apollonius of Tyana's Passage to India." *GRBS* 42 (2001) 185–99.
———. "Some Letters of Apollonius of Tyana." In *Theios Sophistes: Essays on Flavius Philostratus's Vita Apollonii*, edited by Kristoffel Demoen and Danny Praet, 249–62. Mnemosyne Supplements 305. Leiden: Brill, 2009.
Kähler, Martin. *The So-Called Historical Jesus and the Historic, Biblical Christ*. Edited and Translated by Carl E. Braaten. Philadelphia: Fortress, 1964.
Kee, Howard Clark. *Miracle in the Early Christian World: A Study in Sociohistorical Method*. New Haven: Yale University Press, 1983.
Keener, Craig S. *Christobiography: Memory, History, and the Reliability of the Gospels*. Grand Rapids: Eerdmans, 2019.
———. *The Gospel of John: A Commentary*. 2 vols. Peabody, MA: Hendrickson, 2003.
———. *Miracles: The Credibility of the New Testament Accounts*. 2 vols. Grand Rapids: Baker Academic, 2011.
King, Cynthia. *Musonius Rufus: Lectures and Sayings*. Edited by William B. Irvine. Rev. ed. CreateSpace, 2011.
Kim, Lawrence Young. *Homer Between History and Fiction in Imperial Greek Literature*. Cambridge: Cambridge University Press, 2010.
Klauck, Hans-Josef. *The Religious Context of Early Christianity: A Guide to Greco-Roman Religions*. Translated by Brian McNeil. Minneapolis: Fortress, 2003.
Knoles, Thomas Gregory. "Literary Technique and Theme in Philostratus' *Life of Apollonius of Tyana*." PhD diss., Rutgers University, 1981.
Koester, Helmut. *Ancient Christian Gospels: Their History and Development*. Philadelphia: Trinity, 1990.
———. *Introduction to the New Testament*. 2 vols. Philadelphia: Fortress, 1982.
König, Jason. "Training athletes and interpreting the past in Philostratus' *Gymnasticus*." In *Philostratus*, edited by Ewen Bowie and Jaś Elsner, 251–83. GCRW. Cambridge: Cambridge University Press, 2009.
Koskenniemi, Erkki. *Apollonios von Tyana in der neutestamentlichen Exegese*. WUNT 2/61. Tübingen: Mohr Siebeck, 1994.

———. "Apollonius of Tyana: A Typical ΘΕΙΟΣ ΑΝΗΡ?" *JBL* 117 (1998) 455–67.
———. "The Philostratean Apollonius as a Teacher." In *Theios Sophistes: Essays on Flavius Philostratus's Vita Apollonii*, edited by Kristoffel Demoen and Danny Praet, 321–34. Mnemosyne Supplements 305. Leiden: Brill, 2009.
———. *Der philostrateische Apollonius*. Helsinki: Societas Scientiarum Fennica, 1991.
Köstenberger, Andreas J. *A Theology of John's Gospel and Letters*. Grand Rapids: Zondervan, 2009.
Kurz, William. "Effects of Variant Narrators in Acts 10–11." *NTS* 43 (1997) 570–86.
Landry, David T. and John W. Martens, *Inquiry into the New Testament*. Winona, MN: Anselm Academic, 2018.
Lardner, Nathaniel. *A Large Collection of Ancient Jewish and Heathen Testimonies to the Truth of the Christian Religion*. 4 vols. London: Buckland, Longman, and Waugh, 1766.
———. *The Works of Nathanial Lardner*. 5 vols. London: Censley, 1815.
Lesky, Albin. *A History of Greek Literature*. Translated by James Willis and Cornelis de Heer. Indianapolis: Hackett, 1966.
Leslie, Charles. *A Short and Easy Method with the Deists: Wherein the Certainty of the Christian Religion, Is Demonstrated by Infallible Proof, from Four Rules, Which Are Incompatible to Any Imposture That Ever Yet Has Been, or That Can Possibly Be: In a Letter to a Friend*. London: SPCK, 1711.
Levick, Barbara. "Domitian and the Provinces." *Latomus* 41 (1985) 50–73.
Licona, Michael R. *The Resurrection of Jesus: A New Historiographical Approach*. Downers Grove, IL: InterVarsity, 2010.
LiDonnici, Lynn. "'According to the Jews': Identified (and Identifying) 'Jewish' Elements in the Greek Magical Papyri." In *Heavenly Tablets: Interpretation, Identity and Tradition in Ancient Judaism*, edited by Lynn LiDonnici and Andrea Lieber, 87–108. Journal for the Study of Judaism Supplements 119. Leiden: Brill, 2007.
Lightman, Margorie, and Benjamin Lightman. *A to Z of Ancient Greek and Roman Women*. New York: Facts on File, 2008.
Livingston, James D. *Rising Force: The Magic of Magnetic Levitation*. Cambridge: Harvard University Press, 2019.
Luck, George. *Arcana Mundi: Magic and the Occult in the Greek and Roman World*. Baltimore: Johns Hopkins University Press, 1985.
Lucian. *Anacharsis or Athletics. Menippus or The Descent into Hades. On Funerals. A Professor of Public Speaking. Alexander the False Prophet. Essays in Portraiture. Essays in Portraiture Defended. The Goddesse of Surrye*. Translated by A. H. Harmon. Vol. 4. LCL. New York: Macmillan, 1925.
Maclean, Jennifer K. Berenson, and Ellen Bradshaw Aitken. *Flavius Philostratus: On Heroes*. Writings from the Greco-Roman World 3. Atlanta: Scholars, 2002.
MacMullen, Ramsay. *Christianizing the Roman Empire (A.D. 100–400)*. New Haven: Yale University Press, 1984.
Manley, Deborah, and Sahar Abdel-Hakim. *Travelling through Egypt: From 450 B.C. to the Twentieth Century*. Edited by Sahar Abdel-Hakim. Cairo: American University in Cairo Press, 2008.
Manolaraki, Eleni. *Noscendi Nilum Cupido: Imagining Egypt from Lucan to Philostratus*. Trends in Classics Supplements 18. Berlin: de Gruyter, 2013.

Manutius, Aldus. *Philostrati de uita Apollonii Tyanei octo. Iidem libri Latini interprete Alemano Rinuccino. Eusebius contra Hieroclem qui Tyaneum Christo conferre conatus fuerit. Idem Latinus interprete Zenobio Acciolo.* Venice: Manuzio, 1501–2.

Marković, Nenad. "Titus and the Apis Bull: Reflections on the Socio-Political Importance of the Memphite Divine Bull in Roman Egypt." In *Global Egyptology: Negotiations in the Production of Knowledges on Ancient Egypt in Global Contexts*, edited by Christian Langer, 103–16. London: Golden House, 2017.

Marshall, I. Howard. *Acts*. New International Greek Testament Commentary. Grand Rapids: Eerdmans, 1980.

———. *Gospel of Luke*. New International Greek Testament Commentary. Grand Rapids: Eerdmans, 1978.

Marshall, J. *Taxila: An illustrated Account of Archaeological Excavations Carried out at Taxila under the Orders of the Government of India between the Years 1913 and 1934.* 3 vols. Cambridge: Cambridge University Press, 1951.

Martí-Aguilar, Manuel Álvarez. "Talismans against Tsunamis: Apollonius of Tyana and the *stelai* of the Herakleion in Gades (*VA* 5.5)." *GRBS* 57 (2017) 968–93.

Martin, Luther H. *Hellenistic Religions: An Introduction*. New York: Oxford University Press, 1987.

McCarthy, John A. *Christoph Martin Weiland*. Boston: Twayne, 1979.

McDonald, A. H. "Dio Cassius." In *OCD*, 345.

McLean, B. H. *Hellenistic and Biblical Greek: A Graduated Reader*. New York: Cambridge University Press, 2014.

McNiven, Timothy J. "Behaving Like an Other: Telltale Gestures in Athenian Vase Painting." In *Not the Classical Ideal: Athens and the Construction of the Other in Greek Art*, edited by Beth Cohen, 71–97. Leiden: Brill, 2000.

McRay, John. *Archaeology and the New Testament*. Grand Rapids: Baker, 1997.

McVane, Samuel D. "The Bare Necessities: Ascetic Indian Sages in Philostratus' 'Life of Apollonius.'" BA honors thesis, College of William and Mary, 2011.

Mead, G. R. S. *Apollonius of Tyana: The Philosopher Explorer and Social Reformer of the First Century AD*. Chicago: Ares, 1980.

Meier, John P. *A Marginal Jew: Rethinking the Historical Jesus*. Vol 2. New Haven: Yale University Press, 1994.

Meyer, Eduard. "Apollonius von Tyana und die Biographie des Philostratus." *Phil* 52 (1917) 370–424.

Miles, Graeme. *Philostratus: Interpreters and Interpretation*. Image, Text and Culture in Classical Antiquity. New York: Routledge, 2018.

Miller, J. "Die Beziehungen der Vita Apollonii des Philostratuos zur Pythagoras-sage." *Phil* 51 (1892) 137–45.

Mitchell, Margaret M. *The Heavenly Trumpet: John Chrysostom and the Art of Pauline Interpretation*. Louisville: Westminster John Knox, 2002.

Moeser, Marion C. *The Anecdote in Mark, the Classical World and the Rabbis: A Study of Brief Stories in the Demonax, The Mishnah, and Mark 8:27—10:45.* JSNTSup 227. Sheffield: Sheffield Academic, 2002.

Montaigne, Michel de. *Complete Essays of Montaigne*. Translated by Donald M. Frame. Stanford: Stanford University Press, 1958.

More, Henry. *An Explanation of the Grand Mystery of Godliness; or a True and Faithful Representation of the Everlasting Gospel of Our Lord and Saviour Jesus Christ.* Cambridge: Flescher, 1660.

Morgan, John R. "The Emesan Connection: Philostratus and Heliodorus." In *Theios Sophistes: Essays on Flavius Philostratus's Vita Apollonii*, edited by Kristoffel Demoen and Danny Praet, 263–82. Mnemosyne Supplements 305. Leiden: Brill, 2009.

———. "Lucian's *True Histories* and the *Wonders beyond Thule* of Antonius Diogenes." *CJ* 35 (1985) 475–90.

Motto, Anna Lydia. "Seneca on Trial: The Case of the Opulent Stoic." *CJ* 61.6 (1966) 254–58.

Nails, Deborah. "Socrates." In *The Stanford Encyclopedia of Philosophy*. https://plato.stanford.edu/entries/socrates/

Nettlehorst, R. P. "The Genealogy of Jesus." *JETS* 31 (1988) 169–72.

Newman, John Henry. *The Life of Apollonius Tyanaeus: With a Comparison Between the Miracles of Scripture and Those Elsewhere Related, as Regards Their Respective Object, Nature, and Evidence*. Glasgow: Bell & Bain, 1850.

Nicetus, *O City of Byzantium, Annals of Niketas Choniatēs*. Translated by Harry J. Magoulias. Detroit: Wayne State University Press, 1984.

Nichols, Andrew. "The Complete Fragments of Ctesias of Cnidus: Translation and Commentary with an Introduction." PhD diss., The University of Florida, 2008.

Nielsen, C. L. *Apollonios fra Tyana og Filostrats Beskrivelse af hans Levnet*. Copenhagen: Jørgensen, 1879.

Nongbri, Brent. "Finding Early Christian Books at Nag Hammadi and Beyond." *BSR* 45 (2016) 11–19.

Norden, Eduard. *Agnostos Theos: Untersuchungen zur Formengeschichte religiöser Rede*. Leipzig: Teubner, 1913.

Oden, Thomas C. *Early Libyan Christianity: Uncovering a North African Tradition*. Downers Grove, IL: InterVarsity, 2011.

Oleson, John Peter. *The Oxford Handbook of Engineering and Technology in the Classical World*. Oxford: Oxford University Press, 2008.

Origen. *Against Celsus*. In *Ante-Nicene Fathers*, series 2, vol. 4. Edited by Alexander Roberts and James Donaldson. 1883. 10 vols. Reprint, Peabody: Hendrickson, 1999.

Orr, John. *English Deism: Its Roots and Fruits*. Grand Rapids: Eerdmans, 1934.

Parker, Grant. *The Making of Roman India*. Cambridge: Cambridge University Press, 2008.

Parker, Henry, and Brian Warmington. "Aurelius Antoninus, Marcus." In *OCD*, 153.

———. "Julia Domna." In *OCD*, 567.

———. "Plautianus." In *OCD*, 842.

Parker, Samuel. *A Demonstration of the Divine Authority of the Law of Nature and of the Christian Religion*. London: Flesher, 1681.

Pearson, Lionel. "The Diary and the Letters of Alexander the Great." *Historia* 3 (1955) 429–55.

Penella, R. J. *The Letters of Apollonius of Tyana: A Critical Text with Prolegomena, Translation and Commentary*. Mnemesyne Supplements 56. Leiden: Brill, 1979.

———. "An Overlooked Story about Apollonius of Tyana in Anastasius Sinaita." *Traditio* 34 (1978) 414–15.

———. "Scopelianus and the Eretrians in Cissia." *Athenaeum* 52 (1974) 295–300.

Perrin, Norman. "The Christology of Mark: A Study in Methodology." In *The Interpretation of Mark*, edited by William Telford, 95–108. Philadelphia: Fortress, 1985.

———. *The New Testament: An Introduction*. New York: Harcourt Brace Jovanivich, 1974.

Peterson, Joseph H., ed. *The Lesser Key of Solomon: Detailing the Ceremonial Art of Commanding Spirits Both Good and Bad*. York, ME: Weiser, 2001.

Petzke, G. *Die Traditionen über Apollonius von Tyana und das Neue Testament*. Studia ad corpus Hellenisticum Novi Testamenti 1. Leiden: Brill, 1970.

Phillimore, J. S. *Philostratus—In Honor of Apollonius of Tyana*. Oxford: Clarendon, 1912.

Philostratus. *Apollonius of Tyana*. Edited and translated by Christopher P. Jones. 3 vols. LCL. Cambridge: Harvard University Press, 2005–2006.

———. *Heroicus, Gymnasticus, Discourses 1 and 2*. Edited and translated by Jeffrey Rusten and Jason König. LCL. Cambridge: Harvard University Press, 2014.

———. *The Life of Apollonius of Tyana*. Translated by F. C. Conybeare. 2 vols. LCL. New York: Macmillan, 1912.

Philostratus and Eunapius. *The Lives of the Sophists*. Translated by Wilmer Cave Wright. LCL. Cambridge: Harvard University Press, 1921.

Pico, Giovanni (della Mirandola). *Oration on the Dignity of Man*. Translated by A. Robert Caponigri. Washington, DC: Regnery, 1956.

Platt, Verity. *Facing the Gods: Epiphany and Representation in Graeco-Roman Art, Literature and Religion*. GCRW. Cambridge: Cambridge University Press, 2011.

———. "Virtual Visions: *Phantasia* and the perception of the divine in *The Life of Apollonius of Tyana*." In *Philostratus*, edited by Ewen Bowie and Jaś Elsner, 131–55. GCRW. Cambridge: Cambridge University Press, 2009.

Porreca, David. "Apollonius of Tyana through a Medieval Latin Lens." *Magic, Ritual, and Witchcraft* 9.2 (2014) 157–77.

Poklatecki, Stanislaw. *Pogrom, czarnoksięskie błędy, latawców zdrady i alchimickie fałsze jako rozplasza*. Krakow, 1595.

Porter, Stanley E., and Bryan R. Dyer, eds. *The Synoptic Problem: Four Views*. Grand Rapids: Baker Academic, 2016.

Powell, J. Enoch. "The Sources of Plutarch's *Alexander*." *JHS* 59 (1939) 229–40.

Powell, Mark Allen. *Introducing the New Testament: A Historical, Literary, and Theological Survey*. Grand Rapids: Baker Academic, 2009.

Praet Danny. "Pythagoreanism and the Planetary Deities: The Philosophical and Literary Master-structure of the *Vita Apollonii*." In *Theios Sophistes: Essays on Flavius Philostratus's Vita Apollonii*, edited by Kristoffel Demoen and Danny Praet, 283–320. Mnemosyne Supplements 305. Leiden: Brill, 2009.

Priaulx, Osmond de Beauvoir. *The Indian Travels of Apollonius of Tyana*. London: Quaritch, 1873.

Price, Robert M. *Deconstructing Jesus*. Amherst, NY: Prometheus, 2000.

———. "Was There a Historical Apollonius of Tyana?" *Journal of Higher Criticism* 13.1 (2018) 4–40.

Puskas, Charles B., and C. Michael Robbins. *An Introduction to the New Testament*. 2nd ed. Eugene, OR: Cascade Books, 2011.

Puri, B. N. "The Sakas and Indo-Parthians." In *History of civilizations of Central Asia*, edited by János Harmatta et al., 2:184–201. Paris: UNESCO, 1994.

Raynor, D. H. "Moeragenes and Philostratus: Two Views of Apollonius of Tyana." *CQ* 34 (1984) 222–26.
Reardon, B. P. *Courants littéraires grecs des IIe et IIIe siècles après J.-C*. Annales littéraires de l'Université de Nantes 3. Paris: Les Belles Lettres, 1971.
Reasoner, M. "Emperor, Emperor Cult." In *DLNT* 321–26.
Reimer, Andy M. *Miracle and Magic: A Study of the Acts of the Apostles and the Life of Apollonius of Tyana*. JSNTSup 235. London: Sheffield Academic, 2002.
Réville, Albert. *Apollonius of Tyana, The Pagan Christ of the Third Century*. London: Hotten, 1866.
Roberts, J. M. *Antiquity Unveiled: Ancient Voices from the Spirit Realms Disclose the Most Startling Revelations, Proving Christianity to be of Heathen Origin*. Philadelphia: Oriental, 1894.
Robiano, Patrick. "Les gymnosophistes éthiopiens chez Philostrate et chez Héliodore." *REA* 94 (1992) 413–28.
Robinson, Christopher. *Lucian and His Influence in Europe*. Chapel Hill: University of North Carolina Press, 1979.
Roetzel, Calvin J. *The Letters of Paul: Conversations in Context*. 2nd ed. Atlanta: John Knox, 1982.
———. *The World That Shaped the New Testament*. Louisville: Westminster John Knox, 1985.
Rosenmeyer, Patricia A. *The Language of Ruins: Greek and Latin Inscriptions on the Memnon Colossus*. New York: Oxford University Press, 2018.
Rudolph, Kurt. *Gnosis: The Nature and History of Gnosticism*. Translated and edited by Robert McLachlan Wilson. San Francisco: Harper & Row, 1987.
Rutherford, Ian. "Black Sails to Achilles: The Thessalian Pilgrimage in Philostratus' *Heroicus*." In *Philostratus*, edited by Ewen Bowie and Jaś Elsner, 230–47. GCRW. Cambridge: Cambridge University Press, 2009.
Sanders, E. P. and Margaret Davies. *Studying the Synoptic Gospels*. Philadelphia: Trinity, 1991.
Schirren, Thomas. "Irony Versus Eulogy. The Vita Apollonii as Metabiographical Fiction." In *Theios Sophistes: Essays on Flavius Philostratus's Vita Apollonii*, edited by Kristoffel Demoen and Danny Praet, 161–86. Mnemosyne Supplements 305. Leiden: Brill, 2009.
Schmitz, Thomas. "Narrator and audience in Philostratus' *Lives of the Sophists*." In *Philostratus*, edited by Ewen Bowie and Jaś Elsner, 49–68. GCRW. Cambridge: Cambridge University Press, 2009.
Schultz, Celia E., and Allen M. Ward. *A History of the Roman People*. 7th ed. New York: Routledge, 2019.
Schwartz, E. "Eusebios von Caesarea." *RE* 6 (1907) 1370–439.
Scriptores Historiae Augustae. Translated by David Magie. 3 vols. LCL. Cambridge: Harvard University Press, 1921–1932.
Shelton, Jo-Ann. *Seneca's Hercules Furens: Theme Structure and Style*. Hypomnemata 50. Göttingen: Vandenhoeck & Ruprecht, 1978.
Shipley, Donald Richard. "Plutarch's Life of Agelsilaos: response to sources in the presentation of character." PhD diss., University of Newcastle upon Tyne, 1990.
Shirren, Thomas. "Irony versus Eulogy: The *Vita Apollonii* as Metabiographical Fiction." In *Theios Sophistes: Essays on Flavius Philostratus's Vita Apollonii*, edited

by Kristoffel Demoen and Danny Praet, 161–86. Mnemosyne Supplements 305. Leiden: Brill, 2009.

Sidebottom, Harry. "Philostratus and the Symbolic Roles of the Sophist and Philosopher." In *Philostratus*, edited by Ewen Bowie and Jaś Elsner, 69–99. GCRW. Cambridge: Cambridge University Press, 2009.

Smith, Morton. *Jesus the Magician*. New York: Barnes and Noble, 1993. Smith, R. R. R. "Late Roman Philosopher Portraits from Aphrodisias." *JRS* 80 (1990) 127–55.

Smith, V. A. "The Indian Travels of Apollonius of Tyana." *ZDMG* 68 (1914) 329–44.

Solmsen, Friedrich. "Some Works of Philostratus the Elder." *TAPA* 71 (1941) 556–72.

Speyer, Wolfgang. "Zum Bild des Apollonios bei Heiden und Christen." *JAC* 17 (1974) 48–63.

Spivey, Robert A., D. Moody Smith, and C. Clifton Black. *Anatomy of the New Testament*. Upper Saddle River, NJ: Pearson Prentice Hall, 2007.

Stannish, Steven M., and Christine M. Doran. "Magic and Vampirism in Philostratus's *Life of Apollonius of Tyana* and Bram Stoker's *Dracula*." Preternature: Critical and Historical Studies on the Preternatural 2 (2013) 113–38.

Stout, Stephen O. *The "Man Christ Jesus": The Humanity of Jesus in the Teaching of the Apostle Paul*. Eugene, OR: Wipf & Stock, 2011.

Strobel, Lee. *The Case for Christ: A Journalist's Personal Investigation of the Evidence for Jesus*. Grand Rapids: Zondervan, 1998.

Summers, Geoffrey D. "Ecbatana." In *Dictionary of the Ancient Near East*, edited by Piotr Bienkowski and Alan Millard, 99–100. Philadelphia: University of Pennsylvania Press, 2000.

Swain, Simon. "Culture and Nature in Philostratus." In *Philostratus*, edited by Ewen Bowie and Jaś Elsner, 33–36. GCRW. Cambridge: Cambridge University Press, 2009.

———. "The Reliability of Philostratus's 'Lives of the Sophists.'" *ClAnt* 10 (1991) 148–63.

Syme, Ronald. "Journeys of Hadrian." *ZPE* 73 (1988) 159–70.

Taggart, Bruce Lyle. "Apollonius of Tyana: His Biography and Critics." PhD diss., Tufts University, 1972.

Taylor, Thomas. *Select Works of Porphyry: Containing His Four Books on Abstinence from Animal Food, His Treatise on the Homeric Cave of the Nymphs, and His Auxiliaries to the Perception of Intelligible Natures*. London: Moyes, 1823.

Taylor, Vincent. *The Formation of the Gospel Tradition*. London: Macmillan, 1945.

Theissen, Gerd. *The Miracle Stories of the Early Christian Tradition*. Edited by John Riches. Translated by Francis McDonagh. Philadelphia: Fortress, 1983.

Tiede, David Lenz. *The Charismatic Figure as Miracle Worker*. SBLDS 1. Missoula, MT: Scholars, 1972.

Tooke, William. *Lucian of Samosata. From the Greek. With the comments and illustrations of Wieland and others*. London: Longman, Hurst, Rees, Orme, and Brown, 1820.

Treat, Jay Curry. "Barnabus, Epistle of." In *ABD* 1:614.

Twelftree, Graham H. *Jesus the Exorcist: A Contribution to the Study of the Historical Jesus*. Peabody, MA: Hendrickson, 1993.

Unger, Merrill F. *Archaeology and the New Testament*. Grand Rapids: Zondervan, 1977.

Van der Stockt, Luk. "Never the Twain Shall Meet?" Plutarch and Philostratus' *Life of Apollonius*: Some Themes and Techniques." In *Theios Sophistes: Essays on Flavius*

Philostratus's Vita Apollonii, edited by Kristoffel Demoen and Danny Praet, 187–210. Mnemosyne Supplements 305. Leiden: Brill, 2009.

Van Dijk, Gert-Jan. "*The Odyssey of Apollonius: An Intertextual Paradigm.*" In *Philostratus*, edited by Ewen Bowie and Jaś Elsner, 176–202. GCRW. Cambridge: Cambridge University Press, 2009.

Van Minnen, P. "The Greek Apocalypse of Peter." In *The Apocalypse of Peter*, edited by Jan N. Bremmer and István Czachesz, 15–39. Studies on Early Christian Apocrypha 7. Leuven: Peeters, 2003.

Van Voorst, Robert E. *Jesus Outside the New Testament: An Introduction to the Ancient Evidence*. Grand Rapids, Eerdmans, 2000.

Voltaire, F. M. *Essai sur les moeurs et l'esprit des nations*. Vol. 1. Basil: Tourneisen, 1785.

Voss, Angela, ed. *Marsilio Ficino*. Berkeley: North Atlantic, 2006.

Votaw, Clyde Weber. *The Gospels and Contemporary Biographies in the Greco-Roman World*. Philadelphia: Fortress, 1970.

Weeden, Theodore J. *Mark: Traditions in Conflict*. Philadelphia: Fortress, 1971.

Whitmarsh, Tim. "Greek and Roman in Dialogue: The Pseudo-Lucianic Nero." *JHS* 119 (1999) 142–60.

Wieland, Christoph Martin. *Agathodämon: in Sieben Büchern*. Leipzig: Göschen, 1799.

Wilson, John. "The Miracles of the Gospels." *AJT* 9.1 (1905) 10–33.

Winger, Mike. "The 'Other Jesus' Story That Scares Christians: Apollonius of Tyana." YouTube, Nov 28, 2018. https://youtu.be/smAERl96c9E.

Witherington, Ben, III. *Invitation to the New Testament: First Things*. New York: Oxford University Press, 2013.

Woolston, Thomas. *A Discourse on the Miracles of Our Saviour in View of the Present Controversy between Infidels and Apostates*. London: London & Westminster, 1727.

Wright, N. T. *Jesus and the Victory of God*. Christian Origins and the Question of God 2. Minneapolis: Fortress, 1996.

———. *The Resurrection of the Son of God*. Christian Origins and the Question of God 3. Minneapolis: Fortress, 2003.

Yoder, Timothy S. *Hume on God: Irony, Deism and Genuine Theism*. London: Continuum, 2008.

Zambelli, Paola. *White Magic, Black Magic in the European Renaissance*. Studies in Medieval and Reformation Traditions 125. Leiden: Brill, 2007.

Index

Achilles, 149, 171, 172, 280–83
Acts (book of), preserving the historical Jesus, 399
Aelianus, praetorian prefect of Rome, 181, 316
Africanus, Julius, 343
Against Hierocles (Eusebius), on inconsistencies in the *VA*, 419
agendas
    of Julia Domna, 46, 424
    originating with Julia Domna or Philostratus, 324
    of Philostratus II, 46, 140, 309–36, 337, 382
    of the Second Sophistic movement, 116, 313
    of the *VA*, 46–48, 309–38, 339–45, 369, 381–82
Agesilaus (Xenophon), number of words, 257
Agrippina (Nero's mother), 285–86
Alcestis, 357–58, 359
Alcestis Greek tragedy, episode of resurrection in, 357
Alcinous, descendant of, 366
Alexander (disciple of Apollonius), 198, 199–200, 331, 424
Alexander (Lucian), first-tier source for Apollonius, 404
Alexander of Abonoteichus, 196
Alexander Severus, 59, 112, 113–14, 343

Alexander the False Prophet (Lucian), reference to Apollonius, 196
Alexander the Great, 168, 248, 331, 353
Alexandria, timing of Vespasian's arrival in, 290
Alexianus, son of Julia Mamaea, 110
All the Things that Apollonius did in Aegae (Maximus), collection of local traditions, 217
Amenhotep III, colossi of, 294
Anabasis of Alexander (Arrian), 372
Anastasius Sinaita, 77
ancient figures, many only mentioned once, 381
ancient sources
    errors concerning Apollonius, 19, 53, 54
    identifying the genre of the *VA* as biography, 158
ancient world
    resurrection and *Scheintod* accounts from, 356
    sources of power or knowledge, 231
Anderson, Graham
    on the actual existence of Damis, 245
    on Apollonius resembling Scopelian the most, 142–43
    on Damis as a fictional disciple, 245–46
    effort to demonstrate the reality of Damis, 242
    on the genre of the *VA*, 157

INDEX

Anderson, Graham (*cont.*)
  on a historical core to the *empusa* tale, 284
  isolation of the Damis source, 253
  on legendary development, 374
  on Maximus's book as "miraculous drivel," 375
  on Philostratus, 161, 326
  on problematic stories in the *VA*, 241
  salvaging the account of the satyr, 300–301
  on the *Suda* as correct after all, 128–29
  on an unknown source, 254, 307
animals
  bizarre seen by Apollonius, 275
  existence of fabulous, 170
  fictional, 251, 277
annunciation, to Jesus's mother before conception, 351
anti-Christian agenda, of the *VA*, 47–48, 339–45, 369
Antioch of Syria, Julia Domna in, 120
Antipater of Hierapolis, teacher of Philostratus, 119
Aphrodite, Apollonius rebuked a man in love with a statue of, 179
Apocalypse of Peter, discovered in 1887 within a tomb, 249–50
Apocriticus (Macarius of Magnesia), knowledge of the *VA*, 71–72
Apollo, 77, 78, 353
Apollobex, Egyptian magician, 194
Apollonian Decalogue
  devising criteria for, 29–56
  Eusebius anticipated item 6 of, 63
  initiating the analysis of, 187
  keeping and breaking, 32–56
  Lardner on seven items of, 90
  listing of ten issues of, 26, 30–32
  summary and concluding remarks, 380–83
Apollonian Decalogue (Items of)
  Item 1, 38–40, 187, 380–81
  Item 2, 38–40, 187, 380–81
  Item 3, 39–40, 211–31, 381
  Item 4, 38–40, 211–31, 381
  Item 5, 40–44, 232–60, 381
  Item 6, 44–46, 76, 261–308, 381
  Item 7, 46–47, 309–38, 381
  Item 8, 47–48, 330–69, 381
  Item 9, 48–49, 339–69, 382
  Item 10, 49–52, 370–79, 382
Apollonian legends, growing from history into hagiography, 49
Apollonian material, 388, 395
Apollonian research, 57, 98
Apollonian scholarship, specialists in, 30
Apollonius and Philostratus specialists, issues of, 32
Apollonius of Chalcedon, 196
Apollonius of Rhodes, 195
Apollonius of Tyana
  absence from the earliest historical records, 383
  advocate of Hellenism in the *VA*, 124
  affiliated with the Pythagorean cause, 315
  answering a charge of impiety towards Nero, 173
  appearance to his disciples, 360, 362–63
  attempt to rescue Musonius from prison, 359–60
  on blood sacrifices, 207
  Caracalla's high regard for, 108
  as celebrated among the multitude, 207
  confused or conflated with Apollo, 77
  confused with Apollobex, 194
  disappearance from Domitian's court, 24, 304–5
  as a divine man, 96
  Domitian and, 72, 181–82, 201, 202, 414
  early life of, 14, 165–66, 351
  errors in material about, 53–55
  existence of, 383
  final days of, 183–84
  first contact with as unsettling, 8–11
  healing by, 179, 218
  as a historical figure, 383
  human parents and a divine parent, 350–51

interacted with historically verifiable figures, 24, 286
internal consistency of material, 422
Jesus and, 5–8, 11–12, 15, 24, 26, 27, 61, 71, 78, 361, 425
as the largest repository of lore about, 153
letters of, 219, 220, 221, 228
lifespan of, 24
as a magician, 69, 164, 187, 200, 204, 210, 216, 226, 231, 321, 337, 412–13
mother of, 351, 353
no aspirations for wealth or power, 183
no books about still existing except for the VA, 55
no first-century AD sources mention, 189
no genealogy of, 351
no independent evidence verifying, 303
no known writings of, 222
no tomb, 25
not mentioned at all in the first century, 41
only performed one exorcism himself, 364
as a philosopher, 142, 143, 144, 228, 230, 327, 333
positive assessments of, 76
predictions of, 174, 184, 262
promised to appear to Damis, 182
Pythagoras and, 63, 249, 328
"quest" of the historical, 87–93
raised a girl from the dead, 241, 323
raised a woman from the dead, 174
recommended Demetrius to Titus as a teacher, 178
rehabilitating the reputation of, 39
reputation of, 199, 319
rescuing an Ethiopian village from a satyr, 300
research already conducted on, 56
researchers on, 29
restoring practices of Greek cults, 23
resurgence of interest in, 8–9
revered the traditional Greek gods, 22
on sacrifices, 182, 207, 209
sources, 27, 58, 230, 392–93, 404
as spokesman of Philostratus's religious views, 46
talismans installed by, 73
traditions about, 65, 419
transfigured into a saint, 78
travels of, 76–78, 91–92, 169–73, 285, 299, 308, 330
trial of, 182
on a true man pursuing philosophy, 175
as the ultimate sage, 161
undelivered speech of, 182–83
VA as the chief source on, 153
as valuable in his own right, 13–14
Vespasian and, 290, 291
viewed jars of rain and winds, 169
visiting the Gymnosophists, 333
why he matters, 3–28
Apollonius of Tyana (Christian martyr), 54
"Apollonius the Nazarene," Apollonius as, 7
apologetic agenda
originating with Julia Domna or Philostratus, 324
of Philostratus, 319–36
of the VA, 381
Apologia of Apuleius, reference to Apollonius, 193
Apuleius, 69, 189, 193, 356
Archelaus, the king of Cappadocia, execution of, 262
Ardericca, Philostratus's description of, 266
Areopagus speech, of Paul, 93
Aristobulus, engineer, 372
Aristotle, 276, 373
Arrian, 271, 272, 389
Ars Notoria, 79–80
Asclepiades, saved a comatose man, 356
Asclepius (god), 218
Aslan, Reza, 50, 54, 55
assessment, of items in the Apollonian Decalogue, 34

INDEX

astronomy, Apollonius and, 80
Aswan High Dam, 300
Athens, Philostratus's career as a sophist in, 121
athletic training, treatise on, 130–31
audience, intended for the VA, 162–63
Augustine, 69
Augustus (Suetonius), number of words in, 257
Aurelian, made vows to Apollonius, 59
authors
    covering the Apollonian Decalogue, 55–56
    misreading secondary literature about Apollonius, 54
    noting errors in the VA, 44
    Philostratus impressive as, 13
    similarities as a reliable method for evaluating, 130
    of sources not in collusion, 406–11
automata, as servants, 279–80

Babylon, 265, 268–69, 270
Balinas (Apollonius), 76
Balinus (Apollonius), 79
Bar-Jesus, 190
Barnabas. *See also* Epistle of Barnabas
    Old Testament passages about Jesus, 403, 426
    quoting Matthew, 411, 419, 426
Basil of Seleucia, on talismans, 75
Bassianus (better known as Elagabalus), 110–12
Bassus, Gaius Julius, high priest of Baal, 109
bathing habits, of Apollonius, 227
Baur, F. C., 88, 90–91, 189, 236
Beelzebub, dismantling the dominion of, 368
Bell, Albert A., 48–49
Berwick, Edward, 90
biases
    as important in evaluating historicity, 423–25
    of Philostratus, 326, 424
    of sources, 388
Bible Conspiracies streamed video, 11

biblical scholars, treatment of Apollonius, 16, 25, 33, 97–98
biblical scroll, of Origen found in a jar at Jericho, 249
biographers, 4, 52, 372, 373–74, 376
biographies
    of Apollonius, 58, 59, 214, 424
    motives of, 309
    Philostratus working on, 140–41
    of Pythagoras and Apollonius, 328–30
    titles of ancient, 159
    VA as a, 13, 153, 157–60
Bird, Michael F., 47
birds, at Apollo's birth, 353
birth narratives, of Jesus and Apollonius, 350–54
births, accompanied by heavenly phenomena, 350
black magician, presentations of Apollonius as, 77
bleeding trees, compared to the Heliad poplar that bled gold, 288
blood sacrifice, Apollonius opposed, 207, 312
Blount, Charles, 86, 87
bodily resurrection, unknown in Greco-Roman religion, 348
Bolingbroke, Henry St. John, borrowed from Blount, 87
Boring, 42, 50, 54, 236, 388, 425
Bowersock, G. W., 86, 203, 215, 287, 290, 294, 296
Bowie, Ewen, 162, 214, 215, 229, 238, 243–44, 245, 252–53, 259, 290, 291
Boyd, Gregory A., 46, 48, 52, 318, 419, 423
Bultmann, Rudolf, 95–96
Burridge, Richard A., 158, 160, 162
Byzantium, talismans of, 74

Calderini, A., 316
Cambridge Platonists, 83
Capito, Aetius, confused with Cossutianus Capito, 263
Caracalla

INDEX

on Apollonius as a miracle worker and hero, 204
co-emperor along with Geta, 105–6
crimes and misbehavior of, 107
fascinated by Achilles and Alexander the Great, 108
Julia Domna assisted, 110
monument to Apollonius, 59
on Plautianus, 104
visit to Achilles's tomb at Troy, 282
well acquainted with Apollonius, 155
Castillon, B., 87
castration, prohibition of, 303
categories, for sorting materials by timeframe, 394
Caucasus Mountains, 167, 270–71
Cazemier, Annelies, 322, 323–24
Cedrinus, George, 76
Celsus, 90, 196
Chandler, Samuel, 85
Chariton's *Chaereas and Callirhoe*, 161
Christ, 69, 75, 80. *See also* Jesus
Christian detractors, of Hierocles, 60–66
Christian stories, as an influence on Philostratus, 47
Christian texts or ideas, in the *VA*, 345–46
Christian writers, first-century not mentioning Apollonius, 190
Christianity, 31, 60–61, 340, 344
Christians
  on Christ's miracles, 85
  on God had continued to perform miracles, 84
  lost their fear of Apollonius, 72
  range of opinions on Apollonius, 68
  Severan attitudes toward, 343
  on the talismans of Apollonius, 73–76
Christobiography (Keener), on oral tradition, 388
chronology, in Philostratus's narrative, 238
Chrysostom, John, 69
circle of Julia Domna, 110, 234

Cissia, located far away in western Iran, 266
clairvoyant abilities, Apollonius displayed, 202
Clarke, Samuel, 85
classical scholars, 4, 28, 101
classical writers, not mentioning Apollonius, 190
Clemens, Flavius, 183, 306–7
1 Clement letter, traditions about Jesus, 399–400
Clodius Albinus, 103
Cocconas, 197, 199
collusion, 406, 407
consistency, of sources, 387–88
Constitutio Antoniniana, edict of Caracalla, 107
contradictions, in the *VA* compared to Luke-Acts, 422
Corinthian *empusa*, 283–84
Corinthian Isthmus, attempt to dig a canal through, 132
corpus, of Philostratus, 123–24
Cotta, A. L., 85
Crassus, Calpurnius, exile of, 304
Crates of Thebes, 333
Crete, 173, 184, 284, 285
"criterion of multiple attestation." *See* multiple attestation (independent attestation)
Crossan, John Dominic, 411
crown, Titus's rejection of, 301, 302
Ctesias, on the unicorn, 276
Ctesiphon, as Vardanes's capital, 265
Cudworth, Ralph, 83–84

Cyclops's cave, entrance into, 332

Damianus, Flavius, 244
Damis (the Assyrian)
  absence from the narrative, 253
  Apollonius meeting with, 166
  Apollonius promised to appear to him, 182, 183
  Apollonius sent a second letter to Nerva by, 184
  chronological blunders, 287
  competence as an eyewitness, 53, 377

INDEX

Damis (the Assyrian) *(cont.)*
    deficient style, 234
    did not view Babylon in its
        grandeur, 378
    existence of, 150, 242, 243, 260, 381
    on fabulous animals, springs, and
        inhabitants of India, 170
    inaccurate account of, 266
    narrative ended before the death of
        Apollonius, 377
    no consensus about the truth of, 232
    from "the nonexistent city of
        Nineveh," 264
    as a notetaker, 166, 257–58, 389, 390
    relative of brought memoirs to Julia
        Domna, 40–41
    scholars noting controversy over, 42
    sharing in his master's fate, 181
    studied wisdom under Apollonius,
        233
    testimony on sound from the statue
        of Memnon, 295
    unattested as a historical figure,
        241–46
    viewed jars of rain and winds, 169
Damis memoir, 232–60. *See also Scrap*
    Book (*Scraps from the Manger*)
    Apollonian scholarship hinging
        on, 41
    aspects of not aligning with
        Philostratus's viewpoint, 255
    bridging the historical gap with,
        376–79
    challenge to eyewitness character
        of, 273
    as collusion, 408
    delivered to Julia Domna by an
        unknown relative, 90, 247, 250
    described by Philostratus as a
        "journal," "notes," "memoirs,"
        and "tablets," 234
    differences from *Dictys of Crete* and
        The Wonders Beyond Thule, 248,
        250
    emphases not found in the
        Philostratean corpus, 255
    existence of, 41, 240, 405
    as an eyewitness account, 260, 378,
        382, 383
    as inconclusive, 381
    not appearing to be particularly
        biased, 376
    notebooks preserving, 212, 256–58
    Philostratus's claim to have access
        to, 31
    Philostratus's description of, 233
    as a piece of fiction, 249
    presenting Apollonius as a
        philosopher, 379
    as a source in the *VA*, 252
    as unattested elsewhere, 246–47
    VA claiming to be based on, 19
    as a window into the real
        Apollonius, 375
Damophyle, resembling Damis, 243
Dareius, in Herodotus story, 291
Dares of *Acta diurnal belli Troiani*,
    diaries of, 243
Darius II Ochus, 105, 269
date of publication, of the *VA*, 155–56
d'Aussy, J. B. Legrand, 84, 87
the dead, Apollonius raising, 421
death
    of Apollonius, 24–25
    of Philostratus, 118
Decalogue. *See* Apollonian Decalogue
deception, Philostratus guilty of, 408
deeds and characteristics, of Apollonius
    and Jesus as very similar, 6
deeds of power, of Apollonius, 231
Deinias, adventures of, 248
deists, versus theists, 84–87
deity, born as a human being, 350
Delphic oracle, 352
deltoi, Damis document originally
    composed on, 257
Demetrius, 173, 180, 181, 183, 286–87,
    335
demon(s), 77, 81, 364, 365, 367, 368
Demonax, referred to Apollonius of
    Chalcedon, 195–96
Demonax (Lucian), 195, 257
demon-possessed youth, Apollonius
    cast out the demon, 172
Derkyllis, adventures of, 248

INDEX

Dialexis I, discourse in the Philostratean canon, 137
Dialexis II, discourse in the Philostratean canon, 137
Dictys of Crete, diaries of, 242–43, 248
Dictys of Crete: Chronicle of the Trojan War (*Dictys Cretensis Ephemeris belli Trojani*), 248, 250
Didache, 402
diets, of Apollonius compared to Jesus, 23
Dini, in *Marzuban-nameh*, 242
Dio Cassius, 200–205
   on Apollonius as a magician, 189, 216, 380, 412
   on Barnabas quoting Matthew, 426
   on Caracalla, 155
   despised magic, 424
   on Domitilla's exile to Pandateria, 307
   on the execution of Archelaus, 262–63
   not mentioning Domitian exiling Nerva, 303
   reference to Apollonius as a philosopher, 192
   on a shaggy mane not making one a philosopher, 193
   Vespasian and, 176, 291, 292
Dio Chrysostom, 192, 205
Dio of Prusa, 24, 190
Diogenes, Antonius, 248
Diogenes Laertius, 191, 373
Diogenes of Sinope, 333
Dion, 333
Dionysius, 330, 331
Dionysius of Fourna, 77–78
Dionysus, 334, 336, 353
disciples. *See also* followers
   of Apollonius, 14, 210, 414
   of Jesus, 368, 415
   preserving a record of famous teachers, 232
   selecting, 23
discourse, Apollonius's preference for brief, 420
dissimilarity, criterion of, 347–48

distance, between the time of an event and its recording, 393
divine intervention, as a recurrent theme, 353
divine man. *See also* god-man
   Apollonius as, 21, 95–97
divine-human union, Pythagoras and Apollonius as the product of, 351–52
documents, examples of genuine, rediscovered, 249
Domitian
   accusing and acquitting Apollonius, 180–81, 182
   advice to about ruling over barbarians, 227
   Apollonius's acquaintance with, 24
   Apollonius's disappearance from the court of, 304–5
   Apollonius's implausible speech to, 305–6
   Apollonius's remote viewing of the assassination of, 407
   execution of consul Flavius Clemens and his wife Flavia Domitilla, 306–7
   exiling Nerva to the town of Tarentum, 303–4
   inevitability of Nerva one day taking his place, 183
   passing a judicial examination under, 189
   poisoned Titus, 179
Domitilla, Flavia, 183, 306–7
Dzielska, Maria, 208

early Christian authors, 341, 342
earthquake, predicting, 414
Ecbatana, famed walls of, 269–70
Eddy, Paul Rhodes, 46, 48, 52, 318, 419, 423
edicts, of Domitian, 303
education, of Apollonius versus Jesus, 23
Egypt, 175–76, 298
Ehrman, Bart D., 3, 9, 14–15, 20–25, 38, 42, 48, 53, 55, 371, 390–91, 410, 423, 426

449

Ekkehard of Aura, *Universal Chronicle* mentioned the *VA*, 79
Elagabalus (Bassianus better known as), 110–12, 312, 343–44
Eleusinian mysteries, Apollonius and, 172, 175
elm tree, speaking to Apollonius, 177
Elsner, Jaś, on *phantasia* (vivid visualization) evoked, 136
Elymas, 190
Emesene deity, Elagabalus elevating, 111
Empedocles, devices created by, 74
empusa, Corinthian, 283–84
encomiastic agenda, of the *VA*, 319, 326–36, 381–82
enemies, Euphrates and Bassus mentioned in the *VA* and the letters, 226
enigmatic prediction, of Apollonius, 288
Ephesian plague, Apollonius and, 171, 306
ephors of Sparta, Apollonius wrote a letter to restore, 172
Epistle of Barnabas, 403, 411. See also Barnabas
Epistles of Apollonius. See Letters of Apollonius (*Epistles*)
Erechtheion, cleft under, 271
Eretrians, location of, 266–67
Erotic Letters, amatory and non-amatory letters, 133–36
errors
  in ancient sources, 19
  in eyewitness testimony, 250–54
  in material about Apollonius, 53–55
  scholars providing historical, 45
  in the *VA*, 21, 31, 44, 238–40, 250–51, 261–308, 381
Ethiopia, 177, 178, 297, 301
Eumenes, the royal secretary, 372
Euphrates the Stoic
  on Apollonius as a fraud and magician, 39
  as Apollonius's enemy, 176, 214, 215, 229
  as a famous person of his day, 24
  Philostratus slandering, 63, 178
  position held by, 292
  summoned by Vespasian, 291
King Eurystheus, imposed labors on Hercules, 334
Eusebius
  accused Philostratus and Damis of reshaping the story of Apollonius, 64
  on contemporary opinions about Apollonius, 69
  fragment preserved by attributed to Apollonius, 207
  on Julia Avita Mamaea, 343
  on numerous problems in the *VA*, 62–63
  on pagan attempts to promote Apollonius as a rival to Christ, 66
  preserved fragments from Hegesippus, 404
  on Severus, 342
  skeptical that Apollonius had set up talismans, 75
Euxenus of Heracleia, 165
events, influencing future, 421
exorcism(s)
  absent from pagan wonder workers except for Philostratus, 349
  by Apollonius, 365
  by the Indian Wise Man, 368
  of Jesus, 368
  as a rarity in ancient texts, 363–69
  of the *VA*, 363, 369
extrabiblical sources, mentioning Jesus, 50
extra-sensory perception, Apollonius's gift of, 201
eyewitness testimony
  vs. errors and implausible events in the *VA*, 250–54
  increasing odds of reliable information, 376
  Philostratus's claim that he used, 42
  as sometimes unreliable, 373
  superiority of for Christ, 86
eyewitnesses, 150, 151, 388

Facebook, pages dedicated to Apollonius, 11
family background, of Apollonius, 165

fauna, Philostratus's references to non-mystical, 308
Ferguson, John, 39–40, 44, 46
Ficino, Marsilio, 81
fiction, by Philostratus in the VA, 151, 247
fictional characters, 238, 246
fictional correspondence, 151
fictional creatures and animals, in the VA, 251
fictional diary, Philostratus introduced, 248
fictional documents, in the literature of the Second Sophistic, 246–50
fictional elements, in the VA, 141–42, 151
fictive witnesses, Damis as, 242–43, 244
First God, needing nothing, 207
First Sophistic movement, in the VS, 138
first-century and early-second-century sources, absence of Apollonius in, 189–94
first-century eyewitness, would not have made errors in the VA, 250
first-tier sources, for Apollonius and Jesus, 394, 405
Flavian emperors, modeled after Severan rulers, 316
Flinterman, Jaap-Jan
  on Apollonius, 231
  on the chronology of the alleged exile of Nerva, 303–4
  on Damis's diary as a forgery, 237, 260
  on layers of Apollonian tradition, 216
  on Maximus's material, 375
  on parallels between the Flavians and Severans, 316
  on Philostratus, 127, 159, 162, 286
  on Vespasian, 290, 292
followers. See also disciples
  of Apollonius, 200
forgery, theory of, 251, 258
form criticism, development of, 94–95
Forrest Gump, ancient version of, 338
Four Emperors, Year of, 291, 332

Galba, adopting Otho, 291
gaps. See also historical gaps; temporal gap
  closing, 371–74
  in Philostratus's narrative, 238
Gardiera in Spain, Apollonius visited, 332
Geisler, Norman L., 54
genre, of the VA, 156–62
geographical oddities, of the Egyptian travels of Apollonius, 293
geography
  based on Nearchus's Indike, 254
  of the VA, 92
Georgi, Dieter, 96
German language, as an inadvertent barrier, 4
Geryon, bleeding trees of, 288–89
Geta, hated Plautianus, 104
Gildersleeve, Basil Lanneau, 59
god
  previously existing becoming incarnate, 349
  worshipped by the mind in silence, 206, 207
god-man. See also divine man
  born of a mortal woman, 349
Goldhill, Simon, 135–36
Gordian, Antonius, 138
Gospel of Thomas, 402
Gospel writers, 50, 51, 318, 424, 425
Gospels
  as the best sources for studying historical Jesus, 398
  Christ's miracles in, 86
  collusion in, 409
  exorcisms as Jesus's miracles of healing, 363–64
  as an influence on the VA, 48
  letters of Paul predating, 396
  locating borrowings from, 346–69
  oral and written sources behind, 50
  on the origin or nature of demons, 368
  Philostratus and, 32, 351, 369
  pre-dating the VA, 345
  records of Jesus's words and deeds, 398

INDEX

Gospels (*cont.*)
  related a resurrection of Jesus from the dead, 361
  VA as a counterblast to, 31
  VA never directly quoting, 341
Göttsching, Johannes, 112, 316
Greco-Roman literature
  accounts of resurrection as rare, 354
  rarity of exorcists and exorcisms in, 364
Greco-Roman tales, shaped by stories in *VA*, 363
Greece, Apollonius journey to, 171
Greek literary history, rewriting, 326
Greek religion, *VA* seeking to revive traditional, 312, 349
Grossart, Peter, 282
Grosso, Fulvio, 236, 238, 302
Gymnasticus, 130–31, 252
gymnosophists, 297–99, 331, 378

Habermas, Gary R., 45, 48, 393
Hadrian, collection of Apollonius's letters, 221
hair, Apollonius wore long, 421
Harmartolos, George, 77
healer, portraying Apollunius as, 230
healings, common fare in Greco-Roman texts, 347
Hegesippus, 403, 404, 409
Heliodorus the Arab, 120, 297, 298
Helios, 310, 311
Helix, 148
Hellenistic agenda, Philostratus advancing, 312
Hellenistic Christ, Apollonius as, 7
Hellenistic miracle source, *VA* and NT may have shared, 94
Hellenistic religious revival, Philostratus promoting, 312, 344
Lord Herbert of Cherbury, 86
Hercules, 177, 330–31, 334–36, 357, 359, 360
Hermippas of Smyrna, Diogenes accessing early writings of, 373
Herod Antipas, 24
Herodes, sophist, 142
Herodotus, 266, 268, 292

Heroicus, 145–50, 252, 280–81, 288–89, 325
Herzog, M. J. C., 89
Hierapolis, 264
Hierocles, Sossianus, 61, 62, 64, 65, 66, 71, 162, 216
Hilkiah, rediscovered the Book of the Law, 40
Himerius, not mentioning Apollonius, 67
Hindu Kush, referring to as the Caucasus, 270–71
Hippolytus, on Julia Avita Mamaea, 343
hippopotamus, not native to India, 272, 378
Historia Augusta, 113, 237
historical and geographical errors, in the *VA*, 44, 261
historical Apollonius. *See also* Apollonius of Tyana
  building on the pattern of earlier gods and men, 336
  comparing to the historical Jesus, 16
  key issues needing to be discussed in approaching, 380
  as less relevant to his own times, 191
  no solid evidence of interacting with any Roman rulers, 317
  Philostratus and, 294, 313, 322
  quest of, 87–93
  third-century reimaging of, 382
  whether any of the epistles were penned, 222
historical distance, significance of, 371
historical errors, in the *VA*, 21, 238
historical gaps. *See also* gaps; temporal gap
  between Apollonius and the composition of the *VA*, 370–71
  bridging with the Damis memoir, 376–79
  closing, 371–74
historical Jesus, 9–10, 87, 398
historical methodology, 8
historical problems, with the *VA*, 17, 88, 259
historical reasons, for dismissing Damis, 243–44

INDEX

Hobbes, Thomas, Blount shared the century with, 87
holy man, Apollonius as, 40
Homeric heroes, meeting with the ghosts of, 149
Huetius, P. D., 89
Hugo of Santalla, 79
human being, deity born as, 349
human communities, Philostratus's references to non-existent, 308
human languages, Apollonius knew without studying, 166
Hyphasis River, 168, 280

Iamblicus, 54, 67, 191
Iarchas, chief of the Wise Men, 168, 169, 181, 349
Ignatius of Antioch, 403, 410
Iliad, corrections to, 146
imagination, of Philostratus, 336
Imagines (Philostratus), 301, 325
Imagines I, 129, 136–37
Imagines II, 128
imperial advisor, Apollonius as, 317–18
independence, of sources, 387
India, Apollonius's pilgrimage to, 330
Indian bestiary, 275–77
Indian king Porus, 168
Indian sages, 169, 299, 378. *See also* Wise Ones of India
Indika, of Ctesias, 251
Indike, Nearchus's, 254
Indus River, 271–73
Infancy Gospel of Thomas, 402
inheritance, Apollonius gave away, 165
inscription in Sardis, confirmed details in Apollonius's letters, 223
internal consistency, 388, 419
Ionia, Apollonius in, 170–71
Isodore of Pelusium, 75
Isthmus of Corinth, Apollonius's prediction about, 172

Jacquier, E., 411
Jairus's daughter, 354–55
Jambres, opposed Moses, 190
James (book of), 399
James (brother of Jesus), 401, 404

Jandial, location and description of, 273–74
Jannes, opposed Moses, 190
jars, of rain and wind, 277–78
Jerome, 68–69, 70
Jesus. *See also* Christ
  announcing the coming kingdom of God, 23
  Apollonius closely resembling, 5–8
  brothers including James and Jude, 415
  cast out numerous demons, 368
  details of his life confirmed, 414–15
  as a "divine man," 96, 97
  few extrabiblical sources mentioning until the late first century, 50
  as a firstborn son, 351
  as a Jew who revered the one God of Israel, 22
  material attested in multiple sources, 405, 425
  movement grew into a major world religion, 24
  never demanded that demons give proof of their departure, 366
  one of many figures believed to be sons of God, 20–21
  oral traditions about, 388
  overall picture of as consistent, 425
  problematic areas with some traditions about, 417–18
  similarities to the story of Apollonius, 340
  sources for, 52, 395
  titles and designations used by Paul, 397
Jewish Wars (Josephus), 301
John (Gospel of), 398, 409
John the Baptist, immersed Jesus, 415
Patriarch John VII, 77
Jones, Christopher P., 158, 222–23, 264
Jonson, Ben, 136
Joseph, encounter in a dream, 350
Josephus, 190, 365, 401, 409
King Josiah, rediscovering the Book of the Law, 40

INDEX

journeys
    to Greece, 171
    to Mesopotamia, 166–67
    over the Caucasus Mountains, 167
    from Rome to Dicaearchia, 72
Jude's two sons, trial of before Domitian, 404
Julia Domna
    agenda of, 46, 424
    Antipater shared Syrian ancestry with, 119
    circle of scholars dispersed after her death, 121
    common interests with Philostratus, 120
    gave a text to Philostratus, 259
    held out hope for reconciliation, 106
    honored several deities during her lifetime, 311
    as imperial patron of Philostratus, 20, 31
    impetus for a book detailing Apollonius's life, 154, 234, 235, 324
    the most significant woman of Philostratus's era, 109–10
    no personal desire to fight against Christianity, 343
    suicide of, 109, 110
    two sons of, 104
    worship of the Syrian Sun god, 310
Julia Maesa (sister of Julia Domna), 109, 110–11, 112, 113
Julian the Apostate, not mentioning Apollonius at all, 67
Juppiter trageodeus (Lucian), 242

Kee, Howard Clark, 45–46, 270, 280, 314, 360–61
Keener, Craig S., 43, 45, 46, 47, 49, 52, 259, 374, 376
Klauck, Hans-Kosef, 39, 43, 47
Knoles, Thomas Gregory, 315, 317
Koester, Helmut, 411
König, Jason, 131
Koskenniemi, Erkki, 3, 93, 95, 228, 235–36, 287, 341, 354, 357

labors of Hercules, resurrection of a girl related to, 359
Lactantius, rebuttal of Hierocles, 64
Ladner, Nathaniel, 89–90
Laetius, not citing Apollonius, 191
Lake Nasser, 300
Lemnos, Philostratus spent some time on, 117
length, of the *VA* as beyond the upper limit of a biography, 160
Letronne, J.A., 294–95
Letters of Apollonius (*Epistles*)
    on Apollonius as both a magician and a philosopher, 424
    on Apollonius traveling to Babylon and India, 227
    Apollonius's role as a political advisor, 337
    appearing in the *VA* and the Damis memoir, 408
    authors listing in a footnote or endnote, 38
    claiming that multiple deities did not need sacrifices, 210
    dating and authorship of, 375
    listing no secondary literature, 22
    not mentioning Titus's refusal of a literal crown, 302
    positive view of Apollonius as a magician, 412
    as a primary text, 11
    sage's description in, 313
    as the second largest source of Apollonius material, 219–29
    similarities and differences with the *VA*, 226, 381
    as the source for the *VA*, 414
    translation of, 93
    written by Apollonius himself, 58
letters of Philostratus, 135
Leucothea's veil, protected Odysseus from drowning, 332
levitation, 178, 251, 278–79
Libanius, 67
Licona, Michael R., 393
The Life of Apollonius of Tyana (Philostratus). See *VA* (*The Life of Apollonius of Tyana*)

Life of Apollonius the Pythagorean (Sidonius Apollinaris), 72
Life of Pythagoras (Iamblichus), number of words in, 257
light to the Gentiles, as Jesus or Paul, 421
lightning, helped Philostratus in aligning Apollonius's nativity, 352–53
literary corpus, of Philostratus, 26
literary dependence, between the *VA* and the NT, 93–94
literary grounds, researchers dismissing Damis on, 242–43
literary legacy, Philostratus known for, 121
literary relationship, between the *VA* and *Heroicus*, 149
literary sources, historical details dependent on, 254
Lives of the Sophists (Philostratus), 114
Lo Cascio, Ferdinando, 236
London Underground, "mind the gap" warning, 49
lost documents, claims about the discovery of, 249
The Lover of Lies (Lucian), 296
The Lover of Truth (Hierocles), 60–66, 74
Lucian of Samosata, 194–200
  on Alexander as a Pythagorean philosopher, 230
  on Apollonius as a fraud and magician, 39, 199, 216, 380, 412, 426
  on the death of Apollonius, 199
  on the existence of Alexander, 198
  first author in antiquity to mention Apollonius, 189, 194, 195
  negative view of Apollonius, 58, 406–7
  parodying Christians for bullibility, 404
  visited Homer at the Island of the Blest, 282
  writings of as independent, 409
Luke-Acts, 419, 421–22

Lycus, tyrant and usurper of Thebes, 335

Macarius of Magnesia, 70–71, 72
Macrinus, mastermind behind Caracalla's assassination chosen as the new emperor, 109
Maesa, Julia. *See* Julia Maesa (sister of Julia Domna)
Magi of Babylon and Susa, Apollonius meeting with, 166
magic, 75, 76
magical beasts, *VA* containing, 19
magical components, 322, 323
magical deeds, of Apollonius, 68
magical devices, of Apollonius, 64, 73, 74
magical supernatural details, in the *VA*, 251
magical texts, mentioning Apollonius, 79
magical themes, Damis material treating, 240–41
magical urns, report of, 278
magician
  Apollonius as, 39, 40, 199, 231, 322, 337
  in either a pejorative or complementary sense, 215
  as a false charge about Apollonius, 165
  Philostratus countering the charge that Apollonius was, 164
  Philostratus embarrassed by the term, 215
maiden, Apollonius's resurrection of, 354
Mamaea, Julia Avita, mother of Alexander Severus and niece of Julia Domna, 343
Mamea, Julia, 113
Manolaraki, Eleni, 293
Manutius, Aldus, 81
Mara bar-Sarapion, 400–401
Marcellinus, Ammianus, on Old Ninos, 264
Marciana, Paccia, first wife of Septimius Severus, 109

Marcus Aurelius, tutor of, 196
Mark (Gospel of), number of words, 257
marriage and other sexual activity,
    Apollonius abstaining from,
    165–66
Martial, published epigrams to Nerva,
    304
Martialis (a tribune), killed Caracalla,
    108–9
Mary (mother of Jesus), 351
material sacrifice, Apollonius on, 207,
    230
Matthew text, slight departures by
    Barnabas, 411
Maximus of Aegeae
    account of, 218, 219
    book written by, 374–75
    cited by Philostratus in the *VA*, 237
    incorporating work of into the *VA*,
        59
    little is known about, 216–19
    mentioning Apollonius, 404–5
    Philostratus incorporated accounts
        of, 407
    as the source for Apollonius's youth,
        377
Medieval period, historical texts
    mentioning both Apollonius
    and the *VA*, 79
Megabyzus, in Herodotus story, 291
Meier, 43, 46, 48, 49, 52
Memnon, talking statue of, 149, 176,
    294–97, 378
*Memoirs of Apollonius of Tyana,
    Magician and Philosopher*
    (Moiragenes), 213
Menander's fragmentary play *Phasma*,
    284
Menecrates, 132, 245
Menippus of Lycia, 283
Mesopotamia
    Apollonius's journey to, 166–67
    Philostratus's confused geography
        of, 263
messages and lifestyles, of Jesus
    compared to Apollonius, 23
metempsychosis, attributed to the
    Pythagorean Apollonius, 227

meteorological prediction, Indians as
    masters of, 278
Meyer, Eduard, 216, 236, 244, 246, 254
Middle Ages, Apollonius during, 78–80
Miles, Graeme, 146–47, 157
mind, portraying the image of a god, 178
mind of others, Apollonius's ability to
    know, 420
ministries, of Jesus compared to
    Apollonius, 23–24
miracle stories, role in the development
    of form criticism, 94–95
miracles
    of Apollonius, 69, 322, 341, 346–47
    of Christ, 70
    of Jesus, 23
    at the tomb of Apollonius, 77
"mirrors for princes," genre of, 316
mistakes
    as fatal to a sophist's career, 115
    within Damis's accounts, 262
Moeser, Marion C., 195
Moiragenes (or Moeragenes)
    on Apollonius, 31, 404–5
    on Apollonius as a magician, 39,
        214, 215, 412
    biography of Apollonius, 407
    biography of Apollonius by, 212–16,
        321
    blended magical and philosophical
        aspects of Apollonius, 215
    cited by Philostratus in the *VA*, 237
    disparaging the account of, 59
    material difficult to date, 375
monographs, only two written on
    Apollonius, 28n104
Montaigne, Michel de, 82
More, Henry, 83
mother of Apollonius, received a vision,
    350
multiple attestation (independent
    attestation), criterion of, 188,
    412, 413, 419
Musonius (Stoic philosopher), 132, 173,
    174, 225, 335
Mystic Rites or On Sacrifices, by the
    Suda, 205

INDEX

mythical animals, historical inaccuracy of, 277
mythical creatures and flora, Philostratus's references to, 275, 308

Naked Ones of Ethiopia, 176–78, 297, 298, 299
natural magic, based on a manipulation of natural forces, 81, 85
Nearchus, fleet commander, 372
neo-Pythagoreans, notorious for producing forgeries, 237
Nero
    Apollonius and, 24, 290
    attempted to dig the Corinthian canal but failed, 172
    banishment of the philosopher Demetrius from Rome, 286–87
    close call of, 287–88
    described as Cerberus, guardian of Hades, 335
    executed Cossutianus Capito, 263
    forbade the teaching of philosophy in Rome, 174
    mockery of his mediocre singing voice, 132
    overlap in content with the *VA*, 133
Nero, as a brief dialogue, 132–33
Nerva, 180, 183, 184, 303–4
neutral or hostile sources, constituting stronger evidence, 391
New Testament
    authors referenced magicians, 190
    malevolent actions of demons, 366
    parallels between the *VA* and, 346–69
    ramifications for students of, 382
    reliance on the *VA*, 93
New Testament scholars
    effects of a temporal gap on the historical Jesus, 50
    importance of a proper understanding of Apollonius, 25–26
    not communicating historical and literary problems regarding Apollonius, 16

presenting only the Philostratean version of Apollonius, 188
research on Apollonius or Philostratus, 4
understanding of collusion, 408
New Testament studies, 32–56, 93–97
Newman, John Henry, 87, 318
Nile River, 292–94, 300, 378
Nilus of Ancyra, on the power of talismans, 75
Nineveh, 244, 263–64
non-amatory letters, written to members of the Severan household, 134
non-Christian sources, not much about Jesus in the first century, 400
Norden, Eduard, 93–94
novels, comparisons of the *VA* to, 161
numerous sources, comparing to one another, 391–93

Odysseus, 332, 361–63
Odyssey, 361, 366
Old Ninos, referring to Syrian Hierapolis, 264
Olympic Games, history of the, 131
On Sacrifices, 188, 205–10, 231
One Remarkable Life (Ehrman), 14–15, 21–25, 426
Onesicritus, 272, 373
online presence, Apollonius having a strong, 10
oral materials, behind the Gospels, 388
oral sources, as nearly impossible to evaluate, 374
oral tradition, accuracy of, 388
Oration on the Dignity of Man, included Apollonius with philosophers, 81
Orfitus, exiled to islands, 180
Origen, 190, 212–13, 343
origin, of the *VA*, 154–55
Otanes, in Herodotus story, 291
Otho, adoption by Galba, 291

pagan authors, taking note of Jesus, 402
pagan Christ, Apollonius as, 7
pagan culture, 63

457

INDEX

pagan religious agenda, of Philostratus, 310–13
pagan texts
  on Apollonius as a philosopher, 66
  on Jesus as a criminal, 425
pagans
  on the effectiveness of talismans, 74–75
  regarding Apollonius as divine, 67
pages, mentioning items of the Apollonian Decalogue, 55–56
painting and art interpretation, author of *Imagines I* well-versed in, 136
Palamedes, as both living and dead, 419–20
parallels, between the VA and non-Christian materials, 353
paranormal activities, Philostratus's references to, 308
Parker, Samuel (Bishop of Oxford), 89
Parthenis ("the Virgin'), union with Apollo produced Pythagoras, 352
Parthenon, forecourt of, 271
passages, attributed to Damis, 256
Passing of Peregrinus (Lucian), 404
passion narrative of Jesus, traditions from, 416–17
Paul, 125, 395–96, 409
peace, Jesus's coming and, 421
Penella, R. J., 224, 225, 226, 227, 302
Pentheus (tyrant), 336
Pescennius Niger, 103
Petzke, G., 195, 236, 240
phantom, as Philostratean fiction, 284
pharmakos, expulsion of a, 365
Philip the Arab, 113, 343
Phillimore, J. S.
  allusion to Apollonius in Dio's writings, 192–93
  on Apollonius's disappearance from his trial, 304
  on both Damis and his *Scrapbook* as real, 236
  on Julia encouraging Philostratus to write, 108
  on not taking Philostratus' work at face value, 17

on Philostratus, 203, 239
on the silence of first and second-century writers about Apollonius, 190, 194
Philolaus of Citium, 173
philosopher(s)
  Apollonius as a, 327, 337
  Apollonius's friendship with famous, 224
  as conscientious and austere professionals, 115
  dealing with tyranny, 180, 333
  Ethiopian, 176
  Julia Domna's circle of, 154
  not ranking Apollonius among, 64
  not vilified as magicians, 299
  often counseling rulers, 318
philosophical agenda, of Philostratus, 313–15
philosophical details, magnifying or inventing, 322
philosophical education, of Apollonius, 165
philosophical leanings, of Apollonius, 413–14
philosophy
  Julia Domna interested in, 154, 314
  Nero had become hostile to, 173
  without eloquence as nowhere, 116
Philostratean corpus
  advantages of being familiar with the entire, 123–25
  dissimilarities from, 255
  establishing, 129–50
  lessons learned from exploring, 151–52
  trees on tombs associated with their occupants, 288
  VA as the longest work within, 153
Philostrati, 125, 127, 129
Philostratus, Lucius Flavius
  account of Apollonius as inaccurate, 382
  agendas of, 46, 309, 313, 326, 337
  also called ("the Athenian") ("the Second"), 117
  on Apollonius as a philosopher, 216, 413

458

on Apollonius as a traveler, 161
on Apollonius as an advisor to
    kings, 317
on Apollonius as not interested in
    wealth, 199
on Apollonius had raised the
    maiden from the dead, 356
assertion that Apollonius was not a
    magician, 231
associated Apollonius with great
    explorers, 331–32
as author of amatory and non-
    amatory letters, 134
as author of material attributed to
    Damis, 19
authored all or most of the
    Philostratean corpus, 129–30
based his story on a particular
    Greek tale, 357
bias of, 424
biographer of Apollonius, 4
borrowed from earlier stories by
    Lucian, 150
called Damis's account "clear" and
    detailed, 377
capable of writing fiction and
    history, 151
citing Damis as a participant in
    encounters, 235
claimed that Julia had given him a
    document, 376
claims about Damis and his
    Scrapbook, 235
communing with and questioning
    dead warriors, 283
comparison of Apollonius to famous
    philosophers, 322, 333
confusing two men named "Capito,"
    262–63
consistent in his disapproval of
    magic, 325
content of *On Sacrifices* in the
    VA not matching the extant
    fragment, 208
correcting ignorance about
    Apollonius, 162
created at least one other fictional
    witness, 243
creation of the story about Achilles,
    282
Damis as the product of the fertile
    imagination of, 242
defended Apollonius, 199, 319, 324
denied Apollonius was a magician,
    231, 412
description of the city of Babylon,
    268
details favoring authorship of
    Heroicus, 147–48
did not dedicate the VA to Julia
    Domna, 155–56
Dio Cassius as a contemporary of,
    201
directly associated with the
    Severans, 120
disdain for magic, 258, 325
displaying sophistic skills, forensic
    rhetoric, and invention, 319–20
distinguishing him from other
    members of his family, 125
as either the editor or creator of
    Damis's memoir, 381
establishing the corpus of, 129–50
exhibiting his intellect and talent,
    245
far removed from the time of
    Apollonius, 32
hesitant to relate some of Damis's
    tales, 377
as a high-ranking politician in
    Athens before, 118
ignorant of the facts, 286
influenced by Christian culture, 94
intended the VS as a monument to
    himself, 140
introducing with the entirety of his
    writings, 26
letters of Apollonius in the VA, 221
as a literary master, 318
literary theme of the recovery of a
    lost document, 248
magical material in the Damis
    memoir suggesting a source,
    240–41
material from earlier writers, 407

Philostratus, Lucius Flavius (cont.)
  on Maximus agreeing that Apollonius was a philosopher, 219
  may not have borrowed from the Gospels, 357
  modified his views on Apollonius, 205, 210
  on Moiragenes as inaccurate in his assessment of Apollonius, 213
  never mentions Philostratus I as a sophist, 127
  not deeply interested in Pythagoreanism, 315
  not featuring neo-Pythagoreanism elsewhere in his corpus, 229
  not promoting any particular trend in religion, 341
  not providing a witness for miraculous events, 63
  not well-known to Biblical scholars, 101
  not writing about or against Christianity, 342
  as a Platonist, 83–84
  political world of, 102–14
  postmortem appearance of Apollonius, 184
  preserved the story of Apollonius's career, 59, 383
  purpose for writing the VA as biographical, 159
  recasted Apollonius as a philosopher, 216
  received some benefit from Julia, 318
  rehabilitation of Apollonius's reputation, 337
  relating history in the VS, 141
  reliance on works of earlier writers, 30, 269, 274, 275
  reporting mythical flora, 289
  revisionist history of, 379
  on sages of India, 280
  seeking political advancement or financial gain, 318
  similarities with the uncontested works of, 131
  sketch of his life, 117–22
  as a skilled author with wide interests, 151
  sophistic profession of, 114–17
  as a sorcerer in his own right, 58
  sought to please his patroness, 313
  sources of, 30, 211, 237, 252, 374–75, 408
  speech in the VA that Apollonius wrote but did not deliver, 182
  themes of Greek revivalism and nationalism, 116
  on the tradition that Apollonius ascended into heaven, 199
  traditions about how Apollonius may have died, 184
  transformed Apollonius, 116–17, 143, 337
  at Troy as fiction, 283
  version of Apollonius's life not appearing to be accurate, 231
  welcomed into the Severan court, 119
  on whether Apollonius was a sophist or a philosopher, 143
  worked over source material, 255
  working on VS and VA simultaneously, 144
  world of, 101–22
  writings of, 123–52
  wrote the VA over a century after the death of the historical Apollonius, 20
Philostratus and Damis, styles of as indistinguishable, 389
Philostratus I, 127, 128
Philostratus III, 127, 128
Philostratus of Lemnos, 221–22
Phoenician sailor
  in *Heroicus*, 245
  moved from skepticism to belief, 146
Photius, patriarch of Constantinople, on Apollonius, 76
King Phraotes, 167–68, 181, 274
Phyton, 333
Pico della Mirandola, 81
Pillars of Hercules, 174
Piso, adopted by Galba, 291

plague at Ephesus, Apollonius predicted, 182
plague demon, as an expulsion of a *pharmakos*, 365
planetary prophecy, 214, 241
Plato, 18, 333
Plato's *Republic*, number of words of, 160
Platt, Verity, 295, 296
Plautianus, 103–4, 109, 316
Plautilla, forced marriage to Caracalla, 104
Pliny the Elder, 190, 194
Pliny the Younger, 190, 304, 402, 409
Plutarch, 190, 191–92, 213, 372–73
podcasts, focusing on Apollonius, 11
Poklatecki, Stanislaw, 82–83
Polemo (sophist), 142
political agenda, of Philostratus, 315–18
political career, of Philostratus in Athens, 118
political instruction, in the *VA*, 317
political message, in the *VA*, 163
political orators, 114
political world, of Philostratus II, 102–14
Pontius Pilate, 24
poor man, Apollonius helped, 179
Porphyry, 71, 191, 206–7, 222
Porreca, David, 78
post-Philostratean books, penned by Hierocles and Sidonius have perished, 55
Praetorians, hunted down Elagabalus and his mother, 112
pre-Philostratean sources
  about Apollonius, 27, 38
  conclusions for all, 229–31
  on Homer visiting the burial mound of Achilles, 282
  of Moiragenes and Maximus of Aegae have perished, 55
  not used in the *VA*, 380–81
  surveyed, 210
  used in the *VA*, 211–31, 381
pre-Philostratean treatise, *On Sacrifices* as, 206
Priscus, Helvidius, Stoic senator, 292

Proclus of Naucratus, Philostratus studied under, 117–18
prognostications, of Apollonius, 241
prologue and introductory material, in the *VA*, 159, 164–65
Prometheus, cave where he had been bound, 270
pro-Roman Apollonius, of Philostratus, 228
Protesilaus, in *Heroicus*, 146, 149, 150
Proteus, announced his own birth as Apollonius in the *VA*, 351
Proteus (god), in a vision to Apollonius's mother during her pregnancy, 165
pseudepigraph, Damis memoir as, 42, 258–59, 378
Pseudo-Athanasius, on a wise man named Apollo, 77
Pseudo-Justin, on Apollonius creating talismans, 75
Pseudo-Nonnus, on Apollonius's use of magic, 75
Ptolemy, Alexander's general, 372
Pudentilla, Apuleius persuading to marry him, 193
Pythagoras
  Apollonius as the new, 327
  calming the sea, 54
  compared to Apollonius, 164, 328
  journeys of, 299
  not comparing to Apollonius in resisting tyranny, 333–34
  traditions about, 351
  VA modeled after the biography of, 90
Pythagorean lifestyle, Apollonius's defense of, 182
Pythagorean memoirs, practice of preserving, 237
Pythagorean saint, Julia wanted Apollonius portrayed as, 310
Pythagoreanism
  Apollonius as an adherent of, 210, 218, 313, 327, 328
  Apollonius studied under Euxenus of Heracleia, 165
  as the best philosophy, 177

Pythagoreanism (cont.)
    Plutarch wrote about, 191
    of the VA, 314
Pythagoreans, 183, 190–91, 318, 414

Quadratus, claims about Jesus, 403, 409
quantity
    of information versus quality, 390
    of sources, 387
questions, from a first encounter with
    Apollonius, 12–13
Questions and Answers (Anastasius), 77

rabies, Apollonius cured a dog of, 241
Raynor, D. H., 197, 215
realistic fiction, passing for true history,
    147
Reardon, B. P., 156
reasons, for wanting to know about
    Apollonius, 5–14
Reimarus, Hermann Samuel, 88
relative of Damis, brought an unknown
    document to light, 246
reliability, of sources, 419–22
religious heritage, of Julia Domna, 154
religious reformer, Apollonius's role as,
    337
religious sacrifice, Apollonius's view
    of, 227
"religious superficiality," of Philostratus,
    341–42
Renaissance, brought the VA to the
    West, 80–83
Reply to Hierocles, 63, 93
research methodology, on contradictory
    traditions, 188
researchers, repeating blunders of the
    past, 57
Response to Hierocles (Eusebius), 11
resurrection accounts, 354–63
resurrection story, in the VA as unique
    in Greco-Roman literature, 349
resurrections, rare in pagan literature,
    348
Réville, Albert, 85, 86–87, 310
revisionist history, Philostratus writing,
    150, 379

rhetors, needing a capacious and
    accurate memory, 115
rhinoceros, in northern India as
    plausible, 276
Rinuccini, Alemano, Latin translation of
    the VA, 81
Roberts, J. M., on Damis linked to
    Demas mentioned by Paul, 242
Robiano, Patrick, 297–98
Roetzel, Calvin J., 45, 51, 54
Roman citizen, Philostratus as, 119
Roman emperors, doubt that Apollonius
    wrote and received letters from,
    224
Roman History, edited by Paul the
    Deacon retold a few episodes
    from the VA, 79
Roman History (Dio), negative stance
    towards Apollonius, 204
Roman religion, Elagabalus attempted a
    reform of, 111
Roman world, Apollonius traveled
    throughout, 311
romance, genre of, 314
Rome, Apollonius's visit to, 285
Rosenmeyer, Patricia A., 295–96
Royal Journals (the *Ephemerides*), by
    Arrian, 372
Rufus, Musonius, 180, 192
Rutilianus, Publius Mummius Sisenna,
    as verifiable, 198

Sardis, as a cult center for Demeter, 223
satires, Lucian best known for, 195
satyr, an encounter with a, 300–301
scale, of the VA not fitting well with
    biography, 161
Scheintod ("apparent death"), category
    of, 356
Schirren, Thomas, 256, 284
scholars
    checking writings against the
        Apollonian Decalogue, 33–34
    on Moiragenes portrayin Apollonius
        in a negative light, 215
    providing examples of historical
        errors in the VA, 45

skepticism about the Damis
document, 43
Schutz, Hans Joachim, 94
Scopelian, 142–43, 205, 267–68, 352
Scrap Book (*Scraps from the Manger*).
See also Damis memoir
on Apollonius's journeys, sayings,
speeches, and predictions, 239
of Damis, 41, 166, 238, 260, 376
as official title of Damis's memoirs,
234
as a Philostratean fiction, 378
Scythia, Apollonius left unexplored, 330
Second Sophistic literary renaissance,
121
Second Sophistic movement
agenda of, 313
fictional documents abounding in,
247–50
forty-one sophists of in the *VS*, 138
as a Hellenistic project, 312
histories of many well-known
figures, 145
Philostratus as the paragon of, 140
pro-Hellenic agenda but loyal to the
Roman Empire, 116
secondary material, 22, 53
second-tier sources, 395, 404, 406
Seleucus Nicator, 268
Seneca, not mentioning Apollonius,
190, 191
Septimius, Lucius, translated the diary
of Dictys, 248
Septimius Severus
attempted to repair the statue of
Memnon, 294
as a capable ruler and military
leader, 103–5
Christian persecutions during, 342
death from gout in Eboracum
(York), 105
Julia Domna's visit to Tyana with,
154
as a patron and amateur of letters,
119
trip to Egypt with Julia Domna, 293
servants, automata as, 279–80

Severan rulers
allusions in the *VA*, 317
not displaying hostility toward
Christianity, 342
during Philostratus's career as a
sophist, 102
VA intended for the instruction or
entertainment of, 163, 316
Queen of Sheba, on "the (other) half" of
the story, 25
sibling rivalry, of Severus's two sons,
104–5
Bishop Sidonius Apollinaris, 72, 78
sign
of the coming of the three Thebans,
175
of a true philosopher, 333
silence, Apollonius observed five years
of, 166, 327
Silenus, the drunken satyr, capture of,
301
similarities
of Christ and Apollonius, 91
of Pythagoras and Apollonius, 330
between the *VA* and the Gospels, 345
Simon Magus, 190
singly reported tradition, as trustworthy,
412
skepticism, applying to a hypothetical
first-century source, 52
skeptics, finding Apollonius useful
when compared to Jesus, 8
Smith, Morton, 43, 45, 222
snakes, varieties of, 168, 276–77
social leaders, history professors, 116
social position, of sophists, 116
social status, of Jesus versus Apollonius,
22–23
Socrates, 18, 334
Solmsen, Friedrich, 313
Son of God, Apollonius portrayed as, 14
sophist(s)
Apollonius at times portrayed as, 228
combining literary categories, 157
confirmations of Philostratus's
career as, 118
introduction to the lifestyle of,
114–17

INDEX

sophist(s) (*cont.*)
   Philostratus's career as, 102
   of the *VS* treated as practically holy men, 142
   unbalanced treatment in the *VS*, 139
sophist of sophists, Philostratus desiring to portray his hero as, 161
sophistic characteristics, attributed to Apollonius, 151
sophistic erudition, as mastery of Homeric lore, 147
sophistic lore, Philostratus well-versed in oral or written, 144–45
sophistic talents, Philostratus's desire to show off, 319
sophistic work, from the pen of Philostratus in the *VA*, 254
sorcerer
   Apollonius as, 64, 67, 383
   Philostratus as, 58
sorcery, 75, 324
sources. *See also* ancient sources; pre-Philostratean sources
   about Apollonius, 412
   for Apollonius and Jesus compared, 387–426
   biographical, 18, 150
   brief recap of the date of Philostratus's, 374–75
   disagreeing with Philostratus's portrayal of Apollonius, 30
   earlier, 39, 143, 393
   employed in the composition of the *VA*, 251
   identifiable predating Philostratus's *VA*, 211
   for the itinerary of Apollonius, 238–39
   listed by Philostratus at the beginning of the *VA*, 212
   Philostratus's use of historical, 237
   pre-Philostratean and contemporaneous not used or mentioned in the *VA*, 187–210
   scholars not conducting investigations of, 19

supporting Philostratus's claim that Apollonius was a philosopher, 229
Spain, in the *VA*, 174
speech, Apollonius wrote for his trial, 182–83, 305, 321, 420
Speyer, Wolfgang, 259
Spinoza, Blount shared the century with, 87
spiritual or mental flight, as literal levitation, 278
Stephanus, assassinated Domitian, 183
Stobaeus, letters in his anthology under the name of Apollonius, 222
stories, recycled in the *VA* as insertions, 151
Strabo, on Babylon as neglected and in ruins, 268
structure, of the *VA*, 159
Suda (tenth-century Byzantine encyclopedia), 118, 121, 125–29, 137, 206
Suetonius
   Apollonius unknown to, 189
   on the execution of Flavius Clemens and the assassination of Domitian, 307
   ignored Apollonius, 190
   more about the early Christians, 402
   not mentioning Domitian exiling Nerva, 303
   not mentioning Vespasian meeting with three philosophers, 292
   on Titus having no aversion to accepting crowns, 302
   writings of as independent, 409
sun, eclipse occurred simultaneously with a thunderclap, 287–88
Sun cult, no promotion of in the *VA*, 344
Sun god, 310, 311
supernatural deeds, of Apollonius, 210
supernatural phenomena, in the *VA*, 19–20
supernatural powers, 231, 337
supernatural tales, in the *VA*, 251
Swain, Simon, 312, 313

INDEX

swans, encircled Apollonius's mother at his birth, 165
sympathetic view of Moiragenes, concerning Apollonius, 216
Synopsis historion (Cedrinus), invoking beneficent demons, 76
Synoptic Gospels, 397, 398

tablets. *See* wooden tablets
Tacitus, 189, 190, 292, 402, 409
Taggart, Bruce Lyle, 197, 198, 236, 237, 247
talismans, 69, 73–76, 93
talking statue of Memnon. *See* Memnon
Taxila, location and description of, 273–74
teacher, Jesus as, 400
Telesinus, Gaius Luccius, consul of Rome, 173, 286
telesma, not occurring in the *VA*, 73
temple at Jandial, description of as inaccurate, 273
temporal gap. *See also* historical gaps
    between Apollonius and the composition of the *VA*, 49, 52, 370–79
    between Jesus and his biographers, 50, 52
Tertullian, on Severus, 342
Testimonia, pagan and Christian about Apollonius in antiquity, 66–72
Testimonium Flavianum, neutral in its presentation of Jesus, 425
testimony, earliest as most useful, 393
texts, not mentioned by Philostratus, 210
textual similarity, 348, 349–50, 355–56
Thallus, comments of, 400
theists, deists versus, 84–87
Theocratus of Chios, Diogenes having access to early writings of, 373
theriomorphic depictions, of the gods, 178
Theseus, Hercules delivered from the underworld, 335
Thespasian, friend of Apollonius, 181
Thespesion, oldest member of the Naked Ones, 177, 178

"thou shalt mind the gap" commandment, of earlier experts on Apollonius, 49
Thrasybulus, sent sabotage Apollonius's visit, 177
Tigellinus (prefect of the Praetorian Guard), Demetrius and, 173–74, 286
Timasion, guide of Apollonius in Ethiopia, 176
Patriarch Timothy I, 249
Tindal, borrowed from Blount, 87
Titans, Apollonius's affirmation of, 420
title, in Greek of the *VA*, 158
Titus, 24, 178–79, 301, 302
topoi, of Greek literary tradition, 326
traditions, 13, 388, 393, 413
training, of athletes, 130–31
Trajan, at the ruined site of Babylon, 269
transfiguration on a mountain, of Jesus, 416
transmigration of souls, Apollonius endorsing, 420
treasure, finding in a field in the *VA*, 347
Treat, Jay Curry, on Barnabas quoting Matthew, 411
trees, bleeding sap resembling blood, 288, 289
trial, of Apollonius, 180, 182, 304–5, 336, 420
Trojan War, 146
Trophonius at Lebadea, Apollonius visited the cave of, 183
twice-told tales, phenomenon of, 124
tyrants, confrontations of philosophers with, 180

unicorn, mentioned by Ctesias, 275–76

VA (*The Life of Apollonius of Tyana*)
    agendas of, 309–38
    anti-Christian agenda of, 339–45
    on Apollonius escaping execution, 361
    as biography, 160, 162
    book one, 164–67
    book two, 167–68
    book three, 168–70

INDEX

VA (*The Life of Apollonius of Tyana*) (*cont.*)
   book four, 170–74
   book five, 174–76
   book six, 176–79
   book seven, 180–82
   book eight, 182–84
   borrowed directly from certain NT texts, 94
   challenging the historicity of, 152
   Christian texts or ideas in, 345–46
   claims of often taken at face value, 426
   colossal scale or breadth of, 161
   commissioned by Julia, 310
   completed after Julia's death, 260, 318
   composed much later than the Gospels, 21
   contradicting a fragment of *On Sacrifices*, 210
   contradictions within, 413
   as a counterblast to Christianity, 339
   date of, 155–56
   defense of Apollonius, 320
   dependence on the New Testament, 94
   differences from *Dictys of Crete* and *The Wonders Beyond Thule* as, 160
   dormant until Hierocles resurrected it, 60
   drove earlier competitors "off the market," 59
   dwarfed the Gospel accounts in length, 59
   as the earliest extant work, 54–55, 95
   errors, 53, 158, 262–307
   famous characters as associates of Apollonius, 192
   fictional elements in, 151
   first source claiming that Apollonius was a philosopher, 383
   free pass in terms of veracity, 19
   genre of, 156–62
   Gospel influence on, 345
   historical and geographical errors in, 31, 261–308
   historical problems within, 19
   historical questions about, 20
   historical validity of, 281–82
   illusion that the diary was enormous, 257
   inclusion of in the study of Apollonius, 395
   inspiration from the infancy narratives of Jesus as unlikely, 353
   intended audience of, 162–63
   internal contradictions of, 90, 419–21
   introduction to, 153–63
   longer than the VS, 141
   Moiragenes not serving as a major source for, 375
   narrative gaps and chronological errors suggesting a source, 238–40
   never directly quoted the Gospels, 346
   new translations of, 93
   not a first-century version of Apollonius, 382
   not a Pythagorean manifesto, 315
   not having the appearance of a continuous narrative, 239
   not intended as a direct attack upon Christianity, 340, 344
   not presenting an agenda for monarchs, 317
   not the only source on Apollonius, 40
   not widely popular in the third century, 65
   as an often neglected piece of literature, 13
   as the only work of Philostratus to addressing Apollonius at length, 123
   origin of, 154–55
   by Philostratus, 5, 58–60
   Philostratus altered elements of, 114
   Philostratus unclear on sources, 235
   in Philostratus's other writings, 251

INDEX

political discussion involving Apollonius, Dio Chrysostom, and Euphrates, 205
pre-Philostratean sources not used or mentioned in, 187–210
pre-Philostratean sources used or mentioned in, 211–31
as a primary text, 11
problems in, 16–21
promoting good rule and condemns tyranny, 317
provided miracle accounts from pagan sources, 94–95
publication of several editions of during the Renaissance, 81
published before the VS, 138
publishing Eusebius along with, 82
on pure material sacrifices, 208
relating an exorcism by Apollonius and one by the Indian sage, Iarchas, 349
relationship between philosophers and monarchs, 92
scholars should not rely entirely upon, 229, 382
sources for, 212, 229
subjecting to rigorous historical analysis, 20
summary of Apollonius's life, 15
summary of the contents of, 164–84
themes in foreign to the sophist's worldview, 347–48
weaponizing by pagans for polemical purposes, 61
as a work based on a reliable first-century source, 41
written after the death of Julia Domna, 324
Valerius, 224
validity, of the VA, 124
vampire, 241, 284, 364
Van der Stockt, Luk, 191
Van Dijk, Gert-Jan, 332
King Vardanes of Babylon, 166, 167, 181, 265
Vatican, attack on occult arts, 81–82
vegetarian, Apollonius as, 420
Verus, tutor of, 196

Vespasian, 24, 105, 176, 290, 291–92
Vindex, Julius, revolt of, 289–90
vinedresser, in *Heroicus*, 146, 149
Vitellius, as no better than Nero, 176
volcanology, Apollonius's knowledge of, 175
Voltaire (Francois-Marie Arouet), on Apollonius, 84
Votaw, Clyde Weber, 45, 51, 161, 236, 388, 425
VS (*Vitae Sophistarum* or *Lives of the Sophists*)
attributed to Philostratus II with certainty, 121, 138–45, 205
defending two sophists against charges of using magic, 325
on laying up treasures or a physician healing himself, 347
not indicating specific sources, 252
short of the VA in number of words, 160
sophists described in, 117
sources for, 247
statements about Apollonius, 188
written under Gordian I or Gordian III, 156

water, drinking as a cure for rabies, 241
wealth, Apollonius born into great, 23
wealthy young man, Apollonius advised, 179
weather, Indian sages control of, 277
Weeden, Theodore J., 96
the West
Apollonius in during the Middle Ages, 78–80
Apollonius's return to, 170
why Apollonius matters, case for, 4–14
widow of Nain's son, resurrection of, 354, 355
Wieland, Christoph Martin, philosophic novel *Agathodamon*, 89
"wild onager," animal with a single horn, 275
wisdom, Apollonius sought, 333
Wise Man, one rebuked a spirit with a letter, 367

wise men, feats of in the presence of tyrants, 333
Wise Ones of India. *See also* Indian sages
 Apollonius and the magical practices of, 323
 Apollonius's visit with, 166, 169–70
 claims of, 275
 cures by, 169–70, 218
 exorcism performed by in the *VA*, 367
 levitation by, 251
 pale reflection of, 297
 served a meal by automata, 177, 279
The Wonders Beyond Thule, tale of Deinias in, 242–43
wooden tablets, 234–35, 256–58
Woolston, Thomas, 86

world traveler, Apollonius as, 230, 327, 329, 330
Wright, N. T., 115–16, 359
written traditions, problems of, 388

Xenophon's *Cyropaedia*, 160, 161, 316

Year of the Four Emperors (AD 69), 291, 332
Yoder, Timothy S., 86, 87
yogis, levitation trick employed by, 278
YouTube, videos about Apollonius, 10–11

Zatchlas, Egyptian prophet and priest raised a dead man, 356
Zealot, Reza Aslan's NYT bestseller, 9
Zeno of Elea, 333
Zeus, 209, 311, 351